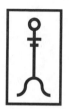

Jonathan Sharp

DIVINING YOUR
DREAMS

How the Ancient,
Mystical Tradition of the Kabbalah
Can Help You Interpret
More Than 850 Powerful Dream Images

Introduction by Dr. Edward Hoffman

A Lark Production

A FIRESIDE BOOK
Published by Simon & Schuster New York London Toronto Sydney Singapore

FIRESIDE
Rockefeller Center
1230 Avenue of the Americas
New York, NY 10020

FIRESIDE and colophon are registered trademarks
of Simon & Schuster, Inc.

For information regarding special discounts for bulk purchases,
please contact Simon & Schuster Special Sales:
1-800-456-6798 or business@simonandschuster.com

Designed by Bonni Leon-Berman

Manufactured in the United States of America

10   9   8   7   6   5   4   3   2   1

Library of Congress Cataloging-in-Publication Data

Sharp, Jonathan.
    Divining your dreams : how the ancient, mystical tradition of the Kabbalah can help you interpret more than 850 powerful dream images / Jonathan Sharp ; introduction by Edward Hoffman.
       p.   cm.
    "A Lark production."
    "A Fireside book."
    1. Dream interpretation—Dictionaries.   2. Cabala—Dictionaries.   I. Title.
BF1091 .S543 2002
135'.3—dc21   2002026806
ISBN 0-7432-2941-X

Many thanks to Victoria, Joanna, and Caroline for giving me the space to write, and many thanks indeed to Willow, 3621, and Watson for inspiring me, and to Frater A. G. and Mary M for being there before, during, and in the future.

JS

In the absence of sages, God reveals wisdom and what is to come in the form of dreams.

—FROM *ZOHAR, OR BOOK OF SPLENDOR*

CONTENTS

INTRODUCTION

A dream uninterpreted is like a letter that is unopened.
—FROM ZOHAR, OR *BOOK OF SPLENDOR*

Dreams have fascinated nearly every culture in recorded history. The ancients regarded dreams with respect and even awe, considering them to herald important messages for our lives. During their golden age, the Greeks built more than three hundred temples in homage to Asclepius, their god of medicine; supplicants would travel long distances to these temples and participate in sacred rituals to elicit useful dreams. In the Far East, dream-incubation temples were similarly erected in serene and peaceful settings. In the West, Native American tribes prized dreams as a wellspring of godlike inspiration. Their shamans would journey deep into the wilderness. Denying themselves food, water, and companionship, they would induce dreams of power or knowledge that they could take back to their people.

With the rise of the Industrial Age, such intuitive wisdom fell on hard times. When Sigmund Freud began to research the medical literature of his day for information on dreams, he found that almost nothing had been written on the topic. Most of his colleagues viewed the entire subject as one of superstition, unworthy of serious attention. Indeed, when in 1899 Freud published his landmark, *The Interpretation of Dreams,* he was greeted with ridicule and derision. For several years, his cogent probings of the hidden meanings of our dreams were rejected as the ravings of a madman or a pornographer.

Eventually, of course, the psychoanalytic movement that Freud spearheaded gained momentum. His revolutionary ideas on the nature of dreams seemed to have an uncanny accuracy. Although the source of his insights remained unknown, Freud's emphasis on dream interpretation as a powerful tool for self-understanding became part of the therapeutic mainstream. In fact, as so often happens with the ideas of great thinkers, his notions acquired the status of dogma among many of his followers. Not until the last twenty years or so have investigators begun to study dreams from new viewpoints. Without disparaging the value of Freud's bold contributions, current experimenters are uncovering more and more information about this still enigmatic human activity.

Although much of this exciting work is happening in laboratories around the world, interested people today are also turning to the ancient spiritual traditions. It has become increasingly clear that these disciplines often incorporated a highly subtle and sophisticated body of knowledge about the human mind. Innovative psychologists have already begun to mine such sources as Yoga, Tibetan Buddhism, Sufism, Taoism, and other age-old approaches for their provocative teachings on dreams. And, most encouragingly, there is growing recognition of the richness and potency of the Kabbalah—Judaism's four-thousand-year-old mystical tradition—on this topic.

For many centuries, the Jewish esoteric system has insisted that dreams have vital importance for our everyday lives. There is convincing evidence that texts such as the *Zohar,* or *Book of Splendor*—which first appeared in the late thirteenth century and is a mystical interpretation of the Pentateuch (the first five books of the Hebrew bible)—may have strongly influenced Freud's seemingly unprecedented theories. Moreover, not only does the Kabbalah predate in many respects our modern-day approach to dreams, but in some ways, this ancient visionary approach offers a more thorough, inclusive viewpoint than typically put forth by contemporary researchers.

Is this surprising? Not really. Although in the United States and many other countries we live in an era of increasingly high technology—with cell phones, faxes, computers, and e-mail—teachers of the Kabbalah have always regarded its insights as timeless and transcendent of place as well. In twenty years of writing, lecturing, and conducting psychotherapy and counseling based on Jewish mystical precepts, I have certainly found this notion to be true. By following these longstanding teachings, we can enhance our individual *tikun* ("life mission" or "purpose") and thereby gain greater clarity, wisdom, and fulfillment in everyday living.

VISIONS OF THE NIGHT

The Kabbalists have always believed that sleep and dreams play a vital role in our lives. They have never condemned sleep as a waste of time but rather have regarded it as directly contributing to our emotional and physical health. In keeping with their image of the human body as beautiful and divine, Jewish mystics have also prized sleep—together with other physical activities such as eating and drinking—as having a crucial spiritual purpose. Through sleep, we replenish our bodily stamina and also open ourselves to higher influences, declares the Kabbalah. We are therefore admonished not to deny ourselves adequate rest—for whatever reason—just as we are advised not to attempt needless fasting or other forms of bodily self-punishment.

The Hasidic masters (Hasidism was a charismatic movement of Jewish self-renewal that arose in eighteenth-century Eastern Europe; the word *Hasid* means "pious" in Hebrew) particularly stressed this idea. Many of their ardent followers sought to keep themselves going during all hours of the day and night, to better attain lofty knowledge. Consequently, their mentors gently but firmly preached that we must maintain satisfactory rest to lead a truly harmonious life. No matter how strongly we may feel the need to busy ourselves in activity, time is needed for respite. Without it, we will quickly begin to lose our inner powers. Thus, the famous Hasid rebbe ("teacher") Zusya declared, "Even sleep has its purpose. One who wishes to progress . . . must first put aside his life-work in order to receive a new spirit, whereby a new revelation may come upon him. And therein lies the secret of sleep."

Interestingly, the early Hasidim judged the mental well-being of their followers according to the quality of their sleep. In a well-known anecdote, one prominent Hasid was asked in his later years what he considered the most valuable instruction from his teacher. His decisive answer was: "How to sleep properly." It is painfully obvious that our society has not yet learned this lesson, as evidenced by the millions of adults who nightly require one or more sedatives in order to fall asleep. From the Kabbalistic perspective, this is a clear sign of the imbalance that exists within many of us.

An intriguing and longstanding practice of the Kabbalah, in this respect, is the midnight prayer or study vigil. Originating at least as far back as the Middle Ages, this method has been much favored by adepts in the Jewish esoteric tradition. At exactly the hour of midnight, the initiate awakens from several hours of sleep. He or she then meditates, sings various holy chants and hymns, and delves into the mysteries of the sacred books. The Kabbalah points out that we are especially receptive to the wisdom of our inner Source at this time, and can confidently expect rapid self-development.

For instance, according to the *Zohar*, King David adhered to this technique because his kingship depended on it, and therefore he was accustomed to rise at this hour. Characteristically, practitioners continue with their exotic pursuits until the break of dawn. In this manner, the *Book of Splendor* goes on to say, the initiate "is encircled with a thread of grace; he looks into the firmament, and a light of holy knowledge rests upon him."

The midnight prayer or study vigil may have particular benefits for us today. Besides the obvious advantages of greater quiet at this hour, we may also gain physically from the increased availability of negative ions in the air. Scientists have become aware that we are acutely affected by the presence of electrically charged particles in the atmosphere. As Fred Soyka reported in his intriguing book, *The Ion Effect* (Bantam, 1978), it is now clear that negative ions exert a helpful influence upon us and typically exist in higher concentrations after the sun goes down.

Further, this cycle of alternating short periods of sleep with waking activities may in itself be of value. From a wide variety of research studies, there is increasing evidence that our creativity is most enhanced when we adopt a daily rhythm involving frequent brief naps. Perhaps intuitively, in modern times, brilliant inventors such as Thomas Edison have made use of precisely this tempo. He would sleep briefly at night and then return to concentrate on his work until the early hours of the morning.

Here again, though, Hasidic leaders issued cautionary advice for us. For example, Rabbi Mordechai of Lekhivitz criticized the tendency of some of his followers to stay up long after dark in pursuit of the higher mysteries of the spiritual world. While he praised the motives behind such practices, he commented: "Many pious folk . . . eat the food of the spirit of sadness [for] their brain is bemused for lack of sleep. This is the wrong way. With sufficient sleep, we may gain a clear head for sacred studies." Similarly, the *Zohar* asserts that without proper attention of mind and piety of heart, the midnight vigil is useless, even self-destructive. In other words, if we are tired and lack the ability to really exert ourselves mentally, we would do well to obtain a good night's rest.

THE DOORWAY OF DREAMS

For the Kabbalists, dreams are the most important aspect of sleep. Again and again, the major visionary writings of Judaism insist that dreams offer us a key avenue for self-exploration, as well as a path to greater wisdom concerning the universe. For instance, the authoritative body of Jewish law and commentary known as the Talmud, compiled between the second and fifth centuries C.E. (common era), contains several cogent discussions on the meaning of dreams. In his well-documented article "Anticipation of Dream Psychology in the Talmud," published in the scholarly *Journal of the History of the Behavioral Sciences* (October 1975, volume II, number 4), Moshe Halevi remarked, "The Talmudic psychology of dreams . . . includes a detailed picture, albeit scattered, among the opinions of many . . . of the nature and mechanics of dreams which anticipates much of the modern experimental observations."

With their masterful insights into our inner makeup, the Kabbalistic thinkers focused intensely on our dreams. Far from seeing them simply as ethereal, inexplicable experiences, they regarded most dreams as reflections of our daily frame of mind. In other words, whatever we most think of as we go about our daily activities—*that* is what will typically occupy our dreams as well. A lucid description of this process can be found in the thirteenth-century *Book of Splendor,* which states, "David was all his life engaged in making war, in shedding blood, and hence all his dreams were of misfortune, of destruction and ruin, of blood and shedding blood, and not of peace."

For the Kabbalists, dreams are meant to be taken seriously. Because they reveal our ordinary emotions, they can provide us with definite pathways into our hidden depths. "A dream uninterpreted is like a letter unopened," the *Zohar* succinctly says. We are to confront our dreams honestly, rather than ignore or dismiss them as irrelevant to our waking life. The *Zohar* stresses even more emphatically, "A dream that is not remembered might as well have not been dreamt, and therefore a dream forgotten and gone from mind is never fulfilled." Throughout the Kabbalah, this teaching echoes: We are to heed closely the messages of our dreams.

The accomplishment of this task requires a decided technique in the eyes of the Kabbalists. Consistent with their peculiarly powerful mixture of rationality and poetic exuberance, they have always insisted that dreams must be interpreted according to certain well-defined rules. These dicta are viewed as inviolate and do not vary from person to person; that is, every human being's dreams—regardless of his or her station in life—can typically be decoded in the same specific manner. Thus, while the Jewish visionary system views dreams as often enigmatic, perplexing, or even inspired by higher powers within us, it does not consider them inherently unfathomable. "All dreams follow their interpretation," we are told. "Because [Joseph] penetrated to the root of the matter, he gave to each dream the fitting interpretation so that everything should fall into place."

The key element in dream interpretation is to understand each separate aspect of our dream. In an approach that remarkably predates classical Freudian theory, the Kabbalah indicates that our minds work during sleep by means of symbols. While texts such as the *Zohar* do not adhere to Freud's overriding emphasis on sexuality as the main symbolic force in our dreams, they do tell us that many features of dreams actually represent abstract thoughts and hidden feelings. Thus, we are informed, "According to the lore of dreams, a river seen in a dream is a presage of peace," and, "every dream which contains the word *tov* ["good"] presages peace, provided the letters are in the proper order." Similarly, the *Book of Splendor* observes that "all colors seen in a dream are of good omen, except blue."

Here, once more, the Kabbalah strikingly anticipates modern psychology, as contemporary research has demonstrated that colors are indeed linked to our deepest emotions. People who typically dream in color—that is, *remember* such dreams—are generally more in touch with their inner world. Furthermore, as the *Zohar* astutely reports, dark colors are associated with feelings of personal unhappiness. In popular English usage, we are well acquainted with "blue Mondays" and "singing the blues."

Though the immensely influential *Zohar* spread the Jewish mystical approach to dream interpretation, it certainly did not originate it. For example, the twelfth-century German-Jewish sage Rabbi Judah the Hasid clearly stated, "Whatever will happen to a person—be it good or bad—is shown to him beforehand in dream symbolism." In a beautiful metaphor he explained, "The symbolic imagery of dreams may be compared to sign language. When a person is traveling to a foreign country, he will meet people whose language he does not understand. They will communicate to him through sign language, much like we communicate with the deaf. A sage can discern what he is being shown in his dream, and why it was shown to him in those symbols, and what the symbols stand for." The Kabbalah has always emphasized that once an element in the dream is correctly unraveled, its meaning will become clear.

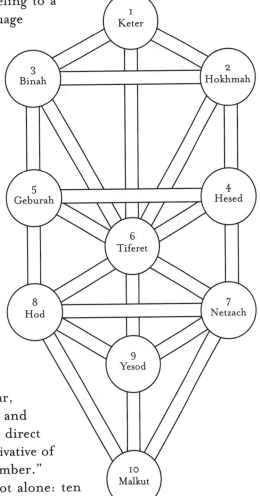

THE TREE OF LIFE

It's vital to know that Kabbalists have always linked dreams to the central mystical symbol of their tradition—known as the Tree of Life. Dating back in written form more than fifteen hundred years to the *Sefer Yetzirah* (*Book of Creation*, an anonymously written mystical text, originating between the third and fifth centuries C.E.), the Tree of Life comprises ten separate but interrelated forces called Sefirot (singular, Sefirah) that underlie all aspects of the cosmos and ultimately come from God. The term has no direct counterpart in any other language and is a derivative of the Hebrew word meaning "to count" or "to number."

The *Book of Creation* tersely states, "Ten Sefirot alone: ten and not nine, ten and not eleven. Understand with wisdom and be wise with understanding. Examine with them and search among them. Know, think, and visualize." However, this ancient tract does not explain what the Sefirot are or how they were created. At least textually, this important feature of the Kabbalah came later; the *Zohar* contains many references to it.

In most Kabbalistic systems—for separate "schools" developed over the centuries—each of the Sefirot is associated with a huge array of attributes and symbols including color, musical notation, and locus within the human body. Generally, the Tree of Life is understood as comprising five levels, starting at the top with Keter (Crown), which is the highest of the forces. So lofty has it been considered that later generations of Jewish mystics sometimes elevated it out of the Sefirotic arrangement entirely. Keter has traditionally been viewed as the primary generative force of the universe. Below, on the right and left respectively, are Hokhmah (Wisdom) and Binah (Understanding). These are seen to correspond to the qualities of active and receptive intelligence.

Directly below Keter, positioned in the middle, is a "shadow" vessel of energy known as Daat (Knowledge). It has often been depicted as an intermediary among the triad above it and may be viewed as the synthesis of those qualities. In the Chabad system of metaphysics taught by the influential, worldwide movement of Lubavitcher Hasidim, the forces of Hokhmah, Binah, and Daat are considered the keys to spiritual mastery.

The second holy triad comprises Hesed (Mercy) on the right, *Geburah* (literally "Strength," but usually translated as "Judgment") opposite it, and *Tiferet* (Beauty) centered below them. The polar attributes of both mercy and judgment or limiting strength are deemed necessary to sustain the universe in equilibrium. Beauty is the vital sphere of energy—described as the highest presence of God we can ordinarily glimpse during earthly life—that underlies several interactive patterns of the Sefirot.

The third triad is composed of Netzach (Victory) on the right, Hod (Glory) on the left, and Yesod (Foundation) in the middle below. While Yesod is typically viewed as the generative power of the material universe, the two other Sefirot are often far more vaguely defined in many Kabbalistic discussions. One perspective is that Netzach refers to the flow of physical energy, such as bodily exuberance involving running, jumping, and laughing, and Hod refers to the containment of this energy, including bodily self-denial and asceticism.

Finally, the Sefirah of Malkut (Kingdom) completes the structure. This energy-essence often symbolizes the realm of nature as well as humanity. Moreover, it refers to the Shekinah, the feminine counterpart of the Deity, said to dwell in exile in our universe. Whenever we act with the right intention and devotion, Jewish mystics have long taught, we convene the Divine presence around us.

It's also worthwhile to know that Kabbalists have identified 32 "pathways" or life situations (such as ecstasy, challenge, blockage, and harmony) that link each Sefirah to those closest to it. Interestingly, the number 32 is exactly the sum reached when we add the 22 Hebrew letters to the 10 Sefirot, and, of course, this is no coincidence. Based on both the numerical value of the Hebrew word that is our dream's central symbol (every Hebrew letter has a specific number associated with it), and the psychological trait associated with that symbol (for example, a crown represents wisdom), we can connect every dream to one of the 32 life situations looming before us. Such is the incredible power of the Kabbalah in interpreting dreams for self-knowledge and growth.

HOW TO INTERPRET YOUR DREAM

Although Kabbalists have been interpreting dreams for hundreds of years, it's not always easy to find a teacher where you live. For this reason, we've created this book to serve as your personal guide in dream exploration. By following a few simple principles, you'll be able immediately to start interpreting—and benefiting from—your nightly dreams.

1. Keep a journal and pen beside your bed every night, so that you can awaken at any time and record your dream—then fall back to sleep. Never rely on the belief that your dream was so fascinating, you'll surely remember it in the morning. If you recall it all, many important details will be forgotten even a few hours later.

2. Record your dream as fully as possible. Details that might seem trivial may prove important, even essential, later on. As you build up a "library" of your dreams, you'll find that certain images or themes repeat themselves. According to Jewish mystics, such repetition is especially significant, even vital, to the message your dreams convey for your current life.

3. Always use the present tense when you describe your dream and be sure to report how you felt in it. For example, "I am sitting in my living room and I hear a knock at the door. It is my college friend Alison, whom I haven't seen in real life for more than twenty years. I feel surprised and happy." Or, "I am driving my car very fast at night and suddenly see that the road ahead is completely blocked. I hardly have time to stop and feel scared."

4. Once you have described your dream, make a list of all the symbols it contains. For example, you are climbing a mountain, flying through the air, making love, or baking bread. Next to each symbol, using an "emotionality scale" of 1 to 5 (1 = minimal emotion, 2 = mild emotion, 3 = moderate emotion, 4 = a lot of emotion, 5 = intense emotion), write down how much emotional impact that symbol has for you.

5. Now, starting with the most emotion-laden symbol, turn to its Kabbalistic interpretation in this book. (See p. 16.) For each symbol, we've provided a lively and helpful description that will not only shed light but enable you to act vibrantly on your dream. Each symbol is discussed in a threefold way: its particular meaning, its significance on the Tree of Life, and its advice for your journey in everyday living.

6. Spend a few minutes to reflect on what you've learned from our Kabbalistic interpretation of your dream's symbols. Now think of one definite message that your dream has given you. Keeping it in mind, go about your day's activities with renewed insight and purpose.

ACTING ON YOUR DREAM'S MESSAGE

A dream is considered to be determined by its interpretation, and once comprehended, it is intended as a springboard for action. Jewish mysticism explicitly teaches that we live in the realm of assiyah (action), where what we actually *do* is the most important aspect of earthly life. So it has always been a vibrant notion that once we understand our dream, we need to act on it—to bring its message into our daily routine as well as our goals and plans. How do we do this? Keeping a journal to record our days' events has been one time-honored means, and another has certainly been to solicit the help and guidance of others we encounter along our life's journey.

But the Kabbalists caution us closely about whom to share our dreams with. In keeping with their view that dreams are hardly trivial matters, they have always stressed that we should not discuss our dreams with just anyone. Strangers or casual companions are likely to distort or misconstrue the significance of our dreams; they may even deliberately downplay an important message conveyed.

For instance, suppose you dream of being very happy after settling in another place—while your co-workers and other acquaintances are opposed to this move. Deliberately or not, they might try to persuade you to disregard this "obviously meaningless" dream. Thus, the *Zohar* flatly states that we should not reveal our dream except to a friend, because the listener may pervert its importance. However, this insightful book is equally emphatic that we should not keep our dreams buried within us: "When one has had a dream, he should unburden himself of it before . . . his friends." Of course, few of us ever share such deeply private feelings, even with our intimates; yet, such behavior might help to bring us closer to one another and avoid future misunderstandings.

The Kabbalistic belief in the importance of dreams as a key inner path is mirrored in the fascinating practice known as the "dream fast." Dating back to Talmudic times, this ancient custom calls for fasting and self-examination after a foreboding dream. We are explicitly instructed to do so on the same day as the dream happened. Rabbinical leaders advised that this custom be observed even on the Sabbath, the traditional Jewish day of rest and worship. They explained that an ominous dream represents a warning, not an irrevocable decree from on high. Thus, by immediately initiating action to face the causes of the disturbing dream, we may be able to rectify the inner imbalance that produced the anxious dream in the first place. And fasting and meditating are quite likely to help us become more in tune with our subconscious feelings.

Typically, this interesting custom involves a group ritual at the end of the dreamer's fast day. Three close friends are assembled around the dreamer; in their comforting presence, he or she then recites several encouraging phrases from the Scriptures—perhaps therein implanting positive self-images in the dreamer's consciousness. Would a contemporary equivalent such as a group phone call or computer chat room be acceptable? Perhaps. But, as a psychologist, I'm convinced that there's an undeniable benefit to face-to-face interaction that would be lost by these more impersonal methods. Still, they are better than not having the dream assemblage at all.

In the sixteenth century, the prominent Kabbalist Joseph Karo dealt specifically with this fascinating spiritual prescription. In codifying past rabbinical dicta on the kinds of dreams after which it is permissible to fast, on the Sabbath, he identified these three: a Torah scroll being burned, the conclusion of Yom Kippur (Day of Atonement) prayers, and one's teeth or the beams of one's house falling out. During a mediumistic trance, Karo experienced an inner voice (known as a *maggid* or "spirit guide") that related, "You have correctly ruled that one should not fast on the Sabbath, except for these." It is intriguing to note that, more than three hundred years later, Freud interpreted the dream of one's teeth falling out as reflective of fears of losing physical vitality, especially sexual potency!

Nearly a century since Freud's formulation, this type of dream remains, in psychoanalytic circles, a classic example of castration anxiety. As for the other sorts of dreams Karo mentioned, their interpretations are similarly not difficult to make—in Judaism, the Day of Atonement is one on which Jews seek forgiveness for their misdeeds and for unexpressed actions that should have been performed. To dream of this religious holiday probably indicates deep guilt feelings about something, the Kabbalists undoubtedly reasoned. Dreams of one's possessions being destroyed—material, or spiritual in the form of the Torah—likewise suggest inner emotional conflicts that need to be resolved.

The Kabbalah therefore admonishes us to take dreams of sickness, death, or destruction quite seriously. "Observe, too, that a man is not warned in a dream without cause," the *Book of Splendor* declares. "Woe to him who has no warning dreams." It is compelling to note that contemporary health researchers are beginning to find a very literal meaning to this Kabbalistic insight. Some investigators have found that our dreams may actually signal our physical well-being, or indicate the lack of it, months or even years before a disease becomes clinically manifest.

As Dr. Patricia Garfield reported in her book *Pathway to Ecstasy* (Prentice Hall, 1990), Russian scientists have been able to predict forthcoming illness with great accuracy based on their patients' dreams. At the Leningrad Institute, they found that dreams of, say, a stomach wound might indicate a liver or kidney ailment before the person was consciously aware of pain or difficulty in that part of the body. In the United States, researchers are similarly discovering that cancer patients frequently have had "warning dreams" about their impending illness, sometimes significantly prior to the actual diagnosis of the dreaded disease. Such examples readily point out the validity of the Kabbalistic view that we should take seriously all of our dreams—and, if we do, the healthier we are likely to be.

Another evocative practice related to dreams that the Kabbalah teaches is that of actively soliciting guidance from them for our daily lives. Several steps in this powerful technique are involved. Perhaps you have been feeling ill lately and want to get in better health. Maybe you have been having doubts about whether to remain at your present job. Before going to bed at night, write down your question, framing it as specifically and briefly as possible. Then, meditate for several minutes, helping to focus the mind with chanting, performing certain rituals, or (as defined later) permutating letters of the Hebrew alphabet. Characteristically, these methods are recommended by the Kabbalists in conjunction with this approach.

Next, you request your dream source to provide an answer to your dilemma. One formula that has come down to us from the twelfth century goes as follows:

> *I adjure you with the great, mighty, and awesome Name of God that you visit me this night and answer my question and request, whether by dream, by vision, by indicating a verse from Scripture, by [automatic] speech . . . or by writing.*

This interesting method is prized by several diverse spiritual disciplines. Known as "dream incubation," the practice of going to sleep to receive a dream of inspiration was valued by the ancient Greeks as well as Native American tribes. In his book *Dream Solutions* (New World Library, 1991) Dr. Henry Reed argues that this technique can be a very potent tool for personal growth. He also reports that shared dream-incubation rituals, involving several people, seem to trigger psychic dreams that resemble telepathy. Today, this exercise has apparently been re-created independently by various psychologists as yet unaware of the Kabbalah's longstanding familiarity with it. Like others who have practiced this self-healing device, I have found it to be most effective when I am at least somewhat lucid before going to sleep, rather than groggy with fatigue: Within a few days, I usually experience a dream that is directly relevant to the question I posed.

Undoubtedly, the most fascinating aspect of Kabbalistic thought about dreams is the belief that they can communicate extrasensory information to us. Such dreams, the Kabbalists insist, are rather rare and not to be expected on a regular basis. They caution us, in fact, that the overwhelming majority of dreams can easily be attributed to mundane thoughts and feelings. For instance, as the *Zohar* repeatedly explains, "There is not a dream that has not intermingled with it some spurious matter, so that it is a mixture of truth and falsehood." In the eighteenth century, Rabbi Moses Chaim Luzzatto similarly observed that it is impossible to have a dream that does not include irrelevant information.

The crucial factor that determines the visionary power of dreams is, then, our frame of mind in daily waking life. The more inwardly serene we are—and the less our sleep is troubled with idle fantasies and restless anxieties—the better able we are to attain "higher" dreams of knowledge. In those lofty states, psychic abilities become manifest, we are told.

For the Kabbalists, dreams are the most pervasive source of paranormal knowledge. The *Book of Splendor* succinctly states, "A dream is more precise than a vision and may explain what is obscure in a vision." Rabbi Luzzatto, again echoing earlier Jewish mystics, declared that dreams are pathways to prophecy. During sleep, the Kabbalah informs us, our minds are far more receptive to our inner wellsprings of creativity; our conscious flow of thought is shut off, thus allowing Divine inspiration to enter—if we are open enough to receive it, rather than being preoccupied with everyday worries and desires. Indeed, about the year 1800, Rabbi Elijah, the *Gaon* ("Genius") of Vilna, told his disciples that sleep exists for the sole purpose of conveying the mysteries of the cosmos through the vehicle of dreams.

INTRODUCTION

In our current era, innovative explorers of the mind are now starting to confirm even this more exotic aspect of Kabbalistic notions about dreams. Freud himself was quite fascinated by cases of apparent extrasensory perception, and in the 1930s he speculated that "telepathy could be the original archaic means by which individuals understand each other." More recently, several psychoanalysts have reported evidence for such communication in the dreams of patients undergoing psychotherapy; their research shows that psychic dreams between patients and their therapists are far from unusual. In fact, the Swiss psychiatrist Carl Jung was even more intrigued by this phenomenon than his mentor Freud, and wrote at length on dreams involving telepathy, precognition, and clairvoyance.

The Maimonides Dream Laboratory at the Maimonides Medical Center in New York City was the site of intensive investigation into the possible paranormal qualities of our dreams. In a series of many experiments, carried out over several years, convincing data were obtained on this issue. In an article titled "Dreams and Other Altered Conscious States" published in the *Journal of Communication* (winter 1975), Dr. Stanley Krippner reviewed the findings of twelve separate studies and concluded, "Telepathy and dreams can be demonstrated in a laboratory setting." His colleague at the Maimonides Dream Laboratory, Dr. Montague Ullman, concluded in the same publication that our dreams sometimes appear able to attract and incorporate information regarding events occurring "at a spatial distance from us, about which we would have no way of knowing."

Even more striking, Ullman noted, was that "they appear to gather information distant in time, as in the case of events which have not yet occurred." As yet, however, such far-sighted researchers are not able to predict *who* will manifest these unusual abilities, for not all of us seem to possess them in equal measure.

Here again, though, the Kabbalah may be of direct relevance to our modern-day inquiries. The Jewish mystical tradition connects extrasensory perception in dreams to our emotional makeup—especially to the emotions of contentment, calmness, and lucidity; freedom from anger and anxiety; and compassion for others. Whether focusing on the most prophetic dreams or the most ordinary, the Kabbalists have always regarded this realm of experience as a potent fountain of understanding. As the *Zohar* aptly tells us, "At night, all things return to their original root and source."

—Dr. Edward Hoffman

NOTES FROM THE AUTHOR

THE WESTERN MYSTERY TRADITION

Your spirituality, like your dream life, is a very personal matter. You may belong to the same spiritual tradition as your friends and relatives, but ultimately you will experience your relationship with the Divine in a unique manner. The analyses provided in this book are not designed to give you the answers but to act as springboards for your personal exploration of the spiritual dimension. The aim of the dream interpretations is to guide rather than direct and encourage you to look for yourself rather than attempt to show you the mystery of the Divine.

The way in which each of us has a unique approach to our spirituality is reflected in the vast number of organized religions and spiritual paths available to us. The Kabbalah, too, has its varied schools of thought.

In writing this book, I have attempted to be true to my spiritual beliefs in the interpretation of these dreams. However, where a different school of thought within the Kabbalistic tradition suggests an alternative analysis, I have included both interpretations. In most cases, the differences are matters of emphasis rather than of substantially differing opinions between various forms of Kabbalistic thought.

My background lies in the Western Mystery Tradition, an approach to spirituality that dates back at least as far as the Middle Ages in Europe. The underlying aim is to try to gain an understanding of the Divine nature of Creation and to fully realize one's spiritual potential. In trying to find ways to achieve these lofty goals, the followers of the Western Mystery Tradition looked to all forms of religious belief and spirituality.

As a follower of the Western Mystery Tradition, I have written this book mainly from the point of view of what is often termed "hermetic Kabbalah." This is the version of the Kabbalah described above: a spiritual system that, while not Judaic in nature, places the central tenets of the Kabbalah at its heart and uses the Tree of Life as the key with which to unlock the secrets within the universe.

The Kabbalah has always promoted study as a route to wisdom and insight into the Divine. The Western Mystery Tradition has a similar attitude toward the need for determination, commitment, and effort. Indeed, the process by which we gradually bring ourselves closer to an understanding of the Divine is known as "the Great Work." You will see many references to this in the dream analyses.

The spiritual belief that underpins the interpretations in this book is one that sees each of us as responsible for our own spiritual advancement and understanding. We should try to accept this responsibility and take up the challenge of the Great Work. If we do set out on that spiritual journey, we must pass through a number of states of consciousness before we reach a level of being that approaches an understanding of the Divine. Each of these possible states is represented by a path on the Tree of Life, and our dreams help us to see not only where we are but how we can move forward to the next stage of our spiritual development.

All spiritual paths are based on the belief in the existence of a soul. In the Western Mystery Tradition, the soul is referred to as the "higher self." The purpose of the Great Work is to try to forge a link between your conscious self and your higher self. This enables your path through life to be more directly guided by that part of your nature which is closest to the Divine. Your higher self is the part of you that is eternal, carrying within it a spark of the Divine.

Even if we are fortunate enough to create a direct link with our higher self, a process that occurs when we reach the Sefirah of Tiferet, our journey is far from over. We must then try to work our way up along the Tree of Life, gradually increasing our understanding of the nature of the Divine as we progress. Of course, the true nature of the Divine is ultimately unknowable. In this sense, the Great Work is paradoxical because we are striving for a level of understanding that will always be beyond us. However, it is the act of reaching for that absolute insight that is important.

METHODOLOGY

This book uses two methods of analysis for interpreting dreams. The first looks at the content of the dream, specifically its surface narrative and embedded symbols. The second, a gematric analysis (from Gematria), considers the letter values of the Hebrew translation.

For the gematric analysis, I translated the title of each dream into Hebrew. In doing so, I did not merely substitute Hebrew for English letters but used the appropriate Hebrew word. The resultant word was then analyzed in terms of the values of the individual letters and the total numerical value of the word. Where appropriate, I also used reductive addition to get yet another number for analysis—342, for instance, yields a value of 9 ($3 + 4 + 2 = 9$). To complete the interpretation, references were made throughout to both traditional and hermetic Kabbalistic associations. In a very few of the interpretations, the traditional and hermetic analyses differ, and the distinctions are interesting and useful.

Having examined the title word, I then looked for similar opportunities for gematric analysis in the dream. For example, a dream of drowning involves analysis of the Hebrew equivalent for the word *drowning*. But if in your dream you are surrounded by fish, you might also look at the Hebrew letter Nun, which means "fish" and has a value of 50.

After completing the numerical analysis, I further considered the dream content. If we accept the idea that dreams offer us a window through which we can glimpse our spiritual potential, it is reasonable to expect that our dreams will be laden with symbols. Although you may not be consciously aware of the meaning of the symbols in your dreams, you should not ignore them, for they represent the attempts of your higher self to communicate with your mundane self.

Jung proposed, and many have accepted, the notion of the collective unconscious. This theory suggests that unconsciously we share certain collective responses and memories. This would, of course, include responses to certain archetypal images and symbols.

When looking at the content of a dream, the analysis must again operate on two levels. At the first level, the surface activity is analyzed in terms of its possible spiritual significance. If you are running in your dream and have a fear of falling, there is a spiritual dimension that suggests you need to focus less on charging ahead in your daily life and should spend more time simply being still with yourself.

At the second level, the dream content is analyzed in terms of embedded symbols. Pairs of items, for instance, would suggest that the dream dealt with the spiritual implications of duality. A dream of sunbathing may not seem symbolic, until you consider the meaning of the Sun in mystical terms as a source of life and associated with the Sefirah Tiferet on the Tree of Life. You would then look at the rest of the dream to see how that symbolic content should be interpreted.

Finally, once the analysis of the raw numbers and the basic and symbolic content of the dream are completed, it is important to look at how all these elements connect with one another to form a coherent interpretation. Once you have interpreted your dream's message about your spiritual state, you can then begin to challenge yourself to move to the next spiritual level.

A NOTE ON THE TAROT

You will notice as you read through this book that some of the dreams contain references to the tarot. This may seem strange, as the tarot comes from a wholly different mystical background than the Kabbalah.

To understand its inclusion, consider the European Renaissance. This was a period when interest in all things esoteric was flourishing. As ever, the mystics of the day were looking for a key to the secret wisdom that underlies the universe in both its physical and spiritual dimensions. It was this period of time that saw the emergence of what can be broadly referred to as the Western Mystery Tradition. The spiritual ingredients that went into the Renaissance melting pot included the Kabbalah, elements of Eastern mysticism, esoteric Christianity, ancient mythology, and ritual, along with the remnants of the European pagan mysteries.

Over subsequent centuries this eclectic mix was handed down through a range of often obscure and deliberately misleading texts, as well as by word of mouth among small groups of spiritual seekers after Truth. The tarot formed part of this wide-ranging body of spiritual lore and wisdom. In order to try to arrive at a more complete understanding, many hermetic philosophers (followers of the Western Mystery Tradition) sought to find the connections between the disparate spiritual traditions that they were using in their spiritual quest. The Kabbalah offered the most complete system, and the Tree of Life, in particular, was seen as a way of representing the various elements of a spiritual universe.

Consequently, it became common to associate an aspect of one tradition with a particular path on the Tree of Life. For instance, the path of Teth is associated with strength of character and will power, so it was linked to the astrological sign Leo, the Egyptian god Horus, and the Greek Vulcan. As there are twenty-two cards in the main part of a tarot deck, it seemed perfectly appropriate to attribute each card to one of the twenty-two letters of the Hebrew Alphabet and, thereby, to one of the paths of the Tree of Life.

This process of spiritual amalgamation was seen as valid on three levels: It symbolized the existence of a kernel of essential Truth in almost all spiritual traditions; it helped to clarify the deep meaning of different aspects of the spiritual universe; finally, it provided a range of images and ideas that would stimulate further meditation. In terms of this book, we can perhaps look at the tarot as rather like illustrations. They do not so much add something wholly new as help to visualize what is already there.

Where a tarot card is mentioned, its significance is also explained; the following table shows the letters of the Hebrew alphabet and their associated tarot cards. It may help your visualizations in certain spiritual states. The images on these cards are not primarily tools for fortune-telling, as is often thought, but are tools for stimulating meditative vision. They have been used in this way for many centuries within the Western Mystery Tradition, but to date there are no widely available books that explain how they can be used to their fullest potential.

—Jonathan Sharp (jon.sharp@uea.ac.uk)

Hebrew Letter	Tarot Card
Aleph	The Fool
Beth	The Magician, Magus, or Juggler
Gimel	The High Priestess, or Papess
Daleth	The Empress
Heh	The Emperor
Vav	The Hierophant, Pope or High Priest
Zayin	The Lovers
Cheth	The Chariot
Teth	Strength, Force, or Power
Yod	The Hermit
Kaph	The Wheel of Fortune
Lamed	Justice
Mem	The Hanged Man
Nun	Death
Samech	Temperance
Ayin	The Devil or Pan
Peh	The Tower, Tower of Destruction, or Tower of God
Tzaddi	The Star
Qoph	The Moon
Resh	The Sun
Shin	Judgment
Tav	The Universe or World

101 SYMBOLS FROM ZOHAR, or Book of Splendor

The following symbols have been identified by Jewish mystical scholars as the most important symbols of the *Zohar*. These symbols are cross-referenced to related or associated dream interpretations. You will find a related *Zohar* symbol for any dream interpretation preceded by the symbol ❧.

1. **Abyss.** Danger in the dreamer's life related to an overly emotional situation. It is important the dreamer be cautious in relating to others in potentially emotion-laden situations.

2. **Academy or Advanced School.** Knowledge, especially of a philosophical or metaphysical nature. The presence of this symbol affirms that deep study would prove beneficial to the dreamer.

3. **Angel.** A higher trait in the dreamer's life, such as the presence of kindness, compassion, or healing. A direct encounter with an angel indicates that strengthening this quality is now of the utmost importance for the dreamer.

4. **Arm.** Strength and prowess. The dreamer has power in a particular situation. An injured arm symbolizes weakened power.

5. **Asp (or any other poisonous snake or insect).** Danger due to something apparently minor or trivial. This symbol warns the dreamer to guard against potential harm through seemingly inconsequential matters.

6. **Baby.** The birth of something in the dreamer's life, most likely a relationship.

7. **Being Lost.** A powerful symbol indicating that the dreamer has gone astray from his/her soul's mission and purpose in life. Being lost also signifies that to gain spiritual bearings is of immediate importance.

8. **Book or Scroll.** Knowledge that can benefit the dreamer. A Torah scroll specifically represents spiritual knowledge; a flying scroll indicates that a course of study will soon gain the dreamer's attention. A prayer book signifies that the dreamer would benefit from the experience of prayer.

9. **Blindness.** The dreamer is either unwilling or unable to see the truth about something current in his/her life. A dream in which one is surrounded by darkness, such as sitting in a dark room, has the same meaning.

10. **Bridge.** A transition from one situation or viewpoint to another. The appearance of this symbol signifies that the dreamer is undergoing a positive shift in life circumstance or outlook.

11. **Candle.** The human soul. A brightly lit candle represents a vibrant soul, whereas a flickering candle indicates present weakness.

12. **Cave.** A place of refuge from a threatening or stressful situation. It is traditionally associated with the act of hiding protectively, as well as with patient waiting for outer circumstances to change for the better in the dreamer's life.

13. **Child.** Innocence and faith unhindered by intellectualization. This symbol affirms the importance of this trait in the dreamer's life.

14. **Climbing.** The dreamer is actively seeking greater fulfillment in his/her life. This is a positive image and signifies inner growth and forward movement.

15. **Coffin, Tomb, or Cemetery.** Something is dead in the dreamer's life. He/she would benefit from accepting this reality and mourning appropriately. (See **Funeral.**)

16. **Comet.** A major change is coming into the dreamer's life. This change may ultimately prove beneficial, but is likely to involve a sudden loss, upheaval, or unexpected turn of events.

17. **Cup or Chalice.** Divine blessing in the dreamer's life. A cup made of silver or gold is especially positive. A broken cup or chalice signifies that the blessing has been willfully refused.

18. **Dagger or Other Weapon.** Personal violence. This indicates that the dreamer has angry, destructive feelings and must therefore bring greater calmness immediately into his/her life.

19. **Dancing.** Physical joyfulness and merriment. A dream in which there is dancing affirms the presence of these qualities in the dreamer's life.

20. **Darkness.** The absence of divinity and holiness; ignorance. The more intense the darkness, the greater its message that the dreamer currently lacks spiritual illumination.

21. **Dawn, Daybreak.** A new start, such as one involving a job or relationship, occurring in the dreamer's life.

22. **Deafness.** The dreamer is ignoring helpful advice, such as that being given by a friend or loved one. More generally, deafness indicates that the dreamer is ignoring a truth being communicated in his/her life.

23. **Demon.** A lower quality in the dreamer's life, such as the presence of jealousy, resentment, or vengeance. A direct encounter with a demon indicates that combatting this trait is now of the utmost importance for the dreamer.

24. **Desert.** Spiritual barrenness in some aspect of the dreamer's life. It would therefore be helpful to take appropriate steps to generate greater fruitfulness or achievement.

25. **Dove.** Peace in general, or a peaceful resolution of a particular situation in the dreamer's life.

26. **Dragon or Monster.** Demonic or spiritually negative forces such as black magic or malevolence. The dreamer should shun anything in his/her life that has such aspects.

27. **Dust.** Humility before God's grandeur. Traditionally associated with the fate of all flesh, the presence of dust in a dream is a reminder to cultivate the qualities of deference and submission.

28. **Eagle.** Imaginative and creative power. A soaring eagle represents a great emergence of this quality in the dreamer's life; an eagle's nest depicts a place of security and rest in which this trait can grow.

29. **Earth.** The world of livelihood, in which all creatures must struggle for existence. This symbol indicates that the dreamer's focus is on mundane matters, such as money or household tasks.

30. **Echo.** Everything we do reverberates in higher, unseen worlds. A dream involving an echo is a reminder of this spiritual truth.

31. **Falling.** The dreamer is dropping to a lower level of consciousness in his/her life, as a result of attitudes such as anger, pride, or fear. This is invariably a negative symbol.

32. **Fire.** Divine judgment concerning the dreamer's flaws and misdeeds. Fire also indicates that he/she must now initiate a thorough moral cleansing for self-purification.

33. **Fish.** Abundance and material blessings in the dreamer's life, such as those involving money, property, and other possessions.

34. **Floating Eye.** God's all-seeingness. This symbol signifies that the dreamer needs greater awareness of this reality in his/her life. A human eye represents that the dreamer has true discernment about a situation, whereas an injured or blind eye symbolizes the opposite.

35. **Flying.** Freedom from mundane concerns. Flying also signifies that the dreamer should use his/her imagination to experience a greater sense of liberation from trivial matters.

36. **Fountain.** Emotional well-being and vitality. The higher the water's cascade, the more vibrant the dreamer's capability of expressing positive emotions, such as gratitude and compassion, in everyday life. In contrast, a broken or poorly functioning fountain signifies emotional blockage.

37. **Funeral.** Something has died in the dreamer's life. This can involve anything—a job, a relationship, or even an important belief—that no longer has any life in it. The dreamer would benefit from recognizing this reality, especially if it involves others. (See **Coffin, Tomb, or Cemetery.**)

38. **Gate.** A barrier that can be overcome by appropriate will and intention. Locked gates symbolize that the dreamer lacks the right attitude to penetrate a certain situation effectively.

39. **Gazelle.** Surety and gracefulness in the dreamer's decision making. This is a very positive indicator.

40. **Genitals (Loins).** The dreamer's generativity; his/her creativity that potently impacts the world. Injured genitals represent an impairment in this function.

41. **Giant.** Egotism, pride, and arrogance. The presence of this symbol indicates that the dreamer is experiencing this quality in him/herself or someone else.

42. **Goat.** Strong coping ability and rugged endurance in the dreamer's life. However, higher qualities of imagination and aesthetic sensitivity are lacking and need to be developed.

43. **Hair.** Virility and sexuality. Full, luxurious hair indicates personal sensuousness, whereas loss of hair is associated with the decline of sensuality. Combing one's hair is often symbolic of vanity.

44. **Hebrew Alphabet.** Each of the twenty-two Hebrew letters has a specific meaning. Whenever one appears in a dream, it is a positive sign of higher communication and a message as well.

45. **Highway, Road.** The dreamer's current path or journey in life. If the highway is inhabited, it indicates that he/she is closely linked with others, whereas a deserted road indicates solitude.

46. **Horizon.** The near future. A dazzling horizon is a depicter of good fortune, whereas one of darkness points to trouble ahead.

47. **House of Worship.** Group religious activity. The presence of this symbol indicates that the dreamer would gain from joining with others in soulful prayer or discussion.

48. **Hunger.** Physical or emotional deprivation. Hunger represents that the dreamer lacks basic satisfaction in his/her bodily and/or emotional needs.

49. **Illness.** The dreamer is lacking balance in his/her life and may soon develop an actual physical or emotional disorder. This is an example of what the *Zohar* calls a "warning dream."

50. **Jewel.** Divine illumination. The more beautiful or dazzling the jewel, the greater the dreamer's sense of spiritual resplendence in his/her life.

51. **Journey.** The dreamer's current path in life. If the journey involves foreign or unfamiliar scenery, it means that that he/she is encountering a new situation or challenge. The presence of companions is a positive sign; their absence indicates potential isolation.

52. **King.** Divine power and judgment. A king's presence in a dream affirms the importance of these qualities in the dreamer's life.

53. **Kiss.** The soul's tasting of the transcendent. A dream involving a kiss suggests that the dreamer—whether fully consciously or not—is experiencing such rapture in some aspect of his/her life.

54. **Ladder.** Character development and growth. The presence of this symbol is a reminder for the dreamer to pay daily attention to his/her traits and their steady improvement.

55. **Lamb.** The traits of meekness and gentleness. The image of a shepherd with a flock signifies that the dreamer is showing appropriate, attentive care in a situation.

56. **Lameness.** The dreamer is failing to use his/her full capability, especially regarding action that must be taken. This lameness may be either self-induced or caused by an external force or situation in the dreamer's life.

57. **Lamp.** Spiritual knowledge and wisdom. The stronger the illumination, the greater are such qualities in the dreamer's life. Interestingly, the *Zohar* also speaks of a lamp of darkness, which is a symbol for evil and disharmony.

58. **Leg.** Endurance, particularly associated with journeys on foot. It signifies that the dreamer has the stamina to deal successfully with a situation that may last for a long time. An injured leg symbolizes weakened stamina.

59. **Light.** Divinity and holiness, as well as wisdom. A major symbol. The more dazzling the light, the greater its significance.

60. **Lion.** Courage and spiritual strength. Traditionally, a lion is also a representation of the Jewish people. The symbol of a lion nuzzling its cubs represents that the dreamer is successfully imparting qualities of courage to others.

61. **Lovemaking.** The soul's ecstasy when it attains union with God. The *Zohar* often presents this image, which emphasizes that each soul has the potential for blissful communion with the Divine.

62. **Marketplace.** Livelihood and the economic necessities of human life. The presence of this symbol indicates that the dreamer is focused on matters pertaining to earning a living.

63. **Moon.** The dreamy, intuitive, and receptive in the dreamer's soul. The moon is traditionally associated with the soul's hidden aspects, such as imagination, creativity's source. The moon is also traditionally linked to femininity and traits associated with it, such as mood and emotion. The full moon represents the fruition or manifestation of these qualities, and the new moon their beginnings.

64. **Morning.** The spiritual state of joyful contentment. It is also associated with physical pleasure, well-being, and healing.

65. **Mountain.** A place of Divine inspiration and revelation. It indicates that the dreamer needs to find such a place in his/her life.

66. **Mouth.** Human speech and its capacity for generating either harmony or conflict. Its presence signifies that the dreamer should examine his/her words and their effects. An injured mouth symbolizes impaired ability to communicate.

67. **Night.** The qualities of somberness and judgment. Night is also generally associated with demonic forces and emotional negativity. **Midnight,** however, represents the time of mystical study and contemplation.

68. **Night Sky (Firmament).** Divine order in the universe, conveying that there is a definite, God-given structure to the cosmos. The firmament also affirms the presence of Divine order in the dreamer's personal life.

69. **Oasis.** A place of rejuvenation and replenishment. The presence of this symbol indicates that the dreamer's sense of spiritual barrenness is ending in a positive way.

70. **Old Man.** Perennial wisdom, particularly from a religious tradition. The presence of this image affirms the importance for the dreamer to seek this quality.

71. **Orchard.** Vibrancy in the dreamer's outlook and beliefs, revealing that he/she has an excellent spiritual perspective on life.

72. **Palace.** The dwelling place of the Divine. The presence of this symbol indicates that the dreamer should seek to become more aware of the sacred in his/her daily life.

73. **Planets.** The subtle, hidden forces that affect the dreamer's life. Traditionally, the planets are viewed astrologically—that is, exerting a definite influence on our day-to-day experiences.

74. **Playing a Musical Instrument.** Spiritual exaltation and delight; also, experiencing the sacred through aesthetic activity.

75. **Queen.** Divine love and compassion. A queen's presence in a dream affirms the importance of these traits in the dreamer's life.

76. **Radiant Star.** Divinity—God's resplendent existence—in the dreamer's life. A radiant star indicates wonderful events and good fortune to come.

77. **Rainbow.** Divine protection and safety. This is a hopeful and encouraging symbol for the dreamer's life.

78. **River, Flowing Stream.** The dreamer's life-spirituality is flowing well. This image affirms that he/she is about to experience positive change and greater momentum.

79. **Rotting Corpse.** Something is dead and decaying in the dreamer's life. It is important that he/she determine what that thing is—such as a job, a living situation, or a relationship—and take immediate action to "bury" it.

80. **Serpent.** Deceit and malevolence, possibly disguised as sincerity or even helpfulness. This image warns the dreamer that there is something or someone potentially dangerous in his/her life.

81. **Singing.** Joyful gratitude. Singing, either by the dreamer or others, affirms that the dreamer has something to gratefully acknowledge and celebrate in his/her life.

82. **Sky.** The world of spirit: the intangible, subtle, and mystical aspects of everyday life. A clear sky signifies clarity in the dreamer's situation, whereas cloudiness indicates confusion. The sky is also associated with purity.

83. **Sleep.** Ignorance, passivity, and withdrawal. Usually this is a negative symbol. In its most positive interpretation, sleep represents unhurried waiting in the dreamer's life. Falling asleep symbolizes loss of awareness and insight.

84. **Stagnant Pool.** The dreamer has become blocked and thwarted in vitality, especially involving his/her spirituality. This image offers a warning to reconnect with one's inner source of aliveness.

85. **Strong Wind.** The force of change. A dream with this element indicates that potent change is sweeping into the dreamer's life. A hurricane connotes that such change is likely to be fierce.

86. **Studying.** The acquisition of knowledge, especially spiritual. This is a positive symbol and indicates that the dreamer is embarking on appropriate inner development.

87. **Stumbling.** The dreamer is impatient and too hurried in daily matters. A sense of calmness and balance are necessary to avoid the calamity of a serious fall.

88. **Sun.** Will, intentionality. A rising sun represents a birth or the emergence of something new in the dreamer's life. (See **Dawn, Daybreak.**) A noonday sun represents a full manifestation of will. A setting sun indicates the ending of something in the dreamer's life. The sun is also traditionally associated with masculinity and traits related to it, such as willfulness, in both its positive and negative aspects.

89. **Swelling Sea.** Pride and arrogance. The dreamer therefore needs to cultivate greater humility.

90. **Teeth.** Physical vitality. Chewing and biting are associated with expressions of bodily energy; a loss of a tooth is a warning about the dreamer's health.

91. **Thirst.** Spiritual longing. This represents that the dreamer is not receiving adequate spiritual fulfillment in his/her life and is yearning for it.

92. **Throne.** The physical manifestation of the Divine. This symbol indicates that the dreamer should seek to become more aware of the sacredness of his/her body.

93. **Tree.** Life and spiritual knowledge (specifically, the Torah). This is a major symbol. A flowering tree also represents worthwhile achievement by the dreamer, whereas a barren tree indicates a lack of attainment.

94. **Turtle.** The Messianic Age in general; also, good fortune coming into the dreamer's life. The *Zohar* says that in the Messianic Age, the voice of the turtle (which is a silent animal) will finally be heard.

95. **Unopened Letter.** An important message that the dreamer has not yet heard. It is therefore necessary that he/she immediately become aware of any possible miscommunication in the present.

96. **Verdant Field.** The dreamer's life is filled with vitality and accomplishment.

97. **Voyage.** Major spiritual growth and transformation. If the ship's movement is on calm and placid waters, the dreamer is likely to encounter little upheaval in daily life. Turbulent waves indicate tension and difficulty in maintaining his/her balance.

98. **Waking up.** The dreamer is now gaining (or regaining) clarity, insight, and personal energy to initiate effective action in his/her life.

99. **Wedding.** A spiritual commitment, such as to a field of study or training or to a long-term endeavor. Generally, depending on the dreamer's gender, a bride or bridegroom represents the personification of this commitment.

100. **Wellspring.** The source of prime vitality and well-being in the dreamer's life. This can be whatever gives personal inspiration—and a sense of flow—such as music, dance, or loving camaraderie with others.

101. **Wilderness.** The absence of civilization, pretense, and security. The wilderness signifies a place of power—and potential danger—where the dreamer can experience the Divine for him/herself.

THE
DREAMS

ABANDONING A CHILD

*hala yeladim-hla yldym-*הלא ילדים-130

MEANING On the surface, this seems to be a dream that does not paint a very pleasant picture of the dreamer. However, unless this dream is a reflection of something that the dreamer has actually done in reality, it is important to remember that the dream is symbolic. In terms of the Kabbalah, the child is a symbol of purity and innocence. In abandoning this part of ourselves, we are reliving our entry into adulthood. While we need worldly experience in order to function well in our practical lives, it is worth remembering that almost all religious systems stress the importance of retaining one's innocence at a spiritual level.

The value of this dream is 130, which reduces to 4, the number of materiality and all things physical. This is significant because it suggests that in abandoning our innocence we are entering a wholly material existence. A world without the element of spirit is a barren existence, so we need to find a way to recover our spiritual innocence. Interestingly, the value of the Hebrew word for "children" reduces to 13. This is the same value as Achad, a Hebrew word that means "unity" and has a strong association with the idea of the Divine.

THE TREE OF LIFE At the spiritual level this dream suggests that there is a need to reawaken yourself to the possibility of the wonderful. It is very easy to allow the certainties of a materialistic outlook to disguise the enormous loss that occurs when we dismiss higher concerns from our life. In terms of the Tree of Life, this dream is solidly placed within Malkut, the Sefirah that represents the fully manifested physical universe. However, because the dream also contains the idea of a child, it points us toward the path of Tav on the Tree, which leads from Malkut to Yesod. In doing so, the dream indicates that we do not have to be trapped in the everyday world, unless we choose to entrap ourselves.

THE JOURNEY If you have had this dream, it is quite possible that you are either very skeptical or are going through a period where you are experiencing significant doubts about your faith. It is notable that the value of the dream can be arrived at by combining the letters Qoph, meaning "head," and Lamed, meaning "ox-goad." The symbology here suggests that the head or rational mind is driving the individual relentlessly. The solution then is to find a way to free your mind from its insistence on viewing the world through wholly rational eyes.

In order to take your first steps on the path toward spiritual realization, you must be able to open yourself to experiences and ideas that run counter to the world of mortgages, offices, and financial concerns. The easiest way to achieve this is to look at life with the eyes of a child, albeit tempered to a degree by adult thoughts. At a practical level, you could consider working with young children on a voluntary basis just to see how fully they immerse themselves in their worlds of imagination. Spiritually, you should try meditating on all the "important" things in your life, such as your job or your financial commitments. The idea is to progress from a view in which you see these things as important to a position where you can realize that in the grand scheme of things they are supremely unimportant.

ABDUCTION

*khateefah-chtyph-*חטיף-107

MEANING Although it may be perceived by many as a relatively recent phenomenon, the idea of abduction by nonhuman beings has a very long history. The fear of being removed from those we love and the places in which we feel comfortable is deep and profound. Today we often hear about alleged alien abductions, but if we go back in time a few hundred years, we see the same fear being played out but with fairies or "the little people" as the perpetrators. In terms of a dream, the theme of abduction is focused on the idea of confusion and worrisome change.

The value of this word in Hebrew is 107. If we use "compression," that is, looking for the fewest letters that will give us this value, we come up with the letters Qoph, meaning "head," and Zayin, meaning "sword." This creates a mental image of the head or mind being in some way attacked or challenged. Interestingly, if we use reductive addition—a process where we add up the individual numbers—we end up with 8 ($1 + 0 + 7 = 8$). The letter Cheth has a value of 8 and means "wall." This suggests that our response to the challenge to our mind is quite literally to put up a brick wall. The dreamer is taking a very defensive position in relation to new ideas that he is being exposed to.

TREE OF LIFE The dreamer who experiences images of abduction is sitting on the path that runs from Malkut to Netzach and is associated with the letter Qoph and the tarot card The Moon. This person is still very much focused on the purely material world, but is beginning to look upward and see that there are greater things in life than career and possessions. However, The Moon card indicates a significant degree of anxiety and possibly melancholy. This negative aspect links to the idea of the dreamer putting up a wall against his spiritual potential.

THE JOURNEY Congratulations! You have taken the first steps toward unlocking your spiritual potential. As the old proverb says: Even the longest journey begins with a single step. It is important that you allow yourself to accept your fears and anxieties because only in doing so can you truly overcome them. It is difficult to try to achieve what we truly want when that means letting go of what we are used to. In your dream, the desire to find something new has become a threat; you are being abducted, taken away from your familiar surroundings against your will. The solution is to inwardly accept that change is positive and ultimately rewarding. Spend some time writing down all the things in your life that would improve if you had a more spiritual outlook, and read that list every night before sleeping. Pretty soon you will find that you are wielding the sword and that it can be used to cut away doubt and fear, rather than cause anxiety and uncertainty.

ABOVE
lemalah-lma'alh-למעלה-175

MEANING This is always a positive element to experience when dreaming. In the broadest psychological terms, the idea of being above carries with it ideas of control, confidence, and achievement. Spiritually, it is entwined with the notion of approaching the Divine. The value of this image is 175, which reduces to 13, a number associated with significant transformation in one's life. Additionally, the number carries the three letters Qoph, Ayin, and Heh, with values of 100, 70, and 5, respectively. As all Hebrew letters have a meaning, we can, with experience, find a tale within a single word. In this case we have a mind that is active and vital, leaping higher and higher to see the light from the Divine.

THE TREE OF LIFE This dream image could be placed on almost any of the paths on the Tree of Life that are associated with positive self-development. Dreams of being above can occur very early in our spiritual journey, spurring us on to greater things or, indeed, in its latter stages as tantalizing glimpses of the final goal. However, placement in Tiferet is probably most appropriate, as this is associated with both the creative energy of the Sun and the powers of Raphael the Archangel of the element Air, which is linked with mental agility and progress.

THE JOURNEY You are making excellent headway in your life both physically and spiritually. It is for us easy to bask in our achievements, though, and when we do this we not only stop moving forward but can start to slip backward. In order to ensure that this does not happen to you, it is important to continue to set goals in all aspects of your life. In terms of your spiritual journey, you should consider focusing on some form of esoteric learning. For instance, you could buy a set of tarot cards and learn not only how to use them but how to meditate on each card in order to find new insights into your soul.

ABROAD
bekhoots la arets-bchvtz lartz-בחוץ לארץ-427

MEANING It is difficult today to imagine just how exotic and exciting foreign travel would have been only a few decades ago. We need to try to imagine this, though, in order to fully appreciate the meaning of this dream. It is worth reminding ourselves that when we dream we are living in the realm of the symbolic, so events and images do not always mean what they would in the mundane world. In a dream, traveling abroad represents the excitement and romance of the new and undiscovered.

Great change is indicated in the value of the dream since it reduces to 13, a value associated with the Death card in tarot. This card is often misunderstood as being a distressing symbol, but it simply refers to the beginning of a new chapter in one's life. It is important to notice that both words in Hebrew end in the letter Tzaddi, meaning "fishhook." This is a mixed message to the dreamer, indicating great opportunity along with the danger of obsession.

THE TREE OF LIFE The dreamer is in both an invigorating and a risk-laden position on the Tree of Life. The path of Tzaddi leads from Yesod to Netzach. It can indicate the movement from an awareness of the spiritual dimension to an incorporation of this awareness into one's emotional relationships with others. This can have other side benefits, such as a blossoming of hidden artistic tendencies.

This path can also represent the influence of the Moon on our emotional sensibilities. When combined with the intense passion and energy of Netzach, this influence can lead to an unhealthy level of obsession. If this happens, it is important that we find ways to keep our feet firmly on the ground.

THE JOURNEY When we first begin to examine the world of the spiritual, it is easy to be overwhelmed by the sheer variety of approaches to the Divine that exist. In addition to the major religions, we have a number of alternative systems to consider. These range from the genuine to the misguided to the exploitative. It is very important that we retain a level of common sense while simultaneously opening ourselves to new experiences. This dream suggests that you are taking the positive step of exploring new ways of looking at the world. At the same time, it offers a timely warning against falling into the trap of seeing any single individual or system as the one true way to the Divine. God has many mansions and can be found in a wonderful array of places. An ideal exercise would be to spend some time reading a variety of different spiritual texts and recognizing that each one holds at least a kernel of truth.

ABUNDANCE

shefa-shpha'a-שפע-450

MEANING One important factor of the Kabbalah is the significance of both individual letters and particular words. In common usage, we often use words almost interchangeably and see little difference between them—for instance, *kind* and *generous*. In the Kabbalah, the subtle differences between words are amplified because each letter counts. When we talk of abundance in a dream, it is worth noting that the theme of the dream is not wealth or riches, but abundance.

The value of this dream is highly significant. It points to an individual who has made major advances in his personal development. The letter Tav, which has a value of 400, indicates a level of self-sacrifice, while the letter Nun, with a value of 50 points, signifies a strengthening of faith emerging from the emotional challenges that have been experienced on the way toward this level of development.

THE TREE OF LIFE We have already learned that the value of this image does not indicate an easy life. The abundance that is referred to is a spiritual and emotional abundance that results from a generosity of spirit and a willingness to accept the difficulties that life throws in our path. This dream places you in the Sefirah Keter, which crowns the Tree of Life and represents the closest we can come to experiencing the Divine. The route to Keter from Malkut, where we all begin our journey, is known as The Serpent Path, and it is significant that

the value of this dream reduces to 9 since the value of the letter Teth, which means "serpent," is also 9.

THE JOURNEY While it is important that you continue to maintain your level of spiritual development, there is now a new role for you to undertake. When you have an abundance of anything, it is always best to share it with those around you. You should now be looking to encourage others to take a close look at their lives and try to fill them with deeper meaning.

ABYSS

tehom-thhvm-תהום-451

MEANING You may recollect, from your childhood, dreams of falling that were both terrifying and exhilarating. Psychologically these dreams relate to the growing realization of our responsibility for and power over our own life and destiny. Similarly, once we reach adulthood, dreams of an abyss represent a growing realization of our responsibility for our spiritual destiny.

The value of "abyss" can be reduced to 10, which represents the completion of a cycle in life. This is wholly appropriate as in esoteric circles the movement from one stage of enlightenment to the next is often referred to as crossing an abyss.

THE TREE OF LIFE This dream occupies a peculiar place on the Tree of Life. It is both a Sefirah and not a Sefirah! The path between Tiferet and Keter has a location known as Daat, meaning "Knowledge." This is situated on the path of Gimel, above the path linking Gevurah and Hesed but below that linking Binah and Hokhmah. This location is known as the Abyss in the Western Mystery Tradition. It is not shown on the Tree of Life because its presence cannot be fully known until one is ready to cross it and enter the final stages of self-development.

THE JOURNEY This is an absolutely critical stage in the life of your soul or higher self, depending on the term you prefer to use. You have already reached a level of significant self-knowledge and understanding and are applying this to your daily life. If you persevere, you will be standing on the brink of a full realization of the power and love of the Divine. It is important that you give yourself some time now to nurture this potential. Ideally, you should schedule some time away from work and family and spend it solitarily in as remote and natural a location as possible. While there, you should simply allow yourself to relax into a state of utter calm and trust in your soul to show you the next steps that you need to take.

See Zohar symbol, Abyss.

ACCELERATOR

*meets-maytz-*מאירץ-141

MEANING In today's corporate world, this would be seen by many as a wholly positive message. It carries with it ideas of speed, competition, and aggression—all qualities needed to succeed in the marketplace. However, from the standpoint of a spiritual seeker, this dream is a warning against focusing too much on living up to demands of the outside world. The value of the dream is 141. When reduced by further addition it takes a value of 6, which is associated with the letter Vav. This letter represents the element of Air, which indicates the need to take a more thoughtful approach in your life. Additionally, the central number is 40, which represents the letter Mem and suggests that you also need to give more space to your emotions.

THE TREE OF LIFE The image of an accelerator is representative of a mind-set that is still trapped in the man-made world of speed, greed, and desire. This places the image within the Sefirah of Malkut. You have yet to really commit yourself to the spiritual quest that is open to those who choose to take up the challenge.

THE JOURNEY If you continue to see only the bright lights and live for the temporary thrill of the moment, you will be missing out on the most valuable aspect of life—the chance to truly understand yourself. This is an opportunity that can only be truly appreciated once you have begun to strive toward it. You should start in a very simple way to change your life, but gradually these small changes will make an enormous impact on your worldview. To begin with, try to spend at least twenty minutes a day in complete silence. That means no radio, TV, or stereo—just you and the silence. You may be surprised at how difficult this is initially, but you will be deeply affected by the results if you persevere.

ACCIDENT

*teoonah-thavnh-*תאונה-462

MEANING According to Jungian psychology, many events that we perceive as accidental are actually examples of synchronicity. This is a situation where seeming coincidences occur for reasons that we are aware of only at an unconscious level. If you asked many occultists in the Western Mystery Tradition, they would tell you that there are no accidents at all—that all events occur for a reason. The message hidden in the value of this dream is that even negative experiences occur for a reason. It is likely that you are experiencing a number of disappointments in your life just now. However, the technique of compression gives us the three letters Tav, Samech, and Beth. The Tav represents the suffering that you are currently experiencing. The letter Samech, however, indicates the support from your higher self that you can gain simply by accepting the events in your life. If you do so, you will have taken a major step toward achieving the goal represented by the letter Beth, which is associated with the tarot card The Magician. The Magician indicates an individual who has balanced himself and is no longer subject to the angst and worry caused by problems in his daily life.

THE TREE OF LIFE The appropriate path for this dream is that linking Tiferet to Yesod. This is the path of Samech, and it connects the world of the astral with the area of consciousness that receives the light of the Divine directly. Moving along this path from Yesod to Tiferet involves eliminating the worries about the practical problems indicated in this dream and moving to a more grounded and balanced perception.

THE JOURNEY The tarot card Temperance belongs to the path of Samech and tells you the goal of this phase of your spiritual journey. Temperance is an old-fashioned term for being emotionally and spiritually balanced. To achieve such balance is never easy. However, you can begin to work toward this goal by actively seeking to see the hidden benefit in each problem that besets you. It may be hard to find, but you can be sure that for every misfortune, you can find some way in which it will help you progress. As Nietzsche points out, "What does not destroy [us] makes [us] stronger."

ACCUSING

*leha asheem-lhashym-*להאשים-376

MEANING In the Old Testament, the figure we now regard as Satan or the Devil has the role of accuser. His function is to challenge our behavior and attitudes on behalf of the Divine. It is only very much later that the figure of Satan takes on the qualities that are now ascribed to him. In this dream, we have a value in which the central number is 70; this is the value of the letter Ayin, which is associated with The Devil card in the tarot. This central number is flanked by numbers indicating the vital energy of the Divine and the central essence of the Divine, respectively. In this dream our higher self challenges our conscious self to address our behavioral faults so that we can come to feel the presence of the Divine.

THE TREE OF LIFE This dream relates to the path that leads us from the primarily rationalistic worldview of Hod to the spiritually integrated state of consciousness that we find in Tiferet. This is the path of Ayin, and, as we have already seen, it is associated with The Devil card in the tarot. This path suggests that you are constraining your relationship with the Divine to an intellectual or abstract level. This means that while your understanding may be growing, the way you relate to others has yet to be adjusted to fit with your greater understanding.

THE JOURNEY The Western Mystery Tradition differs from mainstream religion in a number of ways, but perhaps most significant is the way it places responsibility on us, as individuals, for our spiritual development. This highly individualistic approach can sometimes lead people to take a very insular approach to life. This dream is telling you that while your soul is your responsibility, its development requires that you also have feeling for those around you. It is easy to become self-absorbed when engaged on a spiritual quest, but breaking out of this will pay large dividends in your search for spiritual truth. A good start would be to spend at least one evening a week helping out in a charitable activity. Ideally, this should be for a group of people or sector of society for whom you would normally have little sympathy or understanding.

ACHE

ke'ev–kab–כאב–23

MEANING Surprisingly, this is an extremely encouraging dream, as it indicates that you are making steady progress toward a full understanding of your higher self and your true relationship to the Divine. This in turn will lead to an ability to discover your true purpose in life and achieve your whole potential. In this dream, the sincere seeker so wishes to contact the Divine that he literally aches.

The value of this dream is 23, which is a prime number and suggests that you have a unique personality and nature. This in itself may explain why you are progressing so well in your attempts to develop yourself. When we are slightly at odds with the world

around us, it is often easier to accept ways of thinking that run counter to the accepted worldview.

When we reduce the value by addition we come to the number 5, which is the value of the letter Heh. This letter means "window" and hints at the glimpse of the Divine that is waiting for us.

THE TREE OF LIFE Your progress along the paths of the Tree of Life has been relatively swift and untroubled. You are now standing on the path of Kaph, which takes you from Netzach to Hesed. The Sefirah Hesed represents mercy and the sort of understanding that we would associate with the love of a parent for his or her child. This is a very advanced state of consciousness to achieve and it is now within your grasp.

THE JOURNEY One might expect that in order to fulfill the demands of this part of your spiritual journey, you should be behaving in an obviously religious or pious way. In fact, the opposite is the case. In order to continue to progress you must realize that the practical world is still part of the body of the Divine. The letter Kaph means "hand" and indicates the need for you to engage in some practical work in order to move forward. The Sefirah from which your path begins is Netzach, which is linked to the arts and all creative activity. Thus, the correct response to this dream is to get involved with some community art project; this could be painting a mural or helping with a youth orchestra or even volunteering in an art therapy project.

ACQUAINTANCE

makeer–mkyr–מכיר–270

MEANING Keep an eye on your colleagues and friends, as one of them is about to do you a great service. It may well be that the person will be completely unaware of the help he is providing, but something he says or does will inspire you to greater efforts in your life generally, as well as in your personal development.

There are some clues to the nature of this person in the value of the dream image. The value 270 gives us the two letters Resh and Ayin. Resh is associated with the Sun and is suggestive of a person with a bright disposition and a warm generous nature. Ayin tells us that this person will be an achiever and is also very likely to engage in sports of a physically demanding nature.

THE TREE OF LIFE The inspiration that you are shortly to receive will take quite a while to filter through to your active consciousness. You will be able to fully understand its implications only after considerable thought. Consequently, this dream sits in the Sefirah of Hod, as this relates to the arena of thought. It is appropriate also because the paths of both Resh and Ayin originate in the Sefirah of Hod.

THE JOURNEY Unusually, the way to act on this dream is rather passive. The key thing to do is to pay great attention to everything those around you say or do for the next couple of weeks. This should include chance encounters on the street or while shopping as well as meetings with your closer friends. If something seems that it may have a bearing on your search for your inner being, you should spend considerable time pondering how it may relate to your current position. The long-term benefit of this dream is that it will encourage you to view every interaction, no matter how trivial, as in some way a reflection of your relationship with the Divine.

ADMIRE

*leha'areets-lha'arytz-*לְהַעֲרִיץ-405

MEANING You are someone who genuinely wants to make inroads into understanding your inner nature. Indeed, you have probably attempted to achieve some level of self-insight. However, the value of this dream indicates that up to now you have not met with success.

The main reason for this is that you tend to seek approval from those around you. The final letter, Tzaddi, shows us that you have the ability to be "hooked" by people who have a charismatic personality. This leads you to behave in ways that are designed to appeal to that person, rather than find ways to help yourself to move forward.

THE TREE OF LIFE This dream sits on the path of Teth. This path begins in the Sefirah Gevurah, which is associated with anger, revenge, and the destructive forces in Nature. This seems at odds with the approval-seeking personality described above. However, the need for approval is born from a lack of self-confidence and feelings of inadequacy. As long as we are seeking the approval of others, we will be building up levels of resentment.

THE JOURNEY It should come as no surprise to learn that the key message for you to take away from this dream is that, in order to understand yourself, you must first accept yourself and have a sense of your value as a person. This can be achieved in a

number of ways, from reminding yourself—from a previously prepared list of all your good points—that you are a useful and valuable individual, to ensuring that at least once a week you treat yourself to a small gift. Additionally, you should find a new activity that will involve you in meeting a new circle of people. When you meet this new group, you should consciously remind yourself that you are not to attempt to win their approval but simply to be yourself. If you can do this, you will realize that people like you for who you are and not what you think they might want you to be.

ADOPT

*eemoots-aymvtz-*אִימוּץ-147

MEANING The value of this image reduces to 12, and since the twelfth card of the tarot, The Hanged Man, is associated with the self-sacrifice involved in motherhood, it is a particularly appropriate value for an image of adoption.

Additionally, the central letter in the Hebrew for "adopt" is Mem. This letter is also associated with the tarot card The Hanged Man. Other factors in this dream's value suggest that you are searching for a way to express the spirituality that you already feel very deeply. The key letter indicates a probable solution to that search.

THE TREE OF LIFE The only suitable place to situate this dream is right in the heart of the Sefirah Binah. Binah is also known as The Great Mother, and this dream is all about the maternal instinct that resides within all of us, male and female. It is from Binah that the urge toward definite form emanates; it is, in a sense, the womb of the cosmos. On the individual level, it relates to a desire to empower others in their own lives.

THE JOURNEY Emotionally and spiritually you have an awful lot to give. You know that there is more you could be doing to make the most of your potential, not just for yourself but for others. Given the depth of your understanding, why not simply go out there and talk to people about your experiences? What better way is there to lead than by example? Find a local meditation group or other organization that revolves around the desire to find a spiritual purpose in life, and volunteer to lead one or two sessions just talking about your inner self and your development. Not only will this enable you to help others, but you will find that it clarifies your feelings far more effectively than merely by thinking.

ADULATION

*haratsiah-ha'artzh-*הערצה-370

MEANING This is both a positive dream and potentially one of warning. Adulation is always a dangerous and two-headed beast. On one hand, a dream of adulation suggests that you have reached a position where others can gain from your greater experience. However, it can also point to a risk of being driven by your ego and seeking the admiration of others rather than the solitary achievement of *samadhi* (this is an Eastern term for the achievement of union with the higher self or the Divine force). The value of the dream image is equally double-sided. When reduced it generates the number 10, which indicates successful completion of a phase in your spiritual journey. When we use compression we are left with the two letters Shin and Ayin. While Shin represents the manifested active energy of the higher self, when linked with Ayin (which is linked to The Devil card in the tarot), it suggests that this energy is in danger of turning to self-serving ends.

THE TREE OF LIFE This dream sits on the path of Vav, the third letter of the Tetragrammaton (the four-lettered name of the Divine), which represents the element of Air. You are situated between two very positive Sefirot, those of Hokhmah and Hesed. Both represent aspects of God, as the creative force and as the merciful father, respectively. Such qualities are immensely difficult to embody, but despite the warning, this dream strongly suggests that with effort you are ready to achieve this state of consciousness.

THE JOURNEY To traverse the path of Vav requires deep and personally revealing meditation. Allow yourself to imagine that you are in a position of great power, with vast numbers of people at your command. Now, how exactly do you wield that power? It is important that you do not try to censor the flow of feelings as they come into your head. You may well have all sorts of inappropriate power-hungry ideas that spring up from nowhere. Don't try to hide them; rather, allow them to grow in your mind as you imagine your situation. When you have a good sense of all of your feelings about holding such sway over people's lives, you should list all of the key thoughts that you experienced. Keep the positive thoughts and nurture them, examine the negative ones closely and, in doing so, reverse the imaginative process so that you are now one of the subjects experiencing the nature of your rule. In this way, you will be likely to shake yourself

out of the potential to be ego driven and will be better able to embody the idea that the true ruler is he or she who has no wish to be obeyed.

ADULTERY

*neeoof-nyavph-*ניאוף-147

MEANING A psychological explanation of a dream about adultery would focus on the idea of dissatisfaction with one's current relationship. From the Kabbalistic perspective, the interpretation is radically different. It will be surprising to many to learn that this is actually an encouraging dream. In order to follow a truly spiritual path, we must sever certain ties; this is always difficult and can lead to feelings of guilt and disloyalty. It is worth remembering that Jesus, who was certainly an individual with very deep spiritual insight, reminded his disciples that he came not to bring peace but to set man against wife, brother against brother, and neighbor against neighbor. The value of this dream reduces to 12, and its association with The Hanged Man card from the tarot tells us that this is not a dream about the thrill of an illicit relationship. Rather, it expresses the difficulty of leaving behind what is no longer an integral part of our inner emotional or spiritual life.

THE TREE OF LIFE Lamed represents an unstoppable driving force, meaning as it does "ox-goad" in Hebrew. This is the path to which the dream image of adultery belongs. You are being irreversibly driven in a particular direction, and while you must follow this new course, there are a number of emotional difficulties that must be dealt with. The path of Lamed is a harsh taskmaster and there is no way to avoid its lessons, which may be hard to accept, but they are all part of the solution to our spiritual hunger.

THE JOURNEY Having decided that you wish to uncover your true potential, you now find that many of those who ranked as your close friends seem somehow distant and in some cases completely confused by your change in attitude and values.

To ensure that you are able to continue with your spiritual progress, it is important for you to find some support through the difficult times. You should consider joining a meditation group because not only will you find like-minded people with whom you can discuss your hopes and worries, but the presence of such people will help provide the resolve needed to continue on your spiritual quest.

ADVANCEMENT

*keedoom-kydvm-*כידום*-*70

MEANING When you wake from this dream, you should feel invigorated and full of drive to move forward in your life. Dreams of advancement are our higher self's way of pointing out that we are about to enter a new and more fulfilling phase in life. The dream's value is 70, which connects it to the letter Ayin. This letter represents the vital energy embodied by the mountain goat leaping from rock to rock. It is associated with The Devil card in the tarot, but in this dream it is only the active, thrusting dynamism of The Devil card that is indicated, without any of its negative connotations.

THE TREE OF LIFE Due to its association with progression, it would seem that this dream could belong anywhere on the Tree of Life. However, the importance of the final letter Mem in the dream image indicates that this is about advancement to a greater level of emotional understanding. This factor determines that the dream of advancement lies on the path of Peh, which runs from the Sefirah of Hod to that of Netzach, linking the world of the rational with the world of emotions.

THE JOURNEY Up to now, it is likely that you have been approaching your spiritual development in a way that most people would consider an appropriate manner in which to approach the Divine. In other words, you have spent a lot of time meditating peacefully and thinking reverentially about the nature of the sacred. This is all very valuable, but is far from the whole story.

The quiet, humble, and somewhat melancholy approach to the religious is very much a Western, Christian phenomenon. In other cultures and spiritualities we see the Creator being celebrated in more vibrant and life-affirming ways. In order to achieve greater emotional integration, you should set yourself a very simple target. At least once a week, go out somewhere fun with friends or a partner and make it your primary purpose to spread as much laughter and joy as possible.

ADVENTURE

*harpatkah-hrpthqh-*הרפתקה*-*790

MEANING Your approach to life is to see it as a series of challenges that must be overcome. However, this does not mean that you see this as a negative aspect of your life; rather, you enjoy the whole sense of achievement that comes when you have managed to leap another hurdle and race on to the next opportunity to succeed. The value of this dream can be reduced to 16, a value associated with the tarot card The Tower. This card represents violent and catastrophic change and might be thought to refer to the manner in which you approach life. However, this dream is pointing to a catastrophic change in general that will lead to a new and very different adventure for you.

THE TREE OF LIFE This is a dream about turbulent change and the destruction of the old in order to make way for the new. The Sefirah of Gevurah is responsible for the forces of destruction within the universe, and so this where this dream image resides. It is important to remember that destructive forces are not always negative. In order for new crops to grow, it is necessary for the old crops to die.

THE JOURNEY As a rule, you like life to be exciting and full of events. Part of your desire for constant activity is that it acts as a handy distraction from a deep and thorough examination of your inner nature. It is true that there are an almost infinite number of ways in which to approach a dialogue with the Divine, and that this is in part to ensure that, no matter what our nature, we can find a path that is suitable for us. However, whatever path we take, we can be sure that at some point we will have to engage with the world around us in a way that is totally alien to our normal viewpoint. You have reached that point in your life now. It will be perhaps the greatest challenge you have yet faced, but your goal is to approach life in a calm and measured way. You must learn that we solve our problems through thought and stoic acceptance as much as through determination to change the circumstances in which we find ourselves.

ADVERSARY

*meetnaged-mthngd-*מתנגד*-*497

MEANING It's not easy to feel at one with the cosmos when a colleague or acquaintance makes you want to run amok with a submachine gun! Unfortunately, this world was never designed to be ideal, and what seem like stumbling blocks are actually steps to a higher understanding, if only we look at them in the right way.

Dreaming of an adversary usually means that the source of the dream has really gotten under our skin. The value of this dream reduces to 20, which is the value of the letter Kaph. This letter is associated with the planet Jupiter, which indicates the need to view our adversary in a benevolent manner. Additionally, the letters Mem and Tav in the Hebrew word for "adversary" both point to a necessary level of self-sacrifice and suffering.

THE TREE OF LIFE The need for us to face up to and deal successfully with those who disturb our sense of place in the world can occur at a number of points in our self-development. The fact that this dream is situated on the path of Zayin is a reflection of its function, rather than the position that you have reached within your spiritual development. The letter Zayin means "sword" and indicates that you need to experience a number of challenges to your way of looking at the world in order to achieve further insight into your soul.

THE JOURNEY Read the life story of any famous religious or spiritual figure and you will immediately notice that their lives are anything but easy. Carlos Castaneda in his exploration of the mystical system of the Toltecs noticed that the role of the adversary was extremely important in creating a spiritually developed individual.

As annoying as this person may be, it is your goal to meet his negativity with both a smile and acceptance. In doing so, you will not only disarm him but will embody the notion that only those matters that relate to your inner life are worthy of your fullest attention. When Jesus refers to loving our enemies, his advice is not merely to suggest submission; instead, it gives us an incredibly powerful tool for denying power to those who would seek to reduce us as individuals.

ADVERSITY

ason-asvn-אסון-117

MEANING Life may be tough right now, but remember that just a few hundred years ago the only way to pursue a fully spiritual life was to give up all of one's material possessions and enter a religious community. Some level of material difficulty is inevitable in any life, and you have the advantage of already appreciating that ultimately your wealth, or lack of it, will not matter at all.

The value of this dream has at its center the letter Yod, representing the essential spark of the Divine, which we can look to in our darkest moments. Additionally, when we reduce the value of "adversity" we are left with the number 9, which is associated with the letter Teth and the Strength card in the tarot. This points to the part of our nature on which we need to rely to win through this difficult time.

THE TREE OF LIFE This dreams finds us on the path that is connected to the tarot card The Hermit. The Hermit has cast aside all material concerns, carrying only the staff, which represents his faith in the Divine presence, and his lamp, which signifies the light of his higher self illuminating the way ahead. This path is also the path of Yod, which lies at the heart of the value of this dream image.

THE JOURNEY You should make the most of every situation that comes your way whether it is enjoyable or otherwise, as everything that occurs should be seen as an interaction between yourself and the Divine. The best way to understand the true opportunity that lies hidden in your current difficulties is to meditate on the description of The Hermit given above. Ideally, buy a deck of tarot cards (the Marseilles or Rider-Waite versions are perfect for these purposes) and meditate on your current situation while focusing on The Hermit card. The aim is to visualize yourself into the card so that you are looking with the eyes of The Hermit, rather than your own. From his perspective you will see adversity in a whole new light.

ADVICE

etsah-a'atzh-עצה-165

MEANING You should be feeling very pleased with your progress as this dream indicates that you have achieved some form of contact with your higher self. This is a boon not only in your spiritual development but in your life generally. There is a niche in life for each and every one of us; the key is to find exactly what that niche is. Once you have connected with your higher self, you can find your true way in life that much more easily.

The value of this dream tells us that you have had some significant hardships along the way. This is indicated by the association of the reduced value of this dream with The Hanged Man card in the tarot. The letters that make up the Hebrew word for "advice" suggest that all that suffering is behind you now, as they are all letters that we associate with positive forward-moving energy.

THE TREE OF LIFE When we first make contact with our higher self we are in the Sefirah of Tiferet. This Sefirah has paths reaching out both above and below and thus represents the position of the individual who has integrated his spiritual consciousness into his day-to-day existence.

Your dream places you in a higher position on the Tree of Life as you are receiving advice from your higher self. Consequently, you are sitting in the Sefirah of Hesed receiving advice from Hokhmah, the Sefirah immediately above it. The Sefirah of Hokhmah is one of three Supernals or three uppermost Sefirot that make up the body of the Divine insofar as it can be understood by human beings.

THE JOURNEY This dream doesn't require you to do anything other than to be still and listen. However, this is a lot harder than it may seem. When we talk of being still, we are referring not only to our physical stillness but to our state of mind. In order to receive the advice of the higher self, we must silence all the other competing voices in our mind. The number of conflicting voices varies from person to person, but we are talking about worry, desire, angst, ambition, and all the other ego-driven emotions that beset us.

The best way to achieve stillness is through a simple breathing exercise: Lie on a comfortable surface and expel all the air from your lungs for a count of 4. Next, breathe in for a count of 4, hold that breath for a count of 4, then expel it for a count of 4. Finally, wait for another count of 4 before beginning to breathe in again. The important thing in this exercise is the rhythm, not the length of each breath.

AFFLICTION

*eenooy-a'aynvy-*עינוי-146

MEANING If we were to look at this dream image in a purely psychological light, we would be likely to talk about an individual who felt that he was facing a number of unfair disadvantages in his life, or perhaps a person suffering feelings of sexual inadequacy. However, from a Kabbalistic perspective, this dream is much more complex.

You may not be suffering from any difficulties yourself, but you are concerned with the notion of suffering in general. The value of this dream is 146. The letter Qoph has a value of 100 and relates to the mind and to The Moon card in the tarot. This initial value tells us that you are deeply concerned about some aspect of the world around you. The 46 indicates that this concern is derived from a desire to take some action to improve the lot of others. This is a well-developed way to view the world, but the desire to help others needs to be divorced from any wish to remove all suffering from the world.

THE TREE OF LIFE If there were no suffering in the world we would be incapable of distinguishing a good experience from a bad one. In a world where everyone is content, there is little room for learning or self-development, and one can easily become rather sheeplike and passive.

It is in the sphere of Gevurah that we are exposed to the necessity of destruction in order that the universe may continue to live and grow. With the breakdown of forms that has to occur to provide for the creation of new forms comes an inevitable level of suffering. Right now you are having difficulty reconciling this fact with the notion of a loving God. Consequently, this dream sits on the path of Mem, which runs from Hod to Gevurah and indicates the process whereby you can understand the importance of destruction in the universe.

THE JOURNEY It is a question that is often asked—If God is loving, why does He allow suffering? Your journey will result in your finding the answer to that question. Nobody can give you the answer to this conundrum; like all spiritual insight, it must come from your experience.

One way to explore this issue is simply to go for a walk and make a list of everything you see in the natural world—from grass or insects to the most artificial of products, such as Styrofoam or even junk food! When you return home, your challenge is to try to find any item on your list that could have come into existence without at some point, some other thing having to be destroyed or so radically altered that it was no longer itself. You will not be able to find anything that meets these criteria, and this revelation should help you to meditate on the human condition and why we have to suffer hardship, be it mental, emotional, or physical.

AFFLUENCE

*shofea-shvpha'a-*שופע-456

MEANING From the Koran's insistence on charity to Buddah's dictate that desire is the cause of all sorrow, all major religions agree that attachment to possessions is an obstacle to spiritual growth and understanding. As a broad rule of thumb, it is worth remembering that the further from the spiritual any pursuit becomes, the more temporary and fleeting is the happiness associated with it.

The value of this dream is linked to the Devil card in the tarot, which emphasizes the importance you currently attach to the material world of sensuality and possessions. This is not a terrible state of affairs; it simply reflects the standard mind-set for the early twenty-first century. However, if you wish to realize your potential in a way that goes beyond the transient physical world, you will need to shift your perceptions somewhat.

THE TREE OF LIFE This dream is very much within the sphere of Malkut, as it is wholly concerned with the physical aspects of your life. In terms of your self, this dream belongs to the "guph," which is the lower physical body, as opposed to the Nephesch and the Neschamah, which are increasingly higher levels of the self.

We all begin with our consciousness lodged solely in the lower aspects of our souls. It is the nature of the Great Work to take that initial self and gradually raise it and distil it until we are ready to communicate directly with our higher self.

THE JOURNEY It is relatively easy to accept the essential irrelevance of possessions and money at an intellectual level. However, your task is not to merely recognize it as a truth but to be able to embody that truth in your daily life.

An excellent way to start is to engage in some random acts of kindness. One thing to try is simply to leave a ten-dollar bill on the train or in a shop. The point of this is that not only are you giving away money, but you have no knowledge of who is ultimately going to pick it up and benefit from your kindness. You cannot decide who you think is deserving, nor will you be in a position for anyone to thank you for the gift. In this way, you will be engaging in genuinely selfless behavior. You may well be surprised at how it makes you feel.

AFFRONT

lehaleev-lha'alyb- להעליב-147

MEANING It is never easy to go through life genuinely not caring about how others perceive us. In fact, for most of us it is virtually impossible to achieve. If we are to feel genuinely comfortable with who we are, though, we must at least try not to base our behavior on the expectations of those around us. Similarly, we must learn not to judge others but to accept people as they are.

This dream's value suggests that you still have a desire to change the opinions of others when you regard their views or values as an affront to yourself. While the letter Qoph, which has a value of 100, indicates that our viewpoint should remain merely a thought, the final 7 corresponds to the letter Zayin, meaning "sword," which suggests that you are likely to challenge those whose views differ from yours.

THE TREE OF LIFE It is always difficult to balance the roles of emotions and intellect when dealing with others. When met with opposition, you still have a tendency to let your feelings get in the way of tact and sense. This tendency puts your dream on the path of Peh. Peh means "mouth" in Hebrew,

and it is this aspect of the path that most relates to your dream image. In simple terms, the gift of speech is used not only when you say something but when you choose not to say a word. It is the skill of silence that you need to learn in order to make further progress.

THE JOURNEY Before you can help others you must first understand yourself. You fully understand yourself only when you are able to look at the world from a perspective that is opposed to yours, understand that perspective, and retain your own without feeling the need to change the opposing viewpoint.

This is not an easy goal to achieve and it will take considerable effort and soul searching to meet it. The rewards, though, will far outweigh the work required to get to this point of development. A fun way to get into this process is to make a point of always taking the side that you most vehemently disagree with when in a discussion or debate. Another tactic to use when reading a book or watching a film is to try to empathize with the character who is least appealing to you.

AFTERNOON

akhar ha-tsohorayeem-achr htzhryym- אחר הצהריים-569

MEANING This dream image represents something of a plateau in terms of your inner development. You could perhaps think of it as a rest stop on your spiritual highway. However, this does not mean that there is nothing for you to learn from the experience. When we turn to the value of this dream image, we see that the central number is 60—the value of the letter Samech, meaning "prop." In Kabbalistic terms this represents the protective force of the Divine and should be seen as an indication that you need to take some time off and relax a little.

THE TREE OF LIFE Having achieved an inner realization of the genuine existence of higher levels of perception and consciousness, you have arrived at the Sefirah of Yesod. Further thought and meditation has nudged you onto the path that leads directly from Yesod to Tiferet. This is the path of Samech and is associated with the Temperance card in the tarot. Temperance suggests the need for a careful balance of all the elements that make up your personality. This cannot be achieved in a hurry and is as much a matter of recognizing the wonder in your life as it is about correcting any flaws in your nature that you may discover.

THE JOURNEY "Relax and enjoy the ride" is the simple message of this dream. We are told that the Divine presence will support us, while the Temperance card also suggests an unhurried and calm approach to the task at hand.

When we begin to fully balance our inner self, it is important that we don't let go of the reason behind all this activity. While the work may at times be hard, the aim is to achieve an undiluted appreciation of and connection with the creative force that fills the universe. In order to help you approach this state, your job is to enjoy yourself. Visit some art galleries, wander through some unspoiled countryside, or read a beautiful poem. Anything that calls to mind the wonder and mystery of the Creation is ideal at this point in your development.

AGING

lehazkeen - lhzgyn - לְהַזְקִין *-202*

MEANING To fully appreciate the importance of this dream image, we must first try to rid ourselves of the contemporary attitude about age. Everywhere we look, ads and TV commercials are telling us how we can hide the signs of aging, dye our gray hair, or lose those smile lines. In our society, the loudest voice goes with the largest wallet, so the younger adults have significantly more say and seem more appealing than those with more experience of the world. In older, some might say wiser, times the old were respected and their advice was much sought after.

The initial 200 in the value of this dream represents the letter Resh, which is associated with the head and is suggestive of good judgment. Similarly, the final 2 links to the letter Beth and the tarot card The Magician—another indication of wisdom and power being associated with age.

THE TREE OF LIFE The Sefirah Binah is the most appropriate placement on the Tree of Life for this dream. It is linked with the planet Saturn, which is traditionally the planet of age and wisdom. Additionally, in its role as the Great Mother Binah is inevitably blessed both with age and with a protective understanding of those who come after.

THE JOURNEY To have this dream is to begin to realize that you have reached a level of consciousness where you will be able to help others who are searching for a new spiritual reality. The way in which you can help at this point is embedded in the value and positioning of the dream. What you have to offer is of more value than books or abstract theories—you can offer the experience of having been there. The

best way to get into a position where you can offer such assistance is to find a local meditation class and get involved.

AGONY

yeesooreem - yysvrym - יִיסוּרִים *-336*

MEANING This is a dream about significant pain, not just a nasty ache but genuine agony. Presumably, then, this dream carries a warning in its symbolism. In fact, however, dreams where you experience profound levels of physical discomfort are actually extremely encouraging.

The initial 300, which is the value of Shin, the letter that sits on the so-called biting path, gives us a hint that this particular learning curve is going to be tough. The subsequent 30 gives us the letter Lamed, meaning "ox-goad." This value builds on the sense of dynamism provided by the letter Shin and tells us that this is energy directed at us in what feels like an aggressive manner. However, the final 6 not only indicates that this process is intended to engender reflection by its connection to the letter Vav, but it also connects to the idea of the Divine as the hexagram.

THE TREE OF LIFE When we dream of agony, we are entering "the long dark night of the soul." This is a term used in esoteric circles to refer to the period in which we are about to cross the abyss and enter the strange, missing Sefirah of Daat or "knowledge." (See interpretation of Abyss.) As you are still in the confusion and fear that characterize this phase of spiritual development, this dream does not belong to Daat but to the path of Gimel, within which it is hidden. The High Priestess tarot card is associated with this path and it is The High Priestess who holds the scrolls containing the inner secrets of the universe.

THE JOURNEY There is only one way to respond positively to a dream of agony, and that is to turn yourself to face the fear and anxiety that the dream represents in order to be rid of it once and for all. This is not easy to accomplish, and the meditation recommended here should be tried only when you feel genuinely ready, as it will call up all of your inner demons. You should make sure you have an evening to yourself and find a small enclosed space; it may be a closet or even a small tent put up in your yard. This space must be in complete darkness and there should be no sound at all. All you have to do is sit in this space and try to remember the first time you ever felt really afraid. You will find that once you latch on to an experience, all of your concerns will come flooding out. What you must do is face those worries and accept them without letting them continue to have power over you. You need to be able to visualize yourself as a center of sedate calm amid a swirling chaos of anxiety. When you are able to maintain this state without needing to leave your space or turn on a light you will have made the leap into Daat.

AIR

*aveer-avvyr-*אוויר-223

MEANING As a Kabbalist, the first thing that one notices about this dream image is the value of the word *air*. It has a value of 223, which is a prime number, and since prime numbers can be divided only by themselves and by one, they represent uniqueness. Crowley, a famous English mystic, said that "every man and woman is a star," thereby pointing out the fact that each of us is unique. While he was right to do so, it is also true to say that from time to time we meet people who have something extra to give to the world.

The meaning of the word gives a strong clue to the nature of your particular gift. The element of Air is related to the world of the intellect. This dream suggests that you have an exceptionally active mind and a number of new ways of looking at the world that should be shared with others.

THE TREE OF LIFE The Sefirah of Tiferet is associated with the element of Air, so it seems an appropriate place to position this dream. Additionally, Tiferet represents the highest level of integration of the spiritual and physical; it is the mode of consciousness to which we all should aspire. Since you have a gift that should be shared with the world, you are in the position of Tiferet.

THE JOURNEY Only you can determine exactly where your true talent lies and how best to employ it. A dream can be a pointer. It can even provide a key to a number of different doors, but ultimately it is you who must decide which door to open and what to do once you step over the threshold.

Likely, you have had some dream or ambition that you have never shared with anyone because it seemed too arrogant or too outlandish to be taken seriously. Having experienced this dream, all you need to do is believe in yourself. Whatever that ambition might be, you must now do all you can to achieve your goal, as this dream image is telling you that with persistence you will get there and that the end results will help you as well as numerous others.

AIRPLANE

*klee tayees-kly tys-*כלי טים-139

MEANING A psychological interpretation of this dream would focus on the notion of speedy movement and would probably ask if the airplane was moving away from somewhere or heading toward a new destination, as this would be significant in terms of the dreamer's attitude to the situation.

Kabbalistically, this is also a dream about movement, but it is unquestionably a positive message that your higher self is trying to communicate to your conscious mind. The value of this dream reduces to 13, and so it indicates dramatic change that is about to occur in your life. The presence of both the letter Lamed, meaning "ox-goad," and Teth, meaning "serpent," tells us that this change is unavoidable and will occur suddenly and dramatically.

THE TREE OF LIFE Dramatic and catastrophic change is often associated with the Sefirah of Gevurah. The overwhelmingly encouraging message of this dream suggests a connection to the Sefirah of Tiferet, which indicates a significant level of spiritual achievement. Consequently, this dream sits on the path of Lamed, which links Gevurah and Tiferet, as well as being a key letter in the dream title.

THE JOURNEY Besides indicating a driving force toward an inevitable destination, the path of Lamed is also connected to the tarot card Justice. This connection points you toward the area where you are about to experience a dramatic change. Up to this point you have been very much inwardly focused, seeing your spiritual development as a process that begins and ends with yourself. However, if you are truly to become more spiritually whole, you must also reach out to those around you. This dream indicates that you are about to experience a revelation of the connectedness of all things and all people in the universe, and that this sudden insight will initially upset your current worldview. When this experience hits you, try to put it to good use. Having realized that you are part of a great universal family, act on that knowledge by finding some way to help those family members who are less fortunate than you.

AIRPORT

*neemal teoofah-nml tha'avphh-*נמל תעופה-681

MEANING No one likes being stuck in an airport; they are dull, uninspiring places. Rather like commas in a sentence, we need them in order to know where we are and where we are going, but in themselves they offer little of interest. On your spiritual travels, the airport is a place of transit from one Sefirah and its associated level of development to the next.

This dream may seem mundane, but it is a sign that you are ready to move on in your life. While it might not represent an achievement, it is an encouraging symbol that a significant achievement is now within your grasp.

THE TREE OF LIFE As we have said, all of the Sefirot on the Tree of Life are staging posts on our spiritual journey. Each Sefirah has its particular qualities, but each also functions as a plateau from which we climb up along the path that emanates from it to the next Sefirah and the next stage of consciousness.

The dream of an airport is a very modern and materialistic way of representing such a staging post. It is likely that you are currently in Malkut, the sphere of the physical world, and are about to make your first steps up toward the world of the spiritual.

THE JOURNEY Perhaps the most common pursuit in airports is the buying of paperback books so that we can while away both the wait and the flight. In this way, the dream of an airport is again most appropriate, as at this stage in your quest for inner truth you should be reading as much as possible in order to select the path that works best for you as an individual.

ALCOHOL

kohal-kvhl- כוהל -61

MEANING In certain dreams we have to be careful not to exclude the possibility of a direct link between the literal meaning of the image and the dreamer's life. (See interpretation of Abuse.) If you feel that you have a tendency to drink too much or too often and you have this dream, it is probably a good idea for you to seek counseling or some other type of support.

Even if alcohol does not play a significant role in your life, this dream is still a warning from the higher self and should be heeded. The value of the dream reduces to 7, which is the number of the letter Zayin, meaning "sword." This indicates that some aspect of your life is damaging you and needs to be stopped.

THE TREE OF LIFE While the path of Ayin can be seen as highly positive in that it is dynamic and

individualistic, it also has its negative aspect. This is perhaps most apparent through its association with the tarot card The Devil. In terms of this particular dream image, it is the lower qualities of The Devil card that are relevant. This dream tells you that you are far too focused on physical comforts and not nearly enough on the more important matter of your soul.

THE JOURNEY It is not an obstacle to spiritual enjoyment to have an appreciation of the nice things in life—provided that such pleasures do not control you. Many wise people have pointed out that our possessions own us, rather than the other way around. As long as this remains the case, you will find that your inner development is slow. The initial value of 60 in "alcohol" is connected to the letter Samech, meaning "prop." This suggests that you use material comforts as some form of psychological support. By meditating and visualizing yourself wholly without possessions, you should be able to tell by the anxieties that immediately emerge exactly why it is that you feel this way. Once you know why you feel something, it is much easier for you to do something about it.

ALLEY

seemmtah-smth- סמטה -114

MEANING It is often said that the road to enlightenment is a narrow and winding way as opposed to the broad and easy road of self-indulgence. Perhaps, then, this dream image represents that difficult path to spiritual success. Unfortunately, the image of an alley suggests that we have taken a wrong turn somewhere. In spiritual terms we are, in fact, in a blind alley.

The value of "alley" is the same as that of the Hebrew term for weeping, and also the term for the Qlippoth (Qlippoth is a Kabbalistic term that means the negative or shadow aspect of each Sefirah) of Yesod. The Sefirah Yesod is associated with the astral level of consciousness and in its negative aspect can refer to an attempt to escape the real world by flights of fancy.

THE TREE OF LIFE

You are very open to the possibility of a spiritual reality and this is undoubtedly a good thing. However, your eagerness to have a genuine spiritual experience makes you vulnerable to groups or ideas that are less than useful. Sitting as it does in the Sefirah of Yesod, this dream tells us that you have become trapped in a set of beliefs that seems to offer a solution to the big questions in life, but which in fact is simply preventing you from looking deeper and finding ideas of real value. Yesod is a very seductive place to be, as its dreams are very convincing. It takes a lot to realize when you are fooling yourself, but it is always worth the effort when you succeed.

THE JOURNEY Before you can discover your true path, you must inevitably travel at least some way along a number of paths that are not for you. As long as you remain free to consider other ways of looking at the world, this is not a problem for your long term development. This dream image indicates that you have become fixed in one particular viewpoint. The best way to shift yourself out of this is to spend some time reading about and following the practices of an entirely different belief system.

ALTAR

meezbeach-mzbch-מזבה-58

MEANING We do not have to look far to see the spiritual significance in this dream image. The image itself is wholly religious, but it does have somewhat negative connotations in our modern world. The idea of self-sacrifice is now deeply unpopular both in literal and metaphorical terms. Even many New Age systems are focused more on the benefit to the individual than on the notion of losing one's self in order to gain something far greater—a relationship with the Divine.

The initial 50 in the value of "altar" is connected to the Death card in the tarot, and in this case it points to the need for at least a part of you to die, in order that you can be reborn as a more spiritually aware individual. The reduction of the value of the dream image gives us the number 13, which is also connected to the Death card in the tarot.

THE TREE OF LIFE The act of ego sacrifice is essential for full integration with our higher self. It often takes place in an unconscious way, but this dream strongly suggests an active decision on the part of the dreamer to give himself wholly over to a higher will. Such a choice comes only from a very strong and passionate desire to achieve union with the Divine. Consequently, this dream is placed on the path that runs from the Sefirah of Netzach, which is linked with passion and emotion, to the Sefirah of Tiferet, which represents the point at which the light of the Divine enters the physical body. Interestingly, this path is also known as the path of Nun and is the path of the Death card in the tarot.

THE JOURNEY You are standing on the brink of a new and wonderful chapter in your life. Your hard work and generosity of spirit has led you to a position where you are only inches away from a full realization of the presence of the Divine light.

The value of this dream is equivalent to a "notariqon," meaning "love, kindness, and grace." A notariqon is a Kabbalistic practice in which one takes the initial letters of the words in a phrase to form a new word that represents the import of the original phrase. For example, Paradise in Hebrew is "GNADN," and its letters are the initial letters of the Hebrew words meaning Body (GVPH), Soul (NPhSh), Eternity (AD), Knowledge (DA'ATh) and Truth (NKVN). This phrase sums up very well the qualities that have led you to this level of development. Your task now is to maintain those qualities by ensuring that you retain a sense of community with those around you. This means being even more willing to undertake dull but useful work for others. As the Zen masters say, "Before enlightenment chop wood, carry water; after enlightenment chop wood, carry water."

AMBUSH

meemarav-mmarb-ממארב-283

MEANING You probably bought this book with a certain sense of cynicism—your main reason for reading it is out of curiosity rather than a real sense that you are about to embark on any kind of inner development. However, this dream indicates that all this is about to change.

Rather than meaning that you are about to be attacked in any way, the letters that emerge when we look at the value of the dream image through compression indicate that you are about to have an undeniably spiritual experience. The 200, 80, and 3 relate to the letters Resh, Peh, and Gimel, respectively. These letters tell a story in which you will be exposed to the warm energy of the Sun (Resh), the Divine force that this represents will be communicated directly to you (Peh), and this will set you on the path that leads directly to the Divine (Gimel).

THE TREE OF LIFE In one sense you are very much in the Sefirah of Malkut, as you currently have no belief in the existence of a spiritual reality that can be accessed while still in the material world. However, this dream represents an experience not unlike that of St. Paul on the road to Damascus. As a representation of the impending experience, this dream should properly sit on the path of Tav, which leads us out of Malkut and into Yesod, the first Sefirah within which we become aware of the spiritual presence around us at all times.

THE JOURNEY At this time you have not begun your journey and will not be ready even to accept that you have a quest to undertake, until you have a spiritual experience for yourself. If this dream analysis has made you more open to the possibility of such an event, you could begin to prepare yourself by practicing a daily meditation just for twenty minutes or so.

AMMUNITION
*takhmoshet-thchmvshth-*תחמושת-1154

MEANING There are many, many ways to approach the Divine. The most effective method depends very much on the inner nature of the individual. According to the Taoists, we should be like the willow tree and bend with circumstances in order to be unaffected by them. Other philosophies argue that in order to progress we must be able to impose our will on the world. This dream implies that your path belongs more to the latter approach.

The dream value can be reduced to 11. This is a very significant number in the Western Mystery Tradition, as it represents the integrated human made more than human by the use of spiritual power, or magic as it is sometimes referred to. Clearly then you are making significant progress, and this dream is reminding you that you have the means to achieve still more if you have the will to persist.

THE TREE OF LIFE The breaking down of matter to its essentials is one way of understanding the world and our place within it, both in a physical and in a spiritual sense. This method of gaining understanding requires ammunition in order to blow apart the apparent solidity of things to discover the truth hidden within. The Sefirah of Gevurah is dedicated to the disintegration of forms (a process known in science as "entropy"), and it is this Sefirah that is home to the dream of ammunition.

THE JOURNEY You have the ammunition, but you must have the strength of character to go ahead and use it. The forms that you must destroy are not external; they are the fixed ideas and attitudes that have been created in your mind. To progress, you must begin the process of taking apart your ego consciousness to make way for your higher consciousness. You should begin by making a list of everything that seems absolute and fundamental to your sense of yourself. Then, take each item and meditate long and hard on it, until you can see that in fact it is no more absolute to a deep sense of yourself than is the way you dress or the food you eat.

AMOROUS
*ogev-a'avgb-*עוגב-81

MEANING When we find that our inner life can be so much more vibrant and alive than we had thought possible, the world becomes full of excitement and wonder. However, there is always a danger that this sense of wonder can descend into a sense of personal importance. This dream is a warning against allowing your growing awareness to be misdirected into vanity.

The value of this dream image reduces to 9, which is the value of the Hebrew letter Teth, meaning "serpent." The serpent is, of course, associated with lust in almost all cultures due to its phallic connotations. It is important to remember though that lust without love is primarily about a desire for power, and it is the will to have power over others that the serpent represents in terms of this dream.

THE TREE OF LIFE Power is not a terrible thing when it is used wisely and for the benefit of others. Indeed, part of the aim of the Great Work is to gain power over the ego. It is only when power becomes an object of desire that we begin to get into trouble. Such a feeling is identified with The Devil card in the tarot, so we find this dream on the path of Peh, as this is the path on which The Devil card sits. The path of Peh leads us into the Sefirah of Netzach, whose association with the emotions and creativity encourages us to move toward a more compassionate approach to the world.

THE JOURNEY The value of this dream image is the same as the value of the Hebrew word for "throne." In Kabbalah, words that have the same value are perceived as having a relationship with each other. Consequently, we can use the implications of "throne" to help us interpret the right course of action for you to take. At the moment, you are in danger of placing yourself on the throne because you are attracted to the power that you feel you are developing. However, that power comes from the Divine, and it is the Divine that you should place on the throne of your soul. In order to do this, you need to realize the value of humility and the ugliness of placing others in a position subservient to you. You can fully appreciate this only by experience. You should rent a number of videos that deal with such themes and visualize yourself in the position of the victim. Then, use that understanding and imagine yourself as someone interacting with you as you currently are in order to demonstrate why power is not as appealing as it may seem.

AMPUTATION

*keteeah-qtya'ah-*קטיעה-194

MEANING In Jungian psychology, there is a theory that certain symbols from mythology and religion are embedded in our collective unconscious. These symbols can be used in our dreams even when we have no conscious awareness of their significance. The word for "amputation" in Hebrew has the same value as the words meaning "righteousness" and "justice." Consequently, we associate this dream with a desire to be just, and this is where the idea of the collective unconscious comes into play. In the Bible, we are told that if our eye offends we should pluck it out, and similarly that if our arm offends we should cast it away from ourselves. This link between amputation and justice, having been made in one of the key religious texts in human history, becomes embedded in our psyche. It is interesting, of course, that the very word *amputation* in Hebrew has a value that points us toward this connection with notions of justice.

THE TREE OF LIFE It is the path of Lamed that carries the tarot card Justice, and so it is on this path of the Tree of Life that we place this dream. The path of Lamed leads into the Sefirah of Gevurah, which is also known as the Sefirah of Severity, and so the path of Lamed is doubly appropriate. Additionally, the letter Lamed itself means "ox-goad," which creates images of punishment and obedience to external forces. This dream clearly points you out as someone who is very concerned with behaving in an appropriate way in terms of your relationship with the Divine.

THE JOURNEY While we should expect a somewhat harsh experience as we approach the Sefirah of Gevurah, we also need to remember the lessons learned in Tiferet. In Tiferet we understand that true judgment can come only from the Divine, and that what really matters is our aspiration to be better. After all, without error we would not be human. You now need to learn to extend your forgiving attitude to others toward yourself. The danger in excessive self-criticism is that it becomes strangely comforting—another psychological crutch that takes us away from a focus on the higher. To learn to be self-forgiving, you should make a point of writing down whatever you feel you have done wrong. At least a couple of hours later, go back to that piece of paper, read what you wrote, and then enter a dialogue with yourself as you would if it were someone else who had committed the perceived wrong. In this way, you will be more likely to give yourself the compassion that you deserve.

ANCHOR

*ogen-a'avgn-*עוגן-129

MEANING At times, we all feel as though we have been set adrift on the vast ocean that is life, without a map or even a compass to guide us. Recently you have been feeling increasingly lost and confused, and at times you may have even considered giving up hope of ever finding any form of spiritual insight or guidance. You can begin to cheer up now, as this dream indicates that you are on the verge of quite literally dropping anchor at the shore of a new and more contented way of looking at the world. The value of the word *anchor* is equivalent to the Hebrew word meaning "delight," and that is exactly how you will shortly feel.

THE TREE OF LIFE This dream is located on the path of Tzaddi, which leads from Yesod to Netzach. This path is connected to the tarot card The Star, which represents the arrival of a protective and guiding force from above. If before this dream you were adrift on a blank ocean, you now have a star by which to navigate. While Yesod offers us a glimpse of the spiritual, it can also be a confusing and shadowy place. By contrast, Netzach is a place where our emotions and passions are given free expression, and we are able to ground our awareness of the spiritual in our emotional life.

THE JOURNEY You will be able to enter Netzach only when you have built a foundation of certainty from which you can begin to build your emotional responses to your relationship with the Divine. The best way to take a vague sense of spirituality and make it concrete is by engaging in some practical activity. You should spend some time growing your own herbs. All you need is a window box, so you can do this no matter where you live. Herbs are ideal to grow, as you will be following the whole cycle of birth, growth, death, and ultimately conversion into something new. While you are watering, picking, and even eating your herbs, focus on the fact that at a miniature level the life of the herbs represents your own life.

✿ ANGEL

malakh–mlak–מלאך–91

MEANING To dream of angels is to be very close to achieving the goal of unity with the Divine. When we have such dreams, it is common to wake up feeling incredibly invigorated and full of purpose. Quite often the world you awaken to will seem less real than the world you visited in your sleep. This is to be expected as the reality of the spiritual world is becoming more deeply embedded in your conscious mind. The value of this dream points to its importance; it has the same value as the Hebrew word for "manna"—the substance that fed the Israelites on their flight from Egypt. It also has the same value as the word *amen*. Clearly, this dream has a profound religious significance for anyone lucky enough to experience it.

THE TREE OF LIFE With a dream so caught up in the very highest of our spiritual aspirations there is only one place where it can properly be placed, and that is in the Sefirah of Keter. This first Sefirah, or the "Crown" of the Tree of Life, is the closest that we as humans can come to as an approximation of the Divine. This is not to say that Keter is the Divine, as the Divine itself lies beyond all human understanding. Indeed, it is said by the Kabbalists that we can define the Divine only in terms of what it is not. While Keter is not God, it is still a level of consciousness that lies outside what can be achieved by a person still in his physical vehicle. The placement of the dream in Keter indicates that your inspirations and insights are now coming directly from the Divine, rather than meaning that your whole being resides in this Sefirah.

THE JOURNEY You probably never expected to get this far on your spiritual quest, and now that you have realized—not through the intellect but through direct experience—that there really is a Divine force with which we can communicate, you may well be somewhat confused as to what to do next.

It is likely that in pursuing your spiritual goals you have had less time to spend with family and friends. Ironically, now that you have reached a pinnacle of spiritual integration, you should begin to focus on your physical life. This is not the same as going back to the life you had before. Everything you do now will be touched by your spiritual experiences, from the way you treat people to the way you do your work. By focusing on the everyday, you will provide an excellent example of the potential for all of us to live in a more compassionate and more considerate manner. To help those

around us is perhaps the highest thanks that any of us can offer to the Divine for what we ourselves have gained.

See Zohar symbol, Angel.

ANGER

za'am–za'am–זעם–117

MEANING The past can be an excellent teacher if we know how to use it correctly. Unfortunately, the past can also be a prison for our emotions, and unless we learn how to come to terms with our history, we will be unable to build ourselves a genuinely happy future.

The initial Zayin in the Hebrew for "anger" tells us that we are still fighting certain elements of our unconscious. The following Ayin, with its association with The Devil card, indicates that this is an unhealthy conflict, while the final Mem strongly suggests that this problem emerges from your relationship with your parents.

THE TREE OF LIFE This dream indicates that you are currently on the path of Peh. This path is linked to the tarot card The Tower of Destruction, a card which points to a catastrophic but essential collapse of some aspect of your worldview. This relates to your view of your parents, an emotional straitjacket that you can take off only when you face up to your anger and resentment. Interestingly, the letter Peh means "mouth," and it is ultimately through talking that you will reach some kind of closure.

THE JOURNEY The value of this dream reduces to 9, which is the value of the letter Teth, meaning "serpent" and associated with great force of will. At the moment, this will is being wasted in reinforcing your past emotions. However, with sufficient effort you could take this powerful force and apply it to your life in a positive way. In order to come to terms with your childhood, you should certainly consider some form of counseling, but there are also ways you can help yourself. The key to resolution is talking, but it can be extremely difficult to be honest with those who bother you emotionally. As silly as it may sound, you should try talking to a photograph of your parents. Allow yourself to get as angry as you feel and say all the things you could never say to their face—you will be surprised at how cathartic the experience is. When the anger has faded you can then speak to them in terms of how you want the relationship to operate in the future, without past resentments getting in the way.

ANNOYANCE

meetrad-mtrd- מטרד -253

MEANING Before you considered the possibility of an alternative spirituality, your life was very organized and content; from your work to your home life, it was all running smoothly. At least that is a comforting way to view the past when you are faced with the confusion that the spiritual path throws at you.

The value of this dream image reduces to 10, which indicates a sense of unity and completion. As this dream does not point to the fulfillment of the Great Work, this sense of completion is the false sense of contentment you had before beginning this journey. However, you knew inside that something—namely, your spiritual life—was lacking. Right now a part of you wishes you had never made that discovery, but if you persist, the annoyance will fade and be replaced by a *genuine* contentment.

THE TREE OF LIFE You are no longer trapped in the solely material world of Malkut, but you have yet to arrive at a new level of consciousness. Your intermittent irritation at the lack of progress and the sense of disorder that has been thrust into your life places you and your dream on the path of Shin. This path often causes a sense of frustration and even anger, but it does eventually lead you into the Sefirah of Hod, where you will be able to configure a way of looking at your life that is again rational and logical but is also infused with a sense of the spiritual.

THE JOURNEY The value of your dream tells you a story of your position right now. The initial 200 is the letter Resh and represents the warm light of the Divine awakening you to the possibility of the spiritual. The following 50 stands for your current low state, as it is the value of the letter Nun associated with the difficulties we can experience as we try and move to a deeper understanding of the Divine. However, the final 3 is the letter Gimel connected to The High Priestess card in the tarot. This final letter is a promise of what you can gain if you persist, since The High Priestess is the guardian of secret wisdom. You should set aside an hour each day for quiet meditation. There should be no subject on which you focus at this stage; it is enough simply for you to achieve a sense of stillness and calm.

ANXIETY

kharadah-chrdh- חרדה -217

MEANING Ironically, this dream is almost a mirror image of the dream of annoyance, in that both represent our response to the initial steps on our spiritual quest. For some of us, this leads to a sense of frustration at the loss of certainty. For you, this loss has resulted in feelings of unease.

Once again, the value of this dream reduces to 10, indicating the certainty that you had before you began the search for your inner truth. Similarly, the value begins with 200 pointing to the letter Resh and the emergence of a sense of the Divine. The following value of 10 is the letter Yod, which can be seen as the dynamic force of God. It may be the sudden nature of your realization of the spiritual dimension that has led to your anxiety.

THE TREE OF LIFE The Hebrew word for "air" shares the same value as the word meaning "anxiety." The element of Air is associated with the mind, and thus this connection reinforces the notion of a mental anxiety that is troubling you. Such feelings are represented in the tarot by The Moon card. This card sits on the path of Qoph, where you and your dream image are also placed. It is worth noting that the path of Qoph also runs out of Malkut and is a literal mirror image of the path of Shin, again linking this dream with the dream of annoyance.

THE JOURNEY To a large extent your task right now is the same as that for those who dream of annoyance—to persist in your endeavor in the hope of future contentment. You should practice regular meditation in order to create the necessary sense of calm within your mind, remembering that the more you practice this, the closer you will come to reaching the next level of consciousness. It will help you a great deal if you drink an infusion of mint tea before your meditation as this herb has great pacifying and calming qualities.

APATHY

khasar heetanyenoot-chsr htha'anyynvth- חסר התעניינות -1269

MEANING Apathy does not seem like a quality that should be seen as evidence of a finely developed sense of spirituality. There is a great difference between a lack of attachment, where we can see the ultimately illusory nature of differences, and simply not being concerned one way or the other. In our day-to-day lives there are very few occasions when we are genuinely apathetic. Usually when we feel that we are unconcerned it is an unconscious defense mechanism against the possibility of emotional upset or the fear of failure. Similarly, in a spiritual context we are not really unconcerned but are simply protecting ourselves from negative feelings.

THE TREE OF LIFE When we reduce the value of this dream we find the number 9, which is the value of the letter Teth. In this dream both aspects of the letter Teth are relevant. On one hand, it tells us that you are deceived into thinking that you are not interested in the possibility of a spiritual dimension to your life. On the other, it serves as a reminder that you will need to gather together all your willpower in order to make the spiritual commitment that will move you out of your current position in the Sefirah of Malkut.

THE JOURNEY It is never easy to begin a long journey, especially when you have no idea of what the destination is or indeed if you will ever arrive. The compression of this dream's value begins with the letter Qoph multiplied by a factor of 10, and this emphasizes the level of anxiety that you are currently experiencing. The subsequent letters, Resh and Samech, advise you that the benevolent aspect of the Divine will support and guide you if you try to make a commitment to the Great Work.

APPARITION

*hofaah-hvpha'ah-*הופעה-166

MEANING This dream may, on initial reflection, seem worrisome or even frightening since we tend to associate apparitions with ghosts and nightmarish fears. In fact, this is a very encouraging dream, as it indicates that you are beginning to make contact with your higher self. The apparition you have seen is a shadowy version of your soul trying to communicate to your conscious self. With time, it may be that this apparition integrates with your everyday personality, enabling you to live to your fullest potential.

The value of the word *apparition* indicates the positive nature of this dream image. When we compress the number of letters to the smallest possible number to get the value of the dream image, we find the three letters Qoph, Samech, and Vav. This combination tells us that the macrocosm (Vav) or the Divine is supporting you (Samech) by communicating with your unconscious (Qoph).

THE TREE OF LIFE It is likely that you are still in the Sefirah of Malkut, beginning to work on your inner self, but still very much in the early stages. However, as this dream relates to an urge from your higher self to offer you aid and guidance, the dream itself sits in the Sefirah of Hesed. This Sefirah is associated with Jupiter and Zeus from mythology and it exerts a protective and merciful force. In many ways, Hesed represents the ideal father, and this is a similar role to that currently being played by your higher self.

THE JOURNEY The fact that you even had a dream of an apparition suggests that you may be unusually sensitive to phenomena that lie beyond the reach of mainstream science. You should try to work on this facility as it will increase your general appreciation of the spiritual, as well as increase the strength of your link with your higher self. A good way is to purchase ESP cards—even a deck of playing cards will do—and practice, over and over, predicting the symbol that you are about to turn over until you repeatedly achieve results that exceed what could be scored by chance alone.

ARCH

*keshet-qshth-*קשת-800

MEANING This dream image is all about choice and destiny. The word *arch* is made up of the three letters that name the paths leading directly out of the Sefirah Malkut. They are often referred to as a rainbow because they offer us an opportunity to experience the joy of the Divine, if we simply choose to traverse one of them. The value itself reduces to 8, which is symbolic of infinity and relates to the fact that the opportunity represented by the three initial paths will remain open for eternity for any individual who makes the spiritual leap of faith to become more than a merely materialistic being.

THE TREE OF LIFE Malkut must be the place on the Tree of Life where we locate this dream. You are standing at the departure point for all prospective seekers after truth and simply have to take the first step. The fact that all three initial paths are featured in the title of this dream indicates that you are in the lucky position of being able to take almost any approach to your inner development and still achieve a level of success. Once you have started, the indications are that you will be hooked, and it will be only a matter of time before you are helping others to make their first explorations into the world of the spiritual.

THE JOURNEY You have great enthusiasm for the road ahead and can harness that enthusiasm to ensure that you make the most of your potential. Each of the three paths out of Malkut represents a particular approach to the Divine: Tav indicates a wholly mystical approach involving prayer and meditation; Qoph suggests a process led by intuition and psychic perception; Shin points to a vigorous and active approach, possibly involving activities such as yoga or tai chi to encourage the growth of spiritual understanding. In commencing your journey, you should try to incorporate aspects of all three approaches, as you will learn something different about yourself from each one.

❧ARM

zroa-zrva'a-זרוע-283

MEANING In the Kabbalah, the Tree of Life can be seen as a representation of both the physical and the spiritual universe, as a map of the development of human consciousness, as a guide to the individual attempting to reach back up to the Divine, or even as a symbolic representation of the human body. In a dream about an arm, the mind is being directed to consider the two sides of the Tree of Life, which correspond to the male and female sides of human nature.

The value of this dream image reduces to 4, suggesting that you have balanced the two competing sides of your nature—the male and the female; the passive and the active. Additionally, when we look at the letters that make up both the title of the dream image and the letters generated through compression, we see that they are evenly distributed across the Tree of Life, again pointing to a good sense of balance.

THE TREE OF LIFE The initial analysis of this dream reveals that you have a fully balanced outlook on the world, and this immediately points to a position in the middle pillar of the Tree of Life. The most appropriate placement for this dream is on the path of Samech. Not only does this path sit centrally on the Tree, but it is also connected to the Temperance card in the tarot. The Temperance card refers to the ideal position where all the competing elements of the personality are in harmony with one another.

THE JOURNEY Having achieved a level of emotional stability that anyone could justly be proud of, you are now approaching the Sefirah of Tiferet. This is no small achievement since to arrive at this central Sefirah requires a rare level of integrity and awareness. In order to maintain this awareness and further develop your relationship to the Divine, more refinements are necessary. We can understand ourselves best only when we have experienced living in a way that is contrary to our own beliefs and preferences. Your task over the next few weeks is to select a trait each day that is part of your natural personality and to live the opposite of that trait for the whole day. So, for instance, if by nature you are soft-spoken and retiring, you should spend a day being brash and opinionated.

See Zohar symbol, Arm.

ARMY

tsava-tzba-צבא-93

MEANING To dream of an army should not automatically be seen as an indicator of an internal conflict, as this is a dream of soldiers as opposed to a dream of warfare. Certainly this dream suggests a very active and dynamic approach to your spirituality, and this should be seen in a positive rather than a negative light.

Aleister Crowley, the famous English mystic and hermetic Kabbalist, laid the foundations of a new system of spiritual development that relied very much on an energetic approach to achieving union with one's higher self. It is interesting that the key number in his system was 93—the same number as the value of this dream image.

THE TREE OF LIFE Due both to the vigorous nature of the spirituality suggested by the dream of an army and to the link to Crowley's system—known as Thelema—indicated by the value of this dream, the appropriate path is that of Ayin. The path of Ayin reaches from Hod to Tiferet and thus suggests the use of your intellect to inform the development of your inner self. This coincides with the image of an army in the sense of creating an army of rational reasons with which to tackle any residual doubts about the validity of your spiritual quest.

THE JOURNEY Sometimes you find that your desire for a closer understanding of the nature of the universe is frustrated by what you find in books and among groups that might guide you in your search. You are looking for a system that has more vigor and a little less fluff than you have so far encountered. If you are interested in a rigorous and intellectually stimulating exercise, you might consider looking at some of the works of Aleister Crowley, as the value of this dream suggests that you will find much to interest you in his approach.

AROMA

neekhoakh-nychvch-ניחוח-82

MEANING In the mystical context, when we think of aromas we consider incense and perfumes used in order to raise our consciousness or to assist in creating an environment where that can occur. In the spelling of the dream image, we have a description of the meditation process. The letter Nun represents the sorrow that leads to the desire for union with the Divine, while the letter Yod indicates the Divine spark descending to us. The letter Vav represents the element of Air and, as such, is associated with incense and the dream title itself. This letter is surrounded by two Cheths, which indicate the protective force that emanates from the combined energy of your meditative force and the light descending from the higher.

THE TREE OF LIFE The value of the word meaning "aroma" in Hebrew is equivalent to the Hebrew for the angel Anyal—the angel associated with the planet Venus and the Sefirah Netzach. This dream image suits Netzach particularly well because this Sefirah, as one might expect from its connection with Venus, is linked to the use of incense and perfumes as a means to connect with the Divine.

THE JOURNEY Having moved into the Sefirah of Netzach, you will find that your creative inspiration grows and grows. You may find yourself tempted to take art lessons or to learn to play that instrument you've always promised yourself you would learn. Even if this means spending a little money on yourself, you should go ahead. When you are expressing yourself creatively, you should bear in mind that this is another form of spiritual activity. Allow your innermost feelings a voice; when you do so, you will feel much more rounded and whole as a person.

ARREST

*maasar-masr-מאסר-*301

MEANING If you were to look for a psychological explanation of this dream image, it is likely that the dream analyst would focus on an inner sense of guilt that led to you have a dream in which you are arrested. From a Kabbalistic point of view, this dream also functions as something of an accusation, from your higher self to your ego-driven everyday personality.

Right now you are still very focused on the material aspects of your life. It is of greater concern to you at the moment to lose one of your prized possessions than to miss the opportunity to develop the life of your soul. The value of this dream image reduces to 4, which represents the material world, but on the encouraging side the final number, 1, corresponds to the letter Aleph. This letter represents unity with the Divine and indicates the possibility of success in the future.

THE TREE OF LIFE While we might expect to place this dream on the Sefirah of Malkut, it belongs in fact to the path of Shin. You have yet to make significant progress, but the existence of the value of 300, which relates to the letter Shin, and the fact that your dreams are pointing out to you that you do need to change indicate that you have already begun to move out of Malkut.

THE JOURNEY It is never easy to accept criticism. In a peculiar way, it is particularly difficult to take criticism that comes from within ourselves, possibly because it is so much harder to ignore. If you wish to get through the path of Shin, you must be willing to make some difficult decisions and changes in your lifestyle. The first thing you should do is make a point of giving away a tenth of your disposable income for at least two or three months. The point of this is not just to recognize the importance of charity but to free yourself from your attachment to things rather than to truths.

ARROW

*khets-chtz-חץ-*98

MEANING This dream image is both rare and extremely encouraging. The idea of an arrow immediately creates the image of a perfectly straight and swift flight to a chosen target. This is an excellent description of the current trajectory of your spiritual development. You have immersed yourself in metaphysical matters to an extent where your development toward the Divine has taken on an almost inevitable and unstoppable momentum.

One Hebrew word that holds the same value as the word meaning "arrow" is "white." This carries with it connotations of priesthood and a high level of devotion to a mystical way of life. The connection of this dream's value to The Star card from the tarot further backs up the suggestion of untroubled progression toward the goal of the Great Work.

THE TREE OF LIFE At the apex of the Tree of Life stands Keter, or "Crown." This is the Sefirah that receives the Divine light directly without the imposition of any form or reduction in its purity and power. The color associated with Keter is pure white, and this again links back to the value of the dream image. As human beings we can never achieve a state of consciousness that equates directly to Keter, as it represents a level of spirituality that transcends the physical. However, you have achieved a position where your inspiration and intuition is directly informed by the higher will emanating out of Keter.

THE JOURNEY When you have achieved a certain level of inner balance, you have a duty to use your understanding to help others follow your example. You are in exactly this position and your task is to determine precisely how you should go about honoring that spiritual obligation. The image of the arrow suggests both a narrow focus and a high level of dynamism. If we apply this to possible ways of setting an appropriate example of a fully integrated person, we can narrow down the field of possible areas of activity. The narrow focus implies activity on a local level rather than on any grand scheme. The level of energetic activity combined with the obvious conflict potential of the image of an arrow strongly suggests that you should in some way work to help the disabled and disadvantaged members of your community.

ASCENDING
*aleeyah-a'alyyh-*עלייה-125

MEANING You are making good progress and this dream confirms that. Even in standard psychological terms to dream of ascending indicates a person who feels good about himself and his direction in life. When we place this dream in a Kabbalistic context, the idea of ascending becomes far more literal because it suggests a gradual rising of the soul along the paths of the Tree of Life.

This is a very gradual progression, but it is a pace that you feel comfortable with. The value of this dream reduces to 8, the value of the letter Cheth. The letter Cheth is all about protection and defense. It is likely that its presence in the value of the dream image indicates your need to take things slowly in order to have the ability to accept the changes that occur as your sense of the spiritual increases.

THE TREE OF LIFE One of the ways in which you increase your level of comfort with the concept of spiritual advancement is by seeing it partly as a process where the Divine is reaching out to you, rather than by viewing it solely as a climb upward that you have to make by yourself. This dream is situated on the path of Kaph, which mirrors the view of advancement outlined above. The Sefirah of Hesed lies at the end of the path of Kaph, and Hesed represents the paternal aspect of the Divine. In this way, we can see the energy of Hesed reaching down and helping to pull you up toward the Divine.

THE JOURNEY It is sometimes difficult for you to deal with the notion of spirituality in the abstract. You tend to be a tactile person who likes his world to have a sense of solidity to it. In terms of your spiritual pursuits, you will also prefer practices that have a physical element to them. This preference is indicated by the importance of the letter Kaph to this dream. The letter Kaph means "the open hand" or "palm" and is associated with practical activities. It would be a good idea for you to consider taking up yoga or tai chi, as these pursuits combine the physical with the spiritual and will work very well for you.

ASHES
*efer-aphr-*אפר-281

MEANING We associate ashes with funerals, grief, and a significant sense of loss. However, ashes are also connected with traditional spiritual practices, from the customs of Ash Wednesday for Christians to the rites of the Sadhus of India. This dream reduces to 11, which symbolizes the hermetic arts, and so we should see this dream as an indication of spiritual progress rather than of loss and bereavement.

Additionally, the Hebrew word for "ashes" has an equivalent value to the Hebrew for "crown" and "adornment." Such associated words point to an individual of considerable achievement.

THE TREE OF LIFE The religious connotations of this dream all point to experiences that are contemplative rather than active. They are suggestive of an attempt to understand the Divine at a level that penetrates the whole being spiritually, emotionally, and even physically. This dream sits on the path of Beth, which emanates from Keter or "Crown" and leads into the Sefirah of Binah, also known as the Sefirah of understanding.

THE JOURNEY Your deep spirituality is combined with an equally developed sense of duty and obligation. You always try to ensure that those close to you have their needs met and are well looked after before you give yourself time to spend on your personal needs. While this is an admirable quality, you need to learn to allow yourself a little more personal space. This is particularly important now because in order to move on in terms of your inner development, you need to spend some time alone. Ideally, you should go on a mini-pilgrimage for at least a week or so, visiting a range of places that have personal spiritual significance for you. Spend time absorbing the feelings that emanate from these places and allow those feelings to stay with you and support you in your search for the ultimate truths.

ATTIC

aleeyat gag–a'alyyth gg– עליית גג –526

MEANING According to psychological interpretations, buildings in dreams represent our inner emotional structures. With such an approach, an attic would signify those thoughts and feelings that we try to hide from the world and even from ourselves. From a Kabbalistic point of view a similar interpretation would apply, but in this case the attic represents the seat of our inner understanding of the spiritual realm.

The value of this dream reduces to 13, which points to a major change about to occur in your life. The implication of this dream is that those ideas about spirituality that have been hidden away in your mental attic are about to burst through into your conscious mind.

THE TREE OF LIFE Attics are dark and somewhat spooky places. Even as adults we may feel a slight sense of trepidation as we climb up the ladder into that obscure space filled with spider webs, unseen small creatures, who knows what memories. Of course, once we switch on the light we are comfortable in our new surroundings. Right now you are entering the spiritual attic, but you have yet to find the light. Consequently, this dream sits on the path of Qoph. This path takes us out of Malkut and toward a higher level of consciousness, but it is fraught with worry and anxiety as represented by its connection to the tarot card The Moon.

THE JOURNEY How best to find that light switch to illuminate the truths that lie hidden in your unconscious? You could try the usual approach of groping around in the dark with the hope that eventually your hand will find the right switch. A far better approach is to have a map that will point you in the right direction. You should give some serious thought to joining a meditation group with a respected teacher. After a few sessions of guided meditation, you will find the switch increasingly easy to locate.

ATONEMENT

keepor–kypvr– כיפור –316

MEANING The concept of atonement is crucial to most major religions. It refers to a process whereby we are forgiven for our transgressions on the basis of genuinely regretting our negative behaviors. On a wider scale, the idea of atonement can be seen as a symbolic means of beginning a new chapter in your life. It is at this level that this dream image is relevant to your spiritual development.

When we look at the letters that make up the value of the word, we see a short description of the process that you now need to go through. The initial Shin refers to the energy of the Divine within you coming alive and driving you on toward your spiritual goals. The following Yod indicates the input of the Divine responding to your initial efforts. Finally we have Vav, which, having a value of 6, represents the macrocosm and the ultimate goal of union with the Divine.

THE TREE OF LIFE It is the path of Vav that best represents the positioning of this dream. The path of Vav is connected with the element of Air, and as this relates to our thought processes, it can be associated with the reflection you need to engage in so that you can move up toward a new stage of development. Additionally, the path of Vav carries with it the merciful energy of the Sefirah of Hesed, and it is this aspect of the Divine that is invoked in the process of atonement.

THE JOURNEY Atonement need not be a one-way process. It is certainly true that in order to feel closer to the Divine it is necessary for us to feel comfortable with ourselves and our past actions. As long as we are beset by feelings of regret or guilt, we will find it difficult to believe that we can become more spiritually integrated. However, you can also reflect the mercy that emanates from Hesed in your interactions with others. You should make a list of all the people whom you have hurt or upset in the last year or so and then, over the next month, make a point of doing something special for each of them as a way of redressing the harm.

ATTORNEY

orekh deen–a'avrk dyn– עורך דין –360

MEANING There is no easy road to spiritual insight. No matter what path we take, there will always be the need to carefully distinguish between that which will move us forward and that which has only the appearance of valid spiritual guidance. Unfortunately, we have no other way to decide than to rely on our inner judgment. The value of this dream is all about the exercise of proper judgment. At the most obvious level, the dream title itself refers to a profession where clear judgment and analytical skills are paramount. Additionally, the value of the dream is the same as the value of the word Shin in Hebrew.

This word, meaning "tooth," is also, as we know, one of the Hebrew letters and is associated with the tarot card Judgment.

THE TREE OF LIFE There are a number of pointers in the evaluation of this dream image that indicate that it belongs to the path of Shin. The two most obvious signs are the equivalence of the total value to the word Shin itself and the fact that when we compress the word we find that the initial value gives us the letter Shin. In your case, rather than your feeling the harsh journey that is represented by the so-called biting path, this dream placement relates to your appropriately ruthless treatment of your preconceptions and assumptions regarding the world of the spiritual. The process of discarding outdated conceptions of the world is one that you feel entirely happy with, and so while you are biting you do not feel bitten.

THE JOURNEY Spiritual cleansing is an immensely important part of any journey toward the Divine. In the world of alchemy, we have the expression *"Solve et coagula,"* which effectively means to destroy and re-create. It is this breaking down and rebuilding of the self that sits at the heart of the Great Work. Now that you have begun the job of pulling apart the old frameworks that governed your thoughts, you must be careful that the new frameworks you put in their place are helpful to your quest. The best way to ensure this is to take things very slowly and, with each new idea that you have about the nature of the spiritual, be sure that you carefully balance against its opposite to see if you really are comfortable with all of its implications. On a very positive note, the value of this dream is equivalent to the value of the Hebrew for "messiah," which suggests that you have a good chance of making the right decisions.

AUCTION

*mekheerah-mkyrh-*מכירה*-*310

MEANING Very often the significance of a dream is revealed not only in its obvious content but in certain phrases associated with the subject of the dream. This was recognized by both Freud and Jung, who looked at the importance of puns as they occur in dream narratives. In the case of an auction, we are looking at a scenario where the prize always goes to the highest bidder. From a Kabbalistic standpoint, this could mean the reward of spiritual insight going to the one who strives hardest to achieve it.

However, the value of the dream reduces to 4, and as a result the dream indicates a concern with material goods and possessions. The dream is actually pointing to a tendency in the dreamer to give his attention to the highest bidder, indicating that the dreamer still measures a bid for his attention in terms of its material worth.

THE TREE OF LIFE Not surprisingly, this dream lies within the Sefirah of Malkut, as it is a message to the dreamer that he needs to begin to consider the spiritual realm, rather than simply focus on the world around him. In order to shift his perspective up toward the Divine, the dreamer needs to look not at the value of things but at the things that he values.

THE JOURNEY When someone is deeply wedded to the consumer culture of the modern world, it can sometimes take a real shock to the system to shake him out of his current set of values. If you have this dream, there are some simple ways you can begin to force yourself to reevaluate your way of living. For instance, you could attend an auction, ideally one where very expensive goods are being sold. Having soaked up the atmosphere of wealth, take a drive through the poorest neighborhoods in your community. The contrast should make you consider your values very carefully indeed.

AUTUMN

*stav-sthyv-*סתיו*-*476

MEANING Every season has its own atmosphere and autumn is no exception. When the leaves begin to fall and the nights to draw in, there is a sense of the year pulling to a close, but in a warm and reassuring way, unlike the bitterness of winter. When we look at the spelling of the Hebrew for "autumn," we see that the first two letters replicate this state of affairs. On one hand, we have the letter Tav, signifying the suffering that is associated with the increasing cold of the end of the year, while next to Tav is the letter Samech, which indicates the supportive energy that we feel at this time of year. Symbolically, this dream represents the process whereby we move from the comfort of the physical world to the uncertainty of the spiritual. Reassuringly, the dream image also indicates that the Divine will is there to support us as we make this transition.

THE TREE OF LIFE Your spiritual insight is growing and you are now moving out of Malkut toward Yesod. The path that refers to this dream image is the path of Tav. It is connected to feelings of suffering and melancholy, which you are now likely to experience. Additionally, it is the path of The Universe card in the tarot, which points to a positive completion of a phase in your life.

THE JOURNEY When you begin to explore your inner self, it is very easy to give up before you have achieved very much. Often it will take a considerable amount of time from the initial decision to take your spiritual life more seriously to the point when you feel some form of definite confirmation from the higher self that you have indeed made a sensible decision. While you are waiting for this confirmation, it is important to find some form of reassurance from other sources. Seeking out like-minded people who have traveled further down the road will certainly help. Equally helpful is to consider how many events in the natural world and, indeed, in people's lives can occur in a positive way only when something that initially seemed distressing has fully taken place.

AWAKE
*paeel-pa'ayl-פעיל-*190

MEANING In reading through many mystical texts, it becomes common to see references to "the dead" or "the sleeping." These phrases are not to be taken literally but relate to the state of the spiritual consciousness of people who have not recognized their spiritual level of existence. In this dream, we have the opposite of this reference, so we can infer that the dreamer is someone who has begun to develop his relationship with his higher self.

In the spelling of the dream title, we see that the initial Peh indicates your receiving the word of the Divine. This can be inferred from the relationship between the dream's overall value and the fact that Peh means "mouth" in Hebrew. Similarly, the final Lamed tells us that we are being driven vigorously toward the goal of the Great Work.

THE TREE OF LIFE The compression of this dream's value gives us the letters Qoph and Tzaddi. In terms of the Tree of Life, both of these letters sit on paths that link to the Sefirah of Netzach. Additionally, placing this dream on Netzach makes a great deal of sense when we look at the implications of the content of the dream. Netzach represents the internalization of the spiritual within our emotional makeup and follows on from the Sefirah of Hod, where we establish a rational relationship with the Divine. It is perfectly reasonable to see Netzach

as the point at which we become fully awake to the spiritual in all its forms.

THE JOURNEY Once you have awakened to the reality of the spiritual, the next stage in your attempt to form a link with the Divine is to find a means of contacting your higher self and allowing it to speak through you. When your higher self is directing your actions, you are far more likely to make the right decisions in your life. The Sefirah of Netzach is associated with expression and with emotions. In this dream, Netzach's emotional aspect and its connection with Venus are highlighted. This suggests that you need to review your current relationships in the light of your new spirituality and to listen to your intuition as to which relationships to pursue.

BABY
*teenock-thynvq-תינוק-*566

MEANING

A dream of a baby reflects the innocence and infinite potential possessed by all newborns. The baby represents your current state—you have discovered the chance of being reborn as more than simply a material being. This realization that reality does not begin and end with career, money, and relationships is so significant that to experience it is to be reborn.

The value of this dream is equivalent to the value of the Hebrew for "the shadow of death." This may seem a strange association, but it holds a great and simple truth for all genuine seekers after spiritual insight. It is a fact that from the minute we are born we begin the slow process that ultimately leads to our death. Our mortality is the one certainty that exists from our first to our last breath. From a Kabbalistic point of view, the acceptance that even in our earliest moments we are only a heartbeat away from death is a sign of considerable personal development. It is only from such a position of acceptance that we can truly be said to be as innocent as a baby because innocence requires a lack of fear.

THE TREE OF LIFE Another fundamental aspect of a baby's life is that it is incredibly reliant on others for support and assistance. Without the guidance and teaching of loving parents, a baby is unlikely to grow into a happy and well-rounded individual. In terms of your spiritual progress, you also need a loving guide to show you the way. For this reason, the dream sits on the path of Samech, which leads from Yesod to the Sefirah of Tiferet. This path is appropriate because the letter Samech means "prop" and can be seen as symbolic of the guiding hand or staff of the Divine on which we may lean for support and reassurance.

THE JOURNEY What you should take from this dream is a certainty that there is a higher power watching over you and supporting you in your search for ultimate truths. This does not, of course, mean that your life is suddenly going to run smoothly or that you will never again feel down or doubtful or hurt. However, when you do go through upsetting periods in your life, you should remember that babies are incredibly accepting. If you simply accept what life deals out to you and try to see in it something from which you can learn, you will have made a great leap forward.

See Zohar symbol, Baby.

BAKING
*le'efot-laphvth-*לאפות-517

MEANING In this dream, the image is concerned primarily with our activity. It is worth noting that baking is not quite the same as cooking. When we really think about it, baking implies a particular level of care and attention that may not be present in the daily cooking of meals. In addition, we tend to associate baking with special occasions and special food. These associations are very appropriate to this dream, since it relates to the careful preparation and nurturing of the inner self. The value of this dream reduces to 13, which indicates that a significant life change is on the horizon.

THE TREE OF LIFE To continue the analogy, although you are baking, you have not yet produced any finished products. Right now you are in the Sefirah of Malkut, still embedded in the purely physical but making good progress toward leaping free of the materialistic constraints of the modern worldview. The final 7 in the value of this dream refers to the letter Zayin, meaning "sword," and is suggestive of your view of this process as something of a battle. This is quite appropriate, because you are still attached to the comforts of your existence and are battling to reduce your dependency on such things.

THE JOURNEY First and foremost, you should congratulate yourself because you have already taken perhaps the most difficult step. The decision to try to make more of your life is a great act of bravery. Once you decide that there should be more to life, you run the risk of failing to achieve that something more and are then condemned to a terrible sense of loss. Your nature suggests that your bond with the Divine would be best strengthened by engaging in some practical activity. Since you are in the sphere of Malkut, a good activity would be to take up gardening. As you are planting and digging, you should try to sense the connection between the simple dirt and the complexity of the universe.

BALCONY
*meerpeset-mrpsth-*מרפסת-780

MEANING We can see for what looks like miles; there is a certain sense of relaxation and confidence, of having a fuller view of the world than is available to those beneath us. This is how we often feel when standing on a high balcony looking down at the rest of the world. In many ways, this exemplifies some of the common feelings that we experience as we begin to make real progress in our spiritual search. The value of this dream is connected to the tarot as an entire series of symbols and so represents a state of mind where we feel that we possess a significant store of understanding. However, a note of caution is sounded by the fact that the value of this dream reduces to 15. This number is related to feelings of power and indicates that we must temper any feelings of achievement with an appropriate level of awe in the face of the wonder of the universe.

THE TREE OF LIFE The feeling of standing on a balcony looking down is a very simplified image of the experience of entering the Sefirah of Yesod. A level of spiritual insight has been achieved and it is easy to believe that we have climbed closer to the Divine than is actually the case. It is this phase of consciousness that can lead people to set up their own meditation or other New Age groups. These can be a good thing, but the intoxicating nature of Yesod can lead to pride and self aggrandizement, as seen in the number of self-proclaimed gurus that have emerged over the last few decades.

THE JOURNEY You are at a crucial point in your inner journey, a crossroads, you might say. One direction leads to further development and the gradual accumulation of wisdom, always with a sense of humility and gratitude to the creative force that makes such a journey possible. The other path leads to stagnation and a reliance on the reassurance of others that we are in fact already sufficiently enlightened. As Yesod is associated with the element of Air, the best way to ground yourself and prevent a loss of direction is to draw in the calming and deepening energy of the element of Water. This can be achieved in a number of ways, from literally spending time in the water, either swimming or floating in a relaxed state, to taking a course in developing your emotional skills, which will strengthen the element of Water within you.

BALDNESS

*kereakh-kyrch-*קירח-238

MEANING It is ironic that many men attempt to disguise their baldness, often in ways that are more likely to provoke ridicule than if they openly displayed their hair loss. To dream of baldness and attempts to hide it suggests that you are moving beyond superficial concerns, such as worrying about other people's perceptions of your personal appearance. As the dreamer, your higher self is attempting to reassure you that you are making significant strides in your spiritual work.

THE TREE OF LIFE The sense of seniority that is associated with baldness is reflected in the fact that this dream sits on the path of Heh. This path is linked to the tarot card The Emperor, which represents a figure of authority and respect in the world. In many cases The Emperor is focused primarily on a purely material form of authority. However, in the context of this dream, the card refers to an individual who is to be respected for both his spiritual and his practical wisdom and experience.

THE JOURNEY The final 8 in the value of this dream image points not to a desire to protect yourself but to the fact that you are seen as a protective figure by those around you. Additionally, the initial Kaph, meaning "hand," in the Hebrew for "baldness" indicates that you can offer your support in an extremely practical way. In order to develop spiritually, you need to cultivate this aspect of your personality. You should consider getting heavily involved in community activities and organizations such as the local Scouts association or some other volunteer group.

BALLOON

*kador poreakh-*כדור פורח-524

MEANING When we are children, a party just isn't proper without balloons. As adults, we appreciate that balloons are so appealing partly because they are purely fun, with absolutely no useful purpose whatsoever. What may be harder to hold on to as we grow up is that this lack of function is extremely important. If we are to fully appreciate the wonder of the universe, we must learn to value things for

themselves and not for any useful purpose they may serve.

The value of this dream image contains the values of the letter Kaph in both its normal and "final" forms (20 and 500). The letter Kaph is linked with all kinds of practical activities, and there is a clue here that functionless amusement may have greater importance than we realize. The final 4, which is associated with the letter Daleth, meaning "door," tells us that if we allow ourselves such simple enjoyment, we may open the door to a new level of consciousness.

THE TREE OF LIFE It is easy to get caught up in the idea that a spiritual quest should be very dry, intellectual, and somber. In fact, nothing could be further from the truth. While a certain amount of seriousness is essential to connect with the Divine, we should never forget that the Supreme Law of the Universe is Love and that this can be as playful as it can be serious. This dream lies on the path of Tzaddi, which carries you toward the Sefirah of Netzach, where you can realize the emotive aspect of your spiritual personality. The association of Tzaddi with the tarot card The Star indicates that your progress is being guided and assured from above.

THE JOURNEY In very simple terms, you need to let yourself go. While you have developed a very reverent attitude toward issues of spirituality, this has led you to become rather somber in your outlook on life. It is time to remind yourself that your soul is a joyful being that is at its happiest when reveling in the pleasure of its existence. Children have not yet learned to suppress their drive toward pleasure, and getting involved in a play group or simply spending time with your own children on their terms will pay dividends in terms of your inner development. If you have no children or cannot get involved in a local volunteer group working with young people, why not dig out some of your old toys from the attic and just have fun!

BANISHMENT

*geroosh-gyrvsh-*גירוש-519

MEANING One of the key distinctions of the "hermetic" approach to the Great Work, compared to that taken by the major religions of the world, is the fact that in the Western Mystery Tradition we are individually responsible for forming our relationship with the Divine. This can become a somewhat lonely experience since the very nature of the work is that we begin to develop ways of looking at the world that differ from the views of those around us. This dream image represents that sense of being cut off or banished from the rest of the world. The final Shin of the Hebrew for "banishment" along with the final Teth in the compression of the dream's title point to a difficult and testing time ahead. However, the central letter Yod in the compression of the dream image tells us that at the heart of our difficult experiences we can find the spark of the Divine.

THE TREE OF LIFE As the alchemists would tell us, there are a number of distinct stages to the perfection of the human soul and the completion of the Great Work. While some of these are joyful, others can be emotionally troubling and may even make us wish we had never started on our quest for truth. The key thing to do at these times is to persevere, since this is the best route to success in all things.

This dream sits on the path of Lamed, which leads into the Sefirah of Gevurah. It is in Gevurah that we learn to fully appreciate the necessity of conflict and loss in life, and to understand that in time, all losses become gains and all conflicts lead to resolution. The path of Lamed represents both the potentially traumatic nature of your current position as well as the driving force of the Divine urging you on to achieve your spiritual goals.

THE JOURNEY When we begin to realize that changes in our consciousness have affected our relationships with those close to us, it can be tempting to try to reverse the process in order to maintain those emotional ties. Your task now is to find some quiet time for yourself; drinking an infusion of rosemary tea will help to put you in the right frame of mind. You should then begin to work through all of your friends and loved ones and think of new ways in which you can build relationships with them that do not require you to lose the insights you have gained through your spiritual development.

BANK

*bank-bnq-*בנק-152

MEANING It would seem reasonable to assume that a dream about a bank would relate to financial matters rather than concerns of the soul. However, the key aspect of a bank is that it offers us security. In Kabbalistic terms, this dream is about the desire for security and, to a certain extent, the wish to pass the responsibility for that security to somebody else.

These feelings are perfectly natural, and it may often take a number of years before people are genuinely able to take full responsibility for the state of

their soul. The unwillingness to take on the burden of responsibility is born not of laziness but fear and anxiety. This is emphasized by the reduction of the value of this dream image to 8. The letter Cheth, which is associated with defense and protection, has a value of 8, and right now you are looking for some kind of spiritual protection.

THE TREE OF LIFE Throughout history, cultures have associated anxiety and fear with the influence of the Moon. In the Kabbalah, this symbolism is maintained as The Moon card in the tarot, which represents feelings of concern and uncertainty that may reach unhealthy levels if not dealt with effectively. The Moon card is connected with the path of Qoph and it is on this path that we can locate your dream. The letter Qoph means "head" and can be taken to signify that your fears are destined to remain in your mind rather than to be realized.

THE JOURNEY You need to try to make a connection with your higher self as this will provide some of the reassurance that you seek. In the hermetic tradition, you are solely responsible for your inner development. However, this philosophy also believes that a spark of the Divine exists within each of us. Once you connect with that spark, you are no longer alone. A good way to start is to engage in some quiet meditation, ideally while burning frankincense. Once relaxed, you should ask the questions that are troubling you. If you listen closely enough, you will hear the voice of your higher self telling you the answers you need to hear.

BANKRUPT

*poshet regel-pvsht rgl-*פושט רגל-618

MEANING To be financially bankrupt is a devastating experience, but to be spiritually bankrupt is far worse, since money has only a temporary value. If we fail to give our inner self any value, we run the risk of living this life at the expense of our long-term spiritual existence.

The reduction of the value of this dream gives us 15, which connects to The Devil card in the tarot. In the context of this dream image, The Devil card refers to a conscious decision to reject the spiritual in favor of the physical. This is a tragic mistake for anyone to make since there is no reason why one cannot take a spiritual path through life and still enjoy the physicality and sensuality of his human existence at the same time.

THE TREE OF LIFE Given the absence of a spiritual quest in this dream image, it is clear that your state of consciousness is fixed firmly in the Sefirah of Malkut. Certain elements in the spelling of the dream title indicate that the lack of spirituality stems not from disbelief so much as from some deeply distressing incident in your life that has caused you to reject the possibility of a spiritual reality—almost as a protest against the emotional upset you have suffered. This is understandable, and can be overcome if you are able to move from Malkut to the difficult path of Shin.

THE JOURNEY Until you overcome your sense of the unfairness of the world, you are unlikely to move forward in a spiritual sense. Additionally, your current state of mind is likely to hamper your emotional life and indeed your sense of self-esteem. Life is undoubtedly cruel at times and can seem terribly unfair. However, when you look closely at the world around you, you should see that your experiences, while upsetting, do not indicate an absence of the Divine. In all aspects of the universe, we can see the need for an element of loss in order to gain an element of new growth. Consider, for instance, the process of planting a field. In order to produce five strong plants, you would need to plant perhaps twice that number. You should spend the next few weeks looking at a range of different aspects of the world around you, attempting to see where this "loss leading to growth" relationship occurs.

BANQUET

*meseebah–msybh–*מסיבה*-*117

MEANING We tend to associate banquets with finery, good taste, and the wealthy. The general view is that these are gracious affairs, and many people aspire to this kind of atmosphere by organizing their own dinner parties. However, if we look behind the surface, we see an event that is characterized by excess and superficiality. More food than could possibly be eaten is provided, people talk to others simply because they have been seated adjacent to them, and all conversation is kept to the safest of topics. If we look at the value of the dream, we see that by compression we produce the letters Qoph, Yod, and Zayin. The story they tell is of a central Divine spark (Yod), which, on one hand, is causing you to reconsider your worldview (Qoph), while you, on the other hand, are struggling to fight against this disturbance to your established way of seeing the world (Zayin). The image of a banquet means it is likely that you are distracting yourself with physical pleasures and material indulgences as a way to resist altering your perspective. Nevertheless, we must remember that conviviality and social-

izing, in themselves, are healthy and spiritually appropriate aspects of our lives.

THE TREE OF LIFE This dream represents the effect of entering Yesod without the necessary attention to your continuing spiritual development. At the same time, as you open up to the reality of a spiritual dimension to life, you are also likely to become far more attracted to glamour and sensuality, as these are also associated with the Sefirah of Yesod. While these are not negative in themselves, they can be used as unconscious distractions from your inner development.

THE JOURNEY There are plenty of occasions in your spiritual development when it will be wholly appropriate to enjoy material comforts, but this is not the time. Right now you are too easily distracted and will find it very easy to ignore your spiritual potential because you are simply having too much fun. What you must achieve is a level of discipline in your life. This means setting aside at least two evenings a week to spend alone, quietly meditating or reading. Initially, you will find yourself making any number of excuses to avoid this, but if you persevere you will never look back.

BAPTISM

tveelah le natsroor–tblyh lntzrvth–
מבליה לנצרות*-*832

MEANING When we dream of something that is clearly significant in spiritual or religious terms, it usually points to some profound change in life that will have far-reaching consequences. The dream of baptism is no exception, as is indicated by the fact that when we reduce its value we find the number 13, which is symbolic of significant life-changing events.

Additionally, the initial value of 800 relates to the letter Peh, and this is connected to the tarot card The Tower. While it can be a disturbing experience the Tower indicates a major disruption in our life, either internally or externally, that will have significant and positive long-term results. Clearly, the notion of a baptism hints at the nature of such a life-defining event.

THE TREE OF LIFE The image of baptism signifies the acceptance of an individual into a particular religious path. In the context of your spiritual development, it indicates that you have made a genuine commitment to discovering your inner truth. We must have made this commitment before we can begin to climb the Tree of Life, and so this dream lies on the path of Tau, which is the first path to carry us out the Sefirah of Malkut.

THE JOURNEY When we have made a major decision, such as the one to seriously pursue a spiritual goal, it can be very hard after a few days to maintain our momentum. Very often this is because, in every respect other than our decision, the way we live has not changed at all. You can help to consolidate your decision by positive action if you begin to make some significant alterations to your daily routine. This could be as simple as getting up an hour earlier to practice yoga or as complex as completely reorganizing your home, your diet, and your social life.

BARBER

sapar-sapar-spr-ספר-340

MEANING Traditionally, a barber's role had as much to do with shaving as with cutting hair. It is this traditional role that is important in terms of understanding the spiritual import of this dream image. When we begin to make real progress in our inner development, it could be compared to a very close shave. As we approach a link with our higher self, we are cutting away that which is no longer useful and obscures our vision of our true nature.

The value of this dream can be reduced to 7, which is the value of the letter Zayin, meaning "sword." This association indicates again the need to cut away those things that interfere with our spiritual development. In the same way that we can cut ourselves while shaving, we have to be careful when we engage in spiritual pruning.

THE TREE OF LIFE There are three routes out of the Sefirah of Malkut, and each one brings with it its own difficulties and concerns. The path that links to this dream is the path of Shin. Otherwise known as the "biting path," this path is challenging as it forces us to face ourselves honestly. In order to cross the path of Shin into the Sefirah of Hod, we must strip ourselves of the protective veneer that we build up over our lives in order to avoid dealing with the faults and insecurities that we all possess.

THE JOURNEY The task that lies before us is very straightforward, but that does not mean that it will in any way be easy to accomplish. When we try to think about ourselves objectively, we always face the problem that if an insecurity or failing is significant enough, we may unconsciously screen it out. The best way to avoid this problem is to ask a friend to detail your faults for you, but be warned—you will have to be very persuasive if you want to be certain of an honest reply. Once you have a sense of those areas in your personality that need to be corrected, it will help to visualize being on the receiving end of those particular traits to fully understand why they need to be removed.

BAREFOOT

yakhef-ychph-יחף-98

MEANING Few dreams are more auspicious than that of being barefoot. It is very common in religious worship to remove footwear as a symbol of humility. Additionally, it can be seen as sign of growing out of the need for any trappings of status; the person who happily goes barefoot is more concerned about his relationship with the world and the Divine than anybody else's view of him as an individual.

The value of this dream contains both the letter Tzaddi (90) and the letter Cheth (8). Tzaddi tells us that the dreamer is being guided in his spiritual quest by higher agencies. The letter Cheth indicates that the dreamer is also being protected, and this adds up to a profile of an individual who has much to learn and much to offer his community once he achieves a level of spiritual insight.

THE TREE OF LIFE Since you are receiving an unusual level of guidance and input from above, it is not surprising that this dream's location on the Tree of Life is determined not by your development but by the source of the assistance you are receiving. Consequently, this dream sits in the Sefirah of Keter. Keter is also known as the "Crown" and represents the closest that human understanding can get to a description of the Divine. The symbolic color of Keter is white, and it is wholly appropriate that the value of the Hebrew for "barefoot" is the same as the Hebrew for "white."

THE JOURNEY The hardest part of your journey is learning to accept it as your destiny. To dream of being barefoot means that you are obliged to follow a spiritual quest not just for your benefit but for the benefit of those around you and in your wider community. It will be much easier for you to accept that you are being guided by your higher self when you are able to be consciously aware of its presence. To achieve this, you should meditate in a completely dark room. As you relax, slowly clear your mind of all thoughts except the single question, "Why am I here?" Asking this question over and over, you should eventually hear the answer in your mind. What can only be experienced and not explained is that although you will hear it as a thought in your mind, it will distinctly feel as though it is being spoken by some presence outside yourself.

BARN

*asam-asm-*אסם*-*101

MEANING While we may think of a barn as a slightly dilapidated, somewhat picturesque building, we must remember that this is simply because most people now live in cities and are removed from the reality of rural life. In truth, a barn is simply the agricultural equivalent of a warehouse. A barn is a storage building, designed to protect valuable crops from the harmful elements.

If we think of a barn in this sense, we will have a better understanding of the spiritual message hidden within this dream image. The spelling of the dream title supports the view of a barn as a protective storage space. The initial Aleph represents the ultimate unity of the Divine, which manifests itself as the protective support indicated by the letter Samech. The final letter, Mem, tells us that this support is maternal in nature and will lead to the birth of a new you.

THE TREE OF LIFE This is another dream whose position on the Tree of Life relates to the aspect of the Divine that is attempting to assist you, rather than relating to the level of your consciousness. In this case, the dream is infused with the energy of the Sefirah of Binah. Known as the Great Mother, this Sefirah is the source of the aspect of the Divine force that guides and helps to form your personality as you make your way through life.

THE JOURNEY The key to fulfilling the advice within this dream lies in the function of a barn as a place in which to store things. The suggestion here is that the force emanating from Binah has given you a great deal of insight and understanding, but that the door to this storehouse of knowledge is bolted. In order to open the door, you need to get in touch with the energies associated with the Sefirah of Binah. When you are meditating, you should focus on images associated with water, especially the oceans. Additionally, you could find a nice piece of sapphire jewelery, as this gemstone is also connected to the energy of Binah.

BASEMENT

*komat martef-qvmth mrthph-*קומת מרתף*-*1266

MEANING If we liken our personality and psychological makeup to a house, then the darkest recesses of our unconsciousness would be the basement. It is there that we hide those thoughts and feelings that make us feel most uncomfortable. In order to progress with the Great Work, we have to brave enough to deal with even the darkest areas of our nature.

The value of this dream reduces to 6. Indeed, the number recurs throughout the value of the Hebrew word for "basement." The number 6 occurs twice, while the initial 12 in the dream's value can be seen as two further 6's added together. This is very important because the number 6 is connected to the element of Air. The element of Air relates to mental processes, and this tells us that right now you have an awful lot of thinking to do.

THE TREE OF LIFE With its very distinct focus on your need to organize and analyze your deepest thoughts, this dream sits very definitely in the path of Vav. The letter Vav forms part of the Tetragrammaton, a four-letter name for God with each letter representing one of the elements. The letter Vav represents the element of Air and, in the Tetragrammaton, follows the letter Heh, which represents the element of Water. This arrangement points out the need to recognize our emotions (Water) before we try to analyze ourselves (Air).

THE JOURNEY There are two steps to the path that you now need to take. The first is to fully recognize your innermost fears and feelings. In order to ensure that you have accomplished this, you might consider arranging some sessions with a professional counselor. The second stage is to accept these elements of your personality and decide that you will no longer allow them to control your responses to life. The best way to achieve some resolution as to which choice to make is to try to live consciously for a few days without allowing those darkest feelings to surface. When they do, you should carefully repeat to yourself that you are in control of your destiny and will not allow them to determine the way you react to situations.

BASIN

*keeyor-kyvr-*כיור*-*136

MEANING The next few months are going to be very rewarding for you and for those to whom you feel closest. In terms of the spiritual dimension, the image of a basin represents the washing away of your past as a result of your connection with the Divine. The effort that you have been putting into your development over the last weeks has paid off not only in terms of an increase in your understanding but in terms of your daily life.

The value of this dream image has a number of associations with the planet Jupiter and it is this connection that points to benefits in the areas of material as well as personal development that will shortly appear. Jupiter also has a very cheerful aspect; it is, after all, the planet's name that gives us the term *jovial*. You should expect to be in an exceptionally upbeat mood for quite some time.

THE TREE OF LIFE If one were to write a report card for the dreamer of this dream in terms of his spiritual development, it would probably say, "Steady progress." Having resolved both your intellectual and emotional states in relation to your new spiritual awareness, you are now beginning to move further up the Tree of Life. Specifically, you are now on the path of Kaph, which leads out of Netzach and up toward Hesed. The planet of this path is Jupiter, and its tarot card is The Wheel of Fortune. Both of these associations with the path of Kaph back up the notion that your material life is about to improve quite dramatically.

THE JOURNEY You should have learned by now that you cannot always see the hand of the Divine in your life. You will also have become aware that while you may not be able to see its presence, your higher self is always with you, seeking to guide you in the right direction. As you approach a period of relative ease in your life, you should make a point of always going with your gut instinct, as this is the easiest way for your higher self to communicate with you. If you have the trust to act on this instinct, you will find that your link to your higher self will be made considerably stronger.

BASKET
sal–sl– **סל**-90

MEANING This is a complex dream in that it relates to a range of connected issues involved with the search for spiritual truth. At one level we can look at the image of a basket and see it as a symbol for the way in which we can allow the Divine to carry us at difficult moments. However, when we look at the value of the dream, we find that it is the same as a word meaning "silent" in Hebrew. This aspect of the dream, when linked with the idea of a basket as something in which we would be unseen, indicates a desire on the part of the dreamer to remove himself from socializing with others. Finally, we have the fact that the value reduces to 9, which is associated with the tarot card The Hermit and indicates an individual sincerely seeking Divine inspiration.

THE TREE OF LIFE The letter Tzaddi has the same value as the title of this dream, and it is on this path that we can locate the development of the dreamer. The letter Tzaddi means "hook," and you truly have been hooked by the quest for a link with the Divine. The tarot card The Star is linked to the path of Tzaddi and points to a very strong protective and guiding influence whose purpose is to direct you toward your spiritual goal.

THE JOURNEY When you look back at the meaning of this dream, you can see that it is almost wholly positive, with the exception of your tendency to withdraw from society. While it is a great achievement to be as committed as you are to the task of developing your spiritual aspect, you should not pursue this to the exclusion of your physical health. Over the next few weeks, you need to make a point of going out and socializing, ideally with people who have no great interest in spiritual affairs, since your key function when you go out is to let your hair down and have fun!

BATH
ambat–ambt– **אמבט**-52

MEANING All the signs in this dream image point to an individual who has a great deal to offer the world and has a strong desire to express his general feelings of love in a positive and constructive way. The image of a bath is important because it is a watery image and is therefore associated with the emotions. Additionally, the implicit warmth and the fact that we tend to sink into our baths to relax indicates that you have a wish to allow others to feel supported and relaxed.

The theme of support is continued when we look at the value of this dream image. It is equivalent to the Hebrew for both "mother and father" and the title of the Sephira Binah. Binah is also referred to as the "Supernal" Mother, and this suggests a protective and caring nature. The role that you are seeking in life is clearly one where you take a somewhat maternal approach to those around you.

THE TREE OF LIFE You have succeeded in forming a way of looking at the world that allows for a spiritual dimension while retaining a rational and down-to-earth sensibility. You are now ready to move on to a higher level of understanding, and this dream indicates that you have now moved onto the path of Mem. Not only does the letter Mem mean "water," but it is one of the three so-called Mother Letters. This path is appropriate to the dream in both its obvious and its esoteric significance.

THE JOURNEY Many people have a strong urge to take their lives in a particular direction, but somehow they never manage to take the initiative necessary to make those dreams a reality. This dream is a means by which your higher self is trying to confirm to you that your goals are in conformity with your inner nature. The only to way to respond is to ensure that by the end of the month you have taken some practical steps toward getting involved with your community in a supportive and protective position. This is not just the right career move for you, it is the right spiritual move.

BATTLE

krav-krb- **כרב**-222

MEANING The first thing you notice when you look at the value of this dream image is that it consists of nothing but the number 2 repeated. This is because 2 represents duality, and all conflict is born out of difference. This is why the truly wise person places no difference between any two things, but instead sees all things as part of a complex and interconnected unity.

At the moment, you are still trapped in a dualistic way of looking at the world. Inevitably, this means that you find yourself facing internal conflicts. When you divide the world into right and wrong and black and white, inner peace will always be out of your reach.

THE TREE OF LIFE Conflict is primarily the responsibility of the Sefirah of Gevurah. However, the conflict that is evoked by Gevurah is of an ultimately positive nature and revolves around the need for death in order for life to follow, rather than conflicts that simply destroy both sides. The path that reflects the conflict you are currently feeling is the path of Tav. This path, which leads out of Malkut into Yesod, is characterized by a sense of suffering and loss. As you are struggling to accept that there is a spiritual level to the universe, you are experiencing the very same suffering that defines the path of Tav.

THE JOURNEY At this stage in your development you are not likely to be able to fully internalize the ultimate equivalence of all things. You are certainly not yet ready to try to deal with the equally true but seemingly conflicting truth that each of us is unique. However, you can begin to appreciate some of this truth. One way to see the false nature of duality is to examine a public conflict about which you have no opinion and sympathize with each side until you can see that neither is right and neither is wrong.

BEARD

zakan-zqn- **זקן**-157

MEANING To understand this dream we need to know that in the Kabbalah, the term "beard" is used to describe different aspects of creation. The Kabbalistic tradition refers to the "greater" and the "lesser beard" as terms for the "macrocosm" and the "microcosm," respectively. In other words, the individual in the physical world and the individual as part of the spiritual cosmos are represented as parts of either the greater or lesser beard. Thus, dreams of beards are deeply significant and indicate on the part of the dreamer a deep concern with the spiritual.

As the dreamer, you have progressed very well in your spiritual quest and have gained a commendable level of balance in your outlook on life. This is hinted at by the fact that the value of this dream is equivalent to the Hebrew for both the male and the female generative organs. The inclusion of both genders is symbolic of the way in which you are beginning to reconcile apparent opposites as your understanding increases.

THE TREE OF LIFE You should be very pleased with yourself, as you have achieved a level of insight that often eludes even the most sincere of seekers. With an appropriate sense of balance comes a feeling of good will to all your fellow human beings. It is not surprising then that this dream is located in the Sefirah of Tiferet. Tiferet is symbolized by the warmth of the Sun and this nurturing and powerful force is a good symbol of your state of consciousness.

THE JOURNEY Once we have achieved a deep understanding of our spirituality, it becomes our responsibility to encourage others to take a similar interest in their personal development. You can achieve this in a number of ways, some of which need not even be directly related to spirituality. For instance, you might get involved in career development, and this very mundane role may help give people the confidence to begin to explore their development on a deeper level.

BEAR

dov-dvb- **דוב**-10

MEANING Bears are fearsome animals and since time immemorial have been associated with strength and power. If you are dreaming of bears, then it is likely that your unconscious is trying to show the nature that you need to emulate in order to win in your current situation.

The value of this dream is 10, and this is encouraging as it refers to the letter Yod as well as being symbolically representative of the completion of an important cycle in your life. The letter Yod is encouraging as it represents the energizing spark of the Divine that lies within each of us.

THE TREE OF LIFE If we were to associate bears with a particular planet, it would have to be Mars due to its warlike and vigorous nature. Consequently, this dream sits on the path of Peh, which is the path on which Mars sits in the Tree of Life. The path of Peh links Netzach and Hod and can be seen as the channel along which the sometimes conflicting views of our emotions and our logical outlook interact with each other in order to achieve a resolution.

THE JOURNEY You feel as though you are facing some form of opposition in your life just now. On one hand, your mind is telling you to try to ignore the obstacle and simply rise above it. Conversely, your emotional side would far rather meet the obstacle directly with an equally confrontational response. The correct action is indicated by the path on which this path lies. The letter Peh means "mouth," and this dream is letting you know that the way to really resolve your current difficulties is to talk about them, ideally with whomever it is you see as being the source of the problem. Only then will you have achieved the completion of this cycle in your life as hinted at by the overall value of this dream's title.

BED

*meetah-myth-*מיטה*-*74

MEANING While on the surface this dream may appear to be suggestive of a relaxed state of mind, the obvious image of this dream conceals a far more vigorous symbolic meaning. In the spelling we find that "bed" implies a union of two people, rather than simply a place for sleep. The letters Mem and Heh represent the female and male, respectively, while between them we have the letter Yod, signifying the Divine spark and the letter Teth, meaning "serpent," holding definite sexual connotations. It is this union of male and female that leads to the realization of the Divine spark.

THE TREE OF LIFE We can fully understand the world from a spiritual perspective only when we fully participate in all the positive experiences that

the physical world has to offer. It follows from this that we should make judgments about the world only from a position of full understanding. While this dream points to one of the most positive physical experiences that we can seek, it is concerned also with your role as a judge of the world around you and your capacity to carry out this role with genuine insight. It is for this reason that this dream sits on the path of Lamed. It is no accident that the value of this dream equals the value of Lamed when it is spelled out in full.

THE JOURNEY You are someone who takes his personal development seriously. It is also apparent that you use your experience of the spiritual to inform the way you then look at the world and the people around you. The implication of this dream is that you need to ensure that you are balancing your commendable efforts in the spiritual sphere by full participation in a purely physical life. While the dream uses the most intimate example of physical participation, it could be that you simply need to participate in some other way, such as taking up a team sport. Of course, having an intimate relationship can help your development in all sorts of ways.

BEGGAR

*kabtsan-qbtzn-*קבצן*-*242

MEANING In the Western World, to be a beggar or even to be less than financially secure is seen as a failing worse almost than to have a poor moral character. We live in a society that judges people almost entirely by their social and financial status, so it is especially difficult for us to see why the beggar in this dream is a character whose nature we should seek to emulate.

In the spelling of this dream title we see that while the beggar may be poor in terms of money, he is rich in spiritual possessions. The initial Resh indicates that the energy of the Divine is being received in a warm and approving manner. The central letter, Mem, again points at a nurturing influence surrounding the beggar, while the final Beth tells us that the beggar is already at home in terms of his relationship with the Divine.

THE TREE OF LIFE There are many similarities between the qualities symbolized by the beggar and those represented by The Hermit card in the tarot. For this reason, this dream is allocated to the path of Yod on the Tree of Life. The path is associated with The Hermit and also with a very strong sense of the Divine working through an individual in order to allow him to fulfill his true purpose.

THE JOURNEY What you are being advised to do in this dream is to trust your instincts and believe in the fact that your decision to focus on the spiritual rather than the material is an appropriate one. If at times this seems difficult to remember, try the following simple exercise. First, go to a fancy restaurant and take a really close look at the faces and body language of the diners. You will probably notice a distinct lack of genuine happiness in the people's faces. If you then visit a favorite spot in the country and notice the sense of peace and serenity, you should see that your choice of focus is indeed the best one.

BEING KILLED
*makat mavet–mkth mvvth–*מכת מוות-912

MEANING Inevitably, a dream in which we are killed is an extremely disturbing experience. However, as bad an omen as it might appear, such a dream is very encouraging in terms of one's spiritual development. In alchemy, practitioners often talk of "killing" substances before perfecting them. Similarly, the idea that some form of death must precede any genuine enlightenment is not restricted to the biblical story of the crucifixion. The value of this dream reduces to 12, which is the number associated with The Hanged Man card in the tarot and ideas of self-sacrifice that relate to the content of this dream. Symbolically, the dream of being killed is a form of initiation into a spiritually aware circle the members of which may not be known to one another, but are invisibly connected by their level of understanding and insight.

THE TREE OF LIFE It is very rare to dream of being killed, and this dream's position on the Tree of Life reflects that rarity. It occupies the position of Daat on the Tree. This is a non-Sefirah in that it has no definite position but lies along the path of Gimel leading from Tiferet to the highest Sefirah Keter. It represents the inner knowledge that comes when one has faced all aspects of his nature and reconciled them in the light of spiritual understanding.

THE JOURNEY With this level of inner development, you should perhaps be looking to gain an in-depth knowledge of a particular religious or New Age system. You could look closely at the tradition of the tarot, for example. To take such a significant interest in a specialized area will not only hone your understanding but will also help in offering advice and support to others around you embarking on a similar quest for spiritual insight.

~BEING LOST
*lalekhet le'eebood–llkth laybvd–*ללכת לאיבוד-533

MEANING In this dream we have a situation where a standard interpretation and a Kabbalistic interpretation are enormously different, not in terms of the general meaning but in terms of significance. To be generally lost in terms of your direction in life is a relatively common feature of modern life, but to be wholly lost in terms of your spirituality is a far worse prospect. It is worth noting that the full value of this dream title is equivalent to the Hebrew for the "king of terrors." If we believe in the existence of a soul, then losing it must surely be the worst fate that could befall us.

THE TREE OF LIFE Since the dreamer has completed his way in terms of his spirituality, this dream must be placed in Malkut. It may be that the dreamer has previously progressed somewhat in working his way out of the purely material state of consciousness, but due to some major crisis of faith has found himself newly cynical.

THE JOURNEY The journey you now have to undertake is a difficult one. You need to convince yourself of the possibility of a spiritual level of existence before you even can begin to try to make some kind of contact with your higher self. However, the repetition of the letter Lamed, meaning "ox-goad," in the spelling of the dream title indicates that there is a force which is driving you toward the spiritual quest. A good place for you to begin would be to read the autobiographies of a range of people who did manage to discover some form of personal spiritual truth, as this may help you come to believe that it may also happen to you.

See Zohar symbol, Being Lost.

BEING ORPHANED
*yatom–ythvm–*יתום-456

MEANING To those who have experienced it, being orphaned will live in their memory as quite possibly the worst moment in their lives. It is difficult to imagine the extreme anguish that must be felt by someone who has lost his parents. In Kabbalistic terms, such a dream relates to a feeling of abandonment by God. This is a far worse experience than simply not believing in the existence of a Divine force. It is quite likely that the dreamer originally had some faith in a spiritual reality but now has a sense of terrible doubt due to some major crisis in his life.

THE TREE OF LIFE This dream applies to an individual who has already made some progress up the Tree of Life. Although you may feel very alone right now, you have not lost the significant levels of spiritual understanding that you have gained so far. The path of Nun is appropriate to this dream. It leads out of Tiferet and enters Gevurah, the Sefirah of severity. The path of Nun is associated with the potential for sorrow as we move toward a state of faith from a sense of being alone in an uncaring universe. This emotionally draining period is difficult to get through, but we can learn a great deal from it.

THE JOURNEY In Tiferet you achieved a sense of union with your higher self, and the next step is to try to achieve a similar level of union with the Divine. This inevitably involves a recognition of your mortality and unconsciously provokes the feelings characterized by the dream of being orphaned. One good way to combat these feelings and make them work for you in a positive way is to realize your power as an individual. To encourage such a view of yourself, you need to take on some form of difficult but practical challenge. If you persevere, no matter how difficult it may be, you will realize your value as an individual.

BEING PREGNANT

harah-hrh-הרה-210

MEANING Artists and other creatively talented individuals often refer to their creations as being rather like their children. This dream refers to the sense of your spiritually developed self being an as-yet-unborn child. As this dream relates to being pregnant, it is clear that you are already working toward the achievement of your spiritual goal. It is meaningful that just as when we are pregnant we have to take care of ourselves, when we are working on our inner development we have to have the same concern for our health and state of mind. The creative nature of spiritual advancement is hinted at by the fact that the reduction of the dream's value gives us the number 3, which is traditionally the number of creativity.

THE TREE OF LIFE While we might expect this dream to be located in a part of the Tree that represents motherhood, it is important to bear in mind the overall import of the dream. The real focus is on the experience of being pregnant, the process of in-

ternal creation. It is this that leads the dream to be situated in Netzach. This Sefirah is associated with emotions and creativity and so is an ideal home for this particular dream.

THE JOURNEY As you have come this far in your spiritual quest, you may sense that you could simply continue exactly as you are, and in time your spiritual rebirth would still occur. However, there are certain things to consider that would assist you in the birthing of your new self, and these are implied by this dream image. The key thing for you to do right now is to discover a way to express your creative side. You have a need to express yourself and it will help you enormously to do so.

BELT

khagorah-chgvrh-חגורה-222

MEANING A belt is a significant piece of clothing. It holds up other items of clothing, and in doing so it also saves us from potential embarrassment if those items were suddenly to fall down. When we consider the basis of embarrassment, it becomes clear that our concerns are not so much about the embarrassing event itself but are far more involved with the potential reactions of others. We can infer that a dream of a belt is related to the need to protect ourselves from the negative views of those around us. The fact that the value consists of a string of 2's emphasizes that this dream is concerned with duality, which implies some form of inner conflict.

THE TREE OF LIFE Even when we recognize the existence of a higher agency at work in the world, it can be very difficult to ignore the opinions of others when they conflict with our own. This can be the case even when we are talking about our deepest spiritual beliefs; the views of our peers can exert enormous pressure on our acceptance of our faith. This dream sits on the path of Samech, which is associated with the Temperance card in the tarot. This card is all about balance and the need not to be swayed from that middle path by any outside influences.

THE JOURNEY The task that lies before you now is simply to come to terms with the new you. Part of that process is learning to accept and absorb the opposing views of others without seeing them as personal attacks or allowing them to undermine your position. The letter Samech means "prop," and you should remember that you are now on a very supportive path of the Tree. The next time you feel that your beliefs are slipping, you should breathe deeply and remind yourself that all truths are unique and that each of us is like a unique star in the cosmos. If you focus on this truth you will find that you can feel the support of the Divine.

BENCH

*safsal–sphsl–*ספסל-230

MEANING There are places where we like to sit and relax, and there are places where we tend to go when we need to be contemplative. A bench is more of a thinking and reflecting place, and this is an important factor in the interpretation of the dream. It is also worth noting that a bench, like any other seat, is a support and enables us to take time out in an otherwise busy day. The value of this dream image reduces to 5, which is the value of the letter Heh, meaning "window." In a sense, the bench can be seen as providing the dreamer with a window on the world around him.

THE TREE OF LIFE This dream is concerned with reflection, particularly reflecting on our relationships with those around us in the context of our changing spiritual viewpoint. The association of this dream with our mental processes is emphasized by the fact that the total value of this dream image is equivalent to one of the more esoteric titles of the Sefirah of Hod. It is not surprising then that this dream is positioned within this Sefirah and points to the beginnings of a rationalization of your newfound beliefs.

THE JOURNEY At this stage in your spiritual journey, you have begun to develop a personal system of belief. In order to build on this foundation, you are now in need of a framework in which to fit your beliefs without undermining your sense of the rational. In order to begin this work, you should familiarize yourself with the surprisingly diverse range of equally viable ways of viewing the nature of reality. A beginner's philosophy book would be an ideal place for you to start.

BEQUEST

*eezavon–a'ayzbvn–*עזבון-145

MEANING At first glance this dream might appear to be wholly concerned with material matters. We expect a bequest to be a special heirloom or some other valuable item that we can treasure and then pass on to our own nearest and dearest. However, one can look at the idea of a bequest in a more spiritual way. In many cultures throughout history, wisdom was seen as passing from one generation to the next. The reduction of the value of this dream gives us the number 10, which not only is linked to the idea of inheritance and traditions but refers to the completion of a particular cycle in your life.

THE TREE OF LIFE The bequest that this dream refers to is the bequest of the Divine to the whole of creation. The gift in question is that of spiritual understanding, and it is the most precious present that any of us could ever receive. This dream sits on the path of Heh. This is particularly appropriate because it emanates from the Sefirah of Hokhmah. Hokhmah is the second Sefirah in the Tree of Life and can be seen as the point at which the Divine force first has the potential to be felt by individuals as a specific source of guidance in their lives.

THE JOURNEY The message of this dream is twofold. Initially, it indicates that you are beginning to recognize that you can access a great store of wisdom by learning to listen to your inner self. This part of you is connected to all of human history, and it is your higher self that represents the bequest of the dream. Additionally, the association with the number 10 tells you that once you access this wisdom, you will have completed a significant phase in your development. You can encourage your ability to make this connection by meditating while burning sage incense.

BEREAVEMENT

*shekhol–shkvl–*שכול-356

MEANING At the heart of the spiritual quest is the need to understand that the ultimate truths are contradictory when viewed from anything but a spiritual perspective. This is easier to comprehend when we consider the fact that any definition of God must see Him as omniscient and omnipotent, and yet we also allow the paradoxical existence of free will. To remove either would be to reduce the nature of the Divine or that of the human condition, and so belief in the Divine requires apparent contradiction. The compression of the value of this dream provides the contrasting energies of Shin (300), which is symbolic of the element of Fire, and Nun (50), which is symbolic of the cold aspect of the element of Water. These contradictory forces are ultimately reconciled in the final number 6, which represents the macrocosm or the Divine force.

THE TREE OF LIFE While it is possible to intellectually appreciate the point being made in this dream, it is far more difficult to internalize this level of understanding. Because of the deep levels of spiritual insight that are required to accept all the implications of an ultimate truth that is contradictory in its nature, this dream is positioned very high on the Tree of Life. The path of Gimel is most appropriate, and not only because it is one of three paths that leads into the highest Sefirah of Keter. Additionally, the path of Gimel is connected to The High Priestess card in the tarot. The High Priestess is often depicted as carrying the scrolls of secret wisdom. Most significantly, she is pictured sitting between two pillars. These two pillars, named Boaz and Jachin, represent conflicting but equally important aspects of human nature.

THE JOURNEY The full value of the Hebrew for "bereavement" is the same as the value of the Hebrew phrase meaning "spirits of the living." This simple correlation points out that the appreciation of the contradictory nature of the Divine has to extend all the way to one's own mortality. If you are able to internally accept the fact that your own mortality is a means by which the universe is able to increase the number of living spirits, you are making progress in spiritual terms. Gaining this understanding requires significant amount of time and an extremely open mind. One way to work toward an inner appreciation of the contradictory nature of the universe is to consider why it is that, in nature, the number of seeds planted far exceeds the number of plants that will grow into healthy crops.

BETTING

*heemoor-hymvr-*הימור-261

MEANING In many religions, betting is condemned as an immoral pursuit, but in Western culture betting in various forms is seen as wholly acceptable. Indeed, the nature of stock trading is almost indistinguishable from betting, so we could probably argue that our entire society is funded by gambling on a massive scale. The idea of profiting by speculation is often seen as incompatible with a spiritual outlook and can be viewed as exploiting the very chance nature of reality, which is one of the key factors in ensuring free will in our lives. In terms of a direct link to your inner development, this dream suggests that you need to stop hedging your bets and make that difficult but necessary leap of faith.

THE TREE OF LIFE Here we have another dream whose position relates more to an attitude toward life that you need to acquire, rather than reflecting where you are in your spiritual progress. Your higher self is trying to tell you that you need to

develop a genuinely childlike outlook in terms of your beliefs. What this means is that you should try to achieve a wholly trusting state of mind in relation to the Divine, rather than try to calculate the likelihood of different options being accurate descriptions of the Divine. This wholly trusting aspect is related to The Fool card in tarot and the path of Aleph on the Tree of Life.

THE JOURNEY If you are to achieve a significant level of spiritual awareness, you will have to accept a loss of control in certain areas of your life. Right now, you are only partially accepting this loss, but seeking to compensate by trying to judge the odds of success that may lie in any spiritual activity you might undertake. Your task over the next few months is to join a number of spiritual groups, without any great investigation into their backgrounds or possible pitfalls. It may well be that you leave most of them within a week, but the key thing is to make that leap into a new activity.

BIRD

*tseepor-tzypvr-*ציפור-386

MEANING Since the earliest times, people have looked up to the skies and envied the birds for their ability to fly and the apparent freedom that comes with it. From the myth of Daedalus and Icarus to references in the gospels, birds have always been seen as symbols of unfettered liberation. The importance of birds in the human psyche can be seen in the fact that even individual species of birds have particular symbolic significance, from the wise owl to the majestic eagle. In spiritual terms, we become truly liberated only when we unite with our higher self. The reduction of the value of this dream gives us the number 17, which indicates that our higher self is already helping to guide us toward this goal.

THE TREE OF LIFE The most mystical of all the birds is the mythical phoenix. The phoenix epitomizes the freedom signified by birds because it is free even from death. When a phoenix dies, it rises again from the flames of its funeral pyre. The phoenix is associated with the Sefirah of Tiferet, and as this Sefirah relates to the union of the lower and higher selves, it is a very fitting Sefirah for this dream. Additionally, we should be aware that in Kabbalistic tradition, a bird represents a message from the Divine and should be seen as a very positive sign.

THE JOURNEY Dedication to a spiritual quest requires a great deal of discipline and is an enormous responsibility for anyone to attempt to shoulder. In a world where so many are looking for freedom without responsibility, the seeker after truth is often in a position of great responsibility with very little evidence of any freedom. Your task now is to find those freedoms that become available when one is truly committed to the Great Work. Perhaps the greatest of these is the ability to genuinely appreciate the wonder of the world around you. You should book a weekend away in the country by yourself and spend the time appreciating the beauty of nature. You should notice that with your new sense of the spiritual, the world talks to you in ways it never could before.

BITE

*negeesah–ngysh–*נגיסה*–128*

MEANING When we reduce the value of this dream, we find the number 11. As 11 is the number used to represent magic, we know that we are looking at a dream with significant mystical implications, but also that its message is likely to be hidden from view. A psychological interpretation would likely view a bite or the act of biting as a symbol of aggressive sexual desire. However, the Kabbalistic analysis yields a far more subtle explanation. The obvious act of biting represents a determination to succeed in one's spiritual quest. However, if we look at the number 128, we notice that this number is 2 to the power of 7. The number 2 represents duality, and in the context of this dream it refers to the inner conflict that duality produces until we learn to see the essential unity among all things. The number 7 tells us what is driving this inner conflict. Seven is the value of the letter Zayin meaning "sword." The sword image indicates that the dreamer has a vision of taking up arms against a perceived enemy. Until the dreamer learns not to attack but to accept, any attempt to progress is likely to be frustrated.

THE TREE OF LIFE You are very much in the early stages of the Great Work, and the significant levels of conflict that you are experiencing are entirely normal at this point in your inner development. The decision to seek out the greater truths, so ignored by today's society, will inevitably lead to some troubling experiences. In fact, these negative experiences are not simply to be expected but are a necessary part of your progress. This dream and the feelings associated with it relate to the path of Shin, which is appropriately also known as the biting path.

THE JOURNEY Relaxation is the key to your success right now. In order to feel the Divine working through your higher self, you need to be sufficiently open and calm. It is very important that you find a way to lose all the mental clutter that gets in the way when you try to focus on higher things. You can achieve this by practicing some simple breathing techniques. The most useful way to begin is to establish a steady rhythm to your breathing. Try inhaling for a count of 4; holding it for a count of 4; exhaling for a count of 4; and then counting to 4 before the next inhalation.

BLACK

*shakhor–shchvr–*שחור*–514*

MEANING Colors are always very evocative, and to dream of the color black is likely to cause the dreamer to believe himself either to be depressed or about to experience some form of upsetting event in his life. However, in spiritual terms there is nothing negative about this dream at all. The value of the dream reduces to 10 and so points to a completion of a cycle in your life and the beginning of a new phase of consciousness. The initial letter, Shin, in the spelling of the dream title also points to a considerable amount of energy on your part, so this dream is pointing to a busy and useful time ahead for you.

THE TREE OF LIFE As you know from the introduction to this book, each path on the Tree of Life and each Sefirah has its own color. The color for the Sefirah of Malkut is black, as this color represents the earth. Before we begin our spiritual journey we can be compared to the black earth waiting for the seed of the Divine to take root and start to grow. The compression of the value of the dream also indicates the Sefirah of Malkut. Both the initial and final letters refer to practical activity and the material world, both of which are connected to the Sefirah of Malkut.

THE JOURNEY We can never predict what will lead us to take up the challenge of the Great Work. For some of us it is a journey that we have been on for as long as we can remember. For others it is a slow evolution, and for yet others it is the result of a single life-changing event. In the compression of this dream's value, we have the central letter, Yod, representing the energetic Divine spark. This connects with the energetic times ahead that are indicated by the letter Shin. It is likely then that your interest in the spiritual has been sparked quite suddenly. In order to maintain this interest, you should take up some practical activity that has spiritual overtones. The traditional martial arts would be an ideal avenue for you to explore.

BLACK AND WHITE CHECKS

shakhor ve lavan metooshbats-shchvr v lbn mthvshbtz- שחור ו לבן מתושבץ–1430

MEANING Black and white checks have a very long history of mystical significance. Perhaps most famously, they are used in the temples of Freemasonry: they also appear surprisingly often in older churches and cathedrals in Europe. The symbolism of the checkered pattern is quite simple but no less profound for that. Mainstream religions teach that the Divine and the Devil, for lack of a better word, are enemies and that ultimately God will triumph. This is a very human and dualistic interpretation of the nature of the spiritual universe. In mystical systems, we learn that God and Devil are merely labels, and that at the Divine level of consciousness there is no "good" or "evil" and so there can be no Devil. In the Divine, all is one. The checkerboard represents this truth by placing the opposite-color tiles next to each other emphasizing their equal importance and ultimate equivalence.

THE TREE OF LIFE Spiritual understanding comes to us in a number of ways. Certain ideas may arise through our intuition; others emerge slowly and unseen as we change our way of life to better suit a spiritual outlook. Ideas such as those hidden within the black and white checker design require our intellectual focus before they can become an innate part of our understanding of the universe. For this reason, this dream is associated with the Sefirah of Hod on the Tree of Life. The value of the dream reduces to 8, which is the number of this particular Sefirah.

THE JOURNEY The equivalence of good and evil is just one example of the many mystical paradoxes that we have to struggle with when we are seeking the ultimate truths of the universe. It is, of course, important to remember that while the Divine transcends all dualities, it is crucially important that in our day-to-day lives we try to embody the qualities of compassion and charity and understanding. The transcendence of duality is not in any way a license to dispose with all ethical or moral considerations in our physical lives. This dream should be seen as an indication that you are now ready to tackle some of these more challenging concepts about the nature

of the Divine. This means that you are going to have to do a certain amount of reading on the whole area of spirituality, but if you put in the mental effort, you will assuredly be rewarded.

BLANKET

smeekah-shmykh- שמיכה–375

MEANING It may be a seemingly unimportant image, decidedly humble in nature, but the dream of a blanket is highly significant. When we look at the value of the dream we find that it is equivalent to the Hebrew spelling of "Solomon." As Solomon is most famed for his wisdom in matters of moral complexity, we can assume that the dreamer is someone who has a highly developed moral sensibility. Additionally, the value can be reduced to 6, which in the context of this dream should be seen as representing the macrocosm or the Divine presence.

THE TREE OF LIFE The dreamer is an individual with a great deal of spiritual understanding and insight, someone who has already devoted considerable time and effort to his inner development. This may not even have been an entirely conscious process, as people can be born with an innate sense of higher justice. This dream belongs to the path of Vav because it leads from the Sefirah of Hesed, associated with the qualities of mercy, into the Sefirah of Hokhmah, which represents the quality of wisdom.

THE JOURNEY You are now at a point in your spiritual development where you can best move forward by offering the benefit of your experience to those around you. The emphasis in this dream is very much on your ability to see through complex problems and come up with morally appropriate solutions. You should perhaps consider a career move into a field such as counseling or arbitration, which would allow your skills to be used for the benefit of others.

BLASPHEMY

kheelool hashem-chylvl hshm- חילול השם–429

MEANING One of the Hebrew words that has the same value as "blasphemy" is that meaning "lion cub." While a lion is universally regarded as an impressive, proud, and potentially dangerous beast, a lion cub still has a very long way to go before it achieves such status. This dream is suggestive of someone with considerable promise, but with a lot left to learn. It may appear strange that a dream about blasphemy should be viewed positively. However, we need to remember that in the Western Mystery Tradition we tend to look at religious texts not as literal truths but as symbolic guides. This means that by traditional standards, this form of spiritual quest is by its very nature blasphemous.

THE TREE OF LIFE We can approach the Divine in a number of ways, and it is certainly true that many who prefer the passive, more familiar route of sincere prayer and faith have achieved a significant level of insight. The hermetic path requires a more active mind and a willingness to take on more responsibility for our inner development. This strength of mind is represented by the lion cub association, as well as the fact that the value of the dream reduces to the 9. This number is the value of the letter Teth, meaning "serpent," and is connected to the Strength card in the tarot. Consequently, this dream and the dreamer are both currently sitting on the path of Teth.

THE JOURNEY In blaspheming, to continue with the image from this dream, you are simply rejecting the official interpretation of God's will. What you need to do is begin to formulate your own way of interpreting the Divine. This really is a lifelong task that changes with you as you develop. Right now, you have a great deal of energy, but it is undirected. Over the next few weeks you should develop something like a study plan for yourself to add some rigor and discipline, which will greatly aid your progress.

✸BLINDNESS

eever-a'ayvvr- עיוור-292

MEANING It is common in religious imagery to refer to those who do not hold to our same belief system as being blind. However, the suggestion in such texts is that those blind individuals are willfully refusing to see the truth that is in front of them. In this dream the implication is that the dreamer is blind through no fault of his own. From a spiritual point of view, this dream is a positive step on the way toward a better understanding of the Divine. It is better to realize that you are blind than to assume that what you think you see is all that one could ever perceive.

The spelling of the compression of this dream's value hints at a revelation about to occur in the dreamer's life. We find the letters Resh, Tzaddi, and Beth through compression, which tells us the fol-

lowing story: You are becoming aware of the presence of a Divine force in your life (Resh); this force now has you hooked; you feel compelled to investigate further (Tzaddi) in order to rediscover your spiritual home (Beth).

THE TREE OF LIFE Dreams of blindness tend to occur fairly early in our spiritual development as they relate to feelings of uncertainty about the existence of a higher reality and strong anxieties about its actual nature, should it exist. In terms of the Tree of Life, this dream places the dreamer on the path of Qoph. This is one of the three initial paths out of Malkut and so refers to the very first steps on the spiritual quest. It is particularly appropriate because the path of Qoph is associated with mental anxieties of the type that occur when we realize that we are not seeing the whole picture.

THE JOURNEY Having realized that you have been blind to the greater spiritual reality, your task now is to find ways to open your eyes. While reading about a range of mystical ideas may certainly help, what you really need now is a concrete sign of the higher reality that is within your grasp. There are a number of ways to achieve such an experience, which range from attending a respectable spiritualist session, to exploring yourself through self-hypnosis, to taking up a serious meditation routine on a daily basis.

See Zohar symbol, Blindness.

BLOOD

dam-dm- דם-44

MEANING Throughout history, blood has played a central role in almost all religions. Its lasting significance is ensured, if by nothing else, by its role in the Christian religion, where blood, or a symbolic representation of it, is consumed in ritual fashion. If this description seems bizarre, it is simply because we have a term for this ritual that has separated it in our minds from the actual nature of the symbolism involved. Symbolically, communion in the Christian faith represents the union of the material and the spiritual. This is mirrored in the spelling of the dream title. The initial letter, Daleth, represents the physical world since its value is 4, but because its meaning is "door" it can also be seen as a gateway to the spiritual. The final Mem is associated with the maternal aspect of the Divine, and its value of 40 represents the 4 of Daleth being raised to a higher spiritual level.

THE TREE OF LIFE Certain letters in the Hebrew alphabet have two values: a standard value plus a special value when they appear at the end of a word. This final value, as it is known, is not used as a standard when we gematrically analyze a word or phrase. However, there are times when it can be very instructive to look at the final value. In this case, the dream image sits in the Sefirah of Tiferet because this best fits the concept of the union of the lower and higher worlds, represented by the image of blood. Interestingly, the final value of Mem is 600. This links it directly to the macrocosm or the Divine, which is highly appropriate in terms of its significance in the spelling of "blood" as discussed above.

THE JOURNEY This dream is telling you that you need to prepare for a new level of spiritual consciousness. We each have the potential to achieve personal communion with the Divine, and you have reached a stage where such a communion is possible. To increase the chance of its happening, you should select some simple and familiar spiritual practice that you perform at least three times each day—no matter what. It should be performed at the same time each day and continued until the goal is achieved. The act itself can be as simple as a specific prayer or as complicated as a full-blown ceremonial magic ritual.

BLUE
kakhol-kchvl-בחול-64

MEANING When we think of the color blue we tend to think of sadness and depression since these are the feelings that we now associate with that color. Traditionally, of course, this color was primarily linked with the sea, and it is this elemental connection that is most important in the interpretation of this dream. The element of Water is, unsurprisingly, blue, and this dream is all about the effect of the element of Water in your life. Because the value of this dream reduces to 10, you are in the process of completing one cycle in your life and moving into another. It is likely that this new phase in your spiritual development will involve a focus on the emotions, as it is the emotional life that is governed by the element of Water.

THE TREE OF LIFE There are a number of paths on the Tree of life that are colored blue, so we have to be guided by more than the color alone in order to determine this dream's appropriate location on the Tree of Life. The path of Mem is colored blue but also is associated with the element of Water, and as indicated by its link with The Hanged Man card from the tarot it is also concerned mainly with our higher emotional development.

THE JOURNEY It is very easy to become unintentionally selfish when we pursue the Great Work. We can become so absorbed in our higher development that we neglect those nearest us. This is a negative state of affairs in terms of our daily lives and is unlikely to help our spiritual development in the long run. The Hanged Man card, which is connected to this dream, represents supreme self-sacrifice, and it is this self-sacrifice that you now need to learn in order to move forward. Your task for the next few months is to ensure that at least once a week, when you feel inclined to spend some time working on your development, you make a point of doing something with your nearest and dearest instead.

BLUSHING
somek-svmq-סומק-206

MEANING A psychological interpretation of this dream would probably point to a feeling of awkwardness that could relate either to a lack of sexual experience or possibly to more general feelings of inadequacy. In Kabbalistic terms, this dream is not so much about inadequacy or awkwardness as it is about defensiveness. The value of this dream when compressed reveals both the letter Resh, which refers to the presence of the Divine, and the letter Vav, which symbolizes the Divine or macrocosm. However, the reduction of the value of this dream produces the number 8, which refers to a desire to create a defensive wall around oneself. The implication of this is that the dreamer has the potential to achieve significant communication with his higher self but is refusing to recognize that this potential exists.

THE TREE OF LIFE This dream relates to an individual who is not entirely new to the spiritual quest. Indeed, the union with the Divine that is implied suggests somebody who has already made some form of contact with his higher self. This would put the dream at least as high as the Sefirah of Tiferet. The specific path of this dream image is that of Zayin. This is most appropriate because it is the path on which we find the tarot card The Lovers. Contrary to what people may assume, The Lovers card is not about romance but refers to a need to make a choice between what is comfortable and what is right.

THE JOURNEY If you wish to continue your spiritual journey, you need to choose what is right over that with which you are comfortable. The great fear involved in taking this path is that you may lose the union you had achieved with your higher self without ever gaining any closer union with the Divine itself. However, all the greatest prizes come with a certain amount of risk and fear attached, and you should resolve to take the chance. It would be a good idea to organize some form of meditation workshop or spiritual discussion group so that even if you struggle on the path of Zayin, the comments of those in your group will remind you of the significant strides you have already made.

BOAT

*seerah–syrh–*סירה*–275*

MEANING To dream of boats immediately brings the element of Water into play. However, it is important to note that just as boats sail along the top of the water, this is a dream about moving forward through life without paying close attention to one's deepest emotions. For instance, a dream about swimming or diving would suggest that the dreamer has a far greater recognition of his emotional depths.

The value of this dream reduces to 5, which is the value of the letter Heh, meaning "window." This tells us that while you may not be closely examining your emotions, you are engaged in very close observation of the world around you. This in itself is an encouraging sign for your development, as when you understand others you often find clues to understanding yourself.

THE TREE OF LIFE It is clear from the image of boats skimming across the water that the next key area for you to work on is your emotional life. You will need not only to examine your relationships but also to take a very close and hard look at your deepest feelings about life in general. This means that the Sefirah you are sailing toward is that of Netzach, as this is the Sefirah where we learn to integrate our emotions and passions into a relationship with the Divine. The particular path you are currently on is that of Peh. This represents a vigorous and energetic approach to life and to issues of spirituality.

THE JOURNEY You have managed to formulate a mental or intellectual relationship with the Divine and have accepted the reality of a spiritual life. These are both commendable achievements, but they are only passing points on the spiritual quest. In order to move forward, you now need to look at your emotional life in detail. Given your vigorous nature, it is likely that you find this difficult because there are no solid, definite foundations on which to build your understanding. In the emotional world we are floating in a sea of feelings, and this can be very disconcerting. You will improve your chances of dealing with this new challenge if you book some time in a flotation tank. The experience will help prepare you for the emotional investigations that lie ahead.

BOILING

*reteekhah–rthychh–*רתיחה*–623*

MEANING At first we may be inclined to see this dream as worrisome or as a warning about our temper. To be boiling suggests that we are danger of boiling over, that our feelings will bubble up under the intense heat of our temper and spill out, creating an unpleasant situation for those around us. However, we need to look at this dream in a spiritual context. In alchemy, we are repeatedly told of the need first to destroy the ego and then, from the burned remains, create a new spiritual being by a process of distillation. Distillation, of course, requires the repeated boiling of the source material. In this case, the source material is the self and the distillation is the result of continuing spiritual work.

The reduction of the value of this dream gives us 11. This number has always been symbolic of magic and suggests that a highly significant mystical process is going on in this dream. One way to see the image is to remember that the initial liquid represents the element of Water and that as it boils, the liquid is freed from the world of Water, or emotions, and enters the world of Air, or spirit.

THE TREE OF LIFE In finding a home for this dream on the Tree of Life, we need to locate a path that begins in Water and ends in Air. It should also be a path that leads to a very significant sign of spiritual development. Finally, the transformation is described as vigorous and swift rather than occurring by a gradual evolution of ideas. The ideal path for such a set of ideas is that of Ayin. It is a very energetic path and leads from the watery Sefirah of Hod to the airy Sefirah of Tiferet. Moreover, the Sefirah of Tiferet represents the union of the higher and lower self and so is a very significant stage in the spiritual development of the individual.

THE JOURNEY You are experiencing a wide range of emotional states right now. At times your feelings will seem confusing if not downright contradictory. This is to be expected, as the transition from a primarily material to a mainly spiritual view of the world is always difficult. You can ease your transition by engaging in some very contrasting leisure activities. This will help you to appreciate the possibility of two very contrary states existing side by side. For instance, you could join a fencing club and immediately afterward attend a class in art appreciation. Thus in the same evening you will experience the world through two very different modes of perception.

BONES

*etsem–a'atzm-*עצם-200

MEANING To dream of bones is usually an unsettling experience. This is because bones remind us of our mortality. The realization that we are, indeed, going to die is always emotionally affecting because it is far more immediate than the knowledge in the back of our mind that we will not live forever. The value of this dream is very reassuring, though. Its total value is the same as the that of the letter Resh, which represents the warm and benevolent influence of the Divine. Additionally, in the spelling of the dream title we see that the word ends with the letter Mem, and as Mem represents the maternal aspect of God, we can understand that in one way death is not an end but a return to the Divine womb. The reduction of the word's value gives us the number 2. This number is the value of the letter Beth, which relates to the home and domestic concerns, and so again we are being told that death is a return to our original home and so is not a cause for fear.

THE TREE OF LIFE While the dream may contain a number of hidden messages of reassurance, it is inevitable that dreaming of bones leads to a certain amount of anxiety. In fact, it is necessary to experience this sense of worry and impending loss in order to appreciate fully the sense of homecoming that occurs when we realize that such fears are unfounded. This dream relates to the path of Nun, which is linked appropriately with the Death card from the tarot but which also leads into the safe haven of Tiferet. Bearing all this in mind, you can afford to let yourself cheer up a little and try to enjoy life.

THE JOURNEY We live in a world where mortality and even aging are seen as the great enemies. This current perspective means that the idea of death is significantly more disturbing than it was to our ancestors. Accentuating this uneasiness is the fact that belief in any kind of afterlife is much less common now than in earlier generations. In order to come

to terms with the temporary nature of your physical existence, you should spend some time visiting cemeteries and reading the inscriptions on people's headstones. This will initially be depressing, but eventually the realization that despite being physically no more than bones, each one of them continued to live in the hearts of others should spur you on to greater spiritual understanding of your position.

✧BOOK

*sefereem–sphrym-*ספרים-390

MEANING True spiritual understanding can never be taught or learned or indeed read about. The experience of the Divine is something so momentous that it transcends language and cannot be communicated but only felt by each of us as an individual. Having said that, in the Western Mystery Tradition book learning does play an enormously important part in preparing one for such an experience. It is worth remembering that in ancient times "book" did not mean an actual text but referred instead to a store of wisdom that one might have access to. The importance of this dream as an indication that you are close to achieving your spiritual goal is emphasized by the fact that the value of "books" is the same as the value of "heaven."

THE TREE OF LIFE The High Priestess card in the tarot is the keeper of the books of sacred knowledge and in many sets of tarot cards she is depicted holding these books or scrolls on her lap. It is this card that best represents your position right now because that secret knowledge and understanding is within your grasp. The High Priestess card and this dream both sit on the path of Gimel. It is appropriate that the value of this dream reduces to 3, which is the value of the letter Gimel.

THE JOURNEY At this stage in your spiritual development nobody can prescribe exactly what actions you should take to best improve your chances of some form of gnosis (a direct interaction between the individual and the Divine). As you progress up the Tree of Life, the actions needed to continue your journey become increasingly personal. However, what is certain is that now more than ever you need to set aside some specific time each day for spiritual work. Listen very closely to your instincts and follow them no matter how irrational they seem. The central image of a book makes it clear that you need to spend significant time in deep study of a range of spiritual ideas and philosophies.

See Zohar symbol, Book.

BOOT

*magaf-mgph-*מגף-123

MEANING It is pleasantly ironic that having used the metaphor of a journey to describe the inner development of the soul, we find that a dream about boots is one that indicates a person who has achieved that highest of achievements—a sense of union with the Divine. The total value of this dream is equivalent to a Kabbalistic name of God, which implies the three Supernals: Keter, Chesed, and Binah. It is doubly appropriate, therefore, that the value can be read as 1, 2, 3, thereby labeling the three topmost Sefirot through the value of the dream image.

THE TREE OF LIFE This dream is unusual in that it does not really belong to a single path. As we have already seen, this dream tells us that the dreamer has reached a point of development where he is able to appreciate fully the nature of the Divine. This appreciation comes from a spiritual connection having been made with each of the three Supernal Sefirot, and so the dream straddles all of them. It is perhaps no accident that since we are dealing with more than one path on the Tree we have a dream about a type of footwear that enables us to cover more distance with a single stride than does a normal pair of shoes.

THE JOURNEY You may think this dream means that you have reached your journey's end. However, that is never really the case. We live in a living and not a static universe, and as the Divine is present in all aspects of the universe, It is changing all the time, just as the universe is. Consequently, we need to strive to maintain our relationship with God. The spelling of this dream title tells you what you need to do: You have reentered the symbolic womb of the Divine (Mem) by understanding the hidden wisdom (Gimel) but now need to keep up a dialogue with the Divine through meditation and prayer (Peh).

BOTTLE

*bakbook-bqbvq-*בקבוק-210

MEANING At first, this dream image is likely to cause you to wonder whether the bottles in question contain now or ever contained alcohol of any kind. In fact, unless you are already worried about your level of alcohol consumption, it makes no difference to the Kabbalistic interpretation of the dream. The important thing about bottles, from a spiritual point of view, is that they are vessels waiting to be filled. They represent your consciousness, which, like an empty bottle, is waiting to have wisdom and insight poured into it from above. The reduction of the value of this dream gives us the number 3, which points to the letter Gimel and indicates that you are indeed waiting for wisdom to descend down the middle pillar of the Tree of Life in order to increase your spiritual understanding.

THE TREE OF LIFE A deeper investigation of the value of this dream image reveals its correct position on the Tree of Life. The value of "bottles" is the same as one possible Hebrew word for "sword." Another word that means "sword" is zayin. Zayin is also one of the letters of the Hebrew alphabet, and a path on the Tree of Life. The most important aspect of the path of zayin for your dream is its connection to The Lovers card in the tarot.

THE JOURNEY The Lovers card in the tarot indicates the need to make a crucial choice, very often between that which seems attractive and that which does not appeal but is most beneficial to you in the long run. It is likely that the choice facing you right now is the decision about which source to use to fill your empty bottles with spiritual guidance. At this time there are a plethora of spiritual systems around, all of which will promise to give you the answers you seek. This dream is telling you that the most attractive spiritual system may not give you the answers you really need in the long term.

BOUNDARY

*gvool-gbvl-*גבול-41

MEANING In our normal day-to-day life, boundaries are enormously important, even if we are not conscious of their importance to our sense of well-being. If you think for a moment you will realize that your life is determined by boundaries: boundaries around your loved ones, your property, your home, your sense of personal space in a crowded street, the chain of authority in your workplace—the list is virtually endless. In the world of the spiritual, these boundaries begin to dissolve as we recognize the interconnected nature of the universe. The value of this dream points to this truth. The initial 4 of 41 represents the solidity of the material world with all its boundaries, while the 1 represents the letter Aleph and the essential unity of all creation.

THE TREE OF LIFE At this time you have yet to fully internalize the unity of all life and the fact that the differences between people, things, and even states of being are ultimately illusions created by the material framework through which you view reality. This is not at all problematic since in the world of Assiah (the first of the Four Worlds of the Kabbalah) the universe presents itself to us in a way that encourages the sense of difference and separation. Kabbalistic theory breaks up the universe into four levels of increasing spirituality known as the Four Worlds. This can be applied to the Tree of Life so that Assiah, or the purely physical, coincides with Malkut. However, some Kabbalists would argue that there should be a tree for each world. Indeed, some go as far as to say that each Sefirah contains a Tree of Life within it, thereby creating finer and finer gradations of symbolic significance. The other three worlds are Yetzirah (angelic), Briah (Archangelic), and Atziluth (Divine). In terms of the Tree of Life, this dream sits on the path of Cheth. This path is linked to the idea of defensiveness and the need to place boundaries around various aspects of our lives.

THE JOURNEY The value of this dream reduces to 5, the value of the letter Heh. This letter means "window" in Hebrew, and this is a clue to the task that now lies in front of you. It will take a great deal of time before you are able to remove all the boundary walls that you have erected around your life. However, you can begin to remove at least a few of the bricks to create a window through which you can see how life might be if they were all removed. In order to create these windows, you need to listen to your higher self. A good way to start this process is to meditate in front of a mirror and when you feel completely relaxed and mentally uncluttered begin to ask your reflection any questions that come to mind.

BRANCH

anaf-a'anph-200

MEANING If you are reading through this book dream by dream rather than as a reference source to look up specific dreams you have experienced, you should notice that this dream has the same value as the dream image "bones." In the Kabbalah, words of equivalent value are seen as having a significant relationship to each other, and this dream is no exception. Both dreams are related to issues concerning the nature of mortality and the fact that death, when looked at correctly, is a chance to return to our spiritual home. However, there are differences in emphasis. The image here is of a branch, and in spiritual terms this is a reference to the idea of humanity as a tree itself, on which each of us is a

leaf connected to a branch and ultimately to a central trunk. The final Peh, meaning "mouth," in the spelling of the dream title indicates that we can aid others on the same branch as ourselves by sharing our spiritual understanding with them.

THE TREE OF LIFE This dream belongs to the path of Peh. It is appropriate in a number of ways, not least of which is because this dream is urging you to talk to others about your spiritual experiences. It is also appropriate because it acts as a reconciling channel between the demands of the rational mind, represented by Hod, and the desires of the heart, represented by Netzach. This reconciliation is often found only in death, but the implication here is that you can achieve this sense of balance in life if you persist in your efforts.

THE JOURNEY We can achieve much by private meditation and prayer. However, for some people there are times when a move upward can be achieved only by sharing their experiences with others. You are one of these people; you need the input of others in order to unlock the door that will allow you to set foot on the next stage of your spiritual journey. In order to find some like-minded people with whom to share your ideas, you should look for meditation or yoga groups in your neighborhood. It may be equally rewarding to join a philosophy class since philosophical ideas can often be useful tools in developing our spirituality.

BREAK

leeshbor-lshbvr-לשבור-538

MEANING From a material perspective, to break something is usually not an event to be celebrated. Breakages mean the destruction of possessions, and in a world dominated by material and economic concerns this is a bad thing. However, from a spiritual perspective a break can be extremely positive. This dream refers to a break in your consciousness, which is a moment of crisis but also a moment of revelation. The reduction of the value of this dream gives us 16, which is related to The Tower of Destruction card in the tarot. This card indicates a deeply traumatic event on the horizon, but an event that will ultimately be of great benefit to the dreamer.

THE TREE OF LIFE The hardest step in any journey is always the first, and this dream indicates that you are in the process of taking that first stride into the unknown. You are no longer trapped in the Sefirah of Malkut. You have had some kind of powerful emotional experience that has confirmed for you the existence of a hidden spiritual reality and have determined to set out in search of the nature of this reality. The path of Tav lies before you, and you have already had a taste of the emotional suffering that often accompanies this path, thanks to its connection to the melancholy nature of the planet Saturn.

THE JOURNEY In any endeavor the key to success is persistence. Talent does not guarantee hard work, understanding does not ensure that our new wisdom is put into practice, and even the best teacher cannot be with us twenty-four hours a day. The only assurance of success is persistence, and this is the most important thing for you to hold on to right now. The total value of this dream is equivalent to that of a title of a particular form of divination (fortune-telling), and this may well suggest that you possess a latent psychic ability. This ability will certainly assist you and may even have been the spark that led you to this path, but even this cannot take the place of persistence.

BREATH

*nesheemah–nshymh–*נשׁימה*-405*

MEANING The breath has a very symbolic importance in the Kabbalah and the whole of the Western Mystery Tradition. The breath has often been seen as the means by which the Divine force manifests within us. Additionally, in all meditation practices great stress is placed on the need for correct breathing. Different styles and rates of breathing can produce radically different results in the meditation experience. It is no accident that the word for "breath" is the same as the Hebrew word for "soul." If we look at the compression of this dream's value we find the letters Tav and Heh. This defines breath as the window (Heh) onto the divinity of the universe (Tav).

THE TREE OF LIFE In a number of myths, we see the universe being created either by the word or the breath of God. In a sense, these two ideas are the same because in speaking we are also expelling air. In the Kabbalah we have a similar representation of the emanation of the universe from the Divine source. God breathed life into the universe through the uttering of the Hebrew alphabet. Thus, when we look at the Tree of Life, the path that is appropriate to this dream is that of Aleph. This is because as the first path it is the moment when the breath of the Divine began to create.

THE JOURNEY This dream does not pinpoint your position and it can occur at any time in your spiritual development. The position on the Tree of Life relates to the source of the Divine energy that is currently guiding you in your spiritual quest. A good response to this dream would be to take up meditation seriously, not just in its simplest form but to explore a range of approaches, such as Kundalini yoga, for instance. The fact that the dream value reduces to 9, with the value of the letter Teth meaning "serpent," means that Kundalini yoga would be particularly appropriate. There are other deep mystical implications tied up with the fact that the value of this dream is equivalent to the letter Teth, but they must be discovered through personal meditation.

BREEDING

*neemooseem–nymvsym–*נימוסים*-216*

MEANING There was a time when the concept of breeding, and in particular good breeding, was simply a matter of looking at somebody's parents and making a judgment based on their social status. Thankfully, those days are now behind us and we tend to judge people on their merits. However, we now face a new form of judgment by parentage with the advent of genetics and the rise of the nature-versus-nurture argument.

In spiritual terms the notion of breeding refers to the suitability of an individual for the Great Work. In the spelling of "breeding" we see the letter Mem occurring twice. Its first appearance refers to our physical birth while the second refers to our spiritual birth, and it is important to note that this occurrence is preceded by the letter Samech, which represents the supportive force of the Divine.

THE TREE OF LIFE One word that shares the value of the Hebrew word for "breeding" is the Hebrew for "lion." This is obviously appropriate to a dream about breeding because the lion is often regarded as a particularly aristocratic and noble beast. Even more important is the fact that a lion appears on the Strength card in the tarot. This card is attributed to the path of Teth, so it is this path to which the dream of breeding belongs.

THE JOURNEY The presence of the path of Teth implies that you need to take a very active and vigorous line in pursuing your spiritual development right now. In order to make the most of this burst of energy, you should consider taking part in some form of dedicated spiritual practice such as yoga or guided meditation. The fact that the value of this dream also equals the Hebrew for "oracle" suggests that you may be ideally suited to the spiritual life.

BREWING

*vashel–bshl–*בשל-333

MEANING This dream indicates a person of great verve and vigor who will approach the mystery of the Divine with a sense of humor that most people would find irreverent or inappropriate. However, there are signs in the dream's value that this person is absolutely sincere in his quest for the truth, and if anything his joviality is a sign of the closeness he feels to God. This view is supported by the fact that the total value of this dream is equal to the value of the Hebrew "AYQ BKR." This Hebrew word refers to a complex form of Gematria and suggests someone who is capable of penetrating the deepest mysteries of the Divine.

THE TREE OF LIFE The key characteristic of the person who has this dream is a benevolent and avuncular attitude to the world around him. This attitude typifies the personality associated with the planet Jupiter. This planet is found on the path of Kaph, which is an ideal place to locate the dream of brewing. The tarot card connected to the path of Kaph is The Wheel of Fortune, and this recognition of the chance nature of much that happens in our life is well suited to this dream.

THE JOURNEY The central letter, Shin, in the spelling of this dream title is a sign of the very powerful spiritual energy you possess. What is more, the final Lamed indicates that you have a driving urge to express that spiritual energy. Besides using it to develop your inner sense of the spiritual, you should take that energy and direct it toward helping your local community in a practical way. This will not only benefit those around you but will also encourage your own inner progress.

BRIARS

*dardar–drdr–*דרדר-408

MEANING When someone is waxing lyrical about the beauty of nature in a manner suggesting that the countryside is a soft lush paradise, it is always a good idea to remind him about briars! These thorny plants are infuriating when you are trying to make headway on a country walk, and once you are among them it often seems impossible to find a way out. From a spiritual point of view, to dream of briars is to visually re-create the experience of setting out on a mystical journey; we seem to be beset by problems on all sides and our progress is often painfully slow. The reduction of the value of this dream gives us the number 12, which is associated with The Hanged Man card in the tarot. The Hanged Man relates to acts of self-sacrifice, and the spiritual quest is a sacrifice of the self in the sense that it requires the defeat of the ego in order to find unity with the higher self.

THE TREE OF LIFE This dream is appropriate to someone who is taking his first steps on the spiritual ladder we call the Tree of Life. The spelling of the dream title very closely mirrors the experience of the path of Tav. We have the initial Daleth, representing a locked door, followed by the letter Resh, standing for the Divine force that opens the door— only to be faced by yet another Daleth standing for yet another door!

THE JOURNEY The way to continue now is to do exactly what you would if you were actually faced with a mass of briars. The only way to deal with them is to cut them down. You must find those things that are distracting you from the Great Work and cut them down. This is easier than you might think. Write the word *difficulties* with a large black marker pen on a big card and then simply sit and focus on the word, allowing it to get bigger and bigger in your mind's eye. You should then find that all sorts of difficulties, many of which you may not have recognized, will come into your head. Once you have identified and written them down, you can develop strategies to deal with them.

BRIDE

*kalah–klh–*כלה-55

MEANING To dream of a bride would normally be seen as suggesting a desire for marriage or some other relationship that involves the levels of mutual commitment we expect in a marriage. From a Kabbalistic perspective, this is still a dream about a marriage, but it is one between yourself and the Divine rather than between two people. The reduction of the value of this dream produces the number 10, which suggests that you are about to begin a new cycle in your life. As the dream is of a bride and not a wife, the suggestion is that you have yet to wholly commit to pursuing the Great Work but that the decision to do so is not far off.

THE TREE OF LIFE The number 55 is regarded as the mystical title of the Sefirah of Malkut in the Western Mystery Tradition. The fact that you are about to begin your quest and the fact that Malkut is also known as the "Bride" means that this is the only possible location for this dream on the Tree of Life. The title the Bride refers to the relationship of Malkut to the Sefirah of Keter. A common saying in hermetic philosophy is, "As above, so below"; similarly, from Kabbalistic teachings we have the expression, "Keter is in Malkut but after another fashion." The message in these phrases is that the nature of the Divine is reflected in the nature of the material universe, if we know how to look properly. It is because of this mirror relationship that Malkut is referred to as the Bride of Keter.

THE JOURNEY It is always easiest to work at those things that appeal to us, and the spiritual quest is no different. You will progress with much greater ease if you approach the Divine in a manner that you find comfortable and of interest to you. The idea of a marriage is again relevant here because there is a sense in which you need to fall in love with the idea of the Great Work in order to benefit from it. As in any marriage, there will be difficulties, and the initial letter, Nun, in the dream title indicates the potential for sorrow. However, the final letter, Heh, tells us that we can use that sorrow as a window on the universe.

❧BRIDGE

gesher-gshr- גשר-503

MEANING Bridges are not merely extensions of roads. In most cases they are there to protect travelers from some danger beneath them. More often than not this will be water, and the element of Water is very prominent in the Kabbalistic analysis of this dream. Additionally, a bridge can often act as a link between two very contrasting places. In spiritual terms we can see the image of a bridge as representing a movement from one state of consciousness to another. The fact that the value of "bridge" is equivalent to the value of a Hebrew phrase meaning "cast forth" emphasizes the idea of a bridge as indicating a move into a new spiritual state.

THE TREE OF LIFE In the Western Mystery Tradition there are specific titles for particular roles that relate to the power of the elements. The value of this dream is equal to the value of the title for the individual who symbolizes the element of Water. The watery influence continues in the reduction of the dream's value. The value reduces to 8, which

is the number of the Sefirah of Hod, and it is Hod that represents the element of Water in the Tree of Life. Clearly, this dream and the dreamer belong within this path on the Tree.

THE JOURNEY We tend to associate water with the emotions—with the depths of an individual—and generally this is also true of the element of Water in the Kabbalah. However, in this dream the most important water feature is the Sefirah of Hod. Hod is concerned with the way we mentally relate to the world around us and, of course, to the Divine. With this mixture of the emotional and the mental, the dream is telling you that in order to cross the bridge to a new state of consciousness, you need to find a way to rationalize your emotions. A good way to begin a process of self-analysis is to write a short play or story using all the conflicting aspects of your personality as characters. The idea is to figure out which characters come across as sympathetic and why they do so.

See Zohar symbol, Bridge.

BROKEN TELEPHONE

telefon shavoor-tlphvn shbvr- טלפון שבור-683

MEANING Sometimes when we are looking at the Kabbalistic interpretation of a particular dream we end up with a result that seems entirely counterintuitive—dreams about pain being positive, for instance. In this dream, however, the analysis is almost exactly in tune with the interpretation that common sense would predict. The image of a broken telephone suggests a problem with communication, and in terms of the spiritual, a difficulty in communicating with the Divine. The compression of the dream title emphasizes the communication angle as its central letter is Peh, meaning "mouth."

THE TREE OF LIFE This lack of communication you are experiencing is not a sign that your higher self doesn't care; it is simply a matter of using the right "telephone." It is likely that your failure to gain contact so far is probably because you are trying too hard and then feeling let down when you do not achieve the desired result. This leads to a great deal of anxiety, and for this reason the dream of a broken telephone belongs to the path of Qoph.

THE JOURNEY Qoph is one of three possible paths that can lead us out of Malkut. Each of these paths has its own difficulties, and in the case of Qoph those difficulties tend to be focused on confusion and anxiety. This is one of the reasons why the path of Qoph is connected to the tarot card The Moon. However, one of the positive aspects of The Moon card is that it represents an appreciation of the hidden reality that lies beneath the material world. If you try to pay attention to your instincts now, you will find that your worries will be eased.

BROOM

*matate-mtata-*מטאטא-60

MEANING This dream is about new beginnings and it is likely that a new beginning is long overdue in your life. For all sorts of reasons, you have a tendency to be a hoarder. This can apply to people and ideas just as much as to the tons of stuff you keep in the garage because you just can't bear to throw it out. The initial Mem in the spelling of this dream title indicates the way you like to look after and hold on to anything in your life that has had a special meaning for you. However, the subsequent letters Teth and Aleph indicate the need to make changes in your life and the need to be ruthless in doing so.

THE TREE OF LIFE The path that fits this dream is not so much an indication of your position as it is a sign of the attitude toward life that you need to try to develop. This dream occupies the path of Teth, which is associated with a vigorous and supremely determined approach to life, including an ability when necessary to be extremely tough with yourself and others in order to reach your goals. Teth means "serpent," and it may helpful to visualize such an animal when you are trying to create a mental picture of how to develop your personality.

THE JOURNEY For someone who likes to take a relaxed approach to life, this dream may seem unwelcome and more than a little daunting. However, when we look at the total value of the dream we see that it is 60, the value of the letter Samech, which stands for the supportive guidance of the Divine. What you need to do is to begin to be assertive in taking control of your life. You should start by clearing your home of all the clutter you have found it so hard to throw away. This will be difficult for you, but remember that the force of the Divine is there with you.

BROTHER

*akh-ach-*אח-9

MEANING From time to time we experience a dream that is entirely positive. This does not happen that often, but this is one such dream. When we have

these dreams we can look on them as the Divine patting us on the back and encouraging us to continue our inner development. The brother in the dream is a symbolic image that stands for your higher self. It is a sign that you are very close to achieving a real sense of communication with the part of you that is entirely spiritual in nature. The spelling of the dream title tells us the two key qualities of our higher self: The initial Aleph points to the unity with the Divine that becomes possible once we have connected with our higher self. The final Cheth points to the strong protective force that is exerted by this aspect of ourselves.

THE TREE OF LIFE In the tarot card The Sun we see an image of identical-twin boys playing happily in a walled garden while a benevolent Sun smiles down on them. This card is associated with the path of Resh and is ideally suited to this dream. The twins are yourself and your higher self, while the Sun is the Sun of Tiferet. It is the sense of unity within yourself that awaits you in the Sefirah of Tiferet and that this dream is pointing to as a way of encouraging you to persist in your efforts.

THE JOURNEY Throughout history mystics and magicians have put forward any number of methods for contacting the higher self. They may have used different names for the goal: to some it is the holy guardian angel; to others the higher genius; still others regard this initial contact with the spiritual as a contact with the Divine itself. Whatever the name, the intended outcome is the same. In order to achieve self-integration and understanding, you do not need to follow any elaborate or arcane ritual. It is everyone's potential to make this spiritual leap, and we need only to listen carefully to ourselves in order to see the way forward. One useful technique is to meditate while burning an incense that produces a lot of smoke. You should then visualize your reflection forming in the smoke and begin to talk to it as though it were your higher self. If this is practiced with sufficient sincerity, you will find that you do make contact.

BROWN

*khoom-chvm-*חום-54

MEANING Brown is never going to be the most exciting color in the world. Indeed, if there were a poll for the most unpopular color, brown would probably make the top of the list. However, this is a positive feature in terms of its Kabbalistic significance. When we are moving toward a more spiritual life-style we begin to recognize that glamour and fashion do not really matter, and, most important, we learn that the views of others are not anywhere near as crucial as we had once thought. So, we can allow ourselves to appear to be dull and unexceptional to those around us. When we look at the spelling of the dream title we see that the central letter, Vav, which stands for the macrocosm, is surrounded by two letters referring to protection. This implies that you have connected with the divine spark within you and are protecting it vigorously and lovingly.

THE TREE OF LIFE You have already achieved a sense of union with your higher self and are well on the way to some form of direct experience of the Divine itself. The combined protective forces of a loving and a vigorous nature point to this dream lying on the path of Teth. Teth runs between the martial, severe Sefirah of Gevurah and the merciful, loving influence of Hesed. Appropriately, the value of this dream when reduced is equivalent to the value of the letter Teth.

THE JOURNEY As we have said, brown is a very plain and visually unimpressive color. However, you should remember that many important features of the natural world are brown. The earth itself, from which all life springs, is an ordinary and uninspiring shade of brown. You need to embody the nature of this color in your dealings with others. You should engage in a range of community groups, but always as part of a team rather than as a leader. Additionally, where possible you should give people the benefit of your spiritual experience without referring directly to your work or the insights you have gained.

BRUSH

*meevreshet-mbrshth-*מברשת-942

MEANING If we consider the soul as a dirty house in need of cleaning, there are two ways we can try to make it acceptable. The first is to spend a long time on our knees with plenty of detergent and polish—it is hard work but the sense of achievement once the job is done makes it more than worthwhile. The second way is find a suitably large rug and sweep everything underneath—this is much quicker but even when we have finished we have to endure the nagging voice in the back of our minds pointing out that we haven't really done the job properly. This dream suggests that while you have the brush you are not yet sweeping properly, and this is emphasized by the association with The Devil card from the tarot indicated by the reduction of this dream's value.

THE TREE OF LIFE While The Devil card points to a tendency to avoid the hard work that you need to be engaging in right now, there are also signs that the nagging voice in the back of your mind is gradually getting louder. Before long you will be unable to ignore it and will put in the proper level of effort to your spiritual development. This places you on the path of Lamed, and right now you are experiencing the nagging force of the "ox-goad."

THE JOURNEY The journey you need to make right now is from a state of belief to a state of involvement. It is one thing to accept the existence of a spiritual aspect to life; it is another to decide that you are actively going to pursue the nature of this spiritual life. In order to make a start on this journey, it is best that you find a route that engages your interest and, if possible, has an element of fun to it, as this is more likely to hold your attention. An ideal place to start would be with a pack of tarot cards. Spend time focusing on each tarot card in turn, looking in detail at the symbols and allowing your mind to free associate. You may discover some interesting personal associations with each card.

BUCKLE

*avzem-abzm-*אבזם-50

MEANING Life can seem desperate at times and it is often easy to sink into a feeling of apathy. This can be much more acute when we feel that we have had a glimpse of a higher reality and then had it somehow snatched away from us. This dream represents that feeling of deep melancholy, but in the same way that a buckle holds clothing together, this dream indicates that the energy Divine is still with you and will hold you together when you need that level of support. The final Mem acts as an extra emphasis of this protective and maternal influence of higher forces, while the central letter, Zayin, points to the need to keep working to see the positive aspects of your life.

THE TREE OF LIFE The total value of this dream is 50, which is also the value of the letter Nun. It is the path of Nun that is the proper location of this dream because it fits the melancholic nature of the dream's hidden meaning. We should remember though that the path of Nun leads into the haven of Tiferet and should be seen as the great long night before the most beautiful dawn.

THE JOURNEY It is important now that you manage to retain your belief in the goal of the Great Work even at your lowest ebb. From Jonah being trapped in the whale to Odin hanging from the

World Tree, religions throughout history are filled with tales where the greatest reward follows immediately after the most painful suffering. You can help to maintain your belief by focusing on those things around you that remind you of the bountiful nature of the universe. Keep fresh flowers and herbs in your kitchen, spend time walking in the countryside, or spend some time with nephews and nieces; all these things will help you to keep a positive idea of the Divine.

INSECT

kheepoosheet-chyphvshvth- חיפושות-810

MEANING An insect is an ideal example of the nature of the Divine, in that while it may have an obvious appearance and a nature that many people believe they understand, it is in fact very different from how it appears to the average observer. In one sense, the job of the seeker after truth is to learn to see the bug as it really is. We may regard bugs as annoying, germ-carrying pests, but in fact they are absolutely crucial members of whatever ecosystem they happen to inhabit. The value of this dream reduces to 9, which links to the letter Teth, meaning "serpent." A great mystery is concealed therein, in that our perception of the biblical serpent is as inappropriate as our perception of bugs. The purpose of this dream is to alert you generally to the fact that things are never what they seem.

THE TREE OF LIFE In terms of misleading appearances, the most obvious position on the Tree of Life for this dream is the Sefirah of Gevurah. This Sephirah is connected to the inevitability of the destruction and decay of all forms of life and consequently can often be seen in a negative light. In fact, decay and death are essential in order to provide the raw material from which new life springs.

THE JOURNEY To see beneath surface appearances is a great ability to learn even if one is not pursuing a spiritual goal. If you intend to engage with the Western Mystery Tradition, this ability is an absolute necessity. The works of many Kabbalists and occult scholars exploit this fact and deliberately present their writings with obscure and misleading images and concepts. The purpose behind this is to separate the serious seeker from the merely curious. In order to increase your ability to see through the veils that the world projects, you should begin by reading the likes of Aleister Crowley and Eliphas Levi. (Crowley was an initiate of the Golden Dawn, the most influential occultist of the twentieth century and founded a new religion that focuses on the

need for individuals to discover their true inner will. Levi was a famous French occultist of the nineteenth century. He wrote widely on Kabbalah and reintroduced the tarot as a tool for meditation and magic.)

BUILDING

beenyan-bnyyn- בניין-122

MEANING In broad psychological terms, the image of a building seen in a dream represents the psyche. Indeed, the compression of this dream indicates that in Kabbalistic terms we should also view the image of a building as a way of displaying our psychological makeup. The difference is, of course, that as Kabbalists we also include the notion of a soul. In the compression we have the letters Qoph, Kaph, and Beth. When analyzed, this suggests that the mind of the dreamer (Qoph) is remaking itself (Kaph) in order to find its way home (Beth). The reduction value of this dream is 5, which in the context of this dream refers to the pentagram. The pentagram is a visual representation of the individual as a combination of the four elements surmounted by the element of Spirit.

THE TREE OF LIFE This dream indicates that you are in the process of constructing a mental framework for your psyche as a means of beginning the process of self-analysis, which will ultimately lead to the union of your conscious and higher selves. Kaph is the most practical-minded of the paths and is the appropriate destination on the Tree of Life for this dream. The association of Kaph with the tarot card The Wheel of Fortune indicates that this endeavor is likely to succeed.

THE JOURNEY When one enters the path of Kaph, it is very common for him to develop not only spiritually but in terms of his day-to-day life. The implication of this dream is that besides beginning to better understand your inner self, you are likely to meet with good material fortune in the next few months. In order to make the most of the opportunities offered by the path of Kaph, you should make a habit of listening to your intuition. This should be your guide over the next few months in practical as well as spiritual matters.

BULL

shor-shvr- שור-506

MEANING A common interpretation of a dream centered on the image of a bull would be that the dream is related to issues of power, aggression, and possibly, at a more trivial level, of clumsiness. However, in the Western Mystery Tradition the bull has a far more prestigious role. The importance of bulls can be traced as far back as the Minoans, who held the bull in enormously high regard. The fact that this dream reduces to 11 is a definite sign of its profound significance to the dreamer, as 11 is the number of magic. The bull represents the move from benign kindness to a sense of merciful justice that comes with a significant increase in the level of spiritual insight.

THE TREE OF LIFE The zodiac sign of Taurus is associated with the path of Vav. Given the obvious bull associations, this alone would suggest the path of Vav for this dream. Additionally the value of the Vav is 6, and in the value of this dream we see an initial 5 that eventually becomes a 6, the significance of which is explained below. Finally, the tarot card The High Priest or The Hierophant is associated with the path of Vav. Given the profound nature of the spiritual experience that this dream indicates, the High Priest card is especially appropriate.

THE JOURNEY The key to the journey you are about to undertake lies in the value of this dream. We begin with 50, which reduces to 5 and represents the individual who has become aware of his spiritual nature. The number 5 represents the four elements with the addition of the fifth element of Spirit. The dream's value ends with 6, which represents the macrocosm. Thus, the value of this dream tells us that you are about to pass from a microcosmic to a macrocosmic level of understanding. In layperson's terms, this means that you are about to shift from a link with your higher self to a direct link to the Divine.

BURDEN

*maamasah-ma'amsh-*מעמסה-215

MEANING If we were to visualize our life experience as a weight that we had to shoulder, rather like Sisyphus, then the life of the seeker of truth would have to be represented by a massive boulder. When we decide that we intend to pursue the Great Work, we accept an enormous responsibility. The compression of this dream makes it clear that this is a burden you are very happy to carry. You are aware that the benevolent force of the Divine (Resh) enlivens the Divine spark within your soul (Yod) and enables you to see beyond or beneath the material world (Heh).

THE TREE OF LIFE One of the phrases that has an equivalent value to the Hebrew "burden" is a phrase meaning "narrow path." The relationship here is clear; both words are linked to the idea of constraint and restriction. The important thing for the dreamer to remember is that these constraints are difficult but useful if we wish to increase our level of spiritual understanding. The fact that you are quite happy to bear this burden suggests that you are accustomed to carrying it. The path that fits this dream ideally is the path of Gimel, as it requires a deep spiritual insight to reach this far up the Tree of Life. Appropriately, Gimel means "camel," the traditionally beast of burden in the Middle East.

THE JOURNEY It may seem that the journey is almost over for you. After all, you are walking the path of Gimel with only Keter, the "Crown," ahead of you. However, you need to remember that this dream is associated with "burdens" and "narrow paths," so you should expect a difficult time ahead. In order to continue your progress, it is most important now to remember that while you have worked hard, the source of your greater understanding is the Divine and that without the influence of the higher you would not have increased your wisdom.

BURGLAR

*porets-phvrtz-*פורץ-376

MEANING Burglary is a terrible experience for anyone to have to go through and so we would expect any dream about burglary to be suggestive of difficult times ahead. Indeed, we may even be inclined to take it as a warning of some kind. However, this would be to misunderstand or temporarily forget what is ultimately important. A burglary can deprive us only of our material possessions, and since so often our possessions tend to own us rather than the other way around, this may not be such a bad thing.

The reduction value of this dream leads to the number 16. This number points to The Tower of Destruction card in the tarot, so it is likely that you are about to experience some form of catastrophic event. However, The Tower indicates that this will be spiritual rather than physical and that ultimately it will be greatly to your benefit.

THE TREE OF LIFE Aspects in the spelling and value of this dream title indicate that the traumatic experience that awaits you has the capacity to catapult you into a new level of spiritual awareness. Consequently this dream sits in Daat on the Tree of

Life. Daat is never labeled on the Tree because it occupies a position somewhere between Tiferet and Keter along the path of Gimel. Crossing through Daat is always difficult and is often referred to as crossing the abyss. It is this experience that the dream of burglary represents.

THE JOURNEY Your entire system of belief is likely to be significantly challenged over the next weeks or even months. In order to maintain your progress toward your ultimate spiritual goal, you will need to rely on the ideas you constructed in Hod and Netzach. These will help you to rebut any challenges to your beliefs that are thrown up by your unconscious at this time. It is worth remembering that the Hebrew "shalom" has the same value "burglary." This indicates that the peace of Keter follows shortly after the catastrophe of the abyss.

BURIAL

*kvoorah-qbvrh-*קבורה*-313*

MEANING Hidden within this seemingly depressing dream image are a number of extremely hopeful symbols. However, as is so often the way with the Kabbalah, we need to look very carefully and closely to understand the nature of the coded message within the dream. The first message lies in the value of the dream itself when looked at as a series of numerals. The number 3 represents the forces of creativity within the universe and appears twice surrounding the number 10, which indicates the completion of a cycle of our existence. What this tells us is that although one creation may end, it is immediately followed by a new life or creation.

THE TREE OF LIFE When we look at the compression value of this dream, we find the letters Shin, Yod, and Gimel. This tells us that the raw energy of the spirit (Shin) when joined with the Divine spark (Yod) will lead us to the secret wisdom (Gimel). The instruction hidden within the dream, then, is to approach our spiritual quest with greater vigor and passion. Consequently, this dream belongs to the path of Zayin. Zayin means "sword" in Hebrew, and this path is connected to an especially active approach to the Divine.

THE JOURNEY So far, we have considered only the hidden meanings within this dream image. The obvious concept of burial is important as an indicator of the journey you now need to take. Currently, you feel as though your life is becoming increasingly solitary, and while your spiritual development may

be going well, your general day-to-day life is suffering. Just as you will be born again in spiritual terms, you need to reinvent yourself in terms of your social life; otherwise you run the risk of losing all the benefits of a well-rounded life-style.

See Zohar symbol, Funeral.

BURNING

*kveeyah-kvvyyh-*בוייה*-57*

MEANING True spiritual yearning is as powerful and overwhelming as any human love. When we genuinely long for a sense of union with the Divine, we feel as passionate about it as we would for a person. This dream is about that overpowering need to achieve the goal of the Great Work and the way that one really can burn with desire. The value of the dream is equivalent to a Hebrew word meaning "consuming," which points to the nature of this desire for union, while the fact that the word's value is also equal to the word meaning "altar" tells us that this longing is genuinely spiritual in nature.

THE TREE OF LIFE It takes a considerable amount of personal development before one can see the Divine with such a concrete sense of reality that the wish to achieve communion with it becomes a driving passion. The path that fits your current state of development and this dream is the path of Yod. The letter Yod can be seen as the spark of divinity that resides within each of us, and in your case this spark is now glowing white-hot!

THE JOURNEY At the moment you have an intense need to feel a direct connection to God but are unsure about how to express it. This is understandable, in part because there is no single way to express those feelings. At the wholly spiritual level, you should try to engage in some active meditation techniques such as drumming or chanting. However, you can also express your desire for union by acting to protect and care for the Divine Creation at some level. This can be as simple as volunteering to tend a neglected area of public parkland.

BUTCHER

*katzav-qtzb-*קצב*-192*

MEANING "Butcher" has so many different contexts that it is hard to use the word without evoking ideas and thoughts of particularly brutal individuals in recent history. However, from a Kabbalistic perspective, "butcher" relates solely to the preparation of meat and the spiritual analogies that this gives rise to. The key role of a butcher is to take something that has died and turn it into a source of life. In doing so the butcher has to look at a physical reality in a way that would make many of us feel uncomfortable.

THE TREE OF LIFE This dream is about the visceral nature of the physical world and the need to recognize that all death leads in some way to new life, even if this is by becoming food that will sustain an already existing life. In the Tree of Life it is the Sefirah of Gevurah that governs the necessary breakdown of forms and it is here that the dream of a butcher belongs.

THE JOURNEY One of the most difficult aspects of the Great Work is to accept that while the Divine is infinitely loving, it a fundamental part of the universal order that all things must decay and die in order that they can live again in another form or another lifetime. In order to face up to this reality, you might consider visiting a slaughterhouse or even buying a fresh-killed rabbit or chicken and preparing it for cooking yourself.

BUTTON

kaftor-kphthvr-כפתור-706

MEANING At the practical level, buttons are simply a means by which we keep our clothes fastened, and this may suggest that this dream relates to ideas of practical comfort or even to decency. However, you will remember from your childhood the delight that could be had from a collection of brightly colored buttons, and that even the most trivial of items could be used as decorations or playthings. It is the idea of buttons in this context to which this dream refers. The reduction value of this dream gives us the number 13, which relates to ideas of major change in one's life. In your case, this indicates a need to shift away from such a serious outlook and allow yourself to have a little more fun.

THE TREE OF LIFE The Hebrew word meaning "rose" has the same value as this dream. The rose is the flower that is most associated with the Sefirah of Netzach. Additionally, as the Sefirah associated with expressing our emotions, Netzach is appropriate as a path on the Tree of Life that can be linked with free expression and unfettered joy.

THE JOURNEY Spiritual growth is undoubtedly a serious business, but we need to remember that the

Divine partakes of all the feelings that are experienced by human beings. As it says in the Kabbalistic texts, Malkut, or the material world, is a reflection of the spiritual world. This means that the Divine needs to approached with humor and joy as much as with humility and devotion. You should make a point over the next month of doing something entirely silly and fun at least once a day.

CAGE

kloov-klvb-כלוב-58

MEANING It is never the solid bars that make a prison a cage but always the attitude with which we view the cell that we happen to be in. Similarly, we can build ourselves a seemingly inescapable jail even when we have all the freedom in the world. This dream is about the tendency to believe ourselves trapped in a routine or a particular environment and the need to break out of that negative mind-set.

When we compress the value of this dream, we produce the letters Nun and Cheth. The letter Cheth, meaning "fence," represents this desire to protect ourselves, which often leads to our building a prison rather than a simple defensive wall. The initial Nun represents the journey toward a deeper faith in the Divine that could free us from this self-imposed imprisonment.

THE TREE OF LIFE This dream not only includes the letter Cheth in its compression but belongs to the path of Cheth on the Tree of Life. The path of Cheth leads out of Gevurah. As Gevurah is a Sefirah that deals with the inevitability of mortality and all aspects of the universe that tend to be characterized as negative, it is easy to see why the dreamer would be in a melancholic state of mind.

THE JOURNEY To travel the path of Cheth is no easy task. It requires you to learn that you cannot build a wall against all the hurts you may experience in your life. Indeed, once you have traversed the path of Cheth you will have reached a point where you no longer need a defensive wall at all, but will be looking to act as a protective force for others. Right now you can ease your feelings of sorrow by spending time helping those in your community who have enormous problems to cope with.

CALM

regeeah-rgya'ah-רגיעה-288

MEANING We live in an incredibly chaotic world, one that is fast, unpredictable, and inordinately stressful. One of the reasons that we are now seeing a resurgence of interest in the spiritual is a need for some kind of certainty and support, as well as a sense of meaning in all this rushing around. The value of this dream reduces to 9, which is the value of the Hermit card in the tarot. This card represents wisdom and also the desire to improve one's level of understanding of the world. The implication here is that you can achieve a level of calm and peace in your daily life by focusing on your search for a sense of deeper understanding about the Divine.

THE TREE OF LIFE This dream belongs to the path of Mem, not so much in terms of its being where you are on the Tree of Life, but in the sense that it is the maternal energy of Mem that will provide you with the sense of tranquility you need to find in your life. Additionally, this path is associated with the energy of the element of Water and so emphasizes the emotional aspect of this dream together with your need to feel that your relationships are free from stress and disorder.

THE JOURNEY Before we can achieve calm within our lives, we need to accept that a sense of peace comes only when we live in a peaceful manner. This means not entering into conflict with others and refers also to the need to ensure that you are nonconfrontational in all of your interactions with others. This includes ideas of competition. For instance, if you try to behave in a cooperative rather than a competitive way at work, you will find that you are not only more productive but significantly calmer than before.

CAMEL
gamal-gml-גמל-73

MEANING In Western culture the camel has very little in the way of mythic stature. Indeed, if it is renowned for anything it is for its supremely stubborn nature. However, in the Kabbalah the symbol of the camel is extremely significant, and if you have such a dream it is a clear indication of your ability to achieve some form of direct communion with the Divine itself. The value of this dream is the same as the value of a Hebrew phrase meaning "the wise one." This again points to the high level of spiritual insight that you have achieved. The fact that the reduction value of this dream leads to 10 indicates that you are in the process of completing a cycle in your life, and it is likely that this will culminate in something of a revelatory experience.

THE TREE OF LIFE The title of the dream tells us exactly which path of the Tree of Life is appropriate. The Hebrew spelling of "camel" is exactly the same as the spelling of the Hebrew letter Gimel. It is therefore inevitable that this dream sits on the path of Gimel. This path leads directly into the Sefirah of Keter and so can be seen as the last stage of your great spiritual quest.

THE JOURNEY the tarot card associated with the path of Gimel is that of The High Priestess. This card is important as it represents the secret wisdom available only to those who have managed to climb the tree and achieve a level of unity with the Divine. This is not a wisdom that can be learned from a book or a teacher; it must be directly experienced. The only advice that you can be given at this highly personal stage of your development is to maintain a rigorous schedule of meditation and prayer, while firmly believing that contact is only a breath away. In time and with sufficient fervor you will be among the few who have such an experience.

CAMERA
matslemah-mtzlmh-מצלמה-205

MEANING When cameras were first introduced to many cultures, there was an enormous suspicion that if you allowed someone to take your picture, you would lose part of your soul to the photographer. While this is clearly not the case, there is a very real sense in which the nature of a camera is about control rather than simple observation. The photographer is free to select exactly which part of any given scene he will reflect. This dream concerns the conflict between the act of observation and that of control or attempting to control. On one hand, we have the fact that the dream title ends in the letter Heh, which means "window" and suggests someone looking out at the world. In contrast, the value of this word is equivalent to a Hebraized version of the title Ra (the all-powerful God of ancient Egypt who, while represented as an eye, exerted total control).

THE TREE OF LIFE When we reduce the value of this dream, we generate the number 7. This is the value of the letter Zayin, which means "sword." This is very appropriate to the nature of this dream as it points to the will to control and also to the essentially confrontational nature of any attempt to exert control over others. The path of Zayin is the rightful place for this dream, and it is interesting that this is also the path where we find the tarot card The Lovers. This card indicates a pressing choice that must be made, which again links to the conflict between controlling and simply watching.

THE JOURNEY It is tempting to see our spiritual development as conveying upon us a right to take a judgmental view of the behavior of others. However, this is to misunderstand the whole purpose of the Great Work, as its purpose is to develop ourselves as individuals and not to take a view on the behavior of others. What you need to do over the next few weeks is to make a point of being in the company of people whose behavior you dislike. The key achievement to strive for is to resist the temptation to make any negative comments to them and ultimately not even to feel the desire to do so.

CAMP

*makhaneh–mchnh–*מחנה*-*103

MEANING No childhood would be complete without going to camp at least once, either with your family or some organization such as the Scouts. However safe it may have been, we always felt that in some way we were coming face to face with raw nature itself, and there was a real sense of survival when we return home free of permanent injury! The dream of a camp represents a similar sense of facing the material world and winning. The value of this dream reduces to 4, which stands for the physical world, and it is against this materialistic culture that we have to struggle.

THE TREE OF LIFE This dream focuses on the ability of the individual to rise above the challenges and attractions of a life focused entirely on material things. The central Cheth in the spelling of the dream title points to the need to erect a mental wall around our psyche to protect us from the lures of the nonspiritual.

THE JOURNEY Learning to see the difference between price and value is an especially hard lesson in a culture that encourages us to think mainly in terms of property rather than long-term spiritual development. This is the task that lies ahead of you now, and initial Mem in the spelling of the dream title indicates that the Divine will be with you to support you in your struggle. The best way forward is to learn to appreciate the true value of the spiritual. This can be achieved by taking a bath each evening after work and, having added some essence of mallow and chamomile, lying back and visualizing a warm globe of golden light passing over your whole body, soothing away the day's stress and concerns.

CANCER

*sartan–srtn–*סרטן*-*319

MEANING If there is one disease that strikes terror into the hearts of most people, it is cancer. This condition is seen as particularly terrifying because it not only damages us but replaces our cells with replicas of themselves. In this way, it replicates fears of being taken over by some external force. This dream should be seen as a warning that you are at risk of allowing your spiritual self to be taken over by negative energy. Within the spelling of the dream title we have both the letter Teth, which represents the serpent and can be seen as a distraction from the route to the Divine, and the final letter, Nun, which represents the sorrow that you will experience if you are unable to find the proper path.

THE TREE OF LIFE This dream is suggestive of someone who has taken the idea of individual responsibility for his own spiritual development too far. It is probable that he has moved from the idea of possessing a Divine spark to the idea that he is free to define the whole nature of the Divine. This is the danger inherent in the path of Ayin. This path is linked to vigorous and robust characters and, provided that this vigor is expressed in conjunction with an awareness of the higher, it is wholly positive. However, this dream warns that you are in danger of believing that your insights have come from within, rather than from the Divine source.

THE JOURNEY You are currently standing at a crossroads and only you can decide which road to take. If you are attracted by the sense of power that you feel when you believe yourself to be the sole arbiter of your fate, then you face the danger of losing the greatest opportunity of your life. In order to remind yourself of your reliance on a higher source for guidance, you should put yourself in a situation where you begin to experience genuine fear. By doing this, you will find that you begin to look to God for support, rather than to yourself. This experience can be achieved without any real danger; simply spending a full day in a small dark closet will create the disorientation necessary to allow your need for the Divine to resurface.

CANDLE

*ner–nr–*נר*-*250

MEANING It should come as no surprise to learn that this is an extremely positive dream. Even at a commonsense level, we would expect an image of a candle to represent illumination and indeed protection. The Kabbalistic interpretation would go along with such an analysis. However, it is important to note that while the candle may belong to the dreamer, the light is provided by the Divine force that emanates down the Tree from the source of Keter. The compression of this dream reveals a key mystery of the nature of spiritual insight. We have the two letters Resh and Nun. Resh indicates the light and protection of the Sun as a metaphor for the warmth of God. In contrast, Nun indicates sorrow, melancholy, and even death. It is easy to use the concepts signaled by Nun as reasons for rejecting God. However, the true seeker of wisdom will attempt to reconcile issues such as mortality to the existence of a benevolent divinity. Indeed, the symbolic value of the path of Nun is a process that ultimately leads to a deepening of one's faith.

THE TREE OF LIFE The existence of a metaphorical candle to light our way toward the goal of the Great Work is a clear indication of a merciful and kindly God. This aspect of the higher source is best represented by the Sefirah of Hesed. One of the paths that emanates out of Hesed is that of Yod. The letter Yod is the initial letter in the mystical Tetragrammaton and is often seen as representing the initial spark of creation. Consequently, Yod is an ideal path on which to place this dream.

THE JOURNEY For a long time you have been earnestly attempting to develop your spiritual understanding. Very often you may have been tempted to give up in the absence of any sign from above or within that your work is actually causing you to progress. This dream tells you that in a short time you will have confirmation that the Divine is indeed there to help you.

See Zohar symbol, Candle.

CANDY

*sookareeyah–svkryyh–*סוכרייה*–*311

MEANING To dream of candy may be seen as an expression of a desire to return to childhood. Candy is associated with the innocent joys of being a child, and while there is a need for us to recognize the responsibility of adulthood, this does not mean that we have to become entirely cynical. The value of this dream reduces to 5, which connects to the letter Heh, meaning "window." The suggestion here is that you tend to look at the world through the eyes of a child. This should not be taken as a negative

characteristic, though, as it indicates that you do not allow preconceptions to cloud your judgment.

THE TREE OF LIFE The initial letter, Shin, in the compression of the dream title points to an enormous amount of energy, while the subsequent Yod tells us that this energy is expressed in a way that is partly determined by the Divine spark within you. Given the emphasis on childhood, this energy is likely to manifest as an insatiable curiosity about the world. These factors place the dream on the path of Resh, especially due to its association with an active exploratory form of intelligence.

THE JOURNEY You should relish your outlook on the world as it will stand you in good stead throughout your life. As long as you maintain a curiosity about the nature of the universe, you will remain open-minded and able to learn. You should consider turning this infectious love of learning to the advantage of those around you. You have an excellent rapport with young people and should perhaps consider a career shift to teaching. This rewarding profession would develop your spiritual understanding, while your enthusiasm might well encourage some students to begin thinking about the bigger questions in life.

CANE

*kaneh–qnh–*קנה*-*155

MEANING While the word *candy* conjures up images of happy childhood experiences, *cane* evokes far less happy childhood memories of corporal punishment. Thankfully, the world has now advanced in its understanding, and as a rule we no longer beat children as a substitute for teaching them. However, although children may respond far better to explanations than coercion, there are times when our higher self can get our attention only by metaphorically caning us. This is in part because our lives are so embedded in material concerns that we no longer know how to listen to our higher self. The reduction value of this dream gives us the number 11, which implies a profound significance in terms of your spiritual development.

THE TREE OF LIFE When we look at the spelling of this dream title we see a story being told about its impact. We are currently in a phase of considerable reflection and thought (Qoph), which is leading us to a state of melancholy (Nun), but some experience is going to open a window on a new way of looking at ourselves and the universe (Heh). The experience in question is the effect of the cane in the dream, so this dream sits on the path of Lamed. This path is appropriate as it relates to the driving and sometimes critical force that can remotivate us at times when we feel despondent.

THE JOURNEY You have a strong desire to develop spiritually, and even though you may be feeling stagnant right now, this dream indicates that you do possess the willpower to come through this lull in your progress. You need to be a strict disciplinarian with yourself right now. This is much easier said than done, but there are some very simple things that you can do to help. As a start, you should draw up a daily plan of activity that schedules in time for meditating and focusing on the spiritual aspect of your life. If you also allow some time at the end of the day for something you really enjoy, you will be additionally motivated to stick to your timetable.

CAPTIVITY
*shvee-shby-*שבי-313

MEANING There is a sense in which all of us are in a state of captivity. As long as we live in ignorance of the spiritual level of existence, we are trapped in a prison of our own making, suffering the emotional pain that accompanies a lack of any ultimate sense of purpose. However, we all have the opportunity to free ourselves from this half life, but it does require an initial effort and sustained work in order to reap the benefits of freedom. The reduction of the dream's value gives the number 7, which is the value of the Hebrew letter Zayin, meaning "sword." This connection tells us that we need to fight vigorously to rid ourselves of the material concerns that dominate our lives.

THE TREE OF LIFE This dream tends to be experienced by people who have yet to grasp the nettle of the spiritual quest. It is likely that they have given considerable thought to the fact that in some ways their lives feel almost empty and have probably begun to realize that this feeling stems from a sense of loss due to the lack of any spiritual connection. The dreamer and this dream belong to the Sefirah of Malkut, as it represents the wholly physical.

THE JOURNEY You should feel encouraged by this dream because it indicates a realization that your life-style is not ultimately fulfilling. The way to address the negative feelings that such a dream evokes is twofold. The first thing to do is to spend time noticing all the aspects of the physical world that are wonderful and mysterious, from the life cycle of a lowly frog to the incredible power of a

thunderstorm. The second thing to do is to spend at least twenty minutes each day in quiet contemplation as a preparation for the work ahead.

CARDS
*klaf-qlph-*קלף-210

MEANING The history of playing cards makes for very interesting reading. Although today they are regarded simply as the means of playing a number of enjoyable games, there was a time when cards were regarded with the utmost suspicion. In the Middle Ages, when cards first originated, it was believed that they were the work of the Devil. This association had more to do with their use in simple fortune-telling than in gambling. To dream of cards indicates that one is attempting to determine his future. The value of the dream reduces to 3, which is the number that represents the creativity of the Divine. The dreamer is attempting to second-guess the creative process of the Divine.

THE TREE OF LIFE When we have reached a certain level of spiritual development, it is quite common to begin to attribute our success and our wisdom to ourselves. While this is true up to a point, it is essential that we never forget that every insight we have gained is a window on the nature of the Divine. If we then continue as though the Divine did not exist, we immediately negate the value of those insights. The path of Ayin represents the individual who wishes to cut his own path through life. It is also the path that in hermetic Kabbalah is associated with The Devil card. In order to avoid the pitfalls of pride associated with The Devil card in the tarot, you need to remember the importance of the Divine in your life.

THE JOURNEY The spelling of this dream title indicates the journey that you need to take now. The initial Qoph points to the need to reflect on your position, while the Lamed should be seen as a sign of the critical and motivating force of the Divine. Ignore this force and you will cease to develop. The final Peh emphasizes the need for you to try to re-open some kind of dialogue or communion with your higher self. The best way to do this is through meditation.

CARNIVAL
*karnaval-qrnbl-*קרנבל-382

MEANING Carnivals are enormous fun, full of color and light and excitement. The key feature of carnivals that is pertinent to a spiritual interpretation of this dream, though, is the fact that they are so utterly different from normal daily life. Stepping into the middle of a carnival can be very much like stepping into another world. The colors are brighter and more intense, the sounds are louder and more vibrant, and you are surrounded by people in strange and garish costumes. From a Kabbalistic perspective, this dream indicates an individual who has his first taste of spiritual reality and is in a state that could be likened to inebriation. The reduction value of this dream provides the number 13, which encourages the idea that the dreamer is going through a very major change in his outlook on life.

THE TREE OF LIFE When we first begin the Great Work, our task is to find a way to escape the material confines of the Sefirah of Malkut. The next Sefirah on the ladder of lights that leads to Keter and the Divine source is that of Yesod. This Sefirah represents a broad range of experience. Indeed, the nearer to the physical world a path on the Tree of Life is, the greater the range of experiences that it may represent. This dream reflects the sense of glamour, excitement, and mystery that typifies the experience of Yesod.

THE JOURNEY For now, you can simply enjoy the sights and sounds of the carnival. However, having achieved this level of development, you also need to begin to move beyond the wonder at the existence of a spiritual reality and toward actively working with it in order to achieve your full potential as a spiritual being. Now would be a good time to examine the possibility of a range of activities, from yoga to tai chi, which would help you in your journey.

CARPENTER

*nagar-ngr-*נגר-253

MEANING To Christians this dream would probably hold enormous spiritual significance, given that Jesus was a carpenter, like his father before him. However, this book attempts to look at dreams from a much more generic spiritual perspective, using the Kabbalah as the basis for its interpretations. It is worth remembering that the story of Jesus was written by Jews, so any symbolic significance of Joseph's occupation may point more to the Kabbalistic insight of the writer than to the truth of the story itself. Certainly the value of the dream title is significant because it is the number we get if we add together the numbers from 1 to 22—in other words, the sum of all the paths of the Tree of Life. Addi-

tionally, the reduction value gives the number 10, which indicates the completion of an important cycle in your life. Given the significance of the total value, the suggestion is that the completed cycle is that of climbing back up the Tree of Life.

THE TREE OF LIFE This is one of the very few dreams located in Keter. This Sefirah is at the very top of the Tree of Life and is as close to the Divine as is possible for anyone to reach. The central letter, Gimel, in the dream title indicates the means by which the dreamer has come to reside in Keter, as this points to the secret wisdom protected by The High Priestess. The initial Nun points to a period of intense self-reflection that must be experienced before reaching Keter and the benevolence of the Divine as represented by the final Resh.

THE JOURNEY The value of this dream is equivalent to the Hebrew word meaning "proselytes." To proselytize is another term for preaching, so the next stage of your journey is indicated in the very title of the dream. In order to maintain your position within Keter it is important that you share with others the benefit of your spiritual understanding. One way of achieving this would be to set up a guided meditation group, or alternatively, to use your insights for work that is not directly spiritual, such as counseling or mediation. You might also consider taking up woodworking or a similar activity as a craft-based way to express your spirituality.

CARS

*mekhoneet-mkvnyth-*מכונית-526

MEANING It is difficult to see where cars would fit in to a spiritually based book about dreams, but it is important to understand that anything that exists also exists in the mind of the Divine, so it can be seen in a spiritual light. If cars symbolize anything, it is the power of man over his environment and his physical limitations. The car enables us to travel much faster than we are naturally designed to. It is worth noting that the value of the dream consists of the value of the Tetragrammaton along with the value of the letter Kaph when positioned at the end of a word. As the Tetragrammaton means "God" and the letter Kaph means "hand" and is connected with practical activity, we see the value as referring to the idea of replacing God through technology. This dream definitely refers to someone who is more concerned with the material than the spiritual.

THE TREE OF LIFE While you believe yourself to be traveling speedily to your chosen destination, this is only because of the perspective from which you are viewing your life. When looked at from a three-dimensional viewpoint, you are indeed moving very swiftly. However, as soon as you add the spiritual perspective it becomes clear that you are not moving at all. Consequently, this dream belongs to the Sefirah of Malkut—the realm of the purely material.

THE JOURNEY This dream's value reduces to 13, a number that always indicates a major change in the dreamer's life. In your case this change will be a moving away from your consumer-driven worldview to a more inward-looking series of concerns. In order to give yourself the best chance of appreciating this change, you can start to alert yourself to the beauty and wonder in the world that you have been missing out on. For a start, try taking walks instead of driving everywhere. This alone will open your eyes to the wonder of Creation.

CASTLE

teerah-tyrh-טירה-224

MEANING This is likely to feel like a very reassuring dream. Castles are strong symbols of power and security, so you will probably feel that this dream indicates that you are in a safe and secure environment. However, we need to remember the fact that in dreams, buildings are ways for our unconscious to represent our inner feelings. When looked at in this way, we see that the dream points to a person who feels a very strong need to protect himself from the outside world. The initial letter, Teth, meaning "serpent," acts as a clue that this dream may not be as positive as you might think.

THE TREE OF LIFE When we reduce the value of the dream, we find the number 8. This number is the value of the letter Cheth, which means "fence." The letter Cheth relates to feelings of defensiveness, so the reduction value shows us that, far from being a strong image, this dream indicates feelings of insecurity and uncertainty. This dream is placed on the path of Cheth, and the need for self-protection that it points to may well stem from the fact that the path of Cheth emanates from the Sefirah of Gevurah, which represents severity.

THE JOURNEY Even though you are currently experiencing a number of grave concerns, it is important that you don't give up on your spiritual quest. You have already made considerable progress and you need to focus on your successes now in order to give you the resolve to continue. You can

help remove the need for such a defensive outlook by spending time helping out in a local wildlife center or simply by looking at the animals in your local park. You should consider how their fate is entirely dependent on circumstances outside their control. You can contrast this with the level of control you have in your life, and you should also be aware of the fact that despite their lack of control, the animals still live their lives to the fullest.

CASTRATION

lesares-lsrs-לסרס-350

MEANING Few fates are more terrifying to a man than the thought of being castrated. This is not just because of the physical pain that would accompany the experience but because to be castrated is to have the basis of much of your sense of self suddenly taken away. As is often the case, what is terrible in life is actually extremely encouraging in terms of spiritual development. The value of the dream title is the same as that of the Hebrew word meaning "vacuum." When one is spiritually castrated, he loses his sense of gender and so is able to approach the Divine in all of its aspects with equal understanding. However, at the psychological level this dream represents a loss of power and in particular a feeling of physical disempowerment. You need to explore any changes in your day-to-day life that might have provoked such a feeling.

THE TREE OF LIFE It takes considerable insight to reach the point where one experiences the dream of castration. It is worth noting that women may also have this dream, and its implications are exactly the same since we are looking at the removal of gender in general. The path to which this dream belongs is the path of Daleth. This is appropriate as it runs between the Sefirot of Binah and Hokhmah, which stand for the archetypal female and male energies, respectively. When we have mastered the path of Daleth we are free to view the world and the Divine from both archetypically male and female perspectives.

THE JOURNEY The letter Daleth means "door" in Hebrew, and the dream of castration is offering you a door through which you can pass to a new level of understanding. Our sexual roles are perhaps the strongest cultural constraints on our ability to expand our consciousness beyond the individual self to a wider level of understanding. In walking through the door that has now opened for you, you will be another step closer to unity with the Divine force. You can begin to develop the ability to see beyond the restraints of your gender by engaging in interests and activities that you would normally associate with the opposite sex. As you try your hand at football or aerobics, for instance, you should try to think yourself into the gender role you are experiencing.

CATHEDRAL

*katedrelah-qthdrlh-*קתדרלה-739

MEANING We have already seen that buildings in dreams are to be seen not as the institutions that they represent but as outward manifestations of the dreamer's inner psychological state. Since you are dreaming of a cathedral, it is clear that your focus is almost entirely spiritual. The spelling of this dream title explains to us how your sense of the spiritual is constructed. Religious experience is very much a mental process (Qoph) and must involve significant sacrifice (Tav) in order to open the door (Daleth) to the benevolence of the Divine (Resh); this belief drives you forward (Lamed) in the hope of glimpsing the truth (Heh).

THE TREE OF LIFE There is no doubt that you are a deeply spiritual individual. It is likely that you have had a strong interest in the nature of the universe from a very early age. Moreover, you have probably been actively pursuing a range of systems designed to give you a glimpse of the higher reality. Unfortunately, you created too much of a link between notions of suffering, self-sacrifice, and spiritual progress. This worrisome aspect of your construction of the spiritual life is reflected in the presence of the letter Teth in the compression of this dream's value. For this reason, the dream sits on the path of Nun due to its association with a melancholy outlook on the world.

THE JOURNEY It is interesting that in representing a highly spiritual outlook your unconscious chose to display a cathedral. The term *display* is important here because cathedrals are public rather than private buildings. There is a danger in unintentionally focusing on an outward display of piety, rather than having a simple but deep relationship with the Divine that is kept wholly private. It is probable that your focus on suffering stems from a concentration on how others may perceive the spiritually committed individual. What you need to do is put yourself in touch with the joy and wonder that emanates from the Divine. You could begin to do this simply by making a point of going out with friends at least once a week and making sure that you learn to laugh again.

CATS

*khatool-chthvl-*חתול-444

MEANING Whenever we have a dream whose value consists of the same number repeated, we are looking at someone who has a very strong and very particular focus in his life. The number 4 relates to the physical world and a materialistic outlook. If we take this in conjunction with the fact that this dream is about cats, which are renowned for their self-interested way of behaving, we are looking at someone who is rather self-absorbed and is focused on bettering his material position rather than his spiritual state.

THE TREE OF LIFE A dream so obviously based in the world of the physical has to be placed in the Sefirah of Malkut. However, the compression of the dream's value reveals that this self-interest is only a temporary phase, and that in the future you may well achieve considerable levels of insight. The dreamer is about to enter a period of self-sacrifice and gloom (Tav), which will lead him to look for the maternal aspect of the Divine (Mem), and this process will open the door to his inner development (Daleth).

THE JOURNEY The value reduction of this dream gives us the number 12, which indicates self-sacrifice. This seems wholly at odds with the personality type that the total value and the dream content suggests. However, the journey you are about to begin is not one that you will initiate, but one that the Divine will drive you to as a result of an undeniably spiritual experience

❧ CAVE

*mearah-ma'arh-*מערה-315

MEANING Plato used the image of a cave when he described the way that what we perceive as reality is but a shadow of a higher reality. In dreaming of a cave, you are putting yourself in the position of seeing only the shadow and not the full reality. This dream does not suggest someone who has never experienced or considered the spiritual aspect of life, but rather someone who has made a degree of progress and then, for some reason, retreated into a cave of shadows. The initial Mem in the spelling of this dream title along with the final Heh, do indicate though that the maternal energy of the Divine is watching over you and that ultimately you will be brought to see the light that is shining in from outside your cave.

THE TREE OF LIFE The path of Nun represents your state of mind right now. You managed to integrate both your mental and emotional natures with a spiritual view of the world, but then you found that your life continued to be beset by problems and anxieties. This has led you to doubt the reality of your beliefs. However, you should pay attention to the fact that the value of this dream reduces to 9, the value of the letter Teth meaning "serpent." This tells you that your fears and doubts should not be listened to and that you should focus on the insight you have already gained.

THE JOURNEY The path of Nun leads into the Sefirah of Tiferet. This is the Sefirah where we make contact with our higher self and can be seen as a well-deserved reward for our efforts thus far. Before we can reap this reward we have to experience something akin to a long dark night of the soul. You may see this as a test or simply as a natural part of your spiritual evolution. You can ease the pain of this phase of your development by focusing on the joy in your life. You could have some friends over and go through your old photo albums to remind you of the importance of your nearest and dearest.

See Zohar symbol, Cave.

CEMETERY

*bet almeen-bth a'almyn-*בת עלמין-602

MEANING It is important to distinguish between a dream of actually being dead and one in which you are simply in the presence of the dead. This dream indicates that you are coming to terms with the nature of mortality, which is a key achievement in making the journey toward a deeper spiritual understanding. While the final Nun in the dream title indicates significant levels of melancholy that accompany the realization of our mortality, the compression of the dream gives us the letters Mem and Beth, which are both connected to the protective and maternal aspects of the Divine.

THE TREE OF LIFE When we begin to progress up the Tree of Life, our first task is to integrate each aspect of our personality into a spiritual framework. Once this is achieved, we may learn to commune with our higher self. This then leads on to a process of climbing gradually closer to the Divine itself. You are currently occupying the Sefirah of Gevurah, which is closely connected to issues of mortality and the inevitability of death.

THE JOURNEY This dream is a cause for congratulations rather than depression, as it indicates that you have made excellent progress. It is still difficult, though, to accept mortality as yet another positive aspect of the Divine. You should spend some time meditating on the nature of death, while keeping in mind the letters Mem and Beth and their meanings. Over time you will begin to see that death is a return to our ultimate home and results from Divine love rather than a lack of any higher being.

CHAINS

*sharsheret-shrshrth-*שרשרת-1400

MEANING Life can be a terrible struggle sometimes, and the spiritual life is no exception. In this dream we see someone who is engaged in a struggle between the material and the spiritual, and this conflict is represented by the chains that are restraining the dreamer. The repeated letters Shin and Resh represent this conflict, with Resh acting as the positive warmth of the Divine and Shin symbolizing the enormous energy within you, which is currently being misdirected. The total value is equivalent to one of the ways in which we write "chaos" in Hebrew. This is a very appropriate summary of how you feel right now about your spiritual development.

THE TREE OF LIFE As we might expect, this dream relates to a person who is still in the very early stages of the Great Work. The predominance of the letter Shin, along with the sense of conflict that this dream carries, places this dream on the path of Shin, which leads from Malkut to Hod. The tarot card associated with this path is Judgment, which points to the need for you to get a clear grasp on the issues you are struggling with and to make an informed decision about how to proceed.

THE JOURNEY The reduction of this dream gives us the number 5, which is the value of the letter Heh. As this letter means "window," we can see this as a reminder that you have the potential to see out of your current state of internal chaos to the clarity that lies in front of you in the Sefirah of Hod. A good way of breaking the mental chains is to actually write down your conflicting feelings, and then advise yourself on those conflicts, as though you were talking to a friend rather than yourself.

CHAIR

*keese-kysa-*כיסא-91

MEANING Nowadays, most of us sit down just as much when we are working as when we are relaxing.

However, traditionally we worked standing up, and chairs were reserved for those times when the work was over for a while. Consequently, dreams of chairs relate to a sense of calm and rest. The value of this dream reduces to 10, which implies that an important chapter in your life is drawing to a close and so a restful period is probably well deserved. Additionally, the value of this dream is also equivalent to the Hebrew words meaning "tent" and "food," so the idea that you are now entitled to a period of rest is implied both in the obvious meaning of the dream and in the value itself.

THE TREE OF LIFE Chairs are not permanent resting places. They are there to provide us with a break so that we may continue our work refreshed. Similarly, this dream does not indicate that you have reached the end of your journey; in fact, you have a long way left to travel. However, you have reached the Sefirah of Yesod and are now on the path of Samech, making the difficult spiritual trek to Tiferet. The letter Samech means "prop" and should be seen as a sign of support and guidance from above. This means that while you are resting you will still be receiving support and encouragement from the Divine.

THE JOURNEY The tarot card Temperance is associated with the path of Samech. This card represents the achievement of balance in our lives. It is a sense of balance that you must strive for now. Without balance there is conflict, and this prevents us from living in a calm and restful manner. We can train our inner self to behave in a balanced way by trying to ensure that our outward life is equally harmonious. In the next few weeks, you should try to achieve equilibrium in all areas of your life. This includes the way you treat people in the office, the need to exercise and also simply to relax, and even the need to eat a balanced diet.

CHALLENGE
etgar-athgr-אתגר-604

MEANING Simply to survive in the modern world is more than enough of a challenge for many people. However, the seeker of truth knows that however tough the challenge may be, the rewards are greater than can ever be imagined. The central letters, Tav and Gimel, represent the difficulty of the spiritual challenge. On one hand we have the suffering and melancholy represented by Tav, while on the other we have the promise of the secret wisdom indicated by the letter Gimel.

THE TREE OF LIFE This dream is experienced by someone who is struggling to come to terms with his decision to follow a spiritual path. It is a positive dream in that its value reduces to 10, confirming that while you may be feeling anxious, your decision to take the route out of Malkut is definite. In fact, this has already been achieved, and the worries that you now feel are those often experienced by people as they traverse the path of Qoph.

THE JOURNEY As you progress up the path of Qoph, your emotions will be more and more difficult to ignore. All those anxieties and moments of self-doubt that you had managed to bury will begin to crawl out of your mental woodwork to disturb you. The solution is not to try to repress them again, as this was never the right approach. Rather, you need to take the initiative and make an appointment with a counselor or therapist so that you can finally lay the ghosts of your emotional past to rest. This will enable you to face the future in a much more positive and empowered way.

CHAMPION
aloof-alvph-אלוף-117

MEANING Always beware of dreams that flatter your sense of self, as they will inevitably be a warning in disguise. If you take this dream as suggesting that you have already achieved a sufficiency of spiritual insight, you will fall into the trap of pride and begin to slip back down toward Malkut. The total value of this dream has the same value as the word meaning "fog" in Hebrew. The implication of this is that you are in danger of being unable to see the correct path to take, and it appears that your overconfidence in your development so far is the root cause of this problem. This interpretation is supported by the fact that the reduction of the value of this dream leads to the number 9. The number 9 is the value of the letter Teth, which means "serpent" in Hebrew and indicates the potential for self-deceit.

THE TREE OF LIFE It is possible to proceed a significant way along the Tree of Life without recognizing the absolute role of the Divine in your success. However, ultimately you reach a point where you have to recognize the position of the higher source in your development or cease to develop at all. The turning points are many, but in your case this crossroads moment is occurring on the path of Ayin. This path is appropriate as it suggests a very strong individual will and also is potentially confrontational in nature.

THE JOURNEY In order to gain meaningful insights into the reality that lies behind the material universe, you need to learn to perceive the world around you in a way that allows for the existence of God. An intellectual approach to this problem is probably best suited to your nature. A good way to do this exercise is to begin to consider a number of conundrums such as: Do infants have feelings and thoughts before they acquire language? From where do we gain our innate sense of fairness? If there is no God, why would we choose to invent one? If evolution was the only process at work in the development of the planet, why do we never find evidence of those new species that were ill-suited to their environment? And, indeed, what is behind the drive to adapt?

CHASING

*redeefah–rdyphh–*רדיפה-299

MEANING In romance, the unwritten rule is that you should never chase the person you really want to catch, as this merely encourages them to keep you at arm's length. In terms of the spiritual quest the same is true, albeit for different reasons. If you exert all your energy chasing a spiritual experience, you will never achieve the receptive state of mind required for such an experience to occur. The initial letter, Resh, in the compression of this dream and indeed in its spelling indicates that you are likely to gain your looked for spiritual connection, but you need to slow down first!

THE TREE OF LIFE It is in one sense encouraging that you are chasing after the goal of the Great Work since it does at least indicate a firm commitment. Indeed, the path of this dream is the path of Tzaddi, which means "fishhook" and tells us that you have been well and truly hooked by a desire for greater understanding. However, the final number, 9, in the value of this dream points to the letter Teth and with it the danger that in your enthusiasm you may be drawn to routes that will lead you not to the Divine but only to self-delusion.

THE JOURNEY The path of Tzaddi leads into the Sefirah of Netzach, which is associated with our emotions and passions. It is therefore not surprising that you are in danger of getting carried away with yourself right now. This danger can be greatly reduced if you involve yourself in a well-established meditation circle or simply set aside some time each day to read from the vast range of books that deal with the development of the spiritual aspect of life.

CHASTISE

*leyaser–lyysr–*לייסר-310

MEANING Even if we dream of other people, our dreams are always an attempt by our unconscious and our higher self to show us a better way in which to live our lives and to approach an understanding of the spiritual. In this dream, even if you dream of chastising another person it is simply yourself visualized as a separate individual. Your determination to achieve some form of union with the Divine is very strong, and this is indicated by the letters Shin and Yod, which make up the compression of this dream image. The letter Shin indicates great spiritual energy being manifested in action, while Yod indicates the Divine spark itself, which ignites that reservoir of energy within you.

THE TREE OF LIFE Throughout history there have been individuals of great spiritual insight who have gone to radical lengths to get closer to the Divine. It was common in the Middle Ages for Christian mystics to physically abuse themselves in a number of ways in order to achieve an altered state of consciousness. This approach to spirituality is mirrored in a number of faiths, from those of the plains Sioux to those of certain Sufi sects within Islam. While you are not going to such extremes, you are being extremely hard on yourself, so this dream belongs on the path of Lamed. It is of course no accident that the dream itself begins with the letter Lamed, meaning "ox-goad."

THE JOURNEY While dedication and commitment are qualities to be greatly admired, there is always a danger in such a disciplined approach to your spirituality that you will forget or lose the benevolent and joyous aspect of the Divine. This would be a terrible shame, as God made the universe from a perspective of love rather than a need to punish. In order to rediscover the wonder of spirituality, you should visit an art gallery, ideally one that displays some devotional art. When you see the beauty and love that is present in such paintings you will remember the great sense of love that first initiated your interest in the spiritual path.

CHEATING

*leramot–lrmvth–*לרמות-676

MEANING The one thing that none of us can ever cheat is death, and of course once we are dead we cannot cheat the judgment of the Divine. It doesn't matter whether we believe that this judgment comes from karma or a choir of angels or the direct decision of God; the point is that we cannot cheat our way out of it. Since this is the end result of all spiritual life, it is clear that to attempt to cheat at any point in our spiritual development is foolish. The value of this dream's title is equivalent to that of the Hebrew word meaning "artificial," and it is artificiality that this dream is about. We may not be cheating in the most obvious sense of the word, but every time we pretend an emotion or simply go through the motions of some act of worship, we are cheating ourselves because we are trying to cheat the Divine.

THE TREE OF LIFE It is likely that when you are engaging in cheating behavior, in the spiritual sense of the word, you are not at all aware that this is what you are doing. It may well be that you regard your behavior as simply practical. Every path has both its negative and positive attributes and in this case you are on the path of Kaph. The positive aspect of Kaph is that it is concerned with practical activity, but when practicality takes precedence over spirituality, we have a negative situation.

THE JOURNEY Some New Age groups will recommend that when meditating or engaging in visualization activities you should "fake it 'til you make it." This is all very well and good until somebody gets to the point where he cannot distinguish the results of an unfettered imagination from a real spiritual inspiration. Consequently, the best way for you to proceed is to take the view that if you experience nothing when meditating, it simply means that the time is not yet right. You will find far better results if you focus on thinking about the nature of the Divine than if you try to find shortcuts to having a spiritual experience.

CHILDHOOD HOME

*bayeet yaldoot–byth yldvth–*בית ילדות-862

MEANING To dream of our childhood home is to dream of a return to innocence. Of course, in a spiritual sense this refers to a return to pure belief or faith, without the cynical doubt that tends to accrue as we grow older and supposedly wiser. This dream also refers to a desire to experience the feeling of being absolutely loved and utterly protected that we had when we still believed that the world began and ended at our own front door. The central letter, Samech, in the compression of the dream's title indicates that you are about to experience such a sense of support and guidance from the Divine.

THE TREE OF LIFE In order to rid ourselves of our cynicism, it is often necessary for us to go through some form of traumatic event that prompts us to turn again to the higher powers for assistance and a sense of purpose. The reduction of the value of this dream gives us 16, which indicates The Tower card in the tarot. The Tower card tells us that a catastrophic event is waiting in the near future but also that this event will ultimately prove beneficial. This card is linked to the path of Peh on the Tree of Life. We also see that the initial value of 800 in the compression of the dream's value refers to the letter Peh, and that this is the path on which this dream sits.

THE JOURNEY You may be dreaming of your childhood home, but one of the obstacles to achieving that yearned-for state of spiritual innocence is the fact that cynicism is both repellent and attractive at the same time. When we are cynical we don't have to question the way in which we live our lives, nor do we have to worry about the impact of our behavior on the state of our soul. What you can do to increase the balance in favor of innocence is to spend some time revisiting the haunts of your youth and reminding yourself of how you used to feel there.

CHIMES

tseeltsool paamon–tzltzvl pha'amvn–
צלצול פעמון-492

MEANING Many of us now have wind chimes hanging on our houses not just as decorative objects but also thanks to the growing popularity of feng shui. In Kabbalistic terms chimes are significant as they allow the air to be given a voice. This has a very profound implication in terms of the idea that the universe was created by the breath of the Divine giving voice to the Hebrew alphabet. The importance of the element of Air to this dream is demonstrated by the reduction of the dream's value. When reduced, we have a value of 6, which is the value of the Hebrew letter Vav, and the letter Vav stands for the element of Air in the Tetragrammaton.

THE TREE OF LIFE The compression of this dream gives us the letters Tav, Tzaddi, and Beth. The path of Tav runs into Yesod from Malkut, while the path of Tzaddi runs from Yesod into Netzach. The letter Beth means "home," and the path of this dream is the common home of both Tzaddi and Tav—the Sefirah of Yesod. It is equally appropriate to place this dream in the Sefirah of Yesod since it too represents the element of Air.

THE JOURNEY This dream is encouraging you to step back and spend a good deal of time thinking about your spiritual development and the direction in which you wish to move. The constant references to the element of Air indicate that the right decision will take considerable mental effort. You should try burning some sage incense while deciding which spiritual system to follow, as this is ideal for clearing the mind and encouraging wise choices.

CHOKING

khenek-chnq- חנק-158

MEANING This dream represents something of a transformation in an individual. While the content of the dream seems worrisome, even disturbing, it is simply a part of a process of personal growth. Before we can enter into a new and more meaningful relationship with the Divine, we pass through a period where our spiritual existence seems excessively restrictive, hence the idea of choking. The value of the dream title reduces to 5, which links it to the letter Heh, meaning "window" and indicating that there is a light at the end of this particular tunnel.

THE TREE OF LIFE The spelling of this dream title provides a simple narrative that explains why you are experiencing this dream of choking. You have had certain spiritual insights that have caused you to erect a defensive wall around yourself (Cheth). This has prevented you from reflecting on your relationship to the Divine (Nun) and is constantly troubling your mind (Qoph). This chain of events is typical of the response to the Sefirah of Gevurah, as it makes us face up to our mortality. The dream of choking indicates that you are now entering the path of Teth, where you must wrestle with these negative thoughts in order to enter Hesed.

THE JOURNEY It may seem an easy excuse to say that the ways of the Divine are beyond our comprehension, but it is only logical that if some form of divinity exists it is by definition beyond the scope of human understanding. Therefore, we should not be surprised when we are unable to see the purpose of some aspect of the universe. Our correct response should be to attempt to understand, but this is not always easy. In order to escape the doubts introduced by the Sefirah of Gevurah, you need to spend some time imagining the world without death or decay or any kind of metabolic breakdown. When you have a clear image of how such a world would actually be, you will see the wisdom in the force exerted by Gevurah.

CHRIST

notsr-nvtzr- נוצר-346

MEANING Unsurprisingly, there is considerable debate in Kabbalah circles about the nature of Christ. There are, for instance, very significant Kabbalistic analyses that can be generated from all the titles for Christ, from the term Christ itself to Messiah to his given name, Jesus. A Christian Kabbalist will tell you that this demonstrates the validity of his faith, a Jewish Kabbalist might maintain that it demonstrates the Kabbalistic skill of the people who constructed the tale, and a hermetic Kabbalist like myself would argue that the important thing, agreed by both the Christian and the Jewish Kabbalists, is to recognize the spiritual truth that lies within the words and to use them to bring ourselves closer to the Divine, no matter what denomination we may be. The reduction value of the dream title indicates that you are about to experience a major change in your life, and the compression of the dream reveals that this change will be enormously beneficial to your spiritual development. We have evidence of a vast amount of spiritual energy (Shin) allied with the protective influence of the maternal aspect of the Divine (Mem), which leads to some form of union with the macrocosmic consciousness (Vav).

THE TREE OF LIFE In the analysis of dreams we are concerned not with the literal truth or function of a given dream image but with its symbolic value and significance. The image of Christ represents an individual with profound spiritual understanding, and this is underwritten by the value of the dream title. Consequently, this dream belongs to the Sefirah of Tiferet. This fits with the narrative provided by the compression of the dream as well as being the point on the Tree of Life where we make definite contact with our higher self.

THE JOURNEY Whatever our faith, there are certainly some positive lessons about behavior that can be learned by studying the story of Christ. The value of the dream is equivalent to that of the word meaning "channel" in Hebrew. It is this aspect of the Christ story that you are now being encouraged to emulate. In the gospels, Jesus is portrayed as acting as a channel or conduit for the wisdom of the Divine. You must also attempt to behave in such a way that your whole manner of being is a channel for the Divine. This means behaving at all times in a charitable, understanding, and loving manner with all those around you.

CIGARETTE

*seegareeyah–sygryyh–*סיגרייה*–*298

MEANING Cigarettes mean only one thing: conscious self-harm. There can be nobody today who is unaware of the dangers of smoking, and yet we continue to buy these little time bombs by the millions. Not only are they incredibly dangerous, but they also remove our self-determination. As soon as we become hooked, we have given away a part of our free will, and this is a far worse state of affairs than many of us realize. It is akin to throwing away your most prized possession. This dream is not about cigarettes themselves but about a need, which you have yet to overcome, for some form of comfort. Holding on to this need is impeding your inner development.

THE TREE OF LIFE When we look at the compression of this dream we see that the central letter is Tzaddi, which means "fishhook." This is the path on which the dream is located, but it is the negative aspect of Tzaddi that is being highlighted here. It is perfectly acceptable to be hooked on behaviors or beliefs that increase our level of responsibility and understanding. However, the final Cheth in the compression of the dream points to the fact that you are hooked on the idea of feeling safe and protected. This may not seem a negative characteristic, but in spiritual terms it prevents us from discarding our concerns with the material side of life, as this exposes us to too much risk.

THE JOURNEY Like any addiction, the only solution is to quit and to keep to that decision. It is difficult if not impossible for most of us to wake up one day and decide to live a completely nonmaterialistic life. However, you can gradually wean yourself off this source of reassurance in your life. A good start would be to give away some of your possessions. These should be items that are still valuable to you, otherwise all you will be doing is clearing up as opposed to genuinely making a new start for yourself.

CIRCLE

*khoog–chvg–*חוג*–*17

MEANING Geometric figures have always been important in the Western Mystery Tradition and in almost all other forms of mysticism. The Kabbalah is no exception, and the circle is a particularly profound symbol. The circle has no end and

no beginning and, as such, is an ideal symbol for the Divine itself. The value of this dream reduces to 8, and in the context of the dream content this relates not to the letter Cheth but to a figure 8 as a symbol of eternity. To dream of a circle is to be very close to some form of direct communion with the Divine.

THE TREE OF LIFE The spelling of this dream's title indicates which path on the Tree of Life we should be focusing on. The dreamer has understood the cyclical and spiral nature of infinity (Cheth), is now being guided by the macrocosm itself, and has developed a coherent mental approach to his spirituality (Vav). Having achieved these key goals, he is now on the path that leads to the secret wisdom (Gimel). To be on the path of Gimel is no mean feat, and it is likely that the dreamer has passed through the hidden non-Sefirah of Daat and is now in the latter stages of this final path toward Keter.

THE JOURNEY Dreams not only point out those areas of our life that need development, but also very directly indicate how best to ensure that those developments do indeed take place. In this dream we have the image of a circle and equally noticeable the presence of the figure 8. These two figures with their associated meanings are ideal subjects for prolonged meditation. The significance of these symbols when combined cannot be explained but can be experienced directly. You should carefully draw a figure 8 within a circle on a plain white card and then meditate while focusing on that image. When you achieve an understanding of this symbol you will be in no doubt about the validity of your experience.

CLIFFS

*tsook–tzvq–*צוק*–*196

MEANING There is a popular saying that the higher anyone rises, the farther they have to fall. This is obviously true, but is no less important for that. To dream of cliffs certainly indicates a significant level of spiritual insight or at least a strong desire for spiritual development. However, cliffs are defined not simply by their height but by the fact that they lead to an incredibly steep drop to the unforgiving sea. This dream advises the dreamer that he needs to pay close attention to his progress or there is a danger that he will slip and fall. The total value of the dream is equivalent to that of the Hebrew word meaning "summit," which is another hint at the precarious nature of the dreamer's current position.

THE TREE OF LIFE The reduced value of this dream is 16, which is associated with the tarot card The Tower. This card indicates a catastrophic event in the dreamer's life, but one that will ultimately prove beneficial. The idea of impending catastrophe links to the warnings that are being given in the dream's content. This places the dream on the path of Peh. In the *Sefer Yetzirah*, one of the key Kabbalistic texts, this path is also known as the path of the "exciting intelligence." This may be an indication of the need for you to calm down in order to avoid falling over the edge of the metaphorical cliff.

THE JOURNEY Your desire for truth is to be commended and you have made considerable inroads so far in terms of the Great Work. However, enthusiasm should always be tempered with caution and this is the lesson of this dream. The value of the dream title is 196, which is the square of 14. This is significant when we notice that fourteen is associated with balance and calm. Whatever form of spiritual exercise you are currently engaged in, it would be a very good idea for you to begin to practice yoga, as this will help to give you the necessary sense of calm in your life.

CLOTHES

*begadeem–bgdym–*בגדים־59

MEANING In the Book of Genesis, Adam and Eve's first response after eating the fruit of the Tree of Knowledge of Good and Evil is to become aware of their nakedness. The image of clothes in the Kabbalah is associated very closely with notions of moral awareness. The compression of the word *clothes* can be seen as shorthand for that famous tale of the realization of morality. The letter Teth represents the serpent, while the letter Nun indicates the deepening of faith that can ultimately result from a realization of the implications of free will. However, the dream's value reduces to 5, which is the value of the letter Heh, meaning "window," indicating that even at the most sorrowful moment there is always hope.

Traditional Kabbalists see a dream about clothes as a symbol for material well-being and enjoying life's sensual pleasures. Historically, to dream of fine clothes was a positive symbol of splendor in one's life.

THE TREE OF LIFE The wearing of clothes in the Genesis story marks the first judgment of man by the Divine. This dream relates to the need for you as an individual to recognize your past mistakes, not in order to suffer guilt but in order to leave them behind as you begin your spiritual journey. The tarot card Judgment is connected to the path of Shin. As one of the first paths out of Malkut and given its nature as the biting path, this is the most appropriate place to locate this dream.

THE JOURNEY The value of this dream is equivalent to that of the Hebrew word meaning "wall." The implication here is that you have built a wall around part of your past as a way to avoid having to deal with your emotional history. The path of Shin is a difficult one to work through as it requires you to knock down that protective wall and examine yourself more closely than you ever have before. In preparation for this self-examination, it would be beneficial to have at least few sessions with a professional counselor.

CLOUDS

*anan–a'ann–*ענן־170

MEANING The improvement in communications and the greater movement of cultures between countries means that we now have access to a much wider range of spiritual philosophies. However, if we are to interpret them correctly, it is important that we remember the nature of the places from which they originate. For instance, this dream is about clouds, and to people living in a temperate zone it might seem to have negative connotations. In fact, given the origins of the Kabbalah, cloudy skies would be a very good sign indeed. Similarly, from a spiritual perspective this dream is very positive. The compression of the dream's value suggests that the influence of the Divine on your mental state (Qoph) is encouraging you to progress through life with renewed energy and vigor (Ayin).

THE TREE OF LIFE Clouds are inevitably linked with the element of Water, and this points to the Sefirah Hod as it is closely associated with that element. Additionally, the value of this dream reduces to 8, and Hod is the eighth Sefirah in the Tree of Life. In Hod you will be able to draw on the influence of the Divine in order to construct a way to reconcile your rational manner of looking at the world to a more spiritual outlook.

THE JOURNEY You are entering a phase of consolidation in terms of the Great Work. Before you can continue on your quest with the confidence and vigor suggested by the final letter, Ayin, in the compression of the dream's value, you need to take some time to reflect. You can encourage the influence of the Divine by surrounding yourself with an atmosphere that is conducive to the energies reflected in the Sefirah of Hod. For instance, if you have a room in which you meditate, ensure that you have plenty of orange-colored items there. You can also keep some hawthorn in this room as an aid to success.

CODES

*tsofen–tzvphn–*צופן-226

MEANING Even the briefest of examinations of the Kabbalah reveal it to be a system of wisdom that is unusually dependent on codes in one form or another. In this book we are using only the simplest of forms of Gematria, but the Kabbalah can be as complex as you wish to make it. For instance, there are methods of interpreting sacred texts that require abstruse methods of letter substitution, so that the final interpreted text is wholly different from the initial string of letters to be analyzed. This dream suggests that you have gained considerable insight and are able to see the hidden truths that lie beneath both religious texts and the world itself. The compression of the dream gives us the letters Resh, Kaph, and Vav. The influence of the Divine (Resh) is seen as helping us on a practical level (Kaph), allowing us to reflect on our spiritual journey (Vav).

THE TREE OF LIFE Traditionally, the various methods of cryptology that underlie much of the Kabbalah were handed down to students only when they were deemed sufficiently learned in the overt meaning of the texts. To dream of codes therefore points to your having made real progress in your spiritual development. The path of Beth leads directly out of Keter and so is an appropriate place to locate this dream. This is especially so because it is also the path associated with The Magician card in the tarot, a mercurial figure who is ideally placed to interpret hidden codes.

THE JOURNEY You are now in the rare and privileged position of having achieved a level of contact with your higher self and are capable of achieving an even greater level of spiritual understanding. In order to come to grips with some of the more complex issues that apply to a Kabbalistic view of the Divine, you should consider enrolling in a serious Kabbalah group to further explore the subject matter under the guidance of someone who already understands some of its implications.

⚜COFFIN

*aron meteem–arvn mthym-*ארון מתים-747

MEANING You are unlikely to wake up smiling after having a dream in which the central focus is a coffin! When we perceive the final resting place of a person as a coffin, it tends to draw the mind away from the possibility of consciousness persisting after death and can be seen as a suggestion that this physical life is all that there is. If you come away with this viewpoint, you should consider the value of this dream. When it is reduced it gives us the number 9, which warns us through its connection to the letter Teth, that we should not allow ourselves to be deceived by such negative thoughts.

THE TREE OF LIFE Certain Hebrew letters have different, larger values when they appear at the end of a word. It is not common practice to use these larger values all the time when constructing a value for a whole word or phrase. However, this larger value does affect how we then interpret the overall meaning of the word. In this dream, both the letters Mem and Nun are in their final form. This indicates a conflict in the dreamer's mind between a wish to believe in the maternal, caring aspect of the Divine and a feeling of deep melancholy indicated by the letter Nun. Given the content of the dream, its appropriate placement is on the path of Nun.

THE JOURNEY The compression of the value of this dream gives a strong hint as to the action you now need to take in order to shift your perception of the world from that represented by the path of Nun to one more in agreement with the force emanating from the path of Mem. We have the letters Nun, Mem, and Zayin. As we have already seen, the letters Nun and Mem represent a conflict of feelings, and the key letter is Zayin, meaning "sword." This letter suggests that you need to be quite ruthless with yourself and force yourself into a perception shift. The best way to do this is to create a very strict and busy timetable for yourself. That way, you will be so busy that you will not have time for depressing thoughts, and in time such feelings will naturally pass away.

See Zohar symbol, Coffin, Tomb, or Cemetery.

COINS

*matbea–mtba'a-*מטבע-121

MEANING From a wholly nonspiritual point of view, this might be considered an extremely positive dream as it suggests a general increase of wealth for the dreamer. However, from the Kabbalistic point of view, you should be attempting to move away from such a materialistic focus in your life, so this dream should be seen as something of a warning. The reduction value of this dream leads to the number 4, which is also associated with the physical rather than the spiritual dimension.

THE TREE OF LIFE This dream belongs wholly in the Sefirah of Malkut, as it represents a concern with financial security and prosperity over and above spiritual insight. There is, of course, nothing wrong with hoping to provide a secure environment for your family, but it is important that this desire be kept in proper perspective. Although the letter Teth features in the spelling of the word, indicating that this dream is less than positive, it does begin with the letter Mem. This suggests that if you listen to your inner voice you will be able to find a more fulfilling approach to life.

THE JOURNEY Before we can discard our excessive interest in the rewards of a consumer culture, it is necessary for us to see the rewards that such a change in perception can bring. You can help yourself to see the benefits of a shift in attitude by thinking about the things in life that really are most important to you. When you list them on paper and study them, you can see that they would not be affected in any way by any change in your purely material circumstances.

COLD

kor-kvr- כור-226

MEANING They always say that life at the top is lonely, and there is a definite psychological association between feeling lonely and feeling cold. The lack of emotional warmth can have a palpable effect on a person. The reason for your feelings of loneliness are not that you have no friends but that you have reached a level of spiritual development where there are fewer and fewer people with whom you can share your experiences on equal terms. The reduction value of this dream produces the number 10, which indicates the completion of a cycle in your life, so these feelings are likely to be new to you and thus harder to deal with.

THE TREE OF LIFE The Hebrew word meaning "north" has the same value as this dream title. In the Western Mystery Tradition, the Sefirah of Malkut and the element of Earth are connected with the

northerly direction. However, this dream also has the same value as that of the word meaning "codes," suggesting someone of significant insight, so we cannot place the dream in Malkut. If instead we draw a straight line out of Malkut, we will arrive in Tiferet. This Sefirah could be regarded as the next Earth, but one in which we are in communication with our higher self, so this is the rightful place for this dream.

THE JOURNEY Having gained enormous insight into the nature of the universe, you now need to learn how to deal with that wisdom. It can be difficult not to feel cut off from those around you when you are functioning at a level entirely different from theirs. However, what you need to do is to begin to see your role as that of a facilitator of spiritual insight for others. You must, of course, find ways to do this without being either patronizing or sanctimonious, but when you find the right way to help others you will feel yourself beginning to warm up very quickly.

COLLAR

tsavaron-tzvvarvn- צווארון-359

MEANING On the surface this seems to be a fairly innocuous dream. What, after all, could be worrisome about a collar? However, a closer examination reveals that this dream is urging us to be very careful about our choice of spiritual direction. The nature of a collar, even one that fits properly, is restriction and constraint. This dream indicates that you may be significantly constraining and restricting your inner development. The total value of this dream is equivalent to that of the Hebrew word meaning "Satan." This does not mean that you are about to join a group of Devil worshippers, but it does suggest that the paths that you have been considering are related more to issues of self-aggrandizement and self-indulgence than to genuine spiritual growth.

THE TREE OF LIFE The seeming paradox of the value of this dream is that it is equivalent to that of the Hebrew phrase meaning "sacred wind." This seems to fly in the face of the idea of this dream as a warning. There is a deep mystery in the connection between these two contrary phrases, but there is a simple solution to the conundrum in terms of this specific dream. In the compression of the dream's value we find both the letters Nun and Teth, indicating sorrow and deceit respectively. It seems quite clear then that this dream is indeed a warning, so we place it on the path of Ayin.

THE JOURNEY The path of Ayin is selected because in its negative aspect it represents the types of attitudes that are likely to emerge in someone whose dream is seeking to warn him by the hidden use of the word "Satan." It is likely that you are embarking on a spiritual path that will make you feel very good about yourself but will not actually provide you with any real spiritual insight. The best thing to do right now is to return to an entirely solitary approach to your spiritual growth and allow your private meditations and prayers to show you the way forward.

COLLISION

*heetnagshoot-hthngshvth-*התנגשות-1164

MEANING When we think of collisions we tend to think of them in their destructive context, usually in regard to a traffic accident. In fact, the collisions referred to in this dream are entirely positive and constructive. This may sound bizarre, but consider for a moment the fact that the physical universe was created by a collision of sorts, otherwise known as the Big Bang. At a more intimate level, the creation of each new life is a result of a collision between a sperm and an ovum. Each is destroyed in the encounter, but at the very moment its identity is lost, it becomes part of something new and vital. The reduction value of this dream is 12, a number associated with notions of self-sacrifice. This dream is about the need to lose part of ourselves in order to become something more vital than we were before that moment of self-sacrifice.

THE TREE OF LIFE When we first embark on the spiritual quest, we usually believe that we will keep our sense of self intact and simply add a layer of spiritual awareness on top of an already formed personality. The reality is very different, and there is a point in your spiritual growth where, in order to progress further, you will have to give up your ego-based sense of self and, for all intents and purposes, continue your life as a new person. The idea that life emerges from the mutual destruction of two elements in order to form a new third element contains many profound insights, and for that reason this dream is located in the non-Sefirah of Daat, which lies midway along the path of Gimel.

THE JOURNEY Spiritually speaking, you are standing on the edge of a potentially enlightening collision of ideas. This is not a negative position to be in but it is extremely challenging. If you survive the collision intact and head up toward Keter, you will be engaging in a profound relationship with the Divine force. In order to leap this final hurdle you

will have to accept, not just mentally but internally, a number of seemingly paradoxical truths about the nature of the spiritual universe. Only you can decide how to proceed, and whether you do make that jump will be governed solely by your relationship with the Divine.

COMBING

*lesarek-lsrq-*לסרק-390

MEANING It is sometimes very easy to misinterpret a dream image because we give in to the temptation to look at the most obvious implication of the symbol with which we are presented. It would be easy to see this dream as suggesting a vain nature or an excessive concern with the opinions of others. In fact, this dream refers to a person who is grooming not himself but his spirit in order to better his progress up the Tree of Life. The compression of this dream produces the letters Shin and Tzaddi. Tzaddi indicates the fact that you are wholly dedicated to the spiritual life, while Shin points to the high levels of spiritual energy that you possess.

THE TREE OF LIFE Although the reduction value of this dream gives us the number 12, suggesting a degree of self-sacrifice, the overall atmosphere of the dream image is optimistic and expansive. Because of the enthusiasm that infuses this dream, it is located on the path of Kaph. The attitude of the dreamer is very much in tune with the jovial aspect of the Divine that is expressed through the path of Kaph, influenced as it is by the energy of the planet Jupiter.

THE JOURNEY With such a positive outlook on life combined with a devout spirituality, you are in a position to encourage many others to begin to look at their inner development. It is unlikely that the idea of starting some kind of formal group would appeal to your relaxed and down-to-earth nature. However, you can do your part simply by explaining to your co-workers and friends the basis for your happy and healthy outlook on life.

COMMAND

*tsav-tzv-*צו-96

MEANING The desire to control is as common as it is undesirable. When we attempt to control those things over which we have no power, we inevitably fail and, what is more, we indirectly attempt to negate the will of the Divine. As with so many of our failings, there are numerous tales in all major religions that illustrate the problems of an excessive desire for control. Perhaps the most obvious is the story of the Tower of Babel. This phrase has the same value as that of the Hebrew phrase "the secret counsel of the Lord." The key word in this phrase is *secret,* the point being that we should allow the Divine to deal with those areas of life over which we cannot exert influence without seeking to turn the outcome in our favor.

THE TREE OF LIFE This dream represents the desire to exert overwhelming force over your environment, rather than the more enlightened willingness to accept and adapt to change. In even trying to have this level of structure and order in your life, you are engaging in an unconscious self-deceit about the extent of your power and indeed about your right to hold such power. For that reason, this dream is located on the path of Teth.

THE JOURNEY If you truly wish to develop in a spiritual direction, you must learn to let go and accept that certain things will happen entirely outside your control. In learning to do so, you should consider that the value of this dream reduces to 6, the value of the letter Vav. This is a pointer, to those who are willing to listen, that much more reflection rather than action is needed in your life. The next time you are upset at the idea of events moving outside your control, you should make a list of all the ways in which the change may, even in the long term, be of benefit to you.

COMPANION

*ben lavayah-bn lvvyh-*בן לוויה-109

MEANING The first thing that we should remember when considering this dream is the fact that the key aim of the Great Work is to make some form of contact with our higher self. The title of this dream indicates that you may be very close to making contact with this aspect of yourself, and that you are the companion referred to in the dream title. The value of this dream reduces to 10, which indicates the completion of a major cycle in your life; of course, the achievement of a union with your higher self would certainly fit the bill.

THE TREE OF LIFE This dream belongs to the Sefirah of Tiferet as it is here that we come into contact with our higher self. Additionally, the initial Beth in the spelling of the dream title refers to the idea of home. While our first home is Malkut, once we begin to move up the Tree of Life our next home

is Tiferet, which is an intermediary stage between Malkut and Keter.

THE JOURNEY In order to achieve the desired result referred to in this dream you will need to pay very close attention to any thoughts that emerge during meditation or other relaxation exercises that you practice. It is likely that as you approach the Sefirah of Tiferet you will find that your intuition is much more active. However, the presence of the letter Teth in the compression of this dream title means that you will have to watch for any messages that appear to be especially flattering in terms of the level of your spiritual development, as this will be the result of self-deception.

COMPASS

*matspen-mtzphn-*מצפן-260

MEANING We are always told that the one key item we should take with us when we go camping or hiking is a compass. If you don't have your bearings when you are in a strange place, then you are almost definitely going to encounter trouble. The world of the spiritual is about as strange a place as you could find, and this dream is telling you that you need the equivalent of a spiritual compass. Appropriately enough, the value of this dream has several arithmetical relationships to the number 8. This number is associated with the planet Mercury, and of course the mythical Mercury, being the messenger of the gods, must have had great navigational skills.

THE TREE OF LIFE The need for some kind of directional aid indicates that you are relatively new to the spiritual quest. If we look at the compression of the dream title we have the letters Resh and Samech. We can take this to mean that the path of Resh will take you to the support you need, as Samech represents support and guidance. The path of Resh ends in the Sefirah of Hod. This Sefirah is not only the eighth sphere on the Tree of Life but is also associated with the planet Mercury, so it is doubly fitting.

THE JOURNEY The final Nun in the spelling of the dream title tells us that you are approaching the Great Work with significant unresolved sorrows burdening your heart. We find that the letter Nun is preceded by Peh, meaning "mouth." The implication here is that in order for you to progress you need to deal with those emotional issues, and the letter Peh is a way of telling you that you can only do this fully by talking about those areas that are most distressing to you.

COMPLETION

seeyoom–syvm–םיוס–260

MEANING You are approaching a period of spiritual rest and recuperation. As the title of the dream states, you have achieved the completion of a significant part of your inner journey, and before continuing you have time to reflect on what you have achieved. The spelling of the dream title indicates the process that has brought you to a sense of completion. You opened yourself up to the support of the Divine (Samech), and this activated the Divine spark within you (Yod), leading to a meditative process(Vav) that brought you to maternal aspect of the Divine (Mem).

THE TREE OF LIFE The value of this dream is equivalent to that of a Hebrew word that refers directly to the Sefirah of Hesed. As this Sefirah also represents the paternalistic and forgiving nature of the Divine, it is an appropriate location for this dream and, indeed, a marker for your spiritual progress. It is worth noting that in the compression of this dream title the letters Vav and Yod are connected to the Sefirat of Hesed on the Tree of Life.

THE JOURNEY At the beginning of this analysis we talked about your approaching a period of rest and relaxation. This idea is supported by the fact that this dream has the same value as that of the Hebrew word meaning "doves," and doves are, of course, the bird of peace and rest as exemplified by the dove who discovers dry land in the story of Noah. It is not all rest, though, as this dream also indicates that you need to try to spread that feeling of peace and tranquility among those with whom you live and work on a daily basis.

CONCERT

kontsert–qvntzrt–םרצנוק–455

MEANING Generally we would expect concerts to be enjoyable affairs, as they are a chance for people to get together and share in a joyful and exciting experience. However, the value of this dream indicates a far more dismal experience than that. In the dream's compression, the initial Tav points to some degree of suffering, while the letter Nun points to a heavy feeling of sorrow and melancholy. The clue to this feeling lies in the final letter from the compression, which is Heh, meaning "window." The suggestion is that you have reached a point of development where you cannot help but see a gathering

of people celebrating in a wholly secular way as somehow lacking.

THE TREE OF LIFE Once we have reached a point where we are in communion with our higher self, we tend to have a much less jaundiced view of the world and of people who are quite happy in their solely materialistic lives. However, in the early stages of the Great Work, a mixture of almost evangelical fervor and a certain amount of nostalgia for our previous contentment with the mundane world tends to affect our judgment. These feelings are most suited to the path of Qoph as it represents the range of anxieties and doubts we experience when beginning our inner journey.

THE JOURNEY If you wish both to avoid the weight of melancholy now hanging over you and to continue your quest for the Divine, you need to take what may seem like a step backward. It is vital that you do not lose touch with the everyday things that can bring happiness to people, so you should make a point of maintaining your social life. In fact, there is a case to be made for going out even more, at least until you remember how much fun it can be.

CONSPIRACY

kesher–qshr–רשק–600

MEANING This dream is not at all connected with negative conspiracies but is linked to the idea of conspiracy only in the sense that is a wholly unseen and covert plan. The value of this dream is equivalent to the value of the letter Mem in its final form. As the letter Mem links to the idea of the Divine as mother, this suggests that you have accepted that you will never penetrate the full mystery of the Divine's plans for you and so you will accept its unconditional love without question.

THE TREE OF LIFE Since the value of the dream is equivalent to the value of this letter, our dream must be located on the path of Mem. As such, it is associated with The Hanged Man card in the tarot. This card relates to self-sacrifice, and this very much fits with the concept of accepting of God's plan without any attempt to influence the outcome that is planned for you.

THE JOURNEY This dream indicates that you are, or shortly will be, taking a very enlightened approach to your life. The great Chinese philosopher Lao-tzu advises us to be like the willow and be flexible. When a great swath of water or wind hits a willow, it will bend and not be broken. When the storm has passed, the willow will return to its original shape unharmed by the encounter. In your life you will meet many conflicts and causes for concern or annoyance; whenever you are in such a situation, simply remember the willow and you will come through it a better person.

CONTEMPT
*booz-bvz-*בוז-15

MEANING Every major religion urges us to be compassionate and just in our dealings with others, so a dream about contempt suggests a person who has some way to go before achieving any real level of spiritual development. However, we need to remember that this dream is about self-perception at least as much as it may be about how the dreamer perceives those around him. The final letter, Zayin, in the spelling of the dream title indicates the vigor with which the dreamer is approaching the spiritual quest, and when we consider the normal use of a sword, it is highly likely that the dreamer is being extremely critical toward himself.

THE TREE OF LIFE The number 15 has a profound and complex relationship with the Sefirah Gevurah. Gevurah is the fifth Sefirah, and when we add all the numbers from 1 to 5 we get the number 15. There are four paths that lead in and out of Gevurah, but the one that fits this dream is the path of Lamed. Lamed represents the energy of the Divine as a driving force that acts as a strong motivation toward the goal of the Great Work.

THE JOURNEY It is commendable to have such a strong desire to make progress toward the source of the Divine light, but it is counterproductive if you are so critical of yourself that you begin to believe you are not ever going to succeed or even that you don't deserve to make further progress. In order to strengthen your belief in yourself and your resolve to continue, you should keep a vase of sunflowers on your desk. Sunflowers are associated with the life-giving energy of the Sun and also with the self-confidence of the star sign, Leo. By having them on your desk you increase belief in yourself through an unconscious, sympathetic response to the flowers. If possible, enroll in an assertiveness class.

CORPSE
*gveeyah-gvyyyh-*גוייה-40

MEANING Distressing as it may be to wake from a dream of a corpse, this should not be considered a worrisome image or, for that matter, a warning of some horrible fate about to befall you. The corpse in the dream is purely symbolic, indicating the status of a person who has no spiritual beliefs whatsoever. The Hebrew phrase "the hand of the Eternal" has a value that is equivalent to the value of this dream. The point here is not only that the transformation of a person to a corpse is the result of the hand of the Divine, but that even when we are spiritually dead the hand of the Divine is still being proffered, encouraging us to begin our spiritual journey.

THE TREE OF LIFE Again we have a dream where the value is also the value of one of the paths on the Tree of Life. In this case it is the letter Mem. Since Mem is connected to the maternal aspect of the Divine, it may seem strange that this path is regarded as appropriate for a dream of a corpse. It is perhaps less strange when we remember that in our literal death we are returning to what could be considered our spiritual womb, and that when we are figuratively dead it is often the more gentle aspect of the Divine that encourages us to spiritually awaken.

THE JOURNEY In your dream you are not the corpse itself but are looking down at a corpse. This represents the old you, which, as you have now passed through Tiferet, you have wholly left behind. However, while leaving it behind you should not forget it, nor should you discard everything connected to the way you were. This dream is urging you to closely examine your past and make sure that those aspects of your life and yourself that were most important to you are in some way retained.

COUCH
*sapah-sphh-*ספה-145

MEANING We all love to relax on a couch. True, it may not be quite as comfortable as a bed, but there is something about a couch that somehow adds to the sense that we really are taking time out. From a spiritual point of view, this might mean that we are taking things too easy and need to apply ourselves more to the job at hand. However, this dream has the same value as that of the Hebrew word "bequest," so the suggestion is that this is a well-earned rest. Indeed, the central letter, Mem, in the compression of this dream's value could be seen almost as an invitation to lie back in the arms of the maternal Divine.

THE TREE OF LIFE There is little space for rest on the Tree, especially as this is a representation of the very emanation of the universe. If we look at the spelling of the dream title, the first letter is Samech. Now, Samech means "prop" and relates to the supportive force of higher agencies. So, this dream belongs to the path of Samech, and while there is still work to be done here now, you have a moment to simply enjoy the knowledge that you are making good progress.

THE JOURNEY The total value of this dream is the same as the value of the phrase "the staff of God," and for the next few weeks you must learn to lean on this staff. The way we learn to feel the support of the Divine is by learning to still ourselves. There is often so much noise in our heads that we cannot hear the voice of the Divine. Since you are supposed to be relaxing, try listening to some ambient music and allowing yourself to drift.

COUGH
*sheeool–shya'avl–*שיעול–416

MEANING To see the spiritual significance of a cough seems like a fairly tall order, but, as with any other dream, if we look at the construction of the word itself we are sure to find a clue to its meaning. The reduction value of this dream is II, a number that in esoteric circles has always signified profound mysteries. Additionally, the value of the dream title is equivalent to the value of the Hebrew word meaning "thought" or "meditation." When we add to these facts the idea that a cough is a vigorous exhalation of breath and remember that the energy of the Divine is often characterized as breath, we begin to see what the dream is saying. This dream indicates someone who has a very active and enthusiastic spirituality that he expresses in a forcible manner.

THE TREE OF LIFE The first letter of this dream title underlines the raw energy with which the dreamer approaches his life. The final Lamed also points to a sense of being driven toward the spiritual life by a higher force. All this leads to an almost blind force that possesses an inevitability and unstoppable momentum that is best represented by the path of Teth.

THE JOURNEY The path of Teth is not always negative, despite its association with the serpent and the overtones of deceit and danger that accompany it. In this case, it stands simply for the power of your enthusiasm and determination to achieve your spiritual goals. However, in order to ensure that your vigor does not become proud and selfish, you should make a point of finding time in your busy schedule to engage in some form of volunteer work.

COUNTENANCE
*partsoof–phrtzvph–*פרצוף–456

MEANING To dream of a face always implies a need for communication, which itself suggests that there are various pieces of emotional baggage you need to unpack with the help of a friend or a professional counselor. The need for dialogue is strongly emphasized by the fact the dream title both begins and ends in the letter Peh, meaning "mouth." A very positive aspect of this dream is that right in the center of the spelling is the letter Tzaddi, which tells us that no matter what emotional pain you may be dealing with, your commitment to the spiritual quest is absolute.

THE TREE OF LIFE It would be foolish to associate this dream with any path other than that of Peh. This letter figures so strongly in the dream's spelling and is also very appropriate to the idea of a cathartic discussion about your exploration of your feelings. The tarot card The Tower is connected to the path of Peh. This card indicates some traumatic event, such as the unloading of your emotional history, that will be difficult but ultimately beneficial.

THE JOURNEY The compression of this dream combines the saturnine melancholy of the letter Tav with the potential sorrow and sense of self-realization associated with the letter Nun. Do not be discouraged, though, because it also includes the letter Vav, which indicates that with sufficient reflection you will be able to deal with these painful memories. In order to get help in doing this, you should definitely confide in a close friend or consider the services of a counselor.

COUNTING
*sfeerah–sphyrh–*ספירה–355

MEANING When we finally reach the top of the Tree of Life, one of the things that we realize, not just intellectually but internally, is that everything in the universe right down to the level of the subatomic particle is inextricably linked and a part of a much greater unity. Set in this context, the act of counting is symbolic of not yet recognizing the interconnectedness of all things. Additionally, counting is traditionally a means of evaluating our personal worth in terms of property or wealth. This materialistic aspect is supported by the fact that the value of this dream reduces to 4, the number of the purely material world.

THE TREE OF LIFE As long as our main concerns involve items that can be counted rather than feelings that can only be understood or experienced, we will remain trapped in the Sefirah of Malkut. The total value of this dream is equivalent to the value of the Hebrew word meaning "idea." This is a sign of hope that you may be about to see the essentially hollow nature of a life that is focused on goods rather than feelings.

THE JOURNEY Take your wallet or your purse and go out for a walk, but before you go make sure it contains the number of dollar bills that in a normal week you would spend on nonessentials. Every five minutes as you walk take out a dollar bill and drop it on the ground. When your dollar bills are all gone, go home and imagine the enjoyment you may have provided by this action and how liberating it is to be able to give away money without knowing where it will end up.

COUNTRY

*erets-artz-*אֶרֶץ-291

MEANING Whatever our nationality in this life, when it comes to the spiritual life we all have the same homeland, we are all ultimately from the same country. This dream indicates that you are beginning to understand that regardless of our differences, we all have the same principal goal. We may not realize it and some of us never will, but our most important purpose here is simply to ensure that we are fit to go to our true home after this life is over. The value of this dream reduces to 12, which is connected to ideas of self-sacrifice, so we have a further pointer that you have achieved a considerable level of inner development.

THE TREE OF LIFE The idea of home is represented on the Tree of Life by the letter Beth. This path is characterized by deep understanding of all peoples and a sincere tolerance of all viewpoints. Given the attitudes suggested by the dream's content and value, Beth is an ideal path on which to place this dream.

THE JOURNEY This dream places the dreamer only one path away from Keter, the "Crown" of the Tree of Life. In order to achieve that longed-for sense of union with the Divine, you must ensure that every aspect of your life is imbued with a sense of the spiritual. More than that, you should begin to analyze each event in your life as in some way a reflection of a dialogue between yourself and the universe. This is much harder to achieve than it may

sound and is far more revealing than you may expect.

CRADLE

*areesah-a'arysh-*עֲרִיסָה-345

MEANING At times we all wish that we were back in our mother's arms, unaware of all the trials and tribulations of adulthood. In the compression of this dream's value we have the letter Mem as the central point, emphasizing the desire to return to the protective maternal love that this letter represents. However, the letters that frame this central idea point to both a fiery spiritual energy (Shin) and the chance to use this energy in order to see beyond the veil of this mundane world (Heh).

THE TREE OF LIFE Rather than signifying someone who wishes to give up all responsibility this dream points to an individual who is willing to carry great responsibility on his shoulders. It is the extent and weight of this responsibility that causes you to feel the need to regress into a state of innocence from time to time. The path of Aleph carries the greatest responsibility in the Tree of Life as it is the path that carries the undiluted Divine force from the "Crown" or Keter.

THE JOURNEY The value of this dream is equivalent to that of the Hebrew spelling of "Moses." This is clearly very significant and indicates that the dreamer has the potential for a deep level of spiritual insight. When we think of Moses it is either as the baby cast adrift in the bullrushes or as the dynamic leader of a people building a new civilization. It is worth noting that in the Gematric analysis of this dream we see echoes of both of these views of Moses. All of this indicates that it is now time for you to take on more responsibility in your life, not just for yourself but for those around you.

CRIMINAL

*poshea-pvsha'a-*פּוֹשֵׁעַ-456

MEANING As a rule, criminality is not considered a positive characteristic. Certainly in terms of Kabbalistic analysis this dream should be seen as a warning. The presence of the number 15 in the reduction value of this dream points to a strong tendency toward materialism and a desire to accumulate goods purely for the sake of possessing them. This approach to life can only act as an interference in any attempt to follow a spiritual path.

THE TREE OF LIFE The nature of criminality of all types, whether it is burglary or violence or fraud, is antiauthoritarian. Before we can commit any kind of crime, however small, we must make the moral leap that decides that we are above the law and have no regard for authority. In spiritual terms it is a lack of humility that is being pointed out by this dream, and as such it belongs on the path of Ayin, which is often associated with the goat, as goats are seen as loners as well as being slightly suspect in nature.

THE JOURNEY It seems that this dream is full of doom and gloom, but do not despair, for we can all find ways to achieve a level of spiritual advancement no matter where we start. In fact, the sequence of numbers that makes up the value of this dream shows how this is likely to occur. Right now you are focused entirely on the material (4), but some experience in the future will show you a glimmer of light (5), and this will lead you to entirely rethink your perspective and begin to come closer to the Divine (6).

❧ CRIPPLE

nakheh-nkh-נכה-75

MEANING We would expect this dream to indicate someone experiencing significant difficulties in his life, and in spiritual terms we might expect to find that this dream indicates some kind of block to his progress. However, such a view would reveal more about our attitudes to those with disabilities than about our ability to interpret a dream. This dream does indeed refer to difficulties as suggested by the initial Nun, which indicates sorrow and a sense of loss. However, the subsequent letters Kaph and Heh tell us that with some practical thinking (Kaph), the dreamer will find a satisfactory solution to his problems (Heh). In fact, this dream is trying to tell you that your problems are nowhere near as large or as insurmountable as you believe them to be. You simply need to find a different way of looking at them.

THE TREE OF LIFE It takes a considerable degree of determination to overcome the attitudes of many people and, moreover, the fact that we tend to design environments without much thought to people with disabilities. Similarly, it will take a degree of determination for you to overcome the mental block that is preventing you from developing the spiritual side of your life. However, the dream suggests that you will find the courage and vigor to succeed, so this dream is located on the path of Ayin, which represents just that sort of active enthusiasm.

THE JOURNEY The value of the dream title, "cripple," is equivalent to that of a Hebrew word meaning "colors" or "hues." The message to take from this connection is that while hard work and courage will help you, there is also a need for you to find ways to express yourself creatively. This will help you not only with your confidence but with working through the nature of your block. You should consider treating yourself to a selection of art materials and letting your inspiration run away with you!

CROSS

tslav-tzlb-צלב-122

MEANING Inevitably the image of a cross immediately calls to mind the crucifixion and ideas about Jesus. It is certainly possible to interpret this dream in a wholly Christian manner and indeed there is a branch of Kabbalah that is entirely Christian in its outlook and symbolism. However, this dream can be understood fully without our needing to restrict ourselves to a single religious viewpoint. A cross with its four arms represents the four elements and can be seen as a symbolic representation of the purely physical world. When we at look at the value, though, we find that it reduces to 5. This suggests that the dream of a cross represents the possibility of passing from the solely physical to a state of consciousness where the physical is surmounted and guided by the fifth element of Spirit.

THE TREE OF LIFE One of the beauties of the Tree of Life is that it manages to contain so many different symbolic arrangements within it. If we look at the arrangement of the Sefirot we see that they mirror the transformation referred to in this dream. Taking each Sefirah as a point, we find the spiritual number 5 or pentagram made up of Keter, Hokhmah, Binah, Hesed, and Gevurah. Beneath this we have the cross of the elements made up of Tiferet, Netzach, Hod, and Yesod. Your position right now on the Tree is in Tiferet since this constitutes the head of the elemental cross.

THE JOURNEY It seems quite clear that the key task for you now is to start activating that part of you that is wholly spirit. This should be an easy task to accomplish now that your higher self is guiding you through your intuition. We need to be fully balanced in terms of the elements before we can move on to working purely on the spirit, so you should make a list of all the aspects of your personality in terms of the elements they relate to. Once this is done, you need to ensure that any conflicts between the different aspects can be resolved to your satisfaction. Harmony within yourself increases your chances of contacting that which is harmonious without.

CROWD

hamon-hmvn-המון-101

MEANING The strong influence of the final Nun in this dream title immediately tells us that the dreamer is in a state of sorrow. The initial letter in the compression of this dream is Qoph, suggesting that the cause of concern is primarily mental rather than emotional. When we also consider the content of this dream, it is likely that the dreamer's anxiety comes from a growing feeling of separation from the rest of the world represented by the crowd.

THE TREE OF LIFE When we examine the arrangement of numerals in the value of the dream title we notice that we have two I's separated by a void, represented by the central 0. It is clear that this feeling of "otherness" is quite profound. This is not an uncommon feeling to experience when we begin the Great Work. It is a typical symptom of those traversing the path of Qoph, which is one of the initial paths out of Malkut and carries with it many doubts.

THE JOURNEY It is most important now that you feel comfortable with your decision to pursue a spiritual path. "Crowd" is equivalent in value to the Hebrew word meaning "swallowed" or "destroyed." This demonstrates that there is a dual fear disturbing you right now. On one hand, you feel that to continue as you were in a nonspiritual life would lead to your being you swallowed up by the general view of the world. On the other hand is the fear that a spiritual quest may also lead to an absorption and loss of personality. These fears cannot be dispelled quickly, but you can learn to retain a sense of integration with the "normal" world by joining some club or group that has no higher interest whatsoever—a sports team would be ideal for this purpose. The fear of absorption by the Divine can be dealt with only by perseverance in the Great Work.

CROWN

keter-kthr-כתר-620

MEANING This may seem to be the dream that we should hope to experience, as it represents a contact with the source of the remainder of the Tree of Life and the closest that any person can come to a full interaction with the Divine. However, the closer to the Divine we climb, the more likely we are to have dreams that require considerable interpretation to be fully understood. This dream points to the force emanating from Keter rather to being within Keter itself.

THE TREE OF LIFE You might expect this to be a simple matter of locating the dream in Keter, but in fact the dream belongs to the Sefirah of Malkut. This dream is experienced as a spiritual wake-up call to encourage an individual to begin the Great Work. The fundamental aspect of Keter is that it is a source of Divine love that emanates creatively throughout the Tree of Life, so this dream relates to the experience of receiving that influence and not of connecting to it.

THE JOURNEY The spelling of the dream title tells you in detail the nature and even the destination of the early portion of your spiritual journey. The initial Kaph indicates a need to take some practical steps to changing the way you live your life. The Tav indicates that this will not be easy and you will experience considerable feelings of regret at times; it also points out the first path out of Malkut into Yesod. Finally, the Resh indicates both that you will shortly be feeling the benevolent force of the Divine and the path that you should take out of Yesod into Hod.

CRUELTY

akhzereeyoot-akzryvth-אכזריות-644

MEANING Experienced Kabbalists and mystics of all faiths often point to the paradoxical nature of the reality of the Divine and consequently the paradoxical nature of many of the insights that we gain on our spiritual quest. In this dream image we have such a paradox. The content of the dream seems unequivocally negative, and there is no justification for cruelty. To be cruel is to be more than simply stern or harsh, as it implies that something is being done for its own sake rather than to achieve any beneficial result. The compression of the dream tells a very different story. The letter Mem appears in both its final and standard forms and is followed by the letter Daleth, meaning "door." This suggests that you are being greatly protected and cared for by the Divine in order that you will be able to pass through a doorway into a higher level of understanding.

THE TREE OF LIFE Clarity begins to creep into the picture when we remember that while dreams may be a means for our higher self to guide us, they are always filtered through our consciousness. Consequently, what we perceive to be cruelty is simply severity. The value of this dream reduces to 5, which is the number of the Sefirah of Gevurah. This is the location of this dream, and it is worth noting that one of its qualities is indeed "severity."

THE JOURNEY Your dream of cruelty was one in which you were exposed to the severe aspect of the Divine. This is the part of God that is responsible for mortality and decay and all forms of conflict. It seems to us that these things are to be regretted, but without entropy the physical universe would cease to function in the way that we understand it. Similarly, if there were no conflict there could be no compassion or appeasement or reconciliation, all of which are important ways in which we display our humanity. In showing you this dream your higher self has given you the opportunity to understand the necessity for the unpleasant in life, and in doing so you will open the door to a much deeper level of understanding.

CRYING

bhekheeyah-bkyyh-בכייה-47

MEANING None of us enjoys weeping, but it is one of the hallmarks of being human that we have the capacity to express emotions whether they be happy or sad. Even more important, when we are weeping at the fate of someone else, is the ability to have compassion and empathy. Such traits are essential for anyone wishing to make spiritual progress in his life. The value of this dream reduces to II, so it indicates someone who has already made significant leaps in his inner development. Given the content of the dream, it also suggests that the individual has an enormous capacity for empathy and understanding.

THE TREE OF LIFE The compression of the dream title provides us with the letters Mem and Zayin. The first letter is immediately appropriate as it directly refers to the maternal and protective feelings typified by the dream of crying. It is to the path of Mem that this dream belongs, and this is a reflection of your willingness to try to shoulder the emotional burdens of those around you.

THE JOURNEY The letter Zayin seems somehow out-of-place in the compression of this dream. It means "sword" in Hebrew and so is difficult to see

exactly where it fits into the image of such a motherly personality. The answer lies in the nature of the journey you now need to take. Empathy is a wonderful emotion to possess, but it alone will not reduce the causes of your tears. This dream is telling you to find a cause that you believe in, one that makes you weep and then fight for it vigorously in order to change your tears to smiles.

CUTTING

khatakh-chthk-חתך-428

MEANING The reduction of value of this dream gives us 14, which is related to notions of balance in one's life as exemplified by the tarot card Temperance. Clearly the image of cutting suggests a way of dealing with the lack of harmony in one's life by cutting things out, but this approach is too self-critical and may also lead to a new imbalance in terms of generating an excess of severity in your life. Additionally, the compression of the dream's value reveals through the presence of the letter Tav that you have a number of regrets in your past and that simply cutting them out will not provide a long-term solution.

THE TREE OF LIFE In the Kabbalah there is a negative Tree of Life that, instead of Sefirot, consists of Qlippoth or "shells." The value of this dream is equivalent to the value of the title of the Qlippoth of Hesed. This is known as "The Breakers in Pieces." While this is wholly appropriate in that it backs up the idea that simply breaking up pieces of your past will not help your inner develoment, this is not the position of your dream on the Tree of Life. What you need right now is a practical way of dealing with your emotional baggage. The jovial and practical path of Kaph is there to assist you and is indicated by the final Kaph in the spelling of the dream title.

THE JOURNEY You need to find a way to achieve a sense of balance in your life as illustrated by the Temperance card from the tarot. The path of Kaph indicates that you need to change the way you live your day-to-day life. Furthermore, the dream suggests that your lack of balance stems largely from a self-critical attitude. the tarot card often associated with the path of Kaph is The Wheel of Fortune. This card relates to simply taking life as it comes and accepting the bad with the good while maintaining a generally optimistic outlook. To follow the example of The Wheel of Fortune would do you a world of good.

❧DANCING

*reekoodeem-ryqvdym-*ריקודים-370

MEANING Before it had a role in social entertainment, dancing was used to signify courtship, warfare, or worship. Within the Jewish faith the joyous nature of worship including dancing has long been recognized as important. As the reduction value of this dream produces the number 10, indicating the successful completion of a phase in one's life, we can assume that the dancing in this dream is celebratory. The compression of this dream provides the letters Shin and Ayin, both of which indicate a great deal of creative and spiritual energy being expressed in a very individual manner.

THE TREE OF LIFE The value of this dream is equivalent to that of the Hebrew word meaning "foundation." The Sefirah of Yesod is also known as "foundation" as it is the point from which the potential forms and forces of the physical life are made manifest. Your dancing in the dream represents your sense of satisfaction at having reached Yesod. It is additionally appropriate since Yesod is associated with sexual attraction and dancing has always been intimately connected to courtship rituals.

THE JOURNEY Keep on dancing is perhaps the best advice that you can be given at this stage in your spiritual development. It is quite rare to be able to engage fully with the Great Work and at the same retain an appreciation that the Divine is as keen on joy as it is on seriousness and piety. To advance your inner growth even further, you should try to spread your joy among those around you. That may mean talking to them about the nature of your spiritual feelings or simply allowing your infectious enthusiasm for life to prompt them to look for a higher purpose in their lives.

See Zohar symbol, Dancing.

DANGER

*sakanah-sknh-*סכנה-135

MEANING In the Kabbalah and in Gnosticism, which borrows from both the Kabbalistic and Greek Mystery Traditions, the source of wisdom is often characterized as female. In the Kabbalah this secret feminine source of wisdom is known as the Shekinah. This is important to bear in mind when we consider that the value of this dream is equivalent to the value of a Hebrew phrase meaning "a destitute woman." This dream of danger suggests that our current attitude is leaving the Shekinah destitute, or in other words that we are making ourselves unavailable for her wise assistance.

THE TREE OF LIFE The compression of this dream begins with the letter Qoph, which tells us that the main reason for your spiritual danger lies in the way you are conceptualizing the nature of your spiritual reality. The possibility of self-deception is supported by the fact that the value of this dream reduces to 9. This is the value of the letter Teth, meaning "serpent," and is seen as a strong indicator of deceit and danger. It is because of this association that we locate the dream of danger on the path of Teth.

THE JOURNEY It is in the compression of the dream that you will find the solution to your current spiritual problems. At the moment you are falling into the popular New Age trap of believing that we construct our spiritual reality around what seems appealing rather than by listening to that small voice within us that comes from our higher self. The letter following Qoph in the compression is Lamed, which means "ox-goad." The message here is that you need to be more disciplined in your approach to the Great Work if you wish to achieve results that will open the window on the truth referred to by the final Heh in the compression.

❧DARKNESS

*khashekah-chshykh-*חשיכה-343

MEANING As with any system of mysticism, Kabbalah can be both complex and confusing if we expect it to mirror our interpretations of symbols and signs. We would tend to view darkness as a fearful image implying the absence of hope but in fact this is a very hopeful dream. The value of this dream (343) is equivalent to the result of 7 to the power of 3 ($7 \times 7 \times 7 = 343$). The mystical significance of this mathematical relationship is that the number represents Creation and the number 7 is the quintessential number of mystery. Thus, in the word *darkness* we have the idea of creation of the most mysterious kind.

THE TREE OF LIFE The value of this dream is also equivalent to the value of the phrase "and GOD said" from Genesis. What God said ushered in first the light and then the rest of Creation stage by stage in a steady evolution. This association highlights the fact that darkness should be seen not as an absence but as a pool of potential from which we can create. While this dream is undoubtedly placed in Malkut, it contains within it the promise of a dawning light that will carry you up toward Yesod.

THE JOURNEY In the Creation, according to the Kabbalah, the universe came into existence in a single moment when the Divine managed to create a point that was not Divine. This mysterious process is known as the Tzim Tzum. It is written that Malkut is a reflection of Keter but after another manner, so you need to mirror this process in reverse. This means finding room in yourself for a tiny spark of divinity to take hold. You will be able to progress toward this if you begin a disciplined practice of daily meditation.

See Zohar symbol, Darkness.

DAUGHTER

bt–bth–בת–402

MEANING Before we begin to consider the interpretation of this dream it is important to note that we are talking about the idea in a purely symbolic sense and that the dream itself relates to men and women equally. This dream demonstrates very old-fashioned ideas about the nature of daughterhood, as the spelling indicates that this dream focuses on the way in which domestic matters (Beth) cause you considerable feelings of melancholy (Tav). In spiritual terms we can see this as suggesting that your practical day-to-day life is too busy to allow any time for you to focus on your spiritual development.

THE TREE OF LIFE In Kabbalistic symbolism the Sefirah of Malkut has a number of titles. Many of these are feminine in nature and include the notion of Malkut as the daughter of Keter. Taking this factor into account and the fact that this dream is about practicalities getting in the way of spending time on the Great Work, we can place this dream in the Sefirah of Malkut.

THE JOURNEY When we reduce the value of this dream we get the number 6. This number is the value of the letter Vav, which is representative of the element of Air. In order to find space to begin your inner journey you need to pay heed to the element of Air, because much of the journey takes place inside your mind and also as an indication that if you planned your days slightly differently, you would be able to free up sufficient time to make headway in your spiritual quest.

❧ DAWN

shakhar–shchr–שחר–508

MEANING In the Western Mystery Tradition the dawn has always had a deep mystical importance. It represents the awakening of the soul in the light of the Divine force symbolized by the Sun climbing up into the sky. The reduction value of this dream produces the number 13, which indicates a major change about to occur in your life, and this coincides with the idea of dawn as the beginning of a brand-new and spiritually influenced life. As a symbol, the image of dawn is a definite indication of a hopeful and positive direction in your life.

THE TREE OF LIFE The compression of this dream produces the letters Kaph and Cheth. Kaph is in its final form, which adds additional emphasis to the importance of practical activity in your spiritual life right now. Cheth indicates that you still feel the need for a certain degree of defensiveness when it comes to considering the spiritual aspect of the universe. These factors combine to indicate that you are new to the Great Work. The fact that the dream itself is about the dawning of spiritual awareness helps to confirm the placement of this dream on the path of Tav.

THE JOURNEY The initial Shin in the spelling of this dream title points to vast reserves of energy that have been awakened by the new dawn within your soul. You can use this energy to stimulate your inner development. The importance of the letter Kaph in the compression tells us that you should seriously consider some form of physical activity that has a strong spiritual angle, such as tai chi or some other form of martial arts. This will use your high levels of energy and maintain your interest in the spiritual quest.

See Zohar symbol, Dawn, daybreak.

DAY

yom–yvm–יום–56

MEANING This dream is reserved for the very few who manage to persist in their spiritual practices throughout all the obstacles that fate places in their way. A dream of day is symbolic of the long-awaited union with the Divine, and this hidden meaning is buried within the spelling and the value of the dream title. The reduction value of the dream provides the number 11, which should always be seen as an indication of some profound event about to occur. The spelling of the dream title tells us that you have been inflamed by the Divine spark (Yod) and that this has led to much meditation and thought (Vav), with the result that you are now returning to the arms of the Divine (Mem).

THE TREE OF LIFE The value of this dream can be seen as being made up of the numbers 5 and 6. In Kabbalistic terms the number 5 represents the four elements crowned by the fifth element of Spirit. This is the status of the genuine seeker of truth. The number 6 is even more profound as it represents the macrocosm or the Divine itself. The importance of the number 6 in the Kabbalistic tradition can be seen in the symbolic significance of the hexagram as a mystical symbol. This dream indicates that you are ready to move from a state where you are crowned by the element of Spirit to a state where you are entirely infused by the Divine force. The path of Beth leads into Keter, where such a state of consciousness is possible. It is also appropriate because the reduction of the dream's value to 11 can be further reduced to a value of 2, which is the value of the letter Beth.

THE JOURNEY You are on the brink of an experience that is utterly personal and unique to you. No book can prepare you for the feelings and changes in perception that you are about to experience. However, in general there are certain things that you should remember as you move forward. These are simply that however much insight we may gain, we are still human and we still need to maintain those fundamentally human relationships with others in order to lead a fulfilling life. As the Buddhists say, "Before enlightenment chop wood, carry water; after enlightenment chop wood, carry water."

❧DEAFNESS

*khershoot-chyrshvth-*חירשות*-*924

MEANING If we look closely at all mainstream religions we find references to the idea that the truth is not hidden but people choose not to see or hear it. This dream is very much an echo of that viewpoint as it suggests that the dreamer is willfully deaf to the spiritual guidance that, if they simply opened their ears, would be available to them. The compression of the dream provides a strong clue as to why you are deaf to the help of the Divine. The initial Tzaddi tells us that you are "hooked" in to a certain attitude to life, while the following Kaph indicates that this attitude is one in which practicalities take prior-

ity. Finally, the letter Daleth suggests that you have an excessive attachment to the material world, and as its meaning is "door," it implies that you still have the opportunity to enter the world of the spiritual.

THE TREE OF LIFE If your consciousness is an alarm clock, then this dream is wake-up time! It is a warning from your higher self that you are losing time that could be spent perfecting your soul rather than perfecting your career or the polish on your car. Since you have not yet begun to engage with the Great Work, this dream is positioned firmly within the Sefirah of Malkut. The idea of deafness suggests that you are for some reason not hearing the good advice that is available to you at this time. This may be a conscious choice or be unwitting. You should spend some time trying to determine the source of this advice.

THE JOURNEY Ahead of you lies the most difficult and also the simplest step of the whole spiritual quest. It is merely a matter of unstopping your ears, of allowing the noise in your head to be quiet just long enough for you to hear your higher self calling you to a higher state of mind. While this may be a simple step it can be difficult because it involves changing the whole order of things in your life in terms of their relative importance. To give yourself the mental space to think about these issues, you should take off some time from work and go alone into the countryside where you can genuinely experience some peace and tranquillity.

See Zohar symbol, Deafness.

DEATH OF AN ACQUAINTANCE

*mavet shel makeer-mvth shl mkyr-*מות של מכיר*-*1052

MEANING Our sense of security in the world is to a large extent defined by the people whom we know and love. To dream of one of them dying represents a feeling that we are losing that sense of certainty, that in some way we are becoming alone in a world that is potentially threatening. In Kabbalistic terms this indicates an awareness of a spiritual reality, but a lack of any sense of understanding or belonging to that spiritual world. The reduction value of this dream is the number 8, which is the value of the letter Cheth, meaning "fence." This emphasizes the idea that you feel the need to build some kind of protective wall around yourself.

THE TREE OF LIFE It can be disconcerting to begin seriously to pursue a spiritual path. All of our certainties become merely possible truths and our possibilities become even more uncertain than they were; in short, we can feel that we are in mental and emotional free-fall. This experience is represented by the path of Qoph, and the compression of this dream begins with the value of the letter Qoph multiplied by 10, as if to emphasize this connection.

THE JOURNEY What you need right now is to find some way of grounding yourself without returning to a wholly materialistic way of viewing the world in the process. There are numerous spiritual exercises that will help with this. Perhaps the most effective is the Chinese practice of chi gung. This form of physical exercise has a definite spiritual aspect to it. It is particularly appropriate to your state of mind as it is both relaxing and gives a sense of solidity to the idea of the spiritual.

DEBT

khov-chvb- חוב*-*16

MEANING None of us likes to be in debt. Even if we know we can afford to pay off our bills, the knowledge that we have creditors is always there in the back of our mind, acting like a weight preventing us from moving forward in life. The value of this dream is equivalent to that of the Hebrew word meaning "woe," which indicates that this dream is about the negative emotions associated with the knowledge of being in debt. Of course, the dream of debt represents not a literal debt but the feeling of being tied to our past and the sense of being unable to free ourselves from that connection.

THE TREE OF LIFE You are no longer in the Sefirah of Malkut, as the absolute connection to the purely material has been weakened. However, you are not totally free and this is the source of your anxiety. The value of the dream is mathematically related to the number 4, which represents the physical world, as 4 multiplied by itself is 16. The path of this dream is that of Tav. It leads out of Malkut and so is still attached to the physical, but it leads into Yesod and so the dreamer experiences a sense of sorrow that the connection is not yet wholly broken.

THE JOURNEY Patience is very often the key to successful development of the soul, and your position as indicated by the dream of debt is no exception. While it may be painful, you need to remember that the sense of frustration at not having severed the link to the physical is a huge improvement for the individual who cannot even see the need for the link to be broken. You need to be kind to yourself right now, so when you meditate burn some frankincense and before meditating make sure you bathe in water infused with a soothing herb such as chamomile.

DEMONS

shed-shd- שד*-*304

MEANING We all have our demons and they tend to disturb us when we least expect it. No two people have the same demons, and no matter how trivial our problems may seem to others, they are no less significant to us. The spelling of this dream title is positive in that it shows a strong and powerful spiritual energy (Shin) within us that will help us to open the door (Daleth) to a state of mind that has exorcised its demons. The letter Daleth, with its connection to the material world, also indicates that your demons are related to your day-to-day life and not to any spiritual problem. You should spend some time reflecting of what aspect of your life or indeed which individual might be the potentially damaging influence that has provoked this dream.

THE TREE OF LIFE As we progress up the Tree of Life, we experience a range of emotions, from relief at the realization of the existence of a Divine power to a sense of power as we learn to exert control over our fears and doubts. There are also negative emotions that we must pass through and this dream represents one such phase in your development. The path you are now traversing is that of Lamed. The letter of this path means "ox-goad" and represents a period of self-criticism when we come to terms with those aspects of ourselves that are hardest to recognize and accept.

THE JOURNEY Whatever you do now, you must not give up on the quest for spiritual truth or on yourself as a person, as to do so would be to throw away a wonderful opportunity for growth. The reduction value of this dream gives us the number 7, which is the value of the letter Zayin, meaning "sword." The implication of this is that you need to face your demons head-on and defeat them. You can do this if only you are prepared to honestly accept everything about your past. You will be assisted in this work if before you begin to think about your past you spend a short time meditating on the ultimately and unconditionally loving nature of the Divine.

See Zohar symbol, Demon.

❧ DESERT

*meedbar-mydbr-*מידבר-256

MEANING Throughout history mystics of all religious inclinations have spent time in one wilderness or another, be it literal or metaphorical and this wilderness experience is often the key to their enlightenment. Not only have most of the famous religious figures had their sojourn in the wilderness, but the Native American vision quest requires that the individual spend time alone in the desert in order to encounter spiritual illumination. It seems that in order to fully appreciate the nature of the Divine, you must first fully appreciate the nature of our soul, and you can do this only when you have sufficient solitude to prevent the distractions of the world from encroaching on your thoughts. The reduction value of this dream is the number thirteen, which itself points to a major change in your perception of the world. The compression of the dream's value gives the process that leads to your sojourn in the wilderness. The benevolent force of the Divine (Resh) gives way to an understanding of the true nature of your relationship to the higher (Nun), which in turn allows you to begin to contemplate the macrocosm (Vav) or the Divine itself.

THE TREE OF LIFE Before we can experience a union with the Divine force we must pass through the abyss, which is represented by the non-Sefirah of Daat. The experience of Daat is the spiritual wilderness that the dream of a desert represents. In this metaphorical desert there is no evidence of the Divine or indeed of life at all. The only thing that can carry you forward to the second phase of the path of Gimel is your faith.

THE JOURNEY This is a part of your spiritual journey that you must take alone, since solitude is the nature of Daat. However, the spelling of the dream title may offer some pointers as to how you should approach your spiritual development over the next few weeks and months. The protective maternal aspect of the Divine (Mem) has combined with the energetic masculine aspect of the Divine (Yod) in order to open the door (Daleth) to the secret behind duality (Beth). Once understood, this secret will lead you to the benevolence of the Divine represented by the final letter, Resh.

See Zohar symbol, Desert.

DESPAIR

*yeoosh-yyavsh-*ייאוש-327

MEANING It is easy to feel despairing when you look around at the state of the world today. There seems to be very little evidence of God's love and plenty of evidence of man's inhumanity to man, not to mention the disdain that is being shown to the environment, which we all must share and all should be helping to protect. The reduction value of this dream indicates that the proper response to these feelings of hopelessness is not despair but resolve to do your utmost to help the situation. This resolve is suggested by the number 12, the reduced value, which indicates self-sacrifice.

THE TREE OF LIFE The path that best fits this dream image is that of Mem. This is not the path that you are currently on but is the path to which you should be aspiring, and you will reach it if you act on the message of this dream's content. the tarot card The Hanged Man is connected to the path of Mem, and this again emphasizes the need for self-sacrifice on your part to achieve spiritual growth.

THE JOURNEY How do you set about engaging in selfless activity that will dispel your feelings of despair? The answer lies in the compression of the dream's value. You have vast reserves of spiritual energy (Shin) that you are not currently using, and you should begin to use this energy in a practical (Kaph) project such as a recycling program. In this way you will be fighting (Zayin) and both the problems of the world and your feelings of negativity.

DEVIL

*shaitan-shtn-*שטן-359

MEANING To dream of the Devil, especially if you have a definite spiritual belief, is a deeply distressing experience. However, all things that occur have a purpose, so you need to see what message this dream contains, rather than simply feel relieved that it is over. The final Nun in the spelling of this dream title points to a great deal of sadness and loss in your life. This may well be a recent and significant emotional trauma that can lead to doubts about the existence of a loving God. The central letter, Teth, supports the idea that you may be deceiving yourself in the rejection of the Divine, as the letter Teth represents the lies and deception of the biblical serpent. This figure is repeated in the compression of the dream, where we again have the letter Teth.

THE TREE OF LIFE In the Western Mystery Tradition, The Devil card in the tarot is associated with the path of Ayin. This path indicates a proud and vigorous individual who chooses to find his own way through life. However, this dream is about sorrow and loss, the sense of misery that can allow us to lose faith in the Divine and revert to a wholly materialistic view of the world. It is this tendency that epitomizes the Devil in the Kabbalah. As its central focus is deception, the path that fits this dream is that of Teth.

THE JOURNEY If you are to avoid the pitfalls of the path of Teth you need to rediscover an appreciation of all that is wondrous and joyful in the universe. You can begin this journey in your own backyard. If you spend just a few short minutes each day closely examining the beautiful and intricate nature of the plants that are growing there, you will begin to regain an understanding of the mystery of the Divine force. If a simple plant can be so complex, your own nature must be much more entwined and complicated, so you should not expect to always see the reasons why you go through difficult phases in your life. Additionally, you should make a point of spending time giving a proper level of thanks and appreciation to those people in your life who have been there to offer help and assistance in your times of need.

DEVOTION

*meseeroot-msyrvth-*מסירות-716

MEANING Only those who have made significant progress in their spiritual development are likely to experience this dream. Many of us may feel that we take our spiritual lives seriously, but genuine devotion is a characteristic that is extremely rare, since in its purest form it implies putting aside all concerns for the self in favor of absolute commitment to the Great Work. When we reduce the value of this dream we find the number 14, which is associated with ideas of balance. In order to be truly devoted you need to possess an inner harmony that comes only from considerable time spent on understanding your inner nature.

THE TREE OF LIFE In the tarot, the card Temperance is used to signify the balancing of the elements that is represented by the dream of devotion.

This card sits on the path of Samech, which leads from Yesod to the Sefirah of Tiferet. As we need a sincere level of devotion to reach the comfort of Tiferet, where we achieve a sense of union with our higher self, this path is appropriate for this dream image.

THE JOURNEY Feelings of devotion are highly commendable and indicate that you are making great leaps in your spiritual understanding. The presence of the final Nun in the compression of this dream points to the fact that devotion tends to be born out of and often leads to, bouts of deep melancholy. You can avoid this melancholy by reminding yourself of the joy that is all around you. A good way for you to maintain this awareness would be to engage in some volunteer work with children, especially since one of the equivalents of the value of this dream relates to motherhood.

DEW

*tal-tl-*טל-39

MEANING There are few things in nature that are as beautiful as early-morning dew. In Kabbalistic terms the dew can be seen as representing the jewels that are the wisdom of the Divine. Another feature of dew is its transience; as soon as the world begins to go about its daily business, the dew begins to fade until there is no trace of it left. This is another parallel to the nature of Divine wisdom, in that it often fades from our mind once we return to our normal day-to-day life.

THE TREE OF LIFE This dream refers to someone whose spiritual commitment tends to waver. When he is undeniably in the presence of a spiritual event or experience, his commitment is absolute. However, he is easily distracted by the seeming solidity of the normal and the physical. The letter Teth in the spelling of the dream title indicates a capacity for self-deception, while the letter Lamed indicates the need for you to be stern with yourself in order to ensure that you continue to make spiritual progress. This dream sits on the path of Teth, which carries the stern energy of the Sefirah of Gevurah as well as the forgiving energy represented by the Sefirah of Hesed.

THE JOURNEY Clearly, the biggest problem you face in terms of making progress in the Great Work is your level of commitment. This commitment is endangered by your ability to forget any spiritual experience as soon as you return to a normal state of consciousness. What you need to do is to create a strict routine of meditation, reading, and even prayer. Additionally, you should formally record all your experiences in a diary so that when your commitment begins to wane you have something to read that helps to keep you motivated.

DISCOVERING NEW ROOMS IN A FAMILIAR PLACE

legolot kheder khadash bemakom mookar-

lglvth chdr chdsh bmqvm mvkr-

לגלות חדר חדש במקום מוכר-1447

MEANING If we remember that in dreams, buildings are representations of our psyche, then this dream indicates that the dreamer has discovered a whole new side to his personality that up to now has been hidden from him. Such an experience can be both exciting and rewarding while also being rather unsettling, as we all like to think that we know ourselves quite well. The fact you discovered the rooms rather than had them shown to you is a sign that you are taking responsibility for your spiritual development, and this is a very positive sign.

THE TREE OF LIFE When we reduce the very large value of this dream title we find the number 16. This is connected to the tarot card The Tower and it suggests a major trauma of some kind that will entirely change the way you construct your perception of reality. This card also points to a crisis that will ultimately prove to be beneficial. The path of Peh is connected to The Tower card. Additionally, it runs between the Sefirot of Netzach and Hod, both of which involve the individual in a major reassessment of the way he looks at the world and himself.

THE JOURNEY The compression of this dream is most useful in that it reveals an enormous amount of anxiety on your part about the nature of this newly discovered spirituality. The value of the letter Qoph multiplied by itself begins the compression and is followed by the letter Tav, which also connects to notions of melancholy and concern. If you look to the path that matches this dream, you will see that the answer is to share your feelings with those around you. The letter Peh means "mouth," and in order to progress with confidence you need to engage in discussions with others about your current feelings.

DISCOVERING NEW TALENTS OR SKILLS

legolot keeshron khadash-lglvth kshrvn chdsh-

לגלות כשרון חדש-1357

MEANING Those who would doubt the validity of Kabbalistic dream analysis would do well to consider this dream and the one immediately preceding. Both dreams have very large values because they consist of multiple words. Both deal with new discoveries that represent the realization of a new aspect of the self in a spiritual context. What is noticeable is that both of these dreams have a value that when reduced gives the number 16, relating to a beneficial but traumatic event in our lives.

THE TREE OF LIFE As with the dream of discovering a new room, this dream is placed on the path of Peh due to the connection with a life-changing event and the need for communication. In this dream, the letter Peh refers not just to discussing your feelings with others but to expressing your feelings in a creative manner. This additional meaning is due to the connection of this dream to a new talent that suggests that as your spiritual understanding grows, so too does your ability to express it in an artistic way.

THE JOURNEY Not every aspect of your inner development can be dealt with in an overtly spiritual way. It is clear from this dream that you are developing a talent and an interest in the arts. It is likely that this interest has been sparked by a realization of the Divine harmony that underlies our reality and an associated desire within you to express this harmony in a way that will communicate to others. You should seriously consider taking art classes at this time or learning to play a musical instrument.

DISEASE

*kholee-chvly-*חולי-54

MEANING Illness is now even more of a threat to our sense of well-being than it would have been in earlier times. Not only is our culture excessively focused on physical health and appearance, but we operate in a marketplace economy where illness can be a real threat to our long-term career prospects. In a spiritual sense we can see disease as combining a strong feeling of anxiety with a danger that our worries will lead us to make wrong decisions in the pursuit of higher understanding. This latter danger is indicated by the fact that this dream's value reduces to 9, which is the value of the letter Teth, meaning "serpent."

THE TREE OF LIFE When we are diseased we need expert medical care in order to stimulate our recovery. Similarly, when we are dangerously close to making wrong decisions in terms of our inner journey we need support and guidance from above. We also need protection from those negative forces within ourselves that encourage us to set off down blind alleys and spiritual cul-de-sacs. For this reason, the dream of disease is placed on the path of Cheth. The letter Cheth means "fence," and in the context of this dream it stands for the protective will of the Divine.

THE JOURNEY If we study alone, we are likely to reinforce our initial preconceptions of the universe and the nature of spirituality while at the same time finding it easier to ignore viewpoints for which we have never felt a particular affinity. If you join a meditation group or even take a philosophy class you will be exposed to a dialogue and debate about spiritual perspectives. This broadening of your awareness will assist you in finding a path that not only feels right but is likely to increase your chances of spiritual development.

DISFIGUREMENT

lehashkeet tsorah–lhshchyth tzvrh–

להשחית צורה-1054

MEANING In what seems like a very distressing dream is hidden a very positive message. To be disfigured suggests a state of knowingly being ill-shaped. From a spiritual perspective this implies being aware of a lack of proper balance within yourself. To gain this realization is difficult, but is absolutely necessary in order to allow you to move on to a state of harmonious balance. The reduction of the value of this dream provides the number 10, which indicates that you are about to complete an important phase of your inner journey. The realization of imbalance certainly qualifies as a very important act of closure en route to your spiritual goals.

THE TREE OF LIFE The realization you have achieved is not one that could occur in Malkut, but it is typical of the experience of the Sefirah of Yesod. Having become aware of the existence of a spiritual reality in a very concrete way, you now become aware of the need for a harmonization of the elements within your personality. This is the work that

is undertaken in the next two Sefirot, Hod and Netzach.

THE JOURNEY Before you can begin to advance toward the Sefirah of Hod, where you will balance your mental and rational outlook against a spiritual view of the universe, you need to have an initial understanding of the competing aspects of your personality and how they relate to the four elements. To achieve this, you should list what you consider to be your key traits, viewpoints, and values. These should then be mapped according to the four elements so that you can see more easily where any conflicts lie. Make a list for the elements of Air (your thoughtful side), Earth (your material and physical side), Water (sensitive emotions and creativity), and Fire (passion and confidence). When you have assigned all aspects of your personality to one of the four elements, look to see if you have an imbalance where one element has more traits than the other three.

DISPUTE

*veekoakh–vykvch–***ויכוח**-50

MEANING According to the Buddha, desire is the cause of all sorrow. However, in this dream there is another cause of sorrow and that is the existence of disputes. Arguments are always unpleasant and even if you win there is never a feeling of real satisfaction to be gained. The value of this dream is equivalent to the value of the letter Nun, which is closely associated with all ideas of sorrow and loss.

THE TREE OF LIFE In Kabbalistic terms the idea of a dispute refers to a conflict within ourselves that we cannot resolve and is causing us significant distress. In the spelling of the dream we see the two sides of the argument arranged around the central letter, Kaph. The letters Vav in both pairings indicate thought while the letter Yod suggests a belief in active exploration of the spiritual, the letter Cheth indicates a desire for caution and defensiveness. This inner sense of anxiety places the dream on the path of Qoph.

THE JOURNEY The key to your problem can also be located in the spelling of the dream title. The central letter, kaph, indicates practicality. The suggestion here is that perhaps both sides of the argument are correct, in which case we should remember that caution and unconcerned enthusiasm are called for at different times and in different situations. The path of Kaph is associated with the planet Jupiter, and this indicates that we should rely on our gut instinct to tell us which approach is called for at each time, and once a decision has been made we should stick to it and ignore our anxieties.

DISTANCE

*merkhak-mrchq-*מרחק*-*348

MEANING From a Kabbalistic point of view, geographical distance is irrelevant. The only distance that matters is the distance between yourself and the Divine. The purpose of the Great Work is to gradually close the gap between your state of consciousness and the will of the Divine as emanating from Keter. The fact that you are aware of the distance is itself a sign of some initial insights and should be seen as encouraging. The reduction of the value of this dream produces the number 6. This is the value of the letter Vav, which is associated with thought and with the Divine itself and indicates that you are spending much time in contemplation of the nature of God.

THE TREE OF LIFE Clearly, this dream is focused on a particular form of contemplation. This itself suggests the Sefirah of Hod, as it is there that we align our mental processes to a spiritual context. Additionally, the compression of the dream produces the letters Shin and Mem, both of which are paths that connect to Hod on the Tree of Life. Finally, the last number in the compression is 8, and Hod is indeed the eighth Sefirah.

THE JOURNEY There is no correct answer to the question, How far away is God? Indeed, the answer is, like the nature of the Divine, paradoxical. One one hand, God is never distant as his force is present in every aspect of the universe. On the other hand, as we progress we do become closer to God as our understanding of the universe and our role within it increases. The task for you is not so much to find an answer to the question but to understand, through meditating on the question, why it is important that we ask it and what we may learn about ourselves in trying to determine just what level of understanding we have achieved.

DISTANT SOUNDS

*tsleel merookakh-tzlyl mrvchq-*צליל מרוחק*-*514

MEANING When we first begin our spiritual quest, the voice of our higher self is simply a hope, and the voice of the Divine is no more than a dream. As we progress higher and higher these voices become more and more possible. The value of this

dream reduces to 10, which indicates the completion of a major portion of your spiritual journey. In this case, it is likely that you are now on the verge of being able to hear a voice emerge from what is now simply a beckoning sound in the distance.

THE TREE OF LIFE The voice of the Divine in its undiluted form can never be heard by human ears; it enters the Tree of Life from what is known as the Ain Suph and is gradually diluted as it works its way down the Tree. However, the Sefirah of Hesed can be seen as repesenting an aspect of the Divine that many of us would regard as a personification of God. This is in part because of its connections with ideas of justice and mercy as well its association with the planet Jupiter. The path of Kaph is indicated in the compression of this dream, particularly as Kaph runs from Netzach up to Hesed.

THE JOURNEY You need to be open to the influence of the Divine at this time. At the moment all you can hear is a distant sound to which you are being drawn. In order to successfully traverse the path of Kaph you need to learn to hear the words that are hidden within that sound. The only way to achieve this level of spiritual hearing is through disciplined meditation. If you burn an incense known as dittany of Crete (an herb not unlike sage) while you are practicing your breathing you will find it much easier to achieve the level of inner quiet combined with an alert state of consciousness that is needed for success in this matter.

DIVINE COMMUNICATION

*hodah elohee-hvda'ah alvhy-*הודעה אלוהי*-*142

MEANING To achieve some form of genuine communication with the Divine is the ultimate aim of all spiritual endeavors. This dream suggests very definitely that this is now within your grasp, provided that you continue to maintain your current attitudes and behavior toward those around you. The value of the dream reduces to 7, and we should see this as emphasizing the mystical importance of this dream rather than as a reference to the letter Zayin.

THE TREE OF LIFE The position of this dream on the Tree of Life relates to the state of mind that is required in order for any form of Divine communication to take place. It is always a temporary position as we are not designed to maintain a state of consciousness in the highest reaches of the Tree of Life for long periods of time. The compression of the dream yields the letters Qoph, Mem, and Beth. Qoph indicates that the dream refers to a state of mind, and Mem points to the protective and caring nature of the Divine that is calling to you. The final Beth, which tells you that communion with the Divine is a visit to your ultimate home, is the path of the Tree on which this dream sits.

THE JOURNEY In order to achieve some form of dialogue with the Divine we must be fully prepared. This is not just a matter of assiduous spiritual practice in terms of prayer or meditation, but, even more important, we need to display our spiritual awareness in the way in which we interact with others. If there is anybody in your life with whom you have any lingering conflict, you should make a point over the next few weeks of ensuring that you have done everything you can to resolve the issue.

DIVING
leetslol—ltzlvl—לצלול—186

MEANING We can instantly see that this dream is reserved for those individuals who are intensely self-critical. The spelling of the dream title has no less than three instances of the letter Lamed, which means "ox-goad." As if to emphasize the importance of the effect of the letter Lamed, we also have the letter Tzaddi, whose value is 90, which is equivalent to the value of three instances of the letter Lamed. The image of diving is itself important as it is suggestive of getting under the surface of one's personality. This is very important within the Great Work, but we must avoid being so harsh on ourselves that we cease to believe that we may ever succeed in our spiritual quest.

THE TREE OF LIFE Since Lamed occurs three times in the spelling of the dream title, it seems that the only place where this dream can possibly sit is on the path of Lamed. It is important that the tarot card associated with the path of Lamed is Justice. This is not the same as severity, since justice requires clemency and mercy to temper its harsh edge, otherwise it ceases to be justice and becomes merely cruelty.

THE JOURNEY The reduction of this dream produces the number 6, which is the value of the letter Vav. The letter Vav represents the element of Air in the Tetragrammaton. This indicates that you have a lot of thinking to do. Indeed, the only letter that has no relationship to the letter Lamed in the spelling of the dream is Vav. What you should be doing is trying to place yourself in the position of someone other than yourself, trying to help someone who has the same critical self-image as you currently have. You will find that the advice you would give this person can equally be applied to yourself, and you should try to take your own advice and allow yourself to move forward.

DIVORCE
geroosheem—gyrvshym—גירושים—569

MEANING Nobody enjoys divorce; it is upsetting for all concerned. One of the reasons for much of the animosity that occurs when people divorce is the fact that deep down both individuals feel enormously responsible for the failure of their marriage, and as a result they feel like failures as individuals, no matter how unfair this may be. In Kabbalistic terms the idea of divorce relates to a temptation to reject the spiritual path in favor of a return to a purely material existence. The fact that the compression of this dream ends with the letter Teth, which means "serpent," should be seen as a sign that such a decision would be a grave mistake.

THE TREE OF LIFE There are many places on the Tree of Life where someone might be tempted to throw in the towel. The spiritual quest forces us to face some very difficult facts about ourselves and others, not to mention the requirements it places on us in terms of how we behave toward those around us. A divorce is the result of a formal judgment, and this connection would point us toward the path of Shin. The path of Shin is very difficult as tends to involve an awful lot of self-judging in a brutally honest manner. It is the twentieth path on the Tree, and the value of this dream also reduces to 20.

THE JOURNEY If the compression tells us not to give up on our inner journey, through the inclusion of the letter Teth, it also provides us with some help in determining how we should cope with the difficulties associated with the path of Shin. The initial value of 500 is the value of Kaph in its final form. This strongly suggests that you ought to express your spirituality through some form of physical exercise such as yoga or tai chi. The central letter, Samech, is a reminder that when even the physical expression seems difficult to maintain, the spirit of the Divine is with you, acting as a support on which you can lean.

DOGS
kelev—klb—כלב—52

MEANING When we dream of animals it is their generally accepted characteristics that are important in terms of the symbolic meaning of the dream. Dogs are renowned for their loyalty to their masters, and in Kabbalistic terms this dream indicates a person who is deeply committed to the pursuit of the Divine. This loyalty is emphasized by the fact that the value of this dream is equivalent to the value of the phrase "He is my God" from the Book of Job. Job, of course, was an intensely loyal servant of God, despite his being tested in numerous severe ways.

THE TREE OF LIFE The initial letter, Lamed, in this dream's spelling indicates that, like Job, your loyalty is about to be tested. However, the final letter, Beth, also tells us that you have the ability to come through with flying colors. The letter Beth means "home," and the indication here is that your knowledge of the promise of a spiritual home will help you to persist through a range of hardships. This level of commitment under adverse circumstances puts this dream on the path of Zayin.

THE JOURNEY It is easy to feel a sense of love and trust in the Divine when our lives are going well. However, the real test of our devotion to the Great Work is whether we can maintain that same attitude of belief and faith when we are going through turmoil and disappointment. All the signs in this dream are that you will indeed persevere. You can make your life slightly easier by performing a relaxation ritual each morning and night. You should lie down, and while breathing in a slow and regular manner visualize a golden ball of light moving slowly over your whole body, its warmth removing every last niggle and worry from your body and mind.

DOME

*keepat beenyan–kyphth bnyyn–*כיפת בניין*-632*

MEANING As a dream image a dome seems particularly uninspiring, but when we examine the value of the dream title we begin to see that it has a very specific message for the dreamer. When we reduce the value we produce the number 11, which is itself an indication of a mystically significant aspect to the dream. In addition, the compression of the dream suggests the route that has led you to this particular dream. You have been attracted to the spiritual path as a result of a longing for contact with the protective aspect of the Divine (Mem), in order to achieve this you have accepted the sometimes harsh requirements of the Great Work (Lamed), and you are now approaching a spiritual resting place (Beth).

THE TREE OF LIFE Although you are drawn strongly to the notion of the Divine as mother, you have experienced both harsh self-criticism and significant sorrow, as indicated by the final Nun in the spelling of the dream title. This mixture of pain and joy has provided you with the spiritual grounding necessary to lead you to the Sefirah of Tiferet. This is the spiritual resting place referred to by the letter Beth. It is not the end of your journey, but it does allow you finally to achieve a form of contact with your higher self.

THE JOURNEY Because of the main reasons behind your search for spiritual truth, it will be very tempting for you to stay in the Sefirah of Tiferet. To move on involves yet more feelings of isolation, more moments of confusion and doubt. However, if you choose to stop now, you will find that the advances you have made will gradually be lost. In order for you to feel stronger you should consider joining a Kabbalah school, where mixing with other serious seekers of truth will offer you the support that you need.

DOOR

*delet–dlth–*דלת*-434*

MEANING All major religions talk in one way or another about the door to enlightenment, or to redemption, or to the Divine being open and it is simply a matter of knowing how to walk through. It is most clearly spelled out in the phrase "knock and the door shall be opened," but it is by no means a purely Christian conception. In the Kabbalah, the view is perhaps a little more honest in that the door is definitely there but requires more than simply wanting to walk through to get it to open. If we wish spiritual rewards we must put in the appropriate spiritual effort.

THE TREE OF LIFE In one sense the whole Tree of Life could be seen as a series of doors leading from one state of consciousness to another. However, the word meaning "door" is the Hebrew letter Daleth, and it is this letter and its path to which this dream refers. The path of Daleth runs between Hokhmah and Binah, the two Sefirot that when combined provide both the force and the form that allow for ideas of created existence to come into being. This arrangement is mirrored in the value of the dream: the two 4's that begin and end the value represent the two Sefirot, incapable of creation on their own, but when meeting through the channel or doorway of Daleth they become creative, hence the middle number 3.

THE JOURNEY You must now try to emulate the role of the path of Daleth in your daily life. This means that whenever possible you must encourage positive creativity by the marriage of the impetus to create with the ability to give form to that creative urge. This applies to your own life in terms of balancing your personality but also to the workplace or even among your friends and neighbors.

❧DOVES

*yonah-yvnh-*יונה-71

MEANING When we think of peace the first image that is likely to spring to mind is that of a dove holding an olive branch in its mouth. This international symbol of peace is now far more well known than the story that gave rise to its symbolic meaning. The dove was the bird sent forth by Noah to see if there was sufficient dry land for the Ark to cease sailing. It is important to remember this fact as the dove indicates not just the potential for peace in your life but the fact that the search for this peace will be long and arduous.

THE TREE OF LIFE The value of this dream is equivalent to the value of the Hebrew words for "lead" and "vision." Lead is the metal of the planet Saturn, which is associated with the path of Tav on the Tree of Life. Additionally, the idea of a vision is appropriate to this path as it suggestive of the initial inspiration that sets someone off on his first steps out of Malkut.

THE JOURNEY The number 71 is a prime number and suggests that your spiritual journey is likely to be unique. Additionally, the compression of the value of the dream reveals the letters Ayin and Aleph. This can be taken to mean that a wholly individualistic approach (Ayin) will lead you to unity (Aleph) with the Divine. At the same time, the compression of the dream's value gives us 8. This is the value of the letter Cheth, meaning "fence." The implication here is that even on your wholly unique quest you need to ensure that from the start you find ways to help and protect those around you. A good start would be to involve yourself in some local charity work.

See Zohar symbol, Dove.

❧DRAGON

*drakon-drqvn-*דרקון-360

MEANING When we consider mythical creatures we have to be very careful to keep an eye on which culture we are also considering. In China, for instance, dragons are very positive creatures indicating wealth, health, and happiness. In Kabbalistic symbolism this is simply not the case. The value of this dream contains the number of degrees in a circle, but in the context of this dream it is the fact that there is no progression in a circle that is being emphasized. Unlike a spiral, which moves upward as well as around and around, a circle merely returns us again and again to our starting point.

THE TREE OF LIFE Dragons have been known by a number of different names in different cultures and in different times. One popular alternative term for "dragon" is "serpent." On the Tree of Life, the path of Teth is associated with the serpent. The fact that the value of this dream reduces to 9, which is the value of the letter Teth, supports the idea that this dream should be placed there.

THE JOURNEY The path of Teth in its negative aspect refers to excessive force and to a very narrow viewpoint in one's approach to the Divine. These two tendencies inevitably lead to a false view of spiritual reality, and it is this deception that is the nature of the energy of Teth. To avoid falling into the trap of self-deception, you should follow the advice embedded into the compression of this dream's value. We have the two letters Shin and Samech. Shin refers to the enormous energy that you possess, while Samech indicates that you should allow the Divine to direct you as to how best to express that energy. This means that you need to reflect far more than you are used to on the actions that you take in the name of your spiritual progress.

See Zohar symbol, Dragon.

GETTING DRESSED

*heetlabesh-hthlbsh-*התלבש-737

MEANING To call you a bright spark would be a massive understatement. You have enough energy for three people and you are very keen to devote this energy to the pursuit of the Great Work. The act of dressing can be seen as a process of getting ready to face the day, and this dream represents the mental process of preparation for your spiritual journey. The reduction of this dream's value produces the number 17, which indicates significant help and guidance from your higher self. This may in part account for the high levels of spiritual energy that you possess.

THE TREE OF LIFE The value of this dream is equivalent to that of the Hebrew word meaning a "blaze," and this is a good description of your spiritual character. You approach the Great Work with a burning passion and great enthusiasm. In the compression of the dream's value we see that you have experienced great sorrow as indicated by the letter Nun, but that you have borne all of the harsh experiences along your journey (Lamed) by meeting them head-on (Zayin). It is this final letter, Zayin, that sums up your approach and it is the path of Zayin to which this dream belongs.

THE JOURNEY Your progress so far has been commendable and, thanks to the energy you bring to your spiritual journey, extremely swift. However, you are now approaching the "city walls" of the realm of the Divine itself, so a less brash approach is now called for. The same level of energy as indicated by the final Shin in the spelling of the dream is appropriate. However, you need now to direct this energy inward rather than outward. A good way for you to learn the subtle control of your inner energy would be to take classes on Kundalini yoga.

DRINKING
*leeshtot-lshthvth-*לשתות-1136

MEANING Wisdom is often metaphorically referred to as a stream or river from which the enlightened drink. In this dream it is drinking in the sense of receiving spiritual insights that we are being invited to think about. The reduction value of this dream produces the number 11, whose mystical significance suggests that you are drinking very deeply and that the wisdom you are gaining will sustain you well on your spiritual journey.

THE TREE OF LIFE While you are drinking well you are still in the middle reaches of the Tree of Life, so you should look for a path that is connected to the element of Water; this is the area on the Tree that you should focus on. The most appropriate path is that of Mem. It means "water" in Hebrew and is associated with the element of Water in terms of Kabbalistic correspondences used within the Western Mystery Tradition.

THE JOURNEY When we look at the compression of this dream's value we find that the letter Qoph is repeated twice and that this is followed by the letters Lamed and Vav. This tells us that your mind (Qoph) is wholly occupied with the inner journey that you feel driven (Lamed) to undertake and that you have given it much consideration and thought (Vav). However, there is a sense in which you now need to

move from thought to action. The letters in this dream's compression, with the exception of Lamed, are all related to thinking rather than doing. What is more, all of the elements are represented in the dream's compression except for the element of Fire, which represents activity and passion. What you need to do in order to progress is to transform your passive intake of wisdom into an active and outward practice of the insights that you have gained. This should include involvement with some kind of spiritual-awareness-raising group.

DRIVING
*leenhog-lnhvg-*לנהוג-94

MEANING When we drive our cars we tend to undergo something of a personality transformation. Even those of us who are naturally calm and placid can become aggressive and impatient. A large part of the reason for this change in our attitude and behavior stems from the sense of power that a car bestows upon us. As is so often the case, this feeling of power is both illusory and dangerous. In Kabbalistic terms, the power aspect of the driving image is crucial, as this dream is a warning against feeling not just responsible for your spiritual development but in authority to decide whether you are making good progress or otherwise. The value of this dream is equivalent to the value of the Hebrew word meaning "destruction," and this is what waits for anyone who tries to appropriate power and authority that belong only to the Divine.

THE TREE OF LIFE With feelings of power come associated feelings of pride. This belief in the self to the exclusion of listening to the higher self is symptomatic of the negative aspect of the path of Ayin. Additionally, the path of Ayin is associated with The Devil card from the tarot. This card refers to the attraction to power and pride as well as to a materialistic and wholly sensualist outlook on life. The value of this dream reduces to 4, which symbolizes the purely physical world of the elements, and this is another connection to the path of Ayin.

THE JOURNEY The compression of this dream's value yields the letters Tzaddi and Daleth. On one hand, this tells us that the individual has allowed himself to become hooked on the material world and its physical distractions. However, the path of Tzaddi also suggests that you can harness your desire for control and turn it into a desire for self-control. If you are able to do this, you will then be able to open the doors to spiritual insight, which are represented by the letter Daleth.

DROWNING

*leetboa-ltbva'a-*לטבוע-117

MEANING As you might expect, this dream indicates that your spiritual development is not progressing as smoothly as you would hope. The suggestion here is that you are sinking in a sea of confusion and that this is probably due in part to the plethora of New Age systems out there, all of which promise you genuine spiritual enlightenment. The value of this dream is equivalent to that of the Hebrew word meaning "fog" or "darkness." This association emphasizes the confusion that is clouding your ability to make a sound judgment.

THE TREE OF LIFE In the compression of this dream we find that the first letter is Qoph, which represents mental anxiety and concern, often related to our direction in life. Qoph is the ideal path for this dream as it both represents the feelings that you are experiencing and is one of the first paths out of Malkut. The nature of your concerns is indicative of someone who is very new to the spiritual path. It may also be that you feel overwhelmed in your daily life either by too many commitments or too much pressure. You need to find some way of easing the level of stress in your life.

THE JOURNEY The remainder of the compression points to the way to deal with your current confusion. The letter Yod tells you that you need to rely on the Divine spark within you to guide you in choosing a path that is right for you. The letter Zayin implies that you also need to learn to assert yourself and find ways to say no to people and ideas that do not appeal to you. The fact that this dream's value reduces to 9 is also a warning against those who may try to deceive you with promises of instant enlightenment, for a price.

DRUGS

*sam-sm-*סם-100

MEANING Any substance that affects your perception artificially has the ability to interfere with your understanding of your inner self. In spiritual terms we can view the concept of drugs literally or metaphorically. If we look at the symbolic implications, then the notion of drugs relates to any kind of emotional crutch that we use to avoid dealing with

reality. This, of course, can include religion when we use it as a means of self-validation rather than genuinely looking into what its tenets are actually saying.

THE TREE OF LIFE In the 1960s it was popular to claim that those who took drugs were escaping from their lives but that those who took hallucinogens were exploring their lives. Now we can say with confidence that any mind-altering chemical is an attempt to escape from life. We often feel like escaping when we are in a melancholic state, so this dream is most suited to the path of Nun, as this is deeply linked to the emotions of sorrow and depression.

THE JOURNEY The value of this dream is equivalent to the value of the letter Qoph, so it is clear that your need for some form of emotional crutch stems from deep-seated anxieties. The spelling of the dream title advises you that if you are looking for support (Samech), you should learn to trust in the maternal protective aspect of the Divine (Mem). This doesn't mean that you should expect to have everything go your way, but that you should learn to accept that negative experiences may have long-term value.

❧DRUM

*tof-thvph-*תוף-486

MEANING Since ancient times drums have been used as a religious tool. In most cultures the drum itself was regarded as sacred and only certain individuals were permitted to touch it for fear of weakening its spiritual power. To dream of a drum suggests that your higher self is communicating to you your own level of advancement. The idea is that if you are now entitled to visualize a drum in your dreams, you are approaching a point where you will be able to enter into a dialogue with your higher self.

THE TREE OF LIFE It is in the Sefirah of Tiferet that we achieve a sense of communion with our higher self. You are not yet there, so this dream sits on one of the paths that leads into this Sefirah. The most appropriate path is Samech, as it is linked with a decidedly mystical and harmonious approach to the Divine. This path is also associated with the gods of hunting, and it was common practice in ancient times for any hunt to be preceded by sacred drumming.

THE JOURNEY The spelling of this dream title gives the details of your spiritual journey. You have endured the initial regrets and sense of melancholy (Tav) that come with the spiritual path. This has led you to a point where you are ready to communicate with the Divine (Peh). If you persevere you will be able to receive communication back from the macrocosm (Vav). You should consider enrolling in a sacred drumming class, as this may be a practical way in which you can achieve a state of consciousness where you can indeed enter Tiferet.

See Zohar symbol, Playing a Musical Instrument.

DUMB (SPEECHLESS)
eelem-alm-אלם-71

MEANING From a purely physical point of view we might expect this dream to be negative, since we tend to regard an individual who is dumb as significantly disadvantaged. In Kabbalistic terms, the inability to speak is purely symbolic and relates to the need to be still within and listen to the voice of the Divine rather than to our own thoughts and feelings. When we use the final value of the letter Mem in the value of the dream, we find a value that is equivalent to that of a Hebrew word meaning "concealed mystery." This fits ideally with the notion of dumbness especially when we consider it as a prohibition from speaking rather than an inability to speak.

THE TREE OF LIFE To have a dream regarding a concealed mystery suggests a significant level of spiritual development. This is emphasized by the idea that this wisdom is not something that can be spoken of freely. The Sefirah of Binah is regarded as holding a great and concealed mystery, and her nature as the Great Mother emphasizes her role as holding on to a great secret. The reduction of the value of this dream produces the number 8. This is the number of the letter Cheth, and the path of Cheth runs into the Sefirah of Binah. This path is also appropriate in that it means "fence." To be unable to talk of a particular secret is tantamount to "fencing" it off from the uninitiated.

THE JOURNEY Another word that is equivalent to the value of this dream is the Hebrew word meaning "vision." This suggests that you are likely to be privileged to receive some form of Divine revelation. When this happens, you will be in no doubt that it is wholly genuine. It is then your responsibility to communicate the underlying ideas of this vision to the world at large. It may be that you can achieve this through art or music or simply by talking about your experiences.

DUSK
deemdoomeem-dmdvmym-דמדומים-144

MEANING This is a very significant dream in Kabbalistic terms. It indicates an individual with a well-developed capacity for empathy with his fellow man. The letter Mem is consistently repeated throughout the dream title, which is a sure sign of a willingness for self-sacrifice in order to help others. As if to underline this point, the total value of the dream is 144. This number, which is 12 multiplied by 12, has a direct connection to the letter Mem and ideas of altruistic behavior.

THE TREE OF LIFE This dream seems to sit on the path of Mem. This would seem appropriate, but the number of times this letter is repeated suggests that you have achieved a standard of compassion that exceeds the level indicated by the letter Mem. In fact, it is more appropriate to position this dream within the Sefirah of Hesed. This Sefirah represents the merciful aspect of the Divine. It is the fourth Sefirah on the Tree of Life, and the very first letter Mem in the spelling of this dream title is flanked by the letter Daleth, which has a value of 4.

THE JOURNEY It would be a crime not to make the most of the understanding and compassion that you possess. Your spiritual progress will also continue more smoothly if you put your enviable talent to good use. The compression of this dream tells that your head (Qoph) is full of compassion (Mem) that needs to be manifested in the physical word (Daleth). You might also consider changing your career to some kind of caring profession such as counseling, nursing, or teaching.

DUST
avak-abq-אבק-103

MEANING The reduction value of this dream immediately points to its being the sort of dream that one would experience very early in the spiritual quest. The number 4, which we find in the reduction value of this dream, refers to the purely material world and indicates that you have yet to have any contact with your higher self. Additionally, the image of dust emphasizes the biblical idea that life comes from dust before it can evolve into anything higher.

THE TREE OF LIFE The spelling of this dream title indicates that you are already thinking about your inner self and the possibility of some reality beyond the obvious world of the physical. The letters Aleph and Beth tell us that you have recognized the existence of some higher unity and also that in contacting that unity you will in some way be returning to your spiritual home. However, you have yet to move beyond thinking, so this dream is still placed in Malkut.

THE JOURNEY You have the most exciting and fulfilling journey possible ahead of you and all you have to do is take the very first step and then simply keep walking. The letter Qoph in the dream's compression indicates that you are thinking about taking this step. The final letter, Gimel, suggests that you have the imagination and creative belief to go ahead and make that leap into the unknown. A good way to start would be to buy a book on simple meditation techniques and begin to follow the exercises.

See Zohar symbol, Dust.

DYING

*lamoot-lmvth-*למות-476

MEANING There can be few dreams more unsettling than that of dying. However, an awareness of our mortality is essential for a solid grounding in the spiritual. As long as we hang on to the idea of an eternal physical life, we find it easier to put off thinking about the nature of the Divine. When we reduce the value of this dream we get 17, which is a sign of protection from above, so the death that you are dreaming is not a warning but a symbolic sign of your inner transformation. It may also be a reference to changes occurring in your day-to-day life such as a change of career or life-style.

THE TREE OF LIFE If we reduce the value even further we find the number 8, which refers to the Sefirah of Hod. To reconcile the concept of death is an important part of the intellectual work that we must undertake when we are in Hod. The dream suggests a realization rather than a reconciliation and it is therefore likely that this dream should sit on the path of Shin that runs from Malkut into Hod. As the path of Shin is concerned with judgment from above, it is doubly appropriate that this dream deals with the notion of dying, as most spiritual traditions believe that it is in the moment of death that our souls are judged.

THE JOURNEY The compression of this dream provides some very good advice for dealing with the dream of dying and for crossing the biting path of Shin in general. You will have to endure a pervasive feeling of melancholy (Tav) in order to begin to approach the macrocosm (Vav). You can combat this melancholy by maintaining a vigorous attitude to your inner development (Ayin). It is highly likely that you would benefit from learning some form of spiritually related martial art as a means of combining significant energy with spiritual contemplation.

DYNAMITE

*deenameet-dynmyt-*דינמים-113

MEANING One of the more surprising aspects of Gematria is that even when faced with modern Hebrew words such as the word for dynamite one can still find as many significant relationships between letters and values as we would find in an ancient word from the sacred text of the Torah. Such a factor seems to fit the extreme claim of some Kabbalists that the Torah contains all that will be, has been and could ever be within the universe. On the whole dynamite tends to be used for negative reasons and so we see that the spelling of the dream ends in the letter Teth, which means "serpent" and is generally a sign of the capacity for harm. However the value of the dream reduces to 5, which points to the symbol of the pentagram. This symbol represents a person who has balanced all four elements and is now crowned by the fifth element of Spirit.

THE TREE OF LIFE This dream belongs in the Sefirah of Gevurah, otherwise known as the Sefirah of Severity. This Sefirah is connected to the planet Mars, which has very obvious connections to the nature of dynamite. Additionally, Gevurah is the fifth Sefirah and the value of this dream reduces to 5. Finally, Gevurah requires that you have balanced all the elements within yourself so that you can understand the profound importance of the breakdown of forms; in fact, this is as much a part of the Divine as the creation of forms.

THE JOURNEY The energies of Gevurah can be quite overpowering, so it is important not to get carried away with the benefits of entropy and destruction, otherwise you may find yourself making any number of regrettable choices both in your home life and in your workplace. Each day when you wake, you should remind yourself that it is the desire of all things to grow but that only the Divine will has the right to determine when any given thing should begin to break down. This will encourage you to listen to your Divine spark, indicated by the central Yod in the compression of this dream, when you are considering putting an end to a personal or professional relationship.

✺EAGLES

*nesher-nshr-*נשׁר-550

MEANING To dream of eagles is very promising indeed, as it suggests that you have acquired a considerable degree of spiritual authority in terms of a deep understanding particularly of the moral bases of the universe. The reduction value of this dream is 10, a number that indicates that you are approaching the completion of an important cycle in your spiritual development. The dream of an eagle is a personification in animal form of the state of consciousness that you are approaching.

THE TREE OF LIFE The eagle is regarded as a particularly noble bird and has often been linked with the god Jupiter because of its poise and power. The path of Kaph is also associated with the planet Jupiter and so may seem like a good place to locate this dream image. This is supported by the fact that the compression of this dream produces the letter Kaph in its final form. This adds even more weight to the idea that this dream belongs on the path of Kaph.

A traditional Kabbalist would not see the eagle in this way. This is because the Roman occupation of Judea gave a very definite meaning to the image of an eagle and of the Roman god Jupiter. However, hermetic Kabbalists try to find the universal truths within each system and separate them from those factors that are cultural and historical.

THE JOURNEY The path of Kaph is concerned with practical activity, so this dream is suggesting that you should be looking for practical ways in which to express your spirituality. The path that you are on suggests that this expression should in some way take the form of offering assistance to others in a way that may not be directly related to the Great Work. For instance, you could get involved in Habitat for Humanity or some other volunteer housing project in your area. In doing so you will bring yourself closer to achieving the end of the cycle referred to in the value of the dream and closer to being able to enter the Sefirah of Hesed.

See Zohar symbol, Eagle.

EAR

*ozen-avzn-*אוזן-64

MEANING The first thing we notice about this dream is the final Nun, which indicates that you have experienced a significant level of sorrow in the past. However, the letter Zayin, which precedes it, tells us that you have refused to allow this emotional issue to cloud your commitment to your inner development. The initial Aleph makes it clear that you have a very strong awareness of the essential unity of the universe, and it is this thought that has helped you keep close to a sense of the Divine as represented by the letter Vav even in your darkest hours.

THE TREE OF LIFE The value of this dream title is equivalent to that of a Hebrew phrase meaning "golden waters." This image puts us in mind of a sunset over a calm sea, and as the Sun is the planet of the Sefirah of Tiferet, we are inclined to connect this dream with this destination on the Tree of Life. However, this dream's value is also equivalent to that of the Hebrew spelling of "Venus." The planet Venus is connected with the Sefirah of Netzach. Appropriately enough the path that links these two Sefirot is the path of Nun, which is strongly associated with the level of emotional pain that you have been experiencing.

THE JOURNEY You have shown that you can cling resolutely to your commitment to the spiritual path even in the face of great stress. It is this commitment that has brought you to a point where you are within striking distance of Tiferet. The compression of the dream's value tells all that you need do now: Maintain a regular practice of meditation with a particular focus on trying to listen to the advice or message that is out there for you and is symbolized by the dream image of an ear. If you do this, the support of the Divine (Samech) will open the door (Daleth) to Tiferet.

EARTH (SOIL)

*karka-qrqa'a-*קרקע-470

MEANING Our resolution to begin the Great Work often comes from a realization that living a wholly secular life leaves us in a state of loss. We cannot always define exactly what it is that is missing in our lives, but there is a hollowness in the heart of twenty-first-century humanity, and it is this hollowness that drives much of our escapism through shopping, video games, and other life-style fads. The value of this dream is equivalent to that of a Hebrew phrase for "eternity" in which eternity is represented as an endless repetition of a given cycle. This is a stagnant version of eternity that resonates with the emptiness of modern living and emphasizes the idea that this dream represents a decision to regain the spiritual dimension that you lost.

THE TREE OF LIFE The value of this dream can be reduced to 11, indicating profound moment in your spiritual development. In the compression of the dream's value we see have Tav as the first letter. This letter indicates not only the sense of melancholy that has led you to the Great Work but the fact that you have already taken your first step and are now in the process of traversing the path of Tav.

THE JOURNEY In the spelling of this dream title we have the letter Resh flanked on either side by a Qoph. The letter Qoph indicates the anxiety that is still preventing you from accessing the benevolent energy of the Divine as represented by the letter Resh. It is likely that your anxiety stems from a lingering concern about how others would view your change of direction. The final letter, Ayin, in the compression and in the spelling of this dream tells you that you need to learn to stand alone and not allow the opinions of others to get in the way of your spiritual development.

EATING
leekhol-lakvl-לאכול-86

MEANING The letter Lamed stands at both the end and the beginning of this dream title. This suggests that you are going through a period of intense self-criticism. The dream of eating indicates that the criticism relates to a concern you are overindulging in some way. The reduction of this dream's value gives the number 14. This number is associated with a sense of inner balance and harmony, which you are clearly trying to achieve in your life. Eating is also symbolic of an excessive indulgence in the more material comforts of the world. If you try to cut down in this area you will find that you develop much more of a spiritual outlook.

THE TREE OF LIFE In order to escape the excessive severity to which you are exposing yourself, you need to find some means of allowing yourself to be kinder to yourself. The best way to do this is to find some like-minded people who are also following a spiritual path. If you communicate with them, you will find that they have the same doubts as you have. This will enable you to put your perceived failings into perspective. For this reason, this dream is placed on the path of Peh, as this path is about the need for genuine communication.

THE JOURNEY The total value of this dream is equivalent to the Hebrew for the worshipful "hallelujah." This indicates your high level of commitment to the Great Work. Similarly, we can see that within the spelling of the dream title we have the two letters Aleph and Beth. These are the two initial paths out of Keter and demonstrate that you already have the beginnings of a profound understanding. All you need to do right now is give yourself the mental space and emotional support that will allow you to progress. It may help if you think of yourself as your friend, as you will then give yourself the encouragement you deserve.

ECLIPSE (SOLAR)
leekhoy khamah-lyqvy chmh-ליקוי חמה-209

MEANING Even though we understand the astronomical reasons that cause a solar eclipse, events such as this still draw huge crowds of spectators. Almost everyone who has witnessed a solar eclipse will admit to feeling at least a small shiver of worry as the last sliver of light disappears and the world is plunged into total darkness in the middle of the day. In spiritual terms the symbolism here is less obtuse than in some other dreams, as it refers to the fear that you are losing connection with the Divine force.

THE TREE OF LIFE When you enter the Sefirah of Tiferet you are symbolically bathed in the light of the spiritual Sun. This is a reward for your unstinting effort thus far in the spiritual quest. However, in order to become closer to the Divine source you have to press on up the Tree. What often tends to happen at this point is that the sense of a Divine presence becomes weaker and it becomes more important that you rely on your own belief to keep you motivated. The path of Zayin fits this dream and points to the need to spiritually arm yourself with belief in order to avoid the sense of loss that this path can produce.

THE JOURNEY We all know that the Sun will reappear after an eclipse. We are less certain that our sense of the Divine will return when it seems to fade in our consciousness. The presence of the letter Teth in the compression of this dream indicates the potential for false doubts to creep into your mind at this time. The letter Resh is also in the compression and serves to remind you that the benevolent feelings from above are always there even when they seem hidden. You can help yourself through this difficult period by focusing on some of the self-healing techniques that are now in the public domain, such as shiatsu and Reiki. Such practices will help you recognize that the warmth of the Divine is always with you.

ECSTASY

*ekstazah-aqstzh-*אקסטזוה-182

MEANING To dream of ecstasy in the spiritual sense is to be welcomed into the highest reaches of the Tree of Life. Ecstasy occurs in the moment when a direct link between yourself and the Divine is achieved. This moment has a number of names in a range of different mystical traditions. To some it is enlightenment, to others samadhi, to others the final transformation of lead into gold. The reduction value of this dream produces the number 11, which indicates that you are indeed about to experience a highly mystical and profound change in your perception.

THE TREE OF LIFE In the moment of spiritual ecstasy we experience a paradoxical state of mind, and this is one way in which the moment itself constitutes a communion with the Divine as the Divine nature is itself paradoxical. Simultaneously we are both as innocent as a new baby and as experienced as someone who has lived a hundred or more lives before this incarnation. In this way we mirror the nature of The Fool in the tarot, which is closely associated with the path of Aleph on the Tree of Life. As the path of Aleph is the path that carries the most undiluted aspect of the Divine will, it is a wholly appropriate position for this dream.

THE JOURNEY Having the ecstatic experience is just the beginning of this phase of your spiritual journey. The compression of the dream's value indicates that once the mental experience has occurred (Qoph), you must try to communicate the wisdom you have gained to those around you (Peh). In doing so you increase the chance that they in time will be able to reach their spiritual home (Beth), while at the same time increasing your own preparedness for further dialogue with the Divine force.

EGG

*beytsah-bytzh-*ביצוה-107

MEANING Eggs represent potential life and the uniqueness and complete nature of each individual life. To dream of eggs is to recognize the promise and potential that lies within you. Each one of us has the possibility of being reborn as a spiritual being, and this dream is a chance for your higher self to remind you of this possibility. It is important to note that the value of this dream is a prime number (a number that can be divided only by itself and by one). The significance of this is that prime numbers are rare and indicate uniqueness. As this dream refers to the potential within all of us, it is a way of pointing out that all of us are both interconnected and unique at the same time.

THE TREE OF LIFE When we look around the Tree of Life for a location for this dream it is not immediately obvious where it should be placed, until we begin to consider the titles of the Sefirot themselves. We have said that the egg represents the starting point for the evolution of your spiritual consciousness, and the formal title of the Sefirah of Yesod is "Foundation." This Sefirah is also appropriate because the realization of your potential must precede the balancing of the four elements within you but follow on from the initial decision to undertake the Great Work.

THE JOURNEY In the spelling of the dream title we see reference to the spiritual home (Beth) from which we all spring, the Divine spark that lies within our egg of potential (Yod), and we are also told that to succeed in hatching this egg we will have to be dogged in our persistence (Tzaddi). If we make a point of sticking to a definite plan of spiritual work we will begin to open the window (Heh) that allows the light and warmth of the Divine to shine into our lives.

ELECTRICITY

*khashmal-chshml-*חשמל-378

MEANING While a new discovery in terms of a timeline that stretches all the way back to the Exodus and beyond, the natural force of electricity has been with us for all time. Indeed, one of the terms for the emanation of the Sefirot into the universe is "the lightning flash," and lightning is one of the rawest forms of natural electricity that we can experience. Lightning in this context is an immensely powerful and energetic force. It is a force that can be both beautiful and even life-giving but that also has the capacity for destruction. The value of this dream has the same value as the Hebrew phrase meaning "in peace," so we can assume that it is the live-giving properties of lightning that are being highlighted in this dream.

THE TREE OF LIFE This dream sits on the path of Yod. In the Kabbalah, the letter Yod is seen as representing the Divine spark within each of us and also as the very first creative spark sent forth from the Divine. This is why the letter Yod begins the mystical name of God known as the Tetragrammaton. The implication of this association is that you are in the process of receiving a creative spark from the will of the Divine. This is in part due to your commitment to the Great Work, but also so that you can pursue your destiny.

THE JOURNEY You are receiving such an influx of creative energy so that that you can pass on this awareness of the Divine to others. The compression of the dream tells you quite clearly what your task now is. You have been inflamed with a vast amount of spiritual energy (Shin) and you must now use that energy to formulate a means to encourage others to take up the challenge of the Great Work. Whatever means you devise should be wholly your own (Ayin). In doing this, not only will you help others but you will ensure your place in the eternal light of the Divine as represented by the final number 8 in the compression of this dream.

ELOQUENCE

omanoot ha deboor-amnvth h dybvr-

אמנות ה דיבור-724

MEANING This dream is about the need to correctly focus your energy. To be eloquent means that you can say whatever you wish in a manner that is both clear and convincing. However, truth does not lie in utterance, it lies in that which is spoken. Equally true is the point that wisdom is not dependent on being spoken, as it is felt within the soul. This suggests that you are perhaps more concerned with the impression that an idea initially makes on you and less with the actual substance of the idea. However, the dream of eleoquence also suggests a sincerity in your approach to the Great Work.

THE TREE OF LIFE It may be surprising to learn that this dream sits squarely in the Sefirah of Malkut. However, this says more about the way we tend to judge people in our daily lives than it does about the validity of this analysis. It is much easier to be fooled by fine words than to notice fine deeds, especially since truly fine deeds do not draw attention to themselves. When we reduce the value of this dream we find that it produces the number 4, which represents the world of the purely physical.

THE JOURNEY Up to now you have been confusing the packaging of ideas with their content, and you need to learn to look beyond appearances to see what lies within. If you wish to begin to move out of Malkut, you should pay attention to the message that lies within the compression of this dream. Only those systems that admit to the inevitability of sorrow and melancholy (Nun) in their practice are going to provide you with a genuinely practical means (Kaph) to open the door (Daleth) to the paths that lead up the Tree toward union with the Divine.

EMBARRASSMENT

*mevookhah-mbvkh-*מבוכה-73

MEANING Sometimes a dream has a hidden meaning that seems wholly at odds with the obvious content. The dream of embarrassment is one such dream. We expect this dream to refer to some kind of negative aspect of our spiritual development, when in fact it is extremely positive in terms of what it suggests about our progress. The value of this dream reduces to 10, which indicates the positive conclusion of a key aspect of our spiritual development. It is likely that any literal embarrassment you might feel would come from a sense of modesty about your achievements rather than any sense of shame. This dream should also be taken as a sign that you should try to be more accepting of yourself and more comfortable with who you are as a person.

THE TREE OF LIFE The value of this dream is equivalent to the value of the letter Gimel. This letter belongs to the path that runs straight from Tiferet to Keter. It takes a very strong will and a devoutly spiritual nature to reach this far up the Tree of Life. This means that you can be certain that your embarrassment is indeed born of modesty, as there is no embarrassment in being on the path that leads to the secret wisdom of the ancients. The sense of completion that is represented by the value 10, given by reduction, is the realization that your spiritual consciousness is ready to leave the relative comfort of the Sefirah of Tiferet.

THE JOURNEY The crucial task for you in order to progress up the path of Gimel is laid out in the compression of the dream's value and it is surprisingly simple. The letter Ayin indicates that you need to construct your own very individual way of coping with the emotional and mental stresses that you inevitably meet when traversing this final path toward Keter. The final letter, Gimel, not only emphasizes the path that you are on but points to the fact that you need to think creatively about how best to express your spirituality as you approach a direct communion with the Divine force itself.

EMBRACING

*kheebook-chybvq-*חיבוק-126

MEANING This dream indicates an encouraging level of progress, albeit at a relatively early stage of your spiritual development. To dream of embracing indicates that you are beginning to appreciate that the ultimate nature of the Divine is unconditional love. However, the dream reduces to 9, and this is the value of the letter Teth, which means "serpent." Consequently, this implies that while the Divine may love unconditionally, you need to be a little more circumspect in your affections in order to avoid being exploited by those with less sincere intentions.

THE TREE OF LIFE You are now in the process of arranging your emotional psyche in order to reconcile it to your emerging notions about the nature of the Divine. This development of the soul takes place in the Sefirah of Netzach, and it is there that this dream belongs. The value of this dream is equivalent to that of the Hebrew word meaning "hospitality," and it is this sense of free expression and good humor that, in part, sums up the experience of Netzach in its most positive aspect.

THE JOURNEY Beginning to reorganize our emotions is never easy, since we are caught between the desire to love everyone we meet and the need to show some caution in our behavior in the day-to-day world. The potential dangers of too much unconditionality are demonstrated by the fact that the value of this dream is equivalent to Hebrew words meaning "widow" and "darkness." Now is a time to tread carefully but happily. A good way to express some of that positive emotion in a safe way would be to involve yourself in a charity that helps the elderly; that way, you can be extremely friendly and generous without being in danger of being exploited.

EMERALDS

*eezmaragd-azmrgd-*אזמרגד-255

MEANING Traditionally, emeralds signify wisdom and so to dream of emeralds is, spiritually speaking, a very encouraging sign. The value of the dream is equivalent to that of the Hebrew word meaning "east." This becomes significant when we realize that the element of Air is associated with the east. It is the element of Air that governs all mental processes, so this connection backs up the idea that this dream indicates a significant level of wisdom that you have achieved as a result of your inner development.

THE TREE OF LIFE Each path on the Tree of Life has a precious or semiprecious stone with which it can be associated. The emerald can be connected to a number of paths but the one that is most appropriate is the path of Daleth. The letter Daleth completes the spelling of the dream title, and because it connects the two Sefirot known by the formal titles of "Wisdom" and "Understanding," it is the ideal path on which to site this dream and indeed the level of your spiritual insight.

THE JOURNEY The compression of this dream's value indicates the journey that now lies ahead of you if you wish to continue your spiritual quest. You have achieved a place within the benevolence of the Divine force (Resh) after having been through a great deal of hard work and suffering along the way (Nun). You now have the opportunity to pass on the benefit of your experience to others in order to give them a glimpse through the window (Heh) that opens onto the vista of the Divine reality. You should seriously consider setting up some form of meditation or study group as a result of this dream.

EMPLOYEE

*sakheer-shkyr-*שכיר-530

MEANING We always like the content of our dreams to be in some way complimentary. To dream of yourself as an employee is not an especially flattering experience. However, there is much to learn in simply accepting that there is nothing wrong with being part of a team as opposed to being in charge of it. The value of this dream reduces to 8, which is the value of the letter Cheth. In the context of this dream the meaning of Cheth, which is "fence," refers to the protection and support that is afforded by being part of a group rather than working alone. In spiritual terms, this implies a recognition of the interconnectedness of the whole of Creation.

THE TREE OF LIFE When we look at the spelling of the dream we see the letter Shin, representing enormous amounts of energy, driving the letter Kaph, which indicates practical activity. This still has a very obvious workplace-oriented theme, but if we see the Divine as the employer then our place as the employee begins to make sense. This dream sits on the path of Kaph because it indicates the practical work that we must do in order to manifest the will of the Divine expressed in us through the energy of the letter Shin.

THE JOURNEY If we wish to be good employees of the Divine, then like any other reliable employee we must give our utmost. This idea is reiterated through the presence in the compression of the dream of both the letter Kaph in its final form and the letter Lamed, which suggests the driving force that tries to ensure that we stick to the right path. In practical terms, this dream points to a need for you to take your spiritual work as seriously as your career and to apply the same rigorous discipline to the Great Work as you do to your tasks in the office.

EMPLOYER

*maaseek-ma'asyq-*מעסיק-280

MEANING To be an employer in terms of a spiritual perspective suggests more than just responsibility for the growth of your inner self. It also implies a sufficient level of development for you to have some degree of expertise about how best to further your understanding in order to reach higher up the Tree of Life. The reduction of this value produces the number 10, which points to a completed cycle in your life, and this is probably the source of your authority to take some control over the way in which you advance your spiritual understanding.

THE TREE OF LIFE The degree of authority suggested by this dream would require you to have had some contact with your higher self and to have learned how to listen to its guidance. The pairing of the letter Qoph with the letter Yod in the spelling of this dream title suggests that this has occurred, as your thoughts (Qoph) are now informed by the Divine spark (Yod) within you. Because of its associations with The Emperor card in the tarot as well as its connection to ideas of material control, the path that best suits you and this dream is the path of Heh.

THE JOURNEY The path of Heh reaches up to the Supernal Sefirah of Hokhmah. This Sefirah relates to the raw force or energy in the universe, which must be fashioned into a potential form by the shaping energies of Binah. In order not to be overtaken by the sheer power of Hokhmah you need to learn to take a passive approach to life when appropriate. This need is emphasized by the initial Mem in the spelling of this dream title and by the letter Resh in the compression of the dream's value, as Resh represents the warm benevolent aspect of the Divine. You should put yourself in situations where you would normally feel stressed and try to learn simply to breathe deeply and remind yourself of the ultimate unimportance of whatever the stressful situation is.

ENCHANTMENT

*kesem-qsm-*קסם-200

MEANING As difficult as much of the spiritual quest may be, there is also enormous opportunity simply to wonder at the nature if the Divine and the excitement of having a chance to bring yourself closer to the ultimate truths of human existence. This dream is essentially about those moments of sheer awe that we encounter when we set off on a spiritual journey. The value of this dream is 200, which is also the value of the letter Resh. This letter perhaps more than any other represents the Divine force as a wholly benevolent energy that warms and encourages our higher selves.

THE TREE OF LIFE Although wonder is a semi-constant feature of any successful attempt to understand the nature of a spiritually based universe, the sense of enchantment is very much part of the early stages of the Great Work. The Sefirah of Yesod, which is the location of this dream on the Tree of Life, is often associated with enchantment since it indicates the astral plane of reality—that strange world that is neither of the material world nor entirely free from it. Additionally, the letter Resh ends in the Sefirah of Yesod, and its effect is felt throughout this dream.

THE JOURNEY Having made the first step out of Malkut, you are still enjoying the first flushes of success. However, there are more difficult times ahead when you will face a number of difficult truths about yourself and your past. This dream is encouraging you to take the time to fill your head (Qoph) with the sense of enthusiasm and wonder that currently possesses you. This will then act as a support (Samech) and will allow the maternal aspect of the Divine (Mem) to protect you as much as possible as you continue your quest.

ENEMY

*oyev-avyb-*אויב-19

MEANING We need to remember that whenever we dream of other people, they should be regarded as aspects of our own personality. The final letter, Teth, in the compression of the dream's value indicates a potential for self-deception within the dreamer. This may mean that you are misleading yourself in believing that your problems are caused by forces outside your control. Equally, it may be pointing out that you are not recognizing the fact that you do indeed have some issues that you need to deal with.

Traditional Kabbalists would say this dream suggests an enemy outside one's self.

THE TREE OF LIFE The value of this dream is equivalent to the value of the Hebrew word for "Eve." The important feature of the biblical Eve is that she was tempted into actions that she knew were inappropriate. This suggests that the letter Teth is pointing to a tendency not to recognize your incorrect behavior. The inability to face up to our flaws is a common feature of the Sefirah of Yesod and it is this Sefirah to which the dream belongs. As Yesod is associated with the imagination, it is very easy for us to convince ourselves that we are following a clear spiritual path when in fact we are merely fooling ourselves.

THE JOURNEY In order to continue your progression beyond the Sefirah of Yesod you need to bring an element of discipline to your efforts. It would be ideal for you to draw up a very definite timetable for each week that will lay out exactly when you will spend time focusing on the spiritual aspect of your life. Additionally, you should try to make contact with like-minded people, as they will help to keep you on the straight and narrow.

Traditional Kabbalists would suggest you think about possible enemies in your life and how you might go about reconciling with them.

ENGAGEMENT FOR MARRIAGE

*eyrooseem–ayrvsym–*אירוסים*–*327

MEANING When we decide to get engaged, we are deciding to share the rest of our lives with another person. This means that inevitably there will have to be compromise on both sides in order for the relationship to work over the long term. The spiritual aspect of this dream focuses on the compromise aspect of engagement and the fact that when we are finally married we become part of a unit that is larger than either individual alone but within which both are absolutely crucial. The value of this dream reduces to 12, which indicates self-sacrifice. If you are to achieve a successful marriage of your conscious self and your higher self, it is clear that an element of self-sacrifice will be needed.

THE TREE OF LIFE An engagement is full of promise for the future, but it is not yet a binding agreement. In spiritual terms we can see this as indicating that you are in the very early stages of your inner development. This dream belongs on the path of Tav because it is one of the first paths out of Malkut. It is particularly appropriate since the path of Tav has connections to the idea of self-sacrifice, which is suggested by the dream's value.

THE JOURNEY You are feeling extremely positive right now about your decision to follow a spiritual path. This excitement and anticipation are represented by the letter Shin, which begins the compression of this dream's value. The subsequent letter, Kaph, tells us that you are best suited to a practical approach to the inner journey. This means that initially, at least, you would benefit greatly from a course in tai chi or yoga. The final letter, Zayin, is an advance warning that the route you have chosen will not always be easy and that at times you will need a little inner steel to accompany your good humor.

ENGINE

*manoa–mnva'a–*מנוע*–*166

MEANING This is a dream about unstoppable energy and the need for it to be carefully directed. The reduction of this dream gives us the number 13, which is symbolic of major change. In your case, you have sufficient raw energy to go through any number of major changes in a very short period of time. The goal of the Kabbalist is to ensure that all those changes are positive and lead to an increase in wisdom and understanding.

THE TREE OF LIFE The spelling of this dream title begins with the letters Mem and Nun. As these letters are associated with the element of Water, there is a strong suggestion that you arrived at your current state of drive and determination after a very deeply emotional experience. It may well have been a revelatory experience regarding the definite existence of a spiritual dimension to reality that gave you the burst of energy you are now enjoying. The last letter in the dream title is Ayin. This is the path on which this dream lies not simply because of the energetic nature of Ayin but because, like the dream content, it also points to a need for direction and control.

THE JOURNEY If we shake up a bottle of soda and then pop off the lid, we end up with fizzy liquid squirting uncontrollably in all directions. This is similar to the results you will get in your life if you allow all your energy to simply burst out. The compression of this dream has the central letter, Samech, meaning "prop," flanked by two letters associated with the element of Air. The message in this compression is that you need to control your energy by tempering your gut instincts with a careful thinking process.

ENTERTAINMENT

*beedoor-bydvr-*בידור-222

MEANING It is often said that all entertainment is dependent on conflict or at least tension of some kind. In the Kabbalah, opposition and duality are represented by the number 2, and as befits a dream about entertainment we see that the value is a string of 2's. When the soul achieves union with the Divine, all notions of difference and opposition are dissolved, but as long as we live in the physical world such opposition is esssential simply to ensure that we can differentiate one thing from another.

THE TREE OF LIFE When we reduce the value of this dream we find the number 6, which is the value of the letter Vav. As Vav is associated with matters of the mind, it is likely that you have been thinking about the nature of difference in your spiritual work. Such speculation is often the province of the path of Kaph. Kaph has very practical concerns and it is likely that you have been trying to reconcile ideas of spiritual unity to the reality of day-to-day life. The path of Kaph is also connected with the tarot card The Wheel of Fortune, which emphasizes the need to accept the hand that fate deals with us.

THE JOURNEY If the path of Kaph is attempting to teach us acceptance of what may at times seem unfair situations, then it is important that you develop ways in which you can do just that. One good approach is to try to remember an event from your past that seemed wholly negative at the time. You should then try to follow events from that point until you reach—as you certainly will—a point where something extremely positive occurred that could not have happened unless the negative event had also occurred. The initial letter, Resh, and the final letter, Beth, in the compression of the dream's value show that the warmth of the Divine will enable you to return to your spiritual home, at which point the duality of this world will disappear.

ENVY

*keenah-qnah-*קנאה-156

MEANING As anyone who knows the Bible is aware, envy is one of the seven sins. It should not be seen as entirely negative that you have had a dream of envy, but should instead be seen as a sign that you are making progress in terms of your self-knowledge. The compression of this dream reveals the letters Qoph, Nun, and Vav. This indicates that you have significant anxieties, no doubt about your capacity for envy, which have caused you sorrow and upset. The final Vav points out that you are now beginning to reflect on your attitudes and indeed that this reflection will lead to their correction.

THE TREE OF LIFE Before we can approach the Divine we must forge a relationship with our higher selves. In order to do this we must also balance our personalities and achieve a level of inner harmony. The Sefirot of Hod and Netzach are responsible for balancing our minds and our emotions, respectively. This dream, with its focus on the need to remove negative emotional states, is clearly based in the Sefirah of Netzach.

THE JOURNEY Admitting to our faults is a very difficult and often painful experience. It is often more difficult to admit our shortcomings to ourselves in a deep and meaningful way than to simply admit them to others. The value of this dream is equivalent to the value of the Hebrew meaning "viper." This connection points to the existence of poisonous emotions that we need to root out and remove; it also points to the fact that this must be done in a swift and vigorous manner.

EPIDEMIC

*magefah-mgypha-*מגיפא-134

MEANING The reduction of this dream's value gives the number 8, which is the value of the letter Cheth, meaning "fence." A perfectly natural response to an epidemic is to want to fence yourself and your loved ones off from the danger. In Kabbalistic terms the idea of an epidemic represents the sense of a range of threatening and worrisome emotions interfering with your spiritual progress. While it may be tempting to simply shield yourself from their effect, the only real solution is to examine those concerns and deal with them.

THE TREE OF LIFE The value of this dream's title is equivalent to the value of the Hebrew word meaning "burning." This is suggestive of a fierce and vigorous challenge to your well-being. However, what may seem a threat may actually be for our benefit. Medicine of whatever kind can be most unpleasant to take, even though it will ultimately lead to our recovery. The path of Lamed best suits this dream because its vigorous and challenging nature is reflected in both the content and the hidden meaning of the dream.

THE JOURNEY Nobody has ever achieved a significant level of spiritual insight without going through some harsh and revealing self-examination along the way. The compression of this dream indicates that you are deeply troubled (Qoph) by the insights about yourself that the path of Lamed is showing you. The letter Lamed is indeed central in the compression but it is followed by Daleth, meaning "door." In facing up to your negative side, you will be able to open the door to the next phase of your spiritual development. You need to balance the harshness of Lamed with some moments of self-validation. It would be a good idea to set aside at least one night a week to indulge yourself in a hobby or pastime that you thoroughly enjoy.

ERRAND

shleekhoot-shlychvth- שליחות-754

MEANING If we fail to take responsibility for our inner development, we will never begin to make progress in the Great Work. The implication of this dream is that you feel your spiritual development has not really begun. The idea of running errands highlights a sense of frustration and possibly resentment that nothing you perceive as spiritually important has happened to you. The value of this dream reduces to 7, which is the value of the letter Zayin. This letter means "sword" and is a way for your higher self to urge you to be more proactive in securing some inner progress for yourself.

THE TREE OF LIFE The letter Nun appears twice in the compression of this dream. It is there in both its normal and its final forms. This emphasizes the level of melancholy and suffering that you are currently going through. This might point to the dream's being located on the path of Nun, except for the fact that the dream's content indicates a very early point in your spiritual journey. The final value of 4 in the compression should be taken in this context as signifying the four elements and the Sefirah of Malkut. It is there that this dream is located.

THE JOURNEY You must start to believe in your ability to make progress and you must link this to an obvious commitment to the Great Work. Spiritual insight does not just happen, it has to be worked at and often fought for. The first two letters in the spelling of this dream, Shin and Lamed, tell us that you have plenty of energy and that your higher self is

trying to spur you into action. It is likely that you need to find a very low-key way of beginning your spiritual quest. One possible route would be to start visiting art galleries or perhaps reading poetry, as the beauty of art often prompts a recognition of the wonder of the Divine.

ESCALATOR

maaleet-ma'alyth- מעלית-550

MEANING As you might expect, this dream is designed to encourage you in your spiritual work. The reduction value of this dream produces the number 10, which indicates that you are about to complete a major cycle in your life. If we look at the image of an escalator, it is likely that this major cycle involves your moving up from one phase of consciousness to another, and the presence of the number 10 acts to support this interpretation.

THE TREE OF LIFE The compression of this dream's value produces the letters Kaph and Nun. While Nun indicates that you have experienced significant emotional suffering in the recent past, Kaph as it appears in its final form far outweighs the negative aspects of Nun. There is a great deal of energy in this dream and it ideally fits the path of Kaph. The path of Kaph runs up to the Sefirah of Hesed, which is indeed a major stepping stone in your inner development.

THE JOURNEY It is no easy task that lies ahead of you now. The path that leads to the Sefirah of Hesed is very energetic, but it also requires great stoicism on your part. In order to gain the levels of mercy and understanding that are associated with Hesed, you need to learn to accept all that life throws at you. You can help yourself learn to be accepting by paying attention to nature and noticing that those items that bend with the forces of nature survive much longer than those that try to stand stiffly against them. For instance, you can compare the erosion of a cliff with the way in which a willow grows successfully in an area of high wind.

ESCAPE

hekhaltsoot-hychltzvth- היחלצות-549

MEANING In the modern world it is often believed that religion and spirituality in general are nothing more than an attempt to escape reality. In fact, this could not be further from the truth. The spiritual path is an attempt not to escape but to examine as closely as possible every last facet of our nature. In addition, we then need to find a way to fit our nature to the Divine will. The reduction value of this dream gives us the number 9. This is the value of the letter Teth, which means "serpent." This letter is associated with self-deceit and suggests that you are in danger of falsely seeing your spiritual path as an escape.

THE TREE OF LIFE This dream is about self-doubt, particularly doubts about the validity of your inner journey. We can experience these worries at any time in the Great Work, but the path that is most associated with such anxiety is that of Qoph. It is worth noting that one form of reduction produces the value of 18. This value is associated with The Moon card in the tarot, which within the Western Mystery Tradition, is linked to the path of Qoph.

THE JOURNEY The central letter in the spelling of this dream title is Lamed. It stands out both because of its central position and because of its shape relative to the other letters in the dream title. This letter points to the need for you to maintain your studies in spite of your doubts. One way to maintain a positive attitude to your inner journey is to keep a journal of how your spiritual work is affecting your physical well-being. If nothing else, you should find that the improvement in your well-being helps to convince you of the validity of your spiritual quest.

EVENING

*erev-a'arb-*ערב*-272*

MEANING Mornings are hectic times, nights can be either exciting or sleepy, and evenings tend to be the most relaxing part of the day. As the Sun begins to set and everybody is finishing his work for the day, there is a wonderful sense of calm about the evening. This relates in Kabbalistic terms to the feeling that your level of insight is progressing well. You are making steady but solid progress and there is a real sense that the Divine is acting to protect and encourage you. The reduction of this dream's value leads to the number 11, which indicates a growing awareness within you of the mystical nature of your journey. Evening is a time associated with intuition and sensitivity, so you should focus on this aspect of your inner development at this time.

THE TREE OF LIFE The letter Ayin, which begins the spelling of this dream title, suggests a considerable degree of raw power and energy driving your spiritual work. It also indicates a person who is

by nature something of a loner, one who likes to plow his own furrow in life. The final letter, Beth, indicates a very different person indeed. This is someone who likes to have a close and warm circle of friends and who approaches life with a calm certainty. The central letter, Resh, is the explanation for this transformation in your nature. It is the path of Resh that this dream belongs on, and it is a path where we learn to develop not through harsh lessons but through the calm and warm love of the Divine.

THE JOURNEY Right now your personality is typified by the letter Ayin and you need to move to a position where you are typified by the letter Beth. The key aspect that you can focus and work on is to improve your level of inner tranquillity. Learning to calm and still ourselves is not easy but is enormously useful. A good exercise for you to try is this: Lie on your back and breathe in, using your diaphragm muscle to pull in the air and then allowing your chest to fill with air; as you exhale, breathe out using your chest and then push out the remaining air with your diaphragm muscle. Breathing like this regularly will help you to bring much more peace into your state of mind.

EXCHANGE

*hakhlafah-hchlphh-*החלפה*-128*

MEANING Here we have a dream whose Kabbalistic significance has very little to do with its obvious content. The idea of exchange is suggestive of a person who is keen to share experiences with others. While this is probably true of the dreamer, it does not go to the heart of the dream. The central letters in the spelling of the dream title refer to the journey that you have already taken. You have moved from a point where you were seeking to defend yourself from any threat to your stability (Cheth) to one where you are actively seeking a dialogue with the Divine (Peh). This movement has been achieved by the harsh but fair experience of Lamed.

THE TREE OF LIFE This shift in your consciousness from defensiveness to an open and eager approach to the Great Work has opened windows onto the nature of spiritual reality for you. Appropriately enough, this dream is on the path of Heh, and the letter Heh indeed means "window." The zodiac sign associated with this path is Aries and this indicates a very enthusiastic and dynamic individual. You are now only a step away from the Supernals within the Tree of Life, so your enthusiasm is more than justified.

THE JOURNEY The compression of the dream's value tells you the journey that now lies ahead of you. Your state of consciousness has gone through some profound realignment, and the journey so far has been largely a journey in your mind (Qoph). Having achieved your current level of understanding, you are being encouraged to express your spirituality in a very practical (Kaph) way. The final letter, Cheth, now refers not to your defensiveness but to your ability to protect those around you. The implication is that you should get involved in some kind of volunteer group helping vulnerable members of your community.

EXILE
geroosh-gyrvsh- גירוש-519

MEANING It's never easy to feel completely alone and cut off from those about whom you care. To experience this sense of absence when you are also struggling to come to terms with a newfound attitude toward spirituality is extremely difficult. This dream is one that is experienced early in your spiritual journey. While it may refer to a difficult experience, it is important to note that the reduced value of this dream is 6, a number that refers to the macrocosm or the Divine itself, so the overall impact of the dream is positive.

THE TREE OF LIFE When we set out from the physical world of Malkut we can travel along one of three paths. Of these three, the path of Shin is the one that best suits this dream. The path of Shin is very energetic and creates the sense of being driven that one would associate with being exiled. Additionally, the path of Shin is regarded as very harsh in terms of its encouragement of self-judgment; this is in part why it is referred to as the biting path.

THE JOURNEY In your search for some kind of confirmation of the existence of a spiritual dimension to life you may be tempted to allow yourself to be taken in by a number of systems of dubious merit. This possibility is indicated by the presence of the letter Teth at the end of the compression value of this dream. The solution is found in the rest of the compression. The letter Yod tells you to rely on the spark of the Divine within you to point out the systems that will be most useful to you. Finally, the letter Kaph is a reminder that at all times you should take a pragmatic and commonsense approach to your spiritual development.

EXPLOSION
heetpotstsoot-hthphvtztzvth- התפוצצות-1077

MEANING A little learning can be a dangerous thing, as the old saying goes. This is not to be seen as an endorsement of stupidity, though, as the saying goes on to say that we should "drink deep or not at all" from the spring of wisdom. In Kabbalistic terms this phrase is certainly accurate, as in the early stages of our development it is all too easy for us to believe we are more powerful and more entitled to feel superior than could ever really be the case. The fact that the letter Tzaddi occurs twice, side by side, is an indication that you are well and truly hooked on the spiritual path, but it does not mean that you are following entirely the right road.

THE TREE OF LIFE Explosions are very energetic affairs; they are also uncontrollable and unpredictable. This also sums up the nature of a person who believes his inner development is more advanced than it actually is. We begin to feel proud and aloof and able to go our own way in terms of furthering our quest for the truth. This attitude typifies the negative aspect of the path of Ayin, and it is to this path that the dream of explosions belongs. The reduction value of this dream gives us 15. This number is associated with The Devil card in the tarot, which is associated with the path of Ayin and indicates a proud and haughty approach to the spiritual.

THE JOURNEY As is so often the case, the compression value of this dream shows us the way to solve the problem that this dream highlights. The value of 1,000 should be seen as the letter Qoph emphasized tenfold. This means that you have a great deal of mental work to do and that this will involve a degree of angst on your part. The central letter, Ayin, tells us that the intense energy of the path you are on is positive and helpful. However, the final letter, Zayin, tells you that, like the use of a sword, your use of this energy must be controlled, accurate, and considered. In order to become more considered in your approach, you should join a meditation group and possibly involve yourself in some more mainstream methods of religious practice.

EYE
ayeen-a'ayn- עין-130

MEANING This is an immensely encouraging dream; it indicates that you are making excellent progress toward your spiritual goals. The final letter, Nun, suggests that great sorrow may be ahead. This is because Nun refers to a process by which our faith is ultimately strengthened, and this can involve some difficult self-reflection. In spite of this, you should still feel very positive. It is a fact of the Great Work that as we increase our understanding, we must always face a certain amount of depressing soul-searching to make further gains. These experiences are difficult but very worthwhile, as you will always realize once the moment of sorrow has passed.

THE TREE OF LIFE The title of this dream, "eye," is the name of the letter Ayin. It is almost inevitable, therefore, that this dream is assigned to the path of Ayin. Very often we experience the path of Ayin in its more negative aspect. However, the positive aspect of Ayin is extremely invigorating. This path leads into Tiferet and it is no accident that the value of this dream is equivalent to the value of the Hebrew word meaning "deliverance." This is a very suitable word because the experience of Tiferet is a period of deliverance, as it involves your contacting your higher self.

THE JOURNEY You are full of drive and energy at the moment and this is reflected in the presence of the letter Lamed in the compression of the dream's value. It is also pointed out by the fact that the value of this dream is equivalent to that of a Hebrew word meaning "ladder." Right now you should perceive yourself as climbing a staircase toward the Divine. In order to climb those steps in the most effective way, you need not only to exploit the spiritual energy that you possess but to reflect on your spiritual energy. The need for reflection is pointed out by the existence of the letter Qoph in the compression of the dream's value.

FABLES
*mashal-mshl-*משל-370

MEANING One of the things that makes us human is our need to tell and listen to stories. Especially important in our need for story are myths and fables. Such tales are particularly significant because they help us to form ideas about our ideals and expectations in terms of our behavior and that of those around us. From a spiritual point of view, to dream of fables is an indication that you are beginning to closely examine your behavior. This suggests that you now have a set of ideals against which to measure yourself. The reduction value of this dream produces the number 10, which points to the completion of a major cycle in your life. It is no doubt this completion that has led you to have this dream.

THE TREE OF LIFE Once we leave the Sefirah of Yesod we are in a position to begin to shape both our emotional and our intellectual makeup in a way that suits the spiritual message you have begun to receive. It is in the Sefirot of Netzach and Hod that we do this work, and the major cycle you have completed means that you are now ready begin this task. The path that runs between Netzach and Hod is the path of Peh. This is the appropriate path for this dream especially as the path of Peh is about communication, which clearly suits the content of this dream.

THE JOURNEY To reshape your way of looking at the world is a daunting task. It can be invigorating, stimulating, and greatly rewarding, but it is without doubt an emotionally draining event. However, the compression of this dream reveals the letters Shin and Ayin. Both of these letters indicate a great deal of energy within you, the dreamer. This energy will enable you to succeed in the reintegration of your personality within a spiritual context. You must make sure that you also look after yourself. The initial letter in the spelling of this dream's title tells us that we are allowed to care for ourselves and give ourselves some space for relaxation. This letter, Mem, represents the maternal aspect of the Divine and is telling you that at least once a week you should spend the evening doing nothing but relaxing and pampering yourself.

FACE
*paneem-phnym-*פנים-180

MEANING It is through our faces that others know us and it is from the faces of others that we form our first views of them. It is for this reason that the first letter in the spelling of this dream title is Peh, which means "mouth" and refers to processes of communication. In terms of your Kabbalistic development, this dream indicates that you are beginning to look more closely not only at your identity but at the identity of those around you and even the identities of nonhuman aspects of life.

THE TREE OF LIFE Such a close examination of the nature of things and people as this dream suggests can belong only to one destination on the Tree of Life, and that destination is Hod. This is the Sefirah where we engage with the spiritual nature of reality on an intellectual level. It is worth noting that in the value of the dream, the central numeral is 8, which is the number of the Sefirah of Hod. Additionally, the compression of the dream begins with the letter Qoph, which indicates a great deal of mental activity.

Traditional Kabbalists think Hod does not involve intellect, but rather bodily discipline and also communication.

THE JOURNEY Not only are you now in the process of closely examining the world around you, you are also learning to interpret it in a wholly new light. The world appears very different when we begin to look at it within a spiritual context. As soon as you recognize the spark of divinity that resides within all living things, your whole approach to life will have to shift massively to cope with this realization. The final letter, Peh, in the compression of the dream points out that there is a way for you to deal more easily with these new ways of seeing life. You should begin to read up on as many different spiritual philosophies as possible. You may disagree with some of them, but you will learn a great deal from everything you read.

FAINTING

leheetalef-lhtha'alph- לְהִתְעַלֵף -615

MEANING There can be a number of reasons for fainting, and they range from the extremely negative to the wholly positive. In this dream, the value suggests that the image of fainting is to be taken in an encouraging way. The compression of the dream begins with the letter Mem. This letter is associated with ideas of maternity, and one of the best-known features of being pregnant is the tendency to faint. The spiritual implication of this dream is that you are pregnant with spiritual aspirations. The idea of fainting serves to emphasize the strength of your feelings about your inner journey.

THE TREE OF LIFE When we reduce the value of this dream we find the number 12. This number is connected to ideas of self-sacrifice, which links it to the path of Mem. The path of Mem is linked with the tarot card The Hanged Man, and this association further supports the interpretation that this dream is about selfless behavior in the service of a greater cause. After the letter Mem in the compression of this dream we have the letter Yod, which points to the spark of the Divine operating in your life. It is this Divine spark that is responsible for your being about to "give birth" to a new and profound understanding of the world. The final letter,

Heh, in the compression tells us that this revelation will act like a window on the nature of the Divine.

THE JOURNEY The path of Mem leads out of Tiferet, and it can be very difficult to find the motivation to move forward from this very appealing area of the Tree of the Life. The spelling of the dream title contains two instances of the letter Lamed, which tells us that the energy of the Divine is there to ensure that you maintain your spiritual momentum. While you are going through a deeply spiritual experience to the extent that you are almost overwhelmed by it, the best way for you to move forward along the path of Mem is to engage in some form of practical altruistic activity.

FALLING

leepol-lyphvl- לִיפּוּל -156

MEANING As children, most of us experienced the dream of falling. This is often quite a scary experience for us as youngsters and it tends to occur once we start school and begin to recognize ourselves as in some way separate from our parents. The dream of falling is a representation of the fear of responsibility that is attached to the realization that at some point we have to face the world alone. To have this dream as an adult indicates a realization of that same kind of responsibility for our spiritual progress, and it can be equally unnerving.

THE TREE OF LIFE The value of this dream has a profound mathematical significance. It is the number that is produced when we multiply 12 by 13. In symbolic terms, this can be seen as the energy of self-sacrifice combined with the energy of transformative change. The central letter of the compression of the dream's value is Nun, and this is the path on which we should place this dream. The path of Nun is enormously transforming and carries us up to the Sefirah of Tiferet. Additionally, as it is associated with a degree of suffering, this path is also one that requires a great deal of sacrifice on your part.

THE JOURNEY We began this analysis by pointing out how distressing the dream of falling is for children. You should not then be surprised to learn that the path you are crossing will cause you a certain amount of distress. In order for you to reach the haven of Tiferet, you must come to terms with all of your inner fears and doubts. Only when you are at ease with yourself can you begin to communicate fully with your higher nature. To help you to arrive at this position you should make a list of all those aspects of your nature that worry you. You should then take each one in turn and determine why you feel that way and what changes you would like to make to eliminate that particular anxiety.

See Zohar symbol, Falling.

FAME

*noda-nvda'a-*נודע-130

MEANING At this point in the development of the world, we are living in a culture that is almost entirely dominated by the cult of celebrity. The near obsession with fame that we now face is very unhealthy from the point of view of our spiritual development, since it represents a concern with only the outward trappings of a human being rather than his inner nature. The reduction of this dream's value gives us the number 4. This number 4 indicates the world of the purely physical and emphasizes the fact that this dream is a warning that you need to pay more attention to your inner development.

THE TREE OF LIFE The world of the material is represented by the Sefirah of Malkut and it is there that this dream belongs. The fact that you are dreaming about fame suggests that you have yet to develop the correct attitude to the Great Work. To be successful in your quest for truth, you should have no thought for the way in which other people perceive your attitudes and beliefs. The compression of this dream is more positive since the letter Qoph indicates that you are at least beginning to think about your attitudes and the letter Lamed shows that the harsher energy of the Divine will ensure that this energy will drive you forward.

THE JOURNEY The spelling of the dream title begins with the letter Nun. As this letter points to the process of deepening understanding you may well be aware that to move on in your inner journey you will have to face up to the emotional pain you have gone through. Thankfully, the final two letters remind you that the Divine is willing you to progress (Resh), and that when you take that first step it will begin to open the window (Heh) on the spiritual world. You can encourage this process by seeing a counselor to begin to work on releasing some of your anxieties.

FAMILY

*meeshpakah-mshphchh-*משפחה-433

MEANING One of the key lessons to learn in our spiritual journey is the fact that we are all related to one another; we are all part of the same universal family. The term *we* refers not just to people but to every aspect of the universe. The value of the dream reduces to 10, but in the context of this dream the number 10 has a particular significance. One of the important aspects of family is the issue of inheritance—not of things but of characteristics and aspirations. The number 10 relates to matters of inheritance, and in this dream it refers to the general inheritance we all have that entitles us to reach up toward the Divine.

THE TREE OF LIFE In the tarot, the card The High Priestess represents the secret wisdom that is gained as we travel along the path of Gimel. This secret wisdom is the inheritance to which we all should aspire, so this dream lies on the path of Gimel. The family association is emphasized by the fact that The High Priestess can also be seen as the mother of all us, as far as our spiritual identity is concerned.

THE JOURNEY The value of this dream is a prime number and this is important because it emphasizes the fact that while we are all part of the same family, each is a unique individual. The path of Gimel is always a unique experience. When you achieve this level of spiritual insight it is impossible to predict exactly what will occur as you approach a communion with the Divine. The central letter of the compression of this dream is Lamed, and this tells us that the journey is going to be difficult. You can make your journey slightly easier by spending time with those closest to you. This may not be directly spiritual, but the sense of love and connection you will feel should remind you of the fundamental purpose of the spiritual quest.

FAMINE

*raav-ra'ab-*רעב-272

MEANING In spite of the enormous wealth in the world and the leaps in technology that have been made in recent years, we are still used to seeing pictures of terrible famine on our TV. We all know that famine tends to result from some form of internal conflict and if it continues unchecked it will lead to a complete breakdown of the society in which it occurs. When we try to apply this to a spiritual context we see that a lack of a spiritual dimension in your life can not only cause you inner pain but can lead to your whole life failing to completely fulfill you.

THE TREE OF LIFE The reduction of the value of this dream produces the number 11. This is a mystical number and should be seen as an encouraging sign that while you may be experiencing a spiritual drought, the water of the Divine is available to you as soon as you learn to drink. However, the implication of the dream of famine is that there is currently no spiritual aspect to your life, and so for the moment you and your dream are located in the Sefirah of Malkut.

THE JOURNEY Famine often begins as a result of internal conflict, and in your case the spiritual absence you are experiencing is also due largely to conflicts within yourself. There is a tension between the desire to advance your inner self and a pull toward a modern and rational way of looking at the world. The compression of the dream tells us how we should deal with such a conflict. In the back of your mind (Resh) you are aware that you need to ignore the common view and make your own decision as to whether to follow a spiritual path (Ayin), and if you open your heart to be a home (Beth) for the Divine, you will find that your famine draws to an end.

FAN

*meneefah-mnyphh-*מניפה-185

MEANING Fans used to be commonplace items but are now rarely seen except in very formal circumstances. It may seem hard to find a spiritual aspect to a fan, but when we think about the function of a fan we see that it is there to stir the air. In spiritual terms, the element of Air represents thinking processes. If we are stirring our thoughts, we are in the process of challenging our established way of looking at the world. This indicates that you are on the way to achieving some level of spiritual insight.

THE TREE OF LIFE Fans always used to be associated with glamour and also a sense of mystery, as they were historically used to conceal the faces of aristocratic ladies at social events such as balls or masquerades. This points to the Sefirah of Yesod, which is also appropriate since it relates to an early point in your spiritual development. The Sefirah of Yesod is connected to the element of Air, which again links it back to the more obvious content of this dream.

THE JOURNEY Before you can move out of Yesod and begin the work of balancing your inner self you need to achieve some basic framework of spiritual belief. The compression of this dream's value shows that this will require a lot of thought that will not always be comfortable for you (Qoph). It

would be very helpful for you to find some like-minded people with whom to discuss your feelings (Peh). If you do this, you will be able to open a window (Heh) on the light of the Divine. This will enable you to move out of Yesod and into the next phase of your spiritual journey.

FAREWELL

beerkat preedah-byrkth prydh-
931-בירכת פרידה

MEANING Goodbyes are never easy, but this is a dream that sees you waving farewell to a life that is no longer satisfying to you. You should feel very pleased to have had this dream as it implies that you are now ready to have a life that is wholly infused by the Divine force. The reduction value of this dream produces the number 13, which supports the view that this dream points to a major change in your life. Of course, if we further reduce the dream's value we find the number 4, which represents the world of the physical. However, in terms of this dream, 4 refers not to the land of Malkut but to the land of Keter, which is the higher reflection of the physical universe.

THE TREE OF LIFE In bidding goodbye to the world of the physical, you are about to enter a direct relationship with the Divine will. This places you on the path of Aleph, which leads directly into Keter. The tarot card The Fool is linked to the path of Aleph, and this contain many qualities that describe you and your level of inner development. The Fool possesses complete faith in the rightness of the universe, and his trust in the Divine is such that he continues to focus on a butterfly in the air before him rather than on the cliff edge to which he is perilously close. This well describes the depth of your belief and is an attitude that should be treasured and maintained.

THE JOURNEY You are only a few steps away from achieving a significant success in your spiritual quest. As the compression of your dream's value shows, you are absolutely hooked on the Great Work (Tzaddi), have continued to persist even in the face of difficulties, and have been continually pushed forward by your higher self (Lamed). You can now begin to approach the essential unity (Aleph) of creation. It is then your responsibility to try to spread an appreciation and understanding of the Divine to those around you. To follow the example of the energy of the path of Aleph, you should encourage others to take up the challenge of the spiritual by showing your joy and love as an example to all.

FARM

meshek khaklaee-mshq chqlay- מֶשֶׁק חקלאי-589

MEANING According to the creation myths of most mainstream religions, the first people were instructed by their God to be farmers, to tend to the earth and all its inhabitants. This creates an immediate mirror relationship between the Divine and humankind, as the Divine looks after Creation as mankind should look after his own small piece of creation. The reduction value of this dream gives the number 4, which indicates that the focus of this dream is on the purely physical aspect of reality. However, this is not a negative factor in the context of this dream, since we are looking not so much at materialism as at the earth as a mirror of the world of the Divine, which is infinitely productive and rich.

THE TREE OF LIFE You are not yet very far along in your spirtual journey, but you are making steady progress. When we look at the path of Tav, which is the first path leading out of the Sefirah of Malkut, we see that it is linked to the planet Saturn. In mythology, Saturn is the planet associated with agriculture, so we have an immediate link from the path of Tav to this dream. It is also fitting that this dream belongs on the path of Tav because when we partially reduce the value of this dream we find the value 22 (5 + 8 + 9 = 22). Tav is the twenty-second path on the Tree of Life.

THE JOURNEY The compression of this dream gives you a very definite sense of direction that, if you follow it, will make your path into Yesod significantly smoother. The initial value in the compression is 500, which is the final value of the letter Kaph. It is therefore very important for you to approach your spirituality from a practical standpoint. Given the farming aspect of the dream's content, it is likely that you will be able to much improve your sense of a link with the Divine by getting closer to nature in some way. This could be as simple as taking up gardening or even growing some herbs in a window box. The remaining letters, Peh and Teth, inidcate that you will need to discuss your progress with others and that when things become more difficult you must rely on your willpower to keep you going.

FAT

shamen-shmn- שָׁמֵן-390

MEANING We live in a world where to be fat is regarded as something of a sin; it is often seen as a character flaw worse than greed or vanity. In fact, to be fat is not something to be ashamed of and certainly this dream is in no sense negative. Historically, to be large would indicate that you were living well and would therefore suggest that you were a successful individual. From the spiritual point of view, this dream also points to someone who is making a success of his inner journey. The level of the insight you have gained is hinted at by the fact that the value of the dream reduces to 12, which represents altruistic self-sacrifice.

THE TREE OF LIFE The spelling of this dream title indicates the journey that you have taken so far in your spiritual life. You began with enormous spiritual energy (Shin), and the maternal aspect (Mem) of the Divine has provided you with encouragement and support. You are now approaching the Sefirah of Tiferet along the path of Nun. This is emphasized by the fact that the letter Nun is in its final form.

THE JOURNEY The path of Nun is not an easy one. You must risk the potential for considerable amounts of suffering and face all of your inner doubts and fears in order to achieve the level of understanding and faith implied by this path. The compression of the dream suggests that you have the ability to achieve this goal, though. The letter Shin points to the powerful spiritual energy that is driving you forward while the letter Tzaddi is a testament to your commitment to the Great Work. You also need to allow yourself some time when you are not focusing on profound matters of the soul. You should remember that while the value of this dream is equivalent to that of the Hebrew word meaning "heaven," you must also retain a sense of day-to-day life. An excellent idea would be to take up a very practical hobby such as woodworking or car mechanics to help keep your feet on the ground.

FATHER (TO DREAM OF A FATHER FIGURE)

av-ab- אָב-3

MEANING To dream of a father is to dream of the Divine. Symbolically, the idea of a father represents the creator of the universe, so this should be seen as a very encouraging dream. Certain Kabbalists have made much of the fact that the value of the word meaning "father" is 3 and that this points to the notion of the trinity as espoused by Christianity. However, the value of 3 was symbolically significant long before the gospels were written. The number 3 represents the nature of creation. The number 1 represents the unity of the Divine. The number 2 occurs when the Divine reflects itself, but creation of something genuinely new occurs with the emergence of the number 3.

THE TREE OF LIFE This dream is an indication that you are about to begin a new phase in your life, initiated by your recognition in this dream of a higher authority than mankind. The dream itself is located across the three supernal Sefirot that make up the energy of the Divine when combined as one force. Your position on the Tree is in the Sefirah of Malkut, as this dream points to the beginning of your journey. The fact that your dream has such a significant value indicates great things for you in the future.

THE JOURNEY The compression of this dream produces the letter Gimel. This letter is the path of the secret wisdom and you should see this as the reward that you are being offered at the end of the very long road ahead of you. The spelling of the dream title refers not only to the unity of the Divine (Aleph) but to the fact that this unity is your true spiritual home (Beth). In order to take your first steps toward this unity you should start practicing some basic meditation exercises and reading up on a range of spiritual beliefs.

FAVOR

*tovah–tvbh–*טובה*-*22

MEANING The value of this dream is highly significant in Kabbalistic terms as it represents the number of letters in the Hebrew alphabet. In the Kabbalah the alphabet is much more than just a string of letters since each letter is associated with a crucial aspect of the emanation of the Universe. To have a value that equates to the total number of letters in the alphabet suggests an individual who has considerable spiritual insight that touches on an understanding of each of the paths on the Tree of Life. As the final letter in the spelling of this dream is the letter Heh meaning "Window," there is an indication that you are now in a position to have a view of the essential nature of the Divine itself. In terms of the actual content of the dream, to dream of someone doing you a favor represents the gift of increasing understanding from the Divine.

THE TREE OF LIFE Normally, the presence of the letter Teth in the spelling of a dream is a sign of some worrying aspect to your current perception of the spiritual dimension of reality. This is because the letter Teth represents the serpent that points to

self deception and misguided force. However, the serpent can also refer to the so-called serpent path. This is the name given to the route back up the Tree of Life toward the Divine, which takes in each Sefirah on its way back to the divine source. It is this positive aspect of the letter Teth that is indicated within this dream, and it is on the path of Teth itself that this dream resides.

THE JOURNEY The value of this dream is equivalent to the Hebrew word meaning *unity*. This is very appropriate for this dream because the path of Teth acts as a balancing channel running between the merciful Sefirah of Cheth and the severe Sefirah of Gevurah. In sitting between these two Sephiroth, you are able to achieve a genuine state of unity where you are able to balance the competing forces of discipline and indulgence of forgiveness and retribution. The value of the dream reduces to 4, which points to a material expression of the ideas contained within this dream. It is likely that you should begin to put your newly balanced outlook into practice in your day-to-day life. So that others can benefit from your wisdom, you should perhaps consider a career shift into an area such as mediation.

FEAR

*pakhad–pchd–*פחד*-*92

MEANING Many mainstream religions have operated on the basis of fear as a way to maintain the obedience and faith of their congregation. The true spiritual path does not require a state of abject terror on the part of the seeker of truth. Instead, a sense of wonder and proper humility is encouraged. However, inevitably there are moments in your inner development when you will experience intense and consuming feelings of fear and anxiety. This is because the path of the spiritual requires you to face yourself and the world around you in a completely honest way and this is never an easy task to achieve.

THE TREE OF LIFE One of the hardest things to accept as we develop a growing understanding of the nature of the Divine is the presence of death and destruction. We cannot simply attribute the decay of forms to mankind's mismanagement of this planet since we can see that the gradual breakdown of all forms of life is built in to the very heart of the physical laws that govern the universe. What we have to do is find a way of reconciling this fact with the notion of a God who is ultimately loving. This reconciliation is the work that we must undertake in the

Sefirah of Gevurah and it is in this Sefirah that we should place this dream.

THE JOURNEY "Ashes to ashes, dust to dust"; this phrase is so well known that we rarely stop to consider its full implication. When you begin to think closely about the idea of returning to dust, the full impact of the nature of mortality begins to affect you. The value of this dream is equivalent to the Hebrew word meaning "mud." The idea that ultimately you may be no more significant than the dirt of the earth is causing you fear and anxiety. What you must try and do at this time is begin to recognize that your physical body may decay but your inner self, your soul, will continue to live and grow. Spending some time in areas regarded as traditionally sacred will help you understand this more fully as you will be able to feel the presence of all the souls associated with that particular sacred space.

FEATHER

*notsah-nvtzh-*נוצה*-151*

MEANING We tend to associate feathers with the element of Air, but the value of this dream suggests that it is not the more obvious ideas connected with feathers that we need to consider. In the bird kingdom, feathers are used as a means of display to potential mates and can be seen as closely linked to ideas of passion and ornamentation. This links up with the fact that the value of this dream is equivalent to the Hebrew word meaning "jealousy." The overall impression of this dream is that you need to work through your stronger emotions and find a way to achieve some form of harmony and balance within yourself.

THE TREE OF LIFE The value of this dream reduces to 7 and this is the value of the word Zayin meaning "sword." This supports the idea that this dream is pointing to the need for you to take up arms against your more unruly emotions. The Sefirah of Netzach is the seventh Sefirah in the Tree of Life and as it is concerned with the balancing of our emotions, it is the ideal location for this dream.

THE JOURNEY You have traveled along the path of Qoph into the Sefirah of Netzach as indicated by the compression of the value of this dream, which begins with the letter Qoph. Having traversed this path, you will have experienced a number of mental anxieties about the spiritual path itself. Now that you have arrived in Netzach, you have to deal with a range of emotional concerns. This will cause you some degree of pain (Nun) but will also enable you

to approach the Divine with much more success (Aleph). For the next few months, whenever you find yourself reacting in a negative emotional manner to anybody, you should try and turn the situation around so that you imagine yourself as the person about whom you are feeling hostile emotions. This will help you to see things from the other person's point of view.

FENCE

*cheth-chyth-*חית*-418*

MEANING This is a profoundly mystical dream and indicates a high level of spiritual understanding on the part of the dreamer. The dream reduces to 13, which indicates a major change in your life that is about to occur, suggesting that you are on the verge of still more spiritual insights. The central letter Yod in the spelling of this dream tells us that the energy of the Divine is at the very heart of everything that you do. In this context, the fence of the dream is not a defence put up by you against the realities of the world, but rather a protective shield that emerges from the close relationship you have with the Divine. The image of a fence can also relate to the need to protect yourself from negative influences within your life.

THE TREE OF LIFE When we find a dream title that exactly corresponds to the name of one of the paths on the Tree of Life, as is the case with this dream, we often find that the dream itself belongs on that path. This is certainly the case here as the path of Cheth leads from the Sefirah of Gevurah, which is concerned with the harsher aspect of the Divine to the Sefirah of Binah, which can be regarded as the great Universal Mother. This transition certainly suits the suggestion that you are about to experience a major change in your perception of the spiritual universe.

THE JOURNEY The compression of this dream tells us of the journey that you are now undergoing. You have experienced the melancholy that comes with the realization of the inevitability of death and decay (Tav), but this has not in any way dampened your enthusiasm for the Divine (Yod). You can now use this enthusiasm as a protective force (Cheth) for those around you. The total value of this dream is the result of 22 multiplied by 19, Twenty two is the number of the paths on the Tree of Life and 19 is a number that is associated with intellectual endeavours. The suggestion here is that you can now put your wisdom to good use by setting out to teach others the lessons of the paths on The Tree of Life.

FEVER

*khadakhat-qdchth-*קדחת-512

MEANING A common symptom of serious fever is a tendency to hallucinate or become delusional. To a purely scientific mind, the whole process of spiritual belief and development may well seem like a prolonged and feverish delusion. The fact that you are presenting the spiritual work to yourself as a fever in your dreams suggests that you are still very new to the Great Work and still retain certain reservations about your commitment to a spiritual path. The existence of reservations is also emphasized by the fact that the reduction of the value of this dream gives us the number 8. This is the value of the letter Cheth, and in the context of this dream the letter Cheth meaning "fence" points to a desire within you for some form of self-protection.

THE TREE OF LIFE The spelling of this dream indicates that the path that it lies on. You have begun to conceptualize the potential for some form of spiritual experience. Even though this has caused you considerable angst and concern (Qoph), you do realize that the path that you have chosen will ultimately open the door to a higher level of spiritual understanding (Daleth). Your first steps toward a connection with the Divine are being taken along the path of Tav, which is the final letter in the spelling of this dream.

THE JOURNEY Clearly you still have a long journey ahead of you, and this awareness can cause you to feel almost defeated before you begin your spiritual work. The compression of the dream reveals that the best way to reduce any anxiety is to approach your spiritual work from a practical angle. This is indicated by the letter Kaph, and perhaps you should consider taking up some form of spiritually inclined physical exercise such as tai chi. This will enable the spark of the divine that lies within you (Yod) to be awakened. You will then feel much more confident that your true home (Beth) does indeed lie with the Divine.

FIRE

*esh-ash-*אש-301

MEANING To dream of a particular element indicates that at the present moment in time, your personality is out of balance with an excess of the element that is represented by the image in your dream. In your case, you have an overload of those characteristics that are represented by the element of Fire. This tends to refer to raw energy and passion as well as a certain hastiness and the potential for irritability when interacting with others. The value of this dream reduces to 4, which points to the fact that the element of Fire is making itself felt in your day-to-day life as well as in your spiritual development.

THE TREE OF LIFE All of the elements are represented at various points on the Tree of Life. However, the emphasis on the material world indicated by the presence of the number 4 in this dream tells us that we are looking for a path that is quite low on the Tree. The path in question is the path of Shin. This path leads out of Malkut and is often known as the "biting path" both because the letter Shin means "Tooth," and because the path forces us to begin to confront our natures in a judgmental and vigorous manner. It is this vigorous approach that underlies the association of this path with the element of Fire.

THE JOURNEY We began this analysis by pointing out that to dream of a single element implies an imbalance within ourselves. However, as we begin our spiritual quest, it is necessary that we go through such imbalances. So that we can harmonize all of the elements within ourselves, we must focus on each one in turn. The path of Shin enables you to focus on the element of Fire and you can learn to use its powerful energy to good effect. You should take this opportunity to clarify in your mind all those elements of your lifestyle and outlook that you would like to remove from your life. The raw power of the element of Fire will provide you with the determination and requisite ruthlessness to ensure that you do indeed clear those unwanted aspects of your life away for good.

See Zohar symbol, Fire.

FISH

*nun-nvn-*נון-106

MEANING The image of a fish calls to mind all sorts if profound spiritual ideas from a Christian standpoint, as early Christians would represent Christ through a crude drawing of a fish. From a purely Kabbalistic perspective, this dream is equally profound, as it represents an understanding of the intrinsically sorrowful nature of existence unless that existence is enlivened by a relationship with the Divine. The reduction of the value of this dream gives us the number 7, which is the value of the letter Zayin meaning "sword." This tells us that in order to get through life, we have to struggle against its more melancholic aspects.

THE TREE OF LIFE The letter Nun is one of the paths on the Tree of Life, and so a dream of fish certainly belongs on this path. This is an area of the Tree that is associated with great feelings of melancholy and sorrow. In the spelling of the dream title, the letter Nun is repeated twice, thus emphasising the level of emotional pain that tends to come along with this particular path. However, while this is not a cheerful time in your life, it is a very important phase in your spiritual development. It is only through dealing with your self-doubt and anxiety that you will be able to arrive in Tiferet.

THE JOURNEY What is needed for you to move forward spiritually is a period of reflection. This is emphasized by the fact that the compression of this dream yields the letters Qoph and Vav. Both these letters refer to the act of thinking, and it is only through mentally working through your emotional baggage that you will feel ready to continue on your spiritual quest. It may be a good idea to visit a trained counselor or therapist to help you through this process.

See Zohar symbol, Fish.

FLAG
degel-dgl- דגל *-37*

MEANING Walk down any suburban street in the United States of America and you will see the Stars and Stripes flying proudly in any number of backyards. Flags are a way for us to express our identity in a vigorous and proud manner. Historically, flags were most important in times of warfare, but this dream does not refer to a conflict with any outside force. The flag waving in this dream is undertaken by your higher self and its purpose is to encourage you to stand by your newly spiritual way of looking at the world. The final letter in the compression of this dream, Zayin, indicates that you have a struggle ahead, as part of you still wants to remain loyal to the flag of secular materialism.

THE TREE OF LIFE The value of this word is equivalent to the Hebrew word meaning "flames." All images of fire tend to conjure up ideas of great energy and raw force. This great potential driving force is represented by the letter Lamed in both the spelling and compression of this dream. It is on the path of Lamed that we encounter this dream, as this is a point in life when we need to be vigorously

driven forward in our spiritual quest. It is also a time when you need to begin to fully accept the implications of your growing levels of insight in the way you live your life generally.

THE JOURNEY When we reduce the value of this dream, we find the value 10, and this tells you that you are approaching the completion of a cycle in your life. The positioning of the dream indicates that the completion will be achieved when you regard yourself primarily as a spiritually focused individual and not as a materially focused individual. You can help bring this moment closer by setting aside a regular period of time when you will either read about spiritual matters or spend time meditating or engaging in yoga or some similar form of exercise.

FLOOD
sheetafon-shytphvn- שיטפון *-455*

MEANING Kabbalah is quite probably the single most popular system of mysticism in the Western world. In the process of gaining popularity, it has mutated and been adapted to suit an array of different religious and philosophical systems. We have, for instance, had Christian Kabbalah for over five hundred years. What we should never forget though is that Kabbalah has its origins in the Semitic cultures of the Near and Middle East. This is especially important when we come to consider the implications of the dream of floods, as there are very definite connections to the story of the Deluge. This dream indicates a period of purification and cleansing in order to prepare you for the work ahead. This interpretation is supported by the fact that the dream's value reduces to 10, a number that indicates the completion of an important part of your life. However, the force and speed of a flood also suggests that this dream may be pointing to areas of your life in which you feel overwhelmed or unable to cope.

THE TREE OF LIFE A dream that is so clearly associated with the element of Water belongs on a path that is similarly connected to this element. The path of Mem is connected to the element of Water in its aspect as a symbol of the universal womb. However, this dream links to the path of Nun, whose sorrowful aspect ideally represents the nature of the Deluge, but also acts as a cleansing spiritual force in that it prepares you to face the world without the emotional obstacles that previously hindered your further development.

THE JOURNEY The compression of this dream emphasizes the melancholic nature of this stage of your journey. The planet of Saturn is indicated by the letter Tav and this planet is traditionally regarded as the most sorrowful of the planets. This is followed by the letter Nun which, as we have seen, suggests the possibility of significant emotional upset en route to a deeper and more profound faith. However, the final letter, Heh, points to the glimmer of light that will become visible once you have gone through this difficult period in your life. You can help appreciate the importance of this testing time by reading about and considering the importance of the Deluge tales from the Sumerian epic of Gilgamesh to the more familiar tale of Noah.

FLOUR

*kemakh–qmch–*קמח*-148*

MEANING It is said that man cannot live by bread alone. Traditionally, bread is symbolic of food in the most general sense. While we cannot live fulfilling lives by merely satisfying our physical needs, we cannot exist at all unless we at least have our bread. Flour is the most basic ingredient for making bread and is found in one form or another in almost every culture in the world. This dream is about the need to meet those basic physical needs. The reduction of the value of this dream produces the number 13, which indicates that you are going through a major period of change in your life. Clearly, you need to be sure that in the excitement of all the changes you don't neglect the day-to-day aspects of your life.

THE TREE OF LIFE When we are excited, we can easily forget to eat. Quite often we are buzzing with so much adrenaline that we do not even realize that we are hungry. There are few experiences that can live up to the excitement we feel when we realize that our spiritual work is beginning to pay off and that we are getting slight glimpses of the world beyond the purely physical. This is very much the experience of the Sefirah of Yesod and it is here that you and your dream belong on the Tree of Life.

THE JOURNEY It is wonderful to feel enthusiastic and eager for progress on your inner journey. There are dangers, though, in being overenthusiastic. We can fail to pay sufficient attention to our day-to-day life and this can lead to practical difficulties that will ultimately reduce the time you can spend engaged in the Great Work. Additionally, an intense burst of enthusiasm can easily slip into a complete lack of enthusiasm when results do not appear as quickly as we would like. In order to keep your feet on the ground, you should consider involving yourself in a charitable organization. This

will be very beneficial spiritually, but will also keep you in touch with day-to-day life.

FLOWERS

*perakh–prch–*פרח*-288*

MEANING A psychological interpretation of this dream would probably see evidence of romantic thoughts occupying the mind of the dreamer. However, from a Kabbalistic point of view this dream is not about a romantic attachment to another person. It does involve some of the feelings that are often associated with emotional relationships. This dream indicates a yearning for a union with the Divine and points to a realization within you that the most important aspect of the Divine is its capacity for unconditional love. The reduction of this dream's value to 9 does serve as a warning that you must be careful not to let the strength of your desire for a communion with the higher lead you to mistake a false experience for a genuine moment of revelation.

THE TREE OF LIFE When we look for evidence of the love of the Divine, there is no better place to start than the physical universe itself. It is filled with beauty and wonder; when we know how to look properly, there is not a single aspect of the universe that does not reflect the love of the Divine. Flowers are immediately recognizable as beautiful and so they are especially suited to this dream. We can reflect the love of the Divine by exercising our own creative abilities. The Sefirah of Netzach is associated with the arts and creativity and it is for this reason that Netzach acts as the home of this dream.

THE JOURNEY The value of this dream is equivalent to the Hebrew word meaning "offspring." This reiterates the connection of this dream to ideas of creativity. Very often you will hear artists and authors referring to their creations as their babies or their children. You should find a creative endeavor that appeals to you and set about putting a great deal of energy into constructing a piece of art that reflects your sense of the Divine. The effort you exert should be as great as if you were indeed creating a child rather than a work of art.

FLY (INSECT)

*zvoov–zbvb–*זבוב*-17*

MEANING As unpleasant as it may seem to the lay reader, a dream of flies is an encouraging sign that you are beginning to move forward in your understanding of the nature of the world and of yourself. The compression of this dream reveals the letters Yod and Zayin. While the letter Zayin tells us that you are ready and able to begin the struggle for some form of higher knowledge, the letter Yod indicates that the Divine spark that lies within your soul is also ready to be enlivened by a commitment to the Great Work.

THE TREE OF LIFE Flies are never going to win a contest as the most popular animal on the planet or even as the most popular insect. Our standard image of flies is as disease carrying pests that feast on our waste and gather around our discarded food. In symbolic terms we are faced with a being that draws its sustenance from that which is decaying. It is an image of absolute materialism, but most significantly, it demonstrates the error inherent in focusing purely on the physical side of reality; the physical is subject to decay whereas the soul lives on eternally. This dream quite clearly sits in the material Sefirah of Malkut.

THE JOURNEY This dream shows that you have begun to develop a realization of the hollow nature of any purely material achievement, and the need for a spiritual aspect to your life. You can now move from understanding this to practically changing your life to fit this new insight. The best place for you to start is to learn to see the spiritual that lies hidden within even the lowest material object. Take a few walks in the countryside and look very closely at the way even the tiniest of plants is so delicately and carefully constructed. This type of observation should encourage the sense of wonder that precedes a spiritual journey toward the Truth.

❧FLYING

abar-aleph beth resh- אבר-203

MEANING Dreams of flying are often associated with a great sense of well-being and freedom, and when this is the case, they should be regarded as very positive dreams indeed. The act of flying is very much like the act of dreaming itself, in that we feel detached from and unaffected by the laws that rule the physical world. In our dreams there are many things that happen that would never be possible in the workaday world. There are a number of values associated with dreams of flying. If we look at the transliteration into Hebrew, we find a value of 203. This can be reduced to 5 by Kabbalistic addition (2 + 0 + 3 = 5). Five is the value of the letter Heh, meaning "window," and we can draw from this the idea that a dream of flying is giving a window on

the aims of our higher self. The final letter is Resh, meaning "sun," and we only need to consider the tale of Daedalus and Icarus to see the connection of the sun to flying. In the dream of flight our soul is attempting to return to the source of light and life. Of course, other values also come into play in dream analysis. These are values that are associated with the overall symbology of the dream rather than the single word that labels the dream. Of these other values 21 is the most important. The letters Kaph and Aleph add up to 21 and the word Ka is an Egyptian term for the soul. Flying in dreams represents the soul trying to break free from its earthly bonds. It is significant that with Kaph meaning "hand" and Aleph representing the element of Air, the combination of these two letters also represents the act of grasping upwards for the sky.

THE TREE OF LIFE When we fly, we are lifted just above the earth. We are freer than when held down by gravity, but we are still within the world. Flying is undoubtedly situated in the Sefirah of Yesod, which is immediately above that of Malkut, the Sefirah that represents the physical world. As you will have learned from the Introduction, Yesod is very close to what we might regard as the "astral plane." In other words, it is beyond the purely physical but is not a purely spiritual consciousness. In our dream flight we are likely to feel invigorated, peaceful, and even joyful. It is also common to have a feeling of great self-confidence when flying. We mentioned earlier that the moon is important to flying dreams, and the moon is one of the planets associated with Yesod. It is the lunar energy that provides the wonderful feeling of calm and content we referred to. However, the dream of flying may also be warning us of some of the more negative aspects of this position on the Tree of Life. Yesod is closely associated with lower forms of magic, which are used purely for the personal gain of the individual. That feeling of self-confidence as you soar through the skies needs to be controled or it may become complacency and conceit.

THE JOURNEY Flying is very often a dream associated with the beginning of a new stage of the Great Work, your higher self effectively showing you just how far you can escape the bonds of the material world. At this time in your life you are experiencing the first awakening of your higher self. It is the nature of our higher self to seek the Divine and the dream of flight is a very visual image of that desire to return. On a practical level you should begin to explore your creative side, take up painting, or arrange some music lessons. In beginning to free up your imagination, you will start to break down the barriers in your mind that interfere with your spiritual development. A more directly relevant response to this dream would be to ensure that you set aside at least half an hour each day as spiritual time. Initially, it would be useful to spend this time simply reading up on different forms of spirituality and ways of approaching the Divine.

See Zohar symbol, Flying.

FOG

arafel-a'arphl-ערפל-380

MEANING You might expect from the nature of the dream's content that this is not an enormously encouraging dream. It does certainly indicates a sense of loss and confusion on the part of the dreamer. However, the value of this dream reduces to 11, which suggests that there is a profound significance to this dream. We all go through foggy moments in our life when we are uncertain of the right direction to take. The values within this dream suggest that while you may be uncertain of the route to take, when you do decide on the appropriate path, you will meet with great success in terms of your spiritual development.

THE TREE OF LIFE Once we begin to balance the four elements within ourselves in terms of our physical needs, our emotions, our passions, and our intellect, we are much less likely to lose our way. We may get confused from time to time, but nothing to the extent that is suggested by the image of fog. The relevant path for this dream is that of Qoph. This is one of the first paths out of Malkut and represents your first steps on the spiritual journey toward Truth. The path of Qoph is connected with the tarot card The Moon, which points to anxieties and worries. In your case, these worries relate to your uncertainty about the huge step you have just taken.

THE JOURNEY As you travel along the path of Qoph, you may feel alone and at times wonder if you are being foolish in trying to achieve some form of spiritual insight. However, if you pay attention to the compression of the value of the dream, you will see that you are not being at all misguided in your attempts to contact your higher self. You have enormous amounts of spiritual energy (Shin) and all you need to do is find an appropriate way of communicating (Peh) with the spiritual forces around you. You might like to try some form of active spiritual practice such as sacred drumming or chanting.

FOOD

mazon-mzvn-מזון-103

MEANING The world can be a very alienating place for all of us at times. Even when on the outside life seems to be going fine for us, we can be suffering on the inside. As Noel Coward once famously said "duchesses suffer, too." In other words, it doesn't matter what our social position is, we can still be exposed to great upset. When this happens, many of us turn to some form of comfort activity, and for the majority of us this usually involves a big bowl of something decidedly unhealthy like ice cream or popcorn or possibly even both! This dream is about feeling a need for material comforts and this is emphasized by the fact that the value of this dream reduces to 4, the number that represents materiality. However, this dream also refers to the very genuine need that we have for nourishment of both a spiritual and physical nature.

THE TREE OF LIFE This dream's value is equivalent to the Hebrew word meaning "dust" and this association with the most basic form of physical material emphasizes the fact that this dream lies in the Sefirah of Malkut. It is your attachment to comforts that currently prevents you from moving beyond a merely material understanding of the universe. The positive aspect of this value, though, is that it is a prime number. This reminds you that you are a unique individual and that if you find the inner strength to move beyond the trap of the physical, you will be able to realize your full potential in your life.

THE JOURNEY Your current conflict is demonstrated by the compression of the dream's value. On the one hand, we have the letter Qoph representing the fear you have of letting go of the certainties of the physical world. On the other hand, the letter Gimel points to the highest level of spiritual development to which you can aspire as the letter Gimel reaches up to the Crown of Keter and is associated with the secret wisdom that fills us when we achieve a communion with the Divine. Only you can resolve this conflict, but you can help yourself to take the first step upwards by considering those things in life that have caused you genuine joy. You will find that none of them relied on any material goods or comforts, but stemmed from pure emotion.

FOREST

yaar-ya'ar-יער-280

MEANING You are someone who is both attracted by the mystery of the Great Work and are also at times fearful of the unknown and the secrets that lie within a fully developed spiritual understanding. In psychological terms, the image of a forest suggests the unconscious mind and the hidden desires and self-doubts that lurk deep within our personality. In a Kabbalistic analysis, these demons of the mind are still present but the meaning of the dream is increased, as it also relates to a fear of spiritual commitment. The value of this dream is equivalent to the Hebrew word meaning "terror" and this supports the idea of a fear of development.

THE TREE OF LIFE Forests are gloomy and dark places in folklore, within them nature roams free and is wild. In this sense the forest represents the earthiness and unrefined physicality of Malkut. This Sefirah is also appropriate to this dream, as a terror of delving too deep into the spiritual nature of the universe would keep us trapped in the darkness of Malkut. The reduction of the value of this dream produces the number 10, which is connected to the Sefirah of Malkut for two reasons. On the one hand, Malkut is the tenth Sefirah on the Tree of Life. Additionally, the number ten is also associated with coinage in the Western Mystery Tradition, and this is equally symbolic of Malkut.

THE JOURNEY It is clear from your dream that the way forward for you lies in learning to face your fear not only of the spiritual but also your fear of what lies within you. This unwillingness to know yourself in a deep sense may well stem from painful childhood memories that you are trying to avoid. The compression of your dream urges you to go forward with optimism, as the initial letter, Resh, indicates the benevolent aspect of the Divine. The final letter in the compression, Peh, means "mouth." This not only encourages you to attempt to communicate with your higher self, but can also be seen as advice that you need to talk to about your fears to someone who is qualified both to listen and to advise.

FORGETTING WHAT TO SAY

shokeach eyzeh lomar-shkkh ayzh lvmr-

שכח איזה לומר-1025

MEANING We have all had that experience: We are sitting in a meeting or at a gathering of some kind, we have made it quite clear that we intend to say something important, and just as we clear our throat to speak, we realize with dread that we have completely and utterly forgotten what it we were about to say. What follows is a mixture of embarrassment and confusion. In spiritual terms, this experience is very

common. We firmly believe that we have finally gotten a handle on at least the broad implications of our beliefs, when suddenly something happens or a new thought strikes us and we are left flailing again as unsure as ever before. The initial Qoph in the compression of this dream's value represents the feeling of uncertainty and anxiety that this dream represents.

THE TREE OF LIFE One of the Hebrew words that is equivalent in value to the value of this dream is a word that refers to the negative aspect of the zodiac sign Virgo. Since Virgo is associated with social grace and intimate communication, this dream represents an inability to verbalize your feelings in an adequate way. The sign of Virgo sits on the path of Kaph on the Tree of Life and it is on this path that we find this dream.

THE JOURNEY The path of Kaph is associated with practicalities and also with a jovial or good-humored approach to the world around us. Both these aspects of the path of Kaph should be seen as hints as to how you need to act at this point in your spiritual life. The influence of Kaph is also indicated by its presence in the middle of the compression of the value of this dream. If you deal with your confusion in a good-humored way by learning to laugh at your difficulties and mistakes, you will find that your progress becomes far smoother. Additionally while you may not be able to articulate your spirituality with words, you can demonstrate it by the way in which you deal with those around you. As the compression tells us through the final letter, Heh, if you follow this advice you will be able to glimpse the light of the Divine force.

FORK

*mazleg-mzlg-*מזלג-80

MEANING When we analyse dreams from a Kabbalistic standpoint, we always have to be careful to pay very close attention to the exact nature of the dream's content. In this dream, for instance, it is the temptation to think of food or eating that becomes the key to providing a context for analyzing the values hidden within the spelling of the dream's title. However, close examination makes it clear that this dream is not about eating, but about the means by which we convey the food to our mouths. Consequently, in spiritual terms this dream is not about spiritual truth, but about the means by which we access that spiritual truth. The image of a fork strongly suggests that this is a process that we must control and guide, while the initial letter, Mem, in the spelling of this dream tells us that the maternal aspect of the Divine is also present to ensure that, metaphorically speaking, the fork does indeed find your mouth.

THE TREE OF LIFE The image of a mouth is never far away in this dream, and this is in part because you are learning how to access the spiritual nourishment that will help you move toward your spiritual goals. The value of this dream is 80 and this is the value of the letter Peh. It should not be too surprising to learn that the letter Peh means "mouth" in Hebrew. The path of Peh is associated with communication and it is an appropriate path for this dream, as you are now in a position to begin a communication with your higher self.

THE JOURNEY If we reduce the value of the dream we find the number 8, which relates to the protective force of the Divine that surrounds you right now. This protection is also pointed to by the initial letter, Mem, in the spelling of this dream, while the final letter, Gimel, represents the secret wisdom that is your ultimate goal. Between these two protective letters are two letters that represent the sterner, more rigorous aspect of the spiritual path: the letters Zayin and Lamed. These represent your own need to struggle in order to succeed (Zayin) and the driving force (Lamed) of your higher self. This balance between the harsh and the protective also represents the idea of communication in the sense of a constant communication and balancing between these two aspects of the Divine force. In the path of Peh your task is to begin to learn to balance those two competing aspects within yourself.

FRUIT

*pree-pry-*פרי-290

MEANING When we think of fruit in a spiritual sense, we tend to immediately focus on the fruit of the Tree of Knowledge of Good and Evil as eaten by Adam and Eve in the book of Genesis. The value of this dream certainly calls to mind this symbolic event, as it is equivalent to the Hebrew phrase meaning "thine enemy." Clearly, as the eating of the fruit led to the expulsion from the garden, the fruit itself can be seen as the enemy of all people. However, this dream has an overall positive message for you the dreamer, as fruit also symbolizes the wisdom that you are seeking. The reduction of the value of this dream produces the value 11, which indicates that you are about to receive a profoundly spiritual experience.

THE TREE OF LIFE It is important to remember that it is not knowledge that comes under fire in Genesis, but the failure to trust in the Divine that leads to the loss of Eden. Additionally, from a mystical point of view we can see that this fall as an essential precursor to the possibility of full redemption and the achievement of spiritual enlightenment. The point on the Tree of Life that is most associated with knowledge is the Sefirah of Hod. This is the location of this dream and should be seen as positive in that you are now ready to begin to receive spiritually enhanced knowledge. In the spelling of this dream we see both the letters Resh and Peh, which lead into the Sefirah of Hod. The letter Yod represents the Divine spark within you that will be further awakened by the increase in your level of knowledge gained through your time within Hod.

THE JOURNEY As the story of the expulsion from Eden reminds us, knowledge can have its good or bad influences. The task that lies ahead of you is not just to increase your knowledge of the spiritual, but also to put that knowledge to good use. The compression of this dream's value is very encouraging in that it points both to the benevolent force of the Divine that is protecting you (Resh) and also to your own deep commitment (Tzaddi) to the Great Work. In order to have the fullest understanding of the world both in its spiritual and natural aspect, you should begin reading as widely and voraciously as possible on a whole range of subjects.

GARDEN

*gan-gn-*גן-53

MEANING Great beauty can have a peculiar effect on individuals. There is a state of beauty that is simply attractive. However, we can get beyond that to a level of natural beauty that is breathtaking. Such beauty can often shift our response from one of enjoyment to a profound and overwhelming sense of the presence of the Divine. The reduction of this value leads to the number 8. This is the value of the letter Cheth and indicates a desire for protection. This desire for protection stems from the overwhelming power of the Divine force.

THE TREE OF LIFE The spelling of this dream begins with the letter Gimel. This letter is associated with the Tarot card The Empress, which among other things represents great beauty within the universe. Additionally, the letter Gimel lies on the path that leads directly into Keter and thus also represents a high level of spiritual understanding.

However, the second letter, Nun, has much greater force, as it appears in its final form. This is the path to which this dream belongs and indicates a great deepening of your faith that is about to occur.

THE JOURNEY You are at something of a crossroads in your life. The path of Nun leads into Tiferet and this is the Sefirah that holds within it the possibility of direct contact with your higher self. To make the leap from your melancholic feelings to a joyous acceptance of the wondrous nature of the Divine will require significant work on your part. You must learn to become comfortable with the power of the spiritual and this can only be achieved by a regular meditative practice. All you need to do is set aside about half an hour a day and spend that time in quiet meditation. The most important thing to do is to find a regular rhythm to your breathing, as this will help you achieve the required level of relaxation and inner calm. Once you find this clam within yourself, you will begin to feel the power of the Divine force and most importantly you will be able to accept this force without feeling any fear.

❧GATE

*shaar-sha'ar-*שׁעַר-570

MEANING Our spiritual journey is a process of opening a series of gates that lead us upwards into ever more evolved states of consciousness. This dream relates to passing through one such portal. Significant levels of energy are represented by all three letters and this indicates that you are at a particularly crucial stage in your inner development. Additionally, it points to the need for you to be vigorous and forceful in your attempts to deepen your spiritual understanding. The sense of importance and also of great activity is also suggested by the fact that the value of this dream is equivalent to the value of the Hebrew word meaning "earthquake."

THE TREE OF LIFE At first glance, this dream would seem to belong to any of the Sefirot on the Tree of Life. In a very real sense, each Sefirah functions like a gateway to the next stage of heightened insight. A closer examination of the spelling of this dream draws our attention to the fact that two of the three letters are paths that lead out of Malkut. What is more, the value of this dream is also the value of the Hebrew word meaning "ten." Malkut is of course the tenth Sefirah on the Tree Of Life.

THE JOURNEY As this dream belongs to Malkut, it is not surprising that it suggests a significant event about to occur in your life. In any journey, the first

step is always the most eventful and difficult, and this is certainly true of the spiritual journey that you are now contemplating. All you need to open the first gate is the willpower and persistence to make a commitment to the Great Work. There is sufficient fiery energy in the spelling of the dream's title to indicate that you have the potential to make this leap of faith. Before you make any firm decisions, you should spend some time reading up on as many different spiritual and religious systems as you can, so that you find an approach that works for you.

See Zohar symbol, Gate.

GHOST

*rooakh refaeem-rvch rphaym-*רוח רפאים-547

MEANING From a broad psychological perspective, this dream would be noticeable for its connection to the supernatural. As the focus of the dream is a ghost, it would be reasonable for a psychoanalyst to see this dream as an indication of great fear when it comes to those aspects of life that do not have a basis in the material world itself. However, when we look at any dream from a Kabbalistic viewpoint it is intimately entwined with the spiritual nature of reality. The fact that this dream specifies a ghost does not make it any more spiritual in nature than a dream about cheese, for example. However, we should also be aware that in the Kabbalistic tradition, a ghost represents a concern with the reality that lies behind the world of the mundane.

THE TREE OF LIFE It is only in the world of films and mass media that ghosts are almost universally regarded as objects of great terror. Within the Western Mystery Tradition, a ghost or spirit has the same capacity to act for good or evil that people possess when they are alive. The repeated appearance of the letter Resh indicates that you are now under the influence of the benign nature of the Divine. The idea of protection and guidance is also supported by the letter Mem, which completes the spelling of the dream title. Far from being a negative dream or one designating fear on the part of the dreamer, this dream simply points out that you have arrived at a stage in your development where the spiritual aspect to reality can no longer be denied. This realization tends to occur within the Sefirah of Yesod and it is higher that this dream belongs.

THE JOURNEY The first thing we should notice about the value of this dream is that it is a prime number. Prime numbers are those that cannot be divided by any other number except one. Such numbers are relatively rare and become increasingly rare the larger the number. For this reason, prime numbers are seen as an indication of uniqueness on the part of the dreamer. As this is a fairly large number, you have an individuality that is very strong and should be nurtured as you progress toward your spiritual goals. The compression of the dream shows us that you need to keep your feet on the ground and maintain a pragmatic (Kaph) approach to your day-to-day life. The central letter, Mem, implies that you can rely on the maternal aspect of the Divine to encourage you in your efforts. The final letter, Zayin, meaning "Sword" is a reminder that even though you are now well on your way, there are still significant struggles ahead of you.

GIANT

*anak-a'anq-*עִנַק-220

MEANING In almost every culture you will find stories about giants or ogres. With very few exceptions, giants are portrayed as bullying and greedy creatures who famously have very little time for people except perhaps as a nice snack. However, when we analyze dreams it is important to find the single key characteristic of the dream's subject. In this case it is the sheer physical bulk that distinguishes a giant from any other person. On the face of it, this might not seem particularly important, but it does have great symbolic value. The massive size of a giant emphasizes their physical nature and thus their connection to the material rather than the spiritual world. This connection is emphasized by the fact that the value of this dream reduces to 4, which is the number associated with all things material in nature.

THE TREE OF LIFE The value of this dream is equivalent to the Hebrew word meaning "Nephilim." There is no direct English equivalent of this word as it refers to a group of angels, looking like giant men, who visited earth and slept with human women. In the story of the Nephilim, the key point is that these beings decided to ignore the guidance of the Divine. This dream connects a lingering concern with the material comforts of the world with an unwillingness to take advice as to how best to pursue your spiritual goals. These two factors place the dream on the path of Ayin, and it is no accident that the letter Ayin begins the spelling of this dream.

THE JOURNEY The path of Ayin reflects a reasonable level of spiritual development, so your current difficulties should not be taken as an indication that you have not achieved any valid insights so far in your spiritual quest. It is very common among those

who decide to take up the challenge of the Great Work to reach a point where they begin to believe that it is they rather than the Divine that is ultimately the source of their increased understanding. If you fall into this trap and make a giant of yourself, you run the risk of going no farther on the Tree of Life. The compression of the dream's value gives you some good advice as to how best to avoid remaining in this trap. Firstly, you need to recognize the benevolent influence of the Divine (Resh) in your inner development. You can encourage this attitude by taking some practical steps (Kaph) to honor the Divine. This could range from engaging in daily prayer to involving yourself in some local charitable activity.

GIFT (TO RECEIVE A GIFT)

*matanah-mthnh-*מַתָּנָה-495

MEANING In the same way that some of us are born natural athletes or with a particular skill in mathematics or music, there are also those among us who are born with a natural propensity to follow a spiritual path in life. The dream of a gift indicates that you are one of these people who possesses something akin to a sixth sense. This quality should be nurtured, as it will assist you greatly when you try to approach an understanding of the Divine. The value of this dream reduces to 9 and this is the value of the letter Teth meaning "serpent." The historical significance of the serpent is well known, and its inclusion here serves as a warning of the potential to take your gift and turn it to your own ends rather than in service of the Great Work.

THE TREE OF LIFE The warning of Teth aside, this is an enormously positive dream. After all, there are not many people who have the gift of spiritual sensitivity. The compression of this dream tells us that you will need to make a number of emotional sacrifices (Tav) in order to achieve a state of mind that will open a window (Heh) on the inner workings of the universe. It is in the Sefirah of Netzach that we deal with most of our emotional issues. Of the paths that lead into Netzach, the most appropriate in Tzaddi. This path is not right for the dream simply because it is the central letter in the compression of the dream, but also because the path of Tzaddi is connected with a sense of higher guidance and protection.

THE JOURNEY For most of us, the spiritual journey is one where we begin with nothing. In metaphorical terms, we do not even have a pair of shoes. You, on the other hand, by virtue of your innate connection with the supernatural, are starting with the metaphorical equivalent of a pair of stout walking boots. You do need to be careful not to let your gift go to waste, and this means spending the time to cultivate your ability. You do this by something as simple as experimenting with predicting the color that a friend will think of next from a range of six possibilities. The more you work on this in-built facility the easier you will find it to contact your higher self on reaching Tiferet.

GIVING BIRTH
laledet-lldth-ללדת-464

MEANING This is a very complex dream in Kabbalistic terms. As any parent will confirm, childbirth is both a deeply rewarding and an enormously worrying event. It is highly likely that this dream indicates that you are in a transition phase in your life; certain projects or relationships may well be reaching a point at which you feel wholly content. While positive, this dream points to the need to maintain proper levels of planning and responsibility in your life. From the spiritual point of view, this dream indicates a need to focus on a sense of inner harmony, and this is emphasized by the fact that the value of this dream reduces to 14—a number deeply connected to notions of inner balance.

THE TREE OF LIFE Esoteric spirituality is in many ways a creative act, compared to the more mainstream approaches to religious activity. The individual takes responsibility for their own spiritual advancement and redemption rather than relying on any pre-prepared for entry into a communion with the Divine. One of the key tasks to accomplish is to achieve a union with your higher self. This takes a great deal of effort and devotion, and can easily be compared with the task of carrying and ultimately giving birth to a new life. The "birth" of your higher self tales place in Tiferet. The path of Samech leads into this central point on the Tree of Life, and it is on the path of Samech that this dream belongs. The link of this dream to the path of Samech is emphasized by the focus on a sense of harmony that runs through this dream, as this is central to the purpose of Samech.

THE JOURNEY The spelling of this dream begins with the letter Lamed repeated twice. This letter means "ox goad," and indicates a strong and at times harsh driving force that is pushing you toward your spiritual goals. It is now time to listen to that stern inner voice and take your development much more seriously. If you are able to achieve the right level of

commitment, you will indeed open the door (Daleth) to the the glimmer of light (Heh) that acts like a window on the nature of the Divine. Your success will be greatly assisted if you set yourself a strict timetable for meditation and other forms of spiritual practice.

GLASS
zekhookeet-zkvkyth-זכוכית-463

MEANING One of the characteristics of glass is that when it is placed over an object it does not change that object in any way. A painting behind a protective layer of glass is as clear as a painting without any such cover. This in a sense represents what you must be aiming to do in your life. One of the marks of the spiritually developed individual is that they allow their own personal bias to influence the way that they perceive the world. The world is able to present itself to them as unaltered as the painting behind the glass. It may sound easy to see the world as it is and not how we choose to view it, but in fact such a transparent view of the world is extremely difficult to achieve. The value of this dream reduces to 13, which is a number indicating great change, and so it is likely that you are about achieve this level of wise objectivity.

THE TREE OF LIFE When we look at the compression of the value of this dream, we can see that it is made up of the three letters that make up the middle pillar on the Tree of Life—the paths Tav, Samech, and Gimel. In view of the profoundly wise state that is now within your grasp, the dream itself belongs to the topmost of these three paths—the path of Gimel. The inclusion of all the paths from the middle pillar, otherwise known as the "pillar of mildness," is very important. By symbolically representing the whole pillar of mildness, the value of the dream tells us the key characteristic that you will be developing over the next few months.

THE JOURNEY Since the earliest civilizations, mankind has recognized the ideal nature of the objective mind. To Aristotle it was the "golden mean" and even then in Ancient Greece the principles underlying the idea of a "middle way" were the same as they are today. It is only when we remove our own personal preferences for one state of affairs over another that we can judge any situation fairly and wisely. This is a goal that you must now strive toward. You can begin by making a habit of always defending the side you least agree with in any debate or discussion, as this will help you to develop a pure level of objectivity.

❧ GOATS

*tayeesh-thysh-*תיש-710

MEANING If you asked most people whether they would rather be a sheep or a goat, the vast majority would opt for goathood. This is because goats are symbolic of a number of qualities that we find admirable. Where sheep are docile and appear to have little sense of self, goats are dynamic individuals leaping from rocky outcrop to rocky outcrop. In a spiritual context, the image of a goat has long been associated in peoples' minds with the more negative side of the moral divide. However, this is a relatively recent phenomenon based on the Church's objection to pagan fertility Gods and has no basis in Kabbalah symbolism.

THE TREE OF LIFE Although it means "Tooth," the letter Ayin is often associated with goats in the Western Mystery Tradition. This is largely because the letter Ayin represents a vigorous and individualistic approach to life. Additionally, the letter Ayin is linked with the zodiac sign Capricorn, and so we have both the image of a goat in the star sign as well as the element of earth, which is ideally suited to the archetypal image of a goat. It is on the path of Ayin that we find this dream, but this does not mean that your at times aggressively individualistic approach to life is entirely commendable.

THE JOURNEY One of the ways in which the Great Work differs from mainstream religion is that the individual has far greater responsibility for finding their own truth. However, responsibility is not the same as having total freedom to ignore the influence of the Divine. One of the implications of this dream is that you have made yourself deaf to the quiet voice of your higher self. This enables you to follow any path in any way you choose. The reduction of this dream produces the number 8, which is the value of the letter Cheth. The letter Cheth means "fence" and is associated with defensive attitudes and behavior. The suggestion here is that one reason for your fierce individualism is a desire to protect yourself from the overwhelming influence of the Divine. You can escape this excessive self-direction by spending more time meditating before you make any definite decisions of an important nature.

See Zohar symbol, Goat.

GOLD

*zahav-zhb-*זהב-14

MEANING Sometimes we may have a dream that not only seems to be positive but also turns out to be wholly encouraging when analyzed from a Kabbalistic perspective. The value of this dream is 14, and this number is strongly associated with ideas of inner balance and harmony. Additionally, the art of alchemy focused on turning base metal in to gold. While this is a well-known fact, it is less well known that Alchemy was primarily intended as a symbolic rather than a literal practice. The base metal represents the individual before beginning the Great Work, while gold symbolizes the individual once they have achieved a link between themselves and their higher self.

THE TREE OF LIFE If we reduce the value of the dream's title we find the number 5. This number traditionally represents the spiritually awakened individual. We have the four elements, but also the fifth element of Spirit or Soul is present in the individual. The Sefirah of Tiferet is the point on the Tree where we begin to commune with our higher self, and it is to this position that we assign the dream of gold. It is doubly appropriate to place the dream here, as Tiferet is associated with the sun, and by association with gold.

THE JOURNEY The alchemical texts tell us that in order to achieve the transformation into gold we must first destroy the base material completely and then by a slow process of distilling and refining we recover from that crude source a quantity of pure gold. This is an excellent summary of the personal transformation that is required in order to enter Tiferet. In the compression of the dream's value we can see that you have already enlivened the divine spark (Yod) that lies within you and all you now need to do is open the door (Daleth) that lies ahead of you. To open that door requires you to not only believe in the reality of the spiritual aspect of life, but to ensure that your daily life, especially in your dealings with others, is infused with a sense of the Divine presence.

GOSSIP

*rekheeloot-rkylvth-*רכילות-666

MEANING Even non-Christians will immediately recognize the significance of the value of this dream, standing as it does for the Antichrist himself from the book of Revelation. However, if there is any coded significance to the numeration of the "Beast" it will be related to the Greek rather than the Hebrew language. Additionally, we also need to remember that Kabbalah is Judaic in terms of its known origins and so should not expect any direct relationship to Christian symbolism. In terms of the value of the dream, what is important is the repetition of the letter Vav, as this indicates that you are going through a period of intense thought. The image of gossip should be seen as a number of competing ideas that you need to consider.

THE TREE OF LIFE You might expect this dream to be located on the path of Vav due to the repetition of that letter's value in the dream. However, the path of Vav is a very advanced path, and the surrounding context of this dream suggests someone at a relatively early stage of their spiritual journey. The Sefirah of Hod is the place on the Tree of Life where we have to try and organize our thoughts in relation to our newfound spirituality, and this location fits the dream and your own stage of development perfectly.

THE JOURNEY It can be difficult to create a happy balance of the spiritual and the rational, and it has to be said that this is the point where so many people find that their development stagnates. The reduction of the value of this dream produces the number 9, which is the value of the Hebrew letter Teth, and indicates the need to avoid people and ideas that are there to deceive you. This warning emphasizes the difficulties associated with this stage of your spiritual development. An ideal way forward for you at this point would be to join a meditation group so that you have like-minded people around you who can help to clarify your direction.

GRASS

esev-a'ashb- עשב -372

MEANING In a world full of concrete, cars, and computers, it is extremely difficult to picture how life would have been at the time when the tribes of Israel were just receiving the law from Moses. One thing of which we can be sure is the importance of grass. You have to live in a farming community to fully appreciate just how significant grazing land really would have been all those years ago. Bearing this in mind, it begins to be less surprising that this dream is replete with spiritual significance. The value of this dream is equivalent to the value of the Hebrew word meaning "seven." This is a deeply mystical number and is tied up with the wonder of creation itself.

THE TREE OF LIFE To dream of grass implies that you are beginning to tap in to the mysteries underlying the nature of the universe. Specifically, you are gaining insight into the nature of the Divine as a maternal force, and this is pointed to by the final letter, Beth, in the spelling of this dream. As a result, it is likely that you will find yourself feeling far more protective of people in general. When we reduce the value of this dream we find the number 12, which also relates to the idea of maternity through its link to the letter Mem. The path of Mem is the most appropriate location for this dream, as it is deeply connected to the ideas that this dream represents.

THE JOURNEY Although this dream may be about a stereotypically female role of motherhood, the compression of the dream's value indicates that there is plenty of room for individuality in the way that you demonstrate your maternal instinct. It is worth noting that while we are talking about a maternal instinct, this dream applies equally to men and women alike. Both the letters Ayin and Shin in the spelling of the dream indicate great individuality and an ability to plough your own furrow through life. You should start looking for an innovative and unusual way to express your wish to look after those in a less fortunate position than your own.

GRAVE

kever-qbr- קבר -302

MEANING Nobody wants to wake up and recall dreaming of a grave. This is probably even more so today than years ago, as more than ever people have lost their belief in any life continuing after their physical death. A psychological interpretation would probably focus on the idea that this dream indicates feelings of depression or morbidity. A Kabbalistic interpretation looks at this dream from a completely different angle. The initial Qoph in the spelling of the dream does indicate a certain level of anxiety about the next level of existence. However, this is countered by the presence of the final Resh, which points to an awareness of the benevolent nature of the Divine. Additionally, this dream may well refer to the end of some aspect of our day-to-day life, such as the need for us to change careers for instance.

THE TREE OF LIFE In a secular world, the grave is quite literally our final resting place when there is nothing more for us to do or experience. However, from a spiritual point of view the moment of death is a transition rather than an end. The value of this dream's title is equivalent to the Hebrew word meaning "dawn." This is very significant, as it demonstrates the idea that when darkness falls in this lifetime it is simply the moment before the dawn in another state of consciousness. To fully appreciate the implications of this idea requires a considerable level of insight. When we reduce the value of this dream we find the number 5, which corresponds to the letter Heh. This is the path to which this dream belongs, as it indicates that you have managed to open the window on one of the great spiritual truths.

THE JOURNEY Just because death is only a comma rather than a period, we should not take the view that therefore events in this life do not matter. We should perhaps put things in their proper perspective, but it is essential that we still live life to the fullest. The compression of this dream tells us that we should put all our considerable energy (Shin) into the business of living, and that if we do so we will be able to return to our true spiritual home (Beth) when our life here is finally done.

GREETINGS
*brakhah–brkh–*ברכה*–*227

MEANING As you might expect from a dream about greetings, this is a very positive experience for any dreamer. Not only does it indicate that you are moving forward in an optimistic way, it also implies that you are shortly about to have an experience that will have a profound and lasting impact on the way you view the world. This implication is found through the reduction of the value of the dream. The reduced value is 11, and this number is always associated with profoundly mystical experiences.

THE TREE OF LIFE The term *greetings* certainly suggests that you are quite new to the spiritual path. However, the total value of this dream is a prime number. This makes the point that although you have little experience in terms of the realm of the spiritual, you are a unique individual. This should encourage you in your wish to make inner progress. The value of this dream is equivalent to the Hebrew word meaning "remember." Of the paths that run out of Malkut, the one that most fits the idea of looking back at one's past in order to learn spiritual lessons is the path of Tav. It is here that we should place the dream, and as this is the very first path upwards toward the goal of Keter, it is very appropriate in terms of the dream's title.

THE JOURNEY Before we can come to terms with our spiritual self, we have to establish a clear sense of where we have come from, not just as individuals but also as a species. It is interesting to note that one of the words that is equivalent to the value of this dream means a body of water. This is of course the source of all human life, while at the same time the value of this dream also looks forward as another value-equivalent word for "tall." To help assist your spiritual development you should begin reading not just religious texts, but also scientific books looking at the creation of the physical universe and the origins of life on earth.

GROANING
*gneekhah–gnychh–*גניחה*–*76

MEANING Change is never easy, and despite the fact that we live in such a fast moving world, we still have to employ change management consultants to help us or our staff through periods of major change in the workplace. This is because no matter what the speed of our technology, our psychological ability to cope with change takes many many years to adjust. There are no consultants available to help us through change in our personal lives, and the groaning in the title of this dream relates to fact that you are now going through an intense period of adjustment in your inner life. This is borne out by the fact that the value of this dream reduces to 13, which is connected to The Death card in the Tarot and indicates a major shift in your outlook.

THE TREE OF LIFE The value of this dream is equivalent to a Hebrew word meaning "slave," and this sheds light on the nature of the change you are experiencing. As your spiritual understanding increases, you are beginning to realize the alienating nature of a wholly material lifestyle. The initial letter, Gimel, in the spelling of this dream points to this increase in wisdom, while the subsequent letter, Nun, represents the suffering that you are now experiencing. This dream sits on the path of Nun, and although it is a time of emotional distress, it ultimately leads you into a much wiser state of mind.

THE JOURNEY As we realize the importance of the spiritual in our lives, we also become aware that all those things that used to seem so significant no longer matter anywhere near as much as they did before. It can be tempting at this point to decide that you are going to completely opt out of "normal" society and dedicate your whole life to the Great Work.

However, this is more of a response to the negative feelings you have about the secular world than it is about a positive commitment to the spiritual. The compression of this dream tells you that you are right to be spending so much time reflecting on your postion (Vav). It also tells you that you are free to take a wholly individual (Ayin) approach to your life. This does not have to involve throwing away all the beneficial aspects of your day-to-day life, such as friends and community. Rather, what you should be doing is changing the relative importance of all the aspects of your life and acting accordingly.

GUN

totakh-thvthch- תותח *-814*

MEANING It is hard to imagine what possible connection there could be between a weapon and the spiritual path. When we think of the Divine, we are unlikely to link it with violence of any kind. However, symbolically a gun is a means of putting an end to any threat to our well-being. It is in this sense that the image of a gun relates to your inner progress. You are now at a point where you are about to try and destroy those aspects of your life that are preventing you from reaching your full spiritual potential. This interpretation is supported by the fact that the value of this dream reduces to 13, which is a number signifying great change in your life. However, you should also be aware of the possibility that this dream relates to feelings of violence that you may have within yourself toward those who you see as a danger to your sense of well-being.

THE TREE OF LIFE Once we have taken the first steps along the Tree of Life, our progress becomes a steady evolution of consciousness. By contrast, the decision to actually investigate the higher aspects of our inner self is far more momentous and has a much more immediate impact on the way we look at everything. The image of a gun certainly suggests a momentous and life changing event. Additionally, the letter Tav appears twice in this dream, and it is the path of Tav that you now stand upon as you prepare to climb back up toward the Divine source.

THE JOURNEY The imagery of this dream may be violent, but the advice that lies hidden within the compression of the dream's value encourages a very sensible approach to the spiritual. The key to success in the Great Work is communication (Peh). Initially this is communication with your higher self, and often you have to rely on your intuition for guidance. However, even in the earliest stages the spark of the Divine (Yod) is with you. It is by listening to that small inner voice that you will open the door (Daleth) to the next Sefirah on the Tree of Life. Listening to this voice and engaging in meditation will also help to ease any violent feelings that you may be holding on to.

HAIR

sear-shya'ar- שיער *-580*

MEANING Vanity might be the first word that springs to mind when you consider the implications of dreaming about hair. If we added a spiritual connection, then one might be inclined to think about physical strength due to the biblical tale of Samson. Both these possibilities are accurate in that they are concerned with the world of the physical and the nature of appearances. In Kabbalah, the image of hair is seen as a symbol for physical beauty and potency. From a spiritual point of view, this dream relates to the developing ability to distinguish the reality from the appearance of any event or situation. The value of this dream reduces to 13, a number associated with change, and so it is likely that this is a new ability that you are discovering within yourself.

THE TREE OF LIFE A large part of correct perception, from a spiritual standpoint, is the balancing of the rational and emotional elements of our personality through the influence of our higher self or spirit. The path of Peh occupies that balancing position between the rational Sefirah of Hod and the emotional Sefirah of Netzach. This is the path on which we should place this dream and this view is supported by the fact that the compression of this dream produces the letter Peh along with the letter Heh, which represents the four elements crowned by spirit.

THE JOURNEY Now that you have begun to develop the facility for determining the realities that often lie hidden behind obvious appearances, you are in a position to focus that ability on the spiritual realm. This will involve you in reading as widely as possible around the whole area of religious faith, but the spelling of this dream indicates that you have the energy (Shin) and the inspiration (Yod) to persist in this task. You should also take the image of hair as a sign that you should be looking for ways to increase your own sense of potency in all ways within your day-to-day life.

See Zohar symbol, Hair.

HAMMER

*pateesh-ptysh-*פטיש-399

MEANING Subtlety is usually the key to uncovering the mysteries that lie beneath the veil of the material world. There are few things in the world that are less subtle than a hammer, and we are instantly reminded of the old expression about taking a sledge hammer to crack a nut. One implication in the dream's content is that you being too heavy handed in your search for some kind of spiritual truth. This means that you run the risk of obscuring useful insights by your excessively vigorous approach to clearing away all of the material concerns that interfere with your inner progress. However, we can also see the hammer as a tool that can help us break through obstacles and blockages in our spiritual journey. The reduction of the value of this dream produces the number 3. This is a number associated with high levels of creativity, and so there is definite hope here that having realized the inefficiency of your current approach, you will find more suitable ways of discovering your inner self.

THE TREE OF LIFE Although you may have been unsuccessful in your attempts to achieve some form of spiritual insight this has not been due to any lack of effort or indeed of enthusiasm. The central letter in the compression of this dream's value is Tzaddi. This letter means "fish hook" and can be seen as quite literally suggesting that you are hooked on the spiritual path. Of course, such high levels of enthusiasm can lead to over energetic behaviour in your eagerness to access the spiritual insights that you are sure are waiting for you.

THE JOURNEY The biggest danger of over enthusiasm is not that we miss out on a useful kernel of wisdom but that we end up taking the entirely wrong path because it seems to offer more immediate answers to our burning questions. The final letter, Teth, in the compression of this dream's value, and indeed its presence in the spelling of the dream itself, points to the presence of the danger of such self-deception occurring. Your best chance of avoiding such a trap is for you to learn the benefits of relaxation and a slow approach to inner development. You should arrange to have some sessions of Indian head massage or some similar therapeutic treatment as this will help teach you to slow down!

HANDCUFFS

*azeekeem-azyqym-*אזיקים-168

MEANING Depending on your personal preferences, the image of handcuffs will either conjure ideas of arrest and a loss of personal freedom or a rather fun evening! In terms of the spiritual aspects of this dream, it is the idea of constraint and a loss of will that is significant. As is very often the case when we are looking at an individual's state of consciousness, the metaphorical handcuffs are self-imposed and not the result of any other person or higher force trying to prevent your further development. Indeed, we can see the letter Mem at the end of the word, which points to the nurturing energies of the Divine.

THE TREE OF LIFE Once we have broken free of the bounds of a wholly material perspective on the world, we can often feel suddenly overwhelmed by the enormous array of spiritual possibilities before us. There are so many potential explanations of the nonphysical dimension that range from the plausible to the down right wacky. You are now in the position of trying to find your way through this maze of belief, and as such are traversing the path of Qoph, which represents the sense of angst and anxiety that you are experiencing just now.

THE JOURNEY The letter Qoph occupies a central position in the spelling of this dream. While it may represent worry and concern, it is surrounded on each side by the letter Yod. This letter stands for the energizing force of the Divine and the spark that resides within each of us. This should act as a reassurance that you will prevail in your quest for spiritual truth. The means to unlocking your metaphorical handcuffs lies in meditation and a gradual acceptance of the reality of the spiritual. The preceding letter, Zayin, meaning "sword," does point to the need for you to struggle in order to reach your goals, while the initial Aleph tells you that this struggle will be more than worth it as it leads to a realization of the ultimate unity in the universe.

HANDSOME

*yefeh toar-yphh thvar-*יפה תואר-702

MEANING This dream represents both your current position in terms of your inner development and also points the way forward to much greater levels of spiritual insight and understanding. The spelling of the first word in this dream title points out that the Divine spark (Yod) within you is encouraging you to attempt to communicate (Peh) with the Divine in order to open a window (Heh) on the higher levels of reality. The overall value of this first word reduces to 5, and this indicates the state of consciousness to which you should be aspiring. The state of being indicated by this number is one in which the four elements within your inner self are ruled by the fifth element of Spirit.

THE TREE OF LIFE This dream contains references to the highest possible spiritual apsirations, but your current position is still relatively low on the Tree of Life. The purpose behind this dream is to spur you on to greater efforts and achievements. The value of the dream's title reduces to 9, which in the context of this dream relates to the Sefirah Yesod as this is the ninth Sefirah on the Tree of Life. The title itself also points to Yesod as it is in this Sefirah that we become particularly sensitive to the beauty and aesthetic appeal of the world around us.

THE JOURNEY It is certainly tempting to remain in the state of mind that is represented by Yesod. You have an awareness of the spiritual, but only at the level that inspires wonder and enjoyment. This Sefirah also encourages a certain tendency to self-aggrandizement, which while threatening to your further advancement is nonetheless a very pleasant feeling. The compression of this dream points out that in order to return to your spiritual home (Beth), you need to expose yourself to the possibility of great emotional suffering (Nun). In order then to begin to move forward, you should start to examine your own emotional makeup very closely, especially those areas that have caused you pain in the past.

HAT

kova-kvba'a-כובע-98

MEANING The value of this dream is equivalent to the value of the Hebrew word meaning "white." This color has long been associated with spiritual purity and is indeed the color most associated with the Sefirah of Keter. It may seem very strange that a dream about such a seemingly inconsequential item of clothing is connected with such lofty ideas of spirituality. However, we need to remember that in ancient times the wearing of a hat was a sign of authority and most often it was a sign of religious or priestly authority.

THE TREE OF LIFE This dream indicates that you are someone who has made a very definite com-

mitment to pursuing the goals of the Great Work. This is symbolized through the idea of you donning an item of clothing that represents a dedication to the spiritual path. When we reduce the value of this dream, we find the number 17. This number represents the energizing force of the Divine combined with the power of the mysterious. It is also the number of the Tarot card The Star. This card indicates the protection of higher forces and is linked to the path of Tzaddi. Your dream sits well on the path of Tzaddi, as it is all about the idea of being "hooked" on pursuing spiritual truths.

THE JOURNEY One of the words that shares its value with the value of this dream is the Hebrew word meaning "a temporary dwelling." In spiritual terms, this suggests that you will have to pass from one spiritual system to another as you advance in your spiritual understanding. This may also mean that as part of your advancement, you find yourself traveling much more or possibly even relocating. The most important thing for you to be doing right now is to read as voraciously as possible everything you can find in the whole arena of spiritual thought and tradition.

HATE

seenah-shynah-שינאה-366

MEANING There is nothing positive that can be said about the emotion of hatred, it is only ever a destructive state of mind that seeks only to cause harm to the hater and the object of that hatred. The initial letter in the spelling of this dream tells us that you have vast amounts of raw energy. What is more, you are also aware of the energizing Divine spark that lies deep within your soul. However, you have turned all this energy to very negative ends, and as a result your world right now is not a very happy or fulfilling one. This is indicated by the presence of the letter Nun as the central letter in the title of this dream.

THE TREE OF LIFE You are not someone who is unpleasant by nature, and so we need to discover the reason that would lead you to actually feel hatred. The answer lies in the fact that you have great enthusiasm for the spiritual quest as indicated by the presence of the letters Shin and Yod at the beginning of the spelling of this dream. Sometimes our enthusiasm for what is right can lead us to become judgmental of those around us. If this is allowed to go unchecked, then our judgmental feelings become stronger and our attitudes to those we are judging become increasingly hostile. This unfortunate situation is brought about by a false belief that you have the right to judge other people. Consequently, this dream belongs on the path of Teth, as this is the path that deals with issues of deception and the influence of the Serpent.

THE JOURNEY The final two letters in the spelling of this dream tells us that in order to have a glimpse of the Divine light (Heh), we need to appreciate the underlying unity (Aleph) of all aspects of the universe. Once we recognize that we are both separate and intrinsically linked with each and every other individual on the planet, we can see that to hate anyone else is to also hate a part of ourselves. The compression of the dream's value reminds you once again that you possess plenty of energy (Shin) to move forward in your life and also that there are people around you who do support (Samech) you. Your best chance of success is to spend a lot of time reflecting (Vav) on the reasons that you feel such negative emotions and how much better you would feel if you could convert these feelings into an acceptance both of our own imperfections and the imperfections of others.

HAWK

*nets-ntz-*צ̃ני*-140*

MEANING The hawk is a highly symbolic bird and this is a very encouraging dream. The hawk in ancient Egyptian culture represented the God Horus, who was the son of Osiris and went on to avenge the death of his father. In psychological terms, this dream might indicate someone becoming secure with their adulthood and the desire to overthrow their father shifting to a wish to protect him. However, from a spiritual point of view this dream points to your coming of age as a spiritually awakened individual. The value of this dream's title is associated with the value of Hebrew words relating to kingship. In your case the kingdom in question is your inner self.

THE TREE OF LIFE As this dream indicates, a specific aspect of your spiritual development is relatively easy to place it on the Tree of Life. You have reached a point where you could be said to be in control of your inner self. In other words, you have harmonized the four elements within your nature and are now ready to communicate with your higher self in order to come even closer to the Divine force itself. This development takes place in the Sefirah of Tiferet and it is here that we find your dream located.

THE JOURNEY When we reduce the value of this dream we find the number 5. This is a number with a long association with all forms of mysticism including Kabbalah. It is often symbolized by the five-pointed star or pentagram and represents the physical body when it is under the control of the fifth element of Spirit. Your task is to ensure that you maintain that level of control. You can achieve this by getting into the habit of practicing regular meditation. Additionally, you should begin to keep a journal where you analyze the events of each day and your reactions to them. You should assign the nature of your reaction to one of the four elements and check each week that overall you are continuing to manifest each of the four aspects of your nature in a roughly even way.

HEAD

*rosh-rash-*ראש*-501*

MEANING Traditionally, we have associated different parts of the body with particular personality traits. For instance, we would have referred to someone who is known for his moodiness as being "liverish." The head is the seat of the self as it is the location of both the brain and the key organs for interpreting the world and communicating with it, namely the eyes and the mouth. Additionally, the head is the seat of the highest chakra in Eastern meditation systems, and in practical Kabbalistic meditation we attempt to invoke the Divine force from the head downward. This dream suggests an individual with significant spiritual understanding and insight and should be seen as very encouraging.

THE TREE OF LIFE We can look at the Tree of Life in a number of different ways: We can see it as a representation of the emanation of the universe, the evolution of the individual soul, a map of the psyche, or as a representation of the physical body. In dreaming of the head you are unconsciously viewing the Tree of Life from the latter perspective. It is the Sefirah Keter that represents the head, and this is a highly appropriate Sefirah in which to locate this dream. It is not that you have sufficiently evolved in spiritual terms to be in a state of consciousness equivalent to Keter, but that you are so committed to the Great Work that you are receiving the protection and support that comes directly from the Divine itself.

THE JOURNEY The value of this dream is equivalent to that of the Hebrew word meaning "blessedness." This dream indicates that the efforts that you have made have resulted in a special connection between yourself and the higher. The reduction value yields the number 6. This is the value of the letter Vav, which relates to all matters concerning thought and reflection. The implication is that you should capitalize on this special relationship by engaging in regular meditative practice. In particular, you should begin to try to establish some form of dialogue between yourself and your higher self.

HELL

geyheenom-gyhynvm-גיהינום-124

MEANING Even in our secular and modern world, the concept of Hell can cause something to stir deep within us. Since the first people saw threatening shapes in the shadows cast by the flames of their fires on the walls of their caves, we have been adept at creating demons and dark terrors to haunt us. This dream does not require you either to believe or to reject the notion of a literal Hell. However, you should give some thought as to whether there is anything you feel guilty about and how you might resolve that feeling. Its importance as a dream is that it is symbolic of an absence of the Divine and refers to the inner pain associated with that absence. Although that feeling of abandonment can be very painful, you should see this as a positive dream as it is awakening you to the possibility of a spiritual aspect to reality.

THE TREE OF LIFE The value of this dream is equivalent to the value of the Hebrew word meaning "Eden." This may seem a strange analogy to the concept of Hell since Eden was an earthly paradise. However, the main significance of Eden is that humans were cast out of this paradise following their failure to abide by the laws of the Divine. The story of Eden can be taken as a metaphor for our own position in that we are all born into the wholly material Sefirah of Malkut. In this physical realm we are distanced from the Divine, until we choose to begin the slow and arduous climb back up to the crown of the Tree of Life. It is in Malkut that we locate this dream, as it is the position on the Tree that is farthest from the Divine force.

THE JOURNEY Dreaming of Hell is no fun, but it does demonstrate that you are now ready to try to build some kind of relationship with the higher source and to free yourself from a purely material outlook on the world. The compression of the dream indicates the best way for you to move on. Right now you are suffering the anxiety (Qoph) associated with the realization that you have no contact with the Divine. You need to find some practical ac-

tivity (Kaph) that will open the door (Daleth) to a communion with the Divine force. An ideal form of activity would be yoga or tai chi, as these exercises will benefit your body and your state of mind and develop your spiritual awareness.

HIDDEN

moostar-mvsthr-מוסתר-706

MEANING While it tends to be used in an exclusively supernatural context, the term *occult* literally means "hidden." This is because traditionally all forms of esoteric wisdom and knowledge had to be kept secret for fear of persecution of those who held such information. The dream also suggests that you should be looking for evidence of the spiritual within the day-to-day world. The reduction value of this dream is 13, which indicates that you are approaching a period of major change in your life. It is likely that this change will relate to your realizing a number of spiritual truths resulting from your commitment to your inner development.

THE TREE OF LIFE The compression of this dream's value reveals the letters Nun and Vav. While Nun indicates a significant level of suffering over the next few months, the final Vav indicates that your experiences will lead you to some significant reflections on the nature of your existence and your position within a spiritual universe. This dream relates to someone in the initial stages of his inner journey and it fits on the path of Tav. This is the first path that carries you up out of Malkut and, as it is associated with the planet Saturn, indicates a certain degree of melancholy that you will experience as you traverse this first path.

THE JOURNEY When we begin our spiritual journey, it seems that we will never achieve any significant level of insight because all the answers seem so deeply hidden. What is even more disconcerting is that often the questions themselves do not seem clear. Within the spelling of this dream title we see the letters Mem, Samech, and Resh. All of these relate in some way to the supporting and guiding influence of the Divine. You should see this as a sign of encouragement and try to focus on listening to your inner self rather than to your conscious concerns about a lack of obvious progress.

HIDE

or-a'avr-עור-276

MEANING Dreaming of a hide or an animal skin has all sorts of implications in the modern world, where the wearing of furs and skins is seen as highly immoral by the majority of the population. However, we should look at the image of a hide in a much more symbolic way and see it as a representation of a second skin that one might wear to emphasize or hide certain characteristics. It is worth noting that the value of the dream is equivalent to the value of the Hebrew word meaning "Moon." Many cultures associate the Moon with the notion of revealing our hidden and darker aspects. It is this association that leads to the link of the Moon with mythology and lycanthropy.

THE TREE OF LIFE The reduction value of this dream produces the number 6, which is the value of the letter Vav. In the context of this dream, the letter Vav is significant as it represents the element of Air when it appears to the sacred Tetragrammaton or four-letter name of God (YHVH). In looking for an appropriate placement on the Tree of Life, we now have the connection to the Moon and the link with the element of Air on which to base our decision. The Sefirah of Yesod represents the element of Air and is also the symbolic seat of the Moon, as it is concerned with matters of the imagination and the supernatural. This is a doubly appropriate location for this dream because it relates to the idea of trying, on new "skins," and it is in Yesod that we begin to experiment with the implications of a spiritual dimension to our lives.

THE JOURNEY In the compression of this dream's value we have the letter Resh, which represents the benevolent influence of the Divine, along with the letter Ayin, which indicates the ability to determine a very individual path through life. It is interesting and appropriate that both of these letters are also paths on the Tree that lead out of Yesod. The final Vav in the compression is advising you that you now need to make a choice between allowing your inner voice to select the way forward for you and attempting to carve a path based on your conscious ideas.

HISTORY

*heestoryah-hystvryh-*היסטוריה-305

MEANING Dreaming of history indicates an awareness of your links to the rest of the humanity. In spiritual terms, this suggests that you are beginning to understand the interconnected nature of all creation. The value of this dream is the same as that of a Hebrew phrase meaning a "very bright white light," which implies that this realization will come to you quite suddenly, almost like a revelation. The

idea of revelation is reflected in another way in that this dream also has an equivalent value to the phrase referring to "the end of days" in the Book of Daniel in the Hebrew Bible. This suggests that not only are you becoming aware of the continuity between the present and the past but that you are beginning to see that there is an unseen will moving behind the scenes of the world.

THE TREE OF LIFE The insights that you are now experiencing or are on the verge of experiencing are suggestive of a significant level of inner development. When we look at the reduction of this dream's value we see that it produces the number 8, which is the value of the letter Cheth. This letter refers to the need to protect and defend those things that are precious to us. This makes it an ideal path for this dream, as it refers both to the need for you to protect your growing understanding and to the protective force of the Divine.

THE JOURNEY The spiritual path is an arduous one and it does not get easier as you climb up the Tree of Life. However, the compression of this dream's value indicates that you have the spiritual strength (Shin) to achieve that longed-for glimpse (Heh) of the nature of the Divine. What you must do, though, is remember that every spiritual experience is unique to you as an individual. In the same way that you should protect your beliefs and not allow them to be denied by contrary views, you should not see any future experience as a basis for you to encourage others to think exactly as you do.

HOLIDAY

*khag-chg-*חג-11

MEANING With this dream we are again faced with a situation where the traditional meaning of a word differs from our current understanding of its significance. To people today, a holiday implies spending time away from home in new and hopefully sunny surroundings. Years ago, a holiday was only one day, and while it was a time for relaxation and fun, it also had great spiritual significance of some kind. This dream has a value of 11, and throughout the history of esoteric thought and mysticism the number 11 has stood for the most profound of mysteries. We can take from this a realization that this dream is about the holy nature of a holiday rather than the fun and frolics.

THE TREE OF LIFE When we reduce the value of this dream we find the number 2, which represents the notion of dualism. The concept of dualism underpins almost all Western philosophy and thought throughout history, until perhaps the last thirty or forty years. Put simply, it is a way of looking at the world in a very black-and-white way; we are good or we are bad, something is up or it is down, and so on. In order to realize the spiritual nature of reality, we have to move on so that we can see that most things are neither good nor bad and that up or down depends largely on where we are standing. This dream emphasizes the holy or spiritual over the physical and material. It does so in a very complex way that suggests you have already achieved a great deal in your spiritual work. The appropriate path for this dream is the path of Gimel. This is not only the letter that begins this dream title, but is a path where you will learn the secrets hidden behind the symbolism of the number 11.

THE JOURNEY This dream indicates a profound attachment to the Great Work and a real desire to achieve some form of communion with the Divine. When you dream of a holiday, your higher self is pointing out to you the importance of spiritual matters in your life. This is not a reminder to celebrate the religious holidays in your belief system in a proper manner, but a hint that you should see every day as a holiday in the traditional sense of the word. In other words, you should treat every day as a brand-new start and as an opportunity to put right anything that has gone amiss.

HONEY

dvash-dbsh-רבש-306

MEANING As soon as we think of honey in the context of the Kabbalah, we are reminded of the promise to the Hebrew people that they would finally come to a land flowing with milk and honey. It is important to note that while honey is highly nutritious, sweet, and tasty, its function in that ancient text is more symbolic. The value of "honey" is equivalent to the value of the Hebrew phrase meaning "merciful father." Thus, the promise to the tribes of Israel was not so much about the nature of their diet but about a future relationship with the Divine. Similarly, this dream refers to your potential relationship with the higher.

THE TREE OF LIFE This dream is about potential and is intended to spur you on to make a significant commitment to the Great Work. Because of this we can assume that it relates to a fairly early period in your spiritual development. This means that we are looking for one of the lower paths on the Tree of Life. The spelling of the dream title could be taken

to read that there is a door (Daleth) that opens into the house (Beth) of spiritual energy (Shin). This is another way of saying that you are on the threshold of accessing reserves of inner strength that will motivate you to make progress on your journey toward Truth. Of the lower paths that emanate up out of Malkut, the most appropriate to this dream is the path of Shin. It not only figures in both the spelling and compression of the dream's value but it is associated with the element of Fire and so represents a strong motivating force.

THE JOURNEY As is often the case, your way forward is indicated in the compression of the dream's value. You first need to find a way to access the spiritual energy that lies within you (Shin). You will be able to discover the best way to access this energy by reflecting (Vav) on a range of different spiritual systems and meditation techniques to find one right for you. If you begin to practice tai chi or perhaps Kundalini yoga with a qualified instructor, you will very quickly be able to locate the energy that you need. The discipline of yoga will also provide you with a framework within which to start thinking about spiritual matters. You should also remember that honey is sweet and can be seen as a symbol of the joy and enjoyment that you should be trying to find within your spiritual quest.

HOOD

meekhseh-myksh-מיכסה-135

MEANING The immediate response to a dream of a hood is to wonder what it is that is being hidden. Perhaps more appropriately, one wonders *who* is hiding beneath the hood. In this dream there is a definite sense of someone struggling in the darkness to try to discover that which lies veiled from ordinary sight. This is, of course, an excellent summary of the position of the practical Kabbalist. In your quest for spiritual truth you will experience a number of occasions when you feel as though you are floundering completely in the dark. A Hebrew word referring to a destitute female has the same value as this dream has. When we remember that wisdom is often characterized as female, we see that this shared value relates to the fact that right now you feel that in terms of any significant wisdom you are impoverished.

THE TREE OF LIFE Even when we begin our spiritual journey in the lowest Sefirah of Malkut we have access to more insights than we consciously realize. Very often these will present themselves to us as an intuition or simply a gut instinct that something is right. The idea that this dream represents, of being devoid of any understanding, is based on your insecurity rather than on the facts. When we reduce the value of this dream we find the number 9, which is the value of the letter Teth. This letter means "serpent" in Hebrew and always represents the idea of self-deception. It is the path of Teth that is the natural home of this dream. You should now be able to see that in its numerical value this dream is attempting to communicate that you are wrong in your belief that you have not made any advances in the Great Work.

THE JOURNEY While this dream may relate to a range of negative feelings that you are experiencing, it also holds promise for your future perception of your progress. The Hebrew word meaning "congregation" shares its value with the value of this dream. This implies that you will come to realize that rather than being alone and lost, you are part of a wide and unspoken fraternity of individuals all seeking to achieve some form of communion with the Divine. You can help yourself move closer to that realization by looking out for any local spiritual workshops or regular meetings of people interested in the metaphysical aspects of life.

HOOK
keres-qrs-קרס-360

MEANING In all mystical systems, geometric figures have enormous significance. In one sense it is their simplicity that adds something to their profundity as representations of the spiritual nature of the universe. The value of this dream is 360, which is, among other things, the number of degrees in a circle. In Kabbalistic terms the circle represents the oneness and the unity of the Divine, so this dream has great significance to you as a seeker of inner knowledge. In keeping with the paradoxical and unknowable nature of the Divine, this dream's value is equivalent to the value of the Hebrew word meaning "two." The number 2 refers to the way in which people tend to interpret the world as a system of opposites rather than as an interconnected and unified whole.

THE TREE OF LIFE Circles also have a symbolic value as signs of protection, and this dream is pointing you not only in the direction of a realization of the unified nature of creation but toward an understanding that the Divine will is protecting you and guiding you in your journey. The path of Samech represents the notion of the Divine as a guiding force, and this letter appears in the spelling and in

the compression of this dream's value. It is here that this dream is located, and, as this path leads into Tiferet, it is a sign that you are making significant progress.

THE JOURNEY You are in a very fortunate position in terms of your spiritual development right now, as you will find that the depth of your understanding increases out of all proportion to the level of effort you have to put in. This is the thanks to the supportive energies of the path of Samech. However, as the letter Shin within the dream indicates, you need to ensure that you have sufficient energy to keep pace with the insights you will be gaining. At a practical level, it would be a good idea to take a very close look at your diet to ensure that you are maintaining a level of physical fitness that will enable you to cope with the inevitable strain of the growth you are about to experience.

HORSE
soos-svs-סוס-126

MEANING Historically, horses were an indication of nobility for those who were fortunate enough to be able to ride them. In spiritual terms, then, this dream implies a certain standing or high level of insight on your part. However, there is a tendency among those who hold positions of authority in any society to believe themselves to be wiser than they actually are. Similarly, you need to avoid believing yourself to be more aware than you are of the nature of the Divine or of your purpose in spiritual terms. The possibility of this form of self-deception is indicated by the fact the reduction value of this dream is 9, which is also the value of the letter Teth, meaning "serpent."

THE TREE OF LIFE The notion of horses suggests a significant degree of power, but within a framework of control. Whereas some animals can be trained to the extent that they may be regarded as wholly tame, a horse always retains a degree of its wild nature. In this context the dream is very well suited to the path of Ayin. This path is most commonly associated with the goat, which signifies a high level of individuality, but it can equally be applied to a horse. Additionally, the path of Ayin is suggestive of the strength of will that is emphasized by the positive aspect of the letter Teth, which we find in the reduction of this dream's value.

THE JOURNEY Left alone, a horse will run wildly at great speed but with no discernible direction. Similarly, unless it is carefully focused and directed, your energy and enthusiasm will have a tendency to lack direction. You have a certain awareness of this potential as shown by the letter Qoph in the compression of this dream's value, which indicates anxiety and concern. The final two letters of the compression advise you to make sure that you are as thoughtful (Vav) as you are energetic and enthusiastic. A good way to channel that enthusiasm would be a practical (Kaph) project. This could be to construct in your home a particular space for yourself that is set aside solely for spiritual activity.

HOSPITAL
bet kholeem-byth chvlym-בית חולים-506

MEANING None of us likes to feel ill, and we are even less fond of being unwell, particularly to the extent of needing to go to the hospital. This dream can be quite unsettling to us when we first awake. Indeed, it maybe very difficult to shift the notion that in some way this dream functioned as a warning that you are about to become in need of serious medical treatment. This is where a book about dream analysis can be more than simply interesting, as it can stop you from enduring unnecessary stress. This dream is actually about your ability and willingness to care for others rather than about any problem you are about to experience. That said, it would of course be a good idea to get a simple checkup just to alleviate your concerns.

THE TREE OF LIFE When we look at the value of this dream as Kabbalists we see a very significant numerical arrangement. We have the numbers 5 and 6 separated by a 0. The number 5 indicates a person who has balanced the elements within himself and is now ruled by the fifth element of Spirit. The number 6 in this arrangement represents the holy hexagram as seen in Solomon's seal or the so-called Star of David. The circle, or 0, stands for the unknowable nature of the Divine. Taken as a phrase presented to us in symbols, this is a message indicating that you are now ready to move beyond Tiferet and seek to commune with the higher through the agencies of the mysterious Divine. The best location for this dream is on the path of Gimel, which leads directly into the source of the Divine will.

THE JOURNEY The task you must now undertake in order to make the potential experience of the Divine into a reality is laid out for you both in the literal content and in the compression of the value of this dream. You have dreamed of a hospital because in order to refine your higher nature you need to spend time engaging in some activity that is designed

to help and assist others. The letter Kaph in the dream's compression also points to the need for you to get involved in some kind of practical activity, while the final Vav suggests that you also need to reflect carefully on the impact of your help not just on others but on your own sense of self.

HOTEL
malon-mlvn-מלון-126

MEANING The value of the Hebrew word meaning "hotel" is the same as the value of the word meaning "horse," which is discussed above. It is difficult to see what connection there is between a hotel and a horse. However, this is because the appropriate question to ask is, What is the symbolic relationship between a hotel and a horse? We can then see that both are associated with leisure, a certain level of life-style and luxury, and both can, in different ways, be a means to suggest that you need to pay closer attention to the wholly spiritual side of life. Both images are also concerned with transition and travel, which suggests that you have the potential to be in a state of positive spiritual development.

THE TREE OF LIFE The initial letter in the spelling of this dream title is Mem, which we usually interpret as standing for the maternal influence of the Divine. However, one of the aspects of Kabbalah that separates it from other, more recent systems of spiritual analysis, such as numerology, is the fact that one cannot simply read an interpretation out of a formula. Kabbalistic interpretation is both an art and a science, relying on experience and inner insight as much as knowledge for its results. In the context of this dream, the letter Mem refers to the sense of being pampered that comes from indulging yourself in a luxurious life-style. Consequently, this dream belongs in the Sefirah of Malkut, as you have yet to move beyond a concern with the material side of life.

THE JOURNEY The fact that you had this dream indicates that the attraction of the merely physical is beginning to pale. This idea is supported by the presence of the letter Qoph in the compression of the dream's value, as this points to anxiety. The following letter, Kaph, suggests that the way to escape this anxiety and to stimulate some useful reflection (Vav) on the nature of your spiritual makeup would be to take some kind of practical action. As your biggest obstacle is your tie to the luxuries of the world, a good step to take would be to give away some of your favorite luxury items to those around you. Taking the luxury of travel into account, it would also be useful to go away on some kind of spiritual retreat.

HOUSE

bayeet-byth- בית-412

MEANING On the surface this appears to be a very prosaic dream. After all, what can be the importance of dreaming about a pile of bricks and mortar? In fact, this dream is hugely significant and points to the fact that you have already collected a great store of spiritual understanding. The value of this dream is equivalent to that of the Hebrew word meaning "to long for," and it is this powerful desire for some form of enlightenment that has spurred you on in your search for some form of inner truth. Christian Kabbalists would be very quick to point out that the value of this dream is also equivalent to a Hebrew phrase referring to Jesus. However, even without this connection, the dream stands as a symbol of your commendable progress.

THE TREE OF LIFE There is only one path to which this dream can belong. The letter Beth appears in the spelling and in the compression of this dream's value. Further, the letter Beth is the Hebrew word for "house," and so in a sense even the title of this dream is the letter Beth. The path of Beth runs directly into Keter and so represents the potential for direct communion with the Divine itself. You need to prepare yourself as this direct interaction may occur at any time.

THE JOURNEY The path of Beth is very closely linked to ideas of family and domesticity. In spiritual terms this translates as an approach to the Divine that is as concerned with correct and considerate behavior to others as it is with the solitary search for insight. In the value of the dream we have the number 400, which refers to the letter Tav and in this context indicates the sorrow associated with self-sacrifice. Additionally we have the value 12 following the 400, and this is associated with The Hanged Man in the tarot and ideas of altruistic activity. It is clear that in order to encourage a communion with the Divine, you need to find some cause that you can give all your energy to in order to benefit others.

HUGGING

lekhabek-lchbq- להבק-140

MEANING It doesn't happen that often, but in analyzing this dream the Kabbalist and the psychol-

ogist would probably be in general agreement about its significance. To have a dream of hugging is a clear indication that you are comfortable with your emotions and are in touch with your feelings in a very positive way. This dream also indicates that you wish to share your general feelings of benevolence and warmth with everyone around you. The emergence of a capacity for unconditional love is a sure sign that you are making good progress in the Great Work.

THE TREE OF LIFE In one sense, every path is related to some notion of love. This is because the Tree of Life is a means of distinguishing between different aspects of the Divine as it is manifested in the universe. Since the fundamental basis of the Divine is Love, it stands to reason that each path can be seen as a form or type of Divine love. However, in terms of your development, this dream relates to the Sefirah of Netzach. It is there that each of us must learn to balance his emotional makeup in order to move on to Tiferet with a personality that has an inner harmony. There may be someone whom you would like to hug, and you should allow yourself both to do this and to feel comfortable about it.

THE JOURNEY The compression of this dream's value shows us that you are somewhat anxious (Qoph) and that this anxiety stems from a strong desire to express your benevolent feelings in a way that will offer protection and comfort to others (Mem) and make a real difference to their lives. The reduction value shows you what you are aiming to achieve while in the Sefirah of Netzach. The reduced value is 5, which is the number of the individual who has balanced all the elements within himself and is now ruled by the fifth element of Spirit. In order to fully balance your emotional makeup you should seriously consider having at least a few sessions with a therapist, as this will greatly assist your understanding of your emotional nature. Additionally, tai chi is a practice you might consider, as it will help greatly with your sense of physical and emotional well-being.

HUNGER

raav-ra'ab- רעב-272

MEANING One of the key factors of the Kabbalistic approach to mysticism is that it always takes into account the context of whatever situation or words it is seeking to analyze. This is one of the reasons that the Kabbalah is so much richer and complex than many of the New Age systems of mysticism that we see so much of today. This dream highlights the importance of context. To a person viewing the dream from a nonspiritual point of view, the image of hunger would suggest either someone in a state of great suffering or simply a failure to recognize a greedy or gluttonous nature. However, as soon as we put this dream into a spiritual context it becomes clear that it refers to a hunger for some form of revelation of truth, or in other words nourishment for the soul.

THE TREE OF LIFE The value of this dream is equivalent to that of a Hebrew word meaning "injure." While it would be too strong to suggest that this dream indicates that you will be suffering from an injury, there is a definite sense that some external force is goading you on. While the effect of this force is ultimately beneficial, it is not a particularly pleasant experience to deal with. This dream belongs on the path of Lamed because this path relates to the sterner motivating force of the Divine and because the meaning of the letter Lamed is "ox-goad." This is directly relevant to the dream since it revolves around a goading and motivating force.

THE JOURNEY The numerical arrangement of this dream's value indicates your current state of mind. The central 70 connects to the letter Ayin and points to an urge within you to plow ahead on your great journey with a vigorous enthusiasm that has far too much momentum to be interrupted by the views of others. However, flanking this number on both sides is the number 2. In the context of this dream, the repeated 2's relate to the idea of duality. A dualistic vision of the world where things are either on or off, good or bad, true or false is very much the mainstream rational way of looking at the world. Thus, on one hand we have a desire for individualism and on the other a need to follow the accepted way of perceiving reality. What you need to do is find a way to disregard the constraining voices represented by the repeated 2. The energy of the ox-goad will help you by driving you on to look at matters in a spiritual light. You can assist the energy of Lamed by making a point of viewing each event, no matter how trivial, as in some way a symbolic pointer to the nature of the Divine. If you do this or even attempt to, you will find that your hunger begins to be met by an awareness of the presence of the Divine.

See Zohar symbol, Hunger.

HUNTING

*latsood-ltzvd-*לצוד*-130*

MEANING You have a pronounced competitive streak to your nature right now. However, the win-

ning is not nearly as important to you as the excitement of being involved in a clash of wills. This tendency to compete will translate across into your approach to the spiritual quest. You will progress with greater speed if you find a way to view the Great Work as an adventure. The value of this dream is equivalent to that of the Hebrew word meaning "ladder," and this refers to the ladder of the Tree of Life. As long as you can maintain an element of excitement to your approach, you will be able to climb that ladder with relative ease.

THE TREE OF LIFE The letters Lamed and Tzaddi in this dream's spelling indicate a particularly vigorous personality. Although the common perception of the mystical individual is someone of a quiet and introspective nature, there are definite advantages to being more assertive and active. For instance, your vigorous nature means that you have a dogged determination to succeed. The path of Ayin neatly sums up the characteristics that are represented in this dream, and it is no accident that the value of this dream is also equivalent to the value of the Hebrew word Ayin, meaning "eye."

THE JOURNEY In the spelling of this dream title we see the initial letter Lamed, indicating that your abundant enthusiasm comes in part from the driving force of your higher self. The subsequent letter, Tzaddi, encourages you remain committed to your spiritual quest. It is very important, though, that as well as enjoying your adventure in the world of spirit you also find time to reflect (Vav) on the implications of the insights you are gaining. If you engage in some serious thought, you will find that you will be able to open the door (Daleth) to your higher self. An ideal spiritual activity that will both maintain a sense of adventure and encourage some serious reflection would be some form of martial art.

HURRICANE

*soofah-svphh-*סופה*-151*

MEANING The nature of the Divine has been traditionally described in relation to a number of natural forces. The hurricane is no exception to this and in many ways it does represent an excellent depiction of the Divine force. At the center of the hurricane is a space that is perfectly calm, while all around it the most intense forces rage. This signifies the notion that the core of the Divine does not move, no matter how chaotic the world or the universe appears to us from the outside. The value of this dream reduces to 7, which indicates that you are approaching an extremely profound moment in your spiritual development.

THE TREE OF LIFE Mystical experiences can occur in a number of ways, and while we might expect them to be wholly uplifting moments in our lives, the reality is that glimpses of enlightenment are often associated with periods of deep sorrow. When we look at the arrangement of numbers in the value of this dream we see that the number 1, referring to the essential unity of the Divine, stands at both ends of the dream's value. However, the central number is 50, which refers to the letter Nun. The emotional states associated with Nun are melancholy and sorrow. This is the path on which this dream belongs, but it should not be seen as a negative sign, since it is through sorrow that you will be exposed to a spiritual revelation.

THE JOURNEY Although the next few months will be akin to being whirled around on an emotional hurricane, the initial letter Samech tells you that the protective force of the Divine will be there to support you. In order to get through this difficult period you should remember that central core of calm that sits at the heart of every hurricane and try to reflect this in your state of mind. The presence of the letter Peh in the spelling of the dream title should be seen as very good advice that you should talk to those close to you about your feelings.

HURT

leefgoa-lphgva'a-לפגוע-189

MEANING The dream of being hurt is not so much about the actuality of physical harm but about the fear of experiencing pain of some sort. In spiritual terms this dream refers to a strong sense of doubt within the dreamer that he is making any progress in his spiritual quest. It is likely that this doubt stems largely from your wish to discover your own approach to the Divine, as represented by the presence of the letter Ayin in the dream title, which contrasts with the initial letter, Lamed, which points to an external force driving your spiritual approach.

THE TREE OF LIFE When we reduce the value of this dream we find the number 18, which is associated with The Moon card in the tarot. This card represents anxieties and self-doubt. Additionally, it is attributed to the path of Qoph on the Tree of Life. When we look at the compression of the value of this dream we see that the first letter is Qoph. This emphasizes that the correct location for this

dream lies on this path. As the path of Qoph is one of the first routes out of Malkut, you should not feel discouraged that you are having worries about your spiritual development, as this is only normal at this early stage in your journey.

THE JOURNEY The key to coping with the inevitable anxiety associated with your first tentative steps on the ladder out of Malkut lies within the compression of the value of this dream. You need to accept that you have a whole range of doubts and concerns (Qoph). The way to deal with them is to find a group of like-minded people such as a meditation circle and share your anxieties with them. Communication (Peh) will lead to greater understanding of yourself and the nature of the Divine. Finally, the letter Teth warns against allowing your anxiety to lead you into the trap of accepting any system that offers easy but ultimately unfulfilling answers in your spiritual quest.

HUSBAND

baal-ba'al-בעל-102

MEANING From a psychological point of view, this dream would probably be seen as an indication that you are searching for some form of permanent emotional relationship. In Kabbalistic terms, the word *husband* has quite a profound implication. The Sefirah of Malkut is often referred to as the Bride of Keter. This of course suggests that Keter is the husband that those who are beginning to develop a spiritual awareness should be dreaming of. The value of this dream is equivalent to that of the Hebrew words meaning "trust" and "truth." These are, of course, excellent qualities to look for in a spouse but they also reflect the qualities of the Divine that we should seek to emulate in our day-to-day lives.

THE TREE OF LIFE The reduction value of this dream produces the number 3, which is the value of the letter Gimel. The path of Gimel runs directly into Keter, which is the closest that we can come to a direct understanding of the nature of the Divine. However, the title of the dream implies an aspiration rather than an achievement, so the letter Gimel is there to encourage you to persevere in your inner development. The key clue to the location of this dream lies in the status of Malkut as the Bride of Keter, as it is in Malkut that we find this dream, and this Sefirah also represents your current level of spiritual development.

THE JOURNEY It is extremely positive that you are already dreaming about the highest possible spiritual achievement. The presence of the letter Qoph in the compression of this dream's value also indicates that this enthusiasm and optimism is tempered by an understandable degree of anxiety and uncertainty about the path that lies ahead of you. The final letter in the compression is Beth, which literally means "house" and it is to be seen as a promise from the higher that if you persist in your endeavors you will ultimately enter the house of the Divine.

HYPOCRITE

*tsavooa–tzbva'a–*צבוע*-168*

MEANING Nobody likes to be called a hypocrite, but when we are asleep we do not have the presence of our ego to soften the blows of what unconsciously we know is true about our behavior and attitudes. It is worth remembering that while religion can often be used as something of an emotional crutch, the mystical path is a testing and difficult road to travel. In order to successfully complete our journey, we have to be prepared to face ourselves with total honesty.

THE TREE OF LIFE In the normal sense of the word, we expect a hypocrite to be someone who argues for one form of life-style but whose life-style is entirely contrary to the values that he claims to believe in. In a spiritual context, we see this dreaming as indicating that you have reached a level of understanding where you know what is the correct approach to take to your life but have not yet been able to act on this knowledge. When we reduce the value of this dream we find the number 15, which is the number associated with The Devil card in the tarot. This card tends to point to an unhealthy attachment to the physical comforts and desires in life. This leads to a self-deception in which we believe that we are making progress and we do not need to worry about our materialism. For this reason, the dream of hypocrisy belongs on the path of Teth in its negative aspect.

THE JOURNEY The fact that you are dreaming of hypocrisy suggests that you are beginning to realize at least on some level that there is a conflict between your beliefs and your behavior. Within the compression of this dream the letters Samech and Cheth indicate that the force of the Divine is still with you as a source of both support and protection. In order to take advantage of this assistance you must remain committed to the Great Work and all that it requires. This means learning to see the relative unimportance of your possessions. You can rein-

force this insignificance by giving away some of your favorite items to charitable organizations.

ICE

*kerakh–qrch–*קרח*-308*

MEANING When we think of ice we tend to think of the negative aspects of winter. Ice calls to mind the cold, the frostbite, the long dark nights. This is in direct contrast to the mental images that we associate with snow, as snow has much happier and cozy mental associations. However, as is often the case, the Kabbalistic interpretation of the dream is significantly more complex. The value of this dream is equivalent to that of a Hebrew word meaning "daybreak," and this in itself indicates a positive nature to the message hidden with the dream's value. Indeed, it suggests that a higher level of understanding is about to "dawn" on you. However, right now you are in a state of spiritual stagnation and need to find some way to thaw out your approach to the Divine so that you may benefit from the warmth of its presence.

THE TREE OF LIFE Ice is frozen water. The element of Water in the Tree of Life is represented by the Sefirah of Hod. This is the Sefirah that relates to our mental processes, and the suggestion in this dream is that you are about to find a way to refocus your thinking about the world. This shift in thought will lead to a dawning of a better understanding of the Divine. The placement of the dream in Hod is supported by the compression of the dream's value. We are presented with the two numbers, 300 and 8. While the 8 indicates Hod, since this is the eighth Sefirah on the Tree of Life, the number 300 is the value of the letter Shin, which tells the path by which you came to your present position on the Tree.

THE JOURNEY If Hod is associated with water, we have to ask ourselves why in your case the energies of Hod are represented by ice. The transition of a liquid to a solid results from the reduction of movement at the molecular level. One could say the solid form of any element represents its most stable aspect. If ice is water in its most organized and ordered form, the indication is that you need to introduce a greater degree of order and organization into your mental processes. A good way to introduce this stability would be to begin to map out your thoughts and beliefs on paper and try to make links between different ideas. From the point of view of learning to allow yourself to melt a little in the face of the spiritual dimension of the universe it might also be helpful to try a range of relaxation therapies.

IDEA

rayon–ra'ayvn–רעיון–346

MEANING It is a simple truism to say that every good system or product must begin with a good idea. However, in the modern world it is all too easy to forget that every single item we see at the mall was at one time no more than an idea in somebody's mind. One of the distinctive features of a mystical approach to the Divine is that it relies upon us having our own ideas and then testing them out. This is perhaps one of the biggest differences between a Kabbalistic spiritual path and a mainstream religious approach. The value of this dream is equivalent to the value of the Hebrew word meaning a "spring." This connection emphasizes the vital and life-giving nature of ideas. It also suggests a great burst of enthusiasm on your part.

THE TREE OF LIFE If we reduce the value of this dream we find the number 4. This number is associated with all things physical and tends to indicate the Sefirah of Malkut in terms of a position on the Tree of Life. This may seem a peculiar location for this dream, given the immense amount of energy and creativity that is suggested by its value and associated Hebrew words. However, the first step on any journey always requires the greatest effort, so it is actually not surprising that this dream is linked with images of springs bursting from the ground.

THE JOURNEY Congratulations! This dream is a sure sign that you are beginning to awaken to your inner potential. All you need to do is to maintain that level of enthusiasm you feel deep within yourself. The value of this dream is equivalent to that of the Hebrew word meaning "willpower," and this is the key to your future success on your spiritual journey. No matter how talented, enthusiastic, or well placed we may be, the only means to achieve our goal is to persist in our efforts.

IDIOT

metoomtam–mtvmtm–מטומטם–144

MEANING Before assuming that this dream suggests that you lack significant knowledge, you should remember that almost all religious and spiritual texts refer to the wisdom of the fool. This means not that we should aspire to a lack of intelligence but that we should try to retain the innocence and lack of cynicism that both children and the stereotypical fool possess. The value of this dream's title is equivalent to that of the Hebrew word meaning "east," and the east was traditionally the direction one faced when meditating or praying for inspiration. Additionally, as the Sun rises in the east, this can be seen as another subtle pointer to the need to look at everything around you as something new and wondrous.

THE TREE OF LIFE The spelling of this dream title is dominated by the letter Mem. As it appears there three times and again in the compression of the dream, it is appropriate that we locate the dream on this path. This positioning emphasizes the compassionate and giving nature that is associated with an individual in a state of genuine innocence. The path of Mem is associated with The Hanged Man card in the tarot, which also represents deep generosity to the extent of self-sacrifice. It is worth noting that The Hanged Man is the twelfth card in the tarot and this dream's value is equivalent to 12 multiplied by itself.

THE JOURNEY In order to continue your inner progress you need to emulate the qualities that are so strongly emphasized by the values within this dream. You should also be aware that the letter Mem's repeated appearance is matched by the double presence of the letter Teth. Teth warns us to be on lookout for deception usually in the form of self-delusion. In the context of this dream, the most probable risk is that you may begin to believe you are more entitled to spiritual enlightenment than those around you due to your altruistic behavior. To feel like this is to devalue the nature of your unselfish acts, so you should be on your guard against such developing attitudes.

IDLE

batel–btl–בטל–41

MEANING It would be very easy to analyze this dream in psychological terms and view it as a representation of your frustration with a perceived lack of direction in your life. This would seem to make sense from a commonsense point of view. The Kabbalistic interpretation of this dream is rather different, though. The first thing we should notice is that the value of this dream is a prime number (prime numbers can be divided only by themselves and by one). Symbolically, a prime number emphasizes the unique nature of the individual. It requires a certain level of spiritual advancement to reach this position of uniqueness, so the dreamer should not be frustrated with his progress.

THE TREE OF LIFE When we reduce the value of this dream we find the number 5. This number represents an individual who has mastered the four physical elements of Fire, Air Earth, and Water within himself. The fifth element of Spirit is now the ruling influence on such a person's personality. This again indicates a high level of spiritual understanding that would not follow if the dreamer really was idle. However, the Sefirah of Tiferet is a very restful place to stay, as having contacted our higher self we can believe that we have no need to progress further.

THE JOURNEY The value of this dream is equivalent to that of a Hebrew phrase meaning "to go around in circles." This is exactly what you will be doing if you choose not to try to push ahead with the Great Work. The central letter in the spelling of this dream title is Teth, which means "serpent" and is associated with self-deception. In following the letter Beth, which means "house," it is advising that you are wrong to believe that you have already reached your spiritual home. The final letter, Lamed, indicates that you will need a very strong external force to motivate you to continue your search for communion with the Divine. However, while you might not be expecting to experience such a driving force, you can be assured that it will come to you and when it does you will immediately recognize it. It is, however, dependent on your starting the ball rolling by becoming more active and focused in your approach to the spiritual quest.

IDOL
eleel-alyl-אליל-71

MEANING Many of us have heard the story of the Israelites turning to idol worship in the absence of Moses. However, the argument against idol worship is a common one in a great deal of religions. In terms of your spiritual development, the idea of an idol represents the difference between seeking out the Divine as it is and creating a God of your own. It is very tempting to construct an idea of God when we feel certain that our ideas are authentic and valid. However, as soon as we try to create a fixed image or idol of the Divine force, we are unwittingly attempting to reduce its power. One of the crucial aspects of the Divine is that it is utterly beyond human comprehension, and to create an image of God is to reduce the Divine to the status of a prop to human existence. At a more practical level, you should consider whether there is anyone in your life directly or indirectly whom you are in danger of idolizing. This

is not healthy either for you or for the object of your admiration.

THE TREE OF LIFE The letter Lamed appears twice in this dream title, and it certainly would be helpful for you to experience the sterner aspect of the higher right now. However, the dream itself does not belong to the path of Lamed. It is in the compression of the dream that we find the correct path of this dream, which is Ayin. In its positive aspect the path of Ayin points to an individual who is able to carve out his own route to the Divine with great vigor and strength. However, in its negative aspect the path of Ayin refers to someone who insists on clinging to his personal view of the Divine without listening to or considering other interpretations.

THE JOURNEY The Kabbalistic system encourages individuals to form their own opinions about the nature of the universe. However, these views should be formed as a result of sincere prayer or meditation. In this dream we are looking at someone who has preconstructed a notion of the Divine before engaging with the Great Work itself. To have preconceived ideas in any form of investigation is always dangerous as it removes the open-minded attitude that is essential for valid exploration of the inner self.

❧ILLNESS
kholeh-chvlh-חולה-49

MEANING We all hate to be ill, even if it is not a serious condition. Feeling unwell affects not just our body but our ability to work, to have fun, and to live our lives the way we want to. In spiritual terms, the idea of illness should be seen as a sense that in some way we are failing to make the right connections with our higher self. When we reduce the value of this dream we find the number 13. This number relates to change in your life and suggests that you are about to find a way to a more successful relationship with your higher self.

Traditional Kabbalists might view this dream as a health warning, suggesting at a practical level that it would be a good idea to check your health and that of your loved ones.

THE TREE OF LIFE This dream is plainly about anxieties in relation to your spiritual progress. When we first begin to explore our inner selves, we often find that many doubts plague us. These can range from a feeling that we are not suitable for the

Great Work to feeling that perhaps we have let our imagination run away with us. The mental stress that is often experienced by the newcomer to spiritual matters is represented by the path of Qoph, which is where this dream is correctly located.

THE JOURNEY If you pay very close attention to your intuition you will be able to sense a reassuring presence trying to remind you that everybody has the opportunity to achieve some form of communication with his higher self. This encouraging idea is represented by the letter Mem in the compression of this dream's value. However, you also need to be aware of the presence of the letter Teth in the compression. This letter points to the potential for self-deception. You are most at risk from falsely believing yourself to be moving in the right direction at those times when the alternative is to see yourself as failing in some way. The best way to avoid falling into this trap is to find a group of like-minded people and begin to explore the world of the unknown as a team.

ILLUMINATION

*teoorah-thavrh-*תאוורה*-*612

MEANING One of the greatest and longest-running conspiracy theories is that of the Bavarian Illuminati. This mythical body is supposed to be a secret occult fraternity. The term *illuminati* refers to the idea of illumination in the spiritual sense. The use of the term *illumination* refers to the traditional view of spiritual enlightenment as being akin to the light of the Divine descending on the individual. In Eastern mysticism there is also a system of spiritual illumination that relies on the individual energizing his inner soul to leap up rather than on encouraging the Divine light to reach down. It is no accident that in the Kabbalah the path that climbs up along the Tree of Life is known as the Serpent Path and that the value of this dream reduces to the number 9; this is also the value of the letter Teth, which literally means "serpent."

THE TREE OF LIFE When we achieve spiritual illumination we awaken the Divine spark within ourselves. In the sacred Tetragrammaton, as the four-lettered name of God is known, the initial creative spark is represented by the letter Yod. Similarly, in terms of individuals our Divine spark is also represented by the letter Yod. When we look at the compression of this dream's value we see that the central letter is Yod, and this is the path to which this dream belongs. This dream relates to your acti-

vating your soul and the path of Yod refers to that process.

THE JOURNEY You have already made significant progress in the Great Work and are now ready to make a major leap toward some form of direct communication with the Divine. In the compression of the dream's value the two letters that flank the symbol of your soul are Mem and Beth. While Mem points to the protective influence of the higher, the letter Beth should be seen as a reminder that there is a place waiting for you in the house of the Divine. The values in this dream place great emphasis on the idea of achieving spiritual insight by raising one's soul toward God. This is the approach taken by Kundalini yoga and it is likely that you will achieve excellent results if you try this method of meditation. It is important to note the Kundalini yoga must be taught by an experienced practitioner, as it has some very powerful effects that can be distressing or even dangerous if not learned properly.

IMAGE

*demoot-dmvth-*דמות*-*450

MEANING Now more than ever before we live in a world that is often far more concerned with image than with substance. As long as a product looks right, it is guaranteed at least a reasonable level of success. By contrast, there have been plenty of perfectly good products that have failed simply because they did not have the right appearance. If it is important in our day-to-day life to try to spot the difference between the reality and the appearance of things, it is absolutely crucial in the spiritual quest to make this distinction. The value of this dream is equivalent to that of the Hebrew word meaning "cunning," and this is a direct reference to those forces in the universe that would be more than happy for you to be taken in by false appearances.

THE TREE OF LIFE This dream belongs to the Sefirah of Yesod. This Sefirah, also referred to as the "Foundation," is the first resting place we come to on our journey of inner discovery. While Yesod does reflect an initial level of development, it is also the Sefirah associated with the glamour and mystery of the supernatural. If we are not careful, we can be blinded by the glamour and fail to see the more profound messages that lie beneath. The reduction value of this dream gives us the number 9, which is the number of this Sefirah. Additionally, the letter Tav, the path by which you enter the Sefirah of

Yesod, is present in both the compression and the spelling of this dream title.

THE JOURNEY The task that lies before you in order to progress in terms of your understanding is to find the guidance and truths that lie hidden away within a broad range of spiritual and religious writings. The key to finding these truths is to disregard the obvious meaning or image and try to penetrate the words to find their symbolic and universal significance. This is not an easy challenge to take on, and the presence of the letter Nun in the compression of this dream's value indicates that at times you will find yourself doubting that you are getting anywhere. However, at all times you need to remember that this is still a better position to be in than to be falsely believing yourself to be in possession of the truth.

IMITATION
kheekoy-chyqvy- חיקוי -134

MEANING As the saying goes, imitation is the sincerest form of flattery. In terms of our spiritual development, one of the ways in which we can progress is by attempting to develop the qualities and attitudes that we find in individuals who represent high levels of spiritual achievement. When we reduce the value of this dream we find the number 8. This is the value of the letter Cheth, which means "fence" and indicates a desire to protect or defend ourselves. By imitating the behavior of people we believe to be the epitome of spirituality, we are protecting ourselves from the danger of taking the wrong path in our quest for spiritual understanding.

THE TREE OF LIFE As your experience increases you will feel much more confident about your ability to determine your way through the maze of spirituality. This dream suggests that you are still very much in the early stages of your explorations as you still have a very strong need to be guided by the example of others. The path of Peh is associated with all forms of communication. In attempting to follow the examples of others who have gone before you, you are engaging in a communication with those more enlightened individuals, so this is an appropriate path on which to locate this dream.

THE JOURNEY The value of this dream is equivalent to that of the Hebrew word meaning "fire." As one of the four elements, Fire represents our passions and emotions. This numerical connection of the word *fire* to your dream tells us that you have a huge passion for the Great Work, and this suggests that your commitment and enthusiasm will lead you to the accomplishment of your goals. In order to begin to move forward, you should try to rely on your own intuition and ideas to determine the right way to respond to any situation.

INCANTATION
lehaalot beov-lha'alvth bavb- להעלות באוב -552

MEANING Usually when we analyze a dream from a Kabbalistic perspective we are searching for the hidden spiritual relevance within what appears to be a perfectly ordinary dream sequence. In this dream, though, the spiritual aspect is immediately evident. Clearly you are someone for whom the Great Work is of paramount importance. The reduction value of this dream generates the number 12, and this number is associated with self-sacrifice and a surrendering of our own desires and ambitions in favor of the spiritual path or of the needs of those around us. Given the overtly mystical nature of the title of this dream, it is clear that the self-sacrifice relates to a focus on the higher rather than on other individuals.

THE TREE OF LIFE An incantation is an attempt to engage in some kind of dialogue with a spiritual being. The fact that incantations rely on very precise wording and repeated chanting of a predetermined script serves to highlight the verbal nature of this particular attempt to make contact with the Divine. In the Hebrew alphabet each letter has a specific meaning, and the meaning of the letter Peh is "mouth." Additionally, the path of Peh on the Tree of Life is associated with communication in all its forms, so it is the ideal path on which to locate this dream.

THE JOURNEY From your dream it is clear that your higher self is trying to encourage you to be more ambitious in your spiritual work. It is likely that up to now you have been doing much reading and thinking about the nature of the Divine but have steered clear of any attempt to translate your thoughts into definite actions. In the compression of the dream's value we have the letter Kaph in its final form. This acts to emphasize strongly the need for you to take some practical steps toward discovering your higher self. The subsequent letter, Nun, warns you that this will inevitably involve a challenge to your faith, but the letter Beth holds out the promise of a return to your spiritual home as a way of encouraging you to persevere.

INCENSE

*ketoret-qtvrth-*קטורת-715

MEANING It used to be commonly believed that the burning of incense increased the spiritual purity of any event from an act of public worship to a private meditation. This was thought to be because the smell of the appropriate incense was in some way pleasing to the Divine. In the modern world such ideas are often rejected as extremely superstitious. However, incense still has a part to play in the spiritual quest, if only because it still tends to help to put the individual into a state of consciousness that is more amenable to spiritual insight.

THE TREE OF LIFE Many people with years of experience in meditation or other forms of mystical practice will tell you that incense is entirely superfluous to any attempt to contact the higher self. In a sense this is certainly true, as the higher powers have no set of physical conditions that must be complied with before they will deign to appear. However, an enormous part of the spiritual journey is the training of the mind and the inner self to achieve certain states of consciousness. Particularly in the early stages there are a number of "props" that can help you to achieve these crucial mental states. As well as being helpful, they add a certain atmosphere to the proceedings. They encourage you to maintain your commitment to the Great Work and can help you to become hooked on the search for truth. The path of Tzaddi is not only concerned with the idea of total commitment to the spiritual but is connected to the element of Air, which links with the image of incense.

THE JOURNEY You still have a long road ahead of you and it will be some time before you are likely to have significant confidence in your ability to progress. The advice of this dream is that you should not worry about whether any aid you use to improve your spiritual progress is actually necessary; rather, you should simply concentrate on using those aids to improve the level of contact you achieve with your higher self.

INCITEMENT

*hasatah-hsthh-*הסתה-470

MEANING When we reduce the value of this dream we find the number 11. In most cases this would indicate that a profoundly mystical experience was just around the corner. However, the content of this dream and other values within it suggest that we should reduce the value to the number 2, which represents duality. This is because this dream should be seen as a warning against believing that your spiritual truths must apply to everybody else or that those who disagree with you are simply wrong. The nature of the word *incitement* carries with it the implication of trying to coerce others into following your view of the world without question, and this is never an enlightened approach to spirituality.

THE TREE OF LIFE The value of this word is equivalent to that of the Hebrew word meaning "time." From a spiritual point of view, a focus on time is as inappropriate as concentrating on the material aspects of life. When we are behaving in accordance with the Divine will, time ceases to be a consideration since we are looking at reality from the perspective of an eternal soul. However, when we begin to see our spiritual experiences as a blueprint for others to follow, we are unavoidably drawn into issues about control and power, which do not move us forward spiritually. The letter Heh is associated with The Emperor card in the tarot, and this card in its negative aspect refers to a desire for power and control. Consequently, we can place this dream on the path of Heh in its negative aspect.

THE JOURNEY The lesson that you need to learn in order to put your spiritual quest back on track is that each of us must find his own way to contact the Divine force and reach his own personal understanding of the universe. While your ideas and beliefs may be valid for you, there is no reason to suppose that they will work or indeed should work for anyone else. In the compression of this dream's value you are told that your journey will at times be a sad and melancholy one (Tav), but, most important, the letter Ayin tells you that you must be satisfied to move forward alone and follow an individual route toward the higher.

INDEPENDENCE

*atsmaoot-a'atzmavth-*עצמאות-607

MEANING As recently as fifty years ago most of us would have lived in close proximity to our parents, siblings, grandparents, and in-laws. One of the biggest impacts of the technological advances of the last fifty years has been the breakdown not just of the extended family but to a large extent the weakening of the so-called nuclear family. At an individual spiritual level it is important that we find our own way to the Divine. It is one of the paradoxes of the universe that we are both connected to every other entity in the universe and at the same time we need to develop our own unique individuality. This individuality should always be in the context of a healthy and interdependent relationship with a number of individuals. They may not be blood relatives but in one sense they should feel as close as family.

THE TREE OF LIFE The first letter in the spelling of this dream title indicates the path on the Tree of Life to which this dream belongs. The path of Ayin refers to the need within each of us to develop our own personal understanding of the nature of the Divine. It also points to a particularly vigorous approach to life, and this is further emphasized by the following letter, Tzaddi. The path of Ayin affords you the opportunity to make your mark not just in terms of your inner development but in your day-to-day life. You can use that confidence and willpower to construct a life-style that will give you the time and mental space to focus on your spiritual quest.

THE JOURNEY When we reduce the value of this dream we find the number 13. As this number is associated with great change in one's life, this bodes well for the adjustments that you need to make in your day-to-day life in order to make the best possible progress with the Great Work. In the compression of the value of this dream we find the letters Mem and Zayin. Zayin points to the fact that while you have great confidence now, you may still have to struggle in order to achieve your goals. The letter Mem is there to remind you that even when you are struggling, the protective maternal aspect of the Divine is watching over you.

INDIFFERENCE

adeeshoot-adyshvth- אדישות *-721*

MEANING In some ways, a terrible person who at least fervently believes in the moral justification for his behavior is more sympathetic than the individual who is so apathetic that he simply does not care about anything. From a Kabbalistic point of view, the innate rejection of apathy and indifference stems from our deep-seated knowledge that there is a higher purpose to our lives and that it is enormously important that we hold on to our capacity for concern. There is a form of indifference that reflects the highest level of enlightenment, but this occurs only when we recognize that at a very profound level there really is no difference between any possible actions that we might take since ultimately

all actions are equal. It is for this reason that the value of this word is equivalent to that of the Hebrew for the "primordial point," a term referring to the Divine source.

THE TREE OF LIFE It is possible that the dreamer has achieved the supreme state of consciousness where he recognize on a deep and inner level the equivalence of all thoughts, feelings, and actions. However, it is far more likely that this dream reflects a much more common feeling of apathy that you are experiencing right now. This feeling of listlessness results from contemplating the enormity of the task that lies ahead of you, as you are still stuck in the Sefirah of Malkut. However, it is very important that you find a way to move out of this sense of indifference, because one cannot engage with the world of the spiritual without some sense of purpose and inspiration. The reduction value of this dream produces the number 10, and this is the number of the Sefirah of Malkut. The spelling of this dream title begins with the first path (Aleph) of the Tree and ends with the last path (Tav), which represents the vastness of the journey that you are anticipating.

THE JOURNEY It is very easy to feel defeated before you even begin when you seriously start to think about the Great Work. However, the Tree of Life itself offers an ideal way of dealing with the overwhelming size of the challenge. There are thirty-two stages on the Tree of Life and you will find that you progress much more effectively if you allow yourself to consider only the specific stage that lies directly ahead of you at any given time. The first thing to do when you consider exploring your inner self is to establish a routine that sets aside some time for purely spiritual matters. You should make a point of ensuring that you allow yourself that time, no matter what.

INDULGENCE (OF YOURSELF)

heetmakroot-hthmkrvth- התמכרות *-1071*

MEANING Nobody ever said that the spiritual path would be easy. Nor indeed should anyone think that spiritual insights can be gained without some sacrifice on the part of the seeker. This does not mean that you need to give away all your possessions and live in a cave; it means that you need to change the way you prioritize the various elements of your life. The dream of indulgence is a warning that you are too focused on your wants and should concentrate more on what will actually help you to achieve what you need in terms of contacting your higher self.

THE TREE OF LIFE We can indulge ourselves in a range of ways and this dream does not necessarily mean that you are spending your time drinking fine wine, eating chocolate, and generally leading a decadent life-style. Indeed, it is far more likely that you are indulging yourself by failing to critically examine your spiritual development. It is very tempting to interpret every possible spiritual insight or experience as a confirmation of the beliefs that we had when we first began our inner journey. This sort of behavior is just as indulgent as any materialist tendencies. The reduction value of this dream produces the number 9, which is the value of the letter Teth. This letter means "serpent" and is associated with exactly the sort of self-deception that this dream refers to. Consequently, this dream belongs firmly on the path of Teth.

THE JOURNEY There is no easy way to rectify the problem that is indicated by this dream. It requires the strength of will and determination that comes only when you allow yourself to wholly place your trust in the Divine. Fortunately, the positive aspect of the path of Teth relates to the capacity for great determination and willpower in response to trying circumstances. It would be very helpful for you now to join a meditation group and allow the teacher or group leader to work through your experiences with you in order to avoid your tendency to place a wholly uncritical interpretation on them. A meditation group would also help you to build up the necessary self-discipline to succeed in the Great Work.

INDUSTRY

kharoshet-chrvshth- חרושת *-914*

MEANING When we think of the word *industry* today we are likely to envision factories and manufacturing plants and the like. It is very hard to see how a dream about a steel mill, for instance, might relate to your spiritual development. However, we should remember that originally *industry* referred to hard work in general and not just to heavy machinery. This is an encouraging dream and refers to the concerted efforts you have been making to try to contact your higher self.

THE TREE OF LIFE Each stage on the Tree of Life requires a great deal of work if you are to fully reap the benefits of the lessons to be learned on each path and Sefirah. That might lead you to believe that this dream could be placed anywhere on the Tree. However, this dream carries with it the promise of some reward for all that hard labor. Consequently, we are looking at one of the paths that leads into the

Sefirah of Tiferet. When we reduce the value of the dream we find the number 14. This is associated with the Temperance card in the tarot and is also by association linked to the path of Samech. This is one of the paths that carries you to the temporary haven of Tiferet and is the path on which your dream sits.

THE JOURNEY It takes considerable effort and dedication to achieve what you have accomplished in terms of your spiritual journey. The compression of this dream's value indicates the need for you to sustain the level of commitment (Tzaddi) that you have already demonstrated. The subsequent letter, Qoph, tells us that you have a tendency to worry about the level of your increasing insight. However, the final letter, Daleth, in the compression is encouraging you to remember that the door to spiritual understanding is now in front of you and all you have to do is walk through.

INFECTION

zeehoom-zyhvm- ויהום *-68*

MEANING Our first inclination on waking from a dream about an infection would probably be to take a thorough bath or shower. It will come as a great surprise to most readers that this dream is actually extremely positive. When we reduce the value of this dream we find the number 5. This is a hugely significant number in the Western Mystery Tradition and can be seen as a representation of the spiritually integrated human being. The number 5 is symbolic of the four elements of Water, Fire, Air, and Earth, all under the control of the fifth element of Spirit. To find this number in any dream is a sure sign that the dreamer is making good progress in his search for the higher.

Traditional Kabbalists might say a dream of infection is a warning dream, suggesting a poison at work, either physically or spiritually. For traditionalists, the dream might have a connotation too of invasion involving negativity.

THE TREE OF LIFE While our first thoughts concerning the term *infection* tend to be extremely negative, we should also remember that it can be used in a wholly positive manner. For instance, we often refer to people's natures being infectious. This is the context in which we should understand the use of the word infection in terms of this dream. Quite literally you have been infected with the force and energy of the Divine, which has enlivened your higher self. The path that you are currently traversing is the path of Yod, and this path itself represents the spark of the Divine that has been awakened within you.

THE JOURNEY The value of this dream is equivalent to the value of the Hebrew word meaning "wisdom" and it is your acquired understanding of the nature of the universe that will carry you along the path of Yod to the next stage of your spiritual journey. The compression of the value of this dream demonstrates that you are being both guided (Samech) and protected (Cheth) by the Divine force. In order to move forward, you should use this powerful support to assist those around you as well as to develop your inner self. With all your newfound energy, you should seriously consider making some kind of regular contribution to a charity.

INFESTATION
*leeshrots-lshrvtz-*לשרוץ-626

MEANING In the same way as the dream of infection was not at all pessimistic in its spiritual implications, the dream of infestation should not be taken at face value. When we think of an infestation we always think in terms of some form of pest or disease that needs to be exterminated. However, at the level of the soul, when we think of an infestation we should be considering the accumulated emotional baggage that we need to dispose of in order to continue to develop. The reduction value of this dream produces the number 5, and, as we saw in the dream of infection, this suggests as individual who has brought himself under the control of his higher self.

THE TREE OF LIFE The presence of the value 5 in this dream, along with other significant values that can be gleaned from close analysis, points to the fact that this dream relates to an individual who has already made some form of contact with his higher self. The idea of infestation indicates that while you have made enormous progress, you still need to clean house in the sense of ridding yourself of some of the ghosts of your past. This is never easy to do, and the initial Lamed in the spelling of the dream title not only tells you the path on which this dream is situated but lets you know that you will be feeling a very strong need to finally take some action regarding your unresolved emotional issues.

THE JOURNEY Your higher self is the force that is vigorously urging you to address your past so that you can properly look forward to the future. The initial Mem in the compression of the value of this dream lets you know that while you may have painful memories to address, you can rely on a sense of support flowing into you from the maternal aspect of the Divine. The final Vav not only emphasizes the presence of the Divine force by repeating the number 6 (the symbol of the macrocosm) but points to the need for a great deal of quiet reflection. Finally, the central letter, Kaph, suggests that you need to take some practical steps to achieve full closure on these memories. This may mean revisiting some significant locations from your childhood.

INFLUENCE
*hashpah-hshpha'ah-*השפעה-460

MEANING This dream does not happen to many people, and this is due to the high levels of spiritual awareness implied within the Kabbalistic analysis of the values and letter positioning in the dream's title. The reduction value of the dream reveals the number 10, which is an indication that you have achieved the completion of some significant chapter in your life. This is further emphasized by the presence of the letter Heh at both the beginning and the end of the spelling of the title. Not only does this indicate that you are in the process of achieving a glimpse of the nature of the Divine itself, but when we add together the value of both letters, we again find the number ten.

THE TREE OF LIFE This dream is particularly rare because very few people manage to achieve the ultimate goal of climbing all the way up the Tree of Life. The value of this dream is equivalent to the value of a Hebrew phrase from the book of Exodus meaning "holy unto God." The implication is that after much effort you have achieved a deep understanding of all that is holy before the Divine, and you now stand on the path of Aleph, ready to have at least some sight of the nature of the Divine itself.

THE JOURNEY As mentioned above, you have achieved the completion of a major cycle in your life. You may now be thinking that this relates to the completion of the Great Work. However, it is in the nature of the spiritual quest that it can never be fully completed. This is where the title of the dream itself comes into play. Now that you have arrived at the path of Aleph and have an internalized appreciation of the essential unity of the Divine, you should use that knowledge to help others. The compression of this dream indicates that you must now go back to the lowest path on the Tree (Tav) in order to act as a guide and support (Samech) to those around you who wish to begin their own sacred journey.

INHERITANCE

yerooshah-yrvshh- יְרוּשָׁה-521

MEANING There is a sense in which we all share a common inheritance from the Divine, and that is the right, if we choose to act on it, to try to return to a state of consciousness where we have a complete awareness of our spiritual nature. The value of this dream is a prime number, though, and prime numbers always indicate a unique characteristic about the dreamer. Given this fact, the concept of an inheritance is likely to relate to some talent or skill that you have literally inherited and that you can use in the service of your spiritual quest.

THE TREE OF LIFE The value of this dream is the same as the value of a Hebrew phrase meaning "the descending Fire." This phrase suggests fire coming down from the Divine source. In terms of the four elements, Fire is associated with our passions and with creativity. Thus, your inherited ability is some form of artistic talent. On the Tree of Life, the Sefirah of Netzach is linked to the element of Fire and is also the Sefirah that represents the energies and attributes needed for creative expression.

THE JOURNEY The reduction value of this dream produces the number 8, which is the value of the letter Cheth. This letter tends to indicate defensiveness, and in your case it is likely that you are hiding your light under a bushel. This dream is a very direct way of telling you that whatever your creative talent is, you should be making use of it. In doing so, you will not only be helping yourself to understand your inner nature but will be creating a means by which others can also begin to think about the spiritual nature of their own lives.

INITIATION

leezoom-lyzvm- לִיזוּם-93

MEANING The value of this dream holds enormous significance for one particular system within the Western Mystery Tradition. However, it is also a very positive and encouraging dream from a generally Kabbalistic perspective. It is clear that spiritual issues are very much on your mind right now, to the extent that your dream has an overtly mystical content. This is in itself quite unusual, since we would normally expect to have to delve deeply into the hidden meaning of a dream in order to discover its spiritual significance. The initial letter, Lamed, in the spelling of this dream's title suggests that while you have chosen to follow a spiritual route, this is partly because of a very definite feeling that you are being actively driven toward this choice by a strong external force.

THE TREE OF LIFE The process of initiation, especially that of spiritual initiation, is one that takes time. There is a wide range of organizations from the religious to the secular that hold initiation ceremonies. However, this dream is not about a symbolic entrance into a club or an organization but about a very real development of understanding and awareness. Clearly, this dream relates to an early period in your spiritual journey and is positioned on the path of Tav, the first path leading out of Malkut.

THE JOURNEY At this stage in your search for some form of spiritual truth there is little that you need to do beyond maintaining an enthusiastic and open mind. The reduction value of this dream produces the number 12, and this indicates that you will have to sacrifice some of your comforts in order to progress up the Tree of Life. In the compression of the dream's value we have the letter Tzaddi, which reminds you of the need for commitment and persistence, while the final letter, Gimel, is there to let you know of the promise of wisdom that waits for you at the end of your search.

INJURY

petseeah-ptzya'ah- פְּצִיעָה-255

MEANING Waking up from a dream of being injured is not a pleasant experience, and you are likely to spend the first few minutes of your day convinced that you are about to have an accident. This dream should be seen not as prophetic in the sense of foretelling some terrible physical injury that you are going to sustain but as an indication that you have some trying times ahead of you. The value of this dream is equivalent to the value of the Hebrew word meaning "burdensome," and this is a good description of how you are likely to see life over the next few months.

THE TREE OF LIFE There is no such thing as an easy path on the Tree of Life. However, there are some paths that are characterized by the anxieties and difficulties that they cause to the seeker of Truth. One such path is the path of Nun. This is the path that causes us to examine our inner fears and emotional insecurities. It is indeed a burdensome time and you will at times wonder whether you will be able to continue with your spiritual explorations.

When we reduce the value of this dream we find the number 12. This number is associated with self-sacrifice, and in order to fully understand yourself you will need to engage in a certain amount of self-sacrifice.

THE JOURNEY Nun is one of the hardest paths to traverse, due largely to the need to hold up an incredibly honest mirror to every aspect of your personality and your past. If you are able to stick with it, though, you will be amply rewarded, as this path leads into the Sefirah of Tiferet and it is there that you will be able to make some form of contact with your higher self. The only way to deal with this period in your life is to stoically accept that it is not going to be very pleasant and keep reminding yourself of the benefits of undertaking this emotional spring cleaning.

INK

*dyo-dyv-*רֹיד-20

MEANING It seems a highly unlikely candidate for any significant and meaningful analysis and yet there is a great deal of information hidden within this seemingly simple dream of ink. The value of this dream is equivalent to that of the Hebrew word meaning "hand" and is the value of the Hebrew letter Kaph, which itself means "hand." This implies that the dreamer is a practical-minded individual. On the spiritual level, it indicates that you are able to take an issue involved with the most abstract and otherwordly concepts and find a way of explaining it to yourself in a down-to-earth, pragmatic manner.

THE TREE OF LIFE When we have a dream whose value is directly equivalent to the value of one of the paths on the Tree, we tend to position the dream on that particular path. In this case, the dream of ink belongs on the path of Kaph. While we associate the path of Kaph with practicalities, we should also remember that the dream of ink indicates the act of writing. Writing suggests a far more intellectual turn of mind than we might expect from a dream located on the path of Kaph. However, we should remember that the value of the letter Kaph is also a number that in the Western Mystery Tradition is generally associated with the mind and especially with rational judgment.

THE JOURNEY When we look at the spelling of this dream title we see that the letters contain some excellent advice on how to use the energies of the path of Kaph. The letter Daleth indicates that the

door to greater enlightenment is now open for you, and the subsequent Yod tells us that in finding practical applications for your new spiritual insights you will awaken the Divine spark within yourself. The final Vav emphasizes that as well as acting on your spiritual insights, it is important that you reflect on their implications.

INSANITY

*sheegaon-shyga'avn-*שיגעון-439

MEANING The idea of insanity is profoundly frightening, even in today's world, where we are supposed to be tolerant and understanding. It is a telling indictment of society's attitudes that our fear of insanity stems as much from what may happen to us at the hands of others and in terms of their perceptions of us as from a fear of the illness itself. In spiritual terms, we can look at the idea of insanity as simply a symbol of our separation from the world around us due to our different way of looking at reality.

THE TREE OF LIFE The value of this dream reduces to 16, a number associated with The Tower of Destruction in the tarot. This card represents a momentous occasion in one's life that leads to all of his preconceptions being shaken to the core so that a new and more enlightened set of values can take their place. While the long-term outcome is positive, in the short term this can be a very disturbing experience. Indeed, the effects can be so profound as to be akin to the sudden shift in attitude that is often associated with a person suffering the effects of a delusional mental illness. Although the communication from the higher is quite forceful and potentially upsetting, the path of Peh is the rightful place for this dream since it is still a moment of dialogue between you and the Divine force.

THE JOURNEY The lessons that you need to learn from this dream are not so much about doing things as they are about the way in which you respond to and perceive your circumstances. As your interest in the spiritual quest grows, there will be those around you who will mock your sincerity. Worse, they may even suggest that your beliefs are quite literally insane. The compression of this dream's value tells you that while this will be a cause for regret (Tav), you must persevere, and the driving force of your higher self (Lamed) will ensure that you do. Above all, you need to have the determination and willpower (Teth) to stand firm by your beliefs, no matter what anyone else thinks.

INTERPRETER

*toorgeman–thvrgmn–*תורגמן*-*699

MEANING From a broad psychological perspective, this dream would probably be seen as a sign that you tend to act as a mediator in relationships, trying to find ways in which all parties can understand the others' points of view. From a Kabbalistic perspective, your role as an interpreter relates to your ability to look at the mundane world and see in it signs of the Divine presence. The spelling of this dream title begins with the letter Tav, which is associated with melancholy, and ends in the letter Nun, which signifies sorrow. This does not mean that you should spend the next few months in a deep depression, but it does remind you that even when you can see the evidence of the Divine all around you, you are still subject to the same emotional fluctuations as anyone else.

THE TREE OF LIFE We often talk about the spiritual path as a journey, and this is because it requires more than simply learning a series of facts or accepting certain pieces of information. In order to be effective, the spiritual quest must be a holistic experience affecting you in a physical and emotional way. This means that as your understanding develops, your feelings and attitudes change at the same time, to the extent that it is akin to looking at the world from a wholly different perspective or location. This dream opens the door on a way of looking at the world that puts you in direct touch with the energies of the Supernal Sefirot. The path of Daleth not only means "door" but runs between the Sefirot of Binah and Hokhmah and enables you to understand God as a both unstoppable and overwhelming force (Hokhmah) and also as the designer of form and order (Binah). Consequently, it is on the path of Daleth that this dream belongs.

THE JOURNEY It is the nature of interpretation that we translate not only for ourselves but for a group of people. The initial Mem in the compression of the value of this dream points to a desire on your part to use your developing understanding for the benefit of others. By doggedly (Tzaddi) sticking to the spiritual path and using your power strength of will (Teth) to see the evidence of the Divine in every aspect of life, you will create a great fund of wisdom and spiritual experience. You can then share this wisdom with others both by setting an example through your behavior and by acting as an interpreter to translate your experiences into explanations and advice that can be followed by anyone who chooses to listen.

INTOXICATION

*sheekaron–shykrvn–*שיכרון*-*586

MEANING There are many mystical texts that refer to the idea of being intoxicated with the spirit of the Divine. We might expect this dream to be extremely positive given the relatively common usage of images of intoxication to describe the feelings associated with moments when we feel a direct communion with the Divine. However, while not being entirely negative, this dream does not indicate that you are about to achieve some form of direct experience of the higher. The value of this dream is equivalent to the value of the Hebrew word meaning "war trumpet." When we remember the devastating effect of the Hebrew war trumpets on the walls of Jericho, we should realize that this dream does not imply a peaceful time ahead for you!

THE TREE OF LIFE There are a number of distinct stages to intoxication. Initially we may feel happy and full of geniality. This is often followed by a desire to be everybody's friend, a short-lived period that is replaced just as quickly by a need to become depressed and emotional. The final stage of intoxication, and indeed the longest lasting, is a state of near total confusion about where you are, why you are there, and what you are going do next. It is the murky confusion of intoxication that this dream relates to, and consequently this dream belongs on the path of Qoph.

THE JOURNEY In the spelling of the dream title, we see that the letters exemplify various stages of drunkenness, from the feelings of great energy associated with the letter Shin to the mental confusion and sorrow indicated by the pairing of the letters Vav and Nun. In Kabbalistic terms, the task that lies before you is to find some means of ending the confusion that currently besets you. The compression of the value of this dream begins with the final form of the letter Kaph. This makes it very clear that you need to find some practical way to resolve your problem. The subsequent letter, Peh, tells us that communication will be the key, while the letter Vav points to the need for serious reflection. Bearing all these factors in mind, the ideal solution is to try regular meditation combined with various techniques by which you try to visualize your higher self talking to you and giving you advice.

INVENTING

*lehamtsee-lhmtzya-*להמציא-176

MEANING One way in which the Kabbalistic enterprise differs from mainstream religion is the fact that each individual is responsible for his personal development. While there are now a number of groups that can help you try to find the meaning within your life, the ultimate journey must be taken alone with only the Divine for company. The act of invention is also a solitary business, and the fact that you are having this dream strongly suggests that you have now fully accepted the task of developing your spiritual understanding.

THE TREE OF LIFE The value of this dream can be reduced to 14. This number is linked to ideas of balance and harmony, not least because the number can be further reduced to 5, the number of the pentagram. As a symbol, the pentagram or five-pointed star stands for the individual who has brought the four emotional, mental, and physical elements of his nature under the guidance and control of the fifth element of Spirit. The path of Samech represents the guidance and support of the Divine, so it is there that we should locate this dream.

THE JOURNEY As the idea of inventing suggests, you have reached a point in your inner development where you are able to create the frameworks of your beliefs and begin to approach your higher self. This is one reason why your dream is placed on a path that leads into the Sefirah of Tiferet. The compression of the value of this dream suggests that you still have some anxieties (Qoph) about your progress, but your higher self is urging you to have enough belief in yourself to approach the spiritual quest in your own way (Ayin). In the context of the positive message of this dream, the final Vav in the compression, with its value of 6, represents the Divine force itself as symbolized by the number 6 in the hexagram or so-called Star of David.

INVENTOR

*mamtsee-mmtzya-*ממציא-181

MEANING While the dream of inventing puts the dreamer in the position of actively inventing and creating, this dream relates to the idea of an inventor who is someone other than the dreamer. In psychological terms, this dream would suggest someone who tends to rely on others to make his key decisions in life and who tends to lack the initiative to drive his life forward without support. In Kabbalistic terms, this dream relates to the notion of the Divine as the inventor of all life and the universe itself. It symbolizes an awakening of your spiritual awareness and suggests that you are about to take steps to try to understand yourself and the world in which you live a little more deeply.

THE TREE OF LIFE This dream is unusual in that it begins with the letter Mem appearing twice. We might think that this acts as a strong argument for placing the dream on the path of Mem. However, the purpose of this repetition is to emphasize the support that is available to you from your higher self in deciding to find out more about the inventor of your dream. The value of this dream reduces to 10, and this refers to the Sefirah of Malkut, which is where you are currently positioned. However, all the signs are that you will shortly be taking your first step up the ladder toward the Divine source.

THE JOURNEY The realization that there is a creator or inventor of the universe is perhaps the most profound insight that any of us can ever have. We may develop our understanding of what this means, but the realization itself is the key. In the compression of this dream's value we see that you have a number of anxieties (Qoph) about the spiritual path you are about to take. However, if you talk (Peh) to other individuals who are actively engaged in a spiritual quest, you will find that these concerns gradually evaporate. The final letter, Aleph, in the compression relates to the essential unity of the Divine, which, with time and persistence, you will come to experience.

INVITATION

*hazmanah-hzmnh-*הזמנה-107

MEANING Very often our dreams reveal not only what is occurring in our lives right now but what we are like generally as individuals. This dream shows that you are an outgoing and sociable person, as your dream has a party theme to it even though it is about a very serious issue. The value of this dream is equivalent to that of the Hebrew word meaning "egg," and this indicates that there is great potential within you that is just waiting for you to hatch it out. This idea also fits well with the overt title, "invitation," as both suggest some exciting and positive event in the near future.

THE TREE OF LIFE We associate feelings of warmth and benevolence with the energy of the Sun. In the Tree of Life, the Sun is connected to the path of Resh. This path is also linked to the tarot card

The Sun in the Western Mystery Tradition. As well as signifying your open and warm nature, this path suggests an individual with a keen wit and above-average intelligence. You can use both of these qualities in your spiritual quest.

THE JOURNEY The value of this dream reduces to 8 and this is the value of the Sefirah of Hod, the next destination in your spiritual journey. As you travel up the path of Resh you should spend as much time as possible reading up on a range of spiritual philosophies and systems. The compression of the dream's value indicates that the way ahead will involve a certain degree of confusion (Qoph) and that you will have to struggle (Zayin) with a host of conflicting ideas. However, the spelling of this dream title begins and ends with the letter Heh, meaning "window." The significance of this is to remind you that as long as you persevere with your reflections on the nature of the spiritual opportunity now being offered to you, a number of valuable insights will be yours.

ISLAND

*ee-ay-*אֵי*-11*

MEANING At the simplest level, this dream is an attempt by your higher self to remind you of the truth of the old saying, "no man is an island." From a psychological perspective, this dream would suggest somebody who craves solitude in his life. Of course, this is not necessarily a bad thing, but depends on the underlying reasons why the person chooses to be alone. When we consider the dream within a Kabbalistic framework, we find that this dream represents someone very much at a crossroads in his life. On one hand, the dream has the same value as the Hebrew word meaning "haughty," which suggests an individual who has cut himself off from his fellow man. On the other hand, the value of this dream is also equivalent to the Hebrew word meaning "gold," and in spiritual terms this is a very positive sign as gold is associated with spiritual value and progression.

THE TREE OF LIFE As the dreamer you are caught between a path that leads you to great spiritual understanding and inner development and one that leads only to misanthropy and empty pride. The value of this dream consists of the number 1 appearing twice, and as such is almost a pictorial representation of two conflicting and mutually exclusive choices. Additionally, the value of the dream reduces to 2, which emphasizes the dualistic nature

of your current dilemma. It is not so uncommon a problem, though, for people who manage to make a certain amount of headway up the Tree of Life. The path of Ayin in its negative aspect is the location for this dream, as it is there that we become inclined to believe that our way is the one true way and that all our successes are our own without any support from any Divine source.

THE JOURNEY Although this dream does carry with it the possibility of a high degree of arrogance on the part of the dreamer, generally it is a very positive dream. The number 11 itself, while it carries within it implications of dualistic thinking, is also important as it represents the likelihood of a profound experience. Additionally, when we look at the spelling of this dream title we see that the letter Aleph, representing the unity of the Divine, is preceded by the letter Yod, indicating that the Divine spark within you will be awakened in the near future. Consequently, all you need do to avoid pride and a fall is to listen to your intuition.

ITCH

*eektsoots-a'aqtzvtz-*עיקצוץ*-356*

MEANING As the dreamer, you do not have to be told that you are completely hooked on the spiritual quest. The letter Tzaddi, which refers to your total commitment to the Great Work, appears twice in the spelling of this dream title. Your relationship to spiritual matters is very much like an itch in that the more you scratch it, the more it itches. You should be feeling very pleased with yourself, as this dream is a definite indicator that you will achieve the goals you have set yourself, possibly sooner than you had thought.

THE TREE OF LIFE The value of this dream reduces to 5, which is the number of the pentagram, an extremely important symbol in the Westerrn Mystery Tradition. This symbol indicates that you have integrated the four elements within yourself and are ruled by your higher self as indicated by the fifth element of Spirit. The presence of this value indicates that you have already entered the Sefirah of Tiferet. The path that you are now taking is that of Lamed, whose driving force is signified by that itch that will not go away no matter how much you scratch it.

THE JOURNEY You have already traveled a long way in terms of the development of your inner understanding, but you still have a very long way to go. On the positive side the compression of this dream's value indicates quite clearly that you still have plenty of energy and enthusiasm for the Great Work. However, you need to mentally prepare yourself for the fact that there will be difficulties and sorrow (Nun) in the future. When you are faced with difficult emotional moments, you should remember that the final letter in the compression (Vav) refers to the holy hexagram, and that should help to keep that itch firmly in the front of your mind.

JAIL
*kele-chla-*חלא-39

MEANING As long as you are staying on the right side of the law, this dream should not be too disturbing. Of course, what should be the case and what often actually is the case can be two very different things. The experience of this dream is much like the situation of being followed by a police officer on the freeway. We know that we haven't done anything wrong but we can't help feeling guilty! At the spiritual level, this dream is about the concept of atonement. You have dreamed of being in jail because you feel even on an unconscious level that you have something for which you need to atone. At the practical level, it may also refer to a situation in your day-to-day life where you feel restricted or confined, particularly in terms of your personal growth.

THE TREE OF LIFE When we reduce the value of this dream we find the number 12. This may seem surprising since this number is associated with self-sacrifice and unselfish behavior in general. However, the purpose of this value is to show that while you feel the need to atone for some perceived wrongdoing, you actually have no need to feel guilty. These feelings stem from the fact that you are so quick to take responsibility for the pain of those around you. Consequently, this dream belongs on the path of Mem.

THE JOURNEY Usually, our dreams are a means for our higher self to tell us that we need to do more in some way to assist our inner development. Unusually, this dream is advising that if anything, you need to do less! Compassion is a wonderful quality, but like any other trait it can be counterproductive when present in excessive quantities, since then we do not allow ourselves the space to feel good about ourselves. The compression of this dream's value tells you that you need to be on your guard against

self-deception (Teth) when ascribing the strong urge (Lamed) to help others to a Divine source. It will not hurt for you to also examine your life to see if there are any ways in which your spiritual development is being blocked.

JAILER
*kalay-klay-*כלאי-61

MEANING When we dream about an individual, no matter how far removed from us he may seem, the person is a reflection of ourselves. To be more specific, dream figures are reflections of certain aspects of our personality and nature. The value of this dream is equivalent to the value of the Hebrew word meaning "master." Consequently, we can infer that the jailer represents aspects of your personality that exercise control over the way in which you behave and how you perceive the world around you. It may also be that this dream has a more direct reference and that someone or a certain situation is constraining you right now. If that is the case, you should try to find some way of dealing with that obstacle in your development. As usual, meditation will help you to realize the best way forward.

THE TREE OF LIFE From a spiritual point of view, only our higher self should occupy the role of master in terms of how we go about living our life. However, the higher self is a source more of personal empowerment than of spiritual or emotional incarceration. The value of this dream is equivalent to that of the Hebrew words meaning "wealth" and "belly." Both money and food are material comforts. Bearing in mind that this dream is about dominating influences in our personality, this association of words points to a weakness for material comforts and thus places this dream in the Sefirah of Malkut.

THE JOURNEY To recognize our weaknesses is the first step to ridding ourselves of them. Consequently, you should take an optimistic view of this dream as being the first step toward a new and spiritually awakened life. The fact that your higher self refers to your love of the material as a jailer suggests that ridding yourself of these attachments will be a real struggle. It is for this reason that the reduction value of this dream comes to 7, which is the value of the letter Zayin, meaning "sword." You need to create a mental sword fashioned of the strongest willpower and with it defeat your attachment to the merely physical. As the Buddah pointed out, attachment to things is indeed nothing but a cause of great sorrow.

JAM
*reebah-rybh-*רִיבָה*-*217

MEANING Your colleagues and friends might laugh at the idea of a dream about a jam. Indeed, on the surface there is little to suggest any great significance beyond perhaps a morbid fear of traffic congestion! It is only when we start to look at the feelings that we associate with being "stuck in a jam" that we see the spiritual importance of this dream. When the road ahead is clear we are quite relaxed about getting to our destination. However, the moment the traffic begins to slow and we feel that there is some obstacle between us and our goal, we suddenly find that arriving at our destination is now a matter of life-or-death urgency. From a Kabbalistic point of view, this dream represents the enthusiasm and determination that can arise from the experience of an element of difficulty in our inner journey.

THE TREE OF LIFE If we were to pick an insect to represent well-ordered and industrious behavior, we could do a lot worse than selecting the humble bee. It is for this reason that the Hebrew word meaning "bee" shares its value with the value of this dream. The obstacles that you are experiencing are forcing you to take a practical and problem-solving approach to life. While this may require hard work and determination, it is also causes you to emulate the bee in terms of your commitment to the job at hand and your increasing ability to take a structured and ordered approach to the mysteries of the Divine. The path of Kaph represents this practical and organized viewpoint and it is here that we locate this dream.

THE JOURNEY Life is beset with obstacles. The successful person in both spiritual and day-to-day terms is not the one who is lucky enough not to come across any obstacles, but is the person who finds ways to overcome the obstacles in his life. The compression of the value of this dream produces the letters Resh, Yod, and Zayin. It is Resh that promises a safe and warm haven in the future, once you manage to fully awaken the Divine spark (Yod) that resides within you. The final Zayin tells you that to awaken your higher self will require some significant struggling on your part. You can ease this struggle by finding a meditation group in which you can freely and frankly share your experiences.

JAR
*tseentsenet-tzntznth-*צִנְצֶנֶת*-*680

MEANING The image of a jar suggests storage and containment. In psychological terms this implies that you are repressing or trying to conceal some difficult part of your past. The repetition of the letters Tzaddi and Nun suggests a need for you to persevere against some very difficult circumstances. The circumstances in question are difficult memories from your past that have metaphorically been kept sealed away in a jar until now.

THE TREE OF LIFE Not only does the letter Nun appear a number of times in the spelling of this dream title, it is also the correct location for it on the Tree of Life. The letter Nun is associated with sorrow generally, but specifically it is connected to the emotional pain that is a necessary part of exorcising the demons of our past. The fact that the letter Nun appears twice produces the additional value of 100 (50 + 50), and this lets us know that if you did keep your emotional baggage sealed away, that seal has now been broken and you are suffering anxiety as a result.

THE JOURNEY When we reduce the value of this dream we find the number 5, and so although you may be going through a difficult time right now, we know that you have accomplished a great deal in terms of your spiritual development. It is important to remember this now and hang on to the insights you have gained. The compression of the dream's value reveals the two letters Mem and Peh. This lets you know that the maternal aspect of the Divine is still present and that you should be looking to reestablish some form of communication with your higher self to help you through the next few months.

JAWS
*leset-lsth-*לֶסֶת*-*490

MEANING To dream of jaws is not the most pleasant of experiences, but that does not mean that the Kabbalistic implications of the dream are in any way negative. It is often the case that the most encouraging dreams are those with the most apparently negative or seemingly dull themes. At a metaphorical level, this dream can be seen as an indication that you need to bite through some obstacle or block to your spiritual development. The Hebrew word meaning "mouth" is Peh, and this is one of the paths on the Tree of Life. As a path it is associated with all forms of communication. The dream of a pair of jaws implies an enormous mouth and a certain amount of trepidation about getting too close to the owner of that mouth. The values in the dream indicate that this dream is unsettling because it relates to the potential for some form of communion with the Divine itself.

THE TREE OF LIFE The value of this dream is equivalent to that of one of the Hebrew titles for the Sefirah of Binah. This is one of three Supernal Sefirot and as such implies that you really have made commendable progress in your spiritual journey. The Sefirah of Binah is often referred to as the Great Mother of the Tree of Life, and it is evidence of your underlying fear of spiritual failure that you perceive your location on the Tree as a pair of jaws rather than as a return to the womb of the Divine.

THE JOURNEY You are now only one path away from the crown of the Tree, which represents the closest any human can come to a direct appreciation of God. It is wholly understandable that you are now suffering a high degree of anxiety; it is like sitting outside the principal's office, not knowing if you are going to be congratulated or expelled. You should look to the spelling of this dream title to find the encouragement that you need to continue. While the letter Tav is there to represent the origin of your journey and also the melancholy that often accompanies wisdom, we can also see the letter Lamed, telling us that you are being driven ever onward by your higher self. The crucial letter, though, is the central Samech, which tells you that even now you will be guided by the Divine force and so have no need for worries.

JEALOUSY

*keenah-qnah-*קנאה-156

MEANING It is always difficult to separate our positive feelings from our insecurities, as when we feel something it draws on the emotional drives that define our nature. One unfortunate result of this fact of our emotional structure is that so many of us can be incredibly jealous of our partners. This is a classic case of our positive feelings for the one we love getting mixed up with our own insecurities that lead us to worry that we might lose our partner. The real force behind jealousy is not the behavior or feelings of another but our own feelings of inadequacy. Bearing this in mind, we can see how a dream of jealousy might relate to our spiritual quest.

THE TREE OF LIFE There are many times in your exploration of the spiritual aspect of the world

when you may feel that you are not made of "the right stuff." However, in this dream we are looking for a path on the Tree of Life that is concerned primarily with negative and self-deprecatory feelings. In its positive aspect the path of Teth indicates great willpower. However, in its negative aspect this path indicates a tendency for self-deception. The value of this dream is equivalent to the value of the Hebrew word meaning "viper," so it is right to assign this dream to the negative aspect of the path of Teth.

THE JOURNEY Only you can resolve the reasons for your feelings of insecurity about your ability to succeed in your attempts to make some form of connection with the Divine. It is clear from the compression of the dream's value that you are extremely anxious (Qoph) about your suitability for a spiritual path. It is likely that this stems from emotional upsets (Nun) in your childhood; possibly you had overbearing or extremely demanding parents for whom even your best efforts were never enough. The final Vav in the compression is there to remind you that the Divine may be a parental figure in some regards, but that does not mean that the Divine shares the characteristics of your parents.

JEWELS

*even tovah-abn tvbh-*אבן טובה-75

MEANING From a purely psychological point of view, this dream would seem little different from a dream about jewelry. However, from a Kabbalistic point of view, there is a great gulf between the two dreams in terms of their significance. While jewelry is always something that one wears, the term *jewels* can be used as a reference to the Sefirot on the Tree of Life. Consequently, we can see this dream as an indication that you are developing an interest and awareness in the more complex matters of spirituality.

THE TREE OF LIFE The value of this dream reduces to 12, which indicates a willingness to sacrifice those things in life that you enjoy in favor of a higher cause. In your case, this means that you will be spending much more time examining matters of a spiritual nature than you currently do, and this will mean sacrificing some of your leisure pursuits. The value of this dream is equivalent to that of a Hebrew word meaning "colors." There is a subtle suggestion here that you may choose to explore your inner nature through the medium of art. This creativity along with the passion you have for the Great Work place this dream in the Sefirah of Netzach.

THE JOURNEY The letter that stands out in this dream title is Nun in its final form at the end of the first word. This serves to emphasize that as committed as you are to the spiritual quest, you will find it very difficult to maintain your efforts as you begin to deal with some difficult personal issues. However, the compression of the dream's value advises you to remember that you are following your unique (Ayin) path and that if you stay true to your intentions you will be afforded a glimpse (Heh) of the Divine.

JOKES
bedeekhah–bdychh–בדיחה–29

MEANING We tend to regard humor as one of the more shallow arts. For example, it is rare that a comedy play receives the same accolades as a grim and gritty drama. However, there is room for fun within the world of the spiritual. Given that the Divine is loving in nature, there is no reason to suppose that its main purpose is to create people who are dour and humorless. As it says in the *Zohar*, "Whenever a person learns wisdom, it is also incumbent to absorb a bit of folly." In fact, the value of this dream reduces to 11, and this number indicates that you are about to undergo some profound and potentially life-changing event.

THE TREE OF LIFE The value of this dream is a prime number (a number that can be divided only by itself and by one). While there are all kinds of mathematical applications of prime numbers, in Kabbalistic terms the presence of a prime number is an indication of uniqueness. We are each, of course, unique—this is part of the great wonder of the universe—but the dreamer of this dream stands out particularly. This is because the dream about jokes sits on the path of Aleph, the highest path on the Tree of Life. It is very rare for anyone to reach this far in his spiritual journey, so the presence of a prime number in the dream's value is more than amply justified.

THE JOURNEY When you are as close as this to a moment of direct communion with the Divine, it is very difficult if not impossible to advise you on the right actions to take. Since you have reached this far on your own, it is not likely that you will make any terrible mistakes in this final stage of the journey. The tarot card The Fool is connected to the path of Aleph, and of course for all its deep mystical import The Fool is ultimately a court jester. If there is any advice that you could be given it would be to remember that the final path to the Divine is highlighted by

a fool. To lose your sense of humor now would not be an act of piety but would simply indicate that your understanding of the Divine was actually less than was suggested by this dream. In other words, if you keep laughing you will achieve your goals.

JOURNEY
masa–msa'a–מסע–170

MEANING For each dream, we not only attempt to provide an analysis but try to see how this meaning can assist the dreamer in his personal spiritual journey. The idea of the Great Work as being a journey goes back to the earliest mystics, so this dream is about the inner quest as a whole. The value of this dream is equivalent to that of a Hebrew word meaning "staff." The staff is a representation of the support that we can receive from the Divine, provided that we approach the spiritual task with sincerity and commitment.

THE TREE OF LIFE To dream of the journey as a whole rather than as a particular aspect of your spiritual development suggests that you are still relatively new to the spiritual path. Additionally, the presence of a reminder that you can at all times lean on the staff of the Divine for support shows that this dream is suited to someone who is taking his first tentative steps on the Tree of Life, so we place this dream on the path of Tav, which leads from Malkut to Yesod.

THE JOURNEY Since you have been dreaming about it you should already know all the details of your impending journey! At this early stage the most important thing for you to do is to retain a sense of your individuality. There is no set formula for approaching and understanding the Divine. There are guides and advice, but ultimately this is a journey you have to make on your own terms and with your own definitions. The compression of this dream's value recognizes the fact that you are understandably anxious (Qoph). However, even in your most uncertain moments this dream urges you, through the letter Ayin both in the spelling and in the compression of this dream, to find your own way and be true to yourself.

JOY
seemkhah–shmchh–שמחה–353

MEANING For reasons best known to themselves, the organizations behind many mainstream religions seem to have equated the divinity of the creator with an almost morbid level of seriousness. More often than not, there is an unhealthy focus on our less than admirable qualities rather than on our potential to progress as spiritual beings. This dream is a far more endearing interpretation of the Divine since it focuses on the positive and encouraging rather than on the negative and critical.

THE TREE OF LIFE Given the prevalence of somber and decidedly unjoyful approaches to the Divine in Western culture, it is likely that you had made considerable progress up the Tree of Life before you were able to shake off the idea of God as stern and overbearing. The realization that the Divine is wholly joyful is best located in the Sefirah of Hesed. This is the position on the Tree that is linked to the notion of a forgiving and benevolent deity. It is, for instance, linked in the Western Mystery Tradition to the planet Jupiter, a planet regarded as a sign of good fortune and contentment.

THE JOURNEY The value of this dream reduces to the number 11, which is seen as an indication of a profound event about to happen in your life. Its nature is revealed by the compression of this dream. The first and last letters of the compression tell us that your highly energetic enthusiasm (Shin) will carry you even nearer to the secret wisdom of the Divine (Gimel). Part of this secret wisdom is bound up in the central letter, Nun. As this is a dream about the joyful nature of the Divine, we may be surprised to see the letter Nun with its melancholic associations being represented at all. However, spiritual insight does not lead us to deny the reality of the world. The world is at times a very sorrowful place, and the true mystery lies in coming to understand that even when this is so, it does not in any way threaten the overwhelmingly joyful nature of the Divine or the universe as a whole.

JUDGMENT
shfeetah–shphyth–שפיטה–790

MEANING In religious and in philosophical terms generally, the concept of judgment is decidedly difficult to deal with. On one hand, it is important that we take on the responsibility of judging ourselves and our behavior, as well as trying to use rational judgment when making any kind of decision in life. However, when it comes to judging the behavior of others, life becomes much more complicated. This is particularly true in a world where morality is a relative and no longer an absolute concept. There is of course no right answer here, but our attitude toward the judging of others is an important part of our

framework of belief and an area that you now must resolve for yourself.

THE TREE OF LIFE The value of this dream reduces to 16, and in the tarot this is connected to the Tower of Destruction card. The implication here in the context of this dream is that in judging your attitude to life you have realized that you need to make potentially earth-shattering changes to your lifestyle. These changes are perceived as necessary in order for you to feel that the way you are living actually reflects your emerging beliefs. The path for this dream is that of Peh, as it acts as a balancing channel between the emotional concerns of Netzach and the mental concerns of Hod. By finding a middle road between these two aspects of your personality, you will be able to find a way of making changes that satisfies your mind without causing you too much emotional distress.

THE JOURNEY We have already seen that the way forward for you is to find a balanced approach to making changes in your life. Part of this balance is learning not to judge yourself so harshly. The presence of the letter Shin in the spelling of the dream title tells us that you have a lot of energy, and very fiery energy at that. The fact that the letter Teth also appears indicates that this fiery energy could be misdirected in an excessively critical way toward yourself. An ideal way to deal with this potential problem is to always make sure that any criticism you level at yourself is a criticism you would be equally happy to put to someone else.

JUMPING
leekpots–lqphvtz–לקפוץ–306

MEANING The amount of energy indicated in this dream makes it somewhat doubtful that you will even have time to sit down and read this dream analysis! At present, scenery does not exist for you, since you are always so busy focusing on your next destination and never find time to try gazing out the window at the interesting things that are passing you by. While being goal centered can be a good thing in moderation, you are in the position of being so focused on your goals that you will miss out on life completely in your rush to get to the next staging point on your journey.

THE TREE OF LIFE The initial letter in the compression of this dream's value is the Shin, and it is to this path that the dream of jumping belongs. It is worth noting at this point that jumping is a significant choice as opposed to running or rushing.

When we jump, there is the idea of instantaneously moving from one place to another. In other words, we miss out on the journey altogether. One of the potentially negative aspects of the path of Shin is exactly that: You are so full of energized enthusiasm that you forget that the journey and not the destination is the important part.

THE JOURNEY When we reduce the value of this dream we find the number 9, which is the value of the letter Teth. Teth means "serpent" and is associated with self-deception. In your case, the self-deception is the mistaken belief that you are making excellent progress in the Great Work because you are doing everything so quickly. The value of this dream is equivalent to the value of the Hebrew word meaning "Merciful Father." This connection points out the level of genuine commitment that you have to the spiritual quest. It is also a strong hint that you need to be a little more "merciful" with yourself, or, in other words—slow down a little!

JUNGLE

joongel-gvngl- גוּנגּל *-92*

MEANING Some landscapes conjure up feelings of warmth and harmony and others are exciting, but if you are looking for an environment that is likely to case feelings of dread and fear, a jungle is an excellent candidate. In principle, jungles may seem an ideal place for adventure, but in reality they are incredibly dangerous places for animals and people alike. Ironically, they are also the most diverse and prolific of places in terms of the number of different life forms that can be found there. The value of this dream is equivalent to the value of the Hebrew word meaning "mud," and this sums up the nature of the fear that people associate with jungles, their impenetrable and ambiguous nature, with danger ever present but always hidden.

THE TREE OF LIFE The value of this dream is also equivalent to the value of the Hebrew word meaning "terror." This is not only an appropriate word for the feelings associated with this dream but is one of the titles of the Sefirah of Gevurah. It is in this Sefirah that the dream of the jungle belongs. When we are in Gevurah we learn that death is as fundamental to the nature of the Divine as is life or beauty. In the image of the jungle we have the presence not only of death and the fear of death but of the incredible proliferation of life. This is important, as Gevurah teaches us that it is only through death that new life can have the opportunity to come

into existence. At a practical level, though, this dream also suggests that you should be prudent and aware of the potential for danger of a more common kind—within your workplace, for example.

THE JOURNEY As disturbing as it may be at times, the experience of passing through Gevurah is incredibly valuable. When we reduce the value of the dream we find the number 11, which indicates that you are about to undergo a profound and life-changing shift in your perception of the world. This number refers to the realization that death and the fear of death are not simply necessary evils but are actually ways in which the Divine gives us the best chance of living our lives to their full potential. In the spelling of the dream title the letter Gimel appears twice. Gimel is connected to the ultimate truths that are contained within the Divine itself, and its double appearance is a way in which your higher self is reminding you that your time in Gevurah is to be valued and not simply endured.

KEYHOLE

khoor ha manool-chvr hmna'avl-
חוֹר הַמַּנְעוּל *-415*

MEANING Keyholes almost seem designed to be tantalizing. How many movies have you seen where one character just cannot resist looking through the keyhole to see who is doing what to whom? Of course, a keyhole offers us only a very restricted view of whatever lies behind the locked door. In spiritual terms, the dream of a keyhole indicates a feeling that you have achieved a certain level of wisdom but are far from having a complete picture. Indeed, the feeling is almost of being somewhat excluded from the whole truth, but this has not dampened your enthusiasm to discover what that truth is.

THE TREE OF LIFE When we reduce the value of this dream we find the number 10. This indicates that you have completed a significant stage in your inner development. However, given the content of the dream, we also know that you still have a very long way to go before you achieve some form of connection with your higher self. When we are in Malkut we are faced with a closed door. It takes an element of belief and initial effort to open that first door and begin to climb the Tree. You are currently beyond that first door and traveling up along the path of Tav. As the first path, even though you now have a definite awareness of the existence of a spiritual level to reality, there is still much that you cannot see.

THE JOURNEY The initial letter in the compression of this dream's value confirms the notion that you are currently placed on the path of Tav. The subsequent letter, Yod, is a positive encouragement that the spark of the Divine is present within you and merely needs to be enlivened by your continuing commitment to the Great Work. Finally, we have the letter Heh which means "window." The implication is that if you maintain your interest and enthusiasm, the view that you currently have through a mere keyhole will be expanded to the extent that you are looking through a window on the nature of your inner self.

KILLING
laharog-lhrvg- לַהֲרוֹג-244

MEANING If you told a psychiatrist that you were having dreams of killing either yourself or other people, he would likely see this as a worrisome sign of a lack of empathy for those around you or a lack of belief in the purpose of your life. However, the Kabbalistic interpretation of this dream is radically different: Maybe you do have some very negative feelings toward a particular individual that need to be worked on. In most mystical systems you will find the notion that in order to become a fully integrated spiritual being, you must first remove the demands and desires of your ego. In alchemy, the need to do this is put quite explicitly in the context of killing, albeit metaphorical, as chemical substances are substituted for the various elements of your personality. Thus, in order to produce "gold" from base metal, you must first "kill" the base metal.

THE TREE OF LIFE The realization that in order to live a truly fulfilling life you must first kill a part of yourself requires a considerable degree of spiritual awareness. The reduction of this dream produces the number 10, which indicates that you are about to complete a major cycle in your life. This completion relates to the final destruction of the controlling influence of your ego and its replacement by the influence of your higher self. This process takes place in the Sefirah of Tiferet. You are now approaching this Sefirah along the path of Nun, which is intimately connected with notions of mortality.

THE JOURNEY Perhaps the most difficult aspect of the Great Work is the removal of your ego-based attachments. This can be achieved only by concentrated effort on your part. The value of this dream is equivalent to that of the Hebrew word meaning "trance," and this hints at the level of concentration and commitment needed to create an inner space where contact with your higher self is possible. In the compression of the dream's value we have the letters Resh and Mem. These may be seen as the maternal and paternal aspects of the Divine, who are present in order to help you open the door (Daleth) that leads to the completion of this segment of your journey in the haven of Tiferet.

KING
melekh-mlk- מֶלֶךְ-90

MEANING "Delusions of grandeur" is the first phrase that springs to mind when looking at this dream title. Indeed, from a layperson's point of view, this dream is simply an exercise in wish fulfillment. While it may indeed be a very pleasant dream to have, it does have a weighty Kabbalistic significance. To dream of kingship in spiritual terms suggests that you are very close to achieving some form of higher control over yourself. It is important to remember that in our dreams we include only ourselves, so there is no suggestion of kingship over anybody's life but your own. The dream of a king is also symbolic of the notion of majesty as a spiritual quality.

THE TREE OF LIFE The compression of this dream produces only one letter and that letter is Tzaddi in its final form. The letter Tzaddi refers to the commitment and dedication that is needed to achieve any success in your spiritual endeavors. The fact that it appears in its final form emphasizes that your dream is not about the gaining of a privileged position. In fact, it shows that the process of becoming king of your own destiny requires an inordinate amount of hard work. In the tarot The Emperor card is connected to the letter Heh, and it is to the path of Heh that this dream belongs, not least because it carries you into the first of the three Supernal Sefirot.

THE JOURNEY The value of this dream is equivalent to that of the Hebrew word meaning "very silent," so one of the key things you need to remember at this stage is that this transformation is for you only. It is not something that you should share with anyone else. This is in part because in keeping secret the increase in the depth of our understanding, we are demonstrating that our desire for wisdom in no way relates to a desire to feel superior to those around us. You should be working to develop the attributes of the ideal king in your daily life—qualities such as compassion and nobility and generosity of spirit. In the spelling of the dream title the letter Kaph appears in its final form. This letter is associated with ideas of practicalities and physical work. A good way to demonstrate your continuing humility in the face of your spiritual progress would be to take part in some form of regular volunteer work such as running a soup kitchen for the homeless.

See Zohar symbol, King.

KISS
*nesheekah-nshyqh-*נשיקה-465

MEANING Certain dreams that seem deeply pessimistic turn out to be extremely encouraging when looked at from a Kabbalistic perspective. Equally, there are dreams that on the surface appear to be wholly positive in nature but that are actually a warning of some potential problem or downfall in terms of your inner progress. This dream conceals a warning within an image that seems not to carry even the slightest threat. It is perhaps worth mentioning here that the writers of the Gospels almost definitely had knowledge of Kabbalistic wisdom, and when we understand the hidden significance of the word *kiss* we can better understand the reasons for including that infamous kiss in the story of the Garden of Gethsemane.

THE TREE OF LIFE The value of this dream is equivalent to the value of the Hebrew word meaning "a little mouth." Given the importance of communication in the spiritual quest, we can take this as indicating a lack of proper communication. Additionally, the value of this dream is the same as the value that is achieved when we add together all the numbers from 1 to 30 consecutively. The hidden presence of the number 30 also refers this dream to the letter Lamed. The implication is that the force of your higher self is pushing you vigorously in one direction, but that you are choosing not to communicate with your higher self. Indeed, the reduction value of this dream produces the number 15, which tells us that you are still overly concerned with the material and not the spiritual in your life. Consequently, this dream belongs on the path of Ayin in its negative aspect.

THE JOURNEY Unless you learn to listen to your inner voice, your progression with the Great Work will stagnate. It is important that you accept that there will be difficult choices and unpleasant experiences along the route to spiritual achievement.

This fact is supported by the presence of the letter Tav in the compression of this dream's value. The letter Samech, which follows, is evidence that if you are willing to make some sacrifices you will feel the support of the Divine force. Finally, the letter Heh represents the glimpse of the Divine nature that awaits you if make a genuine commitment to your inner development.

KISSING
*lenashek-lnshq-*לנשק-480

MEANING In contrast to the dream of a kiss, the dream of kissing is as positive and encouraging as you would hope and expect from such a pleasant idea. To be kissing rather than simply to give someone a kiss implies some form of communication. Additionally, for two people to be kissing each other there must also be a level of closeness and mutual understanding. In Kabbalistic terms, this dream represents the achievement of a real level of contact between you and your higher self. The dream of kissing should be seen as an expression of pure love and connectivity rather than in any erotic sense. The issue in this dream is closeness as opposed to sexual attraction.

THE TREE OF LIFE When we look at the value of this dream there are a number of equivalent Hebrew words that have some relationship to the Sefirah of Malkut. It might therefore seem reasonable to place this dream on the Sefirah of Malkut; after all, kissing is a physical act and perhaps this is a dream that celebrates the best aspects of the material level of existence. However, to do this would be to fall into the trap of applying the most obvious meaning to the dream. In fact, the dream of kissing refers to a contact with your higher self. This takes place in the Sefirah of Tiferet and it is there that this dream is located. The references to Malkut are there in order to emphasize that once you have arrived in Tiferet, it becomes the equivalent of your new physical home.

THE JOURNEY In order to achieve the goal of communication with your higher self it is necessary for you to make a certain number of sacrifices. This is indicated by the presence of the letter Tav in the compression of the dream's value. The only other letter in the compression is Peh, which means "mouth" and relates to all forms of communication. In this case, it refers directly to the communication between you and your higher self. There is a Kabbalistic concept that the most spiritual of people are taken to Paradise with a Divine kiss, and it is this moment of kissing that you are aiming for in your spiritual work. In the absence of more specific advice, your best means of ensuring that this communication takes place is to set aside an hour a day to meditate and visualize the golden sphere of Tiferet. If you schedule your meditation so that it requires you to give up some leisure activity, you will find that positive results come much more quickly.

KITCHEN

meetbakh–mtbch–מטבח–59

MEANING No matter how egalitarian we are consciously, it is an unavoidable fact that our unconscious mind remains informed by cultural stereotypes long after we can rationally see their ridiculous nature. Once we get to the level of archetypal symbols, it takes even longer for them to become updated to suit a more enlightened society. This is in part because symbols emerge only after they have been embedded in the general unconscious for a considerable length of time. Consequently, when we dream of a kitchen we are focusing on the archetypally female aspects of our spiritual development.

THE TREE OF LIFE In any house, no matter how nice the living room or the den, people have a tendency to gather together in the kitchen. The kitchen is the central hub of the home and this is reflected indirectly by the fact that the value of the word *kitchen* is equivalent to the value of the Hebrew word meaning "brethren." When we combine the idea of domestic gatherings with the archetypally female energy behind this dream, the only path that really fits is the path of Mem. In spiritual terms it indicates a growing desire on your part to reach out to other members of the community in order to enrich their lives in some way.

THE JOURNEY This is an extremely positive dream and indicates that you have achieved a high level of spiritual understanding. You should certainly act on your wishes and get as involved as possible in the wider life of your community. However, there is also a lesson to be learned, and it is as emotionally upsetting as it is useful. In the compression of this dream we have the two letters Nun and Teth. Teth points to the self-deception that you will inevitably engage in, believing that you can make everything better in your community. The letter Nun represents the sorrow that you will experience when you realize you cannot solve everybody's problems.

KNAPSACK

tarmeel gav–thrmyl gb–תרמיל גב–685

MEANING The image of a knapsack fits very nicely with the metaphor of your spiritual development as a journey. Indeed, the letters Gimel and Beth that make up the second word in the Hebrew spelling of knapsack directly to the journey (Gimel) to your spiritual home (Beth). For some people the spiritual quest should be started utterly spontaneously. However, the content of this dream implies that you are a person who likes to take a far more organized approach. The knapsack is a symbol of your need to feel fully prepared with all the appropriate information before you venture into unknown territory.

THE TREE OF LIFE Clearly, you are at an early stage in your journey. The theme here is very much of someone anticipating rather than being fully engaged with his voyage of inner discovery. The value of this dream reduces to 19, and this number is connected to the tarot card The Sun. The Sun card is concerned with the intellect as an outward-looking active force. It is also linked to the path of Resh. The path of Resh is an ideal location for this dream since it is leads out of the Sefirah of Malkut. Additionally, it is a path that relates to themes of meticulous planning and the careful thinking through of any activity.

THE JOURNEY At one level, the only advice you need right now are words of encouragement. You have made a commitment to the spiritual quest and are single-mindedly setting out to ensure that you have the best possible chance of success. However, there is an argument for advising you to relax a little. Planning is very commendable, but you do need to leave some space in your life for the unpredictable. The idea of creative space is very important to any mystical path, and if you try to be totally in control you will not be able to give yourself over to the influence of the Divine.

KNIFE

sakeen–skyn–סכין–140

MEANING It would be very easy to take a negative view of a dream about a knife, especially in the current social climate where knives tend to be associated with petty crime and youth violence. However, as always it is important to look for the symbolic qualities of the dream image. The purpose of a knife is to cut away those things that are no longer of any use to you. It is also worth noting, when analyzing a dream, images that are very similar to the main dream image and what significant differences exist between the two. For instance, in this dream a knife has been selected rather than an ax or a cleaver, and this implies that one of the key features of the knife in this dream is its precision.

THE TREE OF LIFE The compression of this dream reveals the two letters Qoph and Mem. When combined these letters indicate an anxiety about your emotional state. It is therefore clear that the role of the knife in this dream is to cut away those aspects of your emotional makeup that are causing you difficulties. The final Nun in the spelling of this dream title tells us that you are deeply troubled by certain pieces of emotional baggage. The path of Lamed is the appropriate path for this dream because it provides the harsh but helpful force of your higher self, which will enable you to wield the knife with determination.

THE JOURNEY The reduction value of this dream produces the number 5, which is the number of the pentagram. This ancient symbol represents an individual who has united the four elements within himself under the organizing principle of his higher self. This is the promise within the dream of what you can achieve once you have dealt with your emotional issues, or, in mystical terms, once you have harmonized the element of Water within yourself. It may be helpful to consider seeking a professional therapist to assist you in cutting away those undesirable aspects of your emotional makeup.

KNOCKING

lehakeesh-lhqysh-לְהַקִּישׁ-445

MEANING As soon as we think of knocking in a spiritual sense we are likely to recall the phrase from the Gospels that if we knock "the door shall be opened" (Matthew 7:7). While not wishing to cast doubt on the Gospel, experience of the spiritual path suggests that this is far from being the case. One usually has to knock for an awfully long time before anyone even answers, and then it takes just as long before he can be persuaded to actually open the door. Perhaps the words of the Gospels should be read as symbolically as any other mystical text. This is worth mentioning if only to prevent anyone from falsely believing himself to be failing in the Great Work if it takes some time before he achieves any results.

Traditional Kabbalists might emphasize knocking as a symbol for a desire for spiritual growth that is currently blocked or hidden.

THE TREE OF LIFE The Hebrew alphabet can be divided into three sections. We have the three mother letters, seven so-called double letters, and twelve single letters. When we add together the value of all of the single letters, we get 445. This implies that you are on the verge of discovering some of the lesser secrets of the Divine nature, as these are associated with the single letters of the Hebrew alphabet. It is the double and mother letters which represent the more complex and esoteric secrets of the universe. This suggests that all your knocking is about to pay off. As the first of the single letters on the Tree of Life, this dream sits on the path of Qoph.

THE JOURNEY The value of this dream can be reduced to 13, and this number implies a great change in your perceptions of the universe. This ties in directly with the suggestion that you are about to access some initial insights into the Divine and your inner self. In the compression of the dream, the letter Tav advises you that while the change will be positive, it will not be achieved without some level of sacrifice on your part. However, the final letter, Heh, in the compression points to the glimpse of the Divine that will soon be yours.

KNOTS

kesher-qshr-קֶשֶׁר-600

MEANING Very often dreams will use puns and colloquialisms in order to try to pass a message from our unconscious through to our waking, conscious mind. This phenomenon was noted by Freud, but this insight was common knowledge among Kabbalists and within the Western Mystery Tradition in general long before psychoanalysis had been invented. The dream of knots draws on the common phrase "to be tied up in knots" when referring to a state of confusion or a dilemma that one is facing. From a spiritual point of view this interpretation also applies, and we can tell from the dream's content that you are having serious doubts about what step to take next in your spiritual journey.

THE TREE OF LIFE When we look at the spelling of this dream title we notice that the three letters follow each other in terms of their order on the Tree of Life. Their juxtaposition on the Tree means that if a person was at a point where he could begin to traverse the path of Shin, for example, he could also select one of the other two paths. The purpose of this is to emphasize the nature of your confusion. However, the dream does not belong on any of these paths. The path of Vav is concerned primarily with the ideas of choice and reflection, so it is ideally suited to this dream. Moreover, the value of this dream is equivalent to the Hebrew word meaning "six," and this is the value of the letter Vav.

THE JOURNEY The letter Mem is linked to ideas of maternal protection and self-sacrifice. In its final form it has a value of 600, which is the value of this dream. In order for you to move forward in the Great Work, you also need to consider spending some time behaving in a selfless way and concentrating on your inner development. By focusing on the needs of others for a while, you will find that the knots of confusion surrounding your personal quest will untie all by themselves.

LABELS
taveet-thvvyth-תוית-822

MEANING It is always comforting to be able to place labels on things. The act of naming or labeling gives us a sense of control over the world. In our normal day-to-day life it is also very useful as it enables us to share knowledge and experience. Imagine having a conversation about a problem with your car with someone who does not use the same labels as you for the various parts of the engine! However, when it comes to the world of the spiritual, the benefit of labels becomes less clear. The nature of the Divine is that it is beyond human comprehension. As soon as we try to place labels on our spiritual experience, we are in danger of reducing its meaning.

THE TREE OF LIFE Mainstream religion is very good at providing clear labels for every aspect of the Divine, from the definitions of good and evil right down to what food or clothing is acceptable and what is to be avoided at all costs. The mystical path places far more responsibility on the individual to find his own labels for all things spiritual. For this reason, this dream is located on the path of Ayin. This path is about the development of a strong individualistic approach to the Divine.

THE JOURNEY Taking on the challenge of genuinely knowing yourself and developing an understanding of the spiritual dimension of reality is a tough enough task without also having to formulate your own definitions along the way. However, the reduction value of this dream suggests a much more positive way of looking at the situation. The value of this dream reduces to 3, and the number 3 has always been associated with creativity. The message here is that rather than seeing the absence of labels for your higher experiences as a problem, you

should see it as an opportunity to express yourself creatively.

LABOR
laamol-la'amvl-לעמול-176

MEANING Before we embark on an exploration of the higher levels of reality, we are likely to have a romanticized view of what the process of enlightenment involves. The reality of the search for inner truth is that it requires dedication, a willingness to work hard, and, above all, patience. The idea of labor may not seem to be an especially spiritual theme, but in fact it touches on the most important requirement for success in the Great Work. Indeed, as Buddhists point out, "Before enlightenment chop wood, carry water; after enlightenment chop wood, carry water."

THE TREE OF LIFE When we reduce the value of this dream we find the number 14. This number is associated with ideas of balance and inner harmony, which is what we should hope to achieve through our spiritual work. It is also connected, by way of the Temperance card in the tarot, to the path of Samech. This path indicates the support and guidance of the Divine. A literal translation of the letter Samech is "prop." This is the path on which this dream lies and its main function is to act as prop for you to lean on while you work toward a higher level of understanding.

THE JOURNEY The repetition of the letter Lamed in the spelling of this dream title makes it clear that you have little choice right now but to work hard, since the harsh but fair energy of the letter Lamed is currently surrounding you. The compression of this dream shows us that you have some doubts (Qoph) as to whether you have the capacity to succeed, but the subsequent letter Ayin is a sure sign that deep down you have all the vigor and strength of will to persevere no matter how hard the going may get.

LABORATORY
maabadah-ma'abdh-מעברה-111

MEANING Laboratories and mysticism do not seem to be obvious bedfellows. However, the Kabbalah is unusual in that it is both deeply mystical and very rational and scientific in its application. We can also see the dream of a laboratory as a representation of your psyche's being transformed in the laboratory of the Divine. The value of this dream is equivalent to the value of the letter Aleph, and this connection emphasizes the fact that your efforts are designed to bring you ever closer to an understanding of the essential unity of the Divine.

THE TREE OF LIFE There is a sense in which this dream could be located anywhere on the Tree of Life. Whichever path or Sefirah we are on, we are always in a transformative process. The whole underlying principle of the Great Work is that of personal change and development on a spiritual level. However, the energy that drives this change comes from the Sefirah of Keter, and it is therefore not surprising that the value of this dream is equivalent to the value of one of the many Hebrew titles for Keter.

THE JOURNEY Wherever you are on the Tree of Life, you should always be looking to develop your understanding further, and you should always be trying to find your unique approach to the spiritual quest. The value of this dream reduces to 3 which is the number most associated with creativity. The presence of the number 3 serves to remind you that even in the lowest reaches of the Tree of Life you still have a unique soul, and you should bear that in mind as you find creative ways to relate to the world of the spiritual. The initial letter, Qoph, in the compression of the dream's value is an indication of the anxiety that we can feel at any level of our inner development. However, the subsequent letters Yod and Aleph tell us that as long as we stay true to that spark of the Divine within ourselves, we will ultimately come to partake of the unity of the Divine itself.

LACE
*srokh-shrvk-*שרוך-526

MEANING If you spent the night dreaming about lace, you are not likely to wake up the next morning convinced that you have just experienced a profound spiritual moment. In fact, most dreams that involve lace are far from obviously religious in their nature! However, there is a spiritual dimension to this dream if we look close enough. The nature of lace is that it is a particularly fine material, not transparent but still a material through which we can see. In spiritual terms, this very much relates to our position relative to the Divine in that we have a partial view of the spiritual reality.

THE TREE OF LIFE The value of this dream is equivalent to the value of a Hebrew word referring to a very bright light. From a Kabbalistic perspec-

tive, light is symbolic of the Divine energy working its way down the Tree of Life to the world of the physical. Since you are able to observe that light only through a veil, you are not yet in the higher reaches of the Tree. However, given that the veil itself is of the thinnest material, you have achieved a commendable level of insight. The one letter that stands out in the spelling of the dream title is Kaph, which appears in its final form. It is to the path of Kaph that this dream belongs, as it represents an eager and active approach to your spiritual development.

THE JOURNEY The letter Kaph also appears in the compression of this dream's value, both in its final and in its standard form. This implies that you are an extremely practical-minded person in terms of how you understand and relate to the lessons you have learned about the nature of your relationship to the Divine. The final letter, Vav, in the compression of this dream's value refers to the need for you to also engage in some peaceful reflection about your progress. The best way for you to reflect would be through an active form of meditation, such as tai chi or chi gung, as this will suit your very physical approach to life.

LADDER
*soolam-svlm-*סולם-136

MEANING The most famous image of the route up to enlightenment being characterized as a ladder is in the vision of Jacob. In Jacob's case there were angels to guide him. In the matter of your dream there may not have been angels to help you, but the spelling of this dream title does show that you are being assisted in your spiritual quest. The spelling of the title of your dream begins with Samech, which means "prop" and provides you a literal support as you climb up the Tree. Additionally, the spelling ends with the letter Mem, which represents the maternal force of the deity. The ladder is the main Kabbalistic symbol for spiritual development, and it represents the steady step-by-step approach that we should take to our inner journey.

THE TREE OF LIFE The reduction value of this dream produces the number 10, and this indicates that you are about to achieve the completion of a major cycle in your life. The value of the dream itself is equivalent to the value of the Hebrew word meaning "a voice." In terms of the Tree of Life, the path that corresponds to the idea of communication is that of Peh. This path acts as a balancing channel between the emotional focus of Netzach and the intellectual focus of Hod. Because this dream also suggests a completion of a cycle in your life, it is likely that you are on the verge of successfully integrating both the rational and the emotional aspects of your personality.

THE JOURNEY The value of this dream is also connected to the energies of Jupiter, and this suggests that the next few months are going to be very productive for you to the extent that you may find a number of unexpected and lucky circumstances occurring in your life. What you should be doing over the next few months is making the most of the current favorable conditions for your spiritual progress. Indeed, you might consider joining a meditation group or possibly taking some classes on the tradition and practice of Kabbalistic wisdom.

See Zohar symbol, Ladder.

LAKE

agam-agm-❏❏❏-44

MEANING Water is associated with the emotions in the Western Mystery Tradition. To dream of a lake suggests that you are in a state of inner calm and contentment. When we compare a lake to other bodies of water that you could have dreamed about, such as an ocean, we note that the key features of a lake are that it is self-contained and that it does not have tides. Metaphorically, this indicates an individual who is in control of his emotions and is able to respond to difficulties and crises in his life in a calm and mature manner.

THE TREE OF LIFE The value of this dream is equivalent to the value of the Hebrew word for the Zodiac sign Aquarius. This sign indicates a person who tends to have a very tolerant nature, and this continues the suggestions about your nature that are highlighted by the dream of a lake. The sign of Aquarius is linked to the path of Tzaddi, which is concerned with commitment and determination to the spiritual path. As the value of this dream is also equivalent to the Hebrew word meaning "fire" we can see that while you are possessed of an inner calm, you still retain a fiery passion for the Great Work itself.

THE JOURNEY To be as emotionally centered as you clearly are is quite a rare gift. You will be able to enhance your inner development if you use this quality to assist others in their spiritual journeys. The compression of this dream's value also acts as a strong voice in favor of your lending your talents to

support those around you. The letter Mem makes it clear that you have a strong protective urge and a desire to help. The final letter, Daleth, which means "door," makes it clear that you have the potential to enable others to make real progress toward an understanding of the Divine.

LAMB

*keves-kbsh-*ש❏❏-322

MEANING Sheep farming was enormously important to the early Hebrew peoples and so it should not be a surprise that the lamb features so significantly in the symbolism of the Kabbalah. At one level we are all lambs of God, and this dream could be seen simply as a recognition of your relationship to the Divine. It represents an acceptance of the fact that while you have free will and responsibility, ultimately you are dependent on the benevolence of the Divine in order to progress through your life in a successful and fulfilling manner. The lamb is a symbol of humility and meekness, both of which are qualities that, if you develop them, will help you in your spiritual development.

THE TREE OF LIFE Our mental image of lambs tends to be of cute little balls of wool full of life energy and innocence. However, if you are to take on the challenge of the Great Work, you must recognize your dependency on the deity while at the same time accept your responsibility for pushing yourself onward. The reduction value of this dream gives us the number 7, which is the value of the letter Zayin. This letter means "sword" and may seem incongruous in a dream about lambs. However, the image of a sword is a reminder that you need to be prepared to struggle in order to gain your spiritual goals, and this is the path on which your dream sits.

THE JOURNEY As mentioned above, the image of a lamb is a fundamental symbol within the Kabbalah. It is worth noting that the spelling of this dream title is the same as the letters produced by the compression of the dream's value. This is perhaps because it ensures that the symbolic meaning of the term *lamb* is kept as definite and clear as possible. The first letter, Shin, represents the energy and vigor of a young lamb and your ability to drive yourself toward your spiritual goals. The letter Kaph relates to the fact that spiritual activity must have a practical consequence as well as an inner one. You should, for instance, consider taking classes in yoga or some other contemplative physical exercise. If you do so, you will be that much closer to the spiritual home represented by the letter Beth.

✥LAMP

menorah-mnvrh-מנורה-301

MEANING To dream of any light source has profound spiritual implications because the Divine is most often represented by light. This is because light not only is capable of penetrating almost any substance, it also contains all the colors of the spectrum and so symbolizes the totality of the Divine. It is also appropriate that we represent the Divine as pure light given that we now know that the only constant or absolute value in the universe is the speed of light. The value of this dream is also equivalent to that of the Hebrew phrase meaning "My Lord the faithful King," which emphasizes the direct link to the Divine force referred to in this dream.

THE TREE OF LIFE A lamp is a very particular source of light in that it is used specifically to light our way when we are traveling in the darkness. In the tarot card The Hermit we see a robed figure steadily making his way forward with one hand resting on a staff for support while the other holds up a lamp. This card represents the sincere seeker of truth who is putting all his faith in the light of the Divine. This is very much your position right now, so your dream belongs on the path of Yod. This path not only represents the Divine spark that lights your inner lamp but is also linked to The Hermit card in the tarot.

THE JOURNEY Another key feature of a lamp is that it is held in the hand, so this dream is very clearly about the Divine light that we hold within ourselves. The value of this dream is equivalent to that of a Hebrew word meaning "fire." This is Fire in the sense of the element of Fire and relates to the powerful energy that is moving within you and enabling you to make the right choices as you travel closer to an understanding of the Divine. The reduction value of this word produces the number 4, which indicates the world of the material. The suggestion is that you need to find a way to manifest that fiery energy in some form of practical activity that will help you and those around you. You should also see the image as a sign that you ought to be looking to find ways of illuminating the lives of those around you in terms of their spirituality.

LANDSCAPE

nof-nvph-נוף-136

MEANING If a dream of land refers to the humble nature of humanity and our close connection to the earth, a dream of a landscape represents our greatest potential. When we look at the earth we are merely observing, but when we create a landscape we are adding something quintessentially human. A landscape represents our ability to create, and this is an ability possessed only by ourselves and by the Divine. In spiritual terms, this dream indicates that you are beginning to develop an awareness of the spiritual side of your nature and your innate potential to awaken the spark of the Divine within yourself.

THE TREE OF LIFE The key letter in the spelling of this dream title is the letter Peh, which appears here in its final form. This letter literally means "mouth" and is associated with all forms of communication. However, this dream is not situated on the path of Peh. The title of the dream points to the innate creativity within each of us. On the Tree of Life, the Sefirah of Netzach is associated with artistic expression and it is here that the dream belongs. This dream shares its value with the value of the Hebrew word meaning "ladder." While the dream of a ladder refers to an attempt at direct communication with the Divine, this dream is about the expression of your sense of your relationship to the spiritual.

THE JOURNEY While this is a very positive dream in terms of your growing understanding of the nature of the world of the spiritual, it carries with it a certain degree of sorrow. It is very difficult to be creative without having experienced the melancholy side of life. This exposure to the more difficult aspects of emotional experience is represented by the presence of the letter Nun in the spelling of the dream title. In order to make the most of your time in Netzach you should find some form of artistic medium that will allow you to express yourself fully. In doing so, not only will you grow spiritually but you will be able to see the value in even the negative emotional experiences that you have gone through. It would be very useful for you to spend time in the countryside and allow its beauty to develop your understanding of the presence of the Divine within the world.

LAUGHING

leetskhok-ltzchvq-לצהק-234

MEANING Western culture has had the misfortune of being dominated by organized religions that emphasize the serious and the pessimistic rather than point to the joyous and wondrous nature of existence. This dream is a wonderful sign that you have freed yourself from the guilt-ridden approach to the Divine that so often characterizes Western religious practice. The reduction value of this dream produces the number 9. This is the value of the letter Teth. Very often we look at the negative aspect of the letter Teth as a sign of self-deception. However, in the context of this dream, the letter Teth indicates the strength of will that has allowed you to see the deity as capable of enjoying the humorous as much as the serious within humanity.

THE TREE OF LIFE This dream belongs to the path of Resh, which is the first letter in the compression of the value of this dream. This path relates to intelligence of a positive and curious type. Additionally, it corresponds to a jovial outlook on the world. If the path of Resh could be characterized as a person, it would be the jolly and generous uncle who always makes a family get-together fun for everyone and always seeks to see the good in others. You are currently emulating all of these qualities and this bodes well for your future spiritual development.

THE JOURNEY While the initial letter in the compression of this dream title is wholly encouraging, the second letter sounds a slight warning. The letter Lamed represents the harsh, sometimes critical, but always fair force of your higher self. Its role is to push you on in the Great Work. Its presence in this dream suggests that while you fully appreciate the validity of fun and joy as a means of approaching the Divine, you need to spend more time in quiet contemplation in order to develop further. The final letter, Daleth, tells you that if you can combine a degree of seriousness with your exuberant celebration of life, then the door to the Divine will open for you.

LAUGHTER

*tsekhok-tzchvq-*צחוק*-204*

MEANING There is very little difference between the dream of laughing and the dream of laughter. However, the distinction between the two dreams is crucial in terms of their spiritual implications. Whereas the dream of laughing refers to the dreamer's engaging in laughter, the dream of laughter relates to the idea of amusement rather than actively being amused. It is likely that the implication here is that you are making people laugh rather than being involved in the laughter. This is a great gift to possess, as when people laugh they forget their fears and worries. At a spiritual level this dream suggests that you have the capacity to act in a healing capacity to those around you.

THE TREE OF LIFE When we reduce the value of this dream we find the number 6. This relates to the letter Vav and implies that you are a very thoughtful individual. This is further confirmed by the juhtaposition of the letters Qoph and Vav in the spelling of this dream title. The letter Qoph lets us know that your thoughts are often based in anxiety and worry. This is not worry for yourself but for those you care about. The combination of great concern and great thoughtfulness places this dream on the path of Vav.

THE JOURNEY The value of this dream is equivalent to the value of the Hebrew word meaning "the righteous," and this supports the idea of you as someone who has a great deal to offer the world. At one level, you can help people simply through the example you set in the way you behave. Additionally, you should consider looking into some form of natural or alternative therapy training. All the signs are that you could do very well if you pursued Reiki or shiatsu as ways in which to help people.

LAZY

*atsel-a'atzl-*עצל*-190*

MEANING Sometimes dreams can be so enjoyable that when we wake up we feel tempted to go back to sleep, hoping to get back to the dream. Equally, when we are asleep our ego is not on guard to ensure that no negative ideas about ourselves are presented to us. This means that our dreams have the capacity to force us to face our true selves without the justification and excuses that we can usually come up with to rationalize our behavior. This dream is something of a wake-up call for you, and you should determine that you are going to act now to ensure that you can actually develop your inner self.

THE TREE OF LIFE In spiritual terms, the idea of laziness relates to a failure on your part to engage with the Great Work. The value of the dream reduces to the number 10, and normally this value would suggest that the dreamer is about to complete a major cycle in his life. However, the nature of this dream is such that the number 10 refers to the Sefirah of Malkut as it is the tenth Sefirah on the Tree of Life. This position is also appropriate since the dream implies that as yet you have not moved forward beyond the merely physical dimension of reality.

THE JOURNEY The term *lazy* is a very harsh label to apply to anyone. However, it sometimes takes a very vigorous term of criticism to ensure that the person actually takes the critical comments seriously. The compression of this dream explains that your reason for avoiding spiritual work is that you have a deep anxiety (Qoph) about the high level of commitment (Tzaddi) that is required in order to fulfill your spiritual goals. You should consider joining a meditation group because the experiences of your peers will act as an encouragement to you in that you will see the future benefits of taking the Great Work seriously. You might also consider some form of volunteer work as a way to stimulate your enthusiasm and increase your general level of activity.

LEADING
moveel-mvbyl- מוביל-88

MEANING We are, of course, all equal in the eyes of God. However, equality does not imply uniformity. This means that while each of us has the same potential to achieve a union with the Divine, there are different roles that are suited to each of us depending on our personalities and attributes. This dream is a positive one, but it also places a great responsibility on you, since not only are you in charge of your spiritual development but you should be doing your best to encourage those around you to live in a spiritually enlightened manner. The value of this dream reduces to 7, which is equivalent to the value of the letter Zayin, meaning "sword." This refers to the fact that if you are going to lead in any way, you must be willing to struggle to uphold your principles.

THE TREE OF LIFE The value of this dream is equivalent to the value of the Hebrew word meaning "burning." This refers to your passion for the Great Work. This high level of dedication and vigorous enthusiasm places the dream on the path of Tzaddi. However, the idea of burning should also cause you to remember not to act without careful forethought. One of the greatest dangers of being in a position where your word is respected is that you can lose the appropriate sense of humility and caution in what you say.

THE JOURNEY Clearly, you have much to offer and should take this dream very seriously. You may already be in a position to open up a class on meditation or yoga or some such similar practice. If not, you should give serious thought to taking the necessary training to arrive at an appropriate level of expertise in one of these fields. The compression of the dream produces the letters Peh and Cheth. Peh points out that you will be able to lead by

your powers of communication, while Cheth indicates that you have a strong urge to act as a protector both of the spiritual approach to life and of those around you.

LEAKING
nezeelah-nzylh- נזילה-102

MEANING Following a spiritual path is never easy. It requires great honesty, a willingness to think openly and in depth about a broad range of complex issues, and inevitably involves a certain degree of spiritual challenge along the way. The idea of leaking does not suggest that you are facing any major difficulty in your attempts to develop your understanding of yourself and the spiritual. However, it does imply a nagging worry that something somewhere in your approach is not quite working. The value of this dream is equivalent to the value of a Hebrew word meaning "possession," and it may be that this dream is primarily about your need to determine everything that occurs in your life. The idea of a leak represents a worry about the possibility that there may be an aspect of your life over which you have no control.

THE TREE OF LIFE One of the lessons that we must learn as we climb up the Tree of Life is that while we have a responsibility to try to develop our higher nature, we must also accept that the existence of a deity means that we cannot be in charge of our entire life. This dream belongs to the path of Ayin, as this path is concerned with the desire to pursue a wholly individual approach to the Divine. In its negative aspect, as applies here, the path of Ayin represents an individual who has begun to believe that he is wholly the master of his destiny and has made the mistake of trying to remove the influence of the Divine from the equation.

THE JOURNEY The letter Nun at the start of the spelling of this dream title relates to the sense of sorrow you are experiencing due to your struggle (Zayin) to completely control your life. The letter Yod points to the Divine spark and is linked with the following letter Lamed. This combination implies that you need to accept that at times the Divine may choose to send you a lesson that is hard to deal with and is beyond your control. If you can make this leap of faith, you will be able to achieve the glimpse of the Divine nature that is promised in the letter Heh in the compression of the value of this dream. You should remember that the value of this dream is equivalent to that of the Hebrew word meaning "faith," and at all times you should try to allow your faith to calm your worries and anxiety.

LEAPING

deeloog-dylvg- דילוג -53

MEANING Almost all mystical paths will encourage you to pour vast amounts of energy into your spiritual work. This dream is very encouraging as it shows that you are expending a great deal of effort in progressing in the Great Work. Further, the idea of leaping indicates an upward motion emphasizing the sense of reaching toward God. Another important point to make is that leaping is seen as a very exuberant act. Consequently, we can see this dream as suggesting that you are not only striving to increase your inner understanding but are very aware of the joyful and wondrous nature of the universe.

THE TREE OF LIFE When we reduce the value of this dream we find the number 8. This is the number of the letter Cheth, which means "fence." This letter is associated with protection and the defense reflex. However, in this dream we are looking at an individual who is metaphorically leaping over the fence. In other words, you are so confident in your progress that you are happy to jump clear of any protective shield in order to gain the chance of reaching high enough to see the nature of the Divine. The applicable path for this dream is that of Heh, as it is both very close to the Supernal Sefirot and is associated with the vigorous zodiac sign Aries.

THE JOURNEY As positive as this dream is, we can see from the compression of the dream's value that you are not merely brimming with boundless enthusiasm. The letter Nun begins the compression of this dream and it indicates the presence of significant sorrow and melancholy in your life. The fact that you are still able to "leap" up toward God demonstrates a very mature and enlightened understanding. This is confirmed by the presence of the final letter, Gimel, in the compression. The path of Gimel leads all the way into Keter and is associated with the secret wisdom of the Divine that ultimately you will leap high enough to reach.

LEARNING

lemeedah-lmydh- למידה -89

MEANING The goal of the seeker of truth is to learn. Rather than simply accept dogma, the Kabbalist seeks answers for himself and is looking for a direct relationship with the Divine. This dream indicates that you are in the process of taking on the challenge of learning in order to begin to move up the Tree of Life. The value of this dream is equivalent to the value of the Hebrew word meaning "silence." This is perhaps the most important aspect of genuine learning. In order to fully understand new information we need to ensure that we have silenced our own thoughts. Doing this avoids our simply responding to the information on the basis of our preconceptions.

THE TREE OF LIFE The reduction value of this dream produces the number 8, which is the value of the letter Cheth. The letter Cheth signifies a protective force, and this is a very appropriate path for this dream. The more we understand about the nature of the Divine and our relationship to the spiritual level of reality, the more likely we are to make significant progress in the Great Work. The path of Cheth carries you into Binah, and this Sefirah is also known as the Great Mother. The Sefirah of Binah is the source of all the frameworks of wisdom that pass down to the physical world, so it is most important that you have learned as much as possible before entering this point on the Tree.

THE JOURNEY It is, of course, very important to read as much as possible about the whole issue of spirituality in order to increase your understanding of the Great Work. However, you should begin reading philosophy and literature. Indeed, there are few subjects that will not in some way contribute to the development of your inner self. The value of this dream is equivalent to that of a Hebrew word meaning "body," and this draws attention to the learning that is based not in books but in physical experience. If you wish to fully prepare for entering the Sefirah of Binah you need to give some thought to regularly practicing some form of meditative exercise such as yoga.

LEATHER

or-a'avr- עור -276

MEANING In today's world, leather clothing is commonplace. However, in the times when Kabbalistic symbolism was emerging, the wearing of leather indicated that you had some degree of status within your community. The value of this dream is equivalent to the value of the Hebrew word meaning "Moon." The Moon is traditionally associated with the hidden and the unconscious aspect of our personality. This suggests that any idea of status would relate to a position where you were offering advice and emotional support to people, possibly in the context of a spiritual framework.

THE TREE OF LIFE The Moon is assigned to the path of Qoph on the Tree of Life. However, this association relates to the linkage of the Moon to anxiety and fear rather than the more positive lunar aspects such as intuition and empathy. The Moon is also connected to the path of Gimel, and this is where we should locate this dream. Gimel is concerned with the most complex and deep mysteries of the Divine. It is also associated with the High Priestess card from the tarot in the Western Mystery Tradition. This card points to an individual who has the ability to take the secret wisdom and convert it into explanations that everybody can understand.

THE JOURNEY This dream is quite profound in its implications for you and your future. You have nearly reached the highest point on the Tree of Life, but the dream indicates that you now need to use the wisdom you have accumulated to help others. The compression of this dream tells us that you are a quick-witted and expressive (Resh) individual. Additionally, and equally importantly, you are happy to construct your own interpretation of the world and how it applies to your spiritual activity (Ayin). The final letter, Vav, represents the macrocosm or the Divine itself. If you are able to give yourself over to help others reach an understanding of the spiritual world, you will come to achieve a communion with the Divine.

LEAVES

*aleheem-a'alhym-*עלדים-155

MEANING If we categorize the body of spiritual wisdom and understanding as a Tree, then a dream of leaves represents the snippets of wisdom that fall from that Tree in order that we may notice them and be enriched by the experience. The value of this dream reduces to 11, and this indicates that you are about to undergo a profound development in your spiritual understanding. The value of this dream is equivalent to the value of the word "seed," and this indicates that you are in the early stages of your journey.

THE TREE OF LIFE The notion of a seed suggests that while you may be relatively new to the world of the spiritual, you have the potential to grow and achieve a great level of insight. There is also a complex relationship between the leaves that are falling from the Tree of Life and the subsequent transformation of an individual into a seed for spir-

itual growth. This cycle reflects the fact that with death comes the possibility of new life. The full mystery of this cycle is fully revealed in the Sefirah of Gevurah. However, this dream sits on the path of Tav, which requires you to sacrifice at least a part of yourself in order to reach the Sefirah of Yesod. In this way, it prefigures the lesson that is fully learned once you reach Gevurah.

THE JOURNEY As someone new to the idea of the spiritual dimension of reality, your key role right now is to collect as many of those leaves of wisdom as you possibly can. The first thing you need to remember is that you can find wisdom in the most unlikely of places. One thing you should do is to try to spend an afternoon in the park simply looking at everything that passes you by, from the smallest insect to people with their children to the scenery in the park itself. With each thing you see, you should try to find a way in which you can relate it to a spiritual view of the world.

LEAVING

*laazov-la'azvb-*לעזוב-115

MEANING Whether or not we see this dream as positive depends on how we interpret the notion of leaving. If we take this to mean that you are leaving behind the possibility of a spiritual life, then this dream would be a very negative one. On the other hand, if this dream refers to the idea of leaving behind a wholly secular existence, then this dream is extremely encouraging. The advantage that a Kabbalistic interpretation has over a standard psychological approach is that we look not only at the content but at the values behind the title of the dream. The value of this dream is equivalent to that of the Hebrew word meaning "eager," so we can consider this to imply that you are leaving behind the wholly physical world in favor of a spiritual path.

THE TREE OF LIFE The central letter in the spelling of this dream is Zayin. This letter means "sword" and indicates that while your decision to leave the secular world behind is a positive one, you have a number of difficulties ahead that you will have to struggle with. The value of the letter Zayin is also produced when we reduce the value of this dream. This repeated reference to Zayin makes it clear that leaving behind your material concerns and attachments is not easy, and it is the path of Zayin to which this dream belongs.

THE JOURNEY Not surprisingly, you have some doubts and anxieties about your decision, and this is indicated by the presence of the letter Qoph when we compress the value of the dream's title. The subsequent letter, Yod, represents the spark of the Divine that has been awakened within you. No matter how difficult the journey becomes, you will continue on your way toward the glimpse (Heh) of the Divine. When you feel yourself losing confidence, the energy of Yod will excite you and stimulate you to continue with your search for the truth.

❧LEGS
*raglayeem-rglaym-*רגלאים-284

MEANING This dream works on two distinct levels and both of them are equally important in terms of your inner development. The most obvious idea that this dream represents is the notion of freedom. Of course, most of us are more likely to use a car to get around, or indeed we may not have mobility in our legs, but at a symbolic level the image of legs signifies movement. In spiritual terms this indicates that you have a desire to move up along the Tree of Life. The value of this dream is equivalent to the value of a Hebrew word meaning "a small enclosed garden." This emphasizes the desire you have to break out of any feeling of enclosure or restriction.

THE TREE OF LIFE When we look at the position of this dream we need to consider the second level on which this dream operates. The Tree of Life can be seen as a representation of the physical body. The legs are portrayed by the left and right columns on the Tree below the Sefirah of Tiferet. Since your dream relates to both legs, your position on the Tree of Life lies somewhere on the middle pillar of the Tree. When we combine this factor with the idea of needing to move on and up in terms of your spiritual progress, we can locate this dream on the path of Samech. This path is both central on the Tree and leads into the Sefirah of Tiferet, where you will be able to make some form of contact with your higher self.

THE JOURNEY When we reduce the value of this dream we find the number 14. This connects to the path of Samech because of this number's association with the tarot card Temperance, which sits on the path of Samech. We can also further reduce the value to 5, which indicates that you are in the process of ruling the four elements by the fifth element of Spirit. The compression of the dream's value demonstrates that you are receiving the benevolent influence (Resh) of the Divine and that you are able to achieve some level of communication (Peh) with your higher self. Most important, the

final letter, Daleth, indicates that you will be able to open the door to the Sefirah of Tiferet.

See Zohar symbol, Leg.

LENDING
*lehasheel-lhshayl-*להשאיל-376

MEANING To dream of lending things to people is quite unusual. The immediate question that springs to mind is why you would dream of lending rather than simply giving. The key difference, as unpalatable as it might be, is that when you lend something to someone you have a degree of power over him in that he is obligated to you. From a Kabbalistic perspective, this dream suggests that your current reasons for engaging in spiritual pursuits have less to do with a wish to achieve communion with the Divine than with a desire to feel a greater degree of power in your life.

THE TREE OF LIFE To retain a lust for power is to have missed one of the most important lessons of the spiritual quest. That lesson is that in order to become a more spiritual individual, you need to let go of all material concerns. This does not mean just your attachment to money or the comforts of life but to any attractions that are primarily concerned with the physical rather than the spiritual realm. The value of this dream reduces to 7, which is the value of the letter Zayin. This letter means "sword," and in its negative aspect it implies a desire to force your way through life by attacking everything that does not agree with your perspective. Your dream is placed on the path of Zayin in its negative aspect due to your continuing attraction to power.

THE JOURNEY If you wish to move forward and achieve some level of spiritual growth in your life, you should pay attention to the message that lies within the spelling of this dream title. There is a strong force (Lamed) that is trying to push you toward seeing (Heh) the spiritual energy (Shin) behind the unity of the Divine. If you can do this, you will be able to awaken the Divine spark (Yod) within yourself. This will finally lead to your being able to accept the harsh and critical voice (Lamed) of your higher self and in so doing you will begin to develop spiritually.

❧LETTER
*meekhtav-mkthb-*מכתב-462

MEANING To dream of a letter indicates a need for some form of communication. The fact that the dream is of a letter rather than a conversation suggests that the communication you are looking for is relatively formal in nature. From a Kabbalistic perspective, this formal communication implies a wish to gain access to the wisdom that is hidden within the paths of the Tree of Life. It may also suggest that there is a message waiting for you in the higher realm. The value of this dream is equivalent to the value of the Hebrew word meaning "path." This tells us that the nature of the communication you are seeking is some kind of instruction or guidance on how best to access the various paths on the Tree of Life.

THE TREE OF LIFE The concern with instruction, particularly instruction of a formal kind, suggests that you are looking for a rational basis on which to found your spiritual activity. This places the dream squarely in the Sefirah of Hod. This location on the Tree of Life is related to the process where we learn how to integrate a spiritual worldview with a rational understanding of the world. There are strong indications in this dream that while the Sefirah of Hod is just one of the many staging posts on the way to Keter, you are someone who is likely to maintain a largely rational approach to your spirituality throughout your journey.

THE JOURNEY No matter how much it goes against your nature, if you wish to progress up the Tree you will need to compromise on some of your ways of interpreting and interacting with the world. The letter Tav in the compression of the dream's value points to that need to sacrifice a certain amount of your hard-nosed scientific outlook on the world. Instead of pure science, you need to rely on the supportive energies of the letter Samech. You should also consider keeping a journal so that you are able to record the messages from your higher self as and when they occur. If you are able to lean on the "prop" of the Divine, you will find that you are able to return to the house (Beth) of the Divine.

LIAR

shakran-shqrn- שקרן-650

MEANING Nobody likes to be called a liar, so to dream of being a liar is particularly disturbing. When we are awake, our ego has a tendency to protect us from any self-perception that is too critical. However, when we are asleep, our unconscious has free rein to say whatever it wishes, no matter how negative that might be. Moreover, our unconscious has no reason to lie, and what we dream about is al-

ways an honest reflection of our true nature and behavior.

THE TREE OF LIFE While our unconscious is never dishonest, it is often highly symbolic. Consequently, this dream does not necessarily mean you are deliberately setting out to lie. Indeed, at the spiritual level this dream is concerned with you alone, so the concept of lying is much more about the idea of untruth than it is about your misleading anyone. The central letter, Qoph, is the key to this dream as it represents the anxiety that you are feeling. This anxiety is causing you to doubt everything that you hear or read regarding the nature of the spiritual, hence the image of lying.

THE JOURNEY Beginning a journey is always tough and the spiritual journey is the toughest of them all. It is very common to wonder whether you might simply be fooling yourself. It is possible that the dream image of lying refers to a certain degree of self-deception with regard to the Great Work itself or with some other aspect of your life. The letter Nun in the compression of this dream points to your melancholic tendencies right now. However, the other letter in the compression, the letter Mem, indicates that your higher self is trying to help and protect you. You should experiment with some deep-breathing exercises, which may help you to calm down enough to hear the quiet voice of your intuition advising you on the right way to proceed.

LIFEBOAT

seerat hatsalah-syrth htzlh- סירת הצלה-800

MEANING All dreams that involve any form of rescue represent a state of deep confusion and anxiety on the part of the dreamer. The causes of this anxiety may be manifold but as Kabblalists we look to a broad reference of symbols in order to pin down the meaning of this dream more precisely. The fact that your means of rescue is a lifeboat tells us that your main cause of concern is emotional. We can say this with confidence because the element of Water is always concerned with the area of emotion. This dream indicates that you are on the verge of finding some resolution to your emotional difficulties.

THE TREE OF LIFE The value of this dream is equivalent to the value that we would find if we added up the letters of the three lowest paths on the Tree of Life—Tav, Shin, and Qoph—all of which have their origin in Malkut. These three paths terminate in the Sefirot of Yesod, Hod, and Netzach, respectively. Unusually, this dream sits on all three of these paths, and therein lies the root of your emotional distress. You are trying to balance the three competing areas of emotion, intellect, and spiritual awareness within yourself.

THE JOURNEY The task of creating a harmonious balance between all the conflicting elements within your personality is an essential part of the Great Work, but you are attempting this challenge at a very early stage in your inner development. When we look at the compression of this dream's value we find that only one letter is represented. This is the letter Peh in its final form. The letter Peh symbolizes communication in all of its myriad forms. As it is in its final form and stands alone in the compression, this is a clear indication that the key to your rescue lies in talking about your problems. You should make a point of locating a meditation class or some other spiritually focused group so that you can begin to share your experiences with people who have more experience in such things.

❧LIGHT

or-avr-אור-207

MEANING At one time, the connection of light to the Divine was very much a hidden symbolism that would be revealed only to those few dedicated seekers of truth who were deemed worthy of such information. Today, it is common knowledge even among those who have no real interest in spiritual matters that light is a symbol of the outpouring of the Divine force. The image of light is also symbolic of the inspiration that drives any creative process. The spelling of this dream title reveals the means by which the light of the Divine works its way down to the human level of existence. The limitless light originates in the unity of the Lord (Aleph), which must then find a way of entering the minds (Vav) of men. The image of light finds its symbolism in the Sun (Resh), as this is the physical giver of life within our solar system.

THE TREE OF LIFE The value of this dream is equivalent to the value of the Hebrew phrase meaning "Lord of the universe." This association emphasizes the connection of this dream to the Divine itself. When we look for its location, we are actually looking for the source of this dream's energy rather than placing it on the Tree. This dream's location lies outside the boundaries of the Tree of Life as you know it so far. Beyond the Sefirah of Keter, which is the closest anyone can come to a complete communion with the Divine, lies the region known as "Ain Soph Aur." This translates as "limitless light,"

and it is the area of the absolutely unknowable and absolutely undiluted Divine force. By finding ways to be creative in your life, you will encourage a deeper understanding within yourself of the creative nature of the Divine.

THE JOURNEY If we reduce the value of this dream we find the number 9. This is the value of the letter Teth, which means "serpent." It may seem extremely strange that the traditional symbol of evil is intimately connected to the symbol of the absolute Divine. There are certain hermetic Kabbalists who would argue that this shows that the separation of good and evil is a purely human concept and that all is one within the Divine. A less controversial explanation is simply that the letter Teth also stands for strength of will in its positive aspect. What is more, the route up the Tree of Life toward Keter is often referred to as The Serpent Path. The inclusion of a reference to the serpent in this dream is there simply to remind you that even in the presence of the Divine light it still requires great effort on your part to succeed.

LILY

khavatselet-kbtzlth-כבצלת-542

MEANING To dream of almost any flower suggests an individual with a sensitive and emotional temperament. This is certainly the case with the dream of a lily. The lily is a particularly delicate flower and its very delicate white color makes it highly suited to playing a part in spiritual symbolism. The value of this dream reduces to 11, and this indicates that you are about to undergo a profound spiritual experience that is likely to alter your whole outlook.

THE TREE OF LIFE The lily is traditionally associated with funerals and so at first sight may not seem to be a wholly optimistic symbol for you to dream about. However, we need to remember that in spiritual terms this reference to mortality refers not to your higher self but to the ego self, which you must discard in order to achieve your full spiritual potential. The lily tends to be associated with the Sefirah of Malkut, and this is where we should locate your dream. This does not mean that you have not made any spiritual progress; it means simply that this dream is about making the connection between the things of the earth and the Divine.

THE JOURNEY The value of this dream is equivalent to the value of a Hebrew phrase meaning "the unity of Israel." When we take the reference to Israel to include all of humanity, we can see that this dream is urging you to look for the signs of unity and interconnectedness among all things within the world. In learning to see the way in which we and every element in the universe are intrinsically linked, you will be gaining a spiritual insight that will carry you far above the Sefirah of Malkut.

❧ LION

aryeh - aryh - אריה *- 216*

MEANING There are some symbols that resonate extremely deeply within us no matter how far removed from us they are in historical terms. The image of a lion is one such symbol. Even though these are rare animals whose habitat is certainly not in the vicinity of any of our neighborhoods, we all have an instinctive response to the symbol. It represents kingship and power and the overriding strength of will. While the lion may be a killer, it does not create a sense of fear so much as respect in our minds when compared to our immediate response to a tiger, for instance.

THE TREE OF LIFE The tarot card Strength depicts a young woman controlling a large, fierce lion. This picture represents the potential for incredible willpower that lies within each of us. This dream refers to your ability to succeed through sheer willpower and determination. Thus it is located on the path of Teth, as the positive aspect of this path is concerned with individual strength and inner focus. Appropriately enough, the tarot card Strength is also associated with the path of Teth on the Tree of Life.

THE JOURNEY The lion of your dream is rather like the famous lion Aslan in C. S. Lewis's *Narnia Chronicles*. It is a proud and strong animal but one with an innate sense of justice and a wholly benevolent outlook. The letter Resh in the compression of this dream's value indicates that your will to complete the Great Work has not led you to be dismissive or anything but amiable to those around you. The following letter, Yod, shows us that in your attitude to the spiritual quest and to other people you have awakened the Divine spark within you, and, as pointed out by the final Vav in the compression, you will ultimately be rewarded with a glimpse of the macrocosmic Divine itself.

LIPS

safah - shphh - שפה *- 385*

MEANING Sometimes we just don't want to wake up, and to be lying in bed dreaming of someone's

lips is probably far more pleasant than getting up and going to work! As you might expect, this is a dream about the feelings of closeness and intimacy. From a psychological point of view, this dream relates to the desire for a close relationship. When we look at the dream from a Kabbalistic perspective, we should see it as referring to your longing for an in-depth understanding of the nature of the Divine.

THE TREE OF LIFE Your purpose in doing the Great Work is to try to become one with the Divine. Inevitably, this means transcending your physical concerns and attachments. However, the mystical path does not require that you regard the physical as in any way bad in itself. It is the dependency on material comforts that interferes with our spiritual development. An appreciation of the sensual aspect of the world is simply an appreciation of another aspect of the Divine. The value of this dream is equivalent to the value of the Hebrew word for "Assiah," which is another way of referring to the physical dimension of the universe. In terms of the Tree of Life, this dream sits on the path of Tav, which represents the awareness of the spiritual mixing with the appreciation of the positive side of the physical.

THE JOURNEY The value of this dream reduces to 7, which is the value of the letter Zayin, meaning "sword." The message here is that although it is right to enjoy the sensual side of life in a nondependent manner, you also need to be pushing up toward a greater appreciation of the spiritual side of life. The compression of the dream's value reveals the letter Shin, indicating that you certainly have the energy and enthusiasm that can be directed toward spiritual matters. The subsequent letters Peh and Heh suggest that you are most likely to see why you should spend more time contemplating the Divine if you find someone or a group of people with whom you can share your thoughts.

LOAD

masa - msha - משא *- 341*

MEANING Before we even consider the possible Kabbalistic implications of this dream, there is a definite sense that you feel that you are carrying an awesome responsibility. It is quite probable that you have a professional and demanding job, resulting in less mental space for you to consider issues not directly related to your work. The consequence of this is that the task of discovering your inner nature can seem like just another burden, another chore to add to the never-ending list of things to do. This dream may also refer to a personal or financial load such as difficult personal finances or the need to care for a member of your family.

THE TREE OF LIFE When we reduce the value of this dream we find the number 8, which is the value of the letter Cheth, meaning "fence." This letter relates to our defense mechanisms and the need to protect ourselves, and it is the path on which we locate this dream. In the context of this dream, it refers to your tendency to put off thinking about spiritual issues because you have so many other things going on inside your head that you feel you simply cannot take the additional mental load. The value of this dream is equivalent to that of a Hebrew word meaning "guilty," and this lets us know that you also have a strong desire to restructure your life so that you can attend to the Great Work.

THE JOURNEY It is not necessary for you to reorganize your entire life in order to be able to devote sufficient time to trying to forge a link with your higher self. You simply need to set aside an hour every evening and then religiously stick to it. If you add up the time you spend in front of the TV or reading magazines each day, you are bound to be able to construct an hour of free time. In the first half hour, though, you should not think about anything religious or spiritual, in fact you should try not to think at all. The first half of your time should be spent unwinding and genuinely relaxing. You can best achieve this by lying in a warm bath, closing your eyes, and visualizing a warm, golden ball of healing energy moving over your whole body, soothing away all the tension and aches of the day.

LOCK

manool-mna'avl- מנעול *-196*

MEANING In discussing the nature of spiritual progression we often refer to moving up, to paths and to doors. We can extend the metaphor of movement to this dream and see that the idea of a lock indicates some form of block in your spiritual progress. The value of this dream is equivalent to that of a Hebrew word meaning "summit point." This suggests that your progress has been blocked because you believe you have reached as high as you possibly can.

THE TREE OF LIFE The absolute summit of the Tree of Life is, of course, the Sefirah of Keter. However, there is no indication in this dream that you have actually reached that point in terms of the depth of your spiritual insight. Indeed, had you reached the level of wisdom characterized by the Sefirah of Keter, you would know that, far from being at the summit, you still had much more to learn. This dream actually belongs to the Sefirah of Tiferet. It is here that we achieve some form of contact with our higher self, and it is very easy to believe that this indicates the completion of the Great Work.

THE JOURNEY When we reduce the value of this dream we find the value of the letter Zayin, meaning "sword." This is a strong hint from the higher that rather than resting on your laurels, you need to be grappling more forcefully to understand more and more about the nature of the universe. This is confirmed by the letter Tzaddi, which appears in the compression of this dream's value and indicates a need for commitment and dedication. The initial letter Qoph in the compression gives a clue as to why you might feel that you had no farther to climb. The letter Qoph indicates anxiety and worry, and it is the fear of losing what you gained in Tiferet that is holding you back right now. The only way to deal with such fears is to remind yourself of what you would have missed out on if you had allowed your anxieties to rule your behavior when you first started out in the Great Work.

LOCKET

teelyon-thlyvn- תליון *-496*

MEANING Traditionally, we keep a photograph of our loved one in a locket. So, this dream suggests that you are spending a lot of time thinking about your family and close friends right now. In spiritual terms, this dream indicates that you want to forge a close relationship with the Divine. This is a very positive dream in that it represents your view of the Divine as a figure to whom you can relate and feel love toward, as you would to a member of your family. This means that you have moved beyond a perception of the Divine as a being whom you should fear in any way.

THE TREE OF LIFE When we reduce the value of this dream we find the number 19, which relates to The Sun card in the Tarot, which is connected to the path of Resh. This path is a very optimistic and active path that focuses on the development of your perception of the Divine in a way that relates the spiritual to the material world. This process allows you to understand the higher force as a benevolent power in such a way that you could associate it with the feelings we connect with a person whose picture we might keep in a locket. Or, in other words, you may begin to relate to the Divine as you would to a member of your close family.

THE JOURNEY The spiritual quest is ultimately a solitary journey, since no one else can experience your higher self on your behalf and no two people will develop exactly the same relationship with God and the universe. However, as you gain insights into the nature of the Divine you can allow them to inform the way you interact with those around you. This not only helps your development but, as you share your infectious enthusiasm for life, you may also encourage others to look for a deeper meaning to their existence.

LOCUSTS

*arbeh–arbh–*אַרְבֶּה*-*208

MEANING Do not be surprised if you wake up feeling itchy after this dream! Insects in general can make us feel creepy, but locusts have a particularly unpleasant reputation. This is not least because of the part they play in the story of the plagues of Egypt. However, you may be quite surprised to hear that this is a very positive dream. You should remember that the plague of locusts was sent not to trouble the tribes of Israel but to punish the Egyptians. In other words, the locust symbolizes the vigorous removal of those things that threaten your development rather than threaten you as an individual. This dream image can, for instance, relate to the need to remove certain irritants and trivial distractions from your life.

THE TREE OF LIFE The value of this dream is equivalent to the value of the Hebrew word meaning "kill" and "multitude." These associations immediately call to mind the notion of a plague of locusts. The next few months are going to be quite difficult for you because the removal of your current unhealthy attachments will not occur without a degree of upset and doubt. The dream of locusts sits within the path of Lamed, as this path is directly connected to the notion of a strong and sometimes harsh force driving you on to a higher state of consciousness.

THE JOURNEY It is almost inevitable that as you gradually remove all superfluous aspects of your life so that you can focus more clearly on the Great Work, you will experience moments when you seriously consider giving up altogether. It would be ideal to find other individuals who are also attempting to improve the spiritual quality of their lives, because you could offer one another mutual support. The compression of this dream's value attempts to reassure you by pointing out the fact that as tough as things are, your experiences still stem from the benevolent force of the Divine (Resh) and that this process is ultimately for your protection (Cheth).

LODGER

*dayar meeshneh–dyyr mshnh–*דַּיָּיר מִשְׁנֶה*-*619

MEANING The value of this dream is a prime number (a number that can be divided only by itself and by one). Such numbers are quite rare and in mystical terms the presence of a prime number should be seen as indicating that you are an extremely unusual individual. The idea of a lodger when related to your position within the world suggests that you have a feeling of not quite fitting in to the so-called normal world. This feeling of being on the outside looking in occurs because you have a natural sensitivity to spiritual matters, and this leads you to see the world in a very individual manner. However, we cannot live in a vacuum, and this dream also points to your need for companionship in your spiritual quest.

THE TREE OF LIFE In the spelling of this dream title we see the letter Yod repeated. This letter represents the spark of the Divine that exists within each of us. It is a key feature of the spiritual quest that you should awaken that Divine spark so that it can guide you on your route to spiritual enlightenment. The fact that this letter occurs twice points to a very powerful will, especially as the letter Daleth, representing the doorway to the mysteries of the universe, precedes these two letters. It is the path of Daleth on which we should place this dream, as there you can unveil the hidden mysteries both for yourself and for those around you.

THE JOURNEY The route you now need to take is given in the compression of this dream's value. The initial letter, Mem, points to your willingness to try to help others. Although you feel somewhat distanced from other people, you are very keen to use your innate understanding for the benefit of anyone you come into contact with. The central letter, Yod, refers back to the Yod in the spelling of the dream title and serves to emphasize the fact that you do have an unusually strong connection to the Divine. The final letter of the compression is Teth. This has a dual purpose: on one hand, it is a warning not to allow that strong link to blind you from recognizing those moments when you take a wrong turn. At the same time, it is an encouragement to you to use your great strength of character to encourage as many people as possible to begin to examine their inner lives.

LOOKING FOR A PRIVATE PLACE

lekhapes makom pratee-lhphsh mqvm prty-
להפש מקום פרטי-900

MEANING At first sight you might look at the content of this dream and assume that it relates to someone who is trying in some way to escape from his life or society. However, it is important to note that there is no sense of desperation in the content, nor is there any sign of low self-esteem or lack of confidence in any of the values within this dream. This search for a private place relates not to a wish to escape but to a desire to look even more deeply into your inner nature and to find the mental space that will allow you to do so.

THE TREE OF LIFE If we take the value of Lamed and multiply it by itself (in other words, 30 multiplied by 30), we arrive at the value of this dream. This suggests that you are currently experiencing an extremely powerful drive from your higher self to focus on your spiritual development. It is likely that if you do not spend at least an hour a day right now in some way considering matters relating to the Great Work, you will feel that you have let yourself down. However, this dream is located not on the path of Lamed but on that of Tzaddi. The total value of this dream is equivalent to the value of letter Tzaddi in its final form, and this relates to your great commitment to the spiritual quest.

THE JOURNEY The appropriate action to take in relation to a dream is usually very tenuously related, if it all, to the obvious content of the dream. However, in your case, the steps you should now be taking address the theme of your dream completely. It is very important for you to find a private place. In the long term this means finding some mental space, and that is a matter of practicing deep breathing and meditation techniques so that you find a haven of calm no matter where you are. In the short term, you should consider taking a trip on your own so that you have at least a weekend with complete inner silence and peace.

LOSS OF AN OBJECT

*leabed khefets-labd chphtz-*לאבד הפץ-215

MEANING A fundamental premise of the Western Mystery Tradition is that we are all in a state of loss. From a Kabbalistic point of view, the purpose of your life is to try to regain that higher part of yourself—it is essentially a spiritual quest. You know that something is missing, but you don't yet know what it is or how to find it. This dream is essentially your higher self's attempt to prompt you to think more closely about how to regain your connection with the Divine. The value of this dream shows us the way forward to the spiritual quest and details the key problem we face in taking the first great step on the road that lies before us. The value of this dream is equivalent to the value of the Hebrew word meaning "a narrow path" and indicates the need to abide by certain structures in order to succeed in your spiritual quest.

THE TREE OF LIFE As this dream points to the initial realization that there is more to life than the immediate world around us, it is situated right on the bottom of the Tree in the Sefirah of Malkut. Indeed, it could be said that we have not at this stage fully raised our heads to see that there are any other possible planes of existence. It is the dream of loss that suggests to us that we may simply not have been looking properly. In this regard, a dream revolving around a lost object relates to The Hermit card in the tarot. The Hermit is usually depicted on the cards as a solitary figure looking into the darkness holding a lamp before him. For you as the dreamer, the lamp is at this point not properly lit, but you are being encouraged to seek out the source of that light.

THE JOURNEY From a spiritual perspective, to lose material possessions is not seen as a negative experience. Indeed, the less you have, the more fully you own yourself, rather than being owned by the inevitable obligations that come with possessions. Spiritual loss, on the other hand, can be very draining. One practical action that will help you link to the Divine rather than to the mundane is to engage in random acts of kindness. This can be as simple as helping out with some charitable organization or buying cookies for everyone in the office. Most effective, though, is to do a kind service for a complete stranger—carry his shopping, give up your seat on the bus, even the smallest act will help. Now is also a good time for you to begin to come to terms with deeper losses that you have experienced over your lifetime. You will probably feel deep emotional pain that you have never before fully come to terms with, and until you are fully reconciled to the pain and the experience, it will act as a block to your future spiritual development. If you try to face these past hurts now, you will find that you have much greater strength to fully accept them and achieve a genuine sense of closure.

LOVE

ahavah-ahbh-אהבה-13

MEANING A dream of love is one of the most positive dreams that you can experience. The fundamental characteristic of the Divine is love, and to dream of love is to begin to move toward a conscious communion with the Divine itself. The value of this dream is equivalent to the value of the Hebrew word meaning "unity," and this relates to another of the key truths that you will come to understand on a deep level if you persist with your spiritual journey. One of the central paradoxes of the universe is that while each of us is wholly unique, we are all interconnected, and this unity emanates from the Divine source.

THE TREE OF LIFE Each of the paths on the Tree of Life can be seen as representing the force of love since they all carry with them the energy of the Divine. However, to have achieved the level of spiritual understanding that is indicated by the values within this dream, you have clearly reached a high point on the Tree of Life. Indeed, the value of this dream is equivalent to the value of one of the Hebrew titles for the Sefirah of Hokhmah. It is this Sefirah that your dream belongs to, and this suggests that you have a great deal of creative energy that you can use for the benefit of your community.

THE JOURNEY The reduction value of this dream produces the number 4. This number is associated with the world of the material. It may seem surprising to find a reference to the world of the physical in a dream that is placed in such a lofty position on the Tree. However, this does not relate to your level of development. Instead, it is a means for the Divine to encourage you to try to make a practical difference in your community. You should find out which groups in your area need assistance and set up some form of volunteer team to help to turn those people's lives around in a positive way.

LUCK

mazal-mzl-מזל-77

MEANING You should feel very encouraged by this dream because it indicates that your life is about to take a very fortunate turn, not only in terms of your day-to-day life, where you are likely to find any number of lucky coincidences occurring, but also in relation to your inner development. It is striking that the value of this dream consists of the number 7 repeated, and that the number 7 is regarded as the luckiest number. This is true not only in the Judaeo-Christian culture but in spiritual systems as diverse as Taoism and early Celtic paganism.

THE TREE OF LIFE The value of this dream is equivalent to the value of the Hebrew word meaning "overflowing." This emphasizes the sense of great fortune that you are about to experience. In terms of the Tree of Life, this dream is placed in the path of Kaph. This path is associated with the concept luck both by its association with the planet Jupiter and by its connection in the Western Mystery Tradition with the tarot card The Wheel of Fortune.

THE JOURNEY It might be very tempting to see this dream as permission to simply relax and not worry about your spiritual path, since you are clearly going to be lucky regardless of what action you take. However, the value of this dream is equivalent to the value of the Hebrew word meaning "prayed." This association makes it very clear that any luck you experience will occur as a result of your commitment to the Great Work. In the compression of the value of this dream we find the letter Ayin and the letter Zayin. This encourages you to find your own way in terms of your spiritual journey (Ayin), and your current good luck will make this easier for you to achieve. At the same time, you need to continue to struggle (Zayin) to ensure that when your period of good fortune fades you do not lose your commitment to the Great Work.

LUGGAGE

meetan-mta'an-מטען-169

MEANING Freud discovered in his early analysis of people's dreams that very often our unconscious will use symbolism to present a linguistic or metaphorical pun to our conscious mind when we wake up. This dream is a very good example of an image that centers on a pun to make its key point. The dream of luggage is about the need for you to deal with a range of emotional difficulties. This, of course, relates directly to the phrase *emotional baggage,* and this connection with a common phrase helps to emphasize the meaning within the dream.

THE TREE OF LIFE What most stands out in the spelling of this dream title is the final letter, Nun. This letter indicates suffering, and as it appears in its final form there is a suggestion that you are enduring a great deal of emotional suffering. However, this dream is not located on the path of Nun. That would simply underline the suffering in the context of this dream. The path that does fit this dream is the path of Zayin. This path relates to the use of your will to cut away those aspects of your life that are hindering your inner development, and thus it is very appropriate to this dream. Additionally, the reduction of this dream's value produces the value of the letter Zayin.

THE JOURNEY The central two letters in the spelling of this dream title are Teth and Ayin. Both of these letters relate to the use of our willpower and inner strength in order to find new insights and greater understanding. The compression of the dream's value begins with the letter Qoph, which acts as a counterpoint to the positivity within the dream's spelling. However, the final letter, Teth, in the compression of this dream suggests that your strength of character does indeed have the ability to overcome your worries about dealing with your emotional difficulties. You should consider visiting a professional counselor to help you learn to deal with those issues.

LUXURY

*motarot-mvthrvth-*מותרות*-*1052

MEANING To many people, this would seem to be a very favorable dream. Indeed, if someone was told that this dream was prophetic, he would probably be very happy to think that he was about to be introduced to a world of luxury. By contrast, from a Kabbalistic perspective this dream indicates someone who has a significant amount to learn about himself and his inner nature.

THE TREE OF LIFE To be dreaming of luxury is a very clear sign that you are still deeply wedded to the material comforts in life and are unwilling to give them up on the basis of nothing more than a possibility of some form of spiritual enlightenment. The letters Tav and Vav both appear twice in the spelling of this dream title. This points out that you

need to spend a significant amount of time considering the value of the sacrifice that will carry you out of the Sefirah of Malkut and into the path of Tav.

THE JOURNEY When we reduce the value of this dream we find the number 8, which is the value of the letter Cheth. This letter represents feelings of defensiveness on your part. The reason why you feel defensive about the concept of spirituality is revealed in the compression of the value of this dream. The compression begins with the letter Qoph raised tenfold in its value. This tells us that you are completely beset by anxieties that relate to a fear of losing the certainties in your life. The only way to deal with this is to accept that there will be a certain amount of sorrow (Nun) in your life if you follow a spiritual path, but that it is indeed the only way that you can reach back to the spiritual home represented by the letter Beth.

LYING

*leshaker-lshqr-*לשקר*-*630

MEANING To dream that you are being lied to or are in the presence of lying is a very disconcerting experience from a purely personal point of view. When we move into a spiritual context, that sense of unease is far, far worse. Within the spelling of this dream title we see that you feel as though a harsh energy (Lamed) from outside yourself is putting more and more energy (Shin) into the anxiety (Qoph) that you are feeling.

THE TREE OF LIFE If we are to feel comfortable about engaging with the nature of the spiritual universe, we must be at least reasonably confident that we are able to trust the information that is informing our approach to the Divine. Additionally, we need to be able to feel that we can trust our interpretations and intuition. The path on the Tree of Life that relates to the feelings of deception indicated by this dream is the path of Teth. The letter Teth has a value of 9, and this is the number that is produced when we reduce the value of the dream.

THE JOURNEY In the compression of this dream, the letter Lamed, which represents the severe external force referred to above, is preceded by the letter Mem. Since the letter Mem relates to the maternal and protective aspect of the Divine, you can assume that whatever the effect of the energy of Lamed may be, the intention driving it is a positive one. Indeed, the value of this dream is equivalent to that of a Hebrew phrase meaning "the Holy Spirit."

Consequently, you should assume that the troublesome time you are having right now is a test of your faith rather than a threat to your spiritual progress.

MACHINERY

*mekhonah-mkvnh-*מכונה-121

MEANING We associate machinery with the modern world, or at least we tend to think of machinery as not being much in evidence until after the Industrial Revolution. However, we know that as far back as Ancient Egypt the wealthy had access to a range of "magical" apparatus that relied on complex cog-wheel-based machinery to function. If nature represents the untarnished creation of the Divine, then machinery represents a creativity that is wholly human. In spiritual terms, this indicates a sense in the dreamer that perhaps God is either irrelevant or even nonexistent.

THE TREE OF LIFE Not surprisingly, this dream belongs to the Sefirah of Malkut. The value of this dream is equivalent to that of a Hebrew phrase meaning "whirling motions." This gives a sense of dynamic energy that in a spiritual context would be seen as a depiction of the nature of the Divine itself. The fact that this phrase has also been associated with machinery suggests that you are placing man's ingenuity on a par with the mystery of the Creator.

THE JOURNEY Another phrase that is equivalent to the value of this dream is the Hebrew meaning "vain idols." This makes it very clear that from a Kabbalistic point of view, your perception of the world is incorrect. The compression of the dream suggests that you would like to believe in the existence of a Divine being. However, you are deeply worried (Qoph) that the world of the practical (Kaph) is the true center of reality and that there is no higher level of existence. The final letter, Aleph, is a sign of hope, though. You should try to spend some time in the countryside and notice how nature not only functions as well as any machinery but is also beautiful and self-reproducing.

MADNESS

*teroof-tyrvph-*טירוף-305

MEANING At a psychological level, this dream would be rather worrisome and could cause you to wonder if you had been under too much stress lately. However, from a spiritual point of view, this is an extremely positive dream. There is an old saying that genius is next to madness, and it has always been a well-established view that real spiritual insight is often akin to a moment of madness. For instance, the tarot card associated with the highest level of spiritual awareness is The Fool.

THE TREE OF LIFE The value of this dream is equivalent to that of a Hebrew phrase meaning "dazzling white light." Light, especially white light, is a representation of the Divine force, so this dream is clearly connected to an individual who is increasingly in tune with his higher self. In terms of exact location, we can again turn to the value of the dream since it is equivalent to one of the Hebrew titles of the Sefirah Netzach, and it is here that this dream is located.

THE JOURNEY Netzach is concerned with the arts, with creativity, and above all with emotional passion. Consequently, the way for you to develop your spiritual understanding right now is to engage in some form of artistic expression that allows you to communicate your feelings about the Divine and at the same time excites your artistic sensibilities. There is a lot of vigorous energy in this dream, as indicated, for instance, by the letter Shin in the dream's compression. It would be ideal to find some form of art that involves a lot of physical activity such as sculpture or even working at a potter's wheel.

Traditional Kabbalists would say that Netzach is associated with bodily exuberance, such as in dancing and athletics, and not necessarily with the arts other than performing arts. Inclusion of the arts in the hermetic interpretation is as a means of expressing passion.

MAGIC

*keeshoof-kyshvph-*כישוף-416

MEANING It is often assumed that if mysticism is a positive approach to the mysteries of the universe then magic is the opposite and is a dangerous or simply foolhardy pursuit. However, this largely depends on your definitions. In the Western Mystery Tradition, mysticism was seen as a process of approaching the Divine by trying to encourage the energy of the Divine to reach down to the individual. Magic was also seen as an attempt to contact the Divine, but by climbing up to meet the Divine, so this is an active rather than a passive system of spirituality. It is this idea of magic as a positive activity that determines the meaning of this dream in a Kabbalistic context.

THE TREE OF LIFE The value of this dream is equivalent to the value of the Hebrew word meaning "a pledge." This further indicates that you are progressing toward the Divine and have made a definite commitment to the spiritual quest. Commitment to the Great Work is associated with the path of Tzaddi, but in your case your commitment is generated by your enormous enthusiasm and energy. This is indicated by the presence of the letter Shin at a central point in the spelling of this dream title. This is also the path that this dream belongs on, as it relates to the fiery passion that you have for your inner progress.

THE JOURNEY When we reduce the value of this dream we find the number II, and this tells us that you are about to experience a profound spiritual moment in your life. The value of this dream is equivalent to the value of the Hebrew word meaning "meditation," and this means that you need to ensure that you set aside a regular period of time each day to practice meditation. Given the equivalence of the word *meditation* to the value of this dream, it is likely that it will be during meditation that you will experience a spiritual revelation of some form. It is important that when you meditate, you keep your thoughts focused on the possibility of hearing the voice of your higher self.

MAGNET

*magnet–mgnt–*מגנמ*–*102

MEANING In extremely close relationships it can often feel as though there is a magnetic attraction between the two people involved. Not only do you feel a constant pull toward your loved one, but you are often able to sense when he is in trouble or feeling low and in need of cheering up. In a Kabbalistic context, this dream suggests a very close connection to the Divine and a feeling that you are being actively drawn ever higher up the Tree of Life. The value of this dream is equivalent to that of the Hebrew word meaning "faith." We can infer from this that you are extremely committed to the Great Work.

THE TREE OF LIFE When we reduce the value of this dream we find the number 3. This is the value of the letter Gimel. This is the path that is associated with this dream, as it reflects both the sense of trust in the Divine that is indicated by the content of the dream, and the high level of achievement that you have gained. This is thanks to your determination to succeed in your inner journey.

The path of Gimel is connected to the tarot card The High Priestess, which represents the secret wisdom that can be won by sufficient spiritual effort, and you will shortly be in a position to put this wisdom to good use.

THE JOURNEY You have gained a place on the path of Gimel because of your spiritual work and also due to your willingness to help others in a wholly altruistic way, as pointed out by the presence of the letter Mem in the compression of this dream's value. Now that you have access to a great store of wisdom, your level of higher understanding will increase dramatically. In order to maintain your position on the Tree of Life, you should now begin to try to encourage others to take their first steps on the road to self-discovery. This dream suggests that you have sufficient insight and charisma to motivate a wide range of people to begin that journey.

MAGNIFYING GLASS

*zekhookheet hagdeel–zkvkyth hgdyl–*זכוכית הגדיל*–*515

MEANING Whenever we think about a detective, the key symbol that springs to mind is a magnifying glass. This symbol represents an ability to look for the slightest detail in any situation and also points to the qualities of patience and a methodical approach to the world. From the spiritual point of view, this dream represents a desire to progress within the Great Work but to progress steadily and cautiously. You like to know as much as possible about any subject or practice before making a firm commitment, and this attitude to life extends to your approach to the Divine.

THE TREE OF LIFE Religious experiences cannot easily be categorized as intellectual or emotional events in our lives, any more than we can clearly define the mystical path as either an art or a science. Very often the determination of whether a spiritual experience is felt primarily as a mental or as an emotional moment is dependent on the basic nature of the individual. In your case, you are most likely to interact with the higher levels of reality on a mainly intellectual level. This is due mainly to the fact that you need to know a great deal about a subject before you will engage with it in any practical way. This overriding concern with mental matters places this dream in the Sefirah of Hod, as this is the Sefirah that governs rationality and our thought processes.

THE JOURNEY To many people an abstract view of the Divine creates an impression of the higher forces as unapproachable. However, you are far more at home with an abstract intellectual approach. The value of this dream reduces to II, which indicates without doubt that you are due to have some form of deeply spiritual experience. The compression of this dream suggests that once this has occurred, you will begin to take a much more practical (Kaph) approach to your spirituality, because the moment will have awakened the spark of the Divine (Yod) within you.

MAGPIE

leevnee-lbny- לבני-92

MEANING In European folklore, magpies were regarded with great suspicion and regarded as consorts of the Devil. Because of their tendency to gather in large flocks in the bare trees of winter, it was also thought that they held councils and spoke to one another. The magpie's public image is not helped by the fact that it likes bright shiny objects and will steal anything that appeals to its taste for shiny and sparkling objects. In spiritual terms, the dream of a magpie indicates that you are focused too much on the surface show of spiritual and mystical ideas rather than on the depth of their content.

THE TREE OF LIFE The value of this dream is equivalent to a Hebrew word meaning "mud." The spiritual significance of this association is that while you may believe you are winning the spiritual equivalent of shiny jewels, in fact from a content point of view they are no more sparkling than a puddle of mud. In short, this dream shows that you are deluding yourself about the value of the supposedly spiritual systems that you are exploring. This places the dream on the path of Teth as this path is concerned with all forms of self-deception.

THE JOURNEY Rather than progress upward, you are simply circling around and around in the same position. This is because you are attracted to first one New Age scheme and then another, drawn in by their interesting appearance as opposed to any substance that they may have to offer. However, on the positive side, the value of this dream reduces to II, and this tells us that in the near future your aimless ramblings among the range of spiritual systems will be over, as you are about to have an unmistakably genuine experience of the higher levels of reality.

MALL

merkaz kneeyot-mrkz qnyvth- מרכז קניות-833

MEANING If someone wanted to design an altar to the God of materialist consumerism, they would probably build something that looked like a shopping mall! There is only one function to a shopping mall: It is to encourage us to open our wallets or purses and start spending. This suggests that the interpretation of this dream will not be very encouraging from a spiritual point of view. However, the dream of a mall is surprisingly hopeful in what it says about your spiritual progress.

THE TREE OF LIFE When we reduce the value of this dream we see that it produces the number 5. This is a very important number in spiritual terms as it indicates an individual who has mastered the four elements of Fire, Earth, Air, and Water within himself in terms of the different aspects of his personality. Most important, it shows that you are now ruled by the element of Spirit in terms of your behavior and attitudes. If we look at a mall not just as a shopping center but as a place that symbolically is full of windows onto amazing sights, then we can place the dream on the path of Heh. This is sufficiently high on the Tree of Life to reflect not only your level of insight but the potential value of a mall as a metaphor for the wondrous bounty of Creation.

THE JOURNEY While malls may be full of shops, they are also full of people. Malls can be seen as today's equivalent of a bazaar. It is the people element that is focused on in the compression of this dream's value. The initial Peh tells you that you need to start communicating with people in your community, and the mall acts as a symbol of just how many people there are out there. The letter Lamed suggests that you need to be encouraging them, perhaps even in a critical way, to begin to address their materialism and lack of spirituality. The final letter, Gimel, hints at the path you will be able to ascend to if you are able to encourage people to take a second look at their lives.

MAN

eesh-aysh- איש-311

MEANING This dream is not about being a man if you happen to be a woman, nor if you happen to be a man is it a dream about your status as a man. It is a dream that deals with the idea of what it means to be human, what our full potential as spiritual beings really is. The value of this dream is a prime number (a number that can be divided only by itself and by one). In spiritual terms, a prime number is an indication of uniqueness, so this dream is pointing out that each of us is a unique being.

THE TREE OF LIFE The value of this dream reduces to 5. As we saw in the preceding dream, the number 5 is very profound as it points to a person who is living his life under the mastery of the fifth element of Spirit. This is in contrast to the unenlightened person, who tends to live under the control of one or another of the four elements manifested in his personality. It is when we make contact with our higher self that we are able to gain mastery over the elements. This occurs in the Sefirah of Tiferet and it is here that we locate this dream.

THE JOURNEY Having gained some form of contact with your higher self, you are now beginning to wonder exactly what it is that makes us human. The compression of this dream indicates the conclusions that are beginning to formulate in your mind. The three key elements of the spiritually integrated personality are the presence of a great deal of enthusiasm and fiery energy as represented by the letter Shin. This energy allows you to awaken the Divine spark within yourself (Yod). The final and most important facet of being a spiritually aware person is an understanding of the interconnectedness of all people and all entities within the universe.

MANNERS

neemooseem – nymvsym – נימוסים-216

MEANING There is an old saying that "manners maketh the man." This suggests that the way we carry ourselves and the images that we project are as important as what actually lies inside. This may be true in terms of your relationships with other people, but when it comes to your relationship with the Divine, what counts is only your inner nature, not the personality that you show to the rest of the world. The value of this dream is equivalent to the value of the Hebrew word meaning "courage," and this suggests that you should have the bravery to cease caring about other people's perceptions of your nature. However, it is important that you show a proper respect to your fellow man and behave in a well-mannered way with others.

THE TREE OF LIFE In the spelling of this dream title we see that the letters Yod and Mem appear twice. This tells us that you have been able to

awaken the spark of divinity within your soul and that you are being directed by this higher element by the maternal and protective, guiding force of Mem. The value of this dream reduces to the number 9, which is the value of the letter Teth; it is on the letter Teth that we position this dream due to its strong association with willpower and strength of character.

THE JOURNEY We live in a world where appearances count for so much more than they should, and it is extremely difficult to break out of the social pressure to present the "right" appearance. This does not means that good manners or politeness are a sham but rather reflect the concentration on image over substance within modern society. The value of this dream is equivalent to the value of the Hebrew word meaning "anger." This should not be taken to suggest that in refusing to comply with social pressure to present a fake personality to the world, you will be presenting a constantly negative side of your nature. Rather, this value simply points out that when you are attempting to communicate with the Divine, you should display your whole personality. This applies even if you are in a particularly negative state of mind.

MANSION

bet meghoreem le khood – byth mgvrym lchvd – בית מגורים לחוד-759

MEANING It would be tempting to interpret this dream as presenting you with a symbolic representation of your excessive concern with material goods and luxury. From a psychological point of view, this would be the most likely analysis. However, when assessing the significance of this dream we should remember that one of the more memorable phrases from the Gospels is "in my Father's house are many mansions." (John 14:2) Although the Kabbalah precedes the New Testament, the symbolic value of houses and mansions is still important as a means of representing a system of belief.

THE TREE OF LIFE The compression of this dream does not reveal an especially cheerful few months ahead. The letter Nun appears twice, both in its standard and its final forms. This letter represents suffering, specifically the emotional upset that is associated with genuinely examining our inner nature. This process is inevitably upsetting as we have to recognize all of our deepest fears and shortcomings. This dream belongs on the path of Nun, and although this is a difficult path to conquer, it does provide us with some extremely valuable insights.

THE JOURNEY The implication of this dream is that you need to design your own metaphorical mansion, or in other words determine your framework within which to approach the Divine. The reduction value of this dream produces the number 3, which is intimately associated with notions of creativity and will help you to find your unique way of celebrating the spiritual. While the path of Nun tells us that you are going to find the next few months difficult, the final letter in the dream's compression is Teth, and this lets us know that you do have the willpower to succeed.

MANUSCRIPT

ketav yad-kthb yd- כתב יד-436

MEANING Language is the basis for all of our knowledge about the world. There is a very respectable school of thought that believes that without language we would not even be able to think and feel in the way we do now. In other words, our thoughts and feelings are as much a product of our language as they are products of our own unique selves. The written word as always seemed more authoritative than the merely spoken word, and this was even more the case in the ancient world. The implication of this is that you, as the dreamer, have access to a store of very valuable wisdom.

THE TREE OF LIFE Manuscripts are created to be read by others. Although this dream is about you and your personal development, it indicates that you are destined to share what wisdom you may gain with those around you. When we reduce the value of this dream we find the number 4, which is the value of the letter Daleth. This letter means "door" and so supports the idea that you should be offering your support to others on the spiritual path. This dream sits on the path of Daleth, and as you traverse its length toward Hokhmah you will find a number of ways in which you can open the spiritual door for a whole range of people.

THE JOURNEY The value of this dream is equivalent to the value of the Hebrew word meaning "tutor." This is a clear indication that you have a role in life that will involve you in trying to teach others to take up the challenge of the Great Work. A step in the right direction would be to set up a small yoga or meditation class at your workplace. As well as the specified activity, you should take time in each session to introduce some discussion about the nature of the Divine. This will encourage your personal development as well as provide a step up the ladder for those in your group who have yet to make any progress.

MAP

mapa-mphh- מפה-135

MEANING Spiritually speaking, there is no map that can take us to the Divine other than the map that we make for ourselves as we progress in the depth of our understanding. However, while there may not be any source of specific directions, we can access general guidance and support from our higher self. The image of a map is symbolic of the fact that a degree of logical order will be helpful in your spiritual search. This dream focuses on the potential within each of us to make contact with the higher. Once we have made that initial contact, we will be assisted in all that we do in our daily lives as well as in our spiritual quest.

THE TREE OF LIFE The value of this dream is equivalent to the value of the Hebrew word meaning "the congregation." In the context of this dream, the feelings associated with congregations that are relevant are feelings of mutual support and understanding. These feelings link to the idea of a map as a means of guidance. Additionally, if we get lost, a map provides some much-needed moral support. In terms of the Tree of Life, the path that is connected to notions of guidance and support is the path of Samech, and it is here that we locate this dream.

THE JOURNEY Any map is only as good as the map-reading skills of the map user. The more carefully you order and organize your spiritual work, the easier it will be to find a valid route to the Divine. In a spiritual sense, this means that although you are on a part of the Tree of Life that provides a great deal of support, you still need to put in a great deal of work in order to achieve your spiritual goals. The need to sustain hard work is emphasized by the fact that the reduction of this dream's value produces the letter Teth, and this letter is connected with willpower and strength of character. The central letter in the spelling of this dream is Peh. This tells you that in order to get the best available support as you traverse the path of Samech, you should spend time discussing your progress with like-minded individuals.

MARKET

shook-shvq- שוק-406

MEANING Ever since one human being exchanged an item of food for an arrow or other object, markets have been in existence. We tend to see the origins of trade as being relevant only since the advent of mass production. However, since the dawn of civilization our material existence has been dominated by the need to be able to take part in trade of one form or another. To dream of a market is to remind yourself that your main focus in life still lies within the physical rather than the spiritual.

THE TREE OF LIFE When we reduce the value of this dream we find the number 10. Given the content of the dream image, we would expect this to relate to the Sefirah of Malkut. However, the number 10 also represents the completion of a major cycle in your life. It is this latter symbolism of the number 10 that applies to your dream. The value of this dream is equivalent to the value of the Hebrew letter Tav when spelled in full. It is this path to which your dream belongs. The sense of completion relates to the fact that you have made the momentous decision to follow a spiritual path in life.

THE JOURNEY Since you are dreaming about a market, it is clear that you only very recently decided to take up the challenge of the Great Work. The market represents the whole mixture and range of consumer goods that symbolizes the physical attachments that you are now leaving behind. In the spelling of the dream title we see the initial letter Shin, which is responsible for the enthusiasm that has allowed you to make the big decision to explore your inner self. The subsequent letter, Vav, tells us that you have spent a lot of time reflecting on this change in direction. The final letter, Qoph, refers to the extremely understandable feelings of anxiety that you are now going through. You can deal with these initial doubts by spending a day around the shops and noticing how stressed and empty are the facial expressions of most of the people you see.

MARRIAGE

neesooeem-nyshvaym- נישואים-417

MEANING Your analyst would tell you that this dream indicates that you are searching for some kind of committed relationship in your life. If you asked a Kabbalist, he might well agree that you are looking to share your life with a significant other. However, the relationship that you are looking for is with the Divine rather than with another individual. This dream suggests that you are quite fresh to the idea of there being a spiritual dimension to your life and are eager to commit yourself to building on that awareness.

THE TREE OF LIFE If we reduce the value of this dream we find the number 15. This is associated with being attached to the physical pleasures in life. This is not as surprising as it may seem. You dreamed of a marriage rather than of being married. Consequently, you are placed right on the edge between the Sefirah of Malkut and the three paths that lead out of the world of the material. If we further reduce the value of this dream we find the letter Vav. In the context of this dream the letter Vav relates to the macrocosm or the Divine itself.

THE JOURNEY Any marriage requires that both parties put in a lot of effort and try to understand each other. You can rely on the Divine and your higher self to put in the effort and to bend a little to understand your position. The compression of the dream's value lets you know that you will have to make some sacrifices in order to progress (Tav). This will be difficult to do, but it is essential that you do this in order to honor your side of the "marriage." The letter Yod should be reassuring as it reminds you that if you do keep struggling to succeed (Zayin), you will achieve your spiritual goals.

MARTYR

kadosh meooneh-qdvsh ma'avnh- קדוש מעונה-581

MEANING Throughout history there have been those who were willing to suffer for their beliefs and sometimes even die for them. The motivation for such extreme behavior was their love for their fellow man rather than any desire to make an impact for their own gratification in any way. Thankfully, there is no need for you to engage in any literal martyrdom in order to embody the message within this dream. However, you should consider ways in which you can engage in less extreme forms of self-sacrifice. What the dream does indicate, though, is that your development is bound up with your treatment of other people.

THE TREE OF LIFE There is a path that is concerned specifically with all types of altruistic behavior, and that is the path of Mem. The tarot card The Hanged Man is also connected to this path, and this association creates a very direct link with the content of this dream. The path of Mem requires not only that you be willing to help others but that you have a balanced and harmonious nature. The value of this dream can be reduced to the number 14, which points to the presence of a calm and well-integrated personality on your part.

THE JOURNEY The value of this dream is equivalent to the value of the Hebrew phrase meaning "the Ancient One." This serves to emphasize the fact that your desire to help others stems from your relationship with and your respect for the Divine. In order to work out the best way to put this altruistic intent into practice, you need to examine the message hidden within the compression of the dream's value. You need to engage in some practical and useful (Kaph) work, probably as a member of some charitable organization. However, if you wish to progress spiritually as well as make a real change to people's lives, you also need to talk to people (Peh) about the reasons for your behavior. In taking this action you will move one step closer to fully understanding the essential unity (Aleph) of the Divine.

MASKS

*masekhah-mskh-*מסכה-125

MEANING It takes some very careful analysis to tease out the spiritual import of this dream. Any psychologist will tell you that every one of us wears a mask. In fact, we have any number of different masks that we put on depending on the people with whom we are interacting. If you find this hard to accept, you should wonder why it is that many people find it very difficult to attend an office function with their domestic partners. The reason, of course, is that they are suddenly trying to wear two very different masks at the same time. From a spiritual point of view, we should try to go through life simply as ourselves. However, determining exactly who that is is a much harder task than we might realize.

THE TREE OF LIFE The value of this dream reduces to the number 8, which is the value of the letter Cheth. This letter means "fence," and in terms of this dream it relates to the sense of protection and self-defense that we obtain when we face the world through a mask. However, at the same time, this dream sits on the path of Cheth because it represents the protection of the Divine and the realization that thanks to this protection we can afford to take off our masks and discover who we really are.

THE JOURNEY This dream is an encouragement to explore. You should seriously consider spending time with a therapist. This is not because there is anything wrong but because to understand yourself fully is a difficult, if rewarding, task. When we look at the compression of this dream we find the letters Qoph, Kaph, and Heh. The anxiety that leads us to wear a mask in company is shown by the letter Qoph. The letter Kaph makes the point that there can be a practical reason not to show our true selves to everyone we meet. However, the final Heh, which means "window," tells you that it is important for you to know when you are wearing a mask and also to be in control of whether or not you will don a mask.

MASTER

*rosh-rash-*ראש-501

MEANING We all want to be the master of our own fate, as far as that may be possible. This dream suggests that you now perceive yourself at least to be heading toward that position. The value of this dream is equivalent to that of the Hebrew word meaning "blessedness," and this tells us that the dreamer is currently receiving the support of the Divine carrying him toward his spiritual goal. There is no room in any form of sincere spirituality for the domination of others, so it is important that you remember that in dreaming of mastery you are intended to be the master only of yourself and not of anyone else.

THE TREE OF LIFE Sometimes we have to search hard to find the most appropriate path for a particular dream. However, the path that belongs with this dream is spelled out in the letters of the dream title. This is because the Hebrew word meaning "head" is spelled exactly the same as the word meaning "master." The letter Resh means "head," so this is the path to which this dream belongs. The path of Resh represents the benevolent influence of the Divine in your life and is concerned with the processes by which we begin to formulate a coherent structure of belief.

THE JOURNEY When we reduce the value of this dream we find the number 6. In the context of this dream, the number refers both to the letter Vav, indicating that you are spending a great deal of time thinking right now, and to the macrocosm or the Divine itself, which is often symbolized by the number 6, as in the Star of David or Solomon's Seal, for example. The compression of this dream lets us know that you are actively seeking to understand the unity of the universe (Aleph), and while thinking and reflecting are useful, you also need to do some practical work to achieve self-mastery. It would be an excellent idea for you to learn a spiritually informed martial art such as tai chi.

MATCH

*gafroor-gphrvr-*גפרור-489

MEANING Religious or spiritual inspiration is often characterized in terms of light or fire. This probably goes back to the crucial nature of fire and light in our earliest civilizations. The fire was the source of illumination, cooked food, warmth, and protection from predators. The dream image of a match is not equivalent to a dream about fire, but suggests that you are approaching the point when you will start a spiritual fire of your own. You have the matches; it is simply a matter of deciding to strike them.

THE TREE OF LIFE If we reduce the value of this dream we find the number 3. This number indicates a high level of creativity, and of course it can require a creative mind to find a way to strike the match so that it ignites the flame of an active spirituality. Your dream is not located on the path of Gimel, though, despite the fact that Gimel has a value of 3. The path of Gimel would represent the match once it had been lit and was in the process of lighting a fire within your soul. At this stage all we have is the match, and so if we draw a straight line down from Gimel we arrive in the path of Tav, which is where this dream should be placed.

THE JOURNEY The path of Tav appears in the compression of this dream's value. As well as locating the dream, the presence of the letter Tav points to a sense of loss and a certain amount of regret that you will experience when you do strike the match and move into a spiritual approach to the world. To continue the match metaphor, you will be much more aware of how to go about lighting your inner fire if you seek out some like-minded but more experienced individuals and discuss (Peh) your plans and problems with them. The final letter, Teth, in the compression reminds you that in order to keep your match alight you will need all your willpower and strength of character.

MATTRESS

*meezran-mzrn-*מזרון-297

MEANING When you dream of a mattress, your higher self is pointing out that you are in danger of resting too much and need to find a way to motivate yourself to put in the effort needed to achieve some form of spiritual success in your life. The value of this dream is equivalent to the value of the Hebrew

word meaning "a fortified house." This association indicates that you are very concerned about protecting your sense of certainty and security in your life, and this explains your reluctance to make a strong commitment to the Great Work.

THE TREE OF LIFE This dream implies not that you are a lazy person but that you are finding it very difficult to settle down to a concerted examination of your inner self. The sense of anxiety that is responsible for your current state of mind places this dream on the path of Qoph, as this path is concerned with the doubts that commonly beset us when we begin to try to climb the ladder of the Tree of Life. When we reduce the value of this dream we find the number 18, which is connected to the tarot card The Moon. This card is linked to the path of Qoph and serves to emphasize the fact that your inactivity is based on anxiety.

THE JOURNEY The value of this dream is equivalent to the value of a Hebrew phrase that refers to the Sefirah of Gevurah. This Sefirah is also known as the Sefirah of Severity and its presence here suggests that you need to be more stern with yourself in order to stimulate a greater level of spiritual effort. While it is understandable that you have doubts and concerns, sometimes we have to be harsh on ourselves in order to get the desired results. The compression of the dream's value reminds us that we have the benevolent force of the Divine (Resh) behind us, and the subsequent letters point out that you need both to completely commit yourself (Tzaddi) to the quest for truth and to be prepared to struggle (Zayin) in order to get results.

MEALS

*arookhah-arvchh-*ארוחה-220

MEANING We do, of course, need to eat to live, and we could see this dream as simply reflecting a healthy attitude to the physical aspect of our lives. However, we need to look at this dream from a spiritual standpoint. When we do so, our analysis shifts to a position that sees this dream as an indication that you are currently more concerned with the material side of life than with your inner life. Further, this dream points to the fact that your interest in the material relates mainly to indulging in the comforts of the physical rather than to physical necessity.

THE TREE OF LIFE Given the content of this dream, you are clearly placed in the Sefirah of Malkut. Additionally, when we reduce the value of this dream we find the number 4. This number represents the world of the physical and so emphasizes the fact that this dream belongs on the bottom Sefirah of the Tree of Life. The value of this dream is equivalent to the value of the Hebrew word meaning "giants." This association emphasizes the focus on the physical over the spiritual, since the key feature of a giant is his physical size rather than the magnitude of his wisdom.

THE JOURNEY Despite the meaning of this dream, you should not be unduly depressed. The fact that you had this dream makes it clear that you are now ready to move forward and begin the spiritual journey. The value of this dream is equivalent to the value of the Hebrew word meaning "latch." This makes it clear that while you have yet to open the door to the higher levels of reality, that door is not locked. All you have to do is make the decision to lift that latch and walk through to begin your voyage of discovery.

MEAT

basar-bshr-בשר-502

MEANING Food has always been very symbolic, and in assessing the spiritual significance of this dream we need to look at the underlying symbolism of the type of food being dreamed of. Meat was always associated with bravery and courage as well as wealth and luxury, and it was also believed that one absorbed something of the characteristics of the animal that was being eaten. To dream of eating meat indicates that you have a desire to create sufficient strength of will and courage to move forward in your spiritual quest.

THE TREE OF LIFE When we reduce the value of this dream we find the number 7. This number is the value of the Hebrew letter Zayin, which means "sword." This letter relates strongly to the desire, expressed in your dream, to be strong enough to make gains in your spiritual quest. The path of Zayin is the path on which this dream lies, and the fact that the value of this dream is equivalent to that of the Hebrew word meaning "cut" underlines the association of this dream with the sword of Zayin.

THE JOURNEY The spelling of this dream title makes clear your spiritual goals in life. You are seeking to find your way back to your spiritual home (Beth) and are trying to ensure that you have sufficient energy (Shin) to complete this journey. The final Resh is a sign that your efforts will be rewarded, as it represents the benevolent influence of the Divine. The compression of the dream's value again

refers to the communion with the Divine that you are seeking (Beth) and indicated that you need to take some practical steps (Kaph) to increase the chances of your success. Something as simple as a daily meditation would help you work toward your goals.

MECHANIC

mekhonay-mkvnay-מכונאי-127

MEANING We don't generally associate mechanics with spirituality; the tending of machinery and fixing of mechanical problems seems a long way from calm contemplation and meditation. However, when looked at from a spiritual point of view, the machinery becomes our own inner nature and the job of the mechanic is to ensure that each aspect of our personality is functioning in a way that is best placed to achieve success in the Great Work.

THE TREE OF LIFE The value of this dream reduces to 10, which indicates that you have completed an important cycle within your life. This suggests that as the mechanic of your inner self you have managed to realign your personality so that you have balanced all four competing elements of Air, Water, Fire, and Earth within yourself. This places you on a path beyond the Sefirah of Netzach. This is because Netzach is the Sefirah where you balance the emotional side of your nature and relate it to the other three elements of your personality. The appropriate path of this dream is that of Kaph, as this is concerned with a practical approach to spirituality and emanates from the Sefirah of Netzach.

THE JOURNEY You are making excellent progress in your Great Work. The compression of the dream indicates that you still worry about making sufficient progress (Qoph). In order to allay your worries you need to find some way to engage with the Divine that is active and physical (Kaph); in doing so you will feel that you are struggling toward a greater understanding. You are someone who needs to feel engaged in a struggle in order to make the most of your spiritual potential. A martial art such as tai chi would be extremely useful for your inner development.

MEDAL

ot heetstaynoot-avth htztyynvth-אות הצטיינות-987

MEANING This is an extremely positive dream as it indicates that you are approaching a point where you will be rewarded for all your efforts to succeed in the Great Work. It may seem very strange that the image of a medal would be used to mark some form of spiritual achievement. Medals are awarded for bravery in conflict, and we would not expect the Divine to support warfare or even images associated with it. However, the spiritual quest is like a war in that you need to defeat your more materialistic desires and attachments.

THE TREE OF LIFE When we reduce the value of this dream we find the number 6. This relates to the letter Vav and indicates that your progress so far has required a great deal of thought and reflection. The dream suggests that you are on the verge of achieving some form of reward for your efforts. The Sefirah of Tiferet is something of a haven in the Tree of Life, since it is where you contact your higher self. Appropriately enough, as it is the Sefirah where this dream is located, the Sefirah of Tiferet is the sixth Sefirah on the Tree of Life.

THE JOURNEY Perhaps now that you are about to receive a metaphorical medal you can afford to relax and consider your journey finished. Not so! The Great Work is never truly completed. Once you have contacted your higher self you need to work toward achieving communion with the Divine, or in other words a deeper understanding with the final goal being the moment of perfect understanding, or samadhi as it is referred to in yoga terms. In the compression of this dream's value we see that you must maintain your commitment to the quest (Tzaddi) and that your goal now is to find some means of communicating (Peh) with the higher. The final letter, Zayin, acts as a warning that once you leave the Sefirah of Tiferet, you will be facing a difficult struggle in order to continue to move forward.

MEDICAL PROFESSIONALS

meektsoan refooee–mqtzva'an rphvay–
מקצועין רפואי-653

MEANING Nobody who begins the search for religious truth should do so believing that it will be an easy task to complete. It is perhaps the most difficult quest that we can undertake and it affects the seeker on every level. This is because not only are you looking out into the world and the universe, but you must spend a great deal of time looking inward at yourself and your personality. This dream suggests that you are finding the work more difficult than you had suspected and feel in need of support at this time.

THE TREE OF LIFE While each path on the Tree has its particular difficulties and challenges that we must overcome, there is one path in particular that is more likely to involve a definite emotional challenge, as it is a path that leads through self-examination to a deepening faith in the Divine and the Great Work. This is the path of Nun, and it is here that your dream should be located. The letter Nun stands out in the spelling of this dream because it occurs in its final form, underlining the fact that your dream sits on this path. You are at the point in your inner development where you need to face your fears, especially those concerning your ability to achieve your spiritual goals.

THE JOURNEY We should make our spiritual life part of the heart of our community, and in many ways it should be a group activity. However, those moments when we feel the presence of the Divine or have a moment of spiritual intuition are unique to us alone. This does not mean that you should not share your experiences and your doubts with others if that will help you to continue with your inner development. The letter Peh appears in this dream to indicate that you should seek like-minded people with whom to discuss your progress, while the presence of the letter Ayin reminds you not to let anyone else define the way in which you approach the Divine. In the compression of the dream's value we have the central letter, Nun, to emphasize that you are experiencing a challenging period in your life. However, the initial Mem reassures you that the supportive and maternal aspect of the Divine is still with you, and the final letter, Gimel, points to the secret wisdom that you will ultimately gain if you persist in your efforts despite the pain you are now experiencing.

MEDICINE

*troofah–thrvphh–*תרופה-691

MEANING If pharmaceutical products are medicine for the body, the Great Work is medicine for the soul. To dream of medicine is not an indication that you are in any way failing in your spiritual quest. We need to remember that until we have integrated our higher self with our conscious personality, we are in a sense spiritually unwell. Indeed, the entire spiritual quest is designed to heal us so that we can ultimately achieve some form of communion with the Divine. At a practical level, though, you should give some consideration to whether you have any health issues that need to be addressed.

THE TREE OF LIFE Throughout our journey up the Tree of Life we are in need of support from the Divine and our higher self. However, there are two paths that are particularly concerned with the dream of medicine. These two paths are Lamed and Mem. The link with Mem stems from the role that Mem has as a symbol of the maternal and caring aspect of the Divine. It may seem strange to also associate Lamed with this dream, since it indicates a harsh and critical force. However, we need to remember that some medicine is unpleasant to taste but is still very beneficial for us.

THE JOURNEY You are clearly progressing well in that you are at least unconsciously aware that you will be able to progress only if you have some guidance from the Divine or through the influence of your higher self. The compression of this dream's value begins with the letter Mem, which indicates that the support you need is available to you. It is not always obvious that you are receiving support from the Divine at the time when the "medicine" is being administered. This is why it is so important that you persevere (Tzaddi), because only then will you come to experience on a deep level the essential unity (Aleph) of the whole universe.

MELANCHOLY

marah shekhorah – mrh shchvrh – מרה שחורה‎-764

MEANING In the last few years all sorts of New Age systems of belief and practice have sprung up. While many of them have a great deal to offer the sincere seeker of truth, a large number are no more than window dressing, with very little in the way of useful content. One good way to tell if a system is potentially useful is to listen to what its proponents tell you about the likely effect on your life. Those who insist that you will be happier, healthier, and even wealthier should be avoided. This is because sorrow is an inevitable feature of spiritual development. It is a phase that can be overcome, but without it you will not significantly increase your spiritual insight.

THE TREE OF LIFE Without question, this dream belongs on the path of Nun. You should not feel depressed that you are on a path that is connected to emotional upset and depression. By reaching the path of Nun you have achieved a great deal already, and although you now have to experience a degree of upset, it is only so that you can go on to achieve an even greater level of understanding. It is often explained in mystical traditions that there is a point in your spiritual development where you must reach deep down into yourself and exor-

cise your ghosts in order to face your future without the past holding you back.

THE JOURNEY The compression of this dream begins with the letter Nun in its final form. This serves to emphasize that the melancholy phase of your inner journey is unavoidable. On the reassuring side, the subsequent letter is Samech, and this reminds you that no matter how low you are feeling, the supportive force of the Divine is still with you. Further, the final letter in the compression is Daleth, and this tells you that once you have passed through this time of upset, you will be able to open the door to a much greater level of insight about the Divine and also about your inner nature.

MEMORIAL

azkarah – azkrh – אזכרה‎-233

MEANING The value of this dream is equivalent to the value of the Hebrew phrase "the Tree of Life." This association puts this dream in a particularly profound context, as any connection with the Tree of life as a whole implies a deep mystical significance to your dream. Memorials are somber affairs, but their purpose is for us to remember the joy and value that the individual gave to the world. In a spiritual sense, this dream refers to the fact that each of us has the potential for great spiritual achievement and to return to our spiritual home. We may not remember our connection to the Divine, but in making the spiritual quest we are attempting to regain that which we have lost.

THE TREE OF LIFE You might expect this dream to be placed very high on the Tree of Life, but it is important to remember that all paths are equally important and momentous as you experience them. In addition, the first step in any journey is always the most difficult to take, and this is certainly the case as far as the Great Work is concerned. This dream belongs on the path of Tav both because it represents the first realization that there is something of value out there that you should try to reclaim and because the path of Tav is connected with the planet Saturn, which is associated with the past and with memory.

THE JOURNEY Realizing that you want to re-create your innate connection with the Divine is an extremely important moment in your life. The letter Aleph, which begins the spelling of your dream title, and the letter Resh at the beginning of this dream's compression indicate both the unity of the universe and the benign force that is exerting itself in your life. The journey is not an easy one, as shown both by the letter Zayin in the spelling and the letter Lamed in the compression. However, you can make the journey easier by making a point, as you read more about the nature of spirituality, to look at the obvious meaning and to search out any hidden meaning. The need to do this is hinted at by the way in which the meaning of the spelling of this dream is mirrored by the much less obvious but equally important compression of the dream's value.

MENDING

*letaken-lthqn-*לְתִקֵן-580

MEANING The spiritual journey is in a sense a process of mending, only instead of an item of clothing or household appliance it is our soul that is being mended. While we might think that this is a negative dream since it implies that something is broken in your life, this is not at all the case. We all start out in life as potentially spiritual beings, and until we realize that potential we are essentially in need of mending. The reduction value of this dream produces the number 13, which implies that you are about to have a major change in your life.

THE TREE OF LIFE The value of this dream is equivalent to the value of the Hebrew phrase meaning "Angel of Fire." This relates to the intense energy that is needed if you are to fully mend your soul. One of the reasons that you need vast reserves of inner energy is that in the process of self-healing you will have to face some difficult emotional memories, and this is indicated by the presence of the letter Nun in its final form in the spelling of this dream. The Sefirah of Netzach is where we locate this dream, as this is the seat of the emotional and fiery energy that will carry you on along the Tree of Life.

THE JOURNEY The compression of this dream tells you that there are two different tasks that lie before you over the next few months. On one hand, you need to engage in some form of practical activity that embodies your spiritual beliefs. This could be as simple as regularly attending some form of religious service or engaging in some kind of charity work in your community. The letter Peh indicates that as well as taking these practical steps, it is equally important for you to talk about your beliefs with like-minded individuals.

MESSAGE

*meser-msr-*מֶסֶר-300

MEANING In psychological terms, this dream would be seen as a fear that someone is trying to tell you something that you have failed to pick up on. Most often such a dream would be perceived as relating to a missed communication from someone to whom you are very close. However, from a spiritual point of view, this dream is about a message from the Divine. There is no suggestion that you have missed a communication from the higher forces, but simply that you have not yet been able to fully understand the message that is emanating from the Divine source.

THE TREE OF LIFE It is quite understandable that the message of the Divine is not yet clear to you; after all, the whole purpose of the Great Work is to work toward an understanding of the Divine nature, and this takes a very long time. This dream could in principle occur anywhere on the Tree of Life, but the value of the dream and the compression of its value both point to the path of Shin. This is appropriate since it takes a great deal of persistent energy to arrive at a higher level of spiritual insight.

THE JOURNEY The path of Shin is also concerned with the ability to make sound judgments especially in a moral context. This indicates that the first step for you in terms of unraveling the message of the Divine is to establish a clear moral code for yourself. This may not be the same in its entirety as the morality projected by any existing religion, but it should be based on the principles laid out in the spelling of this dream. You should seek to act with compassion and concern for your fellow human beings (Mem) and whenever possible offer support and guidance (Samech). Above all, you should face the world in a positive and benevolent frame of mind.

MESSY

*mevoolbal-mbvlbl-*מבולבל-110

MEANING You might expect this dream to be somewhat critical of the dreamer, but in fact the values within this dream make it clear that you are making good ground in your spiritual work. We have a tendency to think that for something to be working well it needs to be carefully organized. To an extent this is true, but there is also the principle of creative chaos, which applies to individuals who are able to make good progress because they do not have a fixed routine restricting their behavior.

THE TREE OF LIFE The value of this dream is equivalent to the Hebrew phrase meaning "the Father of Faith," so there can be no doubt about the sincerity of your commitment to a spiritual path.

Additionally, the value of this dream can be reduced to the number 11, which indicates that you are about to undergo a profound spiritual experience. The concept of messiness refers simply to the fact that you like to approach the Divine in your own manner, which is one of spontaneity and disorganization. It is your deeply individual approach that places this dream on the path of Ayin.

THE JOURNEY There is absolutely no reason for you to change your approach so that it conforms more closely to the way other people approach the Great Work. You need to be told this because, as the compression of the dream tells us, you worry (Qoph) whether you will be able to awaken the spark of the Divine (Yod) within yourself. In fact, the only way you should change the way you think about spirituality and the way in which you celebrate your relationship to the Divine is that you should stop agonizing over whether you are doing it in the correct manner!

MICROSCOPE

*meekroskop–myqrvsqvph–*מיקרוסקופ*-*602

MEANING It is immediately obvious from the spelling of this dream title that the Hebrew word for "microscope" is borrowed almost directly from the original Latin name. However, as is so often the case, the values behind the spelling of the word still have a value in terms of defining your current spiritual state. The image of a microscope clearly puts us in mind of someone with a very scientific approach to the Great Work. This dream makes it clear that this approach is working very well for you.

THE TREE OF LIFE With a dream that has such an obvious scientific and rationally based theme we would expect the appropriate position on the Tree of Life to be the Sefirah of Hod. This is because Hod is concerned with rationality and our mental processes. This placement on the Tree is supported by the fact that when we reduce the value of this dream we find the number 8, and the Sefirah of Hod is the eighth on the Tree of Life. In addition, the letter Qoph appears twice in the spelling of this dream title. The letter Qoph is also connected to the mind, and while it tends to refer to anxiety and worry, in the context of a dream about the scientific approach to the Divine, we should interpret Qoph as referring to your need to check and recheck your spiritual experiences as though you were conducting some type of experiment.

THE JOURNEY The idea of a microscope suggests that you are trying to look into every last detail of the universe in order to develop your understanding of the Divine. This attitude should be applauded, as it will definitely increase your inner knowledge. Indeed the value of this dream is equivalent to the value of the Hebrew word meaning "brightness," and by your thorough examination of your spiritual experiences you are helping the bright light of the Divine shine into your life.

MILK

*khalav–chlb–*חלב*-*40

MEANING The image of milk has very immediate and obvious connotations. From a psychological point of view, it could be seen as indications that you are still looking for the comfort and protection of a mother. This would be quite negative from a spiritual point of view as it suggests that you are unwilling to take on the responsibility needed in order to progress properly along the Tree of Life. However, if we look at the milk itself as symbolic in spiritual terms, we would see this dream as very positive, since the idea of milk would correspond to the love and spiritual nutrition that emanates from the Divine.

THE TREE OF LIFE We can determine which interpretation of this dream is correct by looking at other words and phrases that share their values with the Hebrew word for "milk." One such phrase with an equivalent value is the Hebrew meaning "the hand of the Eternal." This is quite conclusively supportive of the view that the metaphor of milk relates to the life-giving force that emanates from the Divine. Consequently, you should see this dream as positive and indicating that you are seeking the hand of God to guide you and not to remove your responsibility for your progress. The location of this dream is also given by its value, as it is equivalent to one of the Hebrew titles of the Sefirah of Yesod. This is our first destination after leaving the solely physical world behind us, so it is quite right that you should be seeking out the guidance of the Divine.

THE JOURNEY As someone very new to the Great Work, your next few months of spiritual work should consist largely of reading as much as possible on the subject of religion and spirituality. The spelling of the dream title tells you that you will be able to sense the protective force of your higher self (Cheth), but also that you will feel the harsh force of the Divine (Lamed) at times. This is always a difficult feeling to deal with, but the final letter, Beth, lets you know that ultimately you will be able to return to your spiritual home.

MILL

*takhanah-tchnh-*מחנה-72

MEANING At the time you are reading this analysis, you may be considering giving up on the whole business of the spiritual quest. This is because you are going through a very hard time at the moment. It is likely that in nearly every aspect of your life right now, from the emotional to your work life, you are experiencing some degree of difficulty. This is because you are quite literally being "put through the mill." This is an old expression that means you are putting up with all kinds of obstacles in your life. However, the values within this dream strongly suggest that you should persevere.

THE TREE OF LIFE You might expect this dream to belong on the path of Lamed since that is the path associated with the harsher aspect of the Divine. However, the value of this dream is equivalent to the value of the Hebrew word meaning "mercy." This strongly suggests that even though your life is very difficult right now, there is a point to your difficulties and there is some lesson that you need to learn. Because you currently feel that your problems are not in any way conducive to your inner development, this dream sits on the path of Teth, which is concerned with self-deception of all kinds. Additionally, the value of the dream reduces to 9, which is the value of the letter Teth.

THE JOURNEY The letter Teth also begins the spelling of this dream title, and it is followed by the letter Cheth, which again reminds you that whatever you may think, the higher forces are acting in your best interests. The value of this suffering, represented by the letter Nun in the spelling, is that it will ultimately lead to your being able to focus on those things that are truly important in life. You will then be closer to achieving a glimpse of the Divine, as promised in the final letter, Heh, in the spelling.

MINE

*meekhreh-mykrh-*מיכרה-275

MEANING The process of exploring our inner nature is a difficult one and requires honesty, commitment, and no small degree of courage in order to gain any measure of success. The image of a mine is a very appropriate description of the nature of the Great Work. At the same time as we are climbing up toward the Divine we must also be digging deep into the soil of our unconscious to uncover the valuable nuggets of insight into our personality.

THE TREE OF LIFE When we reduce the value of this dream we find the number 5. This is a very important number as it symbolizes the individual who has managed to bring all the elements of his nature under the organizing control of his higher self. As the content of this dream refers to the act of mining your personality for information and understanding, it is clear that the number 5 relates to a position you will achieve in the future. The path that you are currently positioned on is that of Ayin, and you will need all the vigor that is indicated by this path to achieve the level of self-knowledge that you require to progress to the Sefirah of Tiferet.

THE JOURNEY The road ahead is a tough one, but the presence of the number 5 reminds you that the effort will indeed be worthwhile. In the compression of this dream we have the letter Resh, which reminds you that the benevolent force of the Divine will help you to piece together a comprehensive understanding of your inner nature. At the center of the compression we see the letter Ayin, and this is also an encouraging letter as it tells you that you should have the confidence to follow any spiritual route that feels right to you. If you do so, you will be able to see the haven of Tiferet ahead of you as indicated by the final letter, Heh.

MIRROR

*reee-ray-*ראי-211

MEANING Dreaming of mirrors might cause you to wake up feeling concerned that perhaps you are becoming a little self-centered. There is no need for such concern, though, as there is nothing in this dream to suggest even a hint of vanity or self-obsession on your part. From a spiritual perspective, the image of mirrors relates to the need to be able to see a true reflection both of yourself and of the nature of the Divine. The value of this dream is equivalent to the value of the Hebrew word meaning "a lightning flash." This is a phrase used in the Kabbalah to represent the process by which the Tree of Life emanated from the Divine source. The suggestion in this dream is that you need to try to mirror that process by climbing up the Tree of Life back to the Divine.

THE TREE OF LIFE The value of this dream reduces to the number 4. This number is concerned with the world of the physical, but your dream is not placed in the Sefirah of Malkut. The world of the physical can be seen as extending as high as the Sefirot of Netzach and Hod, since in these Sefirot you are still balancing the four elements within your personality. This dream suggests that this process of internal balancing is almost completed. The path that you are on is the path of Peh. This is the most appropriate path because in order to see a true reflection of ourselves, it is essential that we communicate with others and try to understand how we are seen by those around us.

THE JOURNEY Your task right now is to find a way of balancing the competing elements of the emotional and the intellectual within your personality. Additionally, given the image of a mirror, you need to ensure that you are not allowing any kind of personal vanity to cloud your judgment or your choices right now. When you have achieved this, you will be able to look into a metaphorical mirror of your soul and see yourself as you truly are. The value of this dream is equivalent to the value of the Hebrew word meaning "worthy." The clear implication is that you will complete this task and will be able to continue your attempt to mirror the lightning flash and climb all the way back up the Tree of Life.

MISSING A PLANE

lehakhtee matos–lhchtya mtvs–
להחטיא מטוס-178

MEANING Some dreams don't have to be completely nightmarish to have us waking up in a cold sweat. In fact, if you wake up from a dream of missing a flight, you can find yourself panicking for a few minutes, thinking that you genuinely missed a connection of some kind. From a spiritual point of view, this dream suggests that you have not been paying enough attention to the small voice inside you, otherwise known as your intuition, and that you are now beginning to realize that this may have led you to miss out on some valuable insights that could have moved you closer to your spiritual goals.

THE TREE OF LIFE The value of this dream is equivalent to the value of a Hebrew word meaning "choice." The suggestion here is that you have chosen to ignore the advice coming through your intuition. Our intuition is the way in which our higher self tries to guide us, and to ignore it is effectively to pay no attention to our higher self. This attitude

places the dream on the path of Ayin in its negative aspect. In its negative aspect the path of Ayin represents a determination to find one's own way taken to such an extreme that useful advice and guidance is ignored.

THE JOURNEY The reduction value of this dream leads to the number 16. This number is associated with the tarot card The Tower of Destruction. The implication of this link is that some fairly traumatic event is going to occur that will cause you to realize that you really do need to listen to the advice and guidance of others. This will be some form of spiritual upset rather than any material or physical crisis but will be no less affecting for that. The fact that you are already dreaming of missing a plane means that you are aware of the problem. Indeed, if you take the advice in this analysis and begin to listen to your intuition, you may well avoid the crisis altogether.

MISSING AN APPOINTMENT

lehakhtee meenooy–lhchtya mynvy–
להחטיא מינוי-179

MEANING The value of this dream is a prime number (a number that can be divided only by itself and by one), which indicates that you have a strong sense of individuality. This sense gives you a great deal of energy and enthusiasm for life in general and for the Great Work. However, this dream should be seen as a warning. In missing an appointment in your dream you are creating a symbolic image of missing out on some valuable spiritual insights. You are likely to miss out not because you are too lazy but because you are too focused on following your own vision without reference to any other points of view.

THE TREE OF LIFE We might expect this dream to sit on the negative aspect of the path of Ayin, as was the case with the dream of missing a plane. However, this dream is much more concerned with your anxiety than with your tendency to follow your own agenda at all costs. This dream is a sure sign that you have recognized the error in your current approach to the spiritual. The path that this dream sits on is that of Qoph, as it represents the anxiety that you have about your lack of caution when dealing with the development of your inner self.

THE JOURNEY Although this dream is negative in terms of its description of your current state, there is a very optimistic tone in the compression of this dream. This does not mean that you are not being warned to change your ways, but that the implication is that you will be able to turn things around. The initial letter, Qoph, refers directly to your inner concerns and anxieties. The subsequent Ayin indicates that in the future, your desire to be individual will be tempered by a recognition of the need to think through your actions very carefully. Additionally, you are increasingly aware of your capacity for self-deception, as shown by the presence of the final letter, Teth, in the dream's compression.

MONEY

kesef-ksph-כסף-160

MEANING All of us have to pay attention to the state of our finances when we are awake, and not to do so would be foolish rather than overtly spiritual. However, when we fall asleep we should be able to leave behind our thoughts about money, unless of course we have serious financial difficulties. Assuming that you are no worse off than the next person, we can see this dream in its spiritual context as pointing to an individual who is excessively concerned with monetary gain rather than spiritual progress.

THE TREE OF LIFE The value of this dream is equivalent to the value of the Hebrew word meaning "a rock or stone." This association links the dream not just with money and finance but with the idea of the physical in general. The combination of the purely material in nature along with your continuing attachment to the trappings of materialist culture means that this dream is very firmly placed in the Sefirah of Malkut. The reduction of this dream's value produces the number 7. This is the value of the letter Zayin, which means "sword" and indicates that in order for you to progress, you will have to be willing to struggle with yourself.

THE JOURNEY At the moment, the spiritual journey is still just an idea in your head. If you wish to make it a reality, you need to remember the imagery of a sword found in the dream's reduction. It is clear from the compression of this dream that the key factor holding you is not a love of the material so much as a deep fear (Qoph) of what will replace that material certainty. The letter Samech, which comes at the end of the compression of the dream, indicates that all you have to do is recognize the fact that the support of your higher self is available to you. This should give you the confidence to push on to the next level on the Tree of Life.

❧MONSTER

meefletset-mphltzth-מפלצת-640

MEANING Sometimes we can find a dream whose obvious meaning bears no relation at all to its spiritual significance. The dream of a monster fills us with expectations of all sorts of horrors, and yet the Kabbalistic analysis of this dream is incredibly positive. Indeed, the only way to apply the image of a monster literally to the dream interpretation would be to assume that your spiritual transformation is so major that to a "normal" person you might seem so out of kilter as to be monstrous. The reduction value of this dream produces the letter Aleph, and this represents the essential unity of the Divine and also points very strongly to the high level of your spiritual progress.

THE TREE OF LIFE The central letter in the spelling of this dream title is Lamed. This letter represents a stern and potentially critical force from the higher, which is acting to drive you forward in the Great Work. It is this driving force that has led you to the position that you now occupy on the Tree of Life. The value of this dream is equivalent to the value of the Hebrew word meaning "the Sun." Not only is the Sun supremely important in all mystical systems, but it is the planetary object associated with the Sefirah of Tiferet. The Sefirah of Tiferet is the point in our development where we finally make contact with our higher self, and it is here that your dream is located.

THE JOURNEY When we reduce the value of this dream we find the number 10. In the context of this dream, 10 relates to the completion of some major cycle in your life. The sense of completion that you feel relates to the fact that you have now entered the Sefirah of Tiferet. Having contacted your higher self, you are now in a position not only to further your spiritual development but to assist those around you in their spiritual quest. The need for you to offer caring support to those close to you is indicated very clearly by the fact that the compression of this dream's value contains only the letter Mem in both its standard and final forms.

❧MOON

levanah-lbnh-לבנה-87

MEANING While the Sun is the most important planetary symbol in the Western Mystery Tradition, to most people the Moon is by far the most obviously mystical of the heavenly bodies. This in part because the Sun is associated with the life-giving properties of the Divine, whereas the Moon is associated with the more overtly supernatural aspect of the spiritual dimension. This is a very positive dream and suggests that the traditionally feminine intuitive nature, often associated with the Moon, is an area of your spiritual development that you should be working on at this time.

THE TREE OF LIFE The sphere of the Moon is associated with the path of Qoph, but this is when the Moon is in its negative aspect. It is also linked with the Sefirah of Yesod, and it is here that we should place your dream. The value of this dream is equivalent to the value of the Hebrew word meaning "frankincense." This particular incense is said to encourage deep meditation, and it is such meditative practices that will encourage the development of your intuitive ability. The Sefirah of Yesod is the first Sefirah above Malkut and in many ways can be associated with the world of dreams. The dreamy nature of Yesod perfectly suits the traditional Kabbalistic associations of the Moon.

THE JOURNEY When we reduce the value of this dream we find the number 6. This relates both to the macrocosm or the Divine, to whom you are trying to draw closer, and to the fact that in the early stages of the Great Work we need to spend a great deal of time engaged in quiet reflection. The value of this dream is equivalent to the value of the Hebrew word meaning "determined." This association lets us know that not only have you managed to muster the determination to take the first step into the unknown, but that you will persevere until you achieve the spiritual insight that you are seeking. The Moon is associated with the tidal flow of our emotions, so you should also spend time reflecting on the nature of your emotional relationships, perhaps learning to be more comfortable expressing yourself in an emotional manner.

See Zohar symbol, Moon.

❧MORNING
*boker-bvqr-*בוקר*-*308

MEANING The minute we look at this dream we see that it has a deeply profound significance. This is because when we reduce the value of this dream we find 11. The number 11 is associated with the mystical and mysterious in life, so you should keep your eyes and ears open for anything unusual from which you could gain a useful lesson. Very often, things that initially appear insignificant have a

deeper meaning later in life, so it is worth trying to interpret everything that occurs as a potential insight. Morning is a time for new beginnings and you should see this dream as a positive indication of opportunities ahead.

THE TREE OF LIFE The value of this dream is equivalent to the value of the Hebrew word meaning "investigation." This implies that the appropriate path for this dream is one that relates to looking at the world in great detail, attempting to extract all the possible information from every event. Additionally, the content of this dream suggests that we are looking for a position low on the Tree in order to match the idea of the morning of your spiritual quest. The Sefirah of Hod fits this description perfectly, as it is concerned with the intellectual, rational, and scientific side of our nature.

THE JOURNEY When we look at the compression of this dream's value we see a reflection of your journey thus far. The final number 8 relates to the Sefirah of Hod, where you are currently located, and the initial letter, Shin, is the means by which you arrived at this Sefirah. You are now in the morning of your spiritual day, and this is the time when you can achieve most, since you are at your most energetic and can still draw on the energy of Shin. You should capitalize on the opportunity by setting aside at least an hour each day to critically and analytically read as much you can find on every form of spirituality. The hopeful nature of the symbol of morning suggests that you have a good chance of success if you persevere.

MOSQUITO
yatoosh-ythvsh- יתוש*-*716

MEANING This is the sort of dream that makes us wake up feeling creepy. Insects are not the most popular creatures, even at the best of times. Mosquitoes are particularly unattractive because not only do they possess all the facets that make insects unappealing to the average person, but they carry some terrible diseases. At a spiritual level, the mosquito represents some form of obstacle to your inner progress; in fact, it suggests a factor that is actually trying to make you retreat.

THE TREE OF LIFE The value of this dream reduces to 14, which is associated with the tarot card Temperance. The Temperance card refers to a person who has balanced all the competing elements of his personality. The mosquito image suggests that you have not yet achieved that balance in your life. This becomes relevant when we remember that the Temperance card sits on the path of Samech. The path of Samech is connected to the guidance and support of the Divine. Your dream sits on the path of Samech in its negative aspect. In other words, you are excessively reliant on the support of the Divine. This relates to the mosquito image in the sense that the mosquito takes blood from its victims but also leaves them with a potentially nasty disease.

THE JOURNEY It is clear that what you must do in your life right now is to achieve some level of independence in both your thoughts and your deeds, from a spiritual perspective. The compression of the dream shows the fact that your dependence on the Divine stems from your feelings of melancholy (Nun). However, the subsequent letter, Yod, indicates that the Divine spark within you is ready to be set alight but only if you have the confidence to believe in yourself. The final letter, Vav, relates to the macrocosm or the Divine and is there to encourage you to try to stand alone in order to continue your progress up the Tree of Life.

MOTHER

em–am–▢▢–41

MEANING There are few symbols as important as the image of a mother. This dream indicates that you have a very strong and continually developing appreciation of the nature of the Divine. The value of this dream is equivalent to the value of the Hebrew word meaning "burn." This word lets us know that not only are you growing in wisdom, but that you are filled with a burning passion to succeed in your quest for some form of ultimate truth.

THE TREE OF LIFE We tend to associate motherhood with gentleness and a desire to protect. These qualities, which are certainly present, form part of the your inner spiritual nature and relate to the way in which you interact with the day-to-day world. However, it is worth noting that the image of a mother also implies an unshaking determination to succeed in your aims. The path of Mem is the path on which we should locate this dream as it is directly associated with motherhood and represents the passionate desire to altruistically assist those around you.

THE JOURNEY As you might expect with a dream about being a mother, there are two key tasks ahead of you. One relates to your inner development and the other relates to your need to help those around

you. From your own point of view, you need to take note of the reduction value of this dream, which is the number 5. This is to remind you that you need to make sure that everything you do is carried out under the influence of your fifth element of Spirit. In terms of offering your assistance to others, the most important thing to remember is that all of us are interconnected, as indicated by the presence of the letter Aleph. This means that when you help others you should treat them exactly as you would wish to be treated.

MOUNTAIN

har–hr הר-205

MEANING The image of a mountain is immediately conducive to the notion of spiritual achievement. You have managed to achieve a great deal in your spiritual work, and your dream is telling that you have climbed a good portion of that metaphorical mountain. Mountains can be cold and lonely places and in many ways the long spiritual journey can be a very cold and solitary process. The value of this dream is equivalent to the value of the Hebrew word meaning "splendorous," and this refers to the view and the feeling that you will have when you reach the top of your mountain.

THE TREE OF LIFE This dream places you very high in the Tree of Life and you should be feel very proud of your achievements. The value of this dream is equivalent to the value of the Hebrew word meaning "hero." This points to the fact that you are quite an unusual person in terms of your strength of character. It also relates strongly to the path of Heh, as this is connected to the zodiac sign Aries, which embodies the martial qualities connected with the concept of a hero. The path of Heh is also particularly appropriate since it means "window" and this relates to the view you have from the peak of the mountain.

THE JOURNEY The task ahead of you now is to continue climbing that mountain until you reach the peak of Keter. The reduction of this dream's value produces the number 7, which is the value of the letter Zayin, meaning "sword." This lets you know that even though you are much closer than most to some form of communion with the Divine, you will still have to struggle to achieve a moment of direct contact with the Divine source itself. However, having climbed so high, you should know that the struggle will be more than worth it.

See Zohar symbol, Mountain.

MOURNING
evel-abl- **אבל**-33

MEANING The dream of mourning is much more encouraging than you might think. From a purely psychological point of view, this dream would relate to the loss of a person close to you. It would not necessarily mean that the individual in question had died, but that you had for some reason lost your sense of attachment to him. If we look at the dream from a Kabbalistic perspective, we need to remember that the dream relates not to the loss of someone else but to the loss of some aspect of ourselves.

THE TREE OF LIFE The Great Work is a process both of growing and of pruning. We have to develop the spiritual aspect of our personality while pruning away all those elements of our nature that interfere with this growth. To be mourning the loss of such an aspect of yourself implies that you are new to the spiritual path. Although you have committed yourself to the inner path, you are still attached to the way you used to look at the world. The path of Tav is the first path out of the Sefirah of Malkut, and while it is very positive in that it marks a definite step in the journey, it is also connected to the sense of regret and what you have left behind.

THE JOURNEY At this very early stage in your development your main concern should be to read deeply and widely about spirituality in general and also to begin some exercises in meditation or a similar pursuit. At an inner level you also need to reflect on the effect of this momentous decision on every other aspect of your life. The value of this dream is equivalent to the value of the Hebrew word meaning "spring." This reminds you that while you are losing some aspects of your old personality, you are being filled with a brand-new energy and nature from the fountain of the Divine.

MOVIES
kolnoa-qvlnva'a- **קולנוע**-262

MEANING We live in a world that now has unprecedented levels of entertainment available to all of us. This is, in part, a way in which we compensate for the fact that our lives are far less intense than they would have been even a few hundred years ago. None of us has to hunt our own food anymore and we are protected in a broad range of ways from subsidized health care to welfare. These are all good things in their own right, but they also reduce our sense of responsibility for our own lives.

In taking on the challenge of the Great Work, we are taking back that sense of responsibility, which carries with it the sense of adventure and excitement that are normally restricted to the world of movies.

THE TREE OF LIFE As well as representing the sense of adventure that we gain when we take up the spiritual task, the dream of movies also highlights our role as an observer in life. You are being advised by your higher self to look at the whole world around you and indeed within you with the same close attention as you would pay if you were seeing the action on a movie screen. When we combine the theme of adventure with the notion of an eye for detail, we will find that the path of Ayin is the only path on the Tree that fits both concerns.

THE JOURNEY You have already made good progress in your spiritual work, but there is always room to achieve more success and to come even closer to an understanding of the Divine. The value of this dream is equivalent to the value of the Hebrew phrase meaning "eye to eye." This implies that the closer you look both at the world around you and at your behavior, the more you will understand not just about yourself but about the nature of the Divine.

MUD
bots-bvtz- **בוץ**-98

MEANING To dream of mud is not the sort of experience that will make you wake up full of enthusiasm and inspiration. The image of mud calls to mind our earliest primeval origins and reminds us of our potential to spend our whole lives without once lifting our heads to see the possibility of a higher, more spiritual existence. The value of this dream is equivalent to that of a Hebrew phrase that refers to the notion of concealment. This relates to how you feel at the moment, as you have no sense of the presence of the Divine in your life.

THE TREE OF LIFE We might expect this dream to be found in the Sefirah of Malkut, as this is the position on the Tree that is concerned with a solely materialist life-style. However, although you are not yet aware of any guidance from your higher self, you have already made the great leap to try to move forward spiritually. The letter Tzaddi is very prominent in the spelling of this dream title and it is to the path of Tzaddi that this dream belongs. Tzaddi indicates that you have a very strong and determined commitment to the Great Work, and this is what you need to rely on at this difficult time in your development.

THE JOURNEY When we reduce the value of this dream we find the number 17. This is the number of the tarot card The Star. This card signifies that even if you cannot see it or feel it, you are being protected by higher forces. It is also the tarot card that is associated with the path of Tzaddi. In order to encourage an awareness of the Divine presence, you should stimulate your current state of mind, which is embedded in the physical in a positive way. Some form of spiritually based physical exercise such as yoga or tai chi would be an ideal pursuit for you right now.

MULE

pered-prd- פרד *-284*

MEANING Notoriously stubborn and famously bad tempered, a mule is not an animal that many of us would want to be compared to. If someone did make such a comparison, we would unlikely see the comparison as being in any way complimentary! However, this dream is actually very favorable and it points to an individual who is making good progress in his attempt to rediscover that lost connection with a sense of the spiritual in his life.

THE TREE OF LIFE When we reduce the value of this dream we find the number 14. This number connects with the tarot card Temperance, which relates to a person who has managed to achieve an inner harmony and balance. Such a person is very close to the moment in his spiritual development when he finally makes contact with his higher self. In terms of the Tree of Life, the Temperance card sits on the path of Samech, which leads into the Sefirah of Tiferet, where the longed-for moment of contact takes place. The letter Samech means "prop" in Hebrew and refers to a supporting force. In this sense we can also see the connection of Samech with the image of a mule, since a mule's function is to bear our load for us as we continue on our travels.

THE JOURNEY The value of this dream is equivalent to that of a Hebrew phrase meaning "a small enclosed garden." The idea of a garden is often used to symbolize spiritual enlightenment. The fact that this garden is small and enclosed serves to emphasize that the route to Tiferet is a narrow one beset with obstacles and distractions. The compression of the value of this dream tells you all you need to know if you are to stick to the narrow path of Samech. You must remember that the benevolent force of the

Divine (Resh) is with you at all times. Additionally, you should discuss your feelings with like-minded people (Peh). If you do this, the door (Daleth) to Tiferet will be open for you.

MURDER

retsakh-rtzch- רצח *-298*

MEANING Don't be alarmed if you wake up from a dream of murder—it does not mean that you are about to run amok with a selection of firearms! A psychologist might see this dream as pointing to a seething mass of unresolved tension and resentment, and you should honestly examine your feelings to see if this applies to you. To the Kabbalist, this dream indicates that you are ready to move on to a level of consciousness where your spiritual self begins to take priority over your material, day-to-day personality. This dream's value is equivalent to the value of the Hebrew word meaning "white." This color is associated in the Kabbalah with spiritual purity of the highest kind, so it is quite clear that far from engaging in any illegal activities, the image of murder is symbolic of a shift in perception and consciousness.

THE TREE OF LIFE Throughout the Western Mystery Tradition we find the idea that in order to fully awaken our higher self, our genius, or whatever term is used to represent our spiritual self, we must first destroy our ego-driven concerns. This process is the murder referred to by the dream title. If that description seems a little extreme, we should consider that this very same symbolism was used as far back as the days of the alchemists, who wrote that the base metal could become gold only after it had been killed. The extremely vigorous and harsh undertones of this dream's message place it firmly on the path of Lamed.

THE JOURNEY Before you can remove the influence of your ego-driven concerns you must be able to identify them clearly. You can make a start in this by engaging in a regular meditation each day where you reflect on your behavior and thoughts with a view to isolating those aspects with which you are unhappy. Additionally, you might like to consider getting up some form of professional counseling or therapy, as this will speed up the process of identifying those parts of your personality that need to be worked on. This is particularly appropriate if you have identified feelings of resentment or violent ideas within you in relation to another person or a situation. While the central letter, Tzaddi, in the spelling of this dream title refers to the need for commitment in order to succeed in this difficult task, the initial Resh and the final Cheth both point to the fact that the protective and benevolent aspect of the Divine is with you at all times.

MUSEUM

bet nekhot-byth nkvth- בית נכות-888

MEANING One of the valid translations of the Hebrew word "Kabbalah" is "tradition." Museums are places that are literally stuffed full of tradition. Your dream indicates that you are trying to immerse yourself in the whole tradition and history of the spiritual quest throughout the ages. It is an excellent way to stimulate growth within yourself, because when we see the things that encouraged and inspired others, we begin to find those things and thoughts that will encourage and inspire us to new heights.

THE TREE OF LIFE The most striking thing about this dream is the fact that its value consists entirely of repetitions of the number 8. This number is used as a symbol of eternity itself and so is very appropriate to this dream, given your interest in the tradition of mysticism. Additionally, the number 8 refers to the Sefirah of Hod, as this is the eighth Sefirah on the Tree of Life. Hod relates to our desire to understand the universe from an intellectual and scientific viewpoint. Once again, this aspect of the number 8 suits the dream of a museum. Both your dream and its position on the Tree of Life refer to your desire to increase your knowledge and understanding.

THE JOURNEY The acquisition of knowledge can be a lonely business sometimes. However, as much as we can learn from books, it is in our interactions with others that the lessons of the books are put into practice and take on a much deeper significance. The compression of this dream contains the letter Peh in both its standard and final forms. The letter Peh means "mouth" and is concerned with all forms of communication. The message to you as the dreamer is that you must continue your search for truth, but you should find a way of ensuring that the search includes plenty of discussion with other people.

MUSIC

negeenah-ngynh- נגינה-118

MEANING Throughout history humankind has used music to celebrate life in general and in particular to worship the Divine. There is a divinity in music that can be fully appreciated only when we look into the underlying rules that govern the creation of musical forms. It is no accident that the building up of a piece of harmonious music uses the same mathematical intervals between notes as we find in mathematical formulas used in the construction of sacred sites around the world. Consequently, to dream of music suggests that you are beginning to "tune in" to the underlying formulas that define the presence of the Divine within the physical universe.

THE TREE OF LIFE The value of this dream reduces to 10, which indicates that you have reached the conclusion of a major part of your spiritual quest. The value of the dream is also equivalent to the value of a Hebrew word that refers to one of the spiritual rulers of the element of Air. Given the deeply mystical significance of the dream of music, it is appropriate to further reduce the value of this dream to 1, which is the value of the path of Aleph. This path is related to the element of Air and it is also the path that carries the purest music directly from the Divine source of Keter.

THE JOURNEY You have now tapped in to the spiritual structure of the universe and are able to see that for all the somber truths that we can discover about the nature of the Divine, it is also a force that can best be seen as a wonderful piece of musical creativity to which the whole universe dances. It is for this reason that the path of Aleph is associated with the tarot card The Fool. The truly wise and enlightened individual is so enamored of the pure joy and love that emanates from the Divine that he has no care for the mundane anxieties and worries that tend to govern others' lives. The value of this dream is equivalent to that of the Hebrew word meaning "high priest." In a sense you must now take on the mantle of priesthood as you begin to encourage others to understand and revel in the unbounded love of the Divine.

MUSICAL

mooseekay-mvsyqay- מוסיקאי-227

MEANING While the dream of music refers to an appreciation of the musical structure that governs the universe, this dream is about your innate musicality. From a spiritual perspective, the idea of being musical relates to the notion of creativity in general. Importantly, it also suggests that you have an awareness that this desire to create comes from the influence of the Divine through the agency of your higher self. The value of this dream is a prime number (a number that can be divided only by itself and by one) and this points to your great sense of individuality that you can draw on in your creative efforts.

THE TREE OF LIFE The value of this dream is equivalent to those of Hebrew phrases relating to the element of Fire. The element of Fire is always seen as creative, it is the first element in the sacred Tetragrammaton, and it represents the initial creative burst from which the universe emanated. The Sefirah of Netzach is connected to the element of Fire and also relates to creative enterprises from music to sculpture. It is here that this dream is correctly located.

THE JOURNEY There are any number of ways in which we can celebrate the presence of the Divine. This dream tells us that at this moment it will be most helpful to you to find some creative means to express your unique sense of your relationship to the Divine. The value of this dream is equivalent to the value of the Hebrew word meaning "pond," which serves to point out that although the creative act is typified by the element of Fire, you also need to dig deep into your emotions in order to express yourself in a fully honest manner. In doing so you will not only help yourself to understand your inner nature, you will create a means by which other people can begin to reflect on their relationship to the Divine.

MYSTERY

meestoreen – msthvryn – מסתורין‎-766

MEANING If we look only at the title of this dream, it is not at all clear how to interpret its meaning. This is because a mystery can be intriguing and exciting but equally can be disturbing and worrisome. Obviously the lessons that you can learn about your inner development will differ greatly depending on which form of mystery we use for the analysis. This is the great advantage of a Kabbalistic analysis, as we can look into the structure of the dream title itself. The first thing we notice is that the spelling of this dream title ends with the final form of the letter Nun. This indicates that this dream of mystery relates to a disturbing and worrisome sense of the unknown.

THE TREE OF LIFE In addition to the final letter, Nun, we have the letter Tav placed centrally in the spelling of this dream title. The letter Tav relates a sense of regret and loss, and this is emphasized by the association of this letter with the planet

Saturn, regarded as the oldest and most melancholic of the planets. This sense of loss and confusion defines the mystery of the dream's title. You have begun the Great Work and have started to move up the Tree of Life, but the nature of the Divine remains a complete mystery to you. This sense of worry is connected to the path of Qoph on the Tree of Life and it is here that your dream is situated.

THE JOURNEY Although this dream is characterized by a sense of confusion and doubt, it is important to remember that these feelings are an inevitable part of the process of exploring your spiritual side. The initial letter, Mem, in the spelling of this dream title lets you know that the protective aspect of the Divine is with you even at this difficult stage. Similarly, in the compression of this dream we see the central letter, Samech, which refers to the supportive force of the higher that will help you traverse the path of Qoph and begin to cast off your doubt and confusion.

NAKED IN PUBLIC

arom be farhesyah – a'arvm b phrhsyh – ערום ב פרהסיה‎-678

MEANING Very often we dream of behavior that we would never consider in day-to-day life. This dream certainly fits that definition, for the vast majority of us at least! Many of us would have taken this dream to refer to a concern that we are in some way about to be humiliated or embarrassed, as the idea of being naked in public is one that most of us would not relish. However, the first letter of the spelling of this dream title is the Ayin, which points to an individual who has a great commitment to his individual approach to life. Consequently, the dream of being naked in public may point to your confidence to go against the mainstream viewpoint. Equally, this dream could be a reflection of your sense of vulnerability in the world, in which case the letter Ayin should be seen as an encouragement to try to build up your self-confidence.

THE TREE OF LIFE If you want to find spiritual truth, you have to be prepared to stand out from the crowd and maintain an open mind in the face of a world full of people who have fixed ideas that run contrary to your beliefs. This requires not just confidence in your individuality but a vigorous and energetic approach that will carry you through when you are faced with opposition both internally and externally. For all these reasons, this dream lies on the path of Ayin.

THE JOURNEY While you might not be able to act out the specifics of this dream, unless you live in a very understanding community, you can live out the underlying principle. When we compress the value of this dream we find the letters Mem, Ayin, and Cheth. Mem encourages you to be as idiosyncratic as you feel (Ayin), because no matter how far from the mainstream you stray, the protective force of the Divine will stay with you. The final letter, Cheth, in the compression warns you against becoming defensive in the face of opposition to your beliefs. The reduction of this dream's value gives us the number 3. This number is associated with creativity and so again emphasizes the need for you to follow your own tune. The potential for embarrassment that is associated with being naked in public symbolizes the difficult nature of the task ahead. It is of course not helpful to try to develop your inner self while feeling uncomfortable, and this dream lets you know that it is a good thing to want and to seek support when you need it.

NAKEDNESS

*erom-ayrvm-*אירום-257

MEANING Being naked is highly significant in terms of the Kabbalah. As in many mystical and occult systems, nudity is a symbol both of our intrinsic weakness and of our inner self stripped of any outward or earthly status. To dream of being naked suggests the beginning of some new venture in life, usually of a positive nature. Very often a dream of being naked is a sign that you are beginning to truly make your own way in the world and have the confidence and will to be your own person. In many ways, being naked can be seen as the first step in the process of initiation, the casting off of everything associated with one's previous life in order to begin a completely new life-style.

THE TREE OF LIFE Dreams of nakedness are firmly placed within the Sefirah of Malkut. This is the lowest Sefirah on the Tree of Life and is concerned with the purely material aspects of life. In this dream it is Malkut's association with the element of Earth that is particularly important. In our nakedness we are stripped of all trappings of civilization and sophistication. In some senses this is akin to a state of innocence, and the element of Earth in its lack of intellectual concerns is equally innocent. It is no accident that in many mystical organizations an initiate goes through a ceremony where he is either literally or symbolically naked. The value of this dream is a prime number (a number that can be divided only by itself and by the number one). In spiritual terms, this indicates that even when you are naked you are still a unique individual.

THE JOURNEY As we stand at the very bottom of the Tree, surrounded by the definite and the physical, we have two choices. We can allow our sense of the spiritual to be dulled by the immediacy of material satisfaction. However, if we have the will, we may awaken our inner or higher self and begin to seek out a greater truth. The dream of nakedness suggests that we are making the second and ultimately more satisfying choice. Before we can take a step forward, though, we must strip ourselves of all our existing assumptions and beliefs. Our nudity symbolizes this peeling off of the comfortable certainties of the modern world. It is quite common to feel very vulnerable in this state. This is actually a very positive situation, as it is only through truly relying on faith in our higher self that we open ourselves to the possibility of wisdom.

NATURAL DISASTERS

*ason teevee-asvn tba'ay-*אסון טבעי-208

MEANING When we think about the structure of the universe and try to relate it to the nature of the Divine, we tend to focus on those aspects of Creation that cause us to feel a sense of wonder and joy. However, this is a deep misunderstanding of the nature of God. Since God is by its very nature an unknowable force, we should not expect the universe to conform to our human sense of what is wonderful. To do so would be to try to make God in our own image. This dream indicates that you are beginning to appreciate that the wondrous nature of the Divine is not always immediately obvious to us. The value of this dream is equivalent to the value of the Hebrew word meaning "strife," and this dream introduces you to the idea that strife can be a part of the Divine.

THE TREE OF LIFE The reduction value of this dream leads to the number 10. This refers to the physicality of the dream's subject, but it does not point to the location of the dream being in Malkut. The physicality in this dream is of a very specific type and it relates to the forces of conflict within the universe. An appreciation of the need for these conflicting forces is associated with the Sefirah of Gevurah. This dream is located on the Sefirah of Gevurah, and this is why the least attractive aspects of the physical universe are presenting themselves to your unconscious mind at this time.

THE JOURNEY Perhaps one of the hardest things to accept in the Great Work is that the Divine not only lies behind beauty and wisdom and joy but is responsible for our mortality and the often brutal way in which the natural universe functions, from the smallest particles clashing with one another to produce new elements to the immense power of volcanoes and earthquakes. We need to learn that without mortality we do not have the possibility of the wondrous nature of birth. If you meditate on that simple fact, you will find that the seeming cruelty of the world becomes much easier to understand.

NEED

tsorekh-tzvrk- צורך *-316*

MEANING Our interpretation of need tends to focus on the material needs that drive us. Because of this, we do not usually perceive ourselves as being in a state of need and are likely to extend that label only to individuals who are very clearly lacking in the basic necessities of life. However, when we put our lives into a spiritual context, we should also notice that from the religious point of view we are all deeply in need. Ironically, in fact, the less we are materially in need, the more we tend to become spiritually in need. This is often because the pursuit of material security reduces the amount of time for spiritual security almost to zero.

THE TREE OF LIFE It is encouraging that you are having this dream as it demonstrates an awareness on your part that you are lacking in an important area of your life. The fact that this dream refers to the state of need, and not to any action that you may have taken to address this need, suggests that you have not yet begun your spiritual journey. Additionally, when we reduce the value of this dream we find the number 10, and this number refers to the Sefirah of Malkut, which is the correct location for this dream.

THE JOURNEY Now that you have recognized your need, you need to take some action to start including a sense of the spiritual in your life. In the compression of this dream we see that you certainly have the drive and energy (Shin) to awaken the spark of the Divine (Yod) and begin to approach the Divine (Vav) itself. The value of this dream is equivalent to the value of the Hebrew phrase meaning "to worship," and that is all you have to do in order to start addressing the gap in your life.

NEEDLE

makhat-mcht- מחט *-57*

MEANING Unless you are unusually excited by the prospect of sewing, this dream is likely to seem dull, to say the least. When we remember that our dreams are always in some way a reflection of our natures or our aspirations, we can perceive this dream in a new light. Needles are used to mend clothes when they are torn or broken, so symbolically we can see that a dream of a needle represents a desire to mend and heal. From a spiritual perspective, this points to a wish to both heal your soul and to help those around you heal themselves.

THE TREE OF LIFE When we reduce the value of this dream we find the number 12. This number is associated with self-sacrifice and altruism. This fits very well with the idea of a needle as a symbol of healing and mending at a spiritual level. Additionally, the tarot card The Hanged Man is the twelfth card in the tarot cycle, and this card also relates to the willingness of an individual to place the needs of others before his own needs. Finally, The Hanged Man sits on the path of Mem on the Tree of Life, and this path relates to protective and maternal aspects of the Divine, so it is to the path of Mem that we assign this dream.

THE JOURNEY The value of this dream is equivalent to the value of the Hebrew word meaning "altar." This reiterates the fact that you are moving forward in your spiritual quest. Additionally you can see the image of the altar as supporting the idea that you should behave in a self-sacrificing manner. The compression of the value of this dream tells you that you are going to experience a degree of emotional upset (Nun) as you try to help others, but that you must continue to struggle on (Zayin), as this is the route by which you will come to a communion with the Divine.

NEIGHBOR

shakhen-shkn- שכן *-370*

MEANING The dream of a neighbor may seem like a simple one; after all, you know who lives next door to you, and if you are dreaming about him it is probably due to some memorable conversation or argument you recently had with him. However, every dream has a spiritual aspect to it, as when we sleep our higher self has the best possible opportunity of communicating with us. Further, we should remember that every major religion tells us that every person with whom we share the planet is indeed our neighbor and should be treated as such.

THE TREE OF LIFE The value of this dream is equivalent to the value of the Hebrew word meaning "foundation." The Sefirah of Yesod is also known as "Foundation," so we can confidently place this dream on this position on the Tree of Life. Once we arrive in Yesod, we begin to reflect on the implications of our newfound spirituality. While we do need to consider how we will move forward in our inner life, the decision to take up the spiritual path also affects the way in which we interact with those around us.

THE JOURNEY The spelling of this dream title ends in the letter Nun, which indicates that a challenge to your faith lies on the horizon. You should see this not as a suggestion that you are in any way being singled out for a difficult time but as simply an expression of the suffering that is the lot of us all. Now that you have decided to take up the Great Work, you can see that the letters Shin and Kaph in the spelling indicate that you have the energy to help your neighbors in a practical way with their suffering. In doing so, you will increase your understanding of the Divine.

NEST

*ken-qn-*קן-150

MEANING This is not as uncommon a dream as we might think. Even at the psychological level we can see that it relates to a desire to return to a protected state such as that enjoyed by a fledgling in its nest. This could be a dream about returning to the womb, but even in our dreams there are certain things that we disguise from ourselves. At a spiritual level, this dream works in two directions: on one hand, you want to return to your spiritual home, and on the other, a part of you wants to return to the stage of your life before you discovered the spiritual dimension of your nature.

THE TREE OF LIFE The value of this dream is equivalent to that of a Hebrew word meaning "thine eye." This relates to the eye of God and indicates that you are trying to catch the attention of the Divine. You have realized that you need to try to develop your spiritual nature, but are understandably finding this hard as you have not yet felt any tangible evidence of the existence of a higher force. The anx-

iety that this produces places this dream on the path of Qoph, and this is also the first letter in the dream title.

THE JOURNEY One of the most difficult aspects right now is that you must persevere with the Great Work in the absence of any suggestion that your work is in any way valid. The value of this dream is equivalent to the value of a Hebrew phrase meaning "walking shoe," and this is a way for your higher self to urge you to continue your inner voyage. The compression of this dream's value tells us that what you fear (Qoph) is finding nothing but doubt or challenges to your beliefs (Nun) as a result of your involvement in the Great Work. However, the reduction of the dream's value produces the number 6, which in the context of this dream should be seen as a promise of the ultimate contact you will achieve with the macrocosmic force.

NEWSPAPER

*eeton-a'aythvn-*עיתון-536

MEANING A dream of newspapers would seem to suggest a great concern with the matters of the day-to-day world. We would not necessarily see the dreamer as materialistic in any crass way, but we would see him as more interested in the state of the world than in the state of his soul. However, this would be to misinterpret the spiritual import of this dream. The value of this dream is equivalent to the value of a Hebrew phrase referring to "the world of Assiah." While "the world of Assiah" is indeed a Kabbalistic term for the physical dimension, this dream is interested not in the physical dimension itself but in the messages that can be found within the world of the physical.

THE TREE OF LIFE The value of this dream is also equivalent to the value of a Hebrew phrase meaning "a white cloak." This image emphasizes your spirituality by virtue of the color of the cloak. The cloak itself indicates that you appear to be based mainly in the world of the actual but that your overriding concern is with the hidden spiritual import within the material world. The idea of a newspaper relates to themes of communication, and your approach to the Great Work is similarly an attempt to engage in some form of communication with the Divine. Consequently, this dream belongs on the path of Peh.

THE JOURNEY You will continue to accumulate insights into the spiritual dimension as long as you interpret the world from a spiritual perspective. The value of this dream reduces to 5 which is the value of the Hebrew letter Heh, meaning "window." This tells us that you need to try to look at the world around you as a window onto the nature of the Divine. The compression of this dream's value has the central letter Lamed, which emphasizes the difficulties that lie ahead of you but also points to the force of the Divine (Vav), which will be there to encourage you.

❧ NIGHT

laylah-lylh-לילה-75

MEANING Historically, people have seen the night as a time of fear and insecurity. This stems from our earliest times when the night really was a time of great danger due to the predators prowling around outside the cave with empty stomachs and disturbingly sharp teeth! However, there is no reason to associate the night with spiritual darkness of any kind, and in fact the night can be a wonderful time for meditation and contemplation, due to the peace and quiet that is available to us. Indeed, midnight is traditionally a very sacred time in the tradition of the Kabbalah and is ideal for deep meditation.

THE TREE OF LIFE The value of this dream is equivalent to the value of the Hebrew word meaning "hues" or "colors." This not only reminds us of the positive nature of nighttime by referring to the liveliness that we associate with color but suggests that you have a creative streak that you can use to enrich your spiritual life. The repeated presence of the letter Lamed indicates that you are experiencing the harsh, critical force of the Divine at this time. This dream is situated on the path of Lamed, and this force will encourage you to work on your creative abilities.

THE JOURNEY From your personal point of view, the dream of night relates to the lack of connection you now feel you have to the Divine. But from the point of view of the Divine, the dream of night is a way of suggesting to you that even in the absence of daylight there is still great potential for seeing the presence of the Divine. Your task in the next few months is to use your creative skills to express your relationship to the Divine. This will help you to see its presence in every aspect of the world even in the dead of night.

NOISE

raash-ra'ash-רעש-570

MEANING A dream about noise does not suggest a high level of spiritual insight. In general, we associate noise with chaos, and we do not associate chaos with understanding or enlightenment. The value of this dream is equivalent to the value of the Hebrew word meaning "earthquake," and this adds to the idea that this dream refers to confusion and fear. However, the value of this dream is also equivalent to that of the Hebrew word meaning "ten," and this indicates that you are about to complete a major cycle in your life.

THE TREE OF LIFE When we reduce the value of this dream it leads to the number 12. This number is associated with the concept of self-sacrifice and altruism. At first sight, this seems to run counter to the fact that this dream is full of images of chaos. However, the presence of the number 12 tells us that it is the chaos of other people's lives that is being presented to you in this dream and that you have an altruistic desire to try to introduce some harmony and balance to their lives. For this reason, your dream is situated on the path of Mem, which represents the maternal aspect of the Divine force.

THE JOURNEY Your growing realization that you have a desire to assist others is a novel state of consciousness for you, as in the past you were very focused on your own needs and concerns. When you begin to act on this impulse you will have achieved the completion referred to by the presence of the number 10 in this dream's value. The compression of this dream's value urges you to take some practical steps (Kaph) to manifest this wish. One way to help is to root out any sources of noise and chaos within yourself that are distracting you from your inner development. The final letter, Ayin, in the compression is there to advise you that any volunteer activities you engage in to bring this about should be organized and managed by you rather than an existing charity group.

NOSE

af-aph-אף-81

MEANING It is very tempting to try to see this dream image as symbolic in the colloquial fashion—that is, as an indication of someone who cannot mind his own business. However, the values within the dream title do not support such an interpretation. In fact, this dream indicates a person of great passion and fellowship but not someone who likes to interfere in the lives of others in any way.

THE TREE OF LIFE The value of this dream is equivalent to that of the Hebrew phrase meaning a "hearer of cries," and this certainly points to a person with great empathy for his fellow man. Seemingly in contrast to this the value of the dream is also equivalent to that of a Hebrew word meaning "wrath." However, this allusion to great anger does not imply that you have a bad temper so much as it suggests that in hearing the cries of those in trouble, you have great vigor and passion in offering your assistance. This high level of commitment and passion places this dream on the path of Teth, which in its positive aspect refers to great strength of character and willpower. This path is also indicated by the fact that the reduction value of this dream produces the number 9, which is the value of the letter Teth.

THE JOURNEY Your passionate desire to help should not go to waste, and it is clear from this dream that in order for you to grow as a spiritual being, you need to act on this powerful feeling of empathy. When we look at the compression of the dream's value we can see that the best way for you to help people is not by taking any direct action on their behalf but by communicating (Peh) with them so that you and they can fully understand their situation and find a valid solution. In engaging with others, possibly by seeking a career change to one of the caring professions, you will draw ever closer to a full understanding of the nature of the Divine (Aleph) and of your place within the universe.

NUMBERS

*meesparym-msphrym-*מספרים-430

MEANING The more we learn about the universe, the more the idea that "God is a mathematician" seems a valid definition of the nature of the Divine. As is often the case, science has begun to appreciate a feature of the universe long after mysticism has known it to be the case. It now seems that the physical universe rests almost entirely on mathematical principles rather than on the laws of mechanics, and every mystical system from the Egyptians through the Pythagoreans and right up to the Theosophists of the late nineteenth century has recognized that numbers underlie the structure of the universe.

THE TREE OF LIFE The value of this dream is equivalent to that of the full title of the Sefirah of

Yesod in Hebrew. Consequently this dream belongs in the Sefirah of Yesod, and this links to the title of the dream. In arriving at the first destination on the Tree after the solely physical realm of Malkut, you are beginning to understand the significance of numbers in the realm of the spiritual. Additionally, this dream's value is equivalent to the value of the Hebrew word meaning "twilight," and the Sefirah of Yesod is strongly associated with the feelings that we connect to twilight and dusk.

THE JOURNEY The Kabbalah is concerned, perhaps more than is any other system of mysticism, with the role of numbers in developing an understanding of the Divine. The value of this dream is equivalent to the value of the Hebrew word meaning "concealed." This relates to the fact that the spiritual significance within the Hebrew language is often hidden. The value of this dream reduces to 7, which is the value of the letter Zayin, meaning "sword." In order to progress in the Great Work you need to maintain your struggle to find the spiritual truths no matter how hidden from sight they may be.

OAK

*alon-alvn-*אלון-86

MEANING The oak is a tree that is steeped in mystical associations. While it is perhaps best known for its links with the Druids and other European pagan traditions, it is also an important symbol in a number of other religious traditions. It appears widely, for instance, throughout the Torah as a very significant and symbolic tree. To dream of an oak indicates that you have a very spiritual outlook on life and you are gaining great understanding and insight as you progress on your inner journey. The value of this dream is equivalent to the Hebrew for the well-known cry "Hallelujah," which serves to emphasize your deeply spiritual mind-set.

THE TREE OF LIFE The person who dreams of an oak has made great gains in his understanding both of himself and of the world around him in a spiritual context. The value of this dream is also equivalent to that of a Hebrew phrase meaning "a rustling of wings." This can be seen as suggesting that you are now close enough to some form of direct contact with an angelic force that if you listen closely enough, you may even hear their metaphorical wings beating! When we reduce the value of this dream we find the number 5, which is the value of the letter Heh, and it is the path of Heh on which this dream sits.

THE JOURNEY You are now on one of the paths of the Tree that leads into the supernal Sefirot, and the path of Heh in particular reflects the strength and steadfastness of character that we associate with the oak as well as its deep spiritual importance. The compression of this dream produces the letters Peh and Vav. These tell you that you are now so close to achieving a direct communion with the Divine that you need to begin to pass your wisdom on to others. You should do this by talking (Peh) or possibly writing about your experiences. This will encourage others to reflect (Vav) on their own spiritual potential and will also increase your chances of experiencing the glimpse of the Divine hinted at by the path of Heh.

OAR

mashot-mshvt-משום-355

MEANING Anyone who has seen a professional rowing team in action will tell you that a boat powered by oars can move along at a terrific rate. This dream is about movement, and vigorous movement at that. The fact that you are moving through water in your dream tells us that it is in the sphere of your emotions that changes are likely to occur. Further, the dream's value reduces to 13, and this indicates that you are indeed about to experience a major shift in your way of viewing the world.

THE TREE OF LIFE The value of this dream is equivalent to the value of the Hebrew word meaning "idea," and this suggests that while you are experiencing change on an emotional level, you are heading toward a point where you will focus much more on the abstract intellectual aspect of spirituality than on the emotional side. The position on the Tree of Life that relates to this description is the Sefirah of Hod. The path that you are on, which leads into Hod, is the path of Shin, which is full of the fiery energy represented by the first letter in the compression of this dream's value.

THE JOURNEY In order to deal with the intellectual concepts of Hod, you need to have established at least an initial sense of where you are as emotive individual. This is because even the driest intellectual concept has some resonance for everyone at a deep emotional level. To achieve this early self-knowledge will be difficult, as indicated by Nun, the second letter in the compression of this dream. However, the final Heh is there to reassure you that the more honestly you look at yourself, the better you will be able to glimpse the Divine principles that underlie the structure of the universe.

OATH

shvooah-shbva'ah-שבועה-383

MEANING The growth of technology and the construction of the so-called global village is a two-edged sword in terms of human relationships. On one hand, we can get to know people from all over the world. However, the flip side of this development is that when it comes to more formal relationships, the immense distance between us means that we have to rely on documents and contracts rather than on our word alone. In this modern age the idea of giving an oath has all but disappeared. In the spiritual context, an oath relates to your commitment to the Great Work and to a promise you make to yourself to maintain that commitment.

THE TREE OF LIFE This dream occurs early in your spiritual development. It is an almost conscious separation of your earlier life from your new, spiritually enlivened existence. The central letter within the compression of the value of this dream is Peh. This letter relates to all forms of communication, and this is the path on which this dream lies. The communication in this case is the process by which you consciously dedicate yourself to the task of discovering your higher self.

THE JOURNEY While each of us must in some way make an oath to the Creator fairly early in our spiritual journey, each oath will be individual in its nature and in the way we then act to live up to that promise of commitment. The value of this dream is a prime number (a number that can be divided only by itself and by one), and this serves to emphasize your unique nature. The lesson in this dream is that, having promised to focus on the Great Work, you now need to concentrate not only on finding a means to contact the Divine but on finding a way to fully understand your unique inner nature. The final letter, Gimel, in the compression of this dream tells you that in this act of discovery you should be as creative and innovative as you wish.

OBEDIENCE

tseeyoot-tzyvth-ציוות-506

MEANING We live in a world that encourages us all to try to be as self-reliant as possible. In one sense this is extremely healthy, but in recent years this individualism has begun to lead to a feeling of resentment at the idea of authority. We have, as a culture, started to place the notion of obedience in the same mental brackets as the notion of exploitation or the loss of self. Such dislike and disapproval of the concept of obedience can make spiritual development difficult, as we must accept the right of the Divine to insist on our obedience to its higher wisdom.

THE TREE OF LIFE The value of this dream is equivalent to the value of a Hebrew word referring to the zodiac sign Taurus. The sign of Taurus is connected to characteristics of obedience and a methodical and determined nature. However, Taurus is also linked with a tendency toward a love of the sensual. This points to the fact that obedience need not mean the loss of self or even the loss of self-indulgence at appropriate moments. The sign of Taurus is placed on the path of Vav on the Tree of Life and it is here that we should locate this dream. The path of Vav relates to the reflective side of our nature and this again goes to prove that obedience is not in any way a means of denying your ability to think freely.

THE JOURNEY If we truly wish to form a sense of communion with the Divine, we have to accept that the Divine does indeed stand above us and we are obliged to recognize its ultimate authority. The compression of this dream's value tells us that we need to find some practical means (Kaph) of demonstrating our willingness to put the Divine will (Vav) above our personal wishes. One good way to demonstrate this, and to benefit from the significant insights that will result from this action, is to sacrifice something that you greatly enjoy. For instance, you could make a point of scheduling your regular meditation so that it conflicts with your favorite TV show.

OBITUARY

modaat evel-mvda'ath abl- מודעת אבל-553

MEANING One well-known phrase that perhaps has more relevance to the field of spiritual exploration than any other is the expression, "a little knowledge is a dangerous thing." To gain an understanding of the Divine is quite literally a life's work, but unfortunately it is all too easy to find those who would try to convince you that you can become enlightened in little more than a weekend. Such short-term spiritual projects give birth to any number of myths about the nature of spiritual symbolism. One of the most prevalent is the idea that to dream of your death is a sure indicator that you are not long

for this world. Nothing could be further from the truth, so you should certainly not see anything worrisome in this dream.

THE TREE OF LIFE To dream of your obituary indicates simply that you are recognizing the end of your old, nonspiritual self. The dream of an obituary for this ego-driven aspect of your personality means that you are coming to terms with the need to move on and change in order to grow. The value of this dream reduces to 13, and this indicates that you are experiencing a major change in your life. This change is the movement from a primarily secular to a spiritually based life-style. The Death card in the tarot has the value 13 and is linked to the path of Nun. This path is the location for this dream both in its association with the sense of loss and as it represents the passage into the Sefirah of Tiferet, where you are united with your higher self.

THE JOURNEY Death is always difficult to cope with, but the death of an aspect of yourself, even an unnecessary element of your personality, is doubly difficult to come to terms with. The central letter, Nun, in the compression of this dream points to the path of this dream and to the emotional upset that you will have felt. The initial letter, Kaph, tells you to take some practical action to mark your passage into a new state of consciousness. This should be a creative act (Gimel); for instance, it could involve your disposing of a small number of your possessions that best represent the attitudes and outlook of your old ego-based personality.

OBLIGATION

khovah-chvbh- חובה-21

MEANING Almost every mainstream religion states that there is no penalty applicable to an individual who fails to achieve any relationship with the Divine because he is not given an opportunity to find out about the spiritual nature of the universe. However, they are unanimous in their claim that those who are given the chance of forming that relationship but decide to reject it will in some way suffer once they pass on from their physical incarnation. It is this obligation to take up the chance of enlightenment to which this dream refers. The value of this dream is equivalent to the value of the name "Eheieh," which is the name of God connected to the Sefirah of Keter. This indicates that it is indeed the spiritual obligation that this dream is talking about.

THE TREE OF LIFE Another word that is equivalent to the value of this dream is the Hebrew word meaning "innocence." This word points to the path of Aleph, because this is the first and highest path on the Tree and to be positioned there implies that you have achieved the high level of wisdom that resolves itself to a state of pure innocence. You should feel extremely proud of your spiritual achievements but also be aware that this is not the end of your spiritual obligations.

THE JOURNEY You are now at a point in your spiritual development where your obligations operate in two directions. You still have a commitment to the Divine, and the equivalence of this dream to the value of the Hebrew word meaning "deep meditation" indicates that you must continue to strive to commune with the Divine. At the same time, you now have an obligation to your fellow people. The reduction of this dream produces the number 3, which is the value of the letter Gimel, and this points out that you now need to take your secret wisdom and find a way to spread it to those around you.

✥OCEAN

*okyanos–avqyynvs–*אוקיינוס*–243*

MEANING Our first thought when looking at this dream title is likely to be that this is a dream about your emotional state. This is because the element of Water is associated with the emotions. However, this dream relates to a very active and fiery aspect of our soul. When we consider the values within this dream, we find that the image of the ocean is being used as a symbol of the source of created life within the universe. This is emphasized by the fact that the value of this dream is equivalent to the value of the phrase "created He them" in the book of Genesis.

THE TREE OF LIFE If the ocean represents the metaphorical womb of all physical life in the universe, then the letter Yod is the symbolically male energy that causes the stirring of life within that ocean. Within the sacred four-lettered name of God otherwise known as the Tetragrammaton, the letter Yod represents the element of Fire and is the initiating spark of creation. In terms of the Tree of Life, this dream sits on the path of Yod and represents the fact that you are reaching a point in your life when you can embody the creative force of the Divine in the way in which you approach the Great Work.

THE JOURNEY When we reduce the value of this dream we find the number 9, which is the value of the letter Teth. This letter represents the strength of will that you need in order to progress on your inner journey. Additionally, 9 is the number of the tarot card The Hermit. This emphasizes the paradoxical nature that underlies the energy of the letter Yod. On one hand, it is extremely energetic and dynamic, but at the same time an individual who embodies the energy of Yod also has the capacity to be still both inwardly and in terms of how he interacts with others. You should use this dual nature to both forge ahead in your spiritual quest and to provide yourself with the sense of peace that you need to reflect on your progress.

OFFENSE

*aveyrah–a'abyrh–*עבירה*–287*

MEANING From a purely psychological point of view, this dream would suggest that you have certain feelings about which you feel guilty. Your unconscious is using your sleep as a means of reminding you that you need to face up to your inner feelings and achieve some form of closure. From a spiritual perspective, this dream indicates that you do not believe you are taking the right approach to the Divine. This feeling usually stems from an inner recognition that you have not wholly committed yourself to the Great Work.

THE TREE OF LIFE When we reduce the value of this dream we find the number 8. This is the value of the letter Cheth, which means "fence." The implication of this letter is that for some reason you are acting in a defensive manner in relation to the Divine. The reason for this reluctance to commit openly and completely to the spiritual quest stems from a fear of failure. The value of this dream is equivalent to the value of a Hebrew word referring to the zodiac sign of Cancer. As the sign of Cancer is associated with the path of Cheth, this is further confirmation that this is the path to which your dream belongs.

THE JOURNEY Until you rid yourself of the fear of failure, you will not be able to progress any further in your search for spiritual truth. It is quite common to be so afraid of failing in a pursuit that is very important to us that we unconsciously prevent ourselves from even attempting the task in question, as that way we never have to face the possibility of failure. The compression of this dream reminds you that the benevolent force of the Divine (Resh) is with you. In order to find the courage to fully commit to the spiritual quest, you should discuss your fears (Peh) with like-minded individuals, as this will give you the confidence to undertake the struggle (Zayin) to reach the Divine.

OFFICE

*meesrad-mshrd-*משרד-544

MEANING After a long, hard day at work, the last thing that you want to dream about when you fall asleep is an office. Of course, from a spiritual point of view your dream does not refer to a literal office or even to your career. The image of an office is symbolic of a desire to be organized and efficient in your life. This desire is ultimately driven by a deep-seated need to feel in control of every aspect of your environment, both externally and in terms of your inner self.

THE TREE OF LIFE You have a genuine wish to make progress in your spiritual understanding, but your chances of success are being hampered by your insecurities about the level of control you are able to retain if you fully commit to the Great Work. The value of this dream can be reduced to the number 4, which is the number associated with the physical world and the Sefirah of Malkut. This is the location for this dream, as the wish for organization and control relates to the physical world, whereas in the realm of the spiritual we relinquish our desire to manage our life and inner development.

THE JOURNEY Clearly, you must now learn to relax and let go. Taking up yoga would certainly help greatly. You will not only feel the benefits in your spiritual life, but you will notice that in your day-to-day life, the more you are able to let go, the more smoothly your life will run. The compression of the value of this dream tells you that you need to find some practical activity (Kaph) to move yourself along in the Great Work. You should also consider becoming involved in some form of volunteer work (Mem), as this will also help to open the door (Daleth) to the realm of the spiritual.

OIL

*shemen-shmn-*שמן-390

MEANING From a modern point of view, we would see a dream of oil as probably indicating the accumulation of wealth or possibly suggesting that we are too concerned with material possessions instead of focusing on the really important things in life, such as our relationships with others and with the Divine itself. In fact, this is an extremely positive

dream since it relies on the ancient significance of oil as a medium for anointing an altar. In this context, the dream of oil points to a deeply held commitment and sense of reverence with regard to the Divine.

THE TREE OF LIFE We have all heard the phrase "to pour oil on troubled waters," and this phrase very much reflects the way you tend to interact with other people. Wherever there is discord, you try to introduce a calming force to encourage individuals to resolve their differences. In doing so, you are demonstrating the value of a spiritually based approach to life. You are in a sense offering them a "window" onto the nature of the Divine, and for this reason your dream belongs on the path of Heh.

THE JOURNEY If we reduce the value of this dream we find the number 13. As the number 12 is linked with ideas of compassion and self-sacrifice, its presence in this dream serves to emphasize your caring nature. While reflection and meditation will carry you far along the Tree of Life, it is only when you start to live out the spiritual principles you have absorbed that you achieve great levels of insight. In the compression of this dream's value we are advised that we must maintain this level of commitment to the Great Work (Tzaddi) and that this requires a great deal of fiery energy (Shin). It is therefore most important that you reserve some time in your day just for you.

OLD MAN

*zaken-zqn-*זקן-157

MEANING The value of this dream is a prime number (a number that can be divided only by itself and by one), which immediately alerts us to the fact that the dreamer is an unusual individual. It is of course fundamental to the mystical approach that each of us is unique, so we should take this to mean that you possess unique qualities and characteristics. As the value of this dream is also equivalent to that of the Hebrew word meaning "occult," we can infer that your unusual nature is linked to a natural and innate understanding of many of the mysteries of the Divine.

THE TREE OF LIFE In our society we are not as a rule, very good, to our older citizens. We do not mind leaving them in nursing homes or similar environments as long as we can convince ourselves that it is "for the best." However, in ancient times the older members of the community were treated with great respect because of their accumulated wisdom and experience. To dream of being an old man therefore suggests that you have a great level of insight. This dream belongs in the Sefirah of Hokhmah, as this indicates both the sense of ancient wisdom and the hidden knowledge to which you will shortly have access.

THE JOURNEY You are now within striking distance of the Sefirah of Keter and a direct communion with the Divine. The value of this dream is equivalent to that of the Hebrew phrase meaning "the setting of the Sun." This relates not only to the age aspect of this dream but to the fact that as we get this close to the Divine, we often feel not so much a sense of vibrant joy as the still, inner calm that often falls on us on a mild autumn evening as the Sun sinks behind the horizon.

OLD WOMAN

eeshah kadoom – ayshh qdvm –

אישה קרום-466

MEANING When we look at dreams of an old man or an old woman, it is important to remember that the genders are used in a highly stylized and symbolic manner. The Kabbalah does not set out to differentiate between the capacities and qualities of men and those of women, but simply uses the labels of male and female in its symbolism to represent certain characteristics that could in actuality apply to people of either gender. This dream also represents a great degree of wisdom, but of a different character from that represented by the dream of an old man.

THE TREE OF LIFE When we reduce the value of this dream we find the number 7. This number is associated with the letter Zayin, meaning "sword," which also has a value of 7. This association suggests that you should use your acquired wisdom to help you cut away those aspects of your life which are not helpful to your future development. Symbolically, an old woman represents the age and experience that are contained within the dream of an old man, but this dream additionally indicates a person who has the ability to offer compassionate support and guidance to others. Consequently, not least because its literal meaning is "prop" or "support," this dream sits on the path of Samech.

THE JOURNEY You are now approaching the Sefirah of Tiferet, and when you arrive at this relative haven on the Tree of Life you will be able to make some form of contact with your higher self.

The compression of this dream's value indicates that while you are approaching the Sefirah of Tiferet, you still have a sense of regret (Tav) at leaving behind the world of Malkut. This is because you want to be able to empathize fully with those around you in order to best be of help to them. However, the letters Samech and Vav point out that the Divine force will provide you with the guidance that will enable you to find a means of assisting people to come to their spiritual enlightenment.

OPAL

leshem – lshm – לשם-370

MEANING The opal is a beautiful stone and to dream about one such stone is a very pleasant and reassuring experience. This is because the opal is one of the few precious stones that is not only enormously appealing but has a very warm and comforting resonance. This is in part because its appearance is a mixture of a bright and clear range of shining colors set within a warm, creamy-white background. The appearance of an opal has certain spiritual implications in that it suggests a number of specific revelations set within a general level of confidence about the existence of the Divine.

THE TREE OF LIFE The value of this dream is equivalent to the value of the Hebrew word meaning "creation," and in the context of this dream this refers to your ability to reflect the creative nature of the Divine. The Sefirah of Hod is concerned with the creation of an intellectual structure within ourselves that enables us to reconcile our spiritual beliefs with the rational side of our nature. This is in itself a creative act and it is to this location on the Tree that we should assign this dream. It is no accident that the opal is the precious stone associated with the Sefirah of Hod.

THE JOURNEY The compression of this dream consists of the letters Shin and Ayin. These letters, when looked at as paths on the Tree of Life, both connect to the Sefirah of Hod. As a result, we can see this dream as looking both backward along the path of Shin and forward to the path of Ayin. Your task now is to consolidate the progress you have made so far and use the energy of the path of Shin to prepare yourself for the individualistic and vigorous path of Ayin. It is for this reason that the value of this dream is equivalent to the value of the Hebrew phrase meaning "foundation," as your time in the Sefirah of Hod is designed to provide a basis for the rest of your spiritual journey.

ORANGE

*katom-kthvm-*כתום*-466*

MEANING You should wake up feeling fully refreshed from this dream and ready to enjoy an active and fulfilling day. This is largely because orange is an extremely vibrant color that represents a great deal of positive energy. In terms of your spiritual development this dream indicates that you are about to move forward very quickly, thanks to the driving energy represented in your dream by the color orange.

THE TREE OF LIFE Every path and Sefirah on the Tree of Life has a particular color associated with it. The color orange is linked to a number of different positions on the Tree, so we need to look at the value of this dream in order to clarify the exact location for it. The value of this dream reduces to 7 and this number is connected to the Sefirah Netzach. Netzach is emerald green in color, so we should not assign your orange dream to this Sefirah. Netzach faces the Sefirah of Hod, which is orange in color. The implication here is that your dream sits on the path that runs between the two Sefiroth Netzach and Hod. This is the path of Peh and emphasizes your need to focus on all forms of communication at this time.

THE JOURNEY Over the next few months you should be working to develop your understanding of your inner nature. In doing so you will not only increase your chances of living a fulfilled and contented life, but you will make it much easier for your higher self to make contact with you and for you to recognize this event for what it is, when it does happen. The central letter, Samech, is there to remind you that you will still receive the support and guidance of the Divine to help you continue to move forward along the Tree of Life.

ORATOR

*noem-nvam-*נואם*-97*

MEANING We have largely lost the skill of oratory in the modern world, but before the television age, in order to be a public figure it was absolutely essential to have both charisma and excellent oratorial skills. The value of this dream is a prime number (a number that can be divided only by itself and by one), and this means that you are an unusual person. Given the title of this dream, it is likely that your unique nature relates to your charismatic appeal, which is best revealed through the way in which you speak.

THE TREE OF LIFE The ability to catch people up in your subject when you are speaking is a greatly undervalued art. The Sefirah of Netzach is the location on the Tree of Life that is concerned with all forms of artistic expression. In order to be a good orator, you need to speak with passion as well as eloquence, and Netzach is linked with the planet Venus, which is concerned with passions. Finally, the value of this dream is equivalent to the value of the Hebrew spelling of the name "Archangel Hanael," who is the archangel of the Sefirah of Netzach.

THE JOURNEY Your dream belongs in the Sefirah of Netzach, and at a spiritual level this dream relates to your great passion for the Great Work and your desire to enter into some form of communication with the Divine. The compression of this dream's value emphasizes your yearning to speak to the higher force and underlines your sincere commitment (Tzaddi) to the Great Work. The final letter, Zayin, makes it clear that while you have a charismatic nature that you could use to convince others of the importance of the spiritual quest, you yourself will have to struggle in order to maintain your spiritual progress.

ORCHARD

*boostan-bvsthn-*בוסתן*-518*

MEANING If we were to analyze this dream from a psychological perspective, we would be likely to see the orchard as a symbol of a very fertile imagination and, given the Freudian association of apples, quite possibly a sexually motivated individual. From a spiritual perspective, the orchard represents your inner self and the apples that will grow there are quite literally the fruits of your spiritual efforts. We should also see in this dream the notion of care and protection, because in order for your orchard to be productive, each tree needs careful nurturing. In terms of the Kabbalah, the image of an orchard is a potent symbol of mystical training.

THE TREE OF LIFE When we look at the spelling of this dream title we see that it reveals your spiritual goals and also a way in which they can be achieved. The initial Beth indicates your desire to return to the spiritual home beyond Keter. This will require a great deal of focused meditation (Vav), although you will be assisted in this by the support

(Samech) of the Divine. The subsequent letter Tav is representative of the sense of regret that you will feel as you move away from your old life-style, while the final Nun tells you that this emotional suffering is a necessary precursor to enlightenment. The path of Tav is also the location for this dream as it is linked to the planet Saturn, which is the planet associated with agriculture, and it is also appropriate as this dream indicates that you are new to the spiritual journey.

THE JOURNEY You have taken the great leap forward in your life to commit yourself to the Great Work. It is now important that you capitalize on this decision. Kabbalistic tradition recognizes an orchard as a symbol of deep spiritual study, and you should see this as a clear sign of what you must now do. In the compression of the value of this dream, we see that the first letter is Kaph, and this indicates that you need to find some practical activity to consolidate your spiritual development. An activity such as yoga will help you to awaken the Divine spark (Yod) within you and receive the full benefit of the protective force (Cheth) of the higher forces.

ORCHESTRA
*teezmoret-thzmvrth-*תזמורת-1053

MEANING Music in all its forms has long been associated with giving thanks and praise to the Divine. The dream of an orchestra suggests a very well-organized performance of music. Additionally, orchestral music is very tightly structured, without the opportunity for self-expression that one would find in a more loose musical unit such as a blues band or a folk group. There is a strong sense of anxiety in this dream and it stems from your feeling that you are not suited to such a tightly controlled approach to the Divine.

THE TREE OF LIFE In the compression of this dream we have the initial letter Qoph, but it is represented by a value of 1,000 rather than 100. This change in value is used in the Kabbalah to add extra emphasis to the importance of a particular letter. We can infer from this that your dream belongs on the path of Qoph. This restates the sense of worry and anxiety that you are feeling, and clearly the way for you to progress is to discover some means of resolving your uncertainty around the right spiritual path for you to follow.

THE JOURNEY When we reduce the value of this dream we find the number 9, and this is the value of

the letter Teth. The letter Teth symbolizes a strong character and considerable willpower. You need to discover this strength within yourself right now in order to help you reach a decision and then follow it. It is likely that you are currently involved in a mainstream religious congregation that you feel does not stimulate you spiritually. Once you find the inner strength to decide to make a different type of music in your celebration of the Divine, you will find that your spiritual understanding begins to grow at a much faster rate.

ORPHAN
*yatom-ythvm-*יתום-456

MEANING From a psychological point of view, this dream refers to a deeply seated sense of loss, and it is also likely that you are suffering from a fear of taking responsibility for your personal development. From a spiritual point of view, this dream revolves around your conflicting feelings about the Great Work. On one hand, you have a strong desire to reach up toward some form of contact with your higher self, but at the same time you are trying to hold on to the sense of certainty and security that you find in the material world.

THE TREE OF LIFE It is never easy to make a major change in your life, and a change that affects your outlook as deeply as a shift in your spiritual perceptions is going to be extremely difficult. When we reduce the value of this dream we find the number 15, which is linked to an excessive attachment to physical comforts. This is not because you are particularly materialistic but because you find it very difficult to wholly cut yourself off from the material world at a point in your life when you have not yet had any definite sense of the Divine. This dream is located on the Sefirah of Malkut because until you resolve this problem you will not be able to move forward in your spiritual quest.

THE JOURNEY The only way for you to climb out of the Sefirah of Malkut is to take the risk and make a leap of faith. The compression of the value of this dream begins with the letter Tav, which represents not only the path that you now need to climb but inevitability of the regret that you will feel as you move up. This sorrow, which is a fundamental part of restructuring your inner personality, is represented by the letter Nun. However, the final letter Vav is there to let you know that the Divine is still with you, willing you to succeed.

OUT OF BODY EXPERIENCE

*meetokh goof–mthvk gvph–*מתוך גוף–555

MEANING There are many explanations offered for the phenomenon known as an out-of-body experience. These vary from those that dismiss such events as wholly psychological to those that include all manner of nonhuman entities up to and including the alien abduction theory! From a Kabbalistic point of view, an out-of-body experience would be a moment when your consciousness was sufficiently focused for you to be perceiving directly through the "eyes" of your higher self, at which point you would appear to have left your physical body. To dream of such an experience then indicates that you have a strong desire to achieve a connection with your higher self.

THE TREE OF LIFE The value of this dream is equivalent to the value of the Hebrew word meaning "obscurity." This relates to the fact that at your current level of inner development you are unable to see any evidence of the Divine or of your higher self. This is always the difficulty with the early stages of the Great Work, as it takes time before you begin to see any results. The path for this dream is the path of Peh, as this is the path that refers to all forms of communication, and the key aim for you right now is to find some effective method of communication with your higher self in order to reassure yourself that you are moving in the right direction.

THE JOURNEY The compression of this dream's value tells you not only how you feel right now but how you should approach your current dilemma. The central letter, Nun, in the compression refers to the feelings of upset and the sense of absence that you are experiencing by not yet being in touch with the higher forces. This is an unavoidable part of the spiritual journey but you can help yourself by finding a practical method (Kaph) to increase your chances of making a connection with the Divine. For instance, if you go to some yoga and visualization classes it will not be long before you are able to see (Heh) at least a glimpse of the presence of the Divine in your life.

PACIFY

lehashkeen shalom–lhshkyn shlvm– להשכין שלום–791

MEANING Almost every religion places great value on the attempt to bring peace and harmony to the world. In the famous Sermon on the Mount it is the peacemakers who receive the very first blessing. To dream of being someone who is pacifying others is evidence that your higher self is trying to urge you on to the highest possible spiritual aims. The letter Shin appears twice in this dream, and it is there to emphasize the fact that even when you are trying to spread peace, you must be filled with a great deal of raw spiritual energy.

THE TREE OF LIFE It takes a considerably advanced level of insight into both your inner nature and the underlying moral imperatives of the universe to be able act as a force for peace in the world. When we reduce the value of the dream we find the value 17, which equates to The Star card from the tarot, and this card indicates that the Divine has a particular role for you to fulfill. If we further reduce the value of this dream we arrive at the number 8. This is the value of the letter Cheth, which is the path on which this dream is located and indicates that you are keen to act as a protective force to all of those around you.

THE JOURNEY Caring for another person is an enormous and daunting responsibility. To care for an unspecified number of people is not going to be even remotely easy. The initial letter, Nun, in the compression of this dream's value points to the emotional stress that you will experience in accepting this challenge. The following letter Tzaddi urges you to maintain your commitment to the positive work you are doing. If you continue with your caring and concern, you will bring yourself that much nearer to a full appreciation of the transcendent unity of the Divine.

PAIL

*dlee–dly–*דלי–44

MEANING When we look at the value of this dream we immediately notice that it consists of the number 4 repeated. As the number 4 is associated with all things physical and the element of Earth, we would expect this dream to indicate a very materialistic individual. However, this dream also contains strong references to the other three elements and so indicates an individual who has created an inner harmony and balance. As this dream is about a pail, which is primarily used to carry water, we can see that the element of Water appears through the title of the dream itself, while the element of Air is present by virtue of the fact that the value of this dream reduces to 8, which is the number of the Sefirah of Hod. Finally the value of this dream is equivalent to the value of a Hebrew word meaning "flame," which brings in the element of Fire.

THE TREE OF LIFE Once we have created an equilibrium of the four elements within our personality, we must begin the task of accessing our higher self in order to rule our newly balanced inner nature through the fifth element of Spirit. You have yet to reach this point, so we should place this dream on the path of Samech. This path leads into Tiferet, which is where the union with your higher self will take place.

THE JOURNEY Your task now is clear: You must continue with your spiritual work in order to make definite contact with your higher self. The value of this dream is equivalent to the value of the Hebrew word meaning "captive." You should see this as referring to your commitment to the Great Work, as you are held captive by your desire to succeed in your spiritual journey. The compression of this dream indicates that if you give some of your time to helping those less fortunate than yourself (Mem) you will be able to open the door (Daleth) that leads into the haven of Tiferet.

PAIN
keev-kab-כאב-23

MEANING This is definitely one of those dreams that makes you wish you had never fallen asleep in the first place. It may be difficult to see how a dream about pain could be in any way spiritually useful or illuminating. This is because when we think about a God of love, we tend to define "love" in a very human manner, and we forget that the nature and therefore the Love of the Divine are beyond our comprehension. The value of this dream is equivalent to the value of the Hebrew word meaning "joy." This clearly indicates that however difficult it may be for us to understand, this dream is extremely positive in terms of your spiritual development.

THE TREE OF LIFE The Sefirah of Gevurah is concerned with the aspect of the Divine that is responsible for death and pain and other forms of decay and disorder within the universe. It is here that this dream is located, and it is your difficult task to come to an understanding of how mortality is as essential a part of the wondrous nature of the Divine as is the joy of true love or the beauty of a sunrise. The value of this dream reduces to 5, and Gevurah is the fifth Sefirah on the Tree of Life and so serves to support the idea that this dream belongs to this position on the Tree.

THE JOURNEY The lesson that you must learn from the Sefirah of Gevurah is that without death there can be no life. It is worth noting that the Hebrew word meaning "pain" has exactly the same value as the value of the Hebrew word meaning "life," and so within the title of this dream we have an association of two seemingly opposed concepts. You can help to accept this truth by growing some plants in two equal-sized squares of land in your garden. If you then set fire to all the plants in one square, you will find that the next season the plants that had been burned will grow back even stronger than the ones that were never burned.

PAINTING
leetsboa-ltzbva'a-לצבוע-198

MEANING This dream refers not to a painting by an artist but to the painting of your home. From a psychological point of view, this dream relates to a desire to make a fresh start in your life. In Kabbalistic terms, your dream of painting is not just about starting fresh but is intended to refer to a restructuring of your existing emotional makeup. The reduction value of this dream reveals the number 9, and this is the value of the letter Teth, which represents the strength of character that you will need to succeed in your internal redecorating.

THE TREE OF LIFE The Sefirah of Netzach is concerned with all forms of artistic expression and creativity and the emotions. This dream sits in the Sefirah of Netzach, not because of any artistic connection in this dream but because you are in the process of reconciling your emotional makeup to a spiritual view of the world. The fact that this dream sits in the Sefirah of Netzach is emphasized by the fact that its title in Hebrew is "victory" and the value of this word is equivalent to the value of this dream's title.

THE JOURNEY Dealing with your emotional self is the last phase in the process of reconciling all four elements of your inner self to a spiritualized outlook. It is also the most difficult, as feelings are much harder to adjust and refine than are our thoughts or ways of behaving. The compression of this dream's value tells us that you are worried about your chances of achieving an inner harmony (Qoph), but if you persevere with the task at hand (Tzaddi) you will not only reach a feeling of inner balance but will benefit from the protective force of the Divine as represented by the letter Cheth, which completes the compression of your dream.

PAINTINGS

*temoonah-thmvnh-*תמונה-501

MEANING All forms of art can be viewed as a form of worship. Even if the artist is unconscious of this aspect of his work, true art works on our senses and our souls because it manages to capture something of the underlying truths of the universe that resonate deep within all of us. This is why we very often can be hugely affected by a piece of art without being able to fully express what exactly it is about it that touches us so deeply. From a spiritual point of view, to dream of paintings indicates that you are getting very close to some form of experience of the Divine force.

THE TREE OF LIFE The value of this dream is equivalent to the value of the Hebrew word meaning "blessedness" and this association emphasizes the solid progress that you have made thus far in climbing the Tree of Life. When we combine the idea of being blessed with the notion of seeing paintings as a representation of the Divine nature, we can determine that this dream belongs on the path of Heh. This path relates to the ability to catch a glimpse of the underlying spiritual reality, and that is exactly what this dream is suggesting you are about to achieve.

THE JOURNEY In order to catch a sight of the Divine you need to find some way to externalize your higher self, as it is through this aspect of yourself that you will achieve the longed-for vision that lies at the heart of the Great Work. The compression of this dream tells you that through practical activity (Kaph) of some sort you will be able to appreciate the true unity (Aleph) of the Divine. Given the content of this dream, the ideal practical activity for you would be some form of artwork. You might to try your hand at painting or even something more adventurous such as sculpture.

PALM

*kaf-kph-*כף-100

MEANING In almost every human society the palm is a sign of friendship and trust. When we encounter a stranger, no matter what our specific culture or point in history, the gesture with which we greet him will at some point involve the displaying of the palm of our hand. Additionally, the palm is often said to contain our future and personality within the unique pattern of lines that cross it. When we place all of this in a spiritual context, we see that the dream of a palm refers to a desire to discover our true nature and destiny. Equally it implies a wish to maintain friendly and open relationships with those around us rather than allow our spiritual work to turn us into recluses.

THE TREE OF LIFE The title of this dream is itself one of the titles of a letter in the Hebrew alphabet, and so it is almost automatic that it belongs to this path, namely the path of Kaph. This path is appropriate for a number of reasons, though. Your desire to be sociable and maintain a cheerful relationship with the rest of the world while engaging in your spiritual quest has a close association with the jovial benevolence of the planet Jupiter, which is connected with the path of Kaph. Similarly, the dream of a palm calls to mind the idea that your fortune may be written in your palm, and the tarot card The Wheel of Fortune is also connected with the path of Kaph.

THE JOURNEY Although the path of Kaph is largely concerned with practical activity, it is the letter Peh that really stands out in the spelling of this dream as it appears in its final form. The letter Peh is concerned with all forms of communication. Now, communication itself can be seen as a form of practical activity. This dream is telling you that if you want to discover your destiny and your true nature, you need to make sure that you both talk with and especially listen to the views of those who know you best. Additionally, in taking the time to speak with those around you, you will be ensuring that you maintain good relationships while you are progressing in the Great Work.

PAPER

*neyar-nyyr-*נייר-270

MEANING This may seem a dull dream at first sight, but we need to remember that the invention of paper led to the ability to record a whole range of ideas and philosophies. It was thus that mankind was able to spread new thoughts, which in turn led to the synthesis of wholly new ways of looking at the world. In spiritual terms, a dream of paper represents the potential of the individual to create a new relationship to the Divine. Additionally, as the dream is of a blank piece of paper, it also points to the fact that we are all wholly free to construct our own spiritual frameworks.

THE TREE OF LIFE The value of this dream is equivalent to the value of the Hebrew word meaning "levers." In the same way as paper is the basis of public intellectual expression, the lever is the basis of mechanical invention. The association of this word tells us that our ideas, just like a lever, can be used to change the world in a physical way. This dream sits on the path of Ayin, as it is the path that represents the need to find an individualistic approach to the Great Work and is linked to definite physical activity.

THE JOURNEY In the compression of the value of this dream we see that the letter Ayin is represented. This reminds you that the job ahead of you in the next few weeks is to determine an individualistic approach of your own, a way of approaching the Divine that resonates within you. The initial letter, Resh, tells you that the benevolent energy of the Divine is present to aid in your search for your own spiritual framework.

PARACHUTE

matsneakh – mtznch – מצנח *– 188*

MEANING Parachutes are a relatively recent invention, so we might not expect a dream about them to have any deep spiritual significance. However, both the content and the value of this dream have symbolic meaning that is coherent and relevant to your inner development. The purpose of a parachute is to stop you from hurting yourself when you fall from a great height to the ground. In spiritual terms, this dream image refers to the fact that as you climb higher up the Tree of Life, you need to ensure that you can keep your feet on the ground and maintain a rigorous sense of physical reality. In terms of your day-to-day life, it refers to the possibility that you may feel that you are falling or not in complete control of your life and need some kind of support network to assist you.

THE TREE OF LIFE As we increase our spiritual understanding we inevitably experience a degree of sorrow and emotional stress. This is because part of your growth is dependent on your being wholly honest with yourself about your emotional makeup and the ways in which you interact with others. When we reduce the value of this dream we find the number 8. This is the value of the letter Cheth, which means "fence." This refers to the protective force of the Divine and it is there to ensure that you keep a clear sense of reality that allows you to deal with the range of heightened emotions that you are experiencing. Consequently, we should place this dream on the path of Cheth.

THE JOURNEY Your need for some form of spiritual parachute is clearly indicated by the initial letter, Qoph, in the compression of this dream's value. At the practical level this might mean belonging to a meditation group or even simply reading about issues of spirituality. The following letter, Peh, is there as advice on how you can best obtain the advantage of this protective force. The key, as ever, is to communicate. You need to discuss your spiritual and emotional issues with others as well as with your higher self through regular meditation. It is by entering into conversations with others and indeed with yourself by way of contemplative reflection that you will awaken the protective energies represented by the final letter, Cheth, in this dream's compression.

PARADISE

gan eden – gn a'adn – גן עדן *– 177*

MEANING We might expect that a dream of paradise would indicate that you are making excellent progress in your spiritual work and are getting ever closer to a moment of communion with the Divine. However, we should remember that in the Kabbalistic system, paradise is a state of consciousness that we have left behind, and we should be looking forward to entering Heaven, or in the process of our incarnation we should be attempting to achieve some form of enlightenment. The dream of paradise actually represents a desire on the part of the dreamer to achieve some form of physical comfort and reassurance. However, while there may a degree of wish fulfillment going on in this dream, it is still positive and encouraging that you are focused on the ultimate goals of the Great Work.

THE TREE OF LIFE When we look at the spelling of this dream title we notice that the letter Nun is repeated and on both occasions it appears in its final form. The letter Nun represents a great challenge to your faith, and while you may not consciously feel emotionally low, your spiritual consciousness is certainly suffering. This emphasizes the notion that to wish for paradise is to miss out on the truly spiritual side of life. Your dream is not placed on the path of Nun, though, but belongs to the Sefirah of Malkut, as you have yet to escape the need for physical comfort.

THE JOURNEY The value of this dream is equivalent to the value of the Hebrew phrase meaning "a cry for help." This indicates that some part of you realizes that you do need to find a way to begin climbing out of the wholly material world of Malkut.

The compression of this dream indicates that you have a number of worries (Qoph) about the spiritual journey, and this relates to a feeling that you will not be able to find your own way to relate to the Divine (Ayin). The final letter in the compression is Zayin, which means "sword," and you should see this as way for your higher self to tell you that you need to take a risk and begin to struggle actively to find a way of relating to the Divine.

PARALYSIS

sheetook–shythvq–שיתוק-816

MEANING One of the most worrisome of all possible conditions is that of paralysis. It is an extremely distressing condition to experience as it takes away your control over your own body. If we were viewing this dream from a psychological point of view, we would see this as suggesting that you need to make great efforts to take control of your life. However, from a spiritual perspective this dream suggests that your feeling of paralysis stems from a concern that as you move forward along the spiritual path, you are losing your sense of control and being subsumed by a generalized sense of the Divine.

THE TREE OF LIFE The final letter, Qoph, in the spelling of this dream title makes it very clear that you do have some nagging concerns about the nature of the Great Work. This dream does not sit on the path of Qoph, though. It belongs to the path of Ayin, as your anxiety relates to a desire to follow an individualistic route toward a communion with the Divine and not to feel that you are simply taking a preassigned pathway. The path of Ayin also refers to the need for you to act vigorously to clear any obstacles or blockages to your inner development.

THE JOURNEY When we reduce the value of this dream we find the number 15. This number is associated with The Devil card in the tarot. Its presence in this dream should be seen as a warning that you need to ensure that in finding your own way of looking at the nature of spirituality, you do not fall into the trap of creating a structure that simply flatters your preconceptions. The compression of this dream begins with the final form of the letter Peh, and this points to the fact that you need to discuss your religious ideas with those close to you, especially those who share your interest in spiritual matters. If you engage in these discussions, you will find that you are able to remove the feeling of paralysis and start to climb up the Tree toward the Divine.

PARDON

mekheelah–mchylh–מחילה-93

MEANING It is inevitable that as we progress through life there will be numerous occasions when we offend or hurt others. This may be intentional, but in most cases we do this without intending to or even being aware that we are hurting anyone. From a nonspiritual point of view, we would see this dream as simply a way in which our unconsciousness is attempting to help us deal with our sense of guilt that accumulates over the years. In spiritual terms, this dream is also related to our sense of guilt, but it is concerned with the desire to feel sufficiently free from guilt to progress toward a communion with the Divine.

THE TREE OF LIFE The value of this dream is equivalent to the value of the Hebrew word meaning "incense." This association refers to the fact that you are trying to make a direct appeal to the Divine, as traditionally incense was a way in which one tried to contact the higher forces. The value of this dream reduces to 12, which is associated with the notions of altruism and self-sacrifice. Your willingness to be altruistic will itself ensure that there is no bar to your progress up the Tree of Life. The path of Mem is also connected with the notion of self-sacrifice, and it is this path to which the dream belongs. You should remember that the path of Mem also indicates the maternal aspect of the Divine, and this should reassure you that you do not need to worry about receiving any kind of pardon.

THE JOURNEY The purpose of the Great Work is not to simply try to make amends for past misdemeanors. Indeed, the focus should always be firmly on the future and ensuring that our behavior and our approach are fitting to the spiritual structures that we have found for ourselves. The compression of the dream advises you that the most important thing for you now is to maintain your commitment to the Great Work (Tzaddi). It is this commitment and firm basis of your faith in the existence of a Divine force that will ultimately lead to your accessing the secret wisdom that is represented by the letter Gimel in the compression of the value of this dream.

PARTING

preedah–prydh–פרידה-299

MEANING Dreams of parting would normally be seen as negative, as they are viewed as relating to the loss, albeit temporarily, of someone to whom we feel extremely close. From a Kabbalistic perspective, this dream is also about the loss of a relationship to which we are deeply attached. However, as is so often the case in the spiritual realm, this loss, while hard to accept and emotionally difficult, is ultimately beneficial and indeed essential for you to develop your level of inner understanding.

THE TREE OF LIFE Once we have left Malkut, our spiritual journey is a process of evolution and development. However, the journey out of Malkut is certainly difficult no matter how enthusiastic we are about the Great Work. The compression of this dream tells you that your route out of Malkut lies on the path of Resh, and this is the path on which we should locate this dream. The following two letters, Tzaddi and Teth, serve to remind you that to progess into the Sefirah of Hod will take great commitment and strength of character.

THE JOURNEY When we reduce the value of this dream we find the number 20. This relates to the path of Resh in that Resh is the twentieth path on the Tree of Life. Additionally, the number 20 refers to the tarot card Judgment. This card advises you to begin the process by which you carefully organize and structure your ideas about the nature of the Divine. This advice is spelled out in more detail in the dream title. You need to engage in discussions (Peh) with others in order to fulfill the requirements of the path of Resh (Resh). These discussions will awaken the Divine spark within you (Yod), and this causes the door (Daleth) on the world of the spiritual to open and allow you an initial glimpse (Heh) of the nature of the Divine.

PARTNER

ben zoog-bn zvg- בן זוג -68

MEANING Life is always more fulfilling when we can share our experiences with a partner. The value of this dream is equivalent to that of the Hebrew word meaning "pity." We need to pay close attention to the fact that "pity" does not have to mean feeling sorry for someone but can simply relate to a sense of empathy for a fellow human being. From a spiritual point of view, this dream relates to the search for your higher self, as your higher self represents your ideal partner in the context of a being that is wholly sympathetic and supportive to your quest for truth.

THE TREE OF LIFE The compression of this dream's value begins with the letter Samech, and this is the path on which this dream should be placed. This path is concerned with the support and guidance that comes from the Divine through your higher self and so is particularly appropriate to this dream. When we reduce the value of this dream we find the number 14, and this is linked to the tarot card Temperance, which points to the fact that you have achieved a level of balance and harmony within your inner self. This card is also connected with the path of Samech and suggests that with your partner's support you will achieve even greater equilibrium.

THE JOURNEY While your partner, the higher self, will provide you with a great deal of support, you do have to expect that in reaching the higher levels of the Tree you will experience a degree of emotional upset. This is indicated by the spelling of this dream title in that the first two letters refer to the house (Beth) of suffering (Nun). The subsequent letters tell you that you need to fight (Zayin), using the weapon of reflection and meditation (Vav), to ensure that you are able to reach the point where you can access the secret wisdom (Gimel) of the Divine.

PARTY

meseebah-msybh- מסיבה -117

MEANING There are times in life when we simply take everything far too seriously. This dream is a way for your higher self to reassure you that you do not need to be terribly somber and reclusive in order to succeed in the Great Work. The value of this dream is equivalent to the value of the Hebrew word meaning "fog." This relates to the fact that despite your currently studious attitude to your spiritual quest, you have not achieved a sense of clarity about your search for the Divine. This is due in part to the fact that you need to remember that God created the universe as an act of love and so you should be looking for the Love that lies at the heart of every spiritual text, no matter how dry or abstract it may be.

THE TREE OF LIFE Certain positions on the Tree of Life do require you to take a very serious and even somber approach in order to fully absorb and understand the energies that they represent. Similarly, there are locations that can be fully experienced only when we open ourselves up to the possibility of seeing the joy and wonder in the world. The reduction value of this dream produces the number 9. In the context of this dream's value and content, this relates to the Sefirah of Yesod, which is the ninth Sefirah on the Tree. It is also a Sefirah that encourages you to develop your imagination and your ability to understand the overwhelming wonder that exists in the universe.

THE JOURNEY We can see from the spelling of this dream title that you are being supported in your search for truth both by the energy of your higher self (Samech) and by the maternal aspect of the Divine itself (Mem). These supporting forces will enable you to awaken the Divine spark within yourself (Yod) that will take you to a place (Beth) where you will be able to see (Heh) the hidden nature of the Divine. You also need to bear in mind the fact that the compression of this dream is telling you that once you have reached an understanding of the joy that permeates the universe, you will need to struggle (Zayin) to continue upward on the Tree of Life.

PASSENGER

*nosea–nvsa'a–*נוסע*–*186

MEANING In psychological terms, this might seem like quite an encouraging dream, as the idea of being a passenger suggests that you have sufficient status to be carried by others to your chosen destination and could well be seen as symbolic of success. The value of this dream is equivalent to the value of a Hebrew word meaning "increase," so it might seem that the Kabbalistic interpretation is in agreement with the psychological analysis of the dream. However, we need to bear in mind that in spiritual terms, increases in wealth, status, or power are not goals that should concern us. Our only goal should be to increase our understanding of the Divine. Equally important is the fact that you should never be a passenger in terms of your inner development, as this suggests a passive attitude that lacks any engagement with your need to develop and move forward.

THE TREE OF LIFE The values in this dream indicate that you are neglecting the spiritual side of your life in order to focus on more purely material concerns. For whatever reason, success is extremely important to you, and the final letter Ayin in the spelling of this dream title tells us that you are happy to pursue success in your own vigorous and at times aggressive manner. The path that fits this dream is the path of Lamed in its negative aspect. You are being driven with the level of force that we associate with the letter and path of Lamed, but unfortunately the force is coming from within you rather than being driven by the higher forces.

THE JOURNEY The value of this dream is equivalent to that of the Hebrew phrase meaning "a stone of stumbling." It is clear from the messages that we have already found within the dream that your stumbling block is the excessive concern with material gain of all kinds as well as a failure to be sufficiently active in the pursuit of any spiritual goal. The compression of the dream's value tells us that this concern stems from fear (Qoph). The subsequent letter, Peh, which means "mouth," suggests that the fear you have is that without the trappings of success you will somehow lose the ability to fully communicate your inner self to those around you. We often feel that in order to be ourselves we need a number of props and other forms of self-validation. The final letter, Vav, in the compression of this dream is telling you that you simply need to rely on the support of the Divine, and that if you do, you will progress to ever higher levels of understanding.

PATCH

*tlay–tlay–*טלאי*–*50

MEANING We live in a throwaway society and when something is broken or otherwise damaged, we are not very likely to attempt to mend it but are far more likely to replace it. However, when your soul needs repairing you cannot simply buy a new one, so you have no choice but to try to heal yourself. In a spiritual context, this dream relates to the need that we all have to try to heal our souls. Indeed, the value of this dream is equivalent to the value of the Hebrew word meaning "every," and this reinforces the idea that everyone has some healing work to do on himself.

THE TREE OF LIFE The value of this dream is also equivalent to the value of the Hebrew letter Nun. This letter represents pain and sorrow, and it is this sorrow that you need to patch and heal. Your dream sits on the path of Nun, and right now you are experiencing the emotional pain that is associated with this path. As difficult as it is to deal with, you must try to remember that it is only when you have properly faced your inner fears that you will be able to fully develop yourself as a spiritual being.

THE JOURNEY It is important that when you are faced with a difficult truth about yourself, you force yourself to deal with the issues that it brings up and not try to repress it again. The initial letter, Teth, in the spelling of this dream title tells you that you need a great strength of will to maintain your progress along the Tree of Life. The subsequent letter, Lamed, lets us know that there is a force from outside that will be driving you onward and that this force comes from the Divine itself (Aleph). The more you are willing to walk through this current valley of depression, the closer you will come to waking the Divine spark (Yod) within you.

PEARLS

*peneenah-pnynh-*פנינה*-195*

MEANING Without the benefit of a Kabbalistic analysis, you might think that this dream refers to the potential to acquire great wealth and to enjoy a sense of luxury. When we approach this dream from a Kabbalistic point of view we read a much deeper significance into the dream. We already know that a pearl is formed by a piece of grit irritating an oyster. We could say that a pearl is a thing of beauty formed from concentrated pain or sorrow. In spiritual terms, this suggests that the dream is about the process of learning spiritual truths by experiencing the unalloyed truths of the universe. This can be upsetting but is ultimately rewarding.

THE TREE OF LIFE The spiritual angle on the content of this dream suggests an individual who has achieved a significant level of spiritual insight. The value of this dream is equivalent to the value of the Hebrew word meaning "visitation." This association indicates that you are on the cusp of a truly eventful spiritual experience. The appropriate place for this dream is in the non-Sefirah of Daat. In the Western Mystery Tradition, the location of Daat is known as the Abyss. It is positioned on the path of Gimel and can be seen as the final test before one achieves a true sense of communion with the Divine. Its literal meaning is "knowledge," and it is in Daat that you are flooded with the full knowledge of your inner nature. This is never an easy experience, and thus the idea of beauty born out of sorrow is highly appropriate.

THE JOURNEY The task that lies before you is to try to cross this abyss and find your spiritual home in the communion with the Divine whose nature emanates from the Crown, or Keter. Understandably you are anxious about the impact on yourself of making such a leap into the unknown. This is reflected by the presence of the letter Qoph in the compression of this dream's value. The following letter, Tzaddi, tells you that you need to maintain your commitment to the Great Work, as this is the only way that you will come to achieve a glimpse (Heh) of the Divine itself.

PEN

*et-a'at-*עט*-79*

MEANING As bizarre as it might sound, the image of a pen has a direct connection with the world of magic. Historically, people who had a high level of intelligence were capable of understanding natural processes and basic principles of mechanics, and this allowed them to demonstrate powers that to the person in the street appeared magical or miraculous. The skill of reading and writing has always been the preserve of the intelligentsia, so the image of a pen has a symbolic value that connects with all those manifestations in the material world that appear in some way magical. In your dream, this symbol indicates that you are developing a serious interest in the unexplainable and the mysterious.

THE TREE OF LIFE The value of this dream is equivalent to the value of the Hebrew word meaning "union." If we look at this word in terms of this dream, we are looking at a union or reconciliation of the wondrous and magical with the rational or commonsense view of the world. The integration of a rational worldview with an acceptance of the presence of a Divine force is a process that occurs when we are in the Sefirah of Hod, so it is here that we should locate this dream.

THE JOURNEY When we reduce the value of this dream we find the number 7, which is the value of the letter Zayin. This letter literally means "sword," and in the context of this dream the idea of a sword represents the activity of your mind cutting away all the irrelevant thoughts and ideas that are clouding your ability to see the spiritual truths within the world. Taking the image of a pen, we can also see that it would be very useful for you to keep a journal at this time to record your thoughts and your progress in honing your spiritual ideas. In the compression of this dream the letter Ayin tells you that you must find your own way through the maze that is the Great Work. At the same time, when you are looking at the whole range of anomalous and potentially miraculous phenomena that has been reported over the years you must avoid allowing yourself to be deceived (Teth) by your desire to find the Divine in everything that you consider.

PENALTY

*onesh-a'avnsh-*עונש*-426*

MEANING On awaking from this dream it would be perfectly natural to have a vague sense of guilt that would begin to fade only after you had reassured yourself that there was nothing in your behavior over the last few days that would warrant your suffering any penalty. From the spiritual point of the view, this dream does not necessarily indicate any guilt on your part, but does suggest that you are in the process of suffering some kind of loss. The value of this dream reduces to 12, and this number is associated with self-sacrifice of a positive and altruistic nature. We can now see that the penalty you are suffering is not for any misdemeanor but is some form of privation you going through in order to come to a better understanding of the Divine.

THE TREE OF LIFE The value of this dream is equivalent to the value of the Hebrew word meaning "a medium." The Sefirah of Yesod is traditionally associated with all forms of psychism, so we might think this is where the dream is located. However, the penalty referred to in the dream's title is what you are experiencing so that you may enter the Sefirah of Yesod. Consequently, we place this dream on the path of Tav, which leads into Yesod and is also connected with ideas of regret and melancholy.

THE JOURNEY You have now made the first step in the great voyage of self-discovery, and, as is often the case, you are suffering the confusion and anxiety of a person who has made a deep commitment to an idea without having any tangible evidence of its validity. In the compression of this dream, the initial letter, Tav, refers to this sense of regret at having left behind the certainties of a wholly material world-view, and this is the penalty spoken of in the dream. The final letter, Vav, represents the promise of the Divine that ultimately awaits you. The central letter, Kaph, tells you that you need to find some practical activity that will help you to lose your regret and move forward—a yoga class would be an ideal avenue for you to explore.

PERFUME

*bosem-bvshm-*בושם*-348*

MEANING Today, the idea of perfume relates entirely to the wearing of scent for our own or our partner's pleasure. In ancient times, perfume also had that romantic association but its primary and sacred purpose was its key role in the preparation of an individual for religious ritual. It is this aspect of the significance of perfume that we need to focus on in this dream's analysis. The value of this dream is equivalent to the value of a Hebrew phrase meaning "to arrange in a pattern." This relates strongly to the idea of perfume as a key part of the process by which

we prepare ourselves to try to make some form of contact with our higher self.

THE TREE OF LIFE You are clearly taking your relationship to the Divine very seriously. This dream makes it clear that you should set aside a specific time each day to try to increase your spiritual understanding. Additionally, you should spend a reasonable amount of time working through certain established habits and practices in order to achieve an appropriate state of mind. However, the dream of perfume suggests that you may be becoming more concerned with your preparations and props than with the work itself. This misplaced concern positions this dream in the Sefirah of Yesod, as this is the point on the Tree that relates to the apparatus of the Great Work and contains the danger of being attracted by the "glamor" rather than by the substance of the work.

THE JOURNEY Now that you have established a regular and committed habit of trying to achieve a contact with your higher self, you need to begin to assess the way in which you go about your spiritual practices. It would be a good idea to try meditating without any props at all—no chanting, candles, or incense—just you and the potential presence of the Divine. The compression of this dream tells you that you have all you need for success in the high level of spiritual energy that you possess. In addition, you are lucky in that the Divine is with you both in its maternal aspect (Mem) and as a protective force represented by the letter Cheth.

PERSPIRATION

*hazaah-hza'ah-*הזיעה*-87*

MEANING When we go to sleep we usually expect to wake up feeling refreshed and ready to face a new day. However, if you wake from a dream of perspiration, the chances are that you will feel very much like going back to sleep in order to recover from your nighttime exertions. From a spiritual point of view, we should combine the notion of perspiring with the fact that when you are asleep you are not engaging in any physical activity. Anyone who has practiced the art yogic of breathing will know that in deep meditation one can perspire profusely without exerting any obvious effort, so this dream should be seen as indicating that you are putting a great deal of time into your spiritual quest.

THE TREE OF LIFE To continue the reference to pranayama, or yogic breathing, it is a fact that we perspire long before we receive any form of spiritual revelation. This dream indicates that while you have reached the stage in your practice where your meditations are consuming significant energy, you have yet to have any form of direct experience of higher forces. Consequently, we are looking for a position relatively low on the Tree of Life. The path of Shin is the ideal path for this dream since it refers directly to the raw power and energy that you are putting into the Great Work at this time.

THE JOURNEY The search for spiritual truth can be a very lonely business. However, it does not need to be, and this dream is clearly telling you that an ideal way to increase your level of inner wisdom would be to engage in discussions with likeminded people. This is indicated by the presence of the letter Peh in the compression of this dream's value. Additionally, the final letter, Zayin, in the compression is there to remind you that while communication is the key that will open the door to reassurance and new ideas, you still need to rely on the sword of your own judgment in order to traverse the Tree of Life.

PET

goor shashooeem – gvr sha'ashva'aym –
גור שעשועים-1005

MEANING The idea of keeping a pet is a relatively new concept. People have always kept animals but in the past this was usually for the purposes of food, clothing, or labor. Of course, the wealthy and powerful often kept animals that had no such function, but they were not pets. Such animals had a function as clearly as any farm dog: Their role was to impress visitors and connote a certain status to their owner. What differentiates a pet from any of the animals mentioned above is the fact that we buy them primarily and often solely so that we can care for them and establish some kind of relationship with them. Consequently, when we are searching for a spiritual message in this dream we should be looking for something that relates to a desire to take care of others.

THE TREE OF LIFE When we look at the spelling of this dream title we immediately notice the repeated pairing of the letters Ayin and Shin. Looked at as letters, they tell us that you have an enormous amount of energy (Shin) that is being directed at creating your own spiritual path (Ayin). When we look at the combined value we see that it is equivalent to the value of the Hebrew word meaning "creation." Taken in the context of the content of this dream, there is a suggestion that your desire to

care is bound up with your desire to create your own spiritual path. This places your dream on the path of Mem in its negative aspect, since you are unconsciously looking for outlets for your compassion in order to feel better about yourself rather than simply for the sake of being compassionate.

THE JOURNEY You should not feel bad about the self-interested element of your strong drive to help others. It is a very common motivating force, and the fact that you dreamed about it shows that you have a growing awareness of the problem. This is again hinted at by the presence of the letter Qoph, with its value multiplied by 10, in the compression of this dream's value. The best way to deal with this and to start using your capacity for compassion in a way that is genuinely altruistic and therefore spiritually beneficial is quite simple. You need to find a charitable cause for which you have absolutely no natural sympathy, then devote all your spare time to helping that charity in any way you can. This will not be easy but it will give you some valuable spiritual insights.

PIANO

psanter – phsnthr – **פסנתר**-790

MEANING If you were to think of a single sport to represent all sports, you would probably think of football. It is by far the most popular sport in every state, both for spectators and for participants. Similarly, the piano is probably the first instrument that comes to mind when people are asked to think of a musical instrument. Symbolically, then, this dream refers to the idea of music as a whole. As music was originally used as a means of expressing worship and celebration of the gods, this dream represents your desire to actively engage in celebration of the Divine.

THE TREE OF LIFE The place on the Tree of Life that is concerned with the expressive arts is the Sefirah of Netzach, and this is the correct location for this dream. This is supported by the fact that when we reduce the value of this dream we find the number 7, and the Sefirah of Netzach is the seventh Sefirah on the Tree of Life. This position is also associated with the process of reconciling your emotional makeup with your spiritual view of the world. The dream of a piano, which is a beautifully harmonious instrument, suggests that you are very close to achieving that goal.

THE JOURNEY The compression of this dream begins with the letter Nun, which represents the

249

feeling of sorrow that is associated with the restructuring of your emotions, since this will inevitably involve facing some difficult memories. The following letter, Tzaddi, tells us that you are quite literally "hooked" on the spiritual quest and that you will maintain your commitment despite the difficulties. It would be very helpful for you to take up a musical instrument, as this will enable you to find a new and very satisfying way to express your increasing sense of a close relationship to the Divine.

PICTURE
demoot-dmvth- רמות-450

MEANING This dream is about pictures or images generally. If your dream was specifically about paintings or artworks, you should look at the analysis of the dream "Paintings." From a commonsense point of view we might see this dream as indicating that you have a great love of the world around you, so you like to be surrounded by a range of pictorial images. However, when subjected to Kabbalistic analysis we see that this dream is in fact a warning that you are in danger of being deceived by false promises of enlightenment. This is why the dream is of pictures; you are being presented with an image of a spiritual system rather than something that will actually work and help you gain greater levels of insight.

THE TREE OF LIFE The value of this dream is equivalent to the value of the Hebrew word meaning "craftiness." This in itself is a warning that you may be in the process of being misled by someone who has less-than-honorable intentions. Additionally, when we reduce the value of this dream we find the number 9. This is the value of the letter Teth, which means "serpent." This is the path on which we should position this dream, as it relates directly to the risk of being deceived.

THE JOURNEY The compression of this dream produces the letters Tav and Nun. The letter Tav represents the regret at leaving behind the certainty of the material world, while the letter Nun indicates the sorrow that you will experience as you go through the process of self-development. It is these difficult experiences that make you susceptible to the charlatans that are out there who will offer you enlightenment while taking your money. To avoid the trap that this dream outlines, simply remember that anyone who presents the spiritual quest either as easy or as something that can be completed in a matter of months cannot offer you genuine, spiritually valid guidance.

PILGRIM
oleh regel-a'avlh rgl- עולה רגל-344

MEANING This is a dream with an overtly spiritual theme. The ideal of a pilgrim has very specific significance to Americans, so we should perhaps remind ourselves of the fact that the term *pilgrim* refers to an individual who is making a journey to a specific location that is sacred to his particular religious beliefs. In terms of your inner development, this dream makes it very clear that you have made a conscious commitment to the Great Work and have already progressed some way up the Tree of Life.

THE TREE OF LIFE When we reduce the value of this dream we find the number 11. This number is associated with themes of mystical revelation in almost every known spiritual culture. Additionally, the value of this dream is equivalent to the value of a Hebrew word meaning "garden." Given the association of gardens with a sense of spiritual achievement and a reward emanating from the Divine, we can confidently place your dream on the path of Samech. Further, we can be certain that you are very close to completing the lessons of the path of Samech and entering the haven of Tiferet.

THE JOURNEY The path of Samech is associated with support and guidance from the Divine, so your task in the next weeks is to ensure that you are open to receiving that help when it is offered. This is harder than it may seem, as it requires you to look at every encounter and everything you read as potentially hiding a message or piece of advice from the Divine. The letter Shin at the beginning of the compression of the value of this dream tells us that you certainly have the energy to carry you to the destination of your pilgrimage. Additionally, the letter Mem indicates that you are willing to sacrifice many of the enjoyable aspects of your life in order to focus on the spiritual dimension. In doing so, you will be able to open the door (Daleth) that leads into the garden that is Tiferet and marks the completion of your metaphorical pilgrimage.

PILL
gloolah-glvlh- גלולה-74

MEANING If you looked at this dream and saw in it a reference to the availability of some form of remedy for your current lack of progress in the Great Work, then you would be correct. However, if your idea of a remedy involves some external force simply putting you back on the right track, spiritually speaking, then you are unfortunately mistaken. The Kabbalistic path is a demanding one, and one of its fundamentals is the concept of individual responsibility for your relationship to the Divine. You can be sure that although you are being offered a cure for your current problems, it will be a cure that requires you to work for it to be effective.

THE TREE OF LIFE We can all remember our parents telling us when we turned our noses up at some particularly unpleasant medicine that it was good for us. Indeed, we were told that the foulness of the taste was a sure sign that it was wonderfully effective medicine. When it comes to your spiritual journey the same logic can be applied. You have reached a point where you have lost the motivation to continue exploring your inner self. In order to remotivate you, your higher self will act as a very harsh and critical force that will cause nagging thoughts to enter your mind, ensuring that you will have no peace until you recommence the spiritual quest. The value of this dream is equivalent to the value of the letter Lamed when it is spelled in full. This is the path on which we should place this dream because it both shares its value and because the letter Lamed represents the harsh force referred to in this dream.

THE JOURNEY So far in your spiritual explorations you have been relying on established ideas to inspire and help you to move forward. However, ultimately the Great Work is wholly individual, and the letter Ayin in the compression of this dream is telling you that you need to begin to forge your own approach to the Divine. This is the activity that will help to motivate you again and will also save you from the critical energies of Lamed. Additionally, once you begin to create your own framework of understanding, you will open the door (Daleth) to a greater understanding of the nature of the universe.

PILLOW

*kar-kr-*כר-220

MEANING We associate pillows with sleeping rather than with achieving great gains in our understanding of the spiritual dimension of the universe. Yet, the value of this dream is equivalent to the value of a Hebrew phrase referring to a sense of obligation to the sacred Tetragrammaton. The Tetragrammaton is another name for the Divine. The title of the dream suggests a person who is too busy resting to take on the Great Work, but the value 220 includes the letter Resh, which indicates judgment and the benevolence of the Divine, and the letter Kaph,

which indicates a practical approach to one's inner development. This clearly points to a person who has a real sense of devotion to the spiritual quest.

THE TREE OF LIFE If you separate the idea of sleeping from the idea of a pillow and regard it as simply a resting place for your head, it becomes easier to see how this dream is very positive from the point of view of your inner development. The spelling of this dream title can be seen as telling a story or describing what you are currently doing: You are engaging in very practical work (Kaph) with your head (Resh). This is a clumsy way of referring to the process of thinking. It is because you are thinking so intensely that you need a pillow to symbolically support your head, which is so full of ideas. This focus on ideas places your dream on the path of Resh, a letter that also appears in the compression of the dream's value.

THE JOURNEY The path of Resh leads into the Sefirah of Hod, which is concerned with all kinds of intellectual and rational ideas. The path of Resh is a preparation for this Sefirah and is a time when you should be organizing your thoughts and ideas to analyze them in the context of a spiritual worldview. However, you need to do more than simply think. The value of this dream reduces to 4, which indicates the world of the physical and material. What you must do is to ensure that your ideas about the nature of the Divine and the implications for how you should therefore behave toward others do not remain simply as ideas. Once you have reconciled these ideas in your mind, it is most important that you act out the principles for behavior that are enshrined in those ideas.

PIPE

*meekteret-mqtrth-*מקטרת-749

MEANING Those who smoke cigarettes tend to do so purely out of habit; by contrast, pipe smoking is regarded as a much more genuine pleasure. Additionally, we often associate the smoking of a pipe with the stereotypical academic or other wise individual. Consequently, to dream of a pipe is to dream about relaxed contemplation. From a spiritual point of view, this dream indicates that you have been pursuing the spiritual quest for some time and are in a position to contemplate the nature of the Divine with some degree of insight.

THE TREE OF LIFE When we reduce the value of this dream we find the number 20, which is the value of the letter Kaph. This letter is associated with practical activity, but it is also connected with a very relaxed attitude to life. The tarot card The Wheel of Fortune is linked to the path of Kaph and indicates a person who is happy to accept the ups and downs of life without complaint. Your dream belongs on the path of Kaph, and while you embody the jovial personality that characterizes this path, you do not need to find a way to embody its practical nature.

THE JOURNEY The spiritual journey sometimes involves solitude in order to gain the insights that are available to you along the way. However, in order to make maximum progress you also need to find some way to live out the spiritual principles that you have developed. In the compression of this dream we find the letter Nun, which relates to feelings of sorrow and melancholy. As this is followed by the letter Mem, which refers to compassion and altruism, it is clear that the practical path that lies before you is to find some way to help those around you who are suffering. You should consider getting involved in a local charity, as people will benefit enormously from your cheerful and positive outlook.

PIT
bor-bvr-בור-208

MEANING In almost every religious culture there is some concept of an afterlife, and in almost all systems there is both a paradise and some form of Hell reserved for those who have committed severe transgressions in their lives. Almost without exception, depictions of Hell use the imagery of a pit when attempting to create a visual image of this state of consciousness. You should not start packing your flame-retardant underwear just yet, though, as this dream is not telling you that you are headed straight for the pits of Hell! We can define Hell as the absence of the Divine, and it is the sense of God's absence to which this dream relates.

THE TREE OF LIFE The fact that you have had this dream is in itself a positive sign, since it shows an awareness that right now you do not have any room in your life for the Divine. This lack of spirituality is causing you a degree of distress and concern, as we see that the value of this dream is equivalent to the value of the Hebrew word meaning "strife." When we reduce the value of this dream we find the number 10, which is the number of the Sefirah of Malkut. This Sefirah represents the world of the physical and it is here that your dream is located.

THE JOURNEY It is often said about psychological conditions that the first step toward recovery is recognizing that there is a problem. The same is true of your spiritual makeup. The first stage of the Great Work is recognizing that there is a spiritual reality that you can, potentially, access. The compression of this dream produces the letters Resh and Cheth. Both of these letters are there to reassure you that the nature of the Divine is essentially benevolent (Resh) and that your higher self will act as a protective force (Cheth) while you make your first forays into the world of the spiritual.

❧PLACE OF WORSHIP
mekom tfeelah-mqvm thphylh-מקום תפילה-711

MEANING This appears to be a very spiritual dream as its focus is on a building whose sole purpose is the worship of the Divine. This is not entirely the case, though, as the mystical path requires the individual to find his own way to an appreciation of the true nature of the universe and his place within it. There are a range of sources that can help you, from books to practical exercises, but it is ultimately a task that is accomplished on an individual basis. The idea of a place of worship suggests a group of people being directed by a person or an organization as to how they should forge their relationship with the Divine.

THE TREE OF LIFE When we reduce the value of this dream we find the number 9, which is the value of the letter Teth. This dream sits on the path of Teth in both its negative and positive aspects. From the negative point of view, attendance at a place of worship can involve a denial of your unique responsibility for your inner development and indeed can lead to the self-deception indicated by Teth in that you allow another individual to prescribe your feelings about the nature of the Divine. From a positive angle, we can see the notion of a place of worship as referring not to a building but to your self. In other words, the dream is indicating that you are so focused on the Great Work that your whole self has been turned over to the celebration of the Creator. In this interpretation, the path of Teth is appropriate as it indicates great strength of character and willpower.

THE JOURNEY In the compression of this dream's value the first thing we notice is the letter Nun, which indicates a challenge to your faith and a need to examine your inner nature. This suggests that we should take this dream in its positive aspect, since it is only when we truly turn ourselves over to the Great Work that we can see our inner nature honestly, and this inevitably causes a degree of sorrow. The subsequent Yod also makes it clear that you have awakened the spark of the Divine within yourself, and if you keep that inner flame burning you will progress to a point where you are able to fully appreciate the transcendent unity of the Divine as represented by the final letter, Aleph.

✤PLANET

*kokhav lekhet–kvkb lkth–*כוכב לכת*–*496

MEANING It is an obvious truth, but one that tends not to be at the forefront of our minds, that the earth is a planet just like all the others in our solar system. That we are living on a sphere of rock and minerals hurtling and spinning through the universe at incredible speed is a fact that we all know. However, if you sit down and spend just a few minutes contemplating this information, it does have a very humbling effect. More important, it is likely to lead to some very interesting reflections on the nature of your existence.

THE TREE OF LIFE The value of this dream is equivalent to the value of the Hebrew word meaning "Malkut." This association clearly places your dream on this location on the Tree of Life. However, the other values in this dream tell us that you are very close to leaving the sphere of the material, so you should see this dream as encouraging. The content itself indicates that you are now able to see the realm of the physical in its proper context. Additionally, the value of this dream is the number that we find if we add up all the numbers from 1 to 31 consecutively. This signifies that although you are still within Malkut, you are internally prepared to travel to each of the other thirty-one destinations on the Tree of Life.

THE JOURNEY When we reduce the value of this dream we find the number 10. This relates to the Sefirah of Malkut but also to the fact that you are about to complete a major cycle in your inner development. This completion will come at the point when you make a conscious commitment to the Great Work. The compression of the value of this dream tells us that the only thing holding you back is the sense of regret that you will feel at leaving behind the certainties (Tav) of the material world. However, you are already hooked (Tzaddi) on the idea of the spiritual quest. The final letter Vav in the compression represents the macrocosm or the Divine itself urging you to make that leap.

See Zohar symbol, Planet.

PLANK

*keresh–qrsh–*קרש*–*600

MEANING As Kabbalists, the first thing we do is look very closely at the dream word in order to determine what separates it from other, similar words. In the case of the word *plank,* what distinguishes it from other possible words for "pieces of wood" is that it has a very particular historical significance. In days gone by, the plank was a punishment meted out at sea, whereby you walked along a short length of wood until you reached the end and fell to your death in the waters below. In spiritual terms, we can therefore see this dream as representing a very narrow path that you must walk and which is surrounded by various pitfalls.

THE TREE OF LIFE The most difficult path to traverse is that of Tav. This is because it is the first path to lead out of the wholly physical world of Malkut and therefore has to be crossed with minimal experience of spiritual matters to assist and guide you. All the letters in the spelling of this dream title refer to paths that emanate from the lowest portion of the Tree. This not only emphasizes the fact that you should be looking for a path near the bottom of the Tree but underlines the idea that there are a number of narrow paths that lead out of the physical realm but that of course between each path there is the potential for falling.

THE JOURNEY The task that lies before you is to successfully complete your walk along the plank that is the path of Tav. The compression of this dream produces the letter Mem in its final form, and this should be seen as a strong reassurance that the maternal aspect of the Divine is there to protect you. In the spelling of the dream title we learn that you are anxious about the spiritual journey (Qoph) and that you need to rely on the benevolence of the Divine (Resh) to carry you forward. This will be possible only if you also use the raw spirit (Shin) that lies within you to motivate you to begin exploring the world of the spiritual.

PLANTS

*tsemakh–tzmch–*צמח*–*138

MEANING We are surrounded by plants and yet we pay them very little attention unless they are particularly beautiful. This in itself holds a message for the seeker of truth, in that plants have survived for billions of years and perhaps one of the keys to their survival is the fact that they are unobtrusive. There is much for the spiritually minded individual to learn from the nature of plants, from their innate stillness to their resilience and many other qualities. While it may seem largely a pictorial dream, this dream is very significant in spiritual terms.

THE TREE OF LIFE The central letter in the spelling of this dream title is Mem, and this is the path to which this dream belongs. The Buddha famously and wisely taught that attachment is the cause of all sorrow. A plant, of course, has no attachments and grows unaffected by the world around it. You should try to emulate the lack of attachment of the plant, and should substitute compassion and altruism as represented by the path of Mem in place of your desires and attachments.

THE JOURNEY Anybody who has watched a small weed break its way through a concrete sidewalk can testify to the fact that if nothing else, plants certainly personify persistence. It is this plantlike persistence that will enable you to rid yourself of your attachments and emulate the altruism of the path of Mem. The value of this dream is equivalent to the value of the Hebrew phrase meaning "he shall smite." This positive association strongly suggests that you will succeed and as a result your spiritual understanding will be that much richer.

PLAYGROUND

meegrash—meeskhakeem—mgrsh mshchqym— מגרש משחקים-1041

MEANING As adults, we see the world of the playground as a wonderful place for our children to play and mix with their friends and learn those all-important social skills. However, as most children would tell us if only we would listen, playgrounds are also terrible places where, in the absence of adult authority, the law of the jungle rules, and woe betide the small or the weak or the shy. When considering the significance of a dream of a playground it is important that we recognize it as both a wonderful and a potentially terrifying place, otherwise we will fail to see the meaning hidden in the image. This is not to say that this dream is not positive—as in general it is—but simply that we need to see it in its rich complexity.

Traditional Kabbalists would emphasize the innocence associated with this symbol.

THE TREE OF LIFE When we reduce the value of this dream we find the number 6. This is the value of the letter Vav, and this is the path on which we should locate this dream. The path of Vav is con-

cerned with all matters connected with reflection and contemplation. The experience of this dream is much like a playground in that there is much here that will bring back a fond memory. At the same time, your reflections will also reveal a number of difficult memories that you will have to deal with before you can continue to progress up the Tree of Life.

THE JOURNEY When we are first taken to a playground by our parents, our excitement is tempered if not overwhelmed by a strong sense of anxiety, and this is represented by the letter Qoph in the compression of this dream's value. The following letter, Mem, indicates that the maternal aspect of the Divine will help you to deal with the more difficult feelings that lurk in your unconscious. The final Aleph contains the promise that when you have reconciled your deepest thoughts and feelings to a concept of the Divine, you will be that much closer to a full understanding of the nature of the secret wisdom that you are seeking. Part of that understanding depends on your trying to recover the sense of innocence that you felt in your playground years. There were difficult times, but it was also a time of great enthusiasm, innocence, and playfulness. These are qualities that you should definitely try to recapture.

PLAYING

lesakhek—lshchq— לשחק-438

MEANING When we are exploring the spiritual dimension of the universe it is easy to get carried away with the seriousness of it all. This can lead us to become pompous and self-important in the way in which we view ourselves. Even worse than this is the fact that if we pay attention only to the somber truths of the spiritual realm, we will miss out on a vast amount of understanding about the true nature of the Divine. This dream is extremely encouraging as it suggests that you have reached an understanding of the fact that since the universe is founded on love, we should look for the joy and wonder of the Divine and not just for dry, abstract ideas.

THE TREE OF LIFE The value of this dream is equivalent to the value of the Hebrew phrase meaning "the perfect stone." This may seem unimportant until we consider the fact that in the art of spiritual alchemy, the achievement of a union with the higher forces was referred to as the successful creation of the "philosopher's stone." This philosopher's stone was seen as a symbol of spiritual perfection. So this dream is connected with the idea of contacting the higher forces in order to help perfect yourself. When we reduce the value of this dream we find the number 6. This is the number of the Sefirah of Tiferet and it is here that we contact our higher self, so it is here that we should locate this dream.

THE JOURNEY Gaining an appreciation of the joy that permeates the universe is essential to the successful completion of the Great Work. However, the knowledge that we are all playing a cosmic game does not remove all seriousness from that game. Indeed, the compression of the dream's value tells us that in order to fully learn the lessons of Tiferet, you will experience a degree of regret (Tav). You may need the harsh aspect (Lamed) of your higher self to push you to fully let down your psychological defenses, which are represented by the final letter, Cheth, in the compression of this dream.

POISON
*raal-ra'al-*רעל-300

MEANING Nobody is going to wake up from a dream about poison and decide that quite clearly his spiritual work is coming along very well, thanks to the indications of last night's dream. Nobody, that is, except a trained Kabbalist, as this dream is in fact very positive in terms of its spiritual significance. From a commonsense point of view, this dream relates to a very unpleasant experience and probably the malevolent behavior of a third party. However, in spiritual terms, a poison may kill off one part of your personality in order to free up another aspect of your nature that is closer to your higher self.

Traditional Kabbalists interpret poison as a symbol of danger and harm and suggest the dreamer respond accordingly. The values in the letters suggest something more than the literal symbolism to the hermetic Kabbalist: The dream links to alchemical notions of having to poison and kill the base material or ego in order to produce the gold, or higher self.

THE TREE OF LIFE The value of this dream is equivalent to the value of the letter Shin, and this is the path on which this dream belongs. The path of Shin represents a powerful spiritual force, and the value of this dream is equivalent to the value of the Hebrew phrase meaning "the spirit of God." This energy is both a healing if vigorous salve for your soul and a poison for the ego-driven self.

THE JOURNEY Your task over the next few weeks and months is to cleanse your mind as far as possible in preparation for the work that takes place in the Sefirah of Hod. You need to separate out those ideas about the Divine that are based on intuition and coming to you through your higher self from those that emerge from the desires of your ego-based self. The spelling of this dream title tells you that you will need to use very careful judgment (Resh), relying on both the benevolent assistance of the Divine and your ability to find your own way forward (Ayin). The final letter, Lamed, tells us that while the poison of the dream's title is not harmful to your soul, it can be a harsh experience that you will at times find to difficult to deal with.

POLICE
*meeshtarah-mshtrh-*משטרה-554

MEANING It is a fundamental part of our makeup that no matter how virtuous we are in life, we all have the capacity to be consumed with feelings of guilt. This is especially evident when it comes to the police: In spite of the fact that we have committed no crime, it is always very difficult not to feel at least a little nervous and worried when confronted by an officer of the law. From a Kabbalistic standpoint, the dream of the police is as a metaphorical representation of the part of our consciousness that is constantly monitoring our commitment to the Great Work.

THE TREE OF LIFE When we reduce the value of this dream we find the number 5. This is an extremely positive value as it indicates that you have not only balanced the four elements within your inner nature but are now able to be guided in your life by the fifth element of Spirit. However, our journey does not end in the Sefirah of Tiferet, where the union with our higher self takes place. This dream lies on the path of Lamed, which represents the energy of the Divine urging you to continue with your exploration of the nature of the universe.

THE JOURNEY The central letter in the spelling of this dream title is Teth, which means "serpent." When we combine this with the central letter in the compression of the dream's value, which is the letter Nun, we see that you are in danger of suffering due to some form of self-deception. A common false belief for seekers of truth is that the ultimate goal is to have a conscious sense of the presence of your higher self. In fact, the presence of your higher self is intended to aid you in trying to get closer to the Divine itself. The initial and final letters in the compression of the dream's value tell you that you need to find some form of practical, spiritually related project (Kaph) to put you back on track so that you can open the door (Daleth) to a deeper level of wisdom.

POOL

*brekhah-brykh-*בריכה*-*237

MEANING As discussed in the introduction, the Western Mystery Tradition and indeed almost all spiritual traditions separate the human personality into the four elements of Water, Fire, Earth, and Air. A dream about a pool is clearly based in the element of Water, and this element is concerned with the emotional aspect of our personality. It is important that we remember that when we talk about our emotions we are not referring simply to relationships with others but to the way we feel about our relationship with the Divine.

THE TREE OF LIFE There are a number of locations on the Tree of Life that are linked primarily with the element of Water. We need to look at the value of this dream in order to determine exactly where this dream sits. When we reduce the value of this dream we find the number 12, which is associated with feelings of deep compassion and altruism. Such feelings are also the preserve of the path of Mem. Since the letter Mem means "water," we can safely say that this is the correct location for your dream.

THE JOURNEY It is in the compression of this dream that we can find the appropriate way to respond to this dream. The letter Resh both reassures that our efforts to be altruistic in our relationships with others will be aided by the benevolent force of the Divine and tells us that we need to use careful judgment in determining where to focus our altruistic efforts. If we take too long thinking about it rather than getting on with helping people, though, we will feel the harsher, more critical aspect of the Divine (Lamed). What you should do is look for a cause that is currently experiencing difficulties and could use your mental alacrity to cut away (Zayin) whatever is holding it back from producing the good results for those in need that it was set up to achieve.

PORTRAIT

*dyokan-dyvqn-*דיוקן*-*170

MEANING To dream of a portrait might seem to be a symptom of vanity, especially when we consider the fact that in dreams we are always the subject mat-

ter, so this dream is essentially about a self-portrait. In fact, this dream does not indicate that you are in any way vain or self-indulgent; rather, it represents your desire to understand yourself. This is an absolute essential for anyone wishing to undertake the Great Work. Indeed, the first injunction of any mystical system is that the seeker of truth should first "Know Thyself."

THE TREE OF LIFE It is no easy task to try to fully understand your inner nature. Not only are our unconscious minds very adept at hiding those aspects of our nature that will be upsetting to our conscious selves, but we are also very good at refusing to recognize the more negative aspects of our personalities even when they are being pointed out to us. The value of this dream reduces to 8, which is the value of the letter Cheth. Your dream is located on the path of Cheth as it represents the defensiveness that characterizes our nature when we begin to try to examine ourselves honestly. Additionally, the path of Cheth relates to the fact that the Divine force will be there to protect you when you do see your true nature.

THE JOURNEY The value of this dream is equivalent to the value of the Hebrew word meaning "staff." This association tells you that there is a supportive force available for you to lean on. It is important that you remember that the support is there for you, as the initial letter, Qoph, in the compression of this dream's value lets us know that you have significant worries about how this process will affect you psychologically. However, the final letter, Ayin, makes it clear that it is only through facing yourself that you will be able to create your pathway to the Divine.

POT (FOR COOKING)

*seer-syr-*סיר*-*270

MEANING At a literal level a pot is a container; metaphorically it represents a process whereby you are selecting certain aspects of your personality and life and placing them in a pot marked SPIRITUALITY. This pot of spirituality will provide you with the nourishment you need to help you get through the day and also stimulate your continued interest and development of yet more ingredients to place in your metaphorical cooking pot.

THE TREE OF LIFE The letter Ayin, which completes the compression of this dream's value, is a reminder of the fact that we must all construct our own spiritual frameworks. In order to build your unique relationship to the Divine, represented here by the letter Resh, you need to draw on every aspect of your personality. When we reduce the value of this dream we find the number that is the value of the letter Teth. Your dream is positioned here as it represents the strength of will that is needed to ensure that you can maintain your study of the spiritual to keep your pot boiling happily on the stove of your consciousness.

THE JOURNEY The central letter in the spelling of this dream is the letter Yod, and this represents the Divine spark that lies within you. Your task is to try to awaken this sacred flame so that you can approach the Great Work with your whole body and soul. To continue the metaphor, this flame of inspiration will ensure that your spiritual nourishment is served as warm as possible. The best way to achieve this is to create a rigid schedule of meditation and reading and then to stick to it no matter what unexpected circumstances arise.

POWDER

*avakah-abqh-*אבקה-108

MEANING If we discount our modern knowledge of molecules, atoms, and even subatomic particles such as quarks and leptons, we see why to the ancients the image of powder would represent the finest possible state of matter. When we read in a range of holy books that we come from dust and shall return to it, the significance is twofold. On one hand, it refers to the connection of our physical bodies to the ground on which we live, but, more important, the idea of dust is used to represent the most absolute form of breakdown or decay that could be imagined in ancient times. Consequently, to dream of powder is to realize on a profound level the nature of your mortality.

THE TREE OF LIFE The value of this dream is equivalent to that of the Hebrew phrase meaning "to love very much." This clearly indicates that this dream, while concerned with the nature of your mortality, is not in any way a negative dream. In fact, the key point of this dream is not to emphasize the inevitability of death but to foreground the possibility of eternal life through the continuation of the soul. The value of this dream reduces to 9, which is the number of the Sefirah of Yesod, and this is the position on the Tree where we locate this dream. The Sefirah of Yesod is appropriate not just by virtue of its value but because it is the first point on

the Tree of Life where we realize the inifinite nature of our soul.

THE JOURNEY The realization that you really are going to die is not easy to come to terms with, even when you fervently believe in the potential for life after death. The value of this dream is equivalent to the value of a Hebrew phrase meaning "the fruit of a deep valley." This points to the fact that from the deepest depression can often come the most valuable insights. In your case, the dream of powder may be initially depressing, but it will lead to a positive realization that your physical life is but a preparation for the much more important life of your soul.

POWER STRUGGLE

*koakh maavak-kvch mabq-*כוח מאבק-177

MEANING Dreams about conflict are never about an actual conflict between individuals but are a reflection of inner conflicts that we are experiencing. This dream functions on two levels: On one hand, it is about the struggle between your higher self and your ego-driven self; on the other, it is a dream that is designed to make you aware that conflict is as essential a part of a spiritually informed universe as are joy and unity.

THE TREE OF LIFE This dream lies in the Sefirah of Gevurah. The Sefirah of Gevurah is also known as the Sefirah of Severity. This refers to the fact that Gevurah embodies the aspect of the Divine that is responsible for all forms of conflict, decay, and ultimately death. The value of this dream is equivalent to the value of the Hebrew phrase meaning "the Garden of Eden." This emphasizes the fact that while conflict may be unpleasant, it is, just like the expulsion from the Garden of Eden, an essential part of the universal structure.

THE JOURNEY By the time you have completed your stay in Gevurah you should have come to understand that without conflict and mortality there could be no peace and no new life. Equally important, you should have resolved the conflict between your higher and your lower self. The value of this dream is equivalent to the value of a Hebrew phrase meaning "a cry for help" and it is clear that you are appealing to your higher self to help you to achieve a sense of communion with the Divine. This can occur only when you fully accept that you will have to kill off a part of your old life-style and way of looking at the world.

PRAYER

*tfeelah-thphylh-*תפילה-525

MEANING Most of the time when we are trying to analyze a dream we are attempting to unravel a hidden message within relatively obscure dream images. However, in this dream the spiritual aspect is obvious. This dream makes it clear that you are deeply committed to the spiritual path and that you are actively seeking the assistance of the Divine at this time in order to help you move forward along the Tree of Life.

THE TREE OF LIFE The act of prayer has been around in one form or another since the very first person recognized the possibility that there was a Divine presence in the world and tried to establish some form of contact in order to improve his lot. For most of history, praying has been both a very public and a very dramatic business. It is only recently that we have associated prayer with a very quiet and solitary act. When praying alone, we should find our own words and thoughts to pray with, so prayer is still in a sense an artistic act. The value of this dream is equivalent to that of the Hebrew name for God "Jehovah Tzabaoth," and this name is connected to the Sefirah of Netzach. As this Sefirah is linked with all forms of artistic expression, it is also the location on which we place this dream.

THE JOURNEY When we reduce the value of this dream we find the number 12. This number is associated with themes of self-sacrifice and altruism. The message for you, the dreamer, is that you should certainly be engaging in prayer, but your prayers should not be focused on your physical condition. Instead, you should pray either for the benefit of others or for an increase in your spiritual understanding rather than your material position. If you pray in this fashion, you will find that your level of spiritual insight increases greatly.

PRECIPICE

*tehom-thhvm-*תהום-451

MEANING From any point of view this dream represents a moment in your life that presents you with an opportunity—but an opportunity that is absolutely fraught with danger. In Kabbalistic terms, this dream indicates that you are on the verge of making a poor choice in your life that could relate to your work or your relationships or your inner development. The value of this dream is equivalent to the value of the Hebrew phrase meaning "the essence of man." This suggests that you are doing no more than any other person might; after all, to err is human. However, if you can avoid making a mistake, you should.

THE TREE OF LIFE The value of this dream is equivalent to the value of the Hebrew word meaning "abyss." This is a common term used to describe the position of Daat on the Tree of Life. Daat is not a Sefirah as such, but is a space that lies on the path of Gimel, acting as a final test that separates you from the Divine source of Keter. However, given the content of this dream, we should see the abyss more literally. The literal meaning of the word *Daat* is "knowledge." It is more knowledge that you need right now before you make a hasty decision that you could live to regret.

THE JOURNEY The next few weeks should see you engaged in some serious reflection. Do not make any definite decisions until you have thought through all the possible consequences, even those that may seem unlikely. The central letter, Nun, in the spelling of this dream title indicates that your faith is being challenged. The correct response is to be still and calm in the knowledge that the Divine is with you and to allow yourself the time that you need before making any decisions.

PREGNANCY

*herayon-hryvn-*הריון-271

MEANING From a psychological point of view, this dream could be seen as a reference to a creative desire on your part as the creative process is often referred to as being the metaphorical equivalent of trying to give birth to a child. In spiritual terms, this dream relates to the process of trying to create a viable relationship with the Divine. The reduction value of this dream produces the number 10, which indicates that your spiritual pregnancy is very near its completion.

THE TREE OF LIFE In the Tree of Life, the Sefirah of Binah is also known as the Great Mother and it is the appropriate location of this dream. The title of the Sefirah of Binah is "Understanding," and when you have completed your time is Binah, you will have managed to gain a very rare level of deep spiritual understanding, which will enable you to achieve a direct communion with the Divine itself. It is very unusual for anyone to achieve this level of spiritual enlightenment, and this is represented by the fact that the value of this dream is a prime number. Prime numbers represent the unique nature of each individual because they can be divided only by themselves and by one.

THE JOURNEY The most noticeable feature of the spelling of this dream title is the letter Nun as it appears in its final form. This implies that you will experience a strong challenge to your faith as you pass through the Sefirah of Binah. This is inevitable, as the Great Mother will reveal to you the pain that is present in the world around you since every person who is suffering is one of her children. The compression of this dream encourages you to use your judgment (Resh) carefully when fitting the wisdom you gain from Binah into your individual spiritual framework (Ayin). If you judge correctly, you will be able to come an understanding of the unity of the Divine as represented by the final letter, Aleph.

PRINT
ot-avth-אות-407

MEANING Without print, we would not be living in a technologically advanced society. Indeed, the basis of almost all knowledge that is still in use today relies on the printed word for the fact that it is available to everyone. The value of this dream is equivalent to the value of the Hebrew phrase meaning "the precious oil." This association points very definitely to the importance of the printed word for the development of human understanding and knowledge. From a spiritual perspective, this dream refers to the desire to acquire an in-depth knowledge of mystical thought across the ages.

THE TREE OF LIFE When we reduce the value of this dream we find the number 11, which is associated with mystical and occult matters. Very often this number indicates that the dreamer is about to undergo an experience that will considerably advance his spiritual understanding. This is certainly the case with this dream. The central letter in the spelling of this dream title is Vav, and this letter is associated with all forms of thought and so fits with the general theme of this dream. It also serves to underpin the fact that this dream belongs to the Sefirah of Hod, which is connected to the process of integrating our intellectual ideas with our spiritual frameworks of belief.

THE JOURNEY You have started out well in your spiritual quest, and now that you are in the Sefirah of Hod you have the opportunity to develop your spiritual ideas through a sound, rational way of looking at the world. The compression of this dream's value tells you that you will have some regrets (Tav) as you pare down your wide-ranging ideas about the Divine so that they will make a coherent whole. However, the final letter, Zayin, tells you that in spite of your regrets you need to use the "sword" of your intellect to cut away anything that will not help to further your understanding of the Divine.

PRISON
bet sohar-byth svhr-בית סוהר-683

MEANING This is an uncommon dream. If you experience this dream, it is likely that you will wake with a wholly irrational fear that you are about to be dragged off to jail. When you are fully awake, you will probably be at a complete loss to understand why you would dream of being in prison. However, when we put the dream under the spotlight of a spiritual analysis, we see the prison as a representation of your current state of mind.

THE TREE OF LIFE When we begin to consider the spiritual aspect of reality, it takes us a while before we make a decision to actually commit to the Great Work. In the time that leads up to that momentous decision, we go through a number of mental stages, one of which is the realization that until we open ourselves up to the influence of the Divine we are effectively trapped in a prison of flesh. This dream is placed firmly in the Sefirah of Malkut, as it indicates that you have yet to move out of the wholly material world.

THE JOURNEY Taking that first step out of Malkut is likely to fill you with anxiety. There may be circumstances in your daily life that lead to you feel trapped and constrained. It would be very useful to take some time to reflect on what they may be and how best to deal with them. It is very tempting to try to ease the feeling of anxiety by keeping some part of ourselves separate from the process of spiritual development. The anxiety is caused by an unconscious desire to retain some of the certainties of the material worldview while at the same time wishing to pursue spiritual truth. This desire is reflected by the reduction value of this dream, as it produces the value of the letter Cheth, which indicates a defensive or protective attitude. You need to realize that if you do take up a defensive attitude, you will simply be creating another prison for yourself, as you will inevitably build a metaphorical wall around yourself.

PROMISE

*havtakhah-hbtchh-*הבטחה-29

MEANING Even though it is the job of adults to educate children, it is often the case that we as adults should be listening to and learning from our children. This is particularly true when it comes to the matter of right and wrong behavior. The issue of promises is a very good example. Many adults will make a promise without taking it seriously, whereas any child will tell you that a promise is hugely important and should never be broken. The most important promise that you can make is the promise that you make to yourself to pursue a spiritual path in your life.

THE TREE OF LIFE The value of this dream is equivalent to that of two different ways of spelling the word meaning "broken" in Hebrew. Given the title of this dream, the repeated presence of the word *broken* suggests that you are tempted either to give up or at least to take a break from your spiritual work at this time. This is because the path that you are on is a particularly difficult one. Since you have only recently made your decision to pursue the Great Work, we locate this dream on the path of Shin, which is also known as the biting path because it requires some intense mental effort on your part.

THE JOURNEY As you have now taken your first steps along the Tree of Life, you should do your best to persist in the work. The spelling of this dream title both begins and ends with the letter Heh. The letter Heh means "window" and its function here is to reassure you that you will achieve a glimpse of the nature of the Divine if you persist. In the compression of this dream's value we see the letter Kaph. This letter tells you that you need to engage in some form of practical activity in order to move forward in terms of your spiritual understanding. An ideal activity for you would be to take yoga or tai chi classes, as this will also help to motivate you to continue with the Great Work.

PROPERTY

*rekhoosh-rkvsh-*רכוש-526

MEANING From a psychological point of view, this dream would not be seen as particularly negative; it would indicate simply that, for whatever reason, you are currently spending a lot of time thinking about your long-term financial planning. We can assume that the material focus is on the long term because this dream is about property rather than money itself, and property represents a long-term investment. When considered in a spiritual context, this dream tells us that you need to shift your primary focus from the materialistic to the spiritual.

THE TREE OF LIFE When someone is as concerned with the material side of his life as you clearly are, the only possible location is the Sefirah of Malkut. This is the Sefirah that is associated with the physical word and it acts as the springboard for our spiritual development. When we reduce the value of this dream we find the number 13, which is the number of great change, and it suggests that while you may be languishing in Malkut right now, you will soon be able to move out of the solely physical dimension.

THE JOURNEY The fact that you are dreaming about property tells us that as yet you have not made any real decision to explore your inner nature. However, the initial letter, Nun, in the compression of this dream's value points out that you will shortly become aware of the sorrow that results from failing to explore your spiritual potential. The subsequent letter, Kaph, makes it clear that in order to approach the Divine (Vav) you should begin to take some kind of practical action. The ideal way for you to start would be to obtain as many books as possible on the whole notion of spirituality and begin to read voraciously.

BEING A PROSTITUTE

*zonah-zvnh-*זונה-68

MEANING On the face of it, this dream is not only negative in nature but is deeply unflattering to you as an individual. It seems sensible to interpret this dream as indicating that you are not entering into your relationships for the most appropriate reasons, that you are operating from a calculating rather than a genuinely sincere point of view. However, when we look at this dream from a spiritual point of view, we need to look for the associated reasons why a person would take this approach to life.

THE TREE OF LIFE You are feeling so disheartened about the Great Work that you are considering turning your back on the Divine and returning to a materialistic attitude. This is not uncommon especially in the early stages of our spiritual development, when we have left behind the material world but have yet to see any evidence of the spiritual dimension. In terms of the Tree of Life, this dream belongs on the path of Tzaddi in its negative aspect. Rather than being "hooked" and committed to the spiritual, you are becoming increasingly committed to a materialistic worldview.

THE JOURNEY In order to avoid slipping back down the Tree into Malkut, you need to find some way of reassuring yourself that there really is a spiritual dimension to the universe. The compression of this dream's value indicates that you are about to receive some from of support (Samech) from your higher self. All you need to do in order to be able this strong supportive energy is to take the risk of putting your faith in the Divine. This means making the leap of belief before you receive any proof that it is the correct thing to do. At the moment, the letter Cheth suggests that your desire to protect yourself from failure is getting in the way of your making this brave decision.

PSYCHIATRIST

*pseekheeatr–phsykyatr–*פסיכיאטר*-390*

MEANING There is a certain irony in analyzing a dream about a psychiatrist from a Kabbalistic perspective. This dream should not in any way be seen as a means by which your unconscious can tell you that you ought to seek the advice of a therapist. In fact, this dream is extremely positive about both your state of mind and your progress along the spiritual path. The value of this dream is equivalent to that of the Hebrew word meaning "oil." Traditionally, oils were used both as healing salves and as a feature of many ancient religious rituals. From this we can infer that the dream of a psychiatrist relates to a role that you may be taking on rather than to a person from whom you need to seek therapy.

THE TREE OF LIFE Another common use of the word *oil* is in the phrase to "pour oil on troubled waters." Our dreams often try to put an idea in our conscious minds by using an image or word that figures in a well-known phrase or proverb. In your case, this dream is suggesting that you have the capacity to act as a mediator or calming influence in relationships. This ability stems from your increasing spiritual understanding and confirms the placement of your dream on the path of Mem, as this path is concerned with compassionate self-sacrifice and altruism.

THE JOURNEY When we reduce the value of this dream we find the number 3. This number indicates that not only can you be of great help to those around you but that you have the creative imagination to find new and innovative solutions to people's problems. Additionally, the compression of this dream's value tells us that you have enormous raw energy (Shin) that will enable you to help many people without exhausting yourself. When you engage in this practical expression of your compassion, you will find that your insight continues to grow.

PUBLISHER

*motsee laor–mvtzya lavr–*מוציא לאור*-364*

MEANING Without the input of a Kabbalistic analysis, we might see this dream as representing nothing more than a possible career goal that you may or may not have consciously considered. However, the value of this dream demonstrates that it is far more significant than that. The value of this dream is equivalent to that of a Hebrew phrase meaning "hidden light." As light represents the Divine force, this dream is linked to the revelation of the hidden nature of the Divine. When we consider that the role of a publisher is to release new ideas and information to the public through the medium of the printed word, this association makes a lot of sense.

THE TREE OF LIFE When we reduce the value of this dream we find the number 13, which symbolizes major change. Usually such change is individual, but in the context of this dream it relates to change that you can help bring about in other people by sharing with them the wisdom that you possess. Because of this, we locate your dream on the path of Daleth. The letter Daleth means "door," and this dream is all about opening the door to new spiritual possibilities for other people.

THE JOURNEY The letter Aleph appears twice in the spelling of this dream title; and its function is to remind you that while this dream is about assisting others, you will be helping yourself at the same time. The more you honor your commitment to try to hold open the door to truth for those around you, the closer you will come to experiencing the transcendent unity of the Divine. This is why in the compression of the dream's value the letter Daleth appears at the very end. It represents the door that is being opened for you by your higher self, which leads to a state of consciousness in which you are attuned to the true nature of the universe.

PULSE

*dofek-dvphq-*דופק-190

MEANING This dream presents us with both a problem and its solution. This is very positive since it suggests that at least unconsciously you are growing in self-confidence in both your spiritual development and your day-to-day life. The dream of a pulse is not simply a reminder that you are alive, it is a warning that you are worrying too much and as a result your pulse rate is sufficiently raised for it to merit being the subject of a dream.

THE TREE OF LIFE The value of this dream is equivalent to the value of the Hebrew phrase meaning "the end." This association clearly indicates that you are suffering from a great deal of anxiety at this time. Your anxiety relates to the fact that you have only recently made a decision to begin to explore your inner self. It is quite normal to feel nervous and worried about the possible impact of this journey, and the path of Qoph, on which this dream sits, relates directly to this sense of concern and doubt.

THE JOURNEY The spelling of this dream title tells us how you came to be in this state of anxiety. You made the great leap and opened the door (Daleth) to the world of the spiritual. You then engaged in a great deal of communication about the nature of the Great Work, but these conversations were only with yourself (Peh and Vav). As a result, your feelings of uncertainty gradually compounded and increased, as represented by the final Qoph in the spelling of your dream title. The solution lies in the compression of this dream's value, where we find the letter Tzaddi. This tells you that you need to focus on the work itself and learn more about the world of the spiritual rather than focus on the conceived fears you had before you embarked on your voyage of discovery.

PUNCH

*makat egrof-mkth agrvph-*מכת אגרוף-750

MEANING To suffer a punch in a dream feels extremely distressing. However, you need to remember that the only person in your dreams is you, albeit in a number of guises including your higher self. To receive a punch in your dream means that your higher self is trying vigorously to urge you to pursue your spiritual development. It is also possible that this dream reflects potentially violent urges that you are feeling toward someone or a certain situation in your life.

THE TREE OF LIFE The value of this dream is equivalent to the value of the Hebrew word for "lead." Lead is the metal associated with the planet Saturn, and it represents the sense of melancholy that stems from feeling too old to make any more progress in your life. The idea of melancholy is potentially repeated in the compression of this dream, which consists only of the letter Nun repeated in both its final and its standard forms. The path of Nun is certainly the appropriate location for this dream, but this does not mean that you are right to be feeling so depressed, as the true purpose of the dream is to deepen your sense of faith. While this may be challenging, it is a very positive experience in the long term.

THE JOURNEY Given the presence of the word *lead* in the value of this dream, we know that the primary reason for your sense of sorrow is that you believe it is too late for you to successfully pursue your spiritual goals. This is not at all true, as it is never too late to take up the spiritual path, provided that one is sincerely seeking the truth. In the spelling of this dream title the letter Peh stands out as it appears in its final form. This tells us that the way for you to move forward and leave behind your melancholy outlook is to find a group of like-minded people exploring spiritual issues and discuss with them your fears and doubts. If you are harboring deeply negative or even violent thoughts about a particular individual, the best solution is to try to engage in a discussion with him in order to reconcile your differences.

PURPLE

*argaman-argmn-*ארגמן-294

MEANING All colors have particular ideas and values associated with them, and very often these associations span both time and space. Red, for instance, has been regarded as a color that symbolizes anger and passion in every culture and throughout history. The color purple is linked with ideas of authority and power. In ancient Rome, for instance, the emperor wore a purple tunic as a sign of his status. This color has always hinted at the idea of power that exceeds the merit of the individual wielding that power. It is this association that spawned the expression "purple prose," which refers to writing that is overly dramatic and self-important in the context of its subject matter. From a spiritual point of view, we should note the fact that this dream ends with the letter Nun in its final form, which is a sure sign that ultimately you will not benefit from according yourself greater status than you deserve.

THE TREE OF LIFE This dream indicates that you believe yourself to have a more advanced level of wisdom and spiritual insight than you actually possess. This is a potentially dangerous state of mind as it can lead you to make decisions and follow paths of belief that will take you farther away rather than bring you closer to the Divine. When we reduce the value of this dream we find the number 15. This number is associated with The Devil card in the tarot. As you might expect, this card indicates a person who has decided that he, rather than the Divine, is responsible for the advances that he has so far made in the Great Work. This places your dream on the path of Ayin in its negative aspect, as this path refers to a vigorous pursuit of one's individualistic approach to the spiritual quest.

THE JOURNEY The path of Ayin tends to encourage rash thinking and behavior. If we were to characterize it as a person, we would probably describe a young man or a youth who is full of enthusiasm and arrogance but lacks the experience to make the right choices in life. The value of this dream is equivalent to the value of the Hebrew word meaning "autumn." This suggests that you need the wisdom and experience that is associated with the autumn of our lives. In the absence of sudden aging, what you should do is change your approach to the Divine. You should put your ideas on hold for a while and spend a few months following the ideas and practices of a universally respected mystic. This could be the teachings of the Buddha or the meditations of Ignatius Loyola; the important thing is that you listen to a voice of experience.

PURSE

*arnak-arnq-*ארנק-351

MEANING In Kabbalistic analysis, the specific word or image of a dream is crucially important not just because of the impact on the numerical values used in any analysis but because by its very nature the Kabbalistic approach is very much concerned with details. This dream of a purse, for instance, is extremely positive, whereas a dream of a bank account would not be so encouraging. This is because in terms of the level of your concern for material matters, a purse suggests that you wish to have only the minimum that you need to get by on a daily basis, whereas a bank account suggests a concern with savings and the accumulation of wealth.

THE TREE OF LIFE The fact that this dream is centered around material concerns lets us know that you are still new to the Great Work. Its specific con-

tent also tells us that you have already made a great internal commitment to the spiritual path and are maintaining a minimal interest in the purely physical world only insofar as you need to retain a reasonable day-to-day life. The value of this dream is equivalent to that of the Hebrew spelling of the name "Moses," and of course when he led his people out of Egypt they were able to take only the bare minimum in terms of goods. All religious tales can be seen as metaphors for our individual development, and this dream through its value calls to mind Moses and the Exodus. This further supports the idea that you are only just moving out of Malkut. The value of this dream reduces to 9, the number of the Sefirah of Yesod, which lies immediately above Malkut and is the location of this dream.

THE JOURNEY You have made an excellent start on your inner journey. What you need to do now is to develop a regular routine of spiritual practice. This could mean meditation, the reading of spiritual texts, or simply praying. The New Age culture has led to an increase in the number of mystical systems that talk in terms of the soul but are focused wholly on the individual. You need to ensure that in your spiritual practice you are recognizing the true presence of a Divine force, as it is only through this force that you will achieve enlightenment. The need to do this is hidden in the value of this dream. The value of the Hebrew name for God, "YHVH," is 26, and if we add up all the numbers from 1 to 26, we arrive at the value of this dream.

PURSUIT

*redeefah-rdyphh-*רדיפה-299

MEANING A psychological interpretation of this dream would have to remain vague because it would not be clear whether you are the pursuer or the object of the pursuit. If the former, this dream might be seen as a warning about latent feelings of aggression and frustration; if the latter, it would probably be interpreted as a metaphor for feelings of inadequacy or insecurity. Fortunately, we can look at this dream from a Kabbalistic perspective as well, and say with confidence that you are the pursuer here and are pursuing the greatest prize of all, which is spiritual understanding.

THE TREE OF LIFE There is a great deal of energy in this dream. In terms of the title, "pursuit" suggests a far more vigorous process than "exploration" or "investigation" or even "chase." This vigor stems from your overwhelming enthusiasm for the Great Work. Additionally, the value of this dream reduces to 20, and this could be seen either as the energizing Divine spark of Yod occurring twice or as a reference to the letter Shin, which is the twentieth letter of the Hebrew alphabet. The letter Shin is linked with the element of Fire and understandably it is here that we locate this dream.

THE JOURNEY You are racing toward the Sefirah of Hod, which is the position on the Tree into which the path of Shin leads. Once there, you will have to begin the process of organizing your rational ideas and intellectual conceptions of the nature of the universe in the context of a spiritually integrated view of the world. This is not an easy task, for it requires slow and steady thought as much as it requires enthusiasm. Your task over the next weeks is to learn to maintain that enthusiasm but in a controlled and well-directed manner. This will help you enormously when you reach the Sefirah of Hod.

PYRAMID

peerameedah-pyrmydh-פירמידה-349

MEANING There are few monuments in the world that have received as many articles and texts devoted to their secret significance, or indeed to their lack of mystical import, as the Pyramids. It is for this reason that we can confidently see their presence in this dream as a symbol of all esoteric interests. From a spiritual point of view, we see this dream as representing a growing interest in exploring the wide range of spiritual ideas that might help you in your quest for truth.

THE TREE OF LIFE At its most general level, this dream could be assigned to almost any position on the Tree of Life, since every path is concerned with the exploration of the realm of the spiritual. However, the values within the dream's title help us to pin down an exact position. When we reduce the value of this dream we find the number 7, which is the value of the letter Zayin. This letter means "sword," and it is highly appropriate as the path for your dream since it refers to the need to cut away those ideas about the Divine that are not going to aid your progress.

THE JOURNEY To try to separate the wheat from the chaff when it comes to theories of the Divine and the soul is a daunting task indeed! However, the compression of the value of this dream tells us that you certainly have sufficient raw energy (Shin) to make a good attempt at this challenge. Additionally, the letter Mem indicates that the maternal aspect of the Divine is there to help you. The final letter,

Teth, functions as one last warning to be wary of those spiritual ideas that are attractive because they suggest that you can achieve wisdom in a matter of weeks or because they flatter your sense of importance.

QUARREL

mereevah-mrybh-מריבה-257

MEANING When we think about those individuals whom we regard as the epitome of spiritual insight, we tend not to imagine them as having arguments or entering into any kind of dispute with others. Consequently, we have a tendency to dismiss the whole idea of conflict as being contrary to the Great Work and therefore against the nature of the Divine. The value of this dream is equivalent to that of the Hebrew word meaning "ark." Since we know that the ark was the means by which humans and other animals were protected from extinction in the story of the Deluge, this may seem a strange association, until we realize that conflict is actually an essential part of the Divine and the structure of the universe.

THE TREE OF LIFE We all remember that it was thanks to the ark that mankind survived the great flood. However, most of us do not remember that the flood itself was equally essential to the preservation of a species that would have the potential for spiritual growth. The tale of the Deluge represents the importance of all forms of conflict as a means by which we ultimately arrive at a resolution. This dream sits in the Sefirah of Gevurah since this is the position that corresponds to the aspect of the Divine that is concerned with all forms of conflict.

THE JOURNEY The value of this dream is equivalent to the value of the Hebrew word meaning "magician." We should see this word in its positive sense, as a reference to someone who has sufficient spiritual wisdom to appear to have a miraculous level of insight. The message contained within this associated word is that in order to achieve a truly wise status, you must accept and internalize an understanding of the absolute necessity of quarrels and conflicts.

QUARRY

makhtsavah-mchtzbh-מחצבה-145

MEANING If we did not have the benefit of being able to look at the values of the dreams under analysis, we might make the mistake of seeing this dream as a sign that you are excessively concerned with the material side of life. We tend to associate quarries with mining for valuable ores, so it would be reasonable to view the dreamer as someone very eager to accumulate as much wealth as possible. However, once we look at the values within this dream we discover that this dream relates to an individual who is looking deep within his soul.

THE TREE OF LIFE The value of this dream is equivalent to the value of the Hebrew phrase meaning "the staff of God." This makes it very clear that you are progressing well up the Tree of Life and are not at all focused on the material rewards of life. As the letter Samech means "prop" and refers to the support and guidance of the Divine we can confidently place this dream on the path of Samech. As this path approaches the Sefirah of Tiferet, it is quite right for you to be engaging in deep exploration of your inner nature at this time.

THE JOURNEY Despite your sound progress, you still have some concerns about your suitability for the Great Work, and this is expressed by the letter Qoph at the beginning of the compression of this dream's value. However, the letter Mem tells you that you can rely on the maternal support of the Divine to carry you through. The final letter, Heh, is there to represent the union with your higher self that you will achieve in the Sefirah of Tiferet. The value of Heh is 5, and the symbol for an individual who has learned to rule himself through his higher self is the five-pointed star or pentagram.

QUARTZ

*kvarts-qvvartz-*קוארץ-403

MEANING Stones, especially crystals, were used by almost all ancient peoples in their religious rituals. Additionally, crystals were often used by healers and priests in their attempts to try to cure a range of conditions. Although they were less efficient than the medicines we have available to us today, crystals did and still do have a certain degree of power or "energy" that can be tapped by those who know how to utilize them in their spiritual practices. To dream of quartz indicates that you are beginning to see that even the material world contains more than the merely physical.

THE TREE OF LIFE Over the hundreds of years that Kabbalistic wisdom has been developed by a range of mystical traditions from the strictly orthodox to the frankly bizarre, a whole host of associa-

tions that can be linked with specific positions on the Tree of Life has been developed. For instance, each path is linked with a particular stone or mineral whose symbolic value is sympathetic to the symbolic significance of that path. Quartz is associated with the Sefirah of Malkut, so it is here that we position your dream.

THE JOURNEY Although your dream sits on the path of Malkut, this does not mean that you have yet to begin your spiritual journey. The implication of this dream is that you have made good progress but are now returning to look at Malkut in a new light. In the compression of the dream's value we see the letter Tav, which is the first path out of Malkut, but it is linked to the letter Gimel, which indicates a very high level of spiritual insight. Your task in the months ahead is to reconsider the nature of the physical world with the intention of finding within the material the presence and the wonder of the Divine.

QUEEN

*malkah-mlkh-*מלכה-95

MEANING When we are faced with a dream that is gender specific, we need to remember that the symbolism is ancient and was constructed long before ideas of gender equality had been put forward or accepted. We should also remember that a dream of a queen can apply to a man or a woman and will have exactly the same meaning for both of them. It is worth noting that even when these symbols were first used, there was no suggestion that the gender divisions used to distinguish between aspects of the Divine should apply to the way in which people were actually defined. The dream of a queen is encouraging, as it indicates that you are gaining considerable control and direction over your spiritual quest. Because of the symbolic significance of a queen rather than a king, this dream also suggests that you are using your spirituality to drive a compassionate and generous approach to others.

THE TREE OF LIFE The value of this dream is equivalent to the value of the Hebrew word meaning "the waters." The element of Water is associated with the emotions, so this dream should be located on the path of Mem. The letter Mem means "water" and embodies the compassionate and altruistic behavior that is suggested by the symbol of a queen. It is also of note that in the spelling of this dream title the first letter is Mem, which suggests that the key distinguishing feature of the queen is her generosity of spirit.

THE JOURNEY We should not allow our cultural stereotypes of feminine generosity to color our interpretation of this dream. The compression of this dream's value reveals the letters Tzaddi and Heh, both of which represent very active energy. Specifically, the letter Tzaddi tells you to persist in your charity work and that you should be taking a lead in the organization at least at a local level. The final letter, Heh, indicates that your persistence will be rewarded with a glimpse of the true nature of the Divine.

QUESTION

*sheelah-shalh-*שאלה-336

MEANING Questions lie at the heart of the spiritual quest. In fact, all of our explorations of ourselves and the universe are focused on the one great question: "Why are we here?" This dream tells us not only that you are engaged with a thorough examination of your inner self but that you are already trying to make some form of contact with your higher self. It is worth noting that every number in the value of this dream is a 3 or a multiple of 3. Three is the number of creation, and there is a deep mystery, which can only be experienced and not learned, concealed within this association of the act of creation and the idea of asking a question.

THE TREE OF LIFE In the very early stages of our spiritual journey we need to concentrate on restructuring the way we look at the world both emotionally and intellectually. It is when we have almost completed this task that we can turn our attention more to the Divine itself. The attempt to find an answer to your question must start with some sort of communication, and this is why we locate this dream on the path of Peh, which is concerned with all forms of communication.

THE JOURNEY Even though you are already asking the question of your higher self and the Divine, it can be a whole lifetime or even longer before you receive a complete answer. This is partly because the answer to the greatest questions rely as much on the work that you do yourself as it does on any communication emanating from the higher forces. We can see from the compression of this dream that you have a great deal of energy (Shin). Even so, you will need the harsh force of your higher self (Lamed) to push you on so that you ultimately reach an appreciation of the nature of the macrocosm (Vav) or the Divine.

QUICKSAND

*kholot beetsah-chvlvth bytzh-*חולות ביצה-566

MEANING A psychological interpretation of this dream would probably advise you to look for some area of your life that you feel is taking over and removing both your freedom and your sense of direction in life. A Kabbalistic analysis would to a large extent agree with this view, but rather than look at the world around you for the source of your problems, you should look within yourself to see why you are colluding in the stagnation of your spiritual development.

THE TREE OF LIFE It is an unfortunate fact of human nature that we very often prefer what we are used to, even if it is deeply unsatisfying, to the possibility of failing to achieve a position with which we can be truly content. When we are taking such an approach to life we tend to convince ourselves that we are simply acting to protect ourselves. This fact places this dream on the path of Cheth in its negative aspect, which represents a defensiveness that, rather than protecting you, simply holds you back.

THE JOURNEY The only way to free yourself from the ever-increasing hold of this metaphorical quicksand is to take some form of decisive action. The need for action is supported by the letter Kaph in its final form, which begins the compression of this dream's value. The subsequent letter, Samech, refers to support and guidance, so it would be a good idea for you to join a meditation class or a Kabbalah study group. In doing so, you will begin to pull yourself free and start to move up the Tree again.

RACE

*merots-myrvtz-*מירוץ-346

MEANING In commonsense terms, this dream indicates that you are someone who likes to live fast and has a strong competitive streak. This does not sound like our typical preconceived notion of a spiritually minded person. We might ask from a Kabbalistic standpoint who exactly we are racing against if we are to look at this dream in a spiritual context. The answer is that you are not racing against another person but against the two forces of time and the underlying cynicism of the modern age.

THE TREE OF LIFE It takes considerable persistence to succeed in the Great Work, and this dream suggests that you have realized that there are numerous distractions and forces in the world that would potentially prevent you from making progress. The final letter, Tzaddi in the spelling of this dream title indicates that you have a very strong commitment to your spiritual quest. Additionally, the value of this dream is equivalent to the value of the Hebrew word meaning "willpower," and this associates strongly with your enthusiasm for the spiritual journey. These factors mean that your dream is located on the path of Tzaddi.

THE JOURNEY When we reduce the value of this dream we find the number 13. This number points to great changes in your life, and this relates to the fact that thanks to your persistence you will shortly be entering the Sefirah of Netzach. The compression of this dream's value indicates not only that you are dedicated to reaching an understanding of the Divine, but that you are combining your raw energy (Shin) with a suitably reflective (Vav) turn of mind.

RAGE

*kheymah-chymh-*חימה*-63*

MEANING Established religion tends to frown on the free expression of passionate feelings and seems to prefer its members to express their devotion to the Divine in a much more restrained manner. However, the mystical path encourages you to express your passionate wish for enlightenment. At the same time, this does not mean that the spiritual quest encourages anger and certainly not rage. The value of this dream is equivalent to the value of the Hebrew word meaning "dregs." This not only makes clear the negative nature of this dream but suggests that the image of rage represents some residual aspects of your ego-driven personality.

THE TREE OF LIFE This dream sits on the path of Lamed. The nature of Lamed is to act almost as a scourge on behalf of the Divine. It will certainly help you to remove any vestiges of your old self that are not conducive to the development of a spiritual personality. The harsh nature of the path of Lamed perhaps also explains the reason why this dream has "rage" as its title.

THE JOURNEY While the content may be negative and the path that you are currently traversing is harsh, there are still positive messages within the value of this dream. The initial letter in the compression of this dream's value is Samech, and this

tells you that no matter how difficult it is to face up to the undesirable aspects of your personality, you will be helped in this through the support and guidance of the Divine. If you have feelings of anger toward anyone in particular, you need to understand why you have that anger and then find some way of allowing it to drain away. Anger is never helpful, as it clouds our judgment. The final letter, Gimel, suggests that some form of creative expression such as writing or painting will help you to fully understand which aspects of your nature are interfering with your spiritual progress.

RAIN

*geshem-gshm-*גשם*-343*

MEANING The world never looks as dreary as it does in the middle of a downpour. This might lead you to think that this dream relates to a rather depressing time in your life. However, when we look at the value of this dream we see that it consists of the number of manifestation (4) flanked on each side by the number of creation (3). The implication of this numerical arrangement is that you should look for the Divine in every aspect of the material world—even in the rain. In the Kabbalah, the rain is seen as symbolic of Divine grace, since without the rain the plant life would wither and die, and so rain is a source of life and abundance.

THE TREE OF LIFE When we reduce the value of this dream we find the number 10. This is the value of the Sefirah of Malkut, and since the number of the physical world is also central in the spelling of this dream, it is appropriate to locate your dream in this Sefirah. The value of this dream is equivalent to the value of a Hebrew phrase meaning "a sweet smell." In spiritual terms, this association suggests that you are beginning to sense the presence of the Divine, and this bodes well for your future development.

THE JOURNEY This dream is an attempt by your higher self to awaken you to the omnipresence of the Divine force. The rain should be seen as symbolic of the will of the Divine emanating out of the Sefirah of Keter. In order to begin the long climb back up toward your spiritual home, you need to find some reserves of energy (Shin) and to put your trust in the maternal aspect of the Divine. A simple but effective way to put yourself in tune with the wonder of the natural world and the fact that it is infused wit spirituality would be to take it upon yourself to tend a small area of garden or parkland. Your relationship to the plants will mirror the Divine's relationship to you and prepare you for the Great Work.

❧RAINBOW

*keshet-qshth-*קשׁת*-800*

MEANING Even to a non-Kabbalist the dream of a rainbow is likely to seem full of promise. There is a key difference, though. The nonspiritual interpretation would see the dream of a rainbow as positive because of the common mythology that at the end of a rainbow one will find a pot of gold. The Kabbalist sees this dream as encouraging because it represents the rainbow of promise set over the Sefirah of Malkut by the Divine in order to give us all the chance to climb back up to our spiritual home. At a practical level, it also suggests that a time of good fortune and luck is on its way.

THE TREE OF LIFE The three letters that make up the spelling of this dream title are the first three paths that lead out of the purely physical realm of Malkut. To dream of a rainbow means that you are now ready to begin your spiritual voyage of self-discovery. This dream does not specify which of the three paths you will take, but it is quite clear that you are now committed to the Great Work. Whichever path you choose to take will be a positive step, as you will be that little bit closer to the Divine.

THE JOURNEY The task that lies before you in the next few weeks and months is to make good on your promise to follow the spiritual path. The fact that the promise of the Divine is met with your own promise to commit to the Great Work reflects one of the fundamental truths of the spiritual quest, which is that it is a reciprocal process that involves both you and the higher forces in equal measure. The compression of the value of this dream produces the letter Peh. This letter represents all forms of communication and tells you that it is never too soon to try to make contact with your higher self.

See Zohar symbol, Rainbow.

RAM

*ayeel-ayl-*איל*-41*

MEANING The ram has been used in some cultures, including certain early Christian sects, as a representation of the nature of evil. We are far more used to the image of a goat rather than a ram as a symbol of the evil one, but there was a time when the two were used interchangeably. It is, of course, a complete coincidence that this dream happens to be number 666 in the list of dreams, and just to reassure any readers who may still feel slightly anxious, we can confirm that this dream is in fact very positive. The value of this dream is equivalent to the value of a Hebrew phrase meaning "my God," and this association serves to underline the fact that you as the dreamer are making good progress toward contacting the Divine.

THE TREE OF LIFE When we reduce the value of this dream we find the number 5. This is the value of the letter Heh. The path of Heh is associated with great strength of character, a vigorous will to succeed, and the ability to analyze a situation swiftly and see right through to the heart of the matter. These are among the qualities that are associated with zodiac sign Aries, which is linked with the path of Heh. If this were not enough to firmly place your dream on the path of Heh, the animal that represents Aries is, of course, the ram.

THE JOURNEY The letter Heh literally means "window," and this high up the Tree of Life your goal must be to catch sight of the true nature of the Divine. Part of that nature is encapsulated within the compression of this dream, as we have the letter Mem representing the maternal aspect of God and the letter Aleph representing the unifying force of the Divine. The value of this dream is equivalent to the value of the Hebrew word meaning "to burn." This should be taken to signify your passion for the Great Work. Your success now depends on your ability to use that passion to metaphorically enflame yourself through prayer.

RANSOM

*kofer-kvphr-*כופר*-306*

MEANING An obvious way to analyze this dream would be to see it as an indication that you are interested primarily in accumulating money and that the image of a ransom points to a willingness to go to any lengths in order to increase your wealth. However, such a negative interpretation would not fit well with the fact that this dream's value is equivalent to the value of a Hebrew phrase meaning "Father of Mercy." A far more likely interpretation is that you are so deeply enthusiastic about the Great Work that you would be willing to offer up some form of ransom in terms of your time in order to succeed. Equally, the dream advises you that the Divine does not require sacrifices, merely sincerity.

THE TREE OF LIFE There is at least one other phrase relating to the merciful nature of the Divine that shares its value with the value of this dream. The Sefirah that corresponds to the idea of the Divine as a just and merciful benefactor of mankind is the Sefirah of Hesed, and the path that you are crossing, which leads into Hesed, is the path of Kaph. When we look at the spelling of this dream title we notice that the letter Kaph is also the first letter in the Hebrew word meaning "ransom."

THE JOURNEY We know from the title of this dream that your eagerness for enlightenment is such that you would consider great sacrifices in order to achieve deeper spiritual insight. While the Divine is indeed merciful, the compression of the value of this dream shows that it will take a great deal of positive energy (Shin) to reach Hesed. The path of Kaph is concerned with practical activity, and the final letter in the compression, Vav, represents the more reflective side of your nature. Consequently, an ideal task for you would be to begin a journal that details your key ideas and thoughts about the nature of the Divine.

RAPIDS

mapal mayeem – mphl mym – מפל מים –210

MEANING The element of Water represents the emotions, so this is an extremely emotional dream indeed! This dream represents your emotional drive to come ever closer to the Divine, and quite clearly you have a very strong passion for the Great Work. The value of this dream is equivalent to the value of the Hebrew word meaning "to fly." This association emphasizes the vigor with which you are pursuing your spiritual quest.

THE TREE OF LIFE The letter Mem appears no fewer than three times in the spelling of this dream title, so it is not surprising that this dream is located on the path of Mem. The presence of the powerful water imagery alone would suggest the path of Mem. This path is associated with compassion and altruism along with a maternal approach to those around you. Anyone who would perceive such characteristics as intrinsically passive should consider the raw power and energy that exist in even the least impressive rapids.

THE JOURNEY When we reduce the value of this dream we find the number 3. This indicates that not only are you capable of great empathy for your fellow man but that you should be looking for a creative and innovative means of helping those in need. The compression of the value of this dream tells us that your inspirational willingness to help anyone in need means that you will receive the benefit of the most benevolent aspect of the Divine to help you advance along the Tree of Life. The final letter, Yod, also shows that by sacrificing your desires in favor of the needs of others, you have successfully awakened the Divine spark within yourself.

RATS

khooldah – chvldh – חולדה –53

MEANING If there were a poll to find the most unpopular animal on the planet, rats would have a good chance of topping the list. Rats are notorious for carrying all kinds of diseases including the terrible bubonic plague or Black Death. When we try to consider this dream in a spiritual context, we have to view the rats as a personification of some force within yourself. Since the worst aspect of these animals is their infectious nature we should see them as a vivid metaphor for those aspects of your personality that would seek to disrupt your spiritual work. It is possible that the dream of rats may also represent some external source of disruption and negativity.

THE TREE OF LIFE The value of this dream is equivalent to the value of a Hebrew word meaning "to defend." This association indicates that this dream is not just about the presence of potentially disruptive elements in your personality but is primarily about the need to defend yourself from such threats to your inner journey. When we reduce the value of this dream we find the number 8. This is the value of the letter Cheth, which means "fence." The path of Cheth relates to the defensive force of the Divine and to your ability to protect your soul from negative influences, so this is the path to which your dream belongs.

THE JOURNEY The compression of this dream's value produces the letter Nun, which represents the challenge to your faith that you will experience should those more cynical elements of your nature triumph. The subsequent letter, Gimel, should be seen as a reminder that the wisdom of the Divine is waiting for you if you persevere. The value of this dream is equivalent to that of a Hebrew word meaning "a lover." This may seem like a strange association for this dream until you realize that it refers to your higher self, on whom you should lean to help you to repel your doubts about the validity of your spiritual work.

❧ RATTLE

*sheekshook-shqshvq-*שקשוק-806

MEANING We tend to associate rattles with infants, so we might think that this dream refers to an individual who is somewhat naïve and innocent. In fact rattles are among the earliest forms of musical instruments and were used specifically to try to persuade the appropriate deity to make it rain, bring the sunshine, or fertilize the crops. Bearing this in mind, we should see this dream as representing your attempts to contact the Divine in order to progress in your spiritual development.

THE TREE OF LIFE The initial letter in the compression of this dream's value is the final form of Peh. This letter literally means "mouth," and its presence within the value of this dream reinforces the idea that you are trying to initiate a conversation with the higher forces. The value of this dream reduces to 5, which is the number of the individual who is ruled by his higher self. This places your dream in the Sefirah of Tiferet, as this is the place on the Tree where we are unified with our higher self.

THE JOURNEY Having achieved the integration of your spiritual self, you are now preparing to attempt to make contact with the Divine itself. In the spelling of this dream title we see the repeated pairing of the letters Shin and Qoph. This tells us that while you have sufficient spiritual energy (Shin) to try to communicate, you are troubled by a deep anxiety (Qoph) that you may have reached the pinnacle of your spiritual potential. The letter Vav is present both in the spelling and in the compression of your dream, and this tells you that with sufficient quiet contemplation you will realize that you can continue to climb the Tree all the way to the heights of Keter.

RAZOR

*taar-tha'ar-*תער-670

MEANING In this dream we have another example of the importance of paying close attention to exact words used in any dream's title. We may be inclined to see this dream as simply referring to any sharp blade and would miss out on the key feature of a razor. First of all, a razor is a precision blade, designed to cut without causing injury. Second, but equally important, a razor removes that which is unwanted and in doing so makes us feel better able to face the day ahead. In spiritual terms, this suggests that you are going through a process of refining and

organizing your ideas about the Divine in order to progress with confidence along the Tree of Life.

THE TREE OF LIFE When we reduce the value of this dream we find the number 13, which indicates that you are going through a period of great change. This supports the notion that the image of a razor suggests the cutting away of ideas that are not helpful in order to form a more coherent view of the Divine. In terms of a position on the Tree, this dream belongs on the path of Zayin, as this is the path that involves you in just that process of pruning your spiritual viewpoint as a preparation for reaching the higher branches of the Tree.

THE JOURNEY Most of us find it very difficult to spring clean because we hate to throw away stuff that may have no practical use but to which we have some kind of sentimental attachment. We convince ourselves that wide ties and leisure suits will come back into fashion one day, that the old comics and magazines will be worth a fortune eventually, and so on. Similarly, it is very hard to dispense with ideas that have outgrown their use. This is why the compression of this dream begins with the letter Mem in its final form. This letter tells you that the protective and caring aspect of the Divine will be with you while you are going through this difficult period. The final letter in the compression, Ayin, reminds you of what you are aiming to achieve: a spiritual framework that is uniquely fitted to you and will enable you to stand the best chance of achieving a communion with the Divine itself.

READING

*leekro-lqrva-*לקרוא-337

MEANING Most religions have a single text that its adherents should read and be familiar with so that they can know and understand how to behave and how to perceive their God. The individual seeker of truth has no single book but should read as voraciously as possible on every conceivable subject. This is because your relationship with the Divine is unique, as is your soul, so only you can ultimately determine how best to approach the Great Work. Additionally, the Divine is present in every aspect of the universe, so whether you are reading a nuclear physics text or a cartoon strip, at some level you are increasing your understanding of the universe and consequently coming closer to the Divine.

THE TREE OF LIFE People often characterize reading as an intellectual activity, but in fact it is an activity that should engage all of our senses. Additionally, to read a book fully—that is, to consider it not just as a book but as a window onto the universe—takes a great deal of energy. In terms of the spiritual path, the most intense period of reading should take place quite early in your journey, as the more information you have the better equipped you are to judge your experiences. The most energetic path on the lower branches of the Tree of Life is the path of Shin; it is also the first letter in the compression of this dream's value and so it is here that we locate this dream.

THE JOURNEY When we reduce the value of this dream we find the number 13, and there is no doubt that its association with great change refers to the evolution of your mind and soul that will occur if you persevere with reading in depth about the subject of the Great Work. The second letter in the compression of this dream's value is Lamed, which tells us that there will be times when it will take a nudge from the spiritual to keep you at work. It also suggests that now would be an ideal time for serious study of sacred writings. This is especially the case when you reach the point indicated by the final letter, Zayin, where you have to begin to separate the valuable from the irrelevant in what you have read.

RED

*adom-advm-*אדום-51

MEANING All colors have a specific symbolic significance and red perhaps more than any other color has a universally accepted meaning. No matter where you go in the world, the color red suggests excitement, danger, passion, and, more often than not, conflict. To dream of red is to be in tune with all the emotional states that we associate with that color. In spiritual terms, despite the prominence of associations of conflict in this dream, it suggests that you are moving forward in your spiritual quest.

THE TREE OF LIFE As every color has its symbolic significance, so each Sefirah and each path on the Tree of Life has its associated color. Red is, not surprisingly, the color of the Sefirah of Gevurah. The Sefirah of Gevurah is also known as the Sefirah of Severity, and this fits in well with the emotions that we associate with the color red. The value of this dream is equivalent to the value of the Hebrew word meaning "pain," and this also supports the idea that your dream belongs in Gevurah.

THE JOURNEY The compression of this dream's value produces the letters Nun and Aleph. The combination of these letters tells you that through

an understanding of suffering (Nun), you will approach a better understanding of the essential unity (Aleph) of the Divine. This is perhaps one of the hardest Sefirot to traverse. It requires you to understand that conflict and indeed mortality are as much a part of the nature of the Loving Divine as are any of the more obvious, positive characteristics that come to mind when we imagine the nature of God. When we reduce the value of this dream we find the number 6. This is the value of the letter Vav and is an encouragement to you to meditate on the impact of the inclusion of the Sefirah of Severity in your concept of the Divine.

RELIGION

*dat-dth-*דת-404

MEANING Religion can be found in every culture in the world and has been present in every culture throughout history. It provides a source of comfort and can aid a genuine search for the Divine itself. When we look at the value of this dream, we see the central 0, which represents the undefined nature of the Divine. Flanking this representation of God is the number 4, which signifies the world of the physical. The significance of this arrangement is to show that the substance of religion is removed to a degree from the actual nature of the Divine as it is being shaped by the world of the physical.

THE TREE OF LIFE Whereas religion takes the spiritual and shapes it so that it can be easily conveyed to the majority of the population, the spiritual quest seeks to discover the Divine in an undiluted form. This dream should be seen as something of a warning that in pursuing truth, you should avoid accepting prepackaged answers to what are deeply personal and individual questions. The value of this dream reduces to 8, which is the value of the letter Cheth. This letter refers to a defensive attitude, and religion can be characterized as an organized defense against the uncertainty of the spiritual dimension. This dream sits on the path of Cheth for this reason, and this position is supported by the fact that the value of this dream is equivalent to the value of the Hebrew word meaning "law," since the religious law is a means of protecting us from uncertainty.

THE JOURNEY Religion can often function as a springboard for an individual to begin exploring the nature of the Divine. This inevitably involves moving away to at least some degree from the strict tenets of any single religion. The compression of the value of this dream tells you that you need to move away from the comfort of religion and cope with the regret (Tav) that this will cause in order to open the door (Daleth) to the absolute nature of the Divine.

RENT

*sekheeroot-shkyrvth-*שכירות-936

MEANING This dream initially appears to be concerned with the material side of life. The idea of rent not only calls to mind the concerns of the day-to-day world but is specifically related to issues of money. However, the value of this dream is equivalent to the value of the Sefirah Keter, when we spell each letter in the title of this Sefirah in full. As Keter represents the highest position on the Tree of Life, this dream implies that you have a very strong spiritual focus. Indeed, the idea of rent is a symbolic representation of paying your respects to, or honoring, the Divine force.

THE TREE OF LIFE The value of this dream reduces to the number 9, and in the context of this dream this number relates to the ninth card in the tarot sequence, which is The Hermit. The Hermit card implies not that you are a recluse but that you have a deep dedication to the Great Work. Additionally, the Hermit card is associated with the path of Yod, and this is the path to which this dream belongs. The path of Yod represents the Divine spark, and it is in waking that Divine spark that we can begin to fully honor the Divine.

THE JOURNEY In the compression of this dream the central letter is Lamed, and this suggests that despite your great enthusiasm for all matters spiritual, you also need to devote time to rigorous study of the subject. Since the compression begins with the letter Tzaddi in its final form, which represents the great commitment you have to the Great Work, the need for the harsh force of Lamed has more to do with a lack of organized study than with a lack of commitment. The final Vav in the compression is a reminder to you that to continue your progression up the Tree, you will need to put your thoughts about the nature of the Divine into some kind of order.

REPRIEVE

*arkah-arkh-*ארכה-226

MEANING Before we can receive a reprieve we must be under some form of sentence. From a psychological point of view, this dream would be seen as a prompt for you to consider what event from your past has you so knotted up with guilt that you would dream about gaining a reprieve. The value of this dream is equivalent to the value of a Hebrew word meaning "profound," and this suggests that there is a deeper spiritual significance to this dream.

THE TREE OF LIFE When we reduce the value of this dream we find the number 10, and this points to the Sefirah of Malkut as the location for your dream. Additionally, the value of this dream is equivalent to that of the Hebrew word meaning "north." The Sefirah of Malkut and its element, the element of Earth, are associated with the northerly direction of the compass. The location of this dream in Malkut makes sense of the content of the dream itself. The potential reprieve is the opportunity to free yourself from the bonds of the merely physical.

THE JOURNEY Another word that shares its value with the value of this dream title is the Hebrew word meaning "hidden." This refers to the fact that the escape from Malkut is never easy. The compression of the value of this dream begins with the letter Resh, which points both to the need for you to use careful judgment when deciding how to pursue the spiritual path and to the benevolent influence of the Divine. The central letter, Kaph, makes it clear that the ideal way for you to begin the Great Work would be through some form of practical activity. You should seriously consider learning one of the martial arts that has a spiritual dimension, such as one of the forms of Chinese martial art forms.

RESCUE

*hatsalah-htzlh-*הצלה-130

MEANING In the same way that the dream of redemption relates not to any guilt for your actions but to the release from a nonspiritual existence, the dream of a rescue relates not to any physical act of rescue but to a rescue by engagement with the spiritual quest. The value of this dream is equivalent to the value of the Hebrew word meaning "pillars." In the context of this dream, the term *pillars* relates to the pillars of the Tree of Life, which you need to climb in order to effect your rescue.

THE TREE OF LIFE The value of this dream is also equivalent to the value of the Hebrew word meaning "eye." This word is, of course, *Ayin*, and it is to the path of Ayin that we should assign this dream. This is a path that is concerned with the vigorous pursuit of one's own path through life and specifically the development of one's spiritual framework. This makes it clear that you are not dreaming of a rescue from the prison of the merely material but of a rescue from a spiritual path that relies entirely on the ideas of others.

THE JOURNEY It is very liberating to begin to formulate your own thoughts and theories based on the particular spiritual experiences that you have had thus far in your quest for the Divine. It is also as nerve-racking as it is exciting, and the letter Qoph, which begins the compression of this dream's value, tells us that you are indeed quite anxious about the idea of facing the Great Work alone. The presence of the letter Lamed in the compression of your dream is an indication that, worried or not, you will be pushed to take the risk of thinking for yourself in regard to spiritual matters. The reduction value of this dream produces the value of the letter Daleth, and this advises you that in taking this important step you will be opening the door to the truly spiritual.

RESIGNING

*heetpatroot–hthphtrvth–*הרתפטרות*–*1100

MEANING This dream is not nearly as negative as it might first appear. We live in a world that is excessively concerned with success, particularly in career terms. As a result, the idea of resigning immediately puts us in mind of quitting one's job, so we are unlikely to see this as a bid for freedom but will perceive it as a career-damaging mistake. This dream encourages you to move on to new pastures and accept that those areas of your life that have drawn to a close have done so for a reason. Additionally, this dream refers to the process of resigning yourself to the will of the Divine. This means accepting that the wisdom of the higher forces will ensure that no matter what fate throws at you, as long as you remain committed to the spiritual quest you will ultimately achieve some form of communion with the Divine.

THE TREE OF LIFE It is always hard to hand over control to a third party. It is almost overwhelmingly difficult when you are talking about the control of nearly your whole life. Additionally, our culture teaches us that control and power are the key goals to achieve in order to ensure success. The value of this dream is the number 11 multiplied by 100. The number 11 indicates that you are undergoing a deeply significant spiritual experience, especially as it is present in a form that greatly increases its value. The act of resigning yourself to the Divine will requires a level of spiritual insight that returns

you to a state of almost pure innocence, so we place this dream on the path of Aleph.

THE JOURNEY Standing on the path of Aleph, you are but a step away from the source of the Divine, the Sefirah of Keter. Although you are incredibly close to the achievement of a communion with the Divine, you are still very anxious about how you should go about taking that final step. The letter Qoph is the only letter that appears in the compression of this dream, and this points to the almost all-consuming nature of your uncertainty. However, the solution to your worries lies in the very title of this dream. All you have to do is relax and resign yourself to the force of the Divine and the advice of your higher self, and your intuition will point you in the right direction.

RESTRAINT

*havlagah–hblgh–*הבלגה*–*45

MEANING The value of this dream is equivalent to the value of a Hebrew word that refers to The Fool card in the tarot. As The Fool card is associated with the path of Aleph, we might think that this dream represents a very high level of spiritual achievement. However, when we consider the content of this dream and its other values, we see that this is not strictly the case. In fact, the reference to The Fool card is there to advise you that you need to act with restraint in your spiritual quest at this time in order to avoid literally being foolish.

THE TREE OF LIFE If we add together the numbers from 1 to 9 consecutively, we will arrive at the value of your dream. Additionally, the value of this dream reduces to the number 9. Both of these factors point to your dream's being positioned on the ninth Sefirah on the Tree of Life, which is Yesod. This is supported by the fact that within the Western Mystery Tradition the symbolic number of the Sefirah of Yesod is 45. This location on the Tree of Life is the first that you will come to after leaving Malkut, and very often we can become carried away with our enthusiasm for anything that has even a hint of the spiritual. Consequently, the dream of restraint serves as a timely warning.

THE JOURNEY Having reached the Sefirah of Yesod, you need to begin to formulate some kind of approach to the Great Work. This should certainly involve your reading as much as possible about all systems of spirituality. Equally important, you should make some initial forays into practical expressions of your desire to progress up the Tree of

Life. The compression of this dream advises you that the maternal aspect of the Divine (Mem) will be there to help you avoid following a system that will not actually help you to move forward. The final letter, Heh, means "window" and should be seen as sensible advice that you need to look before you leap into any commitment to a particular approach to the Divine.

RESURRECTION

*tekheeyah–thchyyh–*תחייה*–*433

MEANING Although the idea of resurrection is associated in most people's minds with the Christian religion, it is in fact a common feature of a number of religions, although many of them have now vanished or have a very small number of followers. When we consider the notion of resurrection in terms of a dream analysis, we need to avoid interpreting it simply from a Christian perspective and instead focus on the nature of a resurrection as an event. To die and be brought back to life indicates a complete change of attitude toward life and likely a rearrangement of your inner nature.

THE TREE OF LIFE In terms of your spiritual development, the notion of being killed and then brought back to life fits strongly with many ideas about the experience of contacting your higher self for the first time. The contact itself requires that you rearrange your mental and emotional perceptions in a way that integrates a spiritually based way of looking at the world. Additionally, once you have made contact with your higher self, your ego-based personality is effectively replaced as you allow yourself to be ruled by your soul. The value of this dream reduces to 10, and this indicates the completion of a major cycle in your life. That cycle is the process of approaching Tiferet; you have now arrived in that Sefirah and are ready to be united with your higher self.

THE JOURNEY The value of this dream is a prime number (a number that can be divided only by itself and by one), and this tells us that you are a rare individual. While all of us have the potential to reach the Tiferet, very few people actually have the commitment to achieve this goal. The compression of your dream's value tells us that as positive as this experience is for you, there will be a degree of regret (Tav) at the life you will be leaving behind. Moreover, you will be tempted to see this as the end of your inner journey, and the letter Lamed indicates that the harsh force of the Divine will push you on to find creative (Gimel) ways of approaching the Di-

vine itself. It would be very helpful and instructive on a practical level to learn to let go of some aspect of your day-to-day life. There may be a possession or activity or even an attitude to which you are unhealthfully wedded and you should now try to leave it behind you.

REVENGE

*nekemah–nqmh–*נקמה*–*195

MEANING If you genuinely wish to advance spiritually, you need to be able to rise above such emotional drives as the desire for revenge. While it is perfectly appropriate to wish for justice if you have been wronged, you should not pursue the possibility of revenge. As soon as you allow yourself to be consumed with vengeful thoughts, you have handed over a large portion of your life to the person against whom you bear a grudge. In purely spiritual terms, this dream suggests that you are still carrying various resentments about your day-to-day life and that this is interfering with your spiritual progress.

THE TREE OF LIFE The value of this dream is equivalent to the value of a Hebrew word meaning "flock." The implication here is that in baying for revenge you are allowing yourself to follow a herd instinct rather than having the inner strength to follow those principles that you know are in accordance with the higher will. Resentment and revenge are both examples of the danger of engaging in the judging of others. The path of Shin is associated with the exercise of judgment, so this dream belongs on the negative aspect of the path of Shin.

THE JOURNEY The initial letter, Qoph, in the compression of the dream's value reveals that in truth your vengeful thoughts are born not so much of anger but of fear. In spiritual terms, this suggests that your fear of failure in the Great Work is unconsciously driving you to find aspects of your material life that can be held responsible if your spiritual work does not yield the hoped-for results. Your commitment to the spiritual path (Tzaddi) is not in doubt, but your lack of self-belief puts you in danger of behaving in ways that are counterproductive to your spiritual goals. The final letter in the compression tells you that you need to begin to resolve this problem by taking a very close look through the window (Heh) of your soul. This is so that you can see that you have as many faults to correct as the next person, but also that you have the same potential for success.

REVULSION

*leheetkomem-lhthqvmm-*לההתקומם-621

MEANING Some dreams leave us feeling happy and contented when we wake. Unfortunately, there are also dreams that make us wish that we could crawl away under the nearest stone and hide for a day or two. This dream falls very much into the latter category. The fact that nobody wants to have a dream in which he is revolted does not mean that this dream is negative in terms of its implications about the level of your spiritual development.

THE TREE OF LIFE The letter Mem appears twice in the spelling of this dream title. What is more, the two letters appear side by side, and the second letter is emphasized even more by the fact that it appears in its final form. These factors combine to place this dream firmly on the path of Mem. Since the path of Mem is concerned with a desire to engage in compassionate acts, we can infer that the revulsion in your dream refers to an extreme dislike of all forms of exploitation and inequality. The value of this dream is equivalent to that of the Hebrew word meaning "byways," and this suggests that you really will go out of your way to try to help those in need.

THE JOURNEY When we reduce the value of this dream we find the number 9, which is the value of the letter Teth. This letter points to your great strength of character and willpower, which will help you to cope with the range of difficult sights you will see if you pursue your altruistic concerns. The initial letter, Mem, in the compression of this dream's value certainly urges you to maintain your compassionate attitude, while the letter Kaph tells you that you are right to try to act on your feelings of empathy. Moreover, the final letter, Aleph, hints that if you persevere you will be able to achieve some form of communion with the transcendent Divine itself.

RIB

tsela-tzla'a צלע-190

MEANING Unless you are a fast-food junkie, to dream of a rib does not mean that you are fantasizing about your favorite form of take-out food! In fact, this dream does have a strong tie to the material world, but in a more profound way than to remind you what sort of dinner you prefer. We have all heard or read the story of the creation of the first woman from the rib of the first man. This association refers us back to the nature of our physical

state, especially the fact that despite our creation from material components we are the result of a Divine intervention in the universe.

THE TREE OF LIFE When we reduce the value of this dream we find the number 10. In the context of this dream, this number relates to the Sefirah of Malkut. It is here that we should assign this dream since it relates to a person who has yet to properly begin his spiritual quest. The value of this dream is equivalent to the value of a Hebrew word meaning "inner." This association is an indication that while you are still languishing in Malkut, you are beginning to recognize the existence of an inner life that is far more real and enriching than your normal day-to-day existence.

THE JOURNEY This dream is an attempt by your higher self to awaken you to the presence of the Divine. Your key task over the next few weeks should be to follow up on that wake-up call by spending as much time as possible trying to look at the world from a spiritual perspective and seeking out evidence of the Divine in the everyday world around you. The compression of this dream's value suggests that you may not feel entirely comfortable doing this (Qoph). However, if you persist and demonstrate your commitment (Tzaddi) to the Divine, you will be laying down some firm foundations on which to build your spiritual beliefs.

RIBBON

*seret-srt-*סרט-269

MEANING We associate ribbons with a desire to look attractive or pretty and may be inclined to interpret this dream as indicating an excessive concern on the part of the dreamer with his physical appearance. If we were to look for a deeper spiritual significance, we again might take a negative view of this dream and see it as representing an attempt by your unconscious to put an encouraging dressing on your spiritual progress, which is not as successful as it might be. However, when we begin to delve into the values within the dream, it becomes clear that we are faced with a very positive reflection of your spiritual understanding.

THE TREE OF LIFE A ribbon is often used to wrap a present. From a Kabbalistic point of view, we can see the absorption and accumulation of spiritual insight as a gift that comes directly from the Divine. It is very important that this precious wisdom is protected and treated with the respect and appreciation it deserves. When we reduce the value of this dream we find the number 8, which is the value of the letter Cheth. The letter Cheth refers to the protective force of the Divine and so is highly appropriate to both the content and the spiritual significance of this dream.

THE JOURNEY The image of a ribbon tells us that you are protective of all the ideas and beliefs that you have accumulated as you have climbed your way up the Tree of Life. The compression of this dream's value suggests that you now need to begin to exercise a careful process of organization (Resh) of these various ideas to form a definite spiritual framework. The letter Samech indicates that you will be supported by your higher self in this process, and in undertaking this analysis and organization you will be demonstrating your strength of character (Teth) to the Divine.

RIDDLES

kheedah-chydh- חידה-27

MEANING We do not have to look far to see the spiritual aspect of this dream. The universe itself can be characterized as one great riddle, and our role in life is to try to unravel as much of this mystery as possible. When we reduce the value of this dream we find the number 9, which is the value of the letter Teth. The meaning of the letter Teth is "serpent." The route that leads up from the Sefirah of Malkut to Keter is known as the Serpent Path. When we consider the maze of coils that make up the body of the serpent whose tail is in the physical and whose head rests on the Crown of the Tree, we can see its association with the idea of riddles.

THE TREE OF LIFE The value of this dream is equivalent to that of the Hebrew word meaning "purity." At the spiritual level, almost all of your progress depends on your finding viable solutions to a number of riddles about the nature of the Divine. It takes a very clear head and a firm devotion to the Great Work to have a chance of unraveling the layers of metaphor, symbol, and parable in order to find those rare kernels of truth. The Sefirah of Hod is concerned with all matters intellectual, and as this dream focuses on an intellectual approach to the spiritual it is here that we should locate the dream of riddles.

THE JOURNEY While this dream does concentrate on the use of your mental faculties to succeed in the Great Work, the letter Kaph, which begins the compression of this dream's value, tells us that you

also need to find some practical application for the insights that you achieve. The letter Zayin completes this dream's compression. Its literal meaning is "sword," and this gives a strong hint to the way in which you should apply your hard-won wisdom. Many people lack your ability to cut through the confusing array of information that is available regarding the nature of the spiritual. This dream suggests that you should make a point of trying to help those people to achieve some kind of clarity in their worldview by showing them how to separate the useful from the suspect.

RING

zeerah-zyrh- זיירה-222

MEANING This dream is not about jewelry but relates to a ring in the sense of an arena or perhaps a boxing ring. The first thing that we notice about the value of this dream is that it consists of the number 2 repeated three times. The number 2 represents a dualistic way of looking at the world. In other words, the number 2 suggests a person who has very clear ideas about the nature of right and wrong. When we see the world as a series of oppositions rather than as a place in which distinctions are blurred or fuzzy, we immediately create conditions that are likely to provoke conflict.

THE TREE OF LIFE The value of this dream is equivalent to the value of the Hebrew phrase meaning "I will chase." This tells us that, while your dualistic view of the world runs counter to the spiritually enlightened perception of the nature of difference, you are eagerly pursuing the spiritual goal. The reduction value of this dream produces the number that is the value of the letter Vav. As the letter Vav is associated with contemplative reflection, you are being advised to slow down a little and simply sit and be still. Consequently we place your dream on the path of Vav.

THE JOURNEY The first letter in the spelling of this dream title is Zayin, and this suggests that your approach to the Divine has been a vigorous one where you have hastily cut away any ideas that seem to threaten the clarity of your conception of the spiritual universe. This has unfortunately led you to avoid facing some of the real complexities of the Great Work. The initial Resh in the compression of this dream tells you to try to take a more cautious and careful approach to judging the validity of different spiritual viewpoints. If you can achieve this change in attitude, not only will your practical day-to-day existence be easier (Kaph) but you will have a much better chance of arriving at the home (Beth) of the Divine.

RISING

aleeyah-a'alyyh-עלייה-125

MEANING In almost all cultures, increasing levels of success are symbolized by images of rising or climbing. In a nonspiritual context, this relates to the fact that traditionally the more powerful you were, the higher you would sit when eating or in meetings of any kind. From a Kabbalistic perspective, this dream indicates rising on the Tree of Life or simply climbing out of the world of the physical up to the sphere of the Divine. The earliest Jewish mystics of the Merkabah based their quest for the Divine on a complicated meditation system which used the image of a chariot ascending through the levels of heaven as a meditation tool.

THE TREE OF LIFE When we reduce the value of this dream we find the number 8. In the context of this dream, the number 8 functions in its role as a symbol of eternity. This emphasizes the fact that you are very committed to and focused on the Great Work. The idea of rising suggests a path on the middle pillar of the Tree of Life, as this is the route that ascends from Malkut to Keter. Consequently, we should place this dream on the path of Samech, and this reassures you that you are indeed moving toward a deeper understanding of the nature of eternity.

THE JOURNEY You have a strong desire to reach the haven of Tiferet, where you will be able to make contact with your higher self. However, the dream's compression tells us that you are worried (Qoph) that you may have ascended as far as you can on the Tree. You should find some practical activity (Kaph) such as yoga, as this will increase your awareness of the spiritual and bring you closer to a union with your higher self (Heh) within Tiferet.

RITUALS

poolkhan-pvlchn-פולחן-174

MEANING We all have rituals of one kind or another that structure our lives. They do not have to be spiritual in nature; it could be that you have to get dressed and ready for work in a particular order each day. Although such habits may seem trivial, they can be enormously important in creating a frame of mind that allows us to focus on the business of the day. When we do look at this dream in a Kabbalistic context, it is quite clear that you are taking your inner journey extremely seriously and are attempting to find some formal ways of ensuring positive results from your efforts.

THE TREE OF LIFE In most religions, the rituals that an individual worshiper engages in are prescribed by some authoritative voice or person. However, when you take up the challenge of the Great Work, your role is to construct your own way of approaching the Divine. The central letter in the compression of this dream is Ayin, and this represents the path on which this dream is placed. The path of Ayin is concerned with the vigorous pursuit of one's particular approach to the Divine.

THE JOURNEY When we reduce the value of this dream, we find the number 3. This is the supreme number of creativity within the universe. The reason for its presence in this dream is to advise you to create your own understanding of the Divine rather than simply follow the preordained system of any specific religion. This does not mean that you should not engage in spiritual work on a regular basis, but that the way in which you engage in that work should be unique to you.

RIVAL

meetkhareh-mthchrh-מתחרה-653

MEANING From a psychological point of view, this dream would be seen as an indication that you are being challenged by a colleague or other individual in your life. In a spiritual context, this dream relates more to yourself, so the idea of a rival represents not another person but an aspect of your personality. We spend much of our lives trying to deal with some form of inner conflict. Often we are not even consciously aware of the fact that we are living with conflicting opinions within our minds.

THE TREE OF LIFE The role of the spiritual quest could be seen, at least in part, as a process of self-integration. The intended result is the removal of all areas of inner conflict so that you can progress through life with much greater sense of purpose both spiritually and in terms of your day-to-day existence. Right now the attempt to achieve this integration is being challenged, and this is because in achieving a spiritual consciousness we must face up to all of our inner doubts and fears. This is the work of the path of Nun, so it is here that we position your dream.

THE JOURNEY As difficult as it is to come to terms with the range of painful memories that we all possess, the compression of this dream tells you that you are being supported by the matenal aspect of the Divine. However, you may still have to deal with the melancholy that goes with the challenge to your faith represented by the path of Nun, which occupies the central position of the dream's compression. As a promise of your ultimate reward, the compression ends with the letter Gimel. This refers to the secret wisdom that waits for you if you persevere. The letter Gimel also suggests that you consider a more creative approach to dealing with your inner pain; you could, for instance, try to exorcise your fears by painting them or writing about them.

❧RIVER

nahar-nhr-נהר-255

MEANING At a very simplistic level, the dream of a river calls to mind the element of Water and so suggests that your dream is focused on your emotional state in terms of your relationship to the Divine. However, this dream also uses the technique recognized by psychological dream analysis whereby the subject of a dream refers obliquely to some saying or proverb that relates to the more detailed meaning of the dream. In the case of your dream, the saying in question is that "still waters run deep." This suggests that the emotional issues in this dream are far from straightforward. The power and momentum of a river indicate that you need to make significant changes in your emotional responses to the world, and this probably relates to your sense of personal empowerment.

THE TREE OF LIFE The value of this dream reduces to 12, and this is the number associated with The Hanged Man card in the tarot. Both the number and the card refer to an individual who possesses an altruistic nature and is willing to offer his compasssion and assistance to anyone who needs it. Such characteristics place this dream on the path of Mem. This path is doubly appropriate since its literal meaning is "water," so it also links directly with the content of your dream. It is important that while helping others, you also ensure that you yourself are changing and learning to be more in control of the momentum and direction of your life.

THE JOURNEY The complexity of your emotional state is indicated in the spelling of your dream title. The initial letter, Nun, indicates that your faith is being tested, while the final letter, Resh, suggests an outgoing and optimistic personality. Your personal optimism will possibly be the key

to ensuring that you can accept the need for change in your life and have the confidence to empower yourself. The central letter, Heh, which mediates between the two, represents the opportunity of a glimpse into the true nature of the Divine. It also acts a reminder that you need to learn to use your inner strength in order to allow yourself to see the world from your perspective as well as through the eyes of those around you.

❧ROAD

derekh-drk-דרך-224

MEANING The spiritual quest is a journey, albeit an internal one, so this dream relates directly to the Great Work. Specifically, it suggests that you are dreaming of discovering a definite route to the destination where you will find the answers to your deepest questions. The value of this word is equivalent to the value of the Hebrew word meaning "union." This association emphasizes the whole purpose of the Great Work, which is to achieve a sense of union with the Divine. In order to achieve this it may be necessary for you to undertake a certain amount of travel, as indicated by the content of this dream.

THE TREE OF LIFE When we look at the spelling of this dream title we notice that the letter Kaph appears in it final form. The letter Kaph is associated with practical approaches to the spiritual quest, and since it also occupies the central position in the compression of this dream's value, it is here that we should position your dream.

THE JOURNEY The value of this dream is equivalent to the value of the Hebrew word meaning "male." Symbolically, the male gender represents the attempt to adapt the world around us to suit our needs. This fits both with the practical aspect of the letter Kaph and with the dream image of a road. The practical aspect of the letter Kaph may also refer to the need for you to take a small number of trips in order to deepen your understanding. Your task over the next few months is to try to build yourself a structure of activity that will help you to better understand the nature of Divine. This should include something practical such as building yourself a physical space that will be devoted entirely to the Great Work. The final letter, Daleth, in the compression of this dream indicates that if you can dedicate a space to your inner journey, you will have opened the door to spiritual success.

See Zohar symbol, Highway, Road.

ROCKS
*sela-sla'a-*סלע-160

MEANING The image of rocks does not exactly inspire you or make you feel that your unconscious is trying to tell you that you are making excellent progress in any aspect of your life. In fact, the image of rocks is used by your unconscious exactly because it carries connotations of difficulty and of being halted in your progress. The phrase "stranded on the rocks" is just one of many that represents the negative aspect of this dream. However, as always with such dreams, you should remember that in dreaming of being on the rocks you have already taken a step forward in recognizing that you are not currently increasing your spiritual understanding.

THE TREE OF LIFE Rocks are the basic material of the world and as such they represent the Sefirah of Malkut. This is world of the purely physical, and you must climb free of its restrictions in order to begin the Great Work. A very positive sign is the fact that the value of this dream is equivalent to the value of the Hebrew word meaning "tree." This is a direct reference to the chance you have to climb up the Tree of Life to spiritual freedom.

THE JOURNEY Another Hebrew word that shares its value with this dream is the word meaning "silver." This is the metal that is most associated with the Sefirah of Yesod. As Yesod lies immediately above the Sefirah of Malkut, this association acts as an encouragement for you to begin the journey of self-exploration. The compression of this dream tells us that you are very anxious about beginning the long voyage (Qoph). However, it also tells you, by the presence of the letter Samech, that your higher self will be there at all times to guide you and help you find the right path.

ROGUE
*nokhel-nvkl-*נוכל-106

MEANING There is a world of difference between a rogue and a simple thief or crook. While we unanimously despise thieves for their greed and their lack of honesty and concern for anyone other than themselves, we have a soft spot for rogues. The suggestion of the word is of someone who may be operating on the wrong side of the law but who has an intrinsically charismatic or generous nature. In spiritual terms, this dream indicates that you are not exactly following the spiritual path with absolute rigor but are genuinely eager to develop your un-

derstanding. The value of this dream is equivalent to the value of the Hebrew word meaning "linen thread." The image of a thin thread represents the very fine connection between your approach to the Great Work and an approach that could be considered rigorous or committed!

THE TREE OF LIFE The value of this dream is equivalent to the value of the letter Nun when spelled in full, and it is here that we should position your dream. The path of Nun is associated with a challenge to your faith. This does not seem to fit with your dream, until we realize that your slightly cavalier approach to the Divine is part of that challenge and that in some ways it is coming from within you.

THE JOURNEY When we reduce the value of this dream we find the number 7, which is the value of the letter Zayin. This letter means "sword" and in the context of this dream should be seen as a strong indication of how you should begin to reassess your approach to the Divine. It is essential that you begin to cut away all the activities that you engage in simply to avoid dealing with the spiritual quest. The letter Qoph in the compression of this dream tells us that you are indeed anxious, and this is understandable. However, if you wish to experience the macrocosm or the Divine itself as represented in the compression by the letter Vav, then you need to act now and take a far more disciplined approach to the Great Work. You can achieve this partly by identifying those aspects of your nature that are "roguish" and ensuring that they come into play only when there is a legitimate reason to challenge authority or accepted wisdom.

ROOF
*gag-gg-*גג-6

MEANING It might seem that there should be very little to say in Kabbalistic terms about a dream that has only two letters in its title. In fact, this is a highly portentous dream and indicates a considerable degree of spiritual insight on the part of the dreamer. If you simply look at the content and remember that a house in a dream represents the personality of the dreamer, you will realize in dreaming about a roof you are focusing on the highest aspects of your nature. Furthermore, a roof's function is to protect the rest of the house, and in a similar manner you are concentrating on the development of your soul in order to protect yourself.

THE TREE OF LIFE The spelling of this dream title consits of the letter Gimel repeated. The path of Gimel represents the point in your spiritual development when you begin to access the hidden wisdom of the Divine. This is why the Western Mystery Tradition associates The High Priestess card in the tarot with this path. The value of this dream is equivalent to that of the Hebrew word meaning "gather," and this underlines the fact that your dream belongs on the path of Gimel because it relates to the gathering of wisdom that you are about to undertake.

THE JOURNEY The total value of this dream is 6, and this relates to the macrocosm. "Macrocosm" is another term for the Divine, and we can see the traditional association of the number 6 with the Creator when we look at the seal of Solomon or the Star of David. You are on the verge of having a sense of direct communion with the Divine itself. It is important that you prepare yourself both mentally and spiritually for this event. However, at this stage we cannot prescribe how best to do this. The double presence of the letter Gimel indicates that any preparations should depend entirely on your interpretation of the spiritual realm and your ability to think in creative and innovative ways.

ROOTS

*shoresh-shvrsh-*שורש*-806*

MEANING From a psychological angle, we might see this dream as reflecting a desire within the dreamer to explore his ancestry or heritage, possibly out of curiosity or perhaps to achieve a sense of closure regarding some emotional issue. From a spiritual point of view, this dream refers to your wish to return to your spiritual roots, and this means getting in touch with your higher self.

THE TREE OF LIFE The letter Shin appears twice in the spelling of this dream title, and so we might expect this dream to be placed on the path of Shin. This is not the case, though, as the content of this dream indicates that you have achieved a state of consciousness that is higher on the Tree than the path of Shin. The presence of this letter is meant to tell you that it will take a great deal of raw energy to achieve the longed-for contact with your higher self. The union with your spiritual self takes place in the Sefirah of Tiferet and can be represented symbolically by the five-pointed star or pentagram. The reduction value of this dream produces the number 5 and so suggests that you are very close to your goal. Consequently, we should place your dream on the path of Samech, which leads up into Tiferet.

THE JOURNEY You already know that you will have to draw on all your reserves of spiritual energy in order to make the leap into Tiferet. It will also be very helpful for you to draw on your personal roots. You should try to recall which aspects of spirituality attracted you or made sense to you as a child and begin to revisit those ideas. The compression of this dream presents you with details of how best to work toward that transition. The central O in the value of this dream symbolizes the Divine itself, which you are trying to approach. The initial letter, Peh in its final form, tells you that you need to try to initiate a dialogue of sorts with your higher self in order to succeed. The final letter, Vav, suggests that the best way to establish that dialogue would be through meditation and quiet contemplation.

ROPE

*khevel-chbl-*חבל*-40*

MEANING Without the benefit of Kabbalistic analysis, this dream would be difficult to interpret. The notion of rope does not have any definite implications; it could be viewed as negative in that rope can be a means of tying us down or restricting us. Equally we can see this as a positive dream in that rope can be used to secure important items to prevent them from falling or being blown away. The spelling of this dream title begins with the letter Cheth, which means "fence." This strongly suggests that a protective energy is being represented by this dream, so we now know that it is the idea of rope as a means of securing that which is precious to us.

THE TREE OF LIFE The value of this dream is the same as the value of the letter Mem. This letter means "water" and is connected with ideas of compassion and altruism as well as the more maternal aspect of the Divine. Such associations fit well with the meaning of this dream, and we should place this dream on the path of Mem. The suggestion here is that you are expressing your spirituality by attempting to offer your assistance to those in need. Your willingness to help those around you is in part responsible for the fact that you are currently feeling the protective force of the Divine.

THE JOURNEY The Great Work is essentially a solitary project. Its goal is the refinement of your soul so that you may come closer to understanding yourself and the nature of the Divine. However, in the process of developing your inner nature you should also increase your empathy for your fellow man. The final Lamed in the spelling of this dream tells us that there is a driving force pushing you toward an altruistic approach to life. You should try to find a charity that is in need of volunteers and devote as much of your time as possible to helping your chosen cause.

ROSE

shoshanah–shvshnh–שושנה–661

MEANING The value of this dream is equivalent to the value of the Hebrew name "Esther." Esther is a very significant figure in the Kabbalistic tradition. The festival of Purim in the Jewish calendar was created to celebrate the ridding of the enemies of the Jews thanks to the righteousness of Esther and her uncle Mordechai. This dream should be seen as an indication that you are both spiritually beautiful and scrupulously honest and loyal in your dealings with people around you. At a spiritual level, this dream tells us that you are loyal to the Great Work and to the need to focus on your inner development.

THE TREE OF LIFE One of the terms used to describe the path of Kaph is "The Faithful Intelligence." This is an ideal description of the attitude that is exemplified by this dream and embodied in you in the way in which you behave in your day-to-day life. Additionally, you demonstrate a great faith and loyalty in the way in which you maintain your commitment to the spiritual quest. This loyalty will bring its rewards in the same way as Esther received her reward in the story from the Torah.

THE JOURNEY When we reduce the value of this dream we find the number 13. This is the number that indicates great changes ahead in your spiritual life. These will be positive changes, marked by an increase in your understanding and a sense of greater closeness to the Divine. If you maintain your serious study of spiritual matters you will be rewarded by the encouraging force of the Divine, represented in the compression of this dream by the letter Mem. Additionally, the letter Samech indicates that you will be able to attune yourself to the support and guidance of your higher self. The final letter, Aleph, represents the absolute unity of the Divine that ultimately awaits you.

ROYALTY

malkhoot–mlkvth–מלכות–496

MEANING Since one of the proudest moments in American history was its declaration of independence from England, we might not be inclined to see royalty in a positive light. However, we should remember that in the Kabbalistic tradition royalty is very important. Many of the key figures in the Torah are members of a royal household. Additionally, we can see the idea of royalty in a more abstract sense, as representing nobility of spirit, honor, and a commitment to fulfilling one's destiny in life.

THE TREE OF LIFE The appropriate location for this dream on the Tree of Life is given away by the Hebrew spelling of the dream's title. The Hebrew word meaning "royalty" is the same as the word meaning "kingdom." The literal meaning of "Malkut," the title of the tenth Sefirah, is "kingdom." Further, the reduction value of this dream produces the number 10, which again links directly with the Sefirah of Malkut. Even though this is the bottom Sefirah on the Tree, you should not see this as a negative dream, as it contains much promise for your future development.

THE JOURNEY In many dreams we would see the presence of Malkut as a suggestion that you are too concerned with the purely physical world and not sufficiently focused on the Great Work. However, we also need to take into account the content of this dream. As we have said, royalty is very important in the Kabbalistic tradition, and we should see this dream as indicating a desire on your part to manifest your spiritual ideals in the real world. In other words, you have a sense of obligation to improve the state of the world for your fellow man. This is a very positive response to the realization of the spiritual reality of the universe, and you will find that if you follow your instincts, your spiritual insight will also grow.

RUBBISH

zevel–zbl–זבל–39

MEANING It is hard to see why this dream should be viewed in anything other than a negative light. On a psychological level, dreaming of rubbish suggests a deep dissatisfaction with one's life and sense of direction. On a spiritual level, it would seem to imply either a lack of belief or that you are engaging in practices that will do nothing to enhance your understanding of the universe. However, the value of this word is equivalent to the value of the Hebrew word meaning "dew." Dew falls in the morning and is a beautiful but very transient natural phenomenon. In a spiritual context, dew could be seen as a symbol of the elusive and wondrous nature of wisdom, and so you are being encouraged to persevere in your quest for truth.

THE TREE OF LIFE The reduction value of this dream produces the number 3. This number is associated with creativity, especially the creativity of ideas. While this demonstrates your sincerity, the image of rubbish tells us that your work has not been entirely successful. The letter Lamed appears both in the spelling and the compression of this dream and should be seen as a symbol of the harsh aspect of the Divine urging you to study deeply and think very carefully before pursuing any particular spiritual path. It is to the path of Lamed that we should attribute this dream.

THE JOURNEY The other letter in the compression of this dream's value is Teth, which means "serpent." This points to the danger of your deceiving yourself into thinking that you have found a valid path to the Divine when in fact you are actually standing still. The initial letter, Zayin, in the spelling of this dream title is telling that you need to be very rigorous when considering the range of spiritual philosophies that are out there. Specifically, you need to spend the next few weeks cutting away any ideas that are simply flattering to your sense of self rather than genuinely likely to advance your understanding of the Divine.

RUBY

*even odem-abn avdm-*אבן אודם-104

MEANING All precious stones and gems have symbolic associations, and the ideas that tend to be associated with rubies are generally known even by those who have no interest in matters of an esoteric or spiritual nature. The ruby is strongly linked with passionate feelings and desires. Before we begin to look at the clues within the values of this dream, we can infer that you are someone who has a great passion for the Great Work. When we do look at the value of this dream, we see that it is equivalent to the value of the letter Tzaddi when spelled in full. The letter Tzaddi means "fishhook" and indicates that you are deeply committed to the spiritual quest.

THE TREE OF LIFE Each Sefirah is associated with a range of ideas and objects including gemstones. The ruby is linked with the Sefirah of Gevurah and it is here that we should locate your dream. This Sefirah is also referred to as the Sefirah of Severity, and it represents the martial qualities of the Divine and in particular the necessary decay and entropy of all things in nature. The association with the Sefirah of Gevurah is underlined by the fact that the value of this dream reduces to 5, and Gevurah is the fifth Sefirah in the Tree of Life.

THE JOURNEY The value of this dream is equivalent to the value of the Hebrew phrase meaning "to give up." This might be seen as a negative association, but in fact it refers to the need to surrender to the wisdom of the Divine. It is relatively easy to accomplish this when the will of the Divine appears to coincide with our conscious ideas of the nature of the universe. However, Gevurah forces us to recognize the importance of those aspects of the world that are harder to reconcile to our notion of the Divine. At this time you need to rely on your great passion for the spiritual quest to help you to accept these more difficult aspects of the higher reality.

A RUIN

*khoorbah-chvrbh-*חורבה-221

MEANING The psychological view that buildings in our dreams represent our personalities holds true in Kabbalistic interpretations of dreams. Consequently, to dream of a ruin suggests strongly that your spiritual outlook has recently been severely challenged and substantially damaged. The implication here is that your whole sense of identity feels that it has been broken down. While this is clearly not a good state of affairs if it continues, it is essential to your spiritual development that you be able to destroy your ego-driven self and then begin to build a new spiritually based identity.

THE TREE OF LIFE When we reduce the value of this dream we find the number 5. In the context of this dream's value, we should see this number as a reference to the five-pointed star or pentagram. This symbol refers to an individual who has brought the four elements within his nature under the control of his higher self. This dream tells us that you have yet to achieve this state but have reached the point where you are no longer ruled by the conflicting desires of the four elements. You are working through the path of Lamed, which, while harsh at times, will force you to look very closely at yourself.

THE JOURNEY You are now very close to achieving some form of union with your higher self. First, though, you must go through the process of rejecting many of the ideas that governed your thoughts and behavior before you discovered the spiritual dimension to your life. The compression of the value of this dream gives you some very valuable advice on how best to approach this transitional phase. You should continue to read and investigate widely, but carefully reflect on each new find (Resh). The central letter, Kaph, tells you that in order to have any chance of reaching a full appreciation of the nature of the Divine (Aleph), you need to engage in some kind of physical or practical activity. An ideal activity would be yoga, as it will help greatly to focus your mind and spirit.

RUNNING

*laroots-lrvtz-*לרוץ-326

MEANING Without the benefit of a Kabbalistic analysis it is very difficult to determine the significance of this dream. At a psychological level, this dream could indicate that you are speeding through life full of positive energy. Equally it could be suggesting that you are filled with worry and are running away from a range of concerns. At the spiritual level, we have the advantage of being to able to analyze the values within the dream as well as the content. The value of this dream is equivalent to the value of the Hebrew word meaning "vision." This clearly implies that you are on the verge of experiencing some form of spiritual revelation, so we can see this dream as entirely positive.

THE TREE OF LIFE Since we now know that this is an encouraging dream, we are looking for a path that represents confident progress toward your spiritual goals. The final letter in this dream title is Tzaddi, which means "fishhook" and indicates that you are hooked on the Great Work. This letter appears in its final form, which emphasizes the importance of your deep commitment at this time. Consequently, we should position your dream on the path of Tzaddi.

THE JOURNEY You are still in the early stages of your spiritual journey, but you are striding ahead with confidence and optimism. The compression of this dream tells us that you have great stores of inner energy (Shin), hence the idea of moving ahead at great speed. The central letter, Kaph, in the dream's compression indicates that you should be directing that energy into some kind of practical project that will help you to reflect (Vav) fully on the nature of the Divine. It may be that you should take time to build a permanent space for yourself that you can use for contemplation and meditation.

RUST

*khaloodah-chlvdh-*חלודה-53

MEANING We associate rust with age, so we might initially think that this dream suggests that you have the wisdom of experience. However, a moment's further thought reminds us that rust tends to occur when an item is not in use. The suggestion in this dream, then, is that you are not making sufficient use of your spiritual capacities and that they are in danger of becoming stagnant unless you take some action in the near future.

THE TREE OF LIFE When we reduce the value of this dream we find the number 8. This number refers to the letter Cheth, which means "fence." This suggests that you are seeking to protect yourself in some way. As the content of this dream indicates that you are not actively seeking to pursue the spiritual quest, it is probable that this protection relates to a fear of the unknown. You have not taken the leap of faith to explore your spiritual nature because you think you will not be comfortable with the results. Consequently, we should place this dream in the Sefirah of Malkut, as this represents the solely physical world.

THE JOURNEY The value of this dream is equivalent to the value of a Hebrew word meaning "wall," and this underlines your reluctance to expose yourself to the risks of the spiritual journey. However, this dream's value is also equivalent to the value of a Hebrew word meaning "lover," and this tells you that the force of the Divine is indeed reaching out to you. You should seriously reflect on the wonderful opportunity that you will be missing if you don't accept the challenge of the Great Work. In order to ease your concerns, you should begin simply by reading as much as possible about the subject of spirituality.

SAFETY

*beteekhoot-btychvth-*בטיחות-435

MEANING Those people who do not have any religious beliefs can sometimes regard those who do have faith as in some way weak. They perceive religious belief as something of an emotional crutch, as a way of providing a sense of safety in one's life. However, in reality, making a strong commitment to the spiritual aspect of your nature is a very risky business, since you have no way of knowing exactly how the Divine will respond. Consequently, we should see this dream as referring to a desire for a sense of certainty, but as a desire that arises out of your commitment to the Great Work rather than a wish that would be solved by making that commitment.

THE TREE OF LIFE When we first start out on a quest for truth we are in a very vulnerable position, since the certainties of the material world have been removed without any new set of certainties taking their place. If we were to add up all the numbers from 1 to 29 we would arrive at the value of this dream. This is significant because the twenty-ninth path on the Tree of Life is the path of Qoph. This is a path that is very much associated with the anxieties that we feel as we begin to explore our inner selves and it is here that we should locate this dream.

THE JOURNEY When we reduce the value of this dream we find the number 13, which indicates that great changes are about to occur in your life. You should see this as an encouraging sign that you are on the way to resolving your anxieties about the validity of your spiritual search. It will help you greatly if you spend at least twenty minutes a day meditating or simply contemplating the nature of the universe. The more you do this, the more you will feel comfortable with the idea of the Divine and your quest for some form of relationship with the creative force.

SAILING
*lehafleeg—lhphlyg—*להפליג*-158*

MEANING Our view of sailing tends to be that it is a luxurious leisure activity, so to dream of sailing might seem to indicate that you either have or long for a life of ease and luxury. However, we need to remember that many years ago sailing was a dangerous pursuit that was undertaken in order to bring home much-needed supplies or food. From a Kabbalistic standpoint, it is this traditional view of sailing that is relevant, as this dream is very much about you, the dreamer, taking on some touch challenges in order to provide yourself with essential supplies of a spiritual nature.

THE TREE OF LIFE The value of this word is equivalent to that of the Hebrew word meaning "balances." This is a positive association since it implies that you are at least beginning to understand the need to approach the world from a position of inner balance and harmony. We often associate the idea of balance and harmony with the path of Samech, but this is not always the appropriate path for such ideas. The central letter in the spelling of this dream is Peh, which refers to all forms of communication. It is the path of Peh that should be the location for this dream, as it is by communicating with your higher self that you will gain the safe harbor of spiritual certainty.

THE JOURNEY In the compression of this dream's value we are told that you have a number of

anxieties (Qoph) about your progress in the Great Work. The following letter, Nun, refers not only to the sailing metaphor for the process by which you can ease your worries, but to the fact that in finding a greater depth to your faith you may also experience a significant degree of sorrow as you come to terms with the hidden fears and doubts that we all have within us. However, the final letter, Cheth, is there to reassure you that at all times the protective force of the Divine will be with you to give you the best chance of plotting the correct course.

SALT
*melakh—mlch—*מלח*-78*

MEANING In the modern world salt has been reduced in importance to just one more condiment on the dining-room table. However, it has great spiritual significance, and this dream has profound implications for your spiritual development. The value of this dream is equivalent to the value of the Hebrew word meaning "bread." This emphasizes the importance of salt as a symbol of the life-giving properties of the earth. At a spiritual level, we should be aware that the value of this dream is equivalent to the value of a Hebrew word referring to the influence that emanates from Keter, so the image of salt also points to the spiritual life-giving properties of the Divine source.

THE TREE OF LIFE Perhaps the most well-known reference to salt in the Judaic tradition is the transformation of Lot's wife into a pillar of salt. This distinctly negative association seems to fly in the face of the very positive statements that have been made about the image of salt. In fact, it serves simply to emphasize that the influence from Keter will have an impact that is relevant and appropriate to your approach to the Divine. If you keep a true path, the influence will be wholly positive. When we reduce the value of this dream we find the number 6, and this is the value of the letter Vav. As the path of Vav is associated with reflection and contemplation, it is an appropriate location for this dream.

THE JOURNEY So far you have taken a very sincere approach to the Great Work and have based your practices and developing spiritual ideas on the wisdom that you have read in a range of spiritual texts. The central letter, Lamed, in the spelling of this dream title indicates the rigorous approach that you have taken to your studies. The time has now come for you to begin to develop your individual relationship with the Divine. This is signified by the letter Ayin, which begins the compression of the value of this dream. You may be concerned about this new development because you do not wish to reduce the positive nature of the influence that you are receiving from the Divine. However, the final letter, Cheth, tells us that the influence of the Divine will act as a protective force to help you to make the right decisions about your spiritual direction.

SAND

khol-chvl-חול-44

MEANING When we think of sand we might imagine beaches, sunshine, and the relaxed enjoyment of a long summer's day. From a Kabbalistic perspective, we need to think much more in terms of deserts and the arid, unforgiving nature of a desert landscape. The value of this dream is equivalent to the value of the Hebrew word meaning "captive," and this association underlines the idea that the dream of sand is not a comfortable one. In a spiritual context, the idea of being captive relates to a sense of being trapped in a soulless world. Bearing this in mind, the image of a desert is enormously evocative of the uninspiring nature of an entirely secular lifestyle.

THE TREE OF LIFE The spelling of this dream title can be seen as telling a story about your state of mind: You are currently feeling defensive (Cheth), but future reflections (Vav) and rigorous application to the Great Work (Lamed) will bring you to a greater understanding of the Divine. The value of this dream is equivalent to the value of the Hebrew word meaning "sorrow." The sorrow that you are suffering is the melancholy that is typically associated with the search for a deeper faith, which requires us to face ourselves honestly and openly. Consequently, we should place this dream on the path of Nun.

THE JOURNEY Even at our lowest point we are able to call on the protective aspect of the Divine. The principle creative force in the universe is one of absolute love, so despite the fact that you are going through a difficult time, the compression of this dream's value indicates through the letter Mem that the maternal aspect of the Divine is with you. Equally positive is the final letter in this dream's compression. The letter Daleth means "door" and tells you that if you persevere, you will be able to open the door that leads to a greater relationship with the higher forces in the universe.

SAPPHIRE

sapeer-sphyr-ספיר-350

MEANING During the renaissance, the Kabbalah was popularized by a number of Christian mystics. As might be expected, a significantly different set of ideas emerged and a number of key words were mistranslated. Thus the confusion arose in which the term *Sephira* was associated with the word *sapphire.* While the dream of a sapphire may not be associated with the Sefirot, by sharing a common name it is nonetheless a dream that has profound implications for your spiritual development.

THE TREE OF LIFE In the spelling of this dream title we find the two letters Peh and Yod. This combination suggests that you have not only awakened the Divine spark within yourself but, using the spiritual energy released by this process, have begun to engage in a dialogue with your higher self. This may be largely or even totally unconscious, but you should notice a greater sense of inner understanding. The sapphire is traditionally associated with the Sefirah of Hesed. This Sefirah represents the merciful and benevolent aspect of the Divine. It is in some ways this aspect of the Divine that reaches down to individuals, so the Sefirah of Hesed is an appropriate location for your dream.

THE JOURNEY When we reduce the value of this dream we find the number 8. This is the value of the letter Cheth, and this ties in directly to the notion of Hesed as standing for the merciful aspect of the Divine, as the letter Cheth refers to protection. You have reached a very high point on the Tree of Life, but, as always, there is room for you to advance even further in your spiritual quest. In addition to the letter Cheth, the letter Samech at the beginning of this dream title tells us that you will be supported and guided in your search for greater wisdom. An ideal task for you would be to attempt to collate your ideas and insights into a coherent whole.

SATAN

satan-shtn-שׂטן-359

MEANING Dreams of Satan are few and far between, but when they occur you are likely to have a very anxious response. Even atheists and agnostics can be significantly shaken by a vivid dream about a personification of absolute evil. However, if we put aside all of the popular cultural references to Satan that originate in a largely Christian context, we will see that in the Torah the figure of Satan does not represent the personification of evil but acts something like a prosecuting angel on behalf of the Divine. Consequently, this dream indicates not that you are about to be visited by some terrible evil but that your faith will be tested over the coming weeks.

THE TREE OF LIFE The value of this dream is equivalent to the value of the Hebrew word meaning "sacred wind." This underlines the fact that this dream is not about the absence of God but is about an experience of the Divine that is likely to be vigorous and challenging. In the spelling of this dream title we see that the letter Nun appears in its final form. This letter is associated with the potential for melancholy and sorrow that accompany the attempt to arrive at a depth of faith that allows some form of communion with the Divine. This dream relates directly to the testing of your inner nature that is linked with the path of Nun, so it is here that we should position this dream.

THE JOURNEY The road ahead over the next few weeks will not be easy, but the letters that make up the title of this dream give an indication of the mental and spiritual tools that will help you to come through the experience as a more enlightened and spiritually alive individual. The initial letter, Shin, points to the raw energy and drive that will help to carry you forward. The letter Teth refers to the strength of character and willpower that will allow you to focus that energy toward a specific goal. The final letter, Nun, indicates the difficulty of this phase in your journey but also tells you that you will emerge with a much more profound understanding of yourself and of the Divine.

SAW

*masor-msvr-*מסור-306

MEANING An image of a saw might seem more appropriate to a book about home improvement than to one looking at the spiritual import of your nocturnal visions. However, as is ever the case with Kabbalah, even the most mundane images can conceal great spiritual significance. The value of this dream is equivalent to that of a Hebrew phrase meaning "Merciful Father," and this tells us that this dream is connected to a very deep sense of commitment to the Great Work and a desire for a direct experience of the Divine.

THE TREE OF LIFE While your spiritual aspirations are clearly very deep and sincere, there is

an undeniably practical flavor to this dream. It is always important to remember that we express our spirituality not just through prayer or meditation. Practical acts can have just as much impact on our inner development as any amount of contemplation. While a saw is a cutting implement, its key function is to prepare materials for construction. At a spiritual level, this can be seen as a symbol for the initial shaping of your soul in preparation for further, more detailed work. As the first Sefirah after the purely physical world of Malkut, the Sefirah of Yesod is an ideal location for your dream.

THE JOURNEY We have already noted that this dream suggests that in order to come closer to the Merciful Father referred to in the title of this dream, you need to engage in some kind of practical project. It is also clear that this activity is a preparation for later, deeper work that will further refine your soul and increase your spiritual insight. Yoga is an ideal gateway into serious spiritual work and is an excellent way of preparing your mind, body, and soul for the road ahead. This dream suggests that you should seriously consider enrolling in yoga classes.

SCALDING

*leegrom kveeyot-lgrym kvvyvth-*לגרום כוויות-727

MEANING This is one of those dreams where you wake up not entirely sure whether you have been dreaming or if you should be feeling real pain. It is difficult to see any merit in being scalded, and at a purely psychological level this dream could be interpreted as being no more significant than a fear of suffering severe pain. However, in a spiritual context, the element of Water represents the emotions, and if the water is scalding, this dream indicates the presence of a great passion and extremely intense feelings.

THE TREE OF LIFE Once we have climbed the initial branches on the Tree of Life our progress becomes much more an evolutionary process. Being scalded is a shock, to say the least. This sense of shock suggests a path that is lower on the Tree of Life. Although this is a dream based in the emotions, the idea of scalding introduces the idea of heat and the element of Fire. The path of Shin is ruled by the element of Fire and relates to a very passionate and energetic initial exploration of the world of the spiritual, so this is where we place your dream.

THE JOURNEY It is wonderful that you are beginning your spiritual quest with such unbounded enthusiasm. However, the compression of this dream's value begins with the letter Nun in its final form. This serves as a warning that in pursuing the Great Work you may have to go through a certain amount of melancholy. The subsequent letter, Kaph, suggests that you should engage in some practical activity that will help you to ground your developing beliefs. The final letter, Zayin, which means "sword," indicates that you should look for some form of vigorous activity such as a spiritually based martial art to help develop your inner understanding.

SCALES

mozney kapot—mazny kphvth— מאזני כפות-614

MEANING When we think of a pair of scales we are likely to think either of cookery or the scales of justice. Not surprisingly, the Kabbalistic interpretation of this dream focuses on the image of scales as a representation of balance rather than of bakery, not that the process of feasting doesn't have its own important place in the Kabbalistic tradition. When we refer to balance we are referring to the internal balance of your personality. The Western Mystery Tradition divides the personality into four elements: Air (the mind), Fire (your passions and energy), Earth (the physical body and its drives), and Water (the emotions). The dream of scales suggests that these elements are in harmony with one another.

THE TREE OF LIFE When we reduce the value of this dream we find the number 11. This highly mystical number suggests that you are about to undergo some form of deeply spiritual revelation. The path on the Tree of Life that is associated with a sense of inner harmony and balance is the path of Samech. This path also runs into the Sefirah of Tiferet. It is in Tiferet that we make contact with our higher self, and this is the deeply significant experience referred to by the number 11, and so we should position your dream on the path of Samech.

THE JOURNEY Throughout history, almost all philosophies, whether religious or secular in nature, have advocated taking a balanced or middle path through life. This dream continues that tradition, but, in keeping with the Kabbalistic perspective, this dream also encourages you to seek some form of internal balance. If it is hard to take a balanced approach to the day-to-day world, it is even harder to find a balance within yourself. The central letter in the compression of this dream's value is Yod. This letter suggests that you have awakened the spark of the Divine within yourself. If you wish to find the right route to take in life to achieve this inner harmony, all you need to do is listen to the voice of your intuition.

SCANDAL

sharooreeyah—sha'arvryyh— שערורייה-801

MEANING We do not tend to associate the idea of scandal with anything approaching a spiritual way of looking at the world. Indeed, the usual locations where we would expect to see evidence of scandal are as far removed from a spiritual environment as it is possible to be. We associate scandal with governments and the glamorous world of the movies, not with the serious-minded world of religious exploration.

THE TREE OF LIFE Those who enjoy scandal are interested in the surface details of things far more than the deeper significance of events and relationships. In spiritual terms, this would imply that while you might be attracted to the mystery and intrigue of the spiritual quest, you have yet to commit to the more important task of developing your soul. The compression of this dream's value produces the final form of the letter Peh. This letter means "mouth" and refers to all forms of communication. Given both the title of this dream and the spiritual message that it contains, the appropriate path is the path of Peh.

THE JOURNEY The implication here is that you need to try to engage in a dialogue with the higher forces as represented by the final letter, Aleph, in this dream's compression. Once you start to communicate with your higher self, you will be able to focus on the real substance of the Great Work. Reassuringly, the letter Yod appears twice in the spelling of this dream title, and this indicates that you will be able to awaken the Divine spark within yourself. Additionally, the final letter letter, Heh, which means "window," tells us that with dedication and perseverence you will be able to see something of the Divine nature itself.

SCARCITY

nedeeroot—ndyrvth— נדירות-670

MEANING If we looked at this dream in a non-spiritual context, we would be likely to assume that it represented a fear on the part of the dreamer that he was in danger of running out of money or being in some other way materially damaged. Of course, from a spiritual point of view such concerns are not as pertinent. Indeed, many religions and mystics have taught that it is far easier to progress inwardly when we cease to be worried about our outward progress. As the Buddha stated, attachment is the root cause of sorrow, so when we are free of our attachments we are free of sorrow.

THE TREE OF LIFE The scarcity referred to in this dream is a spiritual one. It is the fear that we will not be able to forge any kind of relationship with the Divine. This is a very common fear among people who are just starting to consider whether to seriously explore their spirituality. The reason it is so scary is that the Great Work requires us to discard the comfortable certainties of the material world before we receive any definite signs from the Divine. As you are still in that state of anxiety, we should place this dream on the path of Qoph, since this path relates to the worries that accompany the early stages of the spiritual journey.

THE JOURNEY When we reduce the value of this dream we find the number 13, which indicates that great change is about to occur in your life. The compression of this dream tells us where that change is likely to occur. The letter Mem appears in its final form in the compression, and this indicates that the maternal aspect of the Divine will be very powerfully present to help you overcome your fears and doubts. The final letter, Ayin, lets us know that as your fears abate, you will be increasingly confident about constructing your own approach to the Divine.

❧SCHOOL

*bet sefer–byth sphr–*בית ספר–752

MEANING The most important tool we possess to help us to develop our soul is our ability to keep an open mind. The worst thing that can happen to anyone is to fall under the spell of the belief that they "know" what life is all about. The moment you allow yourself to believe that you have nothing more to learn, you stop asking questions about yourself and about the nature of the universe. This dream acts as a reminder that we should be learning all our life and that in a sense everything we experience is a part of our spiritual schooling. The image of a school is particularly significant in the Kabbalah because it represents the accumulation of spiritual wisdom through study, which is a cornerstone of the Kabbalistic approach.

THE TREE OF LIFE When we look at the spelling of the Hebrew word meaning "school,"

there are some interesting points to note. The first word means "house," so it is the second word, which defines this house as a school, that should have our attention. It tells us that a school provides us with support and guidance (Samech) through both dialogue (Peh) and, later, reflection (Resh). The most pertinent aspect of this definition of a school in a spiritual context is the idea of thought and reflection. For this reason we should place this dream on the path of Resh.

THE JOURNEY When we reduce the value of this dream we find the number 5. This number is enormously important, as it represents a person who has learned to master the four elements within himself through the fifth element of Spirit, which is manifested in his higher self. In your case, this state of consciousness is still an aspiration, not an achievement. However, its presence in the value of this dream acts to encourage you in your current efforts by holding out a promise of what you can gain in due course.

See Zohar symbols Studying; Academy, Advanced School.

SCISSORS

*meesparayeem–msphryym–*מספריים–440

MEANING The content of this dream has a very direct relationship to its spiritual significance: When we use scissors it is either to cut away that which is not needed or to give a better shape to something. At one level, when we begin to develop our inner self we must take a pair of scissors to some of our initial assumptions about the nature of the Divine and cut some of the ties to our material view of the world.

THE TREE OF LIFE When we reduce the value of this dream we find the number 8. This number refers to the letter Cheth, which means "fence." In the context of this dream, the defensive associations with the letter Cheth should be seen as pointing to your potential to be defensive about removing some attachments that are no longer helpful to your inner progress. This suggests that you are in an early stage of your journey, and the path of Tav would be the most appropriate location for this dream, as it is here that you make your first attempts at moving into a spiritually based perspective.

THE JOURNEY The road ahead of you is a long one that is narrow and difficult to negotiate. However, the understanding and insight that awaits those who persevere is great. The repeated letter

Yod in the spelling of this dream title tells us that the spark of the Divine is already alive within you, spurring you on to greater effort. Additionally, this dream begins and ends with the letter Mem, and the letter Mem is found also in the compression of this dream's value. Consequently, you should feel reassured that the maternal force of the Divine is with you at this early stage in your inner quest.

SCORPION

akrav-aqrb- אקרב-303

MEANING In Kabbalistic tradition, the image of a scorpion represents unpleasant and potentially evil influences, so this dream should be seen as something of a warning. It may be that your spiritual search has led you to consider approaches to the Divine that have the appearance of being useful but are in fact either lacking in spiritual integrity or may actually lead you in a wrong direction. The value of this dream is equivalent to the value of a Hebrew word meaning "putrefaction," which confirms the sense of this dream as suggesting that your progress has been stalled.

THE TREE OF LIFE The scorpion is, of course, usually used to represent the sign Scorpio in the zodiac. However, what is less well known is that the scorpion represents Scorpio in its negative aspect; in its positive and mixed aspects, it is represented by an eagle or a snake, respectively. As this dream represents the wholly negative aspect of the scorpion, we place it on the path of Teth. The path of Teth in its negative aspect relates to the capacity for self-deceit, and this is the position that you are currently in.

THE JOURNEY The compression of this dream's value tells us that you are approaching the spiritual quest with great energy (Shin) and a high degree of creativity (Gimel). However, this is where the potential for taking a wrong turn is at its highest. The spelling of the dream title tells us that you have some worries about the validity of your current ideas about the Divine. In order to put your spiritual work back on track, you need to refocus your thinking (Resh) on the home (Beth) of spiritual truth, which is of course the Divine itself.

SCRATCH

sreetah-shryth- שריטה-524

MEANING A scratch constitutes an injury, although when we notice a scratch it is usually because we see it rather than because we feel any significant amount of pain. Therefore, a dream of a scratch is more about the idea of a mark than it is about discomfort. In a spiritual context, this relates to the idea of being marked as someone following a religious path, attempting to rediscover a link with the Divine. The initial letter, Shin, in the spelling of this dream title tells us that you have a lot of energy to help you pursue your spiritual goals.

THE TREE OF LIFE The sense of a mark as a means of noting the beginning of a new way of life is very common in a range of cultures. If we see this scratch as something significant, as a mark of initiation into the world of the spiritual, then we should look at a path quite low on the Tree of Life. When we reduce the value of this dream we find the number 11, which is associated with the idea of the mysterious, all over the world. It is too early in your journey for this to indicate that a major spiritual event is occurring, so we should assign this dream to the Sefirah of Yesod, as this is the Sefirah that is most associated with ideas of the mysterious.

THE JOURNEY This dream focuses very strongly on the notion of the practical. In the compression of the dream's value, the letter Kaph appears in its final and standard form, which suggests that you need to find some form of practical activity to help you move forward on your spiritual journey. Additionally, the final number in the value of this dream is a 4, which tells us that you need to find some means of manifesting your ideas in the physical world. An ideal practical activity that would meet both of these requirements would be sculpting.

SCREW

boreg-bvrg- בורג-211

MEANING They may be dull and uninspiring, but screws are absolutely essential tools for ensuring that things we build stay together and do not fall apart. From a psychological perspective, it could be said that this dream represents your view of yourself as an unassuming but important member of your community and indeed a person who holds things together. In a spiritual context, this dream indicates a recognition of your smallness in comparison to the wonder of the Divine while also making clear that you are still crucially important. The value of this dream is equivalent to the value of the Hebrew word meaning "fear" in the sense of a fear or wonder at the nature of the Divine.

THE TREE OF LIFE Screws are practical items and their presence as the content of this dream suggests that you are likely to practice your spiritual beliefs in a very down-to-earth manner. This view is supported by the fact that the value of this dream reduces to the number 4, which is the number associated with the physical and practical. The path of Kaph is also linked with the practical expression of your spirituality, so it is here that we should locate your dream.

THE JOURNEY You have a very outgoing nature and a cheerful disposition, as indicated by the letter Resh in the compression of your dream's value. You should use your jovial nature to encourage others to consider their own relationship to the realm of the spiritual. The letter Yod in the compression tells us that you have awakened the spark of the Divine within yourself, and the final letter, Aleph, represents the transcendent unity of the Divine itself. It is through your sincere good humor and helpful nature that you will set an example that may lead others to begin to seek the Divine for themselves.

SCULPT
lefasel-lphsl-לפסל-200

MEANING There are many ways in which we can express our feelings about God and spirituality in general. One of the best ways we can do this is through some form of creative activity. The Divine is interested in us as individuals in our own right, and when we engage in a free expression of our feelings we allow our true, unique identity to shine through. The value of this dream is equivalent to the value of a Hebrew word meaning "archetypal." This emphasizes the idea that you should try to discover the inner self that lies beneath your more obvious personality.

THE TREE OF LIFE We might expect this dream to fall into the Sefirah of Netzach because of its association with artistic expression. However, when we look at the spelling of this dream title we see that it is dominated by the letter Lamed. The letter Lamed means "ox-goad," which is a type of whip used to drive livestock. In spiritual terms, we see this as a harsh force urging you to study deeply the nature of the Divine. We should therefore place this dream on the path of Lamed.

THE JOURNEY It is quite clear that your task over the next months is to study deeply not just ideas about spirituality but your own inner nature. The value of this dream is equivalent to that of the letter Resh, which means "head." This tells us that you should ensure that you allow yourself the mental space and time to reflect on your reasons for pursuing the Great Work and what it is that you are learning about yourself in the process. The central letters Peh and Samech in the spelling of this dream title indicate that you will gain support in your quest if you can find some like-minded individuals with whom you can share your thoughts.

SEA
yamee-ymy-ימי-60

MEANING This is an extremely positive dream, as it indicates a person of great emotional sensitivity. Even from a purely psychological point of view, the sea is regarded as an emblem of the deep emotional consciousness. From a Kabbalistic perspective, the sea is a metaphor for the Great Mother, which is the Sefirah of Binah, one of the three supernal Sefirot. The sea also represents the compassionate and altruistic side of emotional natures. The value of this dream is equivalent to the value of the Hebrew word meaning "excellence," and this confirms the notion that your dream represents an encouraging comment on your inner progress.

THE TREE OF LIFE The value of this dream is equivalent to the value of the letter Samech. This letter represents notions of support and guidance and might initially seem to be an ideal location for this dream. However, when we look at the spelling of this dream title we see that the letter Mem occupies a central position. The letter Mem indicates feelings of compassion and altruism and so is very appropriate to this dream. The letter Mem also represents the element of Water and so refers directly to the title of this dream.

THE JOURNEY Although the letter Samech does not represent the path on which this dream sits, it is very important to a full understanding of the nature of your spiritual progress at this time. It is because of your compassionate approach to those around you that you are receiving the guidance and support of the Divine that is indicated by the letter Samech. The letter Yod, which brackets the representation of the element of Water in the spelling of your dream, also tells us that your acts of altruism are in full accordance with the will of the Divine and are a means by which you can heighten your spiritual understanding.

SEARCHING

*lekhapes-lchphsh-*לחפש-418

MEANING If we did not have the advantage of being able to analyze this dream by referring to the values and symbols that it contains, it would be very difficult to correctly interpret it. We might, for instance, understand the notion of searching to indicate a great sense of worry or concern on the part of the dreamer. However, the values within the dream make it clear that this is a positive dream and one which refers to the quest for inner truth that you have embarked upon. Certain individuals within the Western Mystery Tradition have made much of the symbolic power of the value of this dream, but it is sufficient for us to say that it bodes extremely well for your inner development.

THE TREE OF LIFE When we reduce the value of this dream we find the number 13. This number indicates change and tells you that you are about to undergo a major transformation in your life. The value of the dream is equivalent to the value of the letter Cheth when spelled in full. This letter means "fence" and can be seen as representing the protective force of the Divine. The path of Cheth links the Sefirot of Gevurah and Binah. This tells us that the transformation you are about to experience relates to an increased understanding of the nature of the Divine as an archetypal mother or bringer forth of forms.

THE JOURNEY The road to enlightenment is not simply narrow, it is often dark and overgrown and it can be incredibly difficult to find your way. This dream tells us that you are not being discouraged by the difficulties that you face but are steadfastly continuing with your search. The letter Tav is present in the compression of this dream, which tells us that you have experienced a certain degree of melancholy along the way. However, the subsequent letter, Yod, indicates that this has led to the awakening of the Divine spark within you. The final letter, Cheth, refers back to the path on which you are currently placed and acts as an assurance that your diligence will soon be rewarded with a much deeper understanding of the spiritual realm.

SIEGE

*latsoor al-ltzvr a'al-*לצור על-426

MEANING It takes a great deal of patience and commitment to successfully lay siege to a town or city. It may seem very strange for a metaphor of war to be used in a spiritual context—even more so when we consider that this dream is very positive in terms of the implications it holds for your future spiritual development. The letter Lamed appears twice in the spelling of this dream title, which tells us that your commitment to uncovering the secrets of the universe is based in very dedicated and rigorous study. It is this patient persistence that is indicated by the metaphor of a siege rather than any warlike connotations.

THE TREE OF LIFE The process of spiritual exploration requires a great deal of dedication. However, the path of Tzaddi is specifically related to the notion of commitment to the Great Work and so it is here that we locate your dream. The path of Tzaddi tells us not only that you are dedicated to the quest for truth but that you have a very optimistic outlook and expect to be successful in your search.

THE JOURNEY The path of Tzaddi is one of the earliest paths on the Tree of Life and it is important that you maintain your high enthusiasm. In the compression of this dream, the letter Tav makes it clear that you will have some regrets at leaving behind the certainty of the material world. You are being encouraged to spend a great deal of time in reflecting (Vav) on the nature of the Divine. Most important, you should be seeking some way to put into practice (Kaph) the spiritual insights that you are gaining. It is by living out our beliefs that we fully understand their true significance.

SELLING

*leemkor-lmkvr-*למכור-296

MEANING The world of commerce seems a very long way from the concerns of the spiritual world. Almost every religious culture advises us that in order to progress spiritually, we need to distance ourselves from overtly material interests. This does not mean that we need to consign ourselves to a state of poverty; rather, it means that you should be careful not to place excessive value on the physical comforts of the world. The value of this dream is equivalent to the value of the Hebrew word meaning "of the earth." This reinforces the sense that this dream is warning you against being too caught up in purely physical concerns.

THE TREE OF LIFE This dream is a clear indication that you have yet to fully commit to the Great Work. The title of this dream suggests that the reason for your reluctance to let go of the materialistic side of your life is that you are physically benefiting from your involvement. This dream is located in the Sefirah of Malkut, and in order to begin the journey toward a higher level of understanding you need to find some means of reducing your attachment and dependence on the material comforts of life.

THE JOURNEY When we reduce the value of this dream we find the number 8. This number indicates that you have a defensive outlook on the world. It is quite likely that your defensiveness relates to a fear that if you do focus on the spiritual, you may lose all of your material success without gaining any spiritual insight. The compression of this dream tells us that you will benefit from the benevolent influence of the Divine (Resh) and that this will help you to maintain a commitment to the Great Work (Tzaddi). The final Vav is there to act as an encouraging reminder of the understanding of the Divine that awaits you if you do make the leap to begin the exploration of your inner self.

SEPARATION

*hafradah–hphrdh–*הפרדה–294

MEANING In this day and age we tend to think of separation in terms of couples splitting up. This does not seem to bode well in terms of a spiritual dream, as it seems to indicate all sorts of emotional trauma and upset. However, we need to consider the meaning of the word *separation* in its broadest sense. Even if your dream uses the image of a broken relationship to represent the idea of separation, you should focus on the idea of things being divided into their constituent parts rather than on the sense of distress and pain. In Kabbalistic theory, the world as we experience it is fragmented, while the nature of the Divine is to create unity from the disparate elements that make up the universe. When we are sufficiently in touch with the light of the Divine we can sense that unity for ourselves.

THE TREE OF LIFE When you are developing your spiritual understanding it is important that you learn to look at yourself and the universe as a whole in a holistic way. However, once you are able to conceive of Creation as a single interconnected entity, it is equally important that you be able to appreciate the way in which this single infinite existence can be broken down into its myriad number of individual parts. Additionally, you need to approach an understanding of the necessity for each of those individual parts to ultimately break down.

This understanding is the lesson of Gevurah, and it is here that we should locate your dream.

THE JOURNEY The value of this dream is equivalent to the value of the Hebrew word meaning "purple." Purple tends to be a warlike and masculine color, and this fits in well with a dream about the breaking apart of entities and ideas. However, you should not see this process as a cruel one or even an upsetting one. The presence of the letter Resh in the compression of this dream tells you that the benevolent presence of the Divine is with you and should encourage you to see the positive nature of this constant separation of things. Since the universe is one incomprehensible entity, even when things break down they do not cease to be, they are simply transformed. Without the transformation from life into death, for instance, there would not be the opportunity for future life.

SERENADE

*serenadah–srndh–*סרנדה–319

MEANING Throughout history music has been closely associated with all form of religious activity. Not only has music been used in worship of the Divine, but very often the structure of the universe has been referred to in musical terms. We have the notion of a universal harmony, the music of the spheres, and of course in the Judeo-Christian tradition the abode of the Divine is filled with celestial music. This dream suggests that you feel very close to the Divine, and the specific nature of a serenade indicates that you are actively trying to make some kind of contact with higher forces.

THE TREE OF LIFE The compression of this dream tells us that you have a great deal of positive energy (Shin) that you are bringing to your spiritual quest and that you have awakened the Divine spark within yourself (Yod). You now need simply to rely on your strength of character (Teth) to maintain your progress. This is not very specific in terms of your position on the Tree of Life. However, we know that music is a creative and expressive activity and that the reduction of this dream's value produces the number 3, which is also associated with creativity. As a serenade implies that you are singing *to* someone, we should place this dream on the path of Peh, which deals with all forms of communication.

THE JOURNEY You are making great progress in your self-development and should be encouraged by this dream. It tells us that you are approaching a point where you may be able to engage in some form of dialogue with your higher self. It is important that you maintain a sense of the here and now, though, and not allow your enthusiasm for the spiritual to cause you to lose touch with the day-to-day world. It would be a very good idea for you to join some kind of performance group so that you can express your love of the Divine in a practical and expressive manner.

SERPENT

nakhash-nchsh-נחש-358

MEANING From a psychological point of view, a dream of a serpent would be seen as having a very definite sexual implication. While not a purely Kabbalistic idea, the serpent is regarded as a phallic symbol in many mystical systems, and because of the negative associations of serpents it would be regarded as a dream that indicated a fear with regard to your sexuality. However, serpents have a symbolism that is far deeper than the merely sexual. The serpent represents the potential for self-deceit and the attraction of power as opposed to understanding. The value of this dream is equivalent to the value of the Hebrew word meaning "shame," so we know that we are looking at a dream that is warning you about your current approach to the Divine.

THE TREE OF LIFE The word Nechesh means "serpent" in Hebrew and is the word used to indicate the serpent in the Book of Genesis. The letter Teth also means "serpent," so it is appropriate to locate this dream on the path of Teth. While the path of Teth can refer to the positive aspects of a serpentine nature, when we dream of a serpent it is the negative elements of serpent symbolism that are indicated. This means that you are in danger of taking a wrong turn in your pursuit of the Great Work and need to think very carefully before you make any major decisions.

THE JOURNEY The compression of this dream tells us that you are approaching your inner journey with a great deal of energy (Shin). While this is a good thing generally, it is likely that you need to slow down a little and make sure that you are adequately protecting yourself (Cheth) from rushing into spiritual systems that are misleading or unhelpful to you as a genuine seeker of truth. This is a crucial point in your spiritual journey, and any decisions you make will affect the way in which your personal development progresses in the future. The presence of the letter Nun in the spelling of this dream title indicates that while the road ahead may be difficult, the ultimate effect will be to deepen the nature of your faith and understanding.

SEWING

tfeerah-thphyrh-תפירה-695

MEANING There was a time when every house had a well-stocked sewing basket. This was because we lived in a world where things, including clothes, were repaired any number of times before they were discarded. Much to our detriment, we now live in a world of disposability and few of us actually get our hands on a needle and thread except very occasionally to sew on a button. From a spiritual point of view, the idea of sewing suggests that you have a wish to use your spiritual insight to help heal rifts between people or, for that matter, within your personality.

THE TREE OF LIFE The value of this dream is equivalent to a Hebrew phrase meaning "the moral world." This indicates that your dream of sewing refers to repairing situations where an individual feels that he has behaved in an inappropriate or immoral manner. Such an approach to life indicates a great sense of compassion and empathy. The letter Mem is closely linked with notions of protection and altruism, so it is appropriate to place this dream on the path of Mem.

THE JOURNEY When we reduce the value of this dream we find the number 20. This is the value of the letter Kaph and indicates that you take a very practical approach to all matters spiritual. This has already been hinted at by the meaning of this dream, but its presence in the reduction of the dream's value should reassure you that you are right to try to help others in the way that you do. The letter Mem also appears in the compression of your dream in its final form. The compression tells you that if you persist in your current approach (Tzaddi), you will come to glimpse (Heh) the Divine itself.

❧SEX

meen-myn-מין-100

MEANING From a psychological point of view, this dream would be very interesting to analyze. If a dream about the most mundane things or events is unconsciously related to our sexuality, it begs the question whether a dream about sex should be seen as unconsciously related to more mundane aspects of our life! From a Kabbalistic viewpoint, the focus of this dream should be on the implications of sexual activity. That is, at a spiritual level the sex act represents a union between two individuals that has the potential to create a unique and new individual. The value of this dream is equivalent to the number 10 multiplied by itself. As 10 is the number of completion, this can be seen as referring to the way in which sex creates the potential for a new, complete being.

THE TREE OF LIFE The Sefirah of Yesod is traditionally associated with sexuality. If we were to look at the Tree as a very basic diagram of a person, Yesod would coincide with the loins. Additionally, Yesod is linked with the emotional connections and the sense of desire that drives our sexual feelings. The presence of the number 10 in this dream also references the tenth Sefirah of Malkut. This Sefirah relates to the material world and so is appropriate for this dream, since it refers to the creation of something new within the physical universe. Of course, this does not necessarily refer to the creation of a new life but to a new way of looking at the world or a new conception of the spiritual nature of the universe. This location does not mean that you have yet to begin your spiritual journey but that you are manifesting a part of that journey in the material world.

THE JOURNEY The spelling of this dream title tells us that you are in the process of awakening the Divine spark within your soul, as the central letter in the title is Yod. The initial letter, Mem, indicates that as this is happening and you are bringing forth your new way of looking at the world, you will be assisted by the maternal force of the Divine. The letter Nun also appears in this dream in its final form. Its purpose there is to tell you that while the process of creation can be painful, its final result is to cause a significant increase in the level of your understanding.

See Zohar symbol, Lovemaking.

SHAKING HANDS

leelkhots yadayeem – llchvtz ydyym –
ללחוץ ידיים – 238

MEANING Not all cultures use a handshake as a form of friendly greeting, but it is probably the most well-known way of introducing yourself the world over. This dream tells us that you are an outgoing and friendly individual who likes to make new friends and acquaintances. This open attitude will certainly help you in your search for spiritual truth. From an entirely spiritual point of view, this dream

tells us that you are actively reaching out to try to initiate a close relationship with the Divine.

THE TREE OF LIFE The idea of shaking hands is a relaxed image, and, without the benefit of a Kabbalistic interpretation, we might think that this dream was suggesting that the route to a connection with the higher forces was a smooth and easy one. However, the repetition of the letter Lamed at the beginning of the spelling of this title along with the final form of the letter Tzaddi at the end of the first word tell us that this is far from the case. The letter Tzaddi indicates the need for great commitment to the spiritual path. The repeated letter Lamed tells you that you need to engage in rigorous study in order to achieve a handshake with the higher, and it is on the path of Lamed that we should locate your dream.

THE JOURNEY The reminder that hard work will be needed to move you forward in your spiritual quest is repeated by the central position of the letter Lamed in the compression of this dream's value. On the very positive side, the letter Cheth also appears, which tells you that you are being protected in your studies by the Divine. The initial Resh in the compression points not only to the fact that your studies are moving in the right direction but to the fact that while the work is hard, you must remember to take an optimistic and reflective approach to it.

SHARK

kareesh – krysh – כריש – 530

MEANING Ever since the release of a certain well-known movie and its many sequels, the shark has had a very bad name indeed! It has never been the most loved of fish, not just because of its predatory nature but particularly because of its coldness and the unsettlingly cold appearance of its eyes. Given the feelings that are conjured up when we think of a shark, we can regard this dream as referring to a very definite sense of fear. In a spiritual context, we could see this fear as the concern that the universe itself is essentially dead and unfeeling, consisting of nothing but the promise of a cold and inevitable death.

THE TREE OF LIFE When we reduce the value of this dream we find the number 8. This number refers to the letter Cheth and indicates a defensive outlook. In terms of this particular dream, we see that this is pointing to a defensiveness about the spiritual quest, resulting from your fears that your search will prove fruitless. Such concerns and anxieties are very common in the early stages of a spiritual journey, and they are related to the path of Qoph, which is where we should position your dream.

THE JOURNEY The decision to explore the world of the spiritual is perhaps the biggest decision you will ever make. Inevitably it is accompanied by feelings of grave doubt. It is easier to live with the idea that the spiritual dimension exists if only you looked for it, than to face the notion that, having searched for it, you discover it was just a red herring. The compression of this dream has some sound advice for you that will help to alleviate these very common worries. The letter Kaph appears in its final form and tells you that you should engage in some practical activity to help consolidate your first forays into the Great Work, while the letter Lamed tells you that some intensive study will also help you. An excellent idea would be to enroll in a meditation class or Kabbalah school.

SHAVING
geelooakh–gylvch–גילוח–57

MEANING For those of us who shave, there is a wonderful sense of being cleansed that is associated with the process of removing the night's growth of stubble. Shaving is a ritualistic and deeply important part of the preparation for the day ahead. Of course, in Judaic tradition there were very strict laws regarding shaving and these are still followed rigorously by many. Consequently, from a Kabbalistic perspective the image of shaving becomes even more important as a symbol of careful spiritual preparation.

THE TREE OF LIFE The value of this dream is equivalent to the value of the Hebrew word meaning "altar." This association emphasizes the deeply spiritual associations of this dream. Additionally, it ties the dream to an altruistic and self-sacrificing viewpoint. Consequently, the ideal path on which to locate this dream would be the path of Mem, as this path is also closely linked with such noble and worthy attitudes.

THE JOURNEY When we reduce the value of this dream we find the number 12. This is the number of The Hanged Man card in the tarot, and, appropriately enough, it is also linked with a person who is willing to place the needs of others before his own. If you maintain your caring approach to the world, you will find that your spiritual understanding and your faith deepen as a result of your willingness to expose yourself to the needs and pain of others. This is confirmed by the presence of the letter Nun in the

compression of this dream's value. The final letter, Zayin, in the compression tells us that while compassion is a wonderful virtue, you need to keep yourself mentally alert as well as emotionally engaged.

SHEEP
tson–tzan–צאן–141

MEANING Today, the term *sheep* is often used to indicate someone who lacks independence of thought. When we look at the images in the dreams we are analyzing, it is very important to remember that we are dealing with ancient symbols and therefore we need to consider the meaning that the subjects of our dreams would have held for the ancients. Sheep were a crucial part of the economy of the ancient world and were a solid, reliable basis for the well-being of the people. The value of this dream is equivalent to the value of the Hebrew word meaning "trusty," and this sums up the symbolic significance of sheep. However, the idea of sheep as representing a passive outlook and a preference for the safe and quiet life is also appropriate to this dream.

THE TREE OF LIFE From a spiritual point of view, this dream tells us that you are making steady progress up the Tree of Life and that you have a strong and unwavering faith in the Divine. Another that shares its value with that of the dream is the Hebrew word meaning "oaken." The oak is traditionally associated with the path of Kaph, and this is an ideal path on which to place your dream. The path of Kaph is related to very practical and down-to-earth approaches to the Divine. Additionally, it reaches up to the Sefirah of Hesed, which can be regarded as symbolic of the shepherd aspect of the Divine.

THE JOURNEY If your spiritual development were included in a school report card, it would probably read "steady but continual progress." There is no rush in the Great Work and it does not matter how quickly we develop; the sincerity with which we approach the spiritual quest is all that is important. When we reduce the value of this dream we find the number 6. In the context of this dream, the number 6 represents the macrocosm and serves to reassure you that slowly but surely you are approaching the ultimate goal of all seekers of truth.

SHELTER
meeklat–mqlt–מקלט–179

MEANING Many people turn to religion in order to gain a sense of certainty in an uncertain world. In this way we could see religious belief as a kind of shelter from a spiritually empty world or, from a cynical point of view, as a form of protection from the unpalatable realities of life. However, the genuine seeker of truth is not looking for an easy answer or some kind of escape from the everyday world. Consequently we might see this dream as a warning that you are looking to the spiritual to provide you with a sense of comfort that will not actually help you to move forward in your quest for truth.

THE TREE OF LIFE When we reduce the value of this dream we find the number 8. This is the value of the letter Cheth. The letter Cheth literally means "fence," and in the context of this dream it represents a certain defensiveness in your attitude. The initial letter in the compression of this dream is Qoph, which points to anxiety and uncertainty on your part about the nature or possibly the value of the Great Work. It is this anxiety that leads you to try to see your spiritual beliefs as a source of shelter and as a defense. Consequently, we should place this dream on the path of Qoph.

THE JOURNEY The letters Ayin and Teth also appear in the compression of your dream. These letters tell us the basis of your desire for a protective shield. You have great concerns about taking responsibility for the development of your spiritual understanding (Ayin). This is because you have insufficient faith in your strength of character and willpower (Teth). You can prove to yourself that you are capable of meeting the challenge of the spiritual quest by setting a routine and then sticking to it. This routine may initially be very simple, such as setting aside ten minutes a day to meditate. Once you realize that you can maintain this level of commitment, you can gradually increase the time that you devote to your spiritual studies.

SHIP

*oneeyah–avnyyh–*אונייה–82

MEANING To dream of a ship is extremely positive. You might think that it should indicate that you are about to go on a long physical voyage, perhaps even a cruise. However, the spiritual import of this dream relates to something far more valuable than any physical activity you might undertake. When we reduce the value of this dream we find the number 10. This is a number that relates to the completion of a cycle in your life, and in the context of this dream it represents the achievement of a significant level of spiritual understanding.

THE TREE OF LIFE The value of this dream is equivalent to the value of the Hebrew word meaning "the beloved thing." It is also equivalent to the value of the Hebrew word meaning "white." The color white has often been associated with notions of Divinity, so the beloved thing in question is the Divine itself. The image of a ship represents the journey that you have made so far in order to arrive at a point where some recognition of the "beloved thing" is within reach. The Sefirah of Tiferet is the first point where we make some form of definite contact with higher forces, so it is here that we should locate your dream.

THE JOURNEY The Sefirah of Tiferet is a relative haven on the Tree of Life in that it is a state of consciousness that carries with it the reward of a tangible sense of contact with your higher self. The value of this dream is equivalent to that of the Hebrew word meaning "righteous," and this serves to emphasize that your reward is richly deserved. However, it is also important not to rest on your laurels. The compression of this dream's value reveals the letter Peh, a sure sign that you now need to try to communicate with your higher self. This will enable you to begin the climb to the higher reaches of the Tree and approach the House of God, represented by the letter Beth in this dream's compression.

SHOE

*naal–na'al–*נעל–150

MEANING From a psychological perspective, we might see this dream as referring to a need to travel. The fact that the dream is of a shoe rather than a vehicle of some kind would seem to indicate that your trips would either be short or certainly not expensive to undertake. From a Kabbalistic point of view, we should note that our shoes are the nearest part of our clothing to the ground and that in spiritual terms this would suggest either humility or the fact that you are still residing entirely in the material world of Malkut.

THE TREE OF LIFE When we reduce the value of this dream we find the number 6, which is the value of the letter Vav. This letter is concerned with the element of Air and the notions of thought and reflection. Such an association strongly indicates that you have moved beyond purely physical concerns. The value of this dream is equivalent to the value of the Hebrew word meaning "nest." As a nest is a place where chicks develop into birds, we can assume that you are still relatively new to the Great Work. The path of Tav is the first path that we can walk along and also involves some deep reflections regarding our reasons for choosing a spiritual path, so we can place this dream on the path of Tav.

THE JOURNEY You have made quite probably the most important decision of your life, which was to follow a spiritual path. Now that you are treading the earliest sections of the Tree of Life, you are understandably beginning to suffer doubt and uncertainty about the nature of your spiritual quest. This doubt and worry are represented by the presence of the letter Qoph in the compression of this dream's value. The final letter, Nun, represents both the suffering that you are feeling right now in terms of your anxieties and the fact that this experience of self-doubt will ultimately lead to a deeper faith in the Divine.

SHOP

khanoot-chnvth-חנות-464

MEANING There was a time when shopping was a chore that we did as little and as quickly as possible. The most important aspect of visiting shops was to ensure that we had the supplies we required for the week ahead. However, in recent years we have seen a trend toward the idea of shopping as a leisure activity. It is perhaps a telling comment on the importance of material success that the spending of money has taken on the status of an activity in its own right rather than being simply a means to an end. Spiritually speaking, this dream should be taken as a warning that you are devoting too much time to the material aspect of your life.

THE TREE OF LIFE There are few activities as singularly connected to physical gratification as shopping. To be dreaming of shops is a clear indication that you spend too much time thinking about your physical needs and desires and not enough time focusing on your spiritual needs. In the value of this dream we see that the number 4 both begins and completes the string of numbers. Since 4 is very closely associated with the world of the physical, its presence serves to emphasize the fact that your dream belongs firmly in the Sefirah of Malkut.

THE JOURNEY You have yet to make any kind of firm commitment to the Great Work. However, you should not see this dream as too negative, since it is a step forward that your unconscious is trying to make you aware of the absence in your life. It is never easy to make major changes in life, and a change in values is particularly difficult to achieve. You may find it helpful to join an introductory meditation class,

as this will bring you into contact with others who are new to the process of exploring their inner selves.

SHOUT

tseakah-tza'aqh-צעקה-265

MEANING This is not a dream about anger or rage. We often mistake shouting as a sign that a person is irate. However, regardless of the surface impression, whenever someone feels the need to shout it is because at some level, no matter how well hidden, he feels small and afraid and weak. When we shout it is in an attempt to use the noise to chase away the uncertainties and doubts that are bothering us. When we apply this insight to a spiritual context, we can see that you are suffering a number of worries about your inner journey.

THE TREE OF LIFE The value of this dream is equivalent to the value of the Hebrew word meaning "architect." An architect is someone who takes responsibility for the design of a structure. From a spiritual viewpoint, we see this as referring to your responsibility for constructing your approach to the Divine. This stage of your development is associated with the path of Ayin, so it is here that we should locate your dream. The fact that you still have some grave fears about this challenge tells us that you are only just beginning to experience the lessons of the path of Ayin.

THE JOURNEY When we reduce the value of this dream we find the number 13, which symbolizes great change in your life. The implication here is that you are going to find a way to develop your unique relationship to the spiritual realm, and this should be seen as an encouraging sign. The compression of the dream's value is equally positive. You are under the influence of the benevolent aspect of the Divine (Resh), who will support you (Samech) in your attempts to achieve a sense of ownership of your spiritual voyage. This will ultimately lead to your achieving the much-longed-for glimpse (Heh) of the Divine nature.

SHOVEL

yaeh-ya'ah-יעה-85

MEANING You are making solid progress in your spiritual quest, and this dream is both an encouragement to maintain your efforts and an important lesson on how best to move forward. A dream about a shovel might seem rather uninspiring until we remember the common use of the word *digging* when people are talking about serious introspection. For instance, we dig into our past, we dig up memories, and we might refer to some intense research on a given subject as a period of "serious digging." In Kabbalistic terms, the image of a shovel is symbolic of the digging that we must do within ourselves in order to make spiritual progress.

THE TREE OF LIFE The value of this dream is equivalent to the value of the letter Peh when spelled in full. Additionally, the compression of this dream's value reveals the letter Peh. The letter Peh means "mouth" and is associated with all forms of communication. Very often the best way to dig up information and insights is through conversations with like-minded people, so the path of Peh is a highly appropriate place to position your dream.

THE JOURNEY As well as communicating with those around you, this dream is encouraging you also to begin to try to initiate some form of contact with your higher self. The value of this dream is equivalent to the value of the Hebrew word meaning "circumcision." In Judaism, the act of circumcision is a visible sign of the covenant between the Divine and the individual. This dream is therefore a profound indication that you are now in a position to cement your relationship to the Divine and establish a much deeper sense of the spiritual in your life.

SHOWER

meeklakhat-mqlchth- מקלחת-578

MEANING Almost all religions have a focus on the need to have a sense of purity when attempting to approach the Divine. Very often, part of the requirements to achieve the necessary state of preparedness to worship are related to cleansing. The dream of a shower relates closely to this analogy of external cleanliness to inner purity. At a metaphorical level, the shower represents the washing away of all mundane and material concerns so that you can focus entirely on the Great Work. The fact that you have had this dream tells us that you have a very serious commitment to the spiritual quest.

THE TREE OF LIFE In one sense, every path on the Tree of Life requires you to make efforts to achieve a state of inner cleanliness in order to best benefit from the lessons that it offers. However, the values within this dream tell us that the path in question is the path of Kaph. When we reduce the value of this dream we find the number 20, and this is the value of Kaph in its standard form. In addition, the

compression of this dream's value begins with the letter Kaph in its final form.

THE JOURNEY The path of Kaph is connected with a practical approach to the spiritual journey. This links well with the dream of taking a shower because this also suggests that you are including a spiritual dimension in the practical way in which you live your life. When we look closer at the compression of this dream, we see the letters Ayin and Cheth. Ayin relates to a vigorous and individualistic approach to life, while Cheth refers to the protective influence of the Divine. In practical terms, you are being advised to formulate your own way of expressing your reverence for the spiritual and are reassured that you will be supported in your attempts to achieve this. It is also important that as you develop your ideas you try to share them with those around you.

SHROUD

takhreekheem-thkrykym- תכריכים-700

MEANING We tend to associate shrouds with the dressing of the dead in preparation for burial. Thus, you may expect this dream to have strongly negative implications for your spiritual development. In fact, this dream is extremely positive and suggests that you have made great strides in your spiritual journey. It is important to remember that before you can fully come alive in a spiritual sense you must first allow your ego-driven personality and desires to experience something akin to a death.

THE TREE OF LIFE The value of this dream is equivalent to the value of the letter Nun in its final form. Additionally, the letter Nun is the only letter in the compression of this dream's value. The path of Nun relates to the potential for sorrow that is experienced as we begin to deepen our understanding and increase the strength of our faith in the Divine. If we locate this dream on the path of Nun, we can see the image of a shroud as symbolic of the potential for emotional upset as we struggle toward a clearer view of our spiritual goals.

THE JOURNEY Although we associate shrouds with death and funeral arrangements, a shroud can also signify a veil. This becomes more important when we remember that veils are a common form of clothing in the Middle and Near East. The value of this dream is equivalent to the value of the Hebrew word *Peroketh*. This word refers to the veil that separates the supernal Sefirot from the remainder of the Tree of Life. Any reference to the highest three Sefirot should be seen as deeply encouraging. This dream is telling you that if you persist and refuse to be distracted by any sadness that you may experience at this time, you will be able to draw closer to a state of consciousness where you will be able to penetrate the veil of Peroketh.

SHY

leherata-lhyrtha'a- לֹהירתע-715

MEANING We live in a world where shyness is discouraged. In order to succeed in today's agressive business world, it is essential that we feel capable of pushing ourselves forward for recognition. However, from a spiritual point of view there is nothing negative about being shy in your approach to the Divine. In fact, we can see shyness as an appropriate level of humility in the face of higher spiritual forces.

THE TREE OF LIFE The value of this dream is equivalent to the value of the Hebrew word meaning "secret." This serves to emphasize the importance of the truths that you are seeking and the fact that only a small number of people ever persevere long enough to discover their true nature. While you may be "shy," you do have a high level of commitment to the Great Work, and this is emphasized by the initial letter, Lamed, in the spelling of this dream title. As the path of Lamed represents a very rigorous approach to your studies of the spiritual, it is an ideal position for your dream.

THE JOURNEY When we reduce the value of this dream we find the number 13, which symbolizes a major change that is about to occur in your life. The compression of this dream begins with the letter Nun in its final form, and this tells us that the strength and depth of your faith in the Divine is about to be greatly increased. This will be the result of your awakening the Divine spark within yourself (Yod). The final letter, Heh, acts as a promise of the glimpse of the Divine with which you will ultimately be rewarded.

SICKNESS

makhlah-mchlh- מחלה-83

MEANING Common sense would suggest that a dream about sickness indicates that you are either already feeling under the weather or are about to suffer from some form of illness. At a practical level, you need to be aware that this could be a warning, so you should keep an eye on your health over the next few weeks. However, when we examine the values embedded within the spelling of this dream title, we can see that this dream is highly encouraging and the image of sickness relates not to you but to the world around you. The value of this dream is a prime number. In the Western Mystery Tradition, prime numbers represent uniqueness, and you are blessed with a particular ability to empathize with those who are suffering.

THE TREE OF LIFE The value of this dream reduces to 11, and this number is traditionally associated with all things mystical. The message in this dream is that you will gain an insight into more mystical matters as a direct result of acting on your ability to empathize with the pain of others. The path of Mem is linked to acts of compassion and altruism, so it is the ideal location for your dream.

THE JOURNEY Whereas mainstream religion tends to be focused on acts of community worship, the Great Work is an essentially solitary effort. However, this does not mean that you cannot greatly enhance your depth of spiritual insight by involving yourself in your community. The compression of this dream contains the letters Peh and Gimel. These letters point out that not only can you offer practical help to those in need but that you should try to discuss the spiritual side of reality with them (Peh). Indeed, you have great ability to help other people come to a realization of their need for a spiritual level to their existence, and the letter Gimel is there to urge you to find new and creative ways of trying to convince them of that need.

SIDEWALK

meedrakhah-mdrkh- מדרכה-269

MEANING When we analyze a dream and look at its title, very often it is important not just to consider the implications of the dream content but to consider why other very similar images were not part of the dream. For instance, we need to consider the implications of the use of the word *sidewalk* rather than *road*. This tells us that your approach to the spiritual is relatively relaxed and sedate, that you have no desire to rush toward any particular goal but are content to enjoy the journey itself.

THE TREE OF LIFE The value of this dream is equivalent to the value of the Hebrew word meaning "byways." This suggests that you enjoy the exploratory nature of the spiritual quest. Rather than constantly focusing on raising your consciousness to a higher level, you greatly enjoy looking into a range of ways to approach the Divine and have a genuine curiosity. This attitude suggests that you are relatively new to the Great Work, and, given the considerable interest in the range of spiritual ideas that this dream indicates, we should place this dream in the Sefirah of Yesod.

THE JOURNEY In one sense this is a very positive dream as it tells us that you are very committed to exploring the nature of spirituality. However, the value of the dream hints at a need to begin to try to put some definite direction into your studies of spiritual matters. The reduction of this dream produces the number 8. This is the value of the letter Cheth, and it points to a defensiveness in attitude. In your case, it may be that your reluctance to actually aim for a spiritual goal stems from a fear that if you do so, you will be disappointed. The only way to test this possibility is to actually set a goal and then do your best to achieve it.

SIGH

*anakhah-anchh-*אנכה-64

MEANING Sighs come in many forms, and if we look only at the title of this dream we have very little chance of discovering the significance that lies beneath the dream's surface content. The value of this dream is equivalent to the value of the Hebrew word meaning "justice." This association strongly suggests that you are approaching a more balanced internal state, and this can only bode well for your future spiritual development.

THE TREE OF LIFE We sigh because we are sad, in love, upset, aroused, or struck with wonder. There is nothing in the dream's value that pinpoints which of these emotional states is referred to in this dream. However, the value of this dream is equivalent to the value of the Hebrew word that refers to the planet Venus. This is the planet most associated with all emotional states, so it becomes clear that no single emotion is being specified, because the point of this dream is that you are becoming more aware of all of your emotions. As the Sefirah of Netzach is concerned with passions and is also linked with the planet Venus, it is the most appropriate location for your dream.

THE JOURNEY When we reduce the value of this dream we find the number 10, which tells us that you are approaching the completion of a major cycle in your life. In the context of this dream, it is the achievement of a greater balance in your emotions that is indicated by the presence of the number 10.

This also makes sense of the association of this dream with the notion of justice in its broadest sense. The compression of this dream tells you that you will find a great deal of support (Samech) in achieving this inner harmony and that once completed it will open the door (Daleth) to a deeper relationship with the Divine.

SILK

*meshee-mshy-*מישׁי-350

MEANING We would not normally associate dreams about silk with any kind of deep spiritual significance. In fact, dreams in which silk plays a major part very often revolve around themes that are unlikely to be regarded as particularly religious in nature! However, all the letters in this dream title point to a very positive and energetic approach to the Great Work on your part. The spelling of this dream title contains all but one of the so-called mother letters. These letters, Aleph, Mem, and Shin, represent the three elements of Air, Water, and Fire, respectively, which combine to form the element of Earth. In the spelling of your dream title the airy Aleph is replaced by the dynamic energy of Yod.

THE TREE OF LIFE When we think about the nature of silk it is primarily associated with clothing that is worn next to the skin. It is this intimacy that is important for an understanding of the spiritual import of this dream. To have a sense of intimacy and complete openness in your relationship to the Divine suggests a high position on the Tree of Life beyond the point at which you would have made contact with your higher self. When we combine this with the fact that this dream is full of vigorous energy, the ideal location for your dream is the path of Yod.

THE JOURNEY You are now well on your way to achieving a moment of communion with the Divine energy. In the compression of the value of this dream we find the letter Shin, which again emphasizes the fiery driving energy that is spurring you on to ever greater efforts in your spiritual work. The final letter, Nun, tells you that in order to continue to progress, your energy needs to be tempered by a certain amount of quiet contemplation. This should definitely include an honest appraisal of your nature and personality. While this may involve a degree of sorrow, it is only by fully knowing yourself that you will be able to deepen your spiritual understanding sufficiently to achieve your goals.

SILVER

*kesef-ksph-*כסף-160

MEANING All precious metals have a particular link to one of the paths on the Tree of Life. The metal silver is associated with the Sefirah of Binah. This is one of the supernal Sefirot and is concerned with the potential for form in the universe, and as such it is often regarded as the Great Mother. The values in the dream do not suggest that you have reached this level of self-development. However, the influence of Binah does have an effect on the meaning of this dream. It is clear that you have reached a significant level of self-insight, since dreaming of a lesser metal like silver rather than gold points to a humility that is suggestive of a well-developed nature.

THE TREE OF LIFE When we reduce the value of this dream we find the number 7. This number is the value of the letter Zayin. The literal meaning of Zayin is "sword." In spiritual terms, the idea of a sword refers to your developing ability to cut away the misleading and irrelevant from those pieces of information and insights that are genuinely valuable. The influence of Binah is helpful here in enabling you to see the underlying form and structure within different spiritual ideas. However, the dream is located on the path of Zayin rather than in the supernal Sefirah of Binah.

THE JOURNEY It is clear that the task before you in the next months is to work toward a coherent and clear idea of your spiritual beliefs. This will inevitably involve disregarding some ideas to which you may have been attached. The letter Qoph in the compression of this dream's value tells us that this process may cause you some concerns. You should not worry too much, though, since the final letter, Samech, is a sure sign that you will receive guidance from above in determining what to include and what to discard.

✲SINGING

*lezamer-lzmr-*לזמר-277

MEANING One of the first things that a mathematician would notice about the value of this dream is that it is a prime number (a number that can be divided only by itself and by one). Such numbers are relatively rare and indicate what is unique about an individual. Of course, one of the fundamentals of the spiritual viewpoint is that each of us is unique, but this dream suggests that you have a specific talent that will enable you to achieve great things in terms of your inner development. We should also be aware that singing is symbolic of the joy and praise of the Divine inherent in the universe. We are familiar with the idea of choirs of angels singing in Heaven. In the Kabbalah, the whole universe is seen as singing a song of praise to the Divine. This is particularly interesting when we remember that in scientific terms it is becoming more accepted that the universe consists simply of modulating frequencies or waves, all of which can be represented as sound. Perhaps it is significant that there are twenty-two of these fundamental frequencies—the number of letters in the Hebrew alphabet.

THE TREE OF LIFE The value of this dream is equivalent to the value of a Hebrew word referring to "benevolence." When we consider this in a spiritual context, we should look for a path that relates to the benevolent nature of the Divine. Additionally, as the nature of singing is that it should be a joyous expression of reverence for the Creator, we should also look for a path that relates to the innate sense of wonder at the nature of the universe. An ideal path for this dream would be the path of Resh, which also appears as the first letter in the spelling of this dream title.

THE JOURNEY You are doing very well in your quest for spiritual truth and should see this dream as an encouragement to maintain your current efforts. The value of this dream is equivalent to the value of a Hebrew word meaning "propagate," suggesting that you have a role to play in propagating a desire to seek out the spiritual among others. This also fits with the idea of singing in that one tends to sing to an audience, and it is your role to advocate the spiritual life to any audience that you can find.

See Zohar symbol, Singing.

SISTER

*geesah-gysh-*גיסה-78

MEANING Unless there is some significant issue currently occupying your mind with relation to your actual sister, the image of a sister in this dream has an entirely symbolic meaning. The value of this dream is equivalent to the value of the Hebrew word meaning "pity." This indicates that your dream of a sister relates to a desire for a relationship that will enable you to feel protected and cared for. In spiritual terms, this dream could be seen as your reaching out to make contact with the protective force of the Divine. Such an interpretation is supported by the fact that this dream's value is also equivalent to the value of a Hebrew phrase that refers to the influence of the Divine descending from the Sefirah of Keter.

THE TREE OF LIFE When we reduce the value of this dream we find the number 6. This is the value of the letter Vav and tells us that you have been spending a lot of time reflecting on the spiritual quest and trying to make some kind of important decision. The decision in question is whether or not to act on your wish to pursue the Great Work, and since you have not yet completely committed to the search for truth, we should place your dream in the Sefirah of Malkut.

THE JOURNEY We can be certain that you are still in a state of consciousness that relates to the physical world of Malkut because the value of this dream is the same as the value of the Hebrew words for "bread" and "salt." Both bread and salt are used as symbols of the material level of existence and the element of Earth. The compression of this dream's value begins with the letter Ayin, and this letter is present to urge you to be more vigorous and take the leap into the unknown that is the realm of the spiritual. As a reassurance, the letter Cheth, which stands for the protective higher forces, is also present at the end of the dream's compression.

SKATE
*galgeeleet-glgylyth-*גלגילית*-*486

MEANING This is a very interesting dream in terms of the way in which it conveys its hidden message about your spiritual condition. Psychoanalysis often looks for covert puns or colloquialisms in dreams in order to discern their unconscious significance. With this dream we can do the same to discover the spiritual message. A very common phrase that is connected to skates and skating is the expression that somebody is "skating on thin ice." This expression suggests that an individual is in danger of getting into difficulties due to a lack of appropriate caution.

THE TREE OF LIFE At every stage in our inner development we have to be cautious and ensure that we are genuinely learning the lesson of the path that we are on and not simply accepting those aspects that appeal to our preconceived notions. When we reduce the value of this dream we find the number 9, which is the value of the letter Teth. In its negative aspect the path of Teth refers to our capacity to be

deceived or to deceive ourselves, and it is this danger to which your dream is referring.

THE JOURNEY We discerned that this dream had a warning note by looking at certain colloquial associations. The value of the dream and its reduction helped us to locate the dream. Now we need to turn to the spelling of the dream title itself. Not only are you warned in this dream about the potential to be deceived by a convincing but valueless approach to the spiritual, but you are told how you should go about your quest for truth. The spelling of the dream title tells us that wisdom (Gimel) will come only after rigorous study (Lamed). That wisdom (Gimel) will enable the spark of the Divine (Yod) to come alive within you. Once you are studying (Lamed) under the influence of the Divine within you (Yod), you will achieve the wisdom symbolized by the letter Tav.

SKELETON
*sheled-shld-*שלד*-*334

MEANING For most of us, a dream about a skeleton would fall into the category of a nightmare. Despite the fact that each of has a skeleton, they have an association with the ghostly and the disturbing. In Kabbalistic terms, this dream operates on a number of levels. It could be seen as a reminder of the inevitably temporary nature of our physical life. We could also look at this dream and see it as a reference to the need for you to look to the very core of things, in the same way as a skeleton is the basic core on which our bodies are constructed.

THE TREE OF LIFE When we reduce the value of this dream we find the number 10, which is symbolic of completion. In the context of an image of a skeleton, the theme of completion should be seen as the end of your physical life. This does not mean that you are in any danger of passing away in the near future! It means simply that you are at a stage in your inner development where you need to reflect on the nature of mortality. As this is a dream that encourages you to look at the breakdown of forms, we should place this dream in the Sefirah of Gevurah.

THE JOURNEY The value of this dream is equivalent to that of a Hebrew phrase meaning "a still small voice." This suggests that this dream is making obvious a level of knowledge that has always been there. It suggests the idea that you are beginning to enter into some kind of dialogue with your higher self. The compression of this dream indicates that it will take a great deal of energy (Shin) and rigorous study (Lamed) to initiate this dialogue. You are also being advised that if you persist, you will open the door (Daleth) to a much deeper understanding of the Divine.

SKEPTIC

safkanee-sphqny- סַפְקָנִי-300

MEANING We live in a world where it is now far more acceptable to take a skeptical view than to actually believe firmly in something. This is not true just of religious matters but applies to political and philosophical beliefs, and even our view of morality has become increasingly relativistic. In spiritual terms, to dream of being skeptical suggests that you have yet to fully commit to the Great Work. The value of this dream is equivalent to the value of a Hebrew word meaning "revolution," so we should be aware of the potential for change and transformation that exists within a skeptical point of view.

THE TREE OF LIFE When employed in the right way, a skeptical approach to the spiritual quest can yield positive results and ensure that you do not find yourself fooled into the latest quick-fix approach to spiritual development. However, the value of this dream is also equivalent to a Hebrew word meaning "boundary." The implication here is that you are using a skeptical outlook to put a barrier between yourself and the experience of the spiritual. Such an attitude is born of insecurity and indicates a desire to protect yourself from the consequences of failing in your spiritual quest. The path of Cheth relates to the protective force of the Divine, but the suggestion here is that you are being defensive in a way that will not help you to move forward, so we place your dream on the path of Cheth in its negative aspect.

THE JOURNEY The value of this dream is equivalent to that of a Hebrew word meaning "formation." What you should be doing is taking your basic skepticism and finding a way in which you can use it not to hold back from taking any positive steps toward the Divine but to help you in discerning the valuable from the misleading in the spiritual information that is available to you. It would be very helpful for you to join a Kabbalah class of some sort so that you could discuss your more skeptical positions with others who are coming to terms with a spiritual way of looking at the world.

SKY

shamayeem-shmyym- שָׁמַיִם-400

MEANING This is a dream that usually occurs very early in your spiritual development. Since the very dawn of civilization the sky has been seen as the dwelling place of the gods. There are any number of interesting, unlikely, and downright wacky notions that have been put forward to try to explain this fact. However, the important thing in the analysis of this dream is not why it is the case, but simply to note that in every culture the sky is the place where God, or the most senior gods in some cases, is located.

THE TREE OF LIFE The letters in the spelling of this dream title represent the two forces or elements that are represented by the hexagram. The hexagram is a deeply significant symbol; it is commonly known as the Star of David or the seal of Solomon and it contains within it the symbols of fire and water. These are the two primary forces that make up the nature of the universe and the Divine. The presence of this balance between letters of a fiery and watery nature indicates that you have already begun to think deeply about the spiritual construction of the universe. This means that you have moved beyond the Sefirah of Malkut. The value of this dream is equivalent to the value of the letter Tav, and it is on the path of Tav that we should locate this dream.

THE JOURNEY You should see this dream as a positive encouragement that you are progressing well in your initial steps along the Tree of Life. The presence of the elements of Fire and Water in the spelling of this dream title has a message in it for you in terms of your approach to the Great Work. The Divine creative force of Fire and the ever-present transcendent love for the Creation represented by the element of Water are mysteries that lie before you for exploration. You, of course, represent the element of Earth, and you should approach this mystery by the proper application of the element of Air, which represents thought. In other words, this dream is advising that at all times you should take a very reflective and contemplative approach to the realm of the spiritual.

SLEEPING

radoom-rdvm- רָדוּם-250

MEANING To dream of sleeping has a certain disconcerting quality about it. With many dreams we wake and think that the dream was not real since we were simply sleeping. With this dream it is much harder to distinguish the actual from what was only part of a dream. This is very relevant to the spiritual significance of this dream, as it is about the way in which you need to learn to distinguish the merely physical from the spiritually relevant and the difficulties that are associated with trying to take up this challenge. The idea of sleeping carries a suggestion of passivity and undue inaction. In the world of Assiah, where we are all currently residing, it is our deeds, not the lack of them, that shape and develop us as spiritual beings.

THE TREE OF LIFE The value of this dream is equivalent to the value of the Hebrew word meaning "habit." The implication here is that you live your life according to your established habits. In this way, you are almost living as though asleep. You need to find a way of waking up so that you can look at your life more closely and analytically. The value of this dream can be reduced to 7, which is the value of the letter Zayin, meaning "sword." Your dream belongs on the path of Zayin because the image of a sword refers to the need to cut away the unhelpful and focus on those things that will help you progress spiritually.

THE JOURNEY Do not be discouraged by this dream; there are many people who spend their whole lives without ever waking up properly. The fact that you have had this dream is in itself a positive sign. The value of this dream is equivalent to the value of a title for the Divine that refers to God as "The Living God of the Ages." The symbolic presence of the Divine in the value of your dream should be seen as an encouraging sign. It is also important to note that this is a title of the Divine that suggests a strong degree of vitality and dynamism. You should try to mirror this energy and enthusiasm in the way you approach your day-to-day life and the Great Work itself.

See Zohar symbol, Sleep.

SLING (CATAPULT)
kela-qla'a-קלע-200

MEANING It is always surprising to see a dream of any kind of weapon as having a spiritual significance. However, in order to make sense of any dream in a Kabbalistic context, we need to look beneath its obvious day-to-day meaning, and this is equally the case with a dream in which a weapon is the main focus. The value of this dream is equiva-

lent to the value of a Hebrew word referring to springtime, and this tells us that this dream is hopeful and encouraging in terms of your progress with the Great Work.

THE TREE OF LIFE Of all the seasons, spring is the most optimistic. It is a time when new growth is just beginning to show and we can believe that every shoot will become a strong and healthy plant. Right now you are like a hopeful young shoot and there is every chance that if you maintain your efforts, your spiritual side will blossom. The value of this dream is equivalent to the value of the letter Resh, and it is the path of Resh to which your dream belongs. This path is one of the first on the Tree of Life and is concerned with a positive and optimistic reflective nature.

THE JOURNEY The most famous exponent of the use of the sling as a weapon is probably David. Most people are familiar with the tale of David and Goliath. David's victory is a perfect example of the triumph of faith and thought over brute strength. We could even see the bulk of Goliath as a representation of the material world as a whole, while David represents the potential for the spiritual. This would make the stone emanating from the sling akin to the power of the Divine spark. The spiritual quest may seem daunting and unnerving, and this is reflected by the letter Qoph in the spelling of this dream title, but a rigorous approach to the Great Work (Lamed) will ensure that you can vigorously (Ayin) find your own way to build a relationship with the Divine.

SLIPPERS
naal bayeet-na'al byth-נעל בית-562

MEANING Footwear is never going to be the most exciting imagery to experience in your sleep, and if you were looking for the most innocuous of footwear, slippers would make an excellent choice. The implication of this dream is that you have yet to really make a start on your spiritual journey. However, the value of this dream reduces to 13, which indicates that a great change is about to occur in your life, and this is a positive sign for the future.

THE TREE OF LIFE Slippers are comfortable items of clothing that we wear when we are relaxing around the house. If we try to place this in a spiritual context, the overall impression is of someone who currently prefers that which is comfortable over that which might advance his understanding of the world and of the Divine. Consequently, we should locate this dream in the world of the physical and the Sefirah of Malkut.

THE JOURNEY The task ahead of you is to try to find the inner will to commit to the Great Work. The compression of the dream's value begins with the final version of the letter Kaph. This tells you that it is very important that you take some kind of physical action to initiate your exploration of the spiritual. If you do so, the letter Samech is there to reassure you that you will be guided and supported by your higher self. The final letter, Beth, acts as a promise of the spiritual home that is waiting for you. It would be an excellent idea for you to take up tai chi or a similar exercise as a gentle introduction to the spiritual life.

SMOKE

*ashan-a'ashn-*עשׁן*-*420

MEANING The spiritual significance of this dream can be discerned in part by looking for hidden puns or other linguistic references within the title of the dream. This is a technique that is much used by mainstream psychoanalysis, but there is no reason why it cannot be employed in the search for a spiritual message. One very common expression that uses the title of this dream and also compliments the ideas embedded within the values of this dream is the phrase that "where there's smoke, there's fire." From a Kabbalistic perspective, the smoke represents the belief in a higher power and the fire stands for the Divine itself.

THE TREE OF LIFE If we looked at this dream in terms of the four elements, it would be very firmly placed within the element of Air. Smoke itself certainly fits into the Air category. Additionally, the value of this dream reduces to 6. This is the value of the letter Vav, which is very closely associated with the element of Air. The path of Vav is very much about the need for reflection and making choices based on the results of your reflections. This makes the path of Vav an ideal location for your dream.

THE JOURNEY Your challenge over the coming weeks is to take your belief in the Divine and make it absolute and certain. At the moment your belief is at times shaky, and your dream is trying to tell you that beneath the vague smoke of your faith lies a burning fire that is the reality of the Divine existence. The compression of this dream begins with the letter Tav, and this tells us that you have a certain amount of regret at leaving behind the comforts and certainties of the material world. The final let-

ter, Kaph, in the compression is there to tell you that if you take some practical steps, such as scheduling a regular time each day when you meditate, the world of the spiritual will take on the same air of solidity and certainty.

SNAKE

*leheetpatel-lhthphthl-*להתפתל*-*945

MEANING This is not an analysis of a dream about a snake. If that is your dream, you should refer to the interpretation of a dream of a serpent. This dream refers to snaking as a way of movement. As fearful as many of us are when it comes to an actual snake, there is something about the sinuous winding way in which they move that is strangely appealing. The value of this dream is equivalent to that of one of the traditional titles for the Sefirah of Keter. This association emphasizes the positive nature of this dream and should be seen as a very encouraging sign.

THE TREE OF LIFE In the Kabbalah, the path down from the Sefirah of Keter to Malkut is known as the Lightning Flash. The path that winds its way back up to Keter is referred to as the Serpent Path. This dream relates to this Serpent Path since the route up the Tree is snakelike in its twists and turns. Additionally, when we reduce the value of this dream we find the number 9. This is the value of the letter Teth, which means "serpent" or "snake" and represents great strength of character and willpower. This is clearly an ideal path on which to locate your dream.

THE JOURNEY In one sense, this dream is about the totality of the inner journey as it refers to the Serpent Path as a whole. However, in the spelling of the dream title there are two key issues that you should apply to your spiritual efforts. The letter Tav is repeated, and this emphasizes the regret that you will sometimes feel at leaving behind the certainties of the wholly material world. The letter Lamed introduces and completes the spelling of the dream title. It is interesting that the shape of this letter is itself snakelike, but, most important, it refers to the need to maintain a rigorous attitude to your spiritual work in order to ensure success.

See Zohar symbol, Serpent.

SNOW

*sheleg-shlg-*שׁלג*-*333

MEANING This dream is suggestive of an individual who has made very significant progress in the

Great Work. The first thing that we notice about this dream is the fact that its value consists entirely of the number 3. The number 3 is associated with the potential for creativity, and this itself indicates that you already have well-developed insights into the spiritual realm. However, the idea of snow reminds us of winter, a time of year when all life ceases for a while. To be able to see the creative potential even in the dead of winter suggests that you are very close to achieving some form of communion with the Divine itself.

THE TREE OF LIFE The value of this dream is equivalent to the value of the Hebrew name for a form of Kabbalistic analysis known as the "Kabbalah of nine chambers." This system of Gematria or textual analysis relies on a form of code in order to find new meanings and significance in existing texts. Its presence in this dream indicates that you are beginning to see the truths behind the apparent reality of the physical world. This level of knowledge places this dream in the non-Sefirah of Daat. *Daat* literally means "knowledge," and it is positioned partway along the path of Gimel. It can be seen as a final hurdle on the way to Keter.

THE JOURNEY There is very little specific advice that can be given to you at this stage in your inner development. However, the compression of your dream's value gives some hints as how best to approach the impending communion with the creative source. You will need to put all your energy into this final stage of your journey (Shin) and must not assume that you can afford to stop studying (Lamed) matters of a spiritual nature. If you maintain a rigorous and disciplined approach, you will be able to traverse the path of Gimel and reach the Crown of the Tree of Life.

SOAP

*sabon-sbvn-*סבון-118

MEANING Almost all religions have an injunction to their adherents that they should maintain both physical and spiritual cleanliness. Very often there are a range of complex rules that lay down exactly the level of cleanliness to be achieved. On the surface, this dream would appear to be mainly about the need to be physically prepared for any attempt at establishing a dialogue with the higher forces. However, the values within this dream make it clear that the key focus is on your mental preparation. The value of this dream is equivalent to the value of the Hebrew word relating to the angelic ruler of the ele-

ment of Air, and this emphasizes the importance of thoughts in this dream.

THE TREE OF LIFE When we reduce the value of this dream we find the number 10, which indicates the completion of an important stage in your life. Additionally, the value of this dream is equivalent to that of a Hebrew word meaning "to renew," and this also implies a deepening and strengthening of your relationship to the Divine. In the spelling of this dream title we find the letter Nun in its final form. As the path of Nun relates to the processes by which we increase our understanding of the Divine, it is here that we should locate your dream.

THE JOURNEY The path of Nun can be quite traumatic because in order to better understand the spiritual framework of the world in which we live, we must also better understand ourselves. We can achieve this only by looking honestly at our inner nature, including all of our flaws and fears. The letter Qoph in the compression of this dream points out the anxiety that you may be feeling at this time. However, the subsequent letter, Yod, reveals that you have awakened the Divine spark within yourself, and this will help to ensure that you receive the protection (Cheth) of the Divine as you take up the challenge before you.

SOLDER

*lakham-lchm-*להם-78

MEANING You cannot get much more down-to-earth than solder, and it might be very difficult to see how such a prosaic image could relate to any spiritual activity. However, as is often the way in the Kabbalah, the most mundane objects can have enormously significant symbolic value when looked at in the right way. The value of this dream is equivalent to the value of a Hebrew word referring to the influence of the Divine emanating from the Sefirah of Keter, so we should see this dream as holding very positive implications for your inner development.

THE TREE OF LIFE When we solder anything we are engaging in a process whereby we join together two disparate elements. The influence from Keter is in part responsible for creating the conditions in which we can try to "solder" ourselves together both with other individuals and with the Divine. To achieve this uniting of disparate elements in human society requires a great deal of compassion and understanding. Consequently, the appropriate path for this dream is the path of Mem, as it is strongly connected to ideas of empathy and altruism.

THE JOURNEY This dream's value is equivalent to the value of a Hebrew word meaning "initiation." This suggests that you are undergoing a process of exposure to certain elements of the Divine nature. The more you act on your inclination to be compassionate and act as a mediator, the greater will be your level of understanding. When we reduce the value of your dream we find the number 6. This is the value of the letter Vav, which suggests that as well as helping others, you need to reflect on the spiritual implications of doing so.

SOLDIER
khayal-chyyl-חייל-58

MEANING The Kabbalah has been developed and appropriated by a wide range of faiths and belief systems. However, while it is probable that ideas from other early Middle-Eastern cultures are present, the Kabbalah is intrinsically Judaic in nature. We should not be surprised that the dream of a soldier has a very positive significance when Kabbalistically interpreted, since the Torah is full of battles and wars conducted by the tribes of Israel to secure their future. However, in purely spiritual terms, this dream is advocating not that you take up arms but that you take a determined, disciplined, and courageous approach to the Great Work.

THE TREE OF LIFE The value of this dream is equivalent to the value of Hebrew words that refer to strength and might. We might expect this, but much less expected is the fact that this dream shares its value with a special shorthand way (known as a notariqon) of writing a Hebrew phrase meaning "secret wisdom." We access true wisdom by virtue of the grace of the Divine, and its presence is indicated by the letter Yod in the center of the spelling of this dream. The letter Yod appears twice, and it is the path of Yod to which your dream belongs, since it is about awakening the Divine spark within yourself.

THE JOURNEY The compression of this dream tells you quite clearly that the task ahead of you is to develop and deepen your understanding of the nature of the Divine (Nun). You will be supported in this endeavor by the protective force of the higher powers (Cheth). The final Lamed in the spelling of this dream should be seen as a reminder that although you will be supported in your efforts by the Divine, you must ensure that you are taking a disciplined and well-organized approach to the Great Work. If you do so, the results you achieve will be more than worth the effort.

SON
ben-bn-בן-52

MEANING When we consider family relationships there is always a way in which the physical relationship between two people can be related to an aspect of the spiritual relationship with the Divine. There is for example, a sense in which we all have the same type of relationship to the creative force as a son has to his parents. In dreaming about a son, the focus is not so much on what it means to be a son but on the nature of your relationship to the force that would be symbolized as your parent in this dream.

THE TREE OF LIFE The most important and useful thing we can do for our children is to teach them to think for themselves. If we can do this, all the other important facets of a personality can flow from that ability. Further, a child who loves because he decides to or feels a wish to express that emotion has learned far more about the nature of existence than the child who loves his parent simply because he knows he is expected to. Similarly, the Divine puts us in a situation where we are free to think and learn for ourselves. When we reduce the value of this dream we find the number 7, which is the value of the letter Zayin. This letter can be seen as referring to the ability to discriminate between ideas and actions, so it is the ideal path for this dream.

THE JOURNEY In dreaming of being a son, you have recognized, at least unconsciously, the existence of a profoundly close relationship with the Divine. The value of this dream is equivalent to the value of the Hebrew words meaning "father" and "mother" combined. This supports the idea that the real focus of this dream is on what it is that makes you a "son"—the existence of parents. You should find time over the next weeks to explore the way in which your relationship to the creative force is like that of a child to his parents and try to see how those thoughts can best influence the way in which you approach the Great Work.

SORE
kaoov-kavb-כאוב-29

MEANING To dream of being sore or of suffering from sores is a distinctly unpleasant experience.

Like all dreams, though, no matter how much you might wish you could have avoided it, there is a helpful and significant point being made about the nature of your spiritual development. Being sore or having sores is not simply painful, it can be very distressing and even embarrassing. At a spiritual level, we see this dream as emblematic of feeling that your life's direction is out of your control and seems to be taking a turn for the worse for reasons that you cannot understand.

THE TREE OF LIFE The value of this dream is equivalent to the value of the Hebrew word meaning "to break down." This reinforces the sense of your spiritual life failing to move in the direction in which you wish to take it. However, this is a feeling rather than an actuality. Further, it is a very common feeling for someone who is just beginning to explore his inner self. We should place this dream on the path of Qoph because it represents exactly these initial doubts and anxieties. Additionally, the value of this dream is 29, and the path of Qoph is the twenty-ninth path on the Tree of Life when we count the Sefirot as paths in their own right.

THE JOURNEY In order for you to continue to progress along the Tree it is important that you find some way to remove or at least control your underlying fears. The compression of the dream's value can guide you as to how you should approach the challenge of controlling your anxieties. The letter Kaph tells you that you should find some practical activity to engage in; this could be a meditation or yoga class or simply scheduling a time each day to study spiritual ideas. The final letter, Teth, is there to remind you that ultimately it is your own strength of character that will carry you through this difficult period.

SOUL

nefesh–nphsh-נפש-430

MEANING This is a dream where we do not have to dig too deep to see the spiritual aspect. To be dreaming of your soul is a sure sign that you are extremely eager to make good progress in terms of your inner development. The value of this dream is equivalent to the value of the Hebrew word meaning "concealed," and this emphasizes the fact that even when you are striving to make contact with your higher self, you still face a long and arduous road before success is achieved.

THE TREE OF LIFE You are in a state of longing for a sense of union with your soul, and this is a very encouraging sign. It also tells us that in terms of

your progress, this dream is located somewhere below Tiferet on the Tree of Life. The value of this dream is equivalent to the full title of the Sefirah of Yesod, so this is without doubt the correct location for your dream. Yesod is the first Sefirah that you encounter after leaving Malkut, and it is reasonable that at this point in your journey the desire for contact with your higher self is extremely strong.

THE JOURNEY Having made a commitment to the Great Work and having already reached the first "staging post" on the long trek up to Keter, you are in the difficult position of knowing that the comforts of the material world are largely illusory. At the same time, you do not yet have any tangible sense of the nature of the spiritual reality that lies beyond the physical. The compression of this dream looks both backward and forward in terms of your journey. It looks back to the initial leap of faith of the path of Tav and forward to the rigorous study (Lamed) that will be required in order to continue your growing understanding.

SOUP

marak–mrq-מרק-340

MEANING When we are ill, the one thing that we can still probably manage to eat and that will help to get us back up on our feet is soup. To dream of soup is to dream of a product that is nutritious and warming and easy to swallow. There are some obvious spiritual parallels that can immediately be drawn: The associations that apply to soup could equally be applied to the way in which spiritual truths are presented in most mainstream religious texts. The truths that are presented are nutritious to the soul, they warm our hearts, and when well written they are very definitely easy to swallow.

THE TREE OF LIFE The value of this dream is equivalent to the value of a Hebrew word meaning "lion." The nature of a lion as a symbol is that it is proud, strong, and courageous. The suggestion here is that as well as accepting religious "soup," you need to be a little braver and examine some spiritual ideas that are more "meaty" and complex. This is not a negative statement, though, as it is an indication of your ability to digest more complicated spiritual ideas. The idea of hard study is associated with the path of Lamed, so it is here that we should locate your dream.

THE JOURNEY The compression of this dream's value indicates that it will take a great deal of enthusiastic energy (Shin) on your part to come to grips with the spiritual issues that you are now ready to examine. However, it is also clear that the maternal force of the Divine (Mem) will be with you to ease the way as far as is possible. The value of this dream is equivalent to the value of the Hebrew word meaning "book," so it is quite clear where you should start your studies. There are now lots of stores that carry a broad range of titles on the general subject of spirituality, and it is time for you to start browsing.

SOWING

*leezroa–lzrva'a–*לזרוע-313

MEANING Agriculture is not as visibly important as it was a few hundred years ago, but it is just as fundamental to our well-being. When the Kabbalah was in its infancy, agriculture was at the center of the day-to-day world, and understandably many of the key spiritual symbols were based on terms gleaned from farming. The idea of sowing represents the planting of a spiritual idea or feeling within an individual, so to dream of sowing is to dream of encouraging others to consider their lives in a more spiritual context.

THE TREE OF LIFE The value of this dream reduces to 7, which is the value of the letter Zayin, meaning "sword." This represents the ability to separate the useful and valid spiritual ideas from those that are ultimately unhelpful. This is not the path of this dream, though, since it is the ability represented by the path of Zayin that you are trying to pass on to others. Your dream sits on the path of Heh, meaning "window," since you are close to achieving a glimpse of the nature of the Divine.

THE JOURNEY When we look at the numbers within the value of this dream we see a central 1 bracketed by the number 3. The implication of this is that you should be as creative as possible in encouraging others to engage with spiritual matters and ensuring that the nature of the Divine remains central in all that you say and do. The compression of this dream's value tells us that you will need a great deal of energy to accomplish your goals (Shin), but that the spark of the Divine that is alive within you (Yod) will ensure that you are able to continue on your way toward a full understanding of the secret wisdom.

SPACE

*khalal–chll–*חלל-68

MEANING If we were to believe the tag line of certain science-fiction series, space represents the ultimate barrier that mankind can cross. Certainly this dream symbolizes the achievement of the almost unthinkable. However, in reality the most difficult barrier to breach is not the one that separates us from outer space but the one that separates us from our inner space. The value of this dream is equivalent to the value of the Hebrew word meaning "wisdom," and this dream reflects your desire to possess sufficient wisdom to fully understand your inner nature.

THE TREE OF LIFE When we reduce the value of this dream we find the number 5. This is an enormously significant number in the Western Mystery Tradition, as it represents an individual who has managed to master the four elements within himself under the overall control of the fifth element of Spirit. This is something that we achieve in the Sefirah of Tiferet, where we are able to make contact with our higher self, so it is here that we should locate your dream.

THE JOURNEY The spelling of this dream title highlights the need for a particularly disciplined approach to the study of the spiritual in order to achieve the results that you are aiming for in life. The letter Lamed is repeated, and this represents the sometimes harsh force of the Divine urging you on to ever greater effort. The compression of the dream does contain the letter Samech, which indicates the support you will receive from your higher self. In both the spelling of the dream and in the compression of its value we find the letter Cheth, which represents the protective force of the Divine in your life.

SPARK

*neetsots–nytzvtz–*ניצוץ-246

MEANING Anybody experiencing this dream without a knowledge of the Kabbalah might take it as an indication of great energy or possibly a hint that he was about to experience a number of good ideas in the near future. Even a brief reading of some Kabbalistic ideas will make it clear that the image of a spark has great spiritual significance. The value of this dream is equivalent to the value of the Hebrew word meaning "height." In almost all religions, notions of great height are associated with Divinity, and this dream relates to the influence that descends to us from the Divine.

THE TREE OF LIFE When we reduce the value of this dream it produces the number 12. This number is strongly connected to ideas of self-sacrifice and altruism. It is also the case that those people who are lucky enough to be directly inspired by the creative spark of the Divine tend to behave in a way that places the needs of others over their own. The path of Mem is connected to this commendable approach to the world, and it is here that we should locate your dream.

THE JOURNEY While the letter Mem is also present in the compression of this dream, thereby emphasizing the compassionate and giving nature of your spirituality, the spelling of the dream title also demonstrates a great deal of positive active energy. The letter Tzaddi appears twice in this title, once in its final form, which serves to emphasize its importance. This letter refers to a sense of dedication and commitment to your spiritual work, and as long as you are able to maintain this high level of enthusiasm for the spiritual quest you will have great success in deepening the level of your insight.

SPEAKING
*ledaber–ldbr–*לדבר*-236*

MEANING The key to understanding anything, from politics to spirituality to the workings of your car's engine, is communication. This dream refers to speaking and so represents your attempts to engage in some form of dialogue with the Divine. This does not mean literally attempting to talk with the Divine either through prayer or other means but indicates a desire to achieve the best possible understanding of the nature of the spiritual dimension of the universe.

THE TREE OF LIFE When we reduce the value of this dream we find the number 11. This number is important in many mystical systems and is symbolic of the spiritual as a whole. In the context of this dream, it implies that you are about to experience a spiritually profound moment in your life. There is little doubt that this will result directly from your attempts to find a means of communicating with your higher self. The path of Peh literally means "mouth" and is connected to all forms of communication. Given the content and the significance of this dream, it is ideally positioned on the path of Peh.

THE JOURNEY You should already have a clear sense of the task ahead of you in the coming weeks and months which is to try to build some connections with the higher that will allow you a greater insight into the world of the spiritual. The initial letter, Resh, in the compression of this dream's value is a sign that you are likely to be successful as

you are operating under the benign influence of the Divine. However, this does not mean that it will be easy as the letter Lamed points to the need for rigorous hard work on your part. The final letter, Vav, is a reminder that your studies as disciplined as they might be should also be accompanied by reflection.

SPICE
*letabel–lthbl–*לתבל*-462*

MEANING We think of spices as adding a touch of the exotic to our diet. Consequently, in spiritual terms we might expect the image of spice to indicate that the dreamer is likely to have an interest in the more unusual and esoteric aspects of the underlying truths of the universe. However, it is important that we always remember the origins of archetypal symbols. In the Kabbalah, the image of spice is extremely positive and suggests a sense of sweetness in your relationship with the Divine. Hundreds of years ago, spice was used both to make food more exciting and to preserve food.

THE TREE OF LIFE If we reconsider the significance of this dream in a spiritual context, bearing in mind the original functions of spice, we find a very different underlying meaning. Your dream relates to the attempt to preserve your efforts in the Great Work even at times when you appear to be failing to achieve any results. The path of Teth relates to the strength of character and the willpower that is needed to persist in the spiritual quest, and it is this path to which your dream belongs.

THE JOURNEY There are a growing number of New Age spiritualities that are growing in popularity and prominence. Many of them offer perfectly valid ways to approach the Divine in a style that has been brought up-to-date so that it fits more easily with a twenty-first-century life-style. However, as has always been the case throughout history, there are those that offer an easy or quick route to enlightenment. The unfortunate truth is that, as this dream tells us, the road to success in the Great Work is not an easy one. Even though you may be experiencing difficulties, you should persist, as it is only through dogged determination that the best prizes are ever won.

SPIDER
*akaveesh–a'akbysh–*עכביש*-402*

MEANING Spiders are not the most popular of animals and many people find them positively unsympathetic. It would be tempting to see a dream about spiders as being suggestive of some generally uncomfortable feelings about your spiritual development, but this is not what the values within this dream suggest. The central letter of the spelling of this dream is Beth, which means "house," and in a spiritual context it refers to the house of the Divine. In other words, this dream is about the attempt to gain entrance into the presence of the Divine itself.

THE TREE OF LIFE Whatever you may feel about spiders it is very difficult to look at a spider's web and not be impressed by the intricacy of its design. A spider's web is unique; it is the snowflake of the animal kingdom. No two are the same, yet they possess the same delicate beauty. There are two important spiritual messages contained here. The first is the need to create a complex web of understanding in order to move ever upward on the Tree of Life. The other is the importance of being individual in your approach to the Divine. The initial letter in the spelling of this dream is Ayin, which refers to a vigorous and individual approach to the Great Work, so it is an ideal path on which to locate this dream.

THE JOURNEY However enthusiastic you are to move forward, there is inevitably a certain sense of regret as your level of insight deepens that you can no longer relate so closely to those who do not share your faith in the spiritual. This is indicated by the presence of the letter Tav in the compression of this dream's value. The subsequent letter, Beth, represents the upside of this change in your outlook in that it is bringing you ever close to the home of the Divine.

SPINNING (THREAD)

leetvot-ltvvth-לטוות-451

MEANING In England in the late eighteenth century, the spinning of thread was a thriving cottage industry. Now we think of spinning only in the context either of fairy tales, where spinning tends to feature very heavily, or possibly of the Fates from Greek mythology, who held the thread of each person's life. Even when spinning was a common activity it already had the associations with the thread of life that it has retained through a range of popular tales. It is this mythical and folkloric association with spinning that is relevant to the analysis of your dream. Indeed, the value of this dream is equivalent to the value of a Hebrew phrase that means "the essence of man."

THE TREE OF LIFE This dream is concerned with the whole idea of what it means to be a person, what is the purpose of the lives that we are spinning out day by day. You have made very good progress toward an understanding of the answer to that ultimate question. The value of this dream is equivalent to the value of the Hebrew name for the specific choir of angels associated with the Sefirah of Tiferet. This suggests that we should locate your dream in this Sefirah. The presence of the letter Vav, repeated in the center of the spelling of this dream title, also supports such a positioning. The value of the letter Vav is 6, and the Sefirah of Tiferet is the sixth on the Tree of Life.

THE JOURNEY When we reduce the value of this dream we find the number 10. This number indicates the completion of a major cycle in your life. The cycle in question is the process of seeking and finding your higher self in the Sefirah of Tiferet. However, your journey is far from over, as you must now try to establish some form of communion with the Divine. While it may be very tempting to rest on your laurels, you should make a point of establishing a regular routine of meditation and study so that you continue to deepen your understanding of the spiritual realm.

SPITE

reeshoot-rsha'avth-רשעות-976

MEANING When we interpret a dream it is always important to remember that the events and emotions within that dream relate to the dreamer. Nobody likes to be thought of as spiteful, and to dream of spite might make you worry that a negative side of your personality had been revealed by your unconscious. However, the spite that you are dreaming of is not directed outward but inward at yourself. The values within this dream suggest that you are vigorously attempting to remove those elements of your nature that relate to your ego-based self rather than to your higher self. Consequently, you should see this dream as a positive comment on your inner development.

THE TREE OF LIFE It has been an accepted truth of the vast majority of religions and mystical systems that in order to truly develop, our outward behavior must mirror our inner aspirations. Certainly in terms of those parts of our personality that are ego-based, any change will have a very noticeable impact in the way we live our day-to-day lives. The value of this dream reduces to 4, which is the number of the material world. This association

SPLENDOR

emphasizes the fact that this dream is about change being manifested in the physical world. The path of Kaph is concerned primarily with the practical and actual business of living a spiritually based life, and so this is the path on which we should locate your dream.

THE JOURNEY Your eagerness to rid yourself of the baser side of your nature is certainly commendable, but you must also be careful not to be too hard on yourself, as none of us is perfect nor indeed could anyone ever be. The compression of this dream reveals the letter Tzaddi in its final form, a clear sign of the total commitment that you have to the spiritual quest. The subsequent letter, Ayin, refers to the vigor with which you are pursuing your spiritual goals. However, you should take particular notice of the final letter, Vav, which reminds you of the need for quiet contemplation as well as dynamic self-exploration.

SPLENDOR

hod-hvd-הוד-15

MEANING In a purely psychological analysis, this dream might suggest that the dreamer is somewhat vain or has aspirations to grandeur and wealth. This is because without a Kabbalistic frame of reference, the term *splendor* has no significance beyond its meaning in everyday usage. In the Kabbalah it has a very specific meaning, so this dream points to a very specific stage in your inner development. The key text in the Kabbalah is the *Zohar*, otherwise known as the *Book of Splendor*. It is said that our enlightenment brings with it an innate sense of the splendor in the universe.

THE TREE OF LIFE As you will have noticed from the dream title, the word *splendor* is the literal meaning of the Sefirah of Hod. It is therefore immediately apparent that this is where we should locate your dream. The reason behind the name "Splendor" is too complex for us to examine here, but it does not relate to any earthly concerns with glamour or riches. Rather, it relates to the fact that the Sefirah of Hod is the recipient of the Divine force as transformed by the Great Mother or the Sefirah of Binah. In terms of your practical spiritual development, the Sefirah of Hod is concerned with your mental faculties, and now is an ideal time for you to examine the way in which you approach the Divine in terms of your thoughts.

THE JOURNEY When we reduce the value of this dream we reveal the number 6, which is the value

of the letter Vav. This emphasizes the need for you to spend a good deal of time reflecting on the nature of your spiritual quest. The initial letter, Yod, in the compression of this dream refers to the Divine force, which is responsible for your momentum up the Tree of Life. The final letter, Heh, represents the glimpse of the Divine that you are hoping to gain once you have completed your long journey.

SPLINTER

rasees-rsys-רסיס-330

MEANING From a psychological perspective, this dream would be seen as indicating that you are going through a phase where you have to deal with a number of small but significantly irritating problems. From a Kabbalistic point of view, this dream has a far more positive significance. The key point about a splinter is that it gets under your skin, and though you are constantly aware of its presence, you cannot always see that it is there. The suggestion in this dream is that an awareness of the Divine has, like a splinter, worked its way under your skin.

THE TREE OF LIFE This is a dream that relates to a very early stage in your spiritual journey. The idea of a splinter suggests something unexpected and, of course, something that is small. You are at a point in your inner development where you are not consciously directing your inner growth but are being driven along by a simple awareness. The first path that leads out of Malkut is the path of Tav, and this is a most appropriate location for your dream.

THE JOURNEY As you progress further, the splinter will disappear and be replaced by a very strong conviction and deep understanding of the ever-present nature of the Divine. However, this transformation requires that you apply yourself diligently to the Great Work. The compression of this dream's value advises you that you will need both great energy (Shin) and a willingness to study hard (Lamed) in order to succeed. The reduction value of this dream produces the number 6, which is the value of the letter Vav and reminds you that you will have to set aside a certain amount of time each day to reflect on your progress.

SPOON

kaf-kph-כף-100

MEANING There seems to be very little to say in spiritual terms about a dream in which the main image is a spoon. However, as always, the closer we look the more we can see of relevance to your spiritual development. Of all the different eating utensils that are available to us, the spoon is the easiest to use. It is also the most practical and quickest tool for eating a meal. In spiritual terms, we could see this as indicating that you like to approach the Great Work in a fairly down-to-earth manner. Additionally, it is likely that you do not have the free time to take anything but the simplest of routes to try to achieve some kind of contact with the realm of the spiritual.

THE TREE OF LIFE The spelling of the Hebrew word meaning "spoon" is the same as the spelling of the Hebrew letter Kaph. Consequently, this is a very strong argument for placing your dream on this path. The path of Kaph is concerned with a practical approach to the world and the nature of spirituality, so it also fits the content of this dream. The value of this dream is equivalent to the value of the Hebrew word meaning "exertion," and this makes it clear that although your time is limited, the level of effort you put in is no less than that of someone with significantly more free time.

THE JOURNEY You are making good progress, and your understanding of the spiritual is constantly growing. Further, because of your very practical take on these matters, you are finding ways of bringing your spiritual insights into play within your day-to-day life. The value of this dream is 100, and in the context of this dream the importance of this value is that it is 10, multiplied by itself. The number 10 is associated with completion, and this dream signifies that you are very definitely one of life's finishers. As long as you maintain this level of energy and commitment to the Great Work, you will achieve all of your spiritual goals.

SPRING

aveev–abyb– אביב *-15*

MEANING In the depths of winter life can seem depressing and at times all our best efforts can feel fruitless. However, once the warmth of spring arrives, the world takes on a more optimistic atmosphere and we begin to believe that things may not be so bad after all. In a spiritual context, this dream is also extremely hopeful, as it signifies that you are beginning to grow as a spiritually aware individual. The value of this dream is equivalent to the value of the Hebrew word meaning "overflowing," and this serves to emphasize the encouraging tone of this dream.

THE TREE OF LIFE As spring is the first season of the year, we can safely assume that this dream relates to an early stage of your spiritual development. You have already made a firm commitment to exploring the nature of the universe and are at a point where your enthusiasm is matched by your optimism. The path of Resh has no particular association with the springtime but refers to the eagerness that you feel to explore the nature of the Divine. Additionally, the path of Resh indicates the benevolent aspect of the Divine, and this is very appropriate since the theme of spring suggests that your inner growth is being encouraged by the spiritual equivalent of a warm Sun.

THE JOURNEY The compression of this dream's value produces the letters Yod and Heh. When combined they form one of the names of God in the Kabbalistic tradition. This itself reminds us that you have a very sincere desire to succeed in the Great Work. Taken individually, these letters represent the exact nature of your proper goals at this time. You should first try to awaken the Divine spark within you (Yod). Once this has been achieved, you should be working toward the achievement of at least a brief glimpse of the true nature of the Divine itself.

STAIN

ketem–kthm– כתם *-460*

MEANING To dream of a stain calls to mind ideas of being tainted or shamed in some way. It is extremely difficult to see this dream in anything but a negative manner. However, when we look at the values within this dream, they are all encouraging and suggest that you are making solid progress in your search for spiritual truth. In fact, the value of this dream is equivalent to the value of the Hebrew word meaning "holy unto God," and this serves to emphasize the sincerity of your efforts.

THE TREE OF LIFE If we are not to interpret this dream in a negative manner, then we need to find a different way of perceiving the image of a stain. We should perhaps see the stain as a reference to a symbolic indication that you have made the decision to try to pursue a spiritually focused life. The reduction value of this dream produces the number 10, which tells us that you have completed a major cycle in your life. As this number is referring to your decision to engage with the spiritual, we are looking for a very early path on the Tree of Life, so the ideal location for this dream is the path of Tav.

THE JOURNEY The letter Tav is the central letter in the spelling of this dream title and also appears in the compression of this dream's value. The path of Tav can be a very difficult stage of your inner development. However, the letter Samech completes the compression and is there to remind you that the supportive energies of your higher self will be there to help maintain your commitment to the Great Work. The letter Kaph which begins the spelling of your dream title, suggests that it may be a good idea for you to join a meditation or yoga class in order to give you a concrete basis on which you build your spiritual understanding.

STAIRS

*madregot-mdrgvth-*מדרגות-653

MEANING Any image that involves either height or some form of upward motion can be taken to refer to a desire to rise toward a better understanding of the Divine. The theme of stairs has a long history of symbolic reference within the Western Mystery Tradition. This dream represents your wish to climb up the stairs that are, effectively, the paths on the Tree of Life. When we look at the spelling of this dream title we can see a story of your spiritual direction within the letters. The maternal force of the Divine (Mem) will help you open the door (Daleth) to the benevolence of the Lord (Resh) so that you will be able to access the wisdom (Gimel) of the macrocosm (Vav). This in turn will enable you to see the world (Tav) in a new light.

THE TREE OF LIFE The story that lies within the letters of this dream's spelling indicates that you have already achieved a high level of spiritual insight. When we reduce the value of this dream we find the number 5, and this tells us that you are already in a position where the four elements of your personality are governed by your higher self. The key to the story within the letters is the letter Daleth, which represents the door to a deeper understanding, so we should position this dream on the path of Daleth.

THE JOURNEY If you persist with your current approach to exploring the spiritual nature of the universe, the implications within this dream are that you will soon be reaping some significant rewards for your efforts. The central letter, Nun, in the compression of this dream's value also points to the fact that you are on the verge of achieving a deepening and strengthening of your faith. The value of this dream is a prime number and so is regarded as an indication of uniqueness within the Western Mystery Tradition. The message to take from this is that you should not be afraid to apply your personality to the way in which you build a relationship with the Divine.

STAMMER

*geemgoom-gmgvm-*גמגום-90

MEANING Sometimes we are faced with a dream that would produce significantly different interpretations from a psychological and a Kabbalistic perspective. The dream of stammering is one such dream. The psychologist would be likely to see such a dream as presenting the dreamer with a symbolic representation of his feelings of inadequacy or of his inability to communicate his feelings effectively. From a Kabbalistic point of view, this dream does point to feelings of spiritual unworthiness, but the overall message is that you are engaging with the spiritual quest in a very positive manner. It is well worth remembering that Moses himself was supposed to have a stammer.

THE TREE OF LIFE The notion of stammering suggests a lack of confidence, but the letter Gimel, which is, among other things, associated with creativity and innovation, is repeated within the spelling of this dream title. It is mirrored by the double appearance of the letter Mem. This letter refers to the protective force of the Divine, and the suggestion here is that you should allow this aspect of the higher force to give you the confidence to approach the Divine in the way that feels right for you. The value of this dream is equivalent to the value of the letter Mem when spelled in full, so it is an ideal path on which to position your dream.

THE JOURNEY In terms of individuals, the path of Mem points to a person who has great compassion and is willing to act in an altruistic way for the betterment of others. It is this willingness to place the needs of others above your own that informs your approach to the Great Work. The message in this dream is that in helping others you are also developing yourself spiritually and should not feel that you are in any way unworthy of greater spiritual insight. The value of this dream is also equivalent to the numerical value of the letter Tzaddi, and it is present in this dream to tell you that if you simply continue as you are, your commitment to a spiritually informed life-style will enable you to achieve your goals.

❧ STAR

khokav-kvkb- כוכב *-48*

MEANING As you might expect, a dream of a star has profound and deeply positive implications for your future spiritual development. It is likely that most people are aware of the importance of a star as a herald of great things to come, thanks to the story of Jesus. However, it is important that we remember that the idea of a star was included in the story of the nativity because its symbolic importance was already well established. The star is enormously important in the Kabbalah as an intensely positive symbol of great things to come in terms of your spiritual development. The value of this dream is equivalent to the Hebrew word meaning "mercy," and this suggests that you are being guided at this time by the higher toward the right spiritual direction.

THE TREE OF LIFE The Hebrew word meaning "star" is the same as the Hebrew word for the planet Mercury. This planet has traditionally been associated with the Sefirah of Hod, so it is here that we should locate your dream. The Sefirah of Hod is associated with the attempt to find some means of intellectually understanding the nature of the Divine and of finding a way to communicate that understanding. The value of this dream is also equivalent to the value of the Hebrew word meaning "strength," and this is a sign that you will be able to make sense of the spiritual insights that you will gain.

THE JOURNEY In the Western Mystery Tradition, a star is a sign that you are being protected by higher forces and that you have the potential to achieve great things in terms of your spiritual development. The compression of this dream produces the letters Mem and Cheth. This combination of letters reflects the fact that you are doing your best to mirror the attributes of the Divine in the way that you live your life and bodes well for your ability to learn the lessons of the Sefirah of Hod. The letter Mem refers to your compassion and willingness to help and protect those in need. This is a reflection of the letter Cheth, which refers to the protective influence of the Divine itself.

See Zohar symbol, Radiant Star.

STARVING

raav-ra'ab- רעב *-272*

MEANING This is the sort of dream that seems to have an effect long after you wake. It is likely that you will feel inexplicably hungry despite the fact that this was only a dream. This is because the fear of starvation is so primal and powerful. In spiritual terms, the dream represents an awareness of the absence of the Divine in your life. More than just a realization that your life lacks a spiritual dimension, this dream points to a growing desire on your part to try to rectify the situation.

THE TREE OF LIFE The value of this dream is equivalent to the value of a Hebrew word meaning "brutish." A very strong argument can be made to suggest that it is the existence of a spiritual side to our nature that separates us from brute animals. As you have not yet made the decision to follow your desire to find a spiritual focus in your life, we should place this dream in the Sefirah of Malkut. This view is supported by the fact that the value of the Hebrew word meaning "earth" is also equivalent to the value of your dream.

THE JOURNEY It is clear that your role over the next few weeks is to find the inner will and courage to make a start on your spiritual journey. It will be necessary to make some swift and radical changes to your life-style in order to gain the spiritual nourishment that you need. The reduction of this dream's value produces the number 9, which is the value of the Hebrew letter Teth and relates directly to this need for great strength of character. The letter Ayin at the center of the compression of this dream's value tells you that you need the courage to make a leap of faith, and also need to be willing to develop your own personal relationship with the Divine. If you make a sincere effort to reach out to your higher self, you will find that your faith is duly rewarded.

STATUE

pesel-psl- פסל *-170*

MEANING Language is enormously important to Judaism, and one of the many impressive facts about the Torah is that not a single word or even letter has been changed since it was first transcribed. It is crucial that we bear this in mind when analyzing the significance of this dream. We might be tempted to associate the term *statue* with the idea of an idol, and a traditional Kabbalistic point of view would see this dream as indicative of a reductive and solidifying view of the world that blocks the ability to see the wondrous nature of the Divine. However, they are two distinct concepts, and the word *statue* has only positive implications for your inner development.

The idea of a statue represents a visible symbol of the values to which you are aspiring rather than a graven image.

THE TREE OF LIFE The value of this dream is equivalent to the value of the Hebrew word used to refer to David's staff. The symbolic significance of a staff is that it stands for the support that we can gain from the Divine influence if we maintain our faith and commitment to the Great Work. When we reduce the value of this dream we find the number 8, which is the value of the letter Cheth. This letter refers to the protective influence of the Divine and so fits well with the association of this dream with the staff of David. Consequently, we should place your dream on the path of Cheth.

THE JOURNEY By virtue of already being on the path of Cheth, you have already gone a long way toward achieving your spiritual goals. The advice in this dream is that you need some kind of clearly visible support to help you to continue in your attempts to glean some form of communion with the Divine. The compression of this dream's value indicates that you still have some anxieties about your progress. It may be that you feel that the idea of constructing some kind of reassurance, be it mental or physical, means that you have failed to advance sufficiently. However, the letter Ayin in the dream's compression tells you that you should approach the Divine by whatever way works best for you.

STEEPLE

*tsereeakh-tzrych-*צריח-308

MEANING Although it has been largely appropriated by the Christian faith, there is nothing uniquely Christian about the construction of a steeple on a religious building. The purpose of any steeple is to represent the aspiration of the worshippers to get as close to the Divine as possible. When we reduce the value of this dream we find the number 11. Given the association of the number 11 with all things mystical, it is likely that you are close to achieving some form of spiritual insight.

THE TREE OF LIFE The value of this dream is equivalent to the value of the Hebrew word meaning "approaching." This emphasizes the fact that this dream relates to your attempt to make contact with some aspect of the Divine. The values and associations of this dream suggest that you are very close to entering the Sefirah of Tiferet, where you will be able to make contact with your higher self. We should locate this dream on the path of Samech

since this leads into the haven of Tiferet and, rather like a steeple, can be seen as a guide that directs you to a spiritual communion.

THE JOURNEY You should feel very encouraged by this dream because it is a definite sign that your commitment, indicated by the initial letter, Tzaddi, in the spelling of this dream title, is shortly to be rewarded. The value of this dream is equivalent to the value of the Hebrew word meaning "dawn." This is another appropriate association as the Sefirah of Tiferet is linked with the Sun and also because once you have contacted your higher self, you are able to start a whole new life.

STEPPING

*tsaad-tza'ad-*צעד-164

MEANING It is quite common to refer to the process of spiritual development as some form of voyage. This is in no small part because the experience of a spiritual moment is very much like being in an entirely unfamiliar place. This dream uses the imagery of travel to encourage you to reflect on the nature of your journey of inner discovery. The fact that you are stepping does suggest that your progress is steady rather than speedy but it also contains within it very definite ideas of upward momentum.

THE TREE OF LIFE When we reduce the value of this dream we find the number 11, which indicates that you are about to have a significant mystical experience. If we look at the compression of this dream we see the letters Qoph, Samech, and Daleth. The implication of this sequence is that you have moved from a state of anxiety about your spiritual quest (Qoph) to a position where you are now aware of the support and guidance (Samech) that you are receiving from your higher self. This awareness will allow you to open the door (Daleth) to actual contact with your higher self. The force that is most present at this time is the support from the path of Samech, so it is here that we should position your dream.

THE JOURNEY One of the hardest things to do in the Great Work is to learn to listen to and indeed to trust the voice of your intuition. As you are now traversing the path of Samech, it is particularly important that you try to do this so that you can gain the benefit of the assistance that is available to you. The spelling of your dream tells us that you are very committed to the spiritual quest (Tzaddi) and that if you maintain your vigorous approach you will indeed be able to open the door (Daleth) to a much deeper understanding.

STERN

*khamoor-chmvr-*חמור-254

MEANING If you have a dream where the primary focus is a particular emotional state, it can be quite confusing to try to work out exactly what the target of that emotion may have been in the dream. However, from a spiritual perspective, you do not need to worry about this since whatever the dream content, the real recipient of any emotional expression within a dream is the dreamer himself. The Great Work is not an easy challenge to accept, and there are times when all of us need a little stern nudge from our higher selves in order to ensure that we are maintaining our commitment to the search for truth.

THE TREE OF LIFE When we reduce the value of this dream we find the number 11, and in the context of this dream it refers to the letter Lamed, which is the eleventh letter in the Hebrew alphabet. The letter Lamed means "ox-goad" and is associated with the force that motivates us to engage in diligent and rigorous study. This is the path on which your dream sits, and it is the energy of the path of Lamed that is being represented by the sense of a stern outlook within your dream. The value of this dream is equivalent to the value of the Hebrew word meaning "spear." While this is rather an extreme image, it does convey the sense that you need a very definite spur to ensure your continued efforts.

THE JOURNEY There will be times when the spiritual life is extremely rough. It is very tempting to decide to abandon your inner exploration. However, this would be a tragic waste of your spiritual potential. The value of this dream is equivalent to the value of a Hebrew word meaning "vow." The purpose of this association is to remind you, even in your most trying times, that you have made a definite commitment to the spiritual quest. The letter Nun, which occupies the central position in the compression of this dream, indicates that you have the opportunity to deepen your faith. You will be able to do this only if you remember your promise to follow a spiritual path and are able not to be discouraged by the inevitable worries that there is no basis to support what you believe about the nature of the Divine.

STILTS

*hagbahah kav-qb hgbhh-*הגבהה קב-122

MEANING We usually associate stilts with the circus and so we might think that this dream relates to the idea of finding the comedic within life. In fact, this is a very important dream with a serious message for the dreamer. The key characteristic that defines stilts is that they lift us above our normal height. In spiritual terms, we can see stilts as a metaphor for some tool or practice that brings us closer to the Divine than we could achieve alone.

THE TREE OF LIFE The spelling of this dream title is dominated by the letter Heh. This letter means "window"; in the context of a dream about stilts, we can interpret this as referring to the fact that if you are lifted up to a higher state of consciousness, you will be able to have a clear view of the spiritual nature of reality. When we reduce the value of this dream we find the number 5, which is the value of the letter Heh. It is therefore quite clear that the path of Heh is the appropriate place to position your dream.

THE JOURNEY You should feel encouraged by this dream. It not only points to a very definite aspiration to achieve a glimpse of the Divine but strongly implies that the approach you are taking to the Great Work will yield successful results. The letter Beth is very prominent in the spelling of this dream title and also appears in the compression of the dream's value. The letter Beth means "house," but in a Kabbalistic sense it refers to the domain of the Divine. Its presence in this dream is a reassurance that you are gradually drawing closer to a point where you will be able to enter this domain and experience some form of communion with the Divine itself.

STORM

*searah-sa'arh-*סערה-335

MEANING Storms can be romantic, they can be impressive, and sometimes they can be downright terrifying. However, all storms act as an awesome example of the raw power of nature. When we translate this into a spiritual context, we can see that your dream is about the raw power of the Divine. The value of this dream can be reduced to the number 11, and this number suggests that you are about to undergo a transformative spiritual experience. In this sense, a dream about the raw power of the Divine is appropriate and almost prophetic.

THE TREE OF LIFE One of the most profoundly simple and at the same time complex features of the spiritual dimension is the notion of God as love. We tend to interpret this in line with our own experience and expectations of Love. However, this means that we find it hard to reconcile issues such as the violence within nature, of a storm for example, with the concept of a loving God. The Sefirah of Gevurah is concerned with the aspect of the Divine that is responsible for the breakdown of forms, with mortality and severity. Understanding how these facets of existence are still a part of the nature of the Divine is a very transforming experience indeed. It is this experience that the dream of a storm represents and so we should locate your dream in the Sefirah of Gevurah.

THE JOURNEY Accepting the need for mortality and the apparent chaos that occurs within the world is one of the hardest lessons that we have to learn in our spiritual quest for truth. This is recognized in the compression of this dream's value, as the initial letter, Shin, points to the need for you to have a great deal of inner energy now. Additionally, in order to fully understand how the violence and chaos of a storm relates to the Divine, you will have to apply yourself to your studies diligently (Lamed). If you are able to do this, you will have a rare glimpse (Heh) of one of the more hidden truths about the underlying nature of the universe.

STORY

seepoor-syphvr- סיפור-356

MEANING There are few things as pleasant as being a child tucked up in bed and having a story read to you. From a very early age we intrinsically recognize the value and importance of stories. In early cultures, this attachment to stories continued into adulthood, but sadly there are very few adults today who are still read stories. It is through the medium of stories that we can best begin to arrive at an understanding of the nature of the Divine. The significance of this dream is that it indicates that you are now actively seeking to begin that journey of understanding.

THE TREE OF LIFE The value of this dream is equivalent to a Hebrew phrase meaning "the spirits of the living." This phrase suggests that stories are a way of tapping in to our spirit or higher self. In terms of your dream, it tells us that you are trying to find an effective way of contacting your spirit. Combining this with the surface content of your dream, the ideal path to describe your current stage of development is the path of Peh. The letter Peh literally means "mouth" and its path is concerned with all forms of communication.

THE JOURNEY When we reduce the value of this dream we find the number 5. This number represents an individual who has managed to bring the four elements within himself under the control of the fifth element of Spirit. This is not your position right now but is your aspiration. By paying attention to the meanings within the spiritual "stories" that you are exploring, you will bring yourself ever closer to being able to achieve the goal of self-mastery. The central letter in the compression of this dream is the letter Nun. This tells us that while you might experience some sorrow in the process, the more closely you listen the deeper your faith will become.

STRANGER

zar-zr- זר-207

MEANING Most of us, even in today's increasingly secular world, have a sense of belief in some sort of higher power. However, when we take that vague belief and begin to work with it seriously, we begin to feel very much like a stranger in a foreign land. Ironically, this does not apply just to those moments when we do achieve an undeniably spiritually altered state of consciousness. In fact, very soon after we begin to focus on the spiritual aspect of our lives we find that we feel rather like strangers in the everyday world. The value of this dream is equivalent to the value of the Hebrew word meaning "light," and this should be seen as an encouraging reference to the presence of the Divine, reassuring you that any sense of being a stranger should not worry you. From a traditional Kabbalistic viewpoint, this dream would be seen as representing the unknown nature of the universe, and indeed this is a significant part of the growing sense of otherness that we feel as we begin our spiritual journey.

THE TREE OF LIFE This dream's value is also equivalent to the value of a Hebrew phrase meaning "Lord of the universe." This is a direct reference to one of the many titles for the Divine. It is quite clear that you are making good progress in the Great Work and are drawing ever closer to the Divine itself. When we reduce the value of this dream we find the letter Teth. The path of Teth in its positive aspect is concerned with qualities such as strength of character and willpower. You will need both of these in order to continue despite feeling like a stranger, so we should position your dream on the path of Teth.

THE JOURNEY You have the potential to achieve some very significant insights into the nature of the Divine, and indeed the value of this dream is equivalent to the value of the Hebrew word meaning "grow great." However, success takes a lot of hard work and effort. The compression of this dream's value reassures you that the benevolent aspect of the Divine (Resh) is smiling on your efforts. This letter also indicates the need to reflect on what you learn. Similarly, the final letter, Zayin, is there to remind you that part of your reflections will need to involve the decision as to which pieces of apparent wisdom are valid and which you need to discard.

STRANGLING

*lakhnok-lchnvq-*לחנוק-194

MEANING This is an extremely positive dream and you should feel very encouraged by it, since it indicates an ever-increasing appreciation of the nature of the spiritual realm. It is quite possible that you are now wondering whether the wrong analysis has been printed here—after all, this is a dream about strangling! However, the values in the dream make it clear that what is being strangled is not another person but the lower aspect of your personality.

THE TREE OF LIFE While it may be an extreme image, the theme of strangling is an example of a practical attempt to improve your level of spiritual insight by removing the purely ego-driven side of your nature. The value of this dream is equivalent to the value of the Hebrew name for the planet Jupiter. The sphere of Jupiter is concerned with justice and equity as well as a sense of the pragmatic. It is associated with the path of Kaph on the Tree of Life, and it is here that we should locate your dream.

THE JOURNEY In attempting to bring your baser instincts under control you are taking on one of the most difficult challenges that anyone could attempt to undertake. Understandably, the compression of your dream's value begins with the letter Qoph in order to emphasize the anxiety that you feel about the task that lies before you. However, the subsequent letter, Tzaddi, is there to advise you that if you maintain your strong level of commitment, you will succeed. Indeed, the final letter, Daleth, represents the doorway to understanding, which is now within your reach.

STRAW

*kash-qsh-*קש-400

MEANING The main function of straw in the physical world is to act as bedding for livestock. As a result, it can be seen as a symbol of an absolute lack of luxury. If you are associating yourself with straw, it might be seen as a sign of low self-confidence or self-esteem. However, from a Kabbalistic point of view this dream should be seen as evidence of an encouraging sense of humility in the face of the transcendent wonder of the Divine.

THE TREE OF LIFE It might be expected that such a willingness to humble yourself even in your dreams should indicate a relatively high position on the Tree of Life. However, the value of this dream is equivalent to the value of the letter Tav. In addition, the two letters that make up the spelling of your dream are the titles of the two other paths that lead out of Malkut. This makes it clear that you are at an early stage of your inner journey, so we should place your dream on the path of Tav.

THE JOURNEY As you have begun your spiritual quest with an ideal attitude it is likely that you will be able to progress well up the Tree of Life. Embedded within the value of this dream is a reference to the Sefirah of Yesod, which is the next stage on the way to making contact with your higher self. The initial letter in the spelling of this dream points out that in spite of your ideal level of respect for the task before you, you still have significant anxieties. However, the final letter, Shin, makes it clear that your energy and enthusiasm will carry you through.

STREET

*rekhov-rchvb-*רחוב-216

MEANING If we characterize the Great Work as a journey, we can see the dream of a street as representing the route that you are taking toward the goal of your journey. The spelling of this dream has certain things to say about your journey that are very positive in nature. You are reflecting carefully and rationally on the directions that you are taking (Resh), and the protective force of the Divine (Cheth) is ensuring that your meditations (Vav) take you ever nearer to the destination, which is represented by the letter Beth, or the house of the Divine.

THE TREE OF LIFE Since any of the paths on the Tree of Life could be seen as a street, it is initially very difficult to determine exactly where your dream should be placed. The value of this dream is equivalent to the value of the Hebrew word meaning "courage." This would suggest that the path of Teth is an ideal location. This is further supported by the fact that the zodiac sign Leo is associated with the path of Teth, and the value of this dream is also equivalent to the value of the Hebrew word meaning "lion."

THE JOURNEY It may seem strange to talk of bravery or courage with reference to an exploration of the realm of the spiritual. However, in order to begin to comprehend the Divine, we must also have an honest understanding of ourselves, and this is never an easy feat to accomplish. While the path of Teth represents strength of character, in its negative aspect it can represent a capacity to be deceived. You should be particularly wary at this time of any approaches to the Great Work that appear to offer easy answers that avoid the need for any mental courage on your part, as they are unlikely to offer you any real spiritual insight.

STRETCHING
leheetamets-lhthamtz-להתאמץ-566

MEANING There is nothing quite like a good stretch first thing in the morning. It wakes us up, loosens up our bodies, and takes all the strains and aches out of our muscles. If we were to apply this idea in a spiritual context, we would be looking at an individual who has only just woken up in terms of his awareness of a spiritual dimension to reality. When we reduce the value of this dream we find the number 7, and this is the value of the letter Zayin. This letter refers to the need to separate the useful from the irrelevant in terms of your explorations of spiritual matters. The mental equivalent of a stretch will better prepare you to carry out this task.

THE TREE OF LIFE The final letter in the spelling of this dream is Tzaddi in its final form. This emphasizes the sense of your commitment to your newfound spirituality. However, it is not the path on which we should locate your dream. The idea of stretching suggests a more gentle introduction to the Great Work than the vigorous enthusiasm of the path of Tzaddi. By contrast, the path of Resh is concerned with the initial thoughts and reflections that you might have as you start on this voyage of discovery. It is also linked with the benevolent aspect of the Divine and so is an ideal location for your dream.

THE JOURNEY You have a long journey ahead of you if you wish to achieve some form of communion with the Divine itself. In a sense you are still in the process of warming up and making preparations for the road ahead. The compression of this dream tells us that you should be finding some kind of practical activity (Kaph) to consolidate your commitment to

the quest for truth. Given the reference to stretching and the fact that it is an excellent introduction to the idea of spirituality informing all aspects of your life, you should consider enrolling in a yoga class.

STRUGGLING
maavak-mabq-מאבק-143

MEANING Fundamental to human life is the fact that we must struggle. As a species whose only means of adaptation lies in our ingenuity, rather than in our physical makeup as is the case with other animals, life has always been and always will be a struggle. Anyone who turns to the spiritual life hoping to get away from that essential sense of struggle will be disappointed. Spiritual insight is the greatest of all prizes and so it must be earned through significant effort.

THE TREE OF LIFE The value of this dream is equivalent to the value of a Hebrew word meaning "running waters." Water as an element is associated with the emotions. The letter Mem, which means "water," begins the spelling of this dream. The emotions that we associate with the letter Mem are those of compassion and empathy. This indicates that while the Great Work may require you to struggle, it is in the context of support and protection from above. This is emphasized by the fact that the reduction of this dream's value produces the value of the letter Cheth. Cheth represents the protective force of the Divine, so it is here that we should locate your dream.

THE JOURNEY The voyage to the center of your inner nature is by definition a solitary process. This means that when it gets tough and demanding, it is doubly difficult to maintain your commitment to the work. The letter Qoph, which begins the compression of your dream makes it clear that you worry about the possibility of giving up the struggle for greater insight. However, the letter Mem is central in the compression and shows that you will be protected from abandoning your quest for spiritual growth. The final letter, Gimel, suggests that you can ease the struggle if you try to approach the spiritual realm from a more creative and individual angle.

STUMBLE
leemod-lma'avd-למעוד-150

MEANING This is another dream where it is crucially important to pay close attention to the exact meaning of the dream title. When we stumble we do not necessarily fall over; rather, we lose our footing temporarily. In spiritual terms, this difference is greatly significant as it can represent the difference between someone who completely loses his faith and a person who simply suffers from a degree of doubt or uncertainty about the direction that he is taking.

THE TREE OF LIFE When we reduce the value of this dream we find the number 6. This is the value of the letter Vav, which in the context of this dream refers to the element of Air. The element of Air is concerned with our thoughts, and the reason why you are dreaming of stumbling is that at the moment you are considering a range of different approaches to the Divine. Understandably, this can be deeply confusing at times and may well cause you to lose your metaphorical footing.

THE JOURNEY The value of this dream is equivalent to the value of the Hebrew word meaning "nest." This may seem a strange word to be associated with a dream about stumbling. However, the idea of a nest refers to the fact that right now you are incubating a host of ideas about the nature of the spiritual realm. You may be worried at the moment, as expressed by the letter Qoph in the compression of this dream, that you will not be able to find a single direction to follow on your spiritual journey. However, at some point the right approach for you will appear, and you will find your faith greatly strengthened (Nun) as a result.

See Zohar symbol, Stumbling.

SUBMISSION

*keneeah–knya'ah–*בניעה*-155*

MEANING In today's world the idea of submission is generally frowned upon as a sign of weakness. The overall message of our contemporary culture is that we should strive to be our own masters and not have to pay respects to anyone other than ourselves. A spiritually based approach to life takes a very different point of view, since in order for you to gain any insight into the nature of the Divine it is essential that you have a sense of humility before the transcendent nature of the Creator.

THE TREE OF LIFE When we reduce the value of this dream we find the number 11. This indicates that you are about to experience a deeply significant spiritual insight. The value of this dream is equivalent to the value of the Hebrew word meaning "seed," so it is likely that while now you are metaphorically a seedling in terms of your development, you are about to have an experience that

will cause you to blossom. The central letter in the compression of this dream is the letter Nun, and the path of Nun is where we should locate this dream. It refers to the deepening of your faith, and while this certainly involves a submission of yourself to the will of the higher, which can involve a degree of emotional difficulty, the end result is deeply profound.

THE JOURNEY The value of this dream is equivalent to the value of a Hebrew phrase meaning "Adonai the King" (Adonai is a title for the Divine), and this expresses your relationship to the Divine in your current state of spiritual consciousness. The value of this dream is also equivalent to the value of a Hebrew phrase meaning "faithful friend." Once you have passed through the path of Nun, you will be able to see the Divine much more in terms of this latter phrase without in any way losing reverence for its wondrous power.

SUFFOCATION

*makhnak–mchnq–*מהנק*-198*

MEANING There are many dreams that appear to be very negative when we look at their surface meaning but in fact are extremely encouraging when we look at their values and associated words from a Kabbalistic point of view. This dream is a perfect example of this situation: The content itself is worrisome to say the least, and yet the overall spiritual significance is very encouraging. The value of this dream is equivalent to the value of the Hebrew word meaning "victories," and so whatever the cause of your suffocation, the implication is that you are sure to overcome it.

THE TREE OF LIFE People often talk about feeling suffocated when they are living a life-style that does not suit them. In your case, this sense of being suffocated relates to the fact that you are still very close to the world of the physical and are yearning to be closer to the spiritual realm. However, you should also consider whether there are any aspects of your day-to-day life that are causing you to feel restricted and suffocated. The central letter in the compression of this dream is the letter Tzaddi. This represents your commitment and enthusiasm for the Great Work, and it is on this path that we should locate your dream.

THE JOURNEY In order to escape the feelings of suffocation that you are currently experiencing, you need to continue with your exploration of your inner self and of the spiritual in general. The letter Qoph in the compression of this dream tells us that you have some doubts as to whether this will work, but this is counterbalanced by the enthusiasm represented by the subsequent letter, Tzaddi. Additionally, the final letter, Cheth, in the dream's compression tells you that the protective force of the Divine will be with you in your struggles to climb closer to the creative source.

SUICIDE

heetabdoot-hthabdvth- התאבדות-818

MEANING This book focuses on the spiritual messages behind dreams, but dreams, like people, operate on many levels. If you have been feeling out of sorts or if your friends and colleagues have commented that you seem rather down lately, it would be a very good idea to talk this dream through with someone you feel that you can trust. If you are not going through any significant difficulties in your life right now, then the primary significance of this dream is its spiritual implications.

THE TREE OF LIFE From a Kabbalistic perspective, this dream does not refer to your physical demise but to the voluntary ending of your spiritual life. It is most likely that you have yet to make any commitment to the Great Work and that this dream is a warning against deciding once and for all that you will not make any attempt to explore your inner nature. To refuse to accept the challenge of exploring the true nature of the universe could be categorized as a form of spiritual suicide, as it prevents you from developing an inner understanding. Consequently, we place this dream in the material sphere of Malkut.

THE JOURNEY When we reduce the value of this dream we find the number 8. This is the value of the letter Cheth. In the context of this dream's content, it refers to your defensive nature, which lies behind your reluctance to investigate the possibility of a spiritual dimension in your life. The compression of this dream begins with the letter Peh in its final form. This emphasizes the importance of trying to establish some form of inner dialogue with your higher self. The subsequent letter, Yod, is there as a promise of the Divine spark that you will be able to awaken if you do attempt to open up a line of communication.

SUMMER

kayeets-qytz- קיץ-200

MEANING If the spring is a good metaphor for feelings of hope and optimism for the future, the season of summer represents the time when all that hope is harvested in the form of positive spiritual results. The value of this dream is equivalent to the value of the letter Resh, which is associated with the warmth of the Sun and also points to an optimistic and thoughtful approach to the spiritual quest. You should feel very encouraged by this dream and use it as a motivating force to spur you on to even greater efforts in the Great Work.

THE TREE OF LIFE Although this dream has a value that is equivalent to the value of the letter Resh, this is not where we position your dream. The letter Resh represents the energies that have brought you to where you are now. As we have said, summer represents the fruition of your efforts. The Sefirah of Tiferet is linked to the Sun and the season of summer. It is also the place where you make contact with your higher self, so this is the ideal location for your dream.

THE JOURNEY It is tempting to see the state of consciousness that is represented by the Sefirah of Tiferet as the end of your journey. However, while it does represent a major achievement, there is still much more that you can learn about the nature of the spiritual realm. The spelling of this dream tells us that you have certain anxieties (Qoph) about trying to discover even more, despite the fact that you have awakened the Divine spark (Yod) within yourself. However, the final letter, Tzaddi, tells us that you are quite literally hooked on the Great Work. You may have a rest for a little while but soon enough you will be digging even deeper into the mysteries of the Divine.

SUN

shemesh-shmsh- שמש-640

MEANING As early man discovered agriculture, so the focus of worship shifted from the earth itself to the Sun. This shift resulted from the realization that, far from being a random producer of nourishment, the activities of the earth were dependent on the season of the year and this in turn was determined by the Sun. As more sophisticated ideas about the nature of the Divine emerged, the Sun theme was retained in one covert form or another. If we look at the apparently biographical tale of Jesus, for instance, we see a tale of a son (Sun) who dies, causing a great darkness, only to return alive once more.

THE TREE OF LIFE To dream of the Sun is to dream of the Divine source itself. On the Tree of

Life the Sun is located in the Sefirah of Tiferet. The reduction of the value of this dream produces the number 10, which indicates the completion of a major cycle in your life. In your case, this completion relates to the fact that you have reached a point where you have sufficient force of will to contemplate making some sort of contact with your higher self.

THE JOURNEY At this level of inner development there is little that can be given in terms of specific advice. This is because we must all approach the Divine in our own unique way in order to forge a genuine sense of a relationship with the higher forces. The compression of this dream produces the letter Mem in both its standard and final forms. The letter Mem is concerned with compassion and altruism. The implication here is that in order to continue to progress spiritually, you should spend some time behaving in a charitable and altruistic way toward those in need.

See Zohar symbol, Sun.

SWALLOW
*bleeah—blya'ah—*בליעה-117

MEANING We live in a very sanitized world now, and our food comes prepackaged, processed, and bears very little visible similarity to the animal or vegetable that it is made from. Similarly, we are very coy about all manner of bodily functions, including the business of eating. Thanks to this modern distaste for so many physical activities, we are likely to assume that a dream about swallowing ought to have some vaguely negative spiritual implications. In fact, nothing could be further from the truth, and this dream is very positive about your spiritual development.

THE TREE OF LIFE In physical terms, swallowing is the necessary precursor to digesting. In terms of the Great Work, if we see spiritual insight as the food and digestion as the process of gaining an understanding of that insight, the act of swallowing is a symbol for the means by which we access that spiritual information. This may be meditation, prayer, or reading enlightened texts. Whatever the specific method, all means of swallowing the food of the Divine can be categorized as study, so we should assign this dream to the path of Lamed.

THE JOURNEY If we reduce the value of this dream we find the number 9, which is the value of the letter Teth. This letter is associated with

willpower and strength of character. The presence of this letter tells us that not all the nuggets of truth that you come across will be so easy to swallow. The final letter, Zayin, in the compression of your dream points out that you will need to sort out the nutritious elements from those that are the spiritual equivalent of dressing or decoration. The central Yod in the compression of this dream suggests that the spark of the Divine is alive within you and will help you to ensure that you are getting a spiritually balanced diet.

SWEARING
*leheeshava—lhyshba'a—*להישבע-417

MEANING We do not expect to see a dream about swearing in a book that is devoted to the spiritual aspect of dreaming. Swearing is quite rightly regarded as the last refuge of a person who no longer has an argument to make or the vocabulary with which to put forward a coherent opinion and so resorts to offensive language. This dream is not about the literal act of swearing though, but uses the idea of swearing, as a symbol. We swear when we feel completely frustrated and can think of no constructive way forward. In spiritual terms, this suggests that you feel that you cannot move forward with your spiritual quest and are extremely frustrated by this feeling.

THE TREE OF LIFE Even though it does nothing to improve a situation or to improve our understanding of any situation, swearing requires a lot of energy. Indeed, it takes a lot of energy to maintain a feeling of frustration. When that energy is gone, we cease being frustrated and are likely to become apathetic or depressed. The path of Shin represents the raw energy that in its positive aspect can be used to drive your investigations of the spiritual nature of the world. This dream belongs on the path of Shin but in its negative aspect, since the energy given out is entirely nonconstructive.

THE JOURNEY When we reduce the value of this dream we find the number 12, which is associated with the sense of compassion and altruism that is linked to the letter Mem. The implication here is that you try to translate your feelings of frustration at your apparent lack of success in the Great Work into positive energy. You can then use that positive energy to help others who need some form of support or assistance. In doing so, you will also be bringing yourself ever closer to a point where you will see some results for all your spiritual efforts.

SWEEPING

*sokhef–svchph–*סוחף*–*154

MEANING The psychologist and the Kabbalist might agree on the basic significance of this dream's content but would profoundly disagree on the implications of that meaning. There are not too many genuinely menial tasks left today that have not been made substantially easier by technological innovation. However, sweeping is still a job best achieved by a willing pair of hands and a broom. Most interpretations would agree that to dream of such a lowly activity indicates an absence of vanity. However, while the psychologist might see this as an absence of self-esteem, the Kabbalist would see this as an encouraging sign of suitability for the Great Work.

THE TREE OF LIFE The act of sweeping relates to preparing an area so that it is fit to be used for its given purpose. When translated into a spiritual context this should be seen as referring to a process whereby you prepare yourself mentally and physically for beginning the spiritual quest. When we reduce the value of this dream we find the number 10. Given the preparatory nature of this dream we can see this number as a reference to the Sefirah of Malkut, as it is the tenth Sefirah on the Tree of Life. This is a highly appropriate location for your dream since you have not begun the spiritual quest itself.

THE JOURNEY It is clear from this dream that your task in the next few weeks is to get ready to take your first steps on the long and arduous journey that will ultimately lead you back to the home of the Divine. The letter Qoph in the compression of this dream tells us that you have some anxieties about the road ahead. Chiefly, you are worried about the potential sorrow that you may have to experience (Nun) as you begin to increase your understanding of the Divine. However, you are also aware that you must make the leap of faith and open the door (Daleth) that leads to the spiritual realm.

SWELLING

*tefeekhah–thphychh–*תפיחה*–*503

MEANING This dream might cause you to wake up with a worrying feeling that you ought to see a doctor. This is because we tend to associate the idea of a swelling with physical ailments. However, from a spiritual perspective, we need to consider the idea of a swelling as a reference to some kind of blockage that is getting in the way of your further spiritual development.

THE TREE OF LIFE Dreams have a tendency to play games with words as a means of getting their point across. As well as physical swellings, it is very common to talk of people being swollen with pride or of being so proud that it has made their heads swollen. The danger of pride is far more relevant to your spiritual situation than any possible physical ailment. When we reduce the value of this dream we find the number 8, which is the value of the letter Cheth. This letter refers to your desire to defend yourself from any unsettling influences. The feeling of pride is no more than a defense mechanism designed to stop any contrary influences from affecting your worldview. The path of Ayin is concerned with a vigorously individual approach to the Great Work. This dream suggests that you are taking the individualistic approach to an unhelpful extreme, so this dream is located on the negative aspect of the path of Ayin.

THE JOURNEY The value of this dream is equivalent to the value of the Hebrew word meaning "expelled." It is quite likely that it is a fear of failing in the spiritual quest that is causing you to take the unhelpful stance described above. You will be able to move forward only if you are willing to take the risk of getting things wrong and open yourself up to some form of dialogue with your higher self. It is always worth remembering that the spiritual journey is one that is about learning. Moreover, part of the process of learning is that we make mistakes, but this does not mean that we should not keep trying until we get things right.

SWIMMING

*sekheeyah–shchyyh–*שחייה*–*333

MEANING The number 3 is associated primarily with creativity and innovation. The first thing we notice about this dream is that its value consists of the number 3 three times. The implication is that you are someone with great creative abilities. In spiritual terms, this means that you have the potential to achieve great things if you are willing to commit yourself to the Great Work and maintain a persistent level of effort.

THE TREE OF LIFE We might expect to place this dream on a path that is closely connected with the element of Water due to the fact that the image of water carries with it the idea of water by natural association. However, the spelling of this dream is filled with a fiery energy, and the swimming reference is related primarily to the ease with which you have progressed so far up the Tree of Life.

The letter Yod appears twice in the spelling of this dream, and, as it stands for the original Divine spark of the Creator, it is an ideal location for your dream, given the heavy emphasis on your own innate creative spark.

THE JOURNEY Clearly, with your combination of enthusiasm and inventive nature you have the capacity to travel as far up the Tree of Life as your desire and your commitment to the spiritual quest will take you. The compression of the dream's value reinforces the substantial reserves of raw energy that you have at your disposal (Shin). However, the letter Lamed is placed centrally in the compression. This tells us that while you can afford to take a creative approach to your voyage of self-discovery, you need to provide yourself with a framework in which to operate that is based on a rigorous study of spiritual matters.

SWORD

*zayin–zyn–*זין*–67*

MEANING While we might feel generally uncomfortable about the presence of images of warfare in dreams of a spiritual nature, there is a long and relatively well-known history of the use of swords to represent particular spiritual attributes. In Kabbalistic terms, this is a positive dream that tells us that you are approaching a position where you will be able to begin to formulate your own approach to the Divine. Indeed, the value of this dream is equivalent to the value of the Hebrew spelling of the Sefirah of Binah, whose title is "Understanding." This reinforces the idea that this dream is about an increase in your ability to absorb and digest spiritual ideas.

THE TREE OF LIFE The title of this dream relates directly to one of the letters of the Hebrew alphabet. The letter Zayin is, of course, one of the paths on the Tree of Life and it is here that your dream belongs. The path of Zayin refers to the use of a metaphorical mental sword. In other words, the path of Zayin teaches you to cut away the irrelevant and unhelpful from those nuggets of spiritual insight that will help you to deepen your understanding of the nature of the Divine.

THE JOURNEY The central letter in the spelling of this dream is Yod, and this is important because it makes it clear that while you may be wielding a mental sword, you are using it under the direction and influence of the Divine spark that burns within you.

When we reduce the value of this dream we find the number 13. This is a number that relates to a major change about to occur in your life. If you make good use of the spiritual tool that the path of Zayin provides for you, you will indeed experience a change in your life. Once we are able to strip away all but the genuinely useful elements of a spiritual text or idea, we find that our understanding of the universe develops at a much faster pace.

TABLE

*shoolkhan–shvlchn–*שולחן*–394*

MEANING The table is the focal point of every kitchen, and no matter how cozy the rest of the home, we can usually guarantee that the kitchen is the focal point of every house. If there is something to discuss, people sit around the table to talk about it. If there is a party, the majority of the guests will end up sitting around or near the kitchen table to chat. In spiritual terms, this dream is about the absolute core of what it means to be you, as the table is symbolic of whatever your particular focal point within your nature happens to be. From a traditional point of view, we can also see the table as a symbol of the spiritual nourishment that we need each day and the communal setting in which much of this spiritual nourishment is gained.

THE TREE OF LIFE In one sense, every single path and each of the Sefirot on the Tree of life is about focusing on your core nature. (However, in most cases this is as a means to something else that is the specific message or lesson of that particular path.) However the path of Nun which relates to the deepening of your faith specifically relates to the process of detailed and frank self-examination. The letter Nun appears in its final form at the end of the spelling of this dream title, so we should position your dream on the path of Nun.

THE JOURNEY Just as many of the conversations that we have seated around a table never actually resolve anything, it may be that your experience of the path of Nun does not lead to discovering your essential core self. However, it is the process of exploration itself that is really important. This will not be an easy task, and the letter Shin in the compression of this dream indicates the energy and enthusiasm that you will need. Additionally, the central letter, Tzaddi, makes it clear that you need to maintain a very strong commitment to the Great Work, as this is the only way that you will be able to open the door (Daleth) to yourself and ultimately to an understanding of the Divine.

TAIL

zanav-znb- זנב*-*59

MEANING If there is one bodily part that is undeniably animal in nature, it is a tail. Additionally, it is the one animalistic feature that we are still physically reminded of, thanks to the vestigial tail bone, or coccyx, which is found at the very base of the spine. This dream is an exploration of our relationship to the animal kingdom. In a spiritual context, it relates to your desire to be more spiritual than animal in nature. It should be seen as an encouraging dream that confirms the determination of your unconscious self to pursue the spiritual quest.

THE TREE OF LIFE There is a well-known expression that is used to describe a situation where a minority has control of the majority; we refer to such a state of affairs as "the tail wagging the dog." The dream of a tail is a recognition of the fact that while we may not yet be able to access it, our higher self is the most important of our nature. It should be our spirit and not our ego self that is controlling our actions. It is this realization in its many different forms that leads an individual to set out on the spiritual journey, so we should assign your dream to the path of Tav, as this is the first path that leads out of Malkut.

THE JOURNEY When we reduce the value of this dream we find the number 5. This is a very important symbolic number and refers to an individual who has managed to bring the four elements within his personality under the control of the fifth element of Spirit. The letter Nun in the compression of this dream indicates both the deepening of your spiritual faith that has already occurred and looks ahead to the future as you progress up the Tree of Life. The final letter, Teth, is there to remind you that ultimately your success depends on your own strength, character, and will to succeed.

TALKING

ledaber-ldbr- לדבר*-*236

MEANING In order for us to pursue a spiritual path we must be able to act in a reflective manner. In other words, the Great Work is as much about contemplating what we are doing as it is about any actual activity. With any subject it is always easier and more effective to discuss its implications with at least one other person, or even to enter into a dialogue with oneself. The dream of talking is a direct reference to the fact that we progress best when we try to step out-

side ourselves momentarily and look at what we are doing and how we feel about it.

THE TREE OF LIFE The spelling of this dream relates a simple tale of how the search for spiritual truth works. The first requirement is for rigorous study (Lamed), and this will ultimately open the door (Daleth) to the wisdom held in the domain of the Divine (Beth). When we have access to that wisdom, we will be able to reflect in an informed manner under the benevolent influence of the Divine (Resh). This dream is primarily trying to advise you on the nature of that study, and the key point to remember is that useful studying is not a solitary activity. Once we have taken in any information, we should then discuss it in order to fully understand it. The path of Peh is associated with all forms of communication, so it is here that we should locate your dream.

THE JOURNEY When we reduce the value of this dream we find the number 11. This number is associated with all forms of mystical experience. Its presence here is to encourage you to maintain your commitment to the Great Work by providing you with a promise of the greater insights that await you if you persevere in your work. The compression of this dream reiterates the advice that is present elsewhere in this dream. The central letter is Lamed, which reminds you of the need for rigorous study, while the final Vav emphasizes the importance of contemplation in order to turn that knowledge into a tool for your spiritual development.

TANK (CONTAINER)

meykhal-mykl- מיכל*-*100

MEANING Given some of the truly bizarre things that people dream about, to have a dream where the main focus of interest is a storage tank might lead you to worry that your imagination is in some way lacking. However, you need have no such worries, as this dream is very useful in terms of what it says about your inner development and the underlying reasons for your level of progress with the Great Work.

THE TREE OF LIFE In spiritual terms, to dream of a tank represents the potential that you have for inner development. It also indicates that at this time your potential is stored away and is not being used. Since you are eager to develop your understanding of the nature of the Divine, it is important to discover why this is the case. The value of this dream is equivalent to the value of the Hebrew letter Qoph. The path of Qoph is concerned with the anxiety that we often feel when we begin to explore the spiritual dimension, and it is this anxiety that is holding you back from releasing all that potential energy. Consequently, we should position your dream on the path of Qoph.

THE JOURNEY While it is very important to understand why you are at a particular point in your spiritual journey, it is even more crucial to discover how you can begin to move forward from that position. The spelling of this dream title acts as a brief but useful piece of advice from your higher self that tells you how you should act at this time. Although you are unaware of it, the maternal aspect of the Divine is with you now (Mem). If you trust in its presence, you will be able to awaken the Divine spark within you (Yod). With your newfound energy you should begin putting into practice in the material world (Kaph) the spiritual ideas and values that you have learned through your studies (Lamed) so far.

TAR

*zefet-zphth-*זפת*-*487

MEANING There are many natural substances that are significantly more appealing than tar. Tar is sticky, difficult to wash off, and can be very dangerous; it would be quite reasonable to wonder why you would have a dream about it. However, one of the well-known features of tar is that it contains the remains of animal and plant life from many aeons ago. If we translate this into spiritual terms, the image of tar can be seen as a symbol of the medium through which we can access the knowledge and understanding of our ancestors, so we should see this dream as a positive and encouraging comment on your development.

THE TREE OF LIFE Each path on the Tree of Life enables us to see further and more clearly into the nature of the universe and in particular the spiritual reality that lies beyond the apparently mechanistic physical world that we inhabit. However, we are looking for a path that not only helps us to understand the nature of the Divine but puts us in touch with those who have gone before us. The path of Samech is associated with the general themes of support and advice, so it is an ideal location for this dream.

THE JOURNEY The fact that you are looking back at previous ways in which people constructed their own ideas about the Divine and the nature of the Great Work indicates that you take a very serious approach to the spiritual quest. The letter Tav in the compression of this dream refers to the act of looking back through history and also to the potential for melancholy that this activity carries with it. The subsequent letter, Peh, tells us that your exploration of the past will lead to a form of dialogue with those earlier ideas. Finally, the letter Zayin is a reminder that however interesting you find everything that you discover, you must ensure that you discard anything that is not useful to your future development.

TARGET (GOAL)

*matarah-mtrh-*מטרה*-*254

MEANING We live in a world that is more competitive than ever before. Technological advances and the emergence of a global economy mean that we are all operating under much more pressure than was the case only a few years ago. One very noticeable effect of this has been the increase in goal setting. No matter what your role, the chances are that you have a monthly, a weekly, and even a daily target that you have to meet. However, the spiritual goal is thankfully not a competitive one; it relates only to you, and there is no time limit on when you need to achieve it. Indeed, in many ways it is an aspiration rather than something that you must reach.

THE TREE OF LIFE Even though there is no rush to get there, the notion of a target carries with it a sense of vigorous activity. This is encouraged by the fact that the value of this dream is equivalent to the value of the Hebrew word meaning "spear." Additionally, one of the key factors about a target is that it should be individual, a goal that is personal to you in its nature and in terms of how you try to accomplish it. The path of Ayin is concerned with both an individual and a vigorously active approach to the Divine, so it is here that we should position your dream.

THE JOURNEY The value of this dream is equivalent to a Hebrew word meaning "oath" or "vow." The presence of this associated word is to reinforce the idea that although you have a target to aim for, the most important thing about the Great Work is the sincerity and belief that you have within your soul. It is the commitment rather than the achievement that holds the most value. Your attitude to the spiritual quest is admirable, and the compression of this dream's value makes it clear that you are acting under the benign influence of the Divine. In trying to achieve your chosen target you will deepen your understanding of the spiritual realm (Nun), and this will open the doorway (Daleth) to a route that will lead to your spiritual goal.

TASTING

taam-ta'am-טעם-119

MEANING It is always important to pay attention to exactly what the title of a dream says. It would be easy to equate this dream with the act of eating, but this would then lead to a misinterpretation from a spiritual point of view. This dream is about tasting or in a more general sense sampling a range of different flavors. In a spiritual sense, this relates to a growing interest in matters of a religious nature and suggests that you are exploring a range of possible paths.

THE TREE OF LIFE When we reduce the value of this dream we find the number 11. This suggests that you are on the verge of undergoing a significant spiritual experience. However, this cannot happen while you are still, as it were, trying out the various spiritual flavors. Right now you are still in the Sefirah of Malkut, and in order to progress you need to decide on your choice of food, so to speak, and begin eating it.

THE JOURNEY Not so very long ago we had very little choice about the particular spirituality that we aligned ourselves with, since it was purely a matter of birth and culture. Today we have a plethora of choice and at times this can be rather debilitating. The compression of this dream reveals that you have a number of anxieties (Qoph) about firmly committing to any particular spiritual position, but it also tells us that if you listen to your intuition you can rely on the Divine spark within you (Yod) to guide you in making the right choice. The final letter, Teth, is a reminder that the Great Work requires great strength of character, so you need to take the leap of faith and begin the journey.

TATTOO

ketovet ka'aka–kthvbth qa'aqa'a–
כתובת קעקע-1168

MEANING Until quite recently, tattoos were frowned upon as something that marked a person out as something of an undesirable. Thankfully, this prejudicial outlook has now disappeared and people can wear tattoos without being treated as social outcasts. The history of tattooing makes it quite clear that body art of all forms holds an almost spiritual significance in its own right. They are certainly very

potent symbols of the desire to identify yourself with a particular group or system of beliefs.

THE TREE OF LIFE The spelling of this dream portrays the emotional experience that you are currently going through. The second word in the Hebrew translation of this dream consists entirely of the letters Qoph and Ayin. Ayin represents your desire to construct your personal approach to the Divine. Qoph indicates that you have significant worries about taking such a step forward in your spiritual life, so we should position this dream on the path of Qoph.

THE JOURNEY What you need to try to do over the next few months is to find a way of overcoming your anxieties. The letter Tav is repeated within the spelling of this dream and it indicates a sense of potential regret at the idea of leaving behind the certainties of the secular and physical world. However, you should take heart from the fact that both the letter Samech and the letter Cheth appear in the compression of this dream's value. These letters indicate that you are being supported and protected by your higher self and the Divine.

TEAM

tsevet-tzvvth-צוות-502

MEANING Even those of us who like to operate as individuals have to recognize that in almost all circumstances a good team effort will produce far more far quicker than even an excellent solo effort could hope to achieve. Additionally, the benefits of working as a team extend beyond the increased efficiency, since we also have the opportunity to form friendships and to learn about other people's views and ways of looking at the world. The spiritual quest is one of those few activities that is largely a solitary activity, but the message of this dream is that, where possible, you should be looking to share your experiences with those close to you.

THE TREE OF LIFE Since the beginnings of psychoanalytic theory it has been seeping into the public consciousness that we cannot really talk about ourselves as a single controlling self. We are made up of a number of competing and partial personalities and natures. Bearing this in mind, we can see the reference to a team as referring to a state where all the aspects of our individual nature are pulling in the same direction. When this occurs it is much easier to progress spiritually. The value of this dream is equivalent to the Hebrew word meaning "cutting" and the dream's value reduces to 7, which is the value of the Hebrew letter Zayin, meaning "sword." The suggestion here is that you are able to analyze very efficiently the various spiritual ideas that you come across because you are functioning like a team.

THE JOURNEY The Great Work requires a range of skills and involves a variety of activities. While it is very important to be able to look at information and discard those parts that are not useful, it is equally important that you express your spirituality in a physical manner. The letter Kaph, which begins the compression of this dream's value, is there to make just that point. Given the association in this dream with cutting and swords, you might like to consider joining a martial arts class that also has a focus on the spiritual aspect of the art.

TEARS
deemah-dma'ah-דמעה-119

MEANING Your first response to this dream may be to assume that it has very negative implications for your spiritual development. After all, tears usually indicate a significant level of sadness. However, when we reduce the value of this dream we find the number 11. This is a number that points to some form of mystical experience occurring in your life in the relatively near future, so we should see this dream as a positive message to your conscious self. Additionally, tears are regarded within the Kabbalah as a positive symbol of self-expression and so are not in any way negative.

THE TREE OF LIFE It is certainly true that people can weep for joy, but the value of this dream is equivalent to the value of the Hebrew word meaning "abominable," so it is unlikely that the tears are symbolic of anything other than sorrow. We can therefore infer that your dream relates to your ability to empathize with the sorrow of others. This is an ability that can help you to bring comfort to other people's lives and increase your spiritual understanding at the same time. The path of Mem is associated with compassion and altruism, so this is where we should locate your dream.

THE JOURNEY The spelling of this dream title tells us that you have opened the door (Daleth) to a state of consciousness that allows you to empathize with others (Mem). In doing so, you will be able to begin to develop your unique means of approaching the Divine (Ayin). If you persist in this compassionate approach to those around you, you will ultimately be able to achieve a sight (Heh) of the true nature of the Divine itself.

TEASING
lehakneet-lhqnyt-להקניט-204

MEANING It is a very rare individual who can look at himself and recognize all of his faults. It is even rarer to find someone who can recognize his faults and feel comfortable with them. Consequently, this dream is likely to make you wake up feeling distinctly uncomfortable, as your overwhelming wish will be to try to reassure yourself that you do not tease other people. You can now stop worrying, since this dream does not suggest that you tease those around you; rather, it is symbolic of an attitude that your conscious ego-based self is talking to that part of you that wishes to pursue a spiritual path.

THE TREE OF LIFE The value of this dream is equivalent to a Hebrew word meaning "foreigner." This is how your conscious self sometimes regards the newfound spirituality that is beginning to dominate the way in which you live your life. A tension still exists between that part of you that wishes to make headway in the Great Work and that part of you that cannot help but feel cynical about the whole idea. This dream effectively straddles two paths on the Tree that lead into the Sefirah of Netzach. The path of Tzaddi represents your eagerness for the Great Work, while the path of Qoph refers to your unease, which manifests itself as cynicism.

THE JOURNEY When we reduce the value of this dream we find the number 6. This functions in this dream on a number of levels. On one hand, it stands for the hexagram or Star of David, which represents the Divine and as such is a reminder of the reality of the spiritual dimension. At the same time, it is the value of the letter Vav and relates to the need for you to spend some time in quiet contemplation so that you can resolve the tension in your mind about the spiritual quest. Once this is resolved, you will be able to move on to much deeper and more rewarding levels of spiritual insight.

❧TEETH
shin-shyn-שין-360

MEANING To dream of teeth is to draw attention to one's ability to make sound and clearly decisive judgments. This is obviously appropriate to work contexts and often indicates a need to make some definite career plans, but can apply equally to any area of your life. The Hebrew word meaning "tooth" is *Shin*. Its value is 300, and it is associated with the element of Fire. It is the fiery nature of this dream that gives the aspect of decisiveness to the dreamer.

THE TREE OF LIFE No matter what is happening to the teeth in this dream, the dreamer is clearly located on the thirty-first path of the Tree of Life. This path is also known as the "Path of Perpetual Intelligence" and this refers to the need for constant or perpetual reexamination of ourselves and of our lives. The path runs from Malkut to Hod, and this makes it clear that the dreamer needs to assess the way his material life is progressing from a more objective standpoint.

THE JOURNEY A dream of this type can be relevant at any point in our spiritual development. It is most likely to occur when we are beginning to manage the element of Air, because air is largely intellectual in nature. While we know from the introduction that the first element to master is Earth, we only have to face our intellectual assumptions once we reach the level of Air. When faced with tough choices, if you can simply still your mind long enough you will find that you already know which choice you are meant to take. In order to usher in the positive development that this dream indicates, we need to develop our mental faculties. This does not have to mean enrolling in an evening course on Italian literature or world religions, although this would certainly be useful. Remember always that this is not about trying to be more clever but is about gaining wisdom.

See Zohar symbol, Teeth.

❧LOST TEETH
*shin avood-shyn abvd-*שׁין אבוד-373

MEANING A very common dream involves the loss of teeth. This tells the dreamer that, for one reason or another, he is allowing his sense of control or power over his life to be weakened. You should pay attention to why the teeth are falling out; if, for instance, it is because of someone else, it suggests that you need to assert your power in the workplace. On the other hand, if they simply fall out of their own accord, you need to look deep inside yourself to see why you are unable to act decisively. In spiritual terms, this dream is a warning that you need to take charge of your inner development.

THE TREE OF LIFE Of course, if the teeth are being lost, then so too is one's sense of personal power. The value of this dream reduces to 13, which indicates that significant change is on the way in

your life. However, change requires some input and energy from you as well as from the outside. At the moment, your dream places you on the negative aspect of the path of Shin, since your energy is either dissipated or misdirected. You need to find some way of redirecting your energy in a constructive and helpful way.

THE JOURNEY The presence of the number 3 in the value of this dream also suggests that we are dealing primarily with creative and innovative judgments in this dream. Your intellect is important in your daily life. However, in terms of your spiritual work, a sharpened intellect is essential as a tool to help you achieve a proper level of focus. Developing your intellect is not so much about learning more facts as it is about learning new ways of mentally approaching the world. You should consider visiting a bookstore and buying some introductory books on philosophy. It may be hard going at first, but you will soon find that you are much more able to direct your mental energy in a way that helps you to grow spiritually.

See Zohar symbol, Teeth.

TELEPHONE
*telefon-tlphvn-*טלפון-175

MEANING In traditional Kabbalah, the use of Gematria is restricted to the analysis of the Torah. Organizations and groups that use the Kabbalah in a broader way would still restrict themselves to looking at words that are Hebraic in origin. However, when we look at the value of the Hebrew word meaning "telephone," we find that even in a word that has simply been lifted from the English and transliterated, there are still appropriate Gematric connections. The value of this word, for example, is equivalent to the value of the Hebrew title for the spirit of Mercury, and Mercury of course is the planet that governs communication.

THE TREE OF LIFE When we reduce the value of this dream we find the number 13, which indicates that a great change is about to occur in your life. Undoubtedly this change will be stimulated by the communication that is referred to in the content of this dream. The letter Nun stands out in the spelling of this dream title, since it appears in its final form. The path of Nun is concerned with the deep self-examination that leads to a greater understanding of yourself and of the Divine. It is this dialogue with yourself that the dream relates to, so we should place your dream on the path of Nun.

THE JOURNEY To genuinely examine your inner nature is never an easy task, and the compression of your dream makes this clear by the presence of the letter Qoph, which represents your sense of anxiety at the task ahead of you. The letter Ayin is there to encourage you to have confidence to go ahead with this important aspect of your inner development so that you can formulate your individual approach to the Divine. If you meet this challenge, you will be much closer to achieving a glimpse (Heh) of the nature of the spiritual universe.

TELESCOPE

teleskop – tlsqvph – טלסקופ-285

MEANING When telescopes were first invented they caused more than just excitement. The greater vision that they provided ultimately led to the realization that we live in a heliocentric arrangement of planets. To the authorities who were wedded to the idea of earth being at the center of things this was perceived as the worst kind of heresy. The image of a telescope is not just a symbol of farsightedness but represents an ability to think new and unusual, possibly even controversial thoughts and a willingness to communicate these ideas to the outside world. From a spiritual point of view, this dream also reflects a concern with the bigger picture—a concern with the whole universe—and could be seen as a sign that you should be more cosmic in your thinking about the world.

THE TREE OF LIFE The letter Peh stands out in the spelling of this dream title since it appears in its final form. This emphasizes the importance of communication to your current state of inner development. However, it is not the path on which this dream belongs. Before ideas can be communicated they must be considered and developed. This process is associated with the path of Vav, and this is the path on which your dream sits. This is supported by the fact that when we reduce the value of your dream we find the number 6, which is the value of the letter Vav.

THE JOURNEY When we look at the compression of this dream we see an excellent summary of the nature and purpose of a telescope. It allows our minds (Resh) to communicate (Peh) more effectively with the things we see through the window (Heh) it provides on the universe. Your task over the next few weeks and months is to try to use your mind more like a telescope. In other words, you need to look deeper and further into everything that you engage with so that you might find its spiri-

tual significance and increase your inner understanding.

TELEVISION

televeezyah – tlvvyzyh – טלוויזיה-83

MEANING Television is without doubt the most important cultural medium in the world today. It has its positive aspects in that most people are now able to access information and enjoy drama that without television would not be available to them. However, it also means that for most people, their only exposure to any kind of artistic expression is through a medium that is driven by commercial concerns. This has significant spiritual implications, as people on the whole are more and more concerned with personal enjoyment rather than with finding truth.

THE TREE OF LIFE The value of this dream is equivalent to the value of the Hebrew word meaning "wave." A wave can be something that carries us along or something that drowns us. In a spiritual context, we need to ensure that any spiritual system we investigate will not simply overwhelm us or remove our individual approach to the Divine. You need to be especially vigorous at this time about ensuring that you retain your unique relationship to the Divine, so we should place this dream on the path of Ayin.

THE JOURNEY The compression of this dream produces the letters Peh and Gimel. The combination of these two letters could be read as "creative communication," which, ironically enough, would be an ideal description of television at its best. It is also a valuable piece of advice about how you should approach the Great Work. It is very easy to allow someone else's vision to drive your view of the nature of the spiritual. So it is most important to remember that you do not have to follow anyone else's programme and should stay true to your own beliefs.

TEMPER

mezeg – mzg – מזג-50

MEANING From a psychological point of view, if you are dreaming of having a display of temper it is likely that you are feeling frustrated and blocked in some way in your life right now. A Kabbalistic interpretation of this dream would agree that it indicates a sense of stasis in your spiritual life. The value of this dream is equivalent to the value of the Hebrew word meaning "closed." The sense in this dream is that for some reason, your higher feelings and your ability to communicate spiritually are locked away or being repressed.

THE TREE OF LIFE There are moments in everybody's life when he feels excluded or locked away from the more profound aspects of existence. We might expect to locate this dream in the Sefirah of Malkut, since this relates to the world of the solely physical. However, the value of this dream is equivalent to the value of the Hebrew word meaning "sorrows." When we combine this with the fact that the value of the dream is the same as the value of the letter Nun, we can see that your dream belongs on the path of Nun. This path leads us to a deeper faith and awareness of the Divine. However, it can often involve our passing through a period of sorrow and a sense of absence from the Divine.

THE JOURNEY The most important thing for you to do at this time is to try to maintain your faith in the Great Work and the existence of a spiritual dimension to the world. The spelling of this dream title begins with the letter Mem, and this should remind you that the maternal force of the Divine is still with you. The final letter, Gimel, is an encouragement for you to think creatively about the position you are now in and to try to find innovative ways to stimulate a resurgence of your faith in the Divine. The central letter Zayin makes it clear that you must not allow yourself to lose your analytical rigor when looking at possible answers, no matter how unappealing they may seem.

✤ TEMPLE

meekdash–mqdsh– מקדש *-444*

MEANING It is worth noting right away that this dream title is not the Hebrew word for "synagogue." Rather, a generic term for buildings designed specifically for worship has been used. The first thing that we notice about the value of this dream is that it consists entirely of the number 4. This has two very definite meanings. On one hand, the number 4 is the number of the physical world, and this emphasizes that a temple is a thing of the material rather than the spiritual realm. On the other hand, the value of the letter Daleth is 4, and as Daleth means "door," there is a recognition that a temple is an attempt to construct a doorway into the world of the spiritual.

THE TREE OF LIFE At an individual level, the image of a temple suggests that you have dedicated yourself very fully to the pursuit of the Great Work. Buildings in dreams are representations of the dreamer, and in your case you are being represented by a building whose sole purpose is spiritual. When we reduce the value of this dream we find the number 3. This number is associated with the creative impulse and suggests that you have developed your unique approach to the Divine. The number 3 is also the value of the path of Gimel, and it is here that we should locate your dream.

THE JOURNEY The value of this dream is equivalent to the value of the Hebrew word meaning "sanctuary." Standing on the path of Gimel, you are as close as you can be to a moment of communion with the Divine itself, so the association with the idea of a sanctuary is very appropriate. In terms of your individual progress, the repetition of the number 4 takes on a third level of significance. It does represent the material or physical world but in your case refers to the potential you now have to make your faith in the Divine something as solid and tangible as the earth itself.

See Zohar symbol, House of Worship.

TEMPTATION

peetooy–phythvy– פיתוי *-506*

MEANING There are some ideas that have much more power and significance when we look at them from a spiritual perspective. We now live in an increasingly secular world, and people as a rule associate the idea of temptation with the innocuous possibility that they may not be able to resist that particularly appealing box of chocolates, for example. From a spiritual perspective the dream of temptation is not about whether you indulge the occasional whim but is related to whether or not you manage to maintain your commitment to the Great Work.

THE TREE OF LIFE When we reduce the value of this dream we find the number 11. This number has a well-recognized symbolic significance in a wide range of mystical systems. It suggests that you are about to undergo an experience that will have profound spiritual implications for your future. This is reassuring in that it tells us that you will be able to resist the temptation to stray from the Great Work. The number 11 also relates to the letter Kaph, which is the eleventh in the Hebrew alphabet. This is the path on which we should place your dream, since it is the practical application of your spirituality associated with the path of Kaph that will ensure that you continue to progress.

THE JOURNEY The compression of this dream tells you exactly what you need to do in order to avoid yielding to the temptation before you. The letter Kaph appears in its final form, and this emphasizes the great importance of taking some practical activity to consolidate your commitment to the spiritual quest. Moreover, letter Vav tells us that this activity should also involve a significant element of contemplation or meditation. An ideal solution for you would be to take yoga lessons.

TENT

ohel-avhl- אוהל-42

MEANING As a modern civilization we associate tents with camping trips and holidays. However, in our dreams items take on a symbolic significance that reaches back into ancient history. In terms of the human race as a whole, the use of tents as a leisure accessory is a very recent innovation. The originators of the Kabbalah spent a great deal of their formative years as nomadic peoples, so tents served as their homes. The value of this dream is equivalent to the value of a Hebrew word meaning "loss." This relates to your awareness that you need to rediscover the spiritual aspect of your life.

THE TREE OF LIFE During the Exodus, the tribes of Israel lived in tents a great deal of the time. However, these were not their permanent homes, but were staging points on the way to their ultimate destination. We can apply this to the development of your individual spiritual awareness. You are currently at something of a staging point in your inner journey. The value of this dream is equivalent to the value of a Hebrew word that, due to Kabbalistic associations, refers to a mother who is as yet unfertilized. The symbolic value of this reference is that you have begun the Great Work but have yet to awaken the Divine spark within yourself. An ideal location for this dream is the Sefirah of Yesod, since this is the first staging point beyond the material world of Malkut.

THE JOURNEY The task that lies before you is to continue to grow spiritually so that you may come to make contact with your higher self and ultimately achieve some form of communion with the Divine force itself. The spelling of this dream title begins with the letter Aleph, which represents the absolute unity of the Divine and is your final destination. The subsequent letters, Vav and Lamed, indicate that in order to achieve a glimpse of the true nature of the universe (Heh), you need to dedicate yourself to studying and contemplating deeply the results of your studies.

TERROR

eymah-aymh- אימה-56

MEANING Nightmares are always unpleasant. They take on an additionally worrisome aspect when we begin to see our dreams as in some way functioning as a window onto our soul. To dream of terror does not mean that you are in grave danger or even that you are committing some terrible error in the way you are pursuing your spiritual work. Indeed, the value of this dream reduces to 11, and this suggests very strongly that you are about to undergo a spiritually transforming experience. Traditional Kabbalah would also suggest that you spend some time considering why you are dreaming of a terrifying experience. Perhaps there are aspects of your daily life that are causing you worry and concern.

THE TREE OF LIFE The value of this dream is equivalent to the value of the Hebrew word meaning "beauty." This may seem to be an inappropriate association with a dream whose focus is on terror. However, if we step back a little, we see that both the sensation of terror and the appreciation of beauty require us to engage our passions and our higher emotions. These are marks of what it is to be human, and the reconciliation of our diverse and sometimes conflicting passions takes place in the Sefirah of Netzach, so it is here that we should position your dream.

THE JOURNEY In the spelling of this dream title we find both the letter Aleph, which represents the unity of the Divine, and the letter Yod, which stands for the creative force that emanates from the Divine. This alone is a good indication that your dream should not be taken in a negative way. The Divine force that is moving within you at this time is responsible for your growing ability to reconcile your emotional makeup, and you are being assisted in this task by the maternal aspect of the Divine as represented by the letter Mem in the spelling of this dream title. In order to make the most of the energy that is within you right now, it would be a good idea to consult a professional counselor to help you fully understand your inner nature.

TEST-TAKING

meevkhan-mbchn- מבחן-100

MEANING Nobody likes tests. Even when we know that we have prepared properly, there is still that sense of dryness in our mouths, the unreasonable paranoia that we will be given an incomplete question paper—in short, tests are a complete night-mare! However, there is a sense in which our whole life is a test, but a test in which there are no right answers, only a right approach. In spiritual terms, this dream represents a recognition on your part that you are indeed in the process of being tested and that the reward for success is enlightenment.

THE TREE OF LIFE The value of this dream is equivalent to the value of the Hebrew word meaning "effort," and in order to do well on the test that is your life you will have to put in a great deal of effort. It is easy to think that the Great Work requires only mental and spiritual effort, but if you are to gain really significant insight you will also have to put your spiritual ideas into practice in the way you live your life. The value of this dream is also equivalent to the value of the letter Kaph when spelled in full. The path of Kaph is concerned with the practical application of your spiritual values, so this is where we should locate your dream.

THE JOURNEY One letter that stands out in the spelling of this dream title is the letter Nun in its final form. On one hand, this letter stands for the growth of understanding that you will achieve by practically living out the values that you are now learning. It also points to the potential for sorrow that the Great Work carries with it. The compression of this dream's value produces only the letter Qoph. This letter points out that you are feeling anxiety about your future development. However, the more you live out the ideals of compassion and understanding, the more your worries will gradually dissolve.

TEXT

noosakh–nvsch–נוסח–124

MEANING In Islam, the Muslim, Christian, and Jewish faiths are all referred to as "religions of the book." Within this phrase is a recognition of the importance of sacred scripture to all three religions. However, with the Kabbalah, the Jewish faith has spent far more time and developed more expertise than is the case with the other two main religions when it comes to the close analysis of religious texts. The dream of a text is encouraging you to spend more time looking closely and analytically not just at religious texts but at each aspect of your life.

THE TREE OF LIFE The value of this dream is equivalent to the value of the Qlippoth of Hokhmah, so it is here that we should locate your dream. Every Sefirah has its Qlippoth, and in very

simple terms the Qlippoth represents the negative aspects of the particular qualities of the Sefirah in question. Whole books have been written on the nature of the Qlippoth, but this will suffice for an understanding of your dream. The title of the Sefirah of Hokhmah is "Wisdom," so the implication here is that you need to be very careful that in your studies you do not mistake the misinformation for wisdom.

THE JOURNEY Another word that shares its value with the value of this dream is the Hebrew word meaning "delight." Bearing this in mind, you should be aware that when looking for the spiritual nature of the world around you, it is easy to see what appeals to your sensibilities rather than what is a true reflection of the nature of the Divine. When we reduce the value of this dream we find the number 7, which is the value of the letter Zayin, whose meaning is "sword." It is there to remind you of the sword of analysis that you need to carry whenever you sit down to think about the spiritual nature of the universe.

THAW

hafsharah–hphshrh–הפשרה–590

MEANING Winter can be a wonderful season especially when it snows, since no matter how cold the weather, the landscape has an undeniably beautiful quality. However, even the most ardent fan of winter has to admit to a certain amount of relief when the temperature finally begins to rise and the thaw arrives. When we reduce the value of this dream we find the number 5. This number is very important in the Western Mystery Tradition, as it represents an individual who has taken the four elements of his personality and brought them under the control of the fifth element of Spirit. This is not your current stage of development but is a goal for you to aim toward.

THE TREE OF LIFE In spiritual terms, spring represents the beginning of your inner journey and is full of hope for the future. The thaw can be seen as the moment before you make that commitment to the Great Work. It is a period of time when you begin to think about the spiritual aspect of your life and realize that you should take steps to develop your understanding of the Divine. Consequently, we should place your dream in the Sefirah of Malkut.

THE JOURNEY The value of this dream is equivalent to the value of the Hebrew word meaning "rib." Anyone familiar with Genesis will be aware that it was from a rib that Eve was crafted. This association underlines the fact that this dream is about new beginnings. The compression of this dream's value tells you that you need to find some practical activity (Kaph) that will help to maintain your commitment (Tzaddi) to the spiritual quest. It would be very helpful to you to learn some basic meditation techniques, as they will take you a long way up the Tree of Life.

THEATER

teatron-thyatrvn-תיאטרון-676

MEANING Theater attempts to convince its audience that what they are watching is actually taking place. It is a process of contrivance in which the actors and the audience collude in order to better enjoy and understand the drama unfolding on the stage. When Shakespeare had Macbeth say that life is no more than a stage, he was making a very profound comment about the nature of human existence. From a spiritual point of view, there is a very real sense in which our physical lives are no more than plays, because the truly important aspects of our lives are what happens to our souls, and that, of course, is not visible to anyone else.

THE TREE OF LIFE The value of this dream is equivalent to the Hebrew word meaning "artificial." Additionally, the value of this dream reduces to the number 10, which indicates the completion of a major cycle in your life. When we combine these two factors, we see that you have realized the essential artificiality of your physical life. This realization enables you to see much more clearly into the underlying spiritual reality of the universe, so we should place your dream on the path of Heh.

THE JOURNEY Understanding the illusory nature of the world and its material concerns is a major accomplishment in terms of your inner development. It allows you to have a much deeper appreciation of the nature of the Divine. This is why the value of this dream is equivalent to the number that we produce when we multiply 26 (the value of the Hebrew title for the Divine) by itself. The value of this dream consists of a central number, 70, bracketed by the number 6. The implication here is that you should be forging your personal sense of the spiritual (Ayin) while ensuring that it is set within a framework of belief that emerges from meditation (Vav) and quiet contemplation.

THEFT

gneyvah-gnybh-גניבה-70

MEANING Nobody wants to be thought of as a thief, so this dream is not likely to be one that you enjoy remembering. The associated words that share a value with that of the dream title include "silent" and "night." These certainly suggest the covert and unseen nature of a thief. The image of night also carries with it the sense of unpleasantness that we associated with theft. However, the overall message contained within this dream is a positive one, so we need to consider that the idea of theft may be merely symbolic of an audacious act, in the same way as the myth of Prometheus has him stealing fire from the gods.

THE TREE OF LIFE There are certainly plenty of signs that we should look at in this dream as something of a Promethean metaphor. The value of this dream is equivalent to the value of the Hebrew word meaning "secret." This suggests that you have managed to access some deep insight into the nature of the Divine. Additionally, the value of your dream is the same as the value of the letter Ayin. The path of Ayin is associated with a resolutely individual and vigorous approach to the Great Work, and it is here that we should locate your dream.

THE JOURNEY Far from referring to the unpleasant business of common theft, this dream is about the need for an audacious level of courage in order to be able to climb high into the branches of the Tree of Life. This does not mean that you should lack respect for the Divine or a proper humility in the face of the awesome nature of the underlying spiritual framework of the universe. However, it does indicate that in order to achieve the wisdom you seek, you must be willing to take certain risks and behave with great strength of will.

THERMOMETER

madkhom-mdchvm-מדחום-98

MEANING Although it can have a whole range of uses, we most associate a thermometer with its medical application. When objects appear in dreams, we can normally assume that their symbolic value relates to the functions with which they are normally associated. Consequently, this dream relates to a concern by your higher self about your spiritual temperature. This could mean that you are failing to engage with the Great Work or that you are worrying too much about your spiritual progress.

THE TREE OF LIFE The value of this dream is equivalent to the value of a Hebrew word meaning "white." The color white has long been associated with spiritual purity and is also the color connected to the highest Sefirah of Keter. Consequently, we can infer that if you have a problem with your spiritual quest, it is that you are trying too hard rather than not putting in sufficient effort. The path of Lamed relates to the rigorous study that is needed in order to achieve a full understanding of the spiritual, so it is here that we should place your dream, while noting that perhaps you are studying a little to earnestly.

THE JOURNEY Most dreams involve our higher self trying to advise as to what we should do in order to increase our chances of achieving our spiritual goals. This dream is more concerned with telling you what to do in order to preserve your physical well-being. The compression of this dream reveals the letters Tzaddi and Cheth. Tzaddi is a reminder of the intense commitment that you have to pursuing the spiritual truth, and for this you should be commended. However, the subsequent letter, Cheth, refers to the protective influence of the Divine. In the context of this dream, you should see this as a sign that the higher powers are there to protect you, so you can afford to relax a little and take things a bit more easily for a while.

THIEF

ganav-gnb- גנב-55

MEANING If your dream was about the act of theft, you should consult the entry for "theft" (see p. 335), as the dream in which you see a thief has an entirely different significance. The value of this dream is equivalent to the value of the Hebrew word meaning "pillage." This is a very negative word and it suggests that while you may be developing a number of ideas about the nature of the Divine, you are not building a relationship with the realm of the spiritual. The implication is that you are simply taking in the writings of others without adding in your unique thoughts and feelings.

THE TREE OF LIFE The value of this dream is a number that has been used in a range of Kabbalistic and Neo-Kabbalistic groups to signify the Sefirah of Malkut. Additionally, when we reduce the value of this dream we find the number 10, and this is the number of the Sefirah of Malkut on the Tree of Life. It is quite clear that we should place this dream in the Sefirah of Malkut. This may seem strange since you are obviously already beginning to explore

the spiritual through study. However, in order for your reading to be more than the absorption of data, you must give something of yourself you digest the ideas that are presented.

THE JOURNEY Do not be too disheartened by this dream. In an information age, it is not at all surprising that you would think that you could achieve a level of spiritual insight by learning alone. The spelling of this dream title begins with the letter Gimel. This letter relates to the potential for creativity, and even at this early stage in the Great Work you must be willing to try to think creatively about the spiritual ideas that you come across. It is only once you internalize these ideas and they become feelings rather than thoughts that you will be able to leave the physical world of Malkut.

THIMBLE

etsbaon-atzba'avn- אצבעון-219

MEANING Unless you work in the clothing industry—and indeed only in the more select areas where some stitching is still performed by hand—you are unlikely to have come across a thimble. It is even more unlikely that you have used one. In fact, when we think of thimbles we tend to think only of fairy tales, in which they feature quite prominently in a range of symbolic guises. The purpose of a thimble is to protect our thumbs when we are darning or sewing clothes. In spiritual terms, we see this as a metaphor for the need to ensure that when trying to fix a situation, we are protected ourselves.

THE TREE OF LIFE The value of this dream reduces to 12, and this number is associated with themes of compassion and altruism. The image of a thimble now begins to make more sense. The repairing of clothes is symbolic of your attempts to mend other people's lives, and the thimble indicates your propensity to get too emotionally involved and ultimately hurt in the process. This dream is an attempt by your higher self to encourage you to give yourself the same level of concern that you extend to others. The emphasis on compassion and self-sacrifice places this dream very definitely on the path of Mem.

THE JOURNEY You are unlikely to become any less caring or to be able to turn your back on someone in need. This is a good thing, because in living according to the best spiritual principles you will also be developing your insight into the Divine. However, you will at times feel the strain of all this compassion. It is reassuring to see that in the compression we have both the letter Resh, indicating the benevolent force of the Divine, and the letter Yod, telling us that you have the energy of the Divine spark burning within you. The final letter, Teth, points out that for you to continue in this way will require a great deal of willpower and a very strong character.

❧THIRST

*tsame-tzma-*צמא-131

MEANING The theme of thirst as a spiritual symbol is a common one and has been used in almost all major religions as a way of giving a sense of the tangible to a very abstract and personal feeling. The value of this dream is a prime number (a number that can be divided only by itself and by one). In the Western Mystery Tradition, prime numbers indicate a very individualistic nature, and in the context of this dream it serves to indicate that each of us has a different approach to dealing with our spiritual thirst.

THE TREE OF LIFE The value of this dream is equivalent to that of one of the titles of the Sefirah of Keter. However, this does not mean that your dream is located in this Sefirah; rather, it points to the source of the Divine force that will enable you to quench your thirst. The dream of thirst is one that occurs very early in the Great Work. You have made the initial commitment to the spiritual quest but have yet to experience any evidence of the existence of a Divine presence in the world. Consequently, we should place this dream on the path of Tav, which leads out of Malkut.

THE JOURNEY You have a long road ahead of you if you are to come to achieve some form of communion with the Divine. The value of this dream is equivalent to the value of the Hebrew word meaning "humility," and this is one of the first qualities that you will have to develop if you are to succeed in achieving your goals. You should take heart from the fact that we all have a spiritual thirst. Moreover, the Divine has ensured that there is an oasis for all of us. The letter Qoph in the compression of this dream's value reveals that you have a number of anxieties about the road that lies ahead. However, the subsequent letter, Lamed, is there to make it clear that only committed and rigorous study (Lamed) will lead you to an appreciation of the ultimate unity (Aleph) of the Divine.

See Zohar symbol, Thirst.

THORN

*kots-qvtz-*קוץ-196

MEANING Even without the benefit of a Kabbalistic interpretation, the basic content of this dream can be discerned simply by relying on the tendency of dreams to make references to common expressions. One such expression is to refer to a difficulty or an obstacle in your life as a "thorn in your side." This dream, then, is about the existence of some kind of block that is preventing you from moving forward in your spiritual quest.

THE TREE OF LIFE The value of this dream is equivalent to the number that we get when we multiply 14 by itself. This tells us that the number 14 is important to a full understanding of the dream. This number is associated with a certain degree of stoicism or a temperate attitude to life. This tells us that the reason why obstacles occur in your spiritual life is so that you can learn how to accept adverse circumstances in a constructive way. Additionally, the value of the keyword thorn (14 x 14 = 196) reduces to 7 (1 + 9 + 6 = 16; 1 + 6 = 7) and this is the value of the letter Zayin. The path of Zayin relates to the ability to discard that which is unhelpful in one's life, so this is where we should locate your dream.

THE JOURNEY Learning the critical analytical skills that are associated with the path of Zayin is useful not only for your spiritual development but for your life in general. The letter Qoph in the compression of this dream's value tells us that you have some concerns about the possibility of removing this obstacle. However, the subsequent letter, Tzaddi, is there to reassure you that as long as you maintain your commitment to the Great Work, there is no obstacle that cannot eventually be overcome.

THREAD

*khoot-chvt-*חוט-23

MEANING To dream of a thread is to dream of your life itself. Throughout history human lives have been represented as a thread, and its presence in your dream is a reassuring sign that you are giving some serious thought to your overall direction in life. The value of this dream is equivalent to the value of the Hebrew word meaning "joy," and this indicates that this dream carries very positive implications for your future spiritual development. The idea of weaving a tapestry is very common in Kabbalistic symbolism as a way of representing the way in which the Divine weaves together the strands of reality to form the transcendent unity of creation, so this dream should be seen as very positive.

THE TREE OF LIFE The value of this dream is equivalent to the value of the Hebrew word meaning "life." This certainly reinforces the general association of the image of thread with the life of an individual. From a spiritual perspective, the idea of life does not relate to your physical existence but to the essential life within you that exists before and after your physical incarnation. The path of Yod represents the creative spark of the Divine, the energizing force behind all life, so it is the path of Yod on which we should position your dream.

THE JOURNEY When we reduce the value of this dream we find the number 5. This number represents an individual who has managed to master the four competing elements of Fire, Air, Water, and Earth within his personality. This is achieved by bringing all four into harmony under the control and guidance of the fifth element of Spirit. We can infer from the presence of this number the reason you have been dreaming about your life as a thread. It would be very helpful for you at this time to engage in some meditation focusing on the many different threads that make up your life and your personality. You have recognized the need to address the eternal aspect of your life and make contact with your higher self in order to manifest the internal relationship suggested by the number 5.

THROAT

*garon-grvn-*גרון-259

MEANING It is the throat that allows us to talk. Admittedly our tongues and mouths are quite important to the whole process, but ultimately it is the vocal cords in our throat that allow us to engage in conversation. From a traditional Kabbalistic viewpoint, this dream suggests that you need to find a way to fully express yourself. The image of a throat is a reference to our humanity in terms of those aspects of our nature that distinguish us from other animals. In particular, it is our ability to talk, since talking allows us to share and exchange ideas, which provides for the construction of ever more complex thoughts. In this way, we can see talking as a direct extension of our mental processes.

THE TREE OF LIFE The letter Nun is particularly noticeable in the spelling and in the compression of this dream. However, the path of Nun is not the right location for your dream. The path of Nun

refers to the increased understanding and deepening of your faith that will occur if you engage in the conversations encouraged by the dream of a throat. But first you must take steps to initiate that dialogue. The path of Peh is connected with all forms of communication, so it is here that we should place your dream.

THE JOURNEY Communication is the key to many of life's problems and this is certainly the case when it comes to one's spiritual development. The compression of this dream's value makes it clear that you should have a very hopeful and optimistic outlook (Resh) on your potential for increased spiritual understanding (Nun). All that you need to do is make the effort to communicate with your higher self and as long as you have the strength of character (Teth) to persist in your efforts you will ultimately be rewarded.

➬THRONE

*kes malkhoot-ks mlkvth-*כס מלכות-576

MEANING To dream of a throne would normally be regarded as vain, to say the least. It would seem to suggest ideas of grandeur and self-importance that are unbecoming of anyone who wishes to pursue a spiritual path. However, while the spelling of the dream title itself places the idea of a throne firmly in the world of the physical, in the Sefirah of Malkut, the aspiration that the throne image represents is entirely commendable.

THE TREE OF LIFE Among the earliest Kabbalists were the Merkabah mystics, who tried to achieve a glimpse of the Divine through complex meditation and other spiritual techniques. The dream of a throne hearkens back to those very early mystics, as this dream is not one of vanity but one of spiritual desire. The throne represents the perceived seat of the Divine. When we reduce the value of this dream we find the number 9. This is the value of the letter Teth. The path of Teth relates to the need for a strong character and strength of will in order to succeed in the Great Work. The fact that you are dreaming about experiencing a direct communion with the Divine itself suggests that your dream belongs on the path of Teth.

THE JOURNEY In order to maintain your steady progress up the Tree of Life there are a number of actions that you must accomplish. They are detailed in the compression of the dream's value so that you might come closer to achieving your spiritual goals. The letter Kaph tells you that you should engage in some kind of practical activity that will help you progress up the Tree of Life. It should be something that you choose for yourself (Ayin) and should be fairly vigorous and active, although you must also ensure that you make time to quietly contemplate (Vav) your place within the spiritual universe.

See Zohar symbol, Throne.

THROWING

*leezrok-lzrvq-*לזרוק-343

MEANING It is not at all clear, unless we refer to the values within this dream, exactly what the significance of this dream is. Without the benefit of a Kabbalistic viewpoint, we cannot be certain whether you are throwing something in anger or are engaging in some kind of sporting activity. When we reduce the value of this dream we find the number 10. The number 10 refers to the successful completion of a major cycle in your life. From this we can glean that in fact you are throwing something away. That is, you are disposing of an aspect of your nature that is no longer helpful to you.

THE TREE OF LIFE The value of this dream is equivalent to the value of the Hebrew word meaning "a sweet smell." Your dream also shares its value with the Hebrew word meaning "a garden." These two associated words suggest a place of great beauty. Appropriately enough, the Sefirah of Tiferet has the title "Beauty." It is here that we should locate your dream. Having achieved some form of contact with your higher self, you are now in the position of being able to dispose of your ego-driven personality.

THE JOURNEY You have already achieved a great deal in terms of your spiritual development so it may be tempting to take it easy for a while. However, you are far from the end of your spiritual quest. The compression of this dream's value begins with the letter Shin, and this tells us that you will need a great deal of energy in order to renew your spiritual quest. The subsequent letter, Mem, lets you know that the maternal aspect of the Divine will be with you and will help you to find a creative way (Gimel) of making further progress toward a deeper understanding of the Divine.

THUNDER

*raam-ra'am-*רעם-310

MEANING We can all remember when, as children, we were reassured that the terrifying sound of

thunder was no more than God rearranging his furniture. It is strangely ironic that when we come to look at a Kabbalistic interpretation of the significance of the dream of thunder we discover that it does indeed relate to the involvement of the Divine, in rearranging the nature of your reality if not his own furniture! When we reduce the value of this dream we find the number 4. This number relates to the physical world and makes it clear that this dream is designed to bring about changes in the way you live your day-to-day life. We should remember, though, that just as when we were children, there is nothing worrisome about this dream.

THE TREE OF LIFE The value of this dream is equivalent to the value of the Hebrew word meaning "to trample on" or "to conquer." These are violent images and seem to be a long way from our common understanding of the nature of the Divine. This dream belongs to the Sefirah of Gevurah, as it is here that you learn to appreciate that even the chaotic and the seemingly brutal have a place in the spiritual universe.

THE JOURNEY We tend to think of the Divine only in terms of those aspects of the world and our nature that we find appealing and worthy. However, the spiritual lies behind every aspect of the universe. If there were no death, there could be no birth, for example. If we never engaged in conflict, how could we ever learn the valuable lessons that come with the making of a peace? The Sefirah of Gevurah has some hard lessons for us, but the compression of this dream makes it clear that you have energy (Shin) and the sense of the Divine within yourself (Yod) sufficient to be able to absorb and accept the implications of this aspect of the Divine.

TICKLE

*deegdoog-dgdvg-*דגדוג-20

MEANING It is very easy to get carried away with the idea that the spiritual quest is an entirely somber affair. Indeed, many people with significant experience in such matters, who should really know better, derive an inappropriate sense of self-importance from behaving as though there is no room for fun in a spiritual universe. This dream is about finding the joy in the spiritual and finding the spiritual in a range of things from the simplest daisy to the most complex mathematical formula.

THE TREE OF LIFE Even those paths on the Tree of Life that are undoubtedly connected to the more serious and severe aspects of the Divine nature still have room within them for the genuine seeker of truth to find some evidence of the pure joy and love with which the universe is infused. However, we are looking for a single path on which to position your dream. The value of this dream is equivalent to the value of the letter Kaph. The path of Kaph is concerned with the practical manifestation of spiritual values in the day-to-day world. Additionally, it relates to an attitude to life that does not seek to alter the course of events but accepts whatever fortune brings. This is therefore an ideal path for this dream.

THE JOURNEY In recognizing the potential for joy and even humor within the Great Work, you have already achieved a level of wisdom that many can never accomplish. This is because many people need the idea of severity in order to convey importance. If this dream has a single most-important message, it is that importance or spiritual value cannot be measured by the gravity of the tone that is associated with any given idea. The Divine does not need the trappings of importance, so you should look for the spiritual value in the trivial and the small as well as in the grand and the great.

TIME

*zman-zmn-*זמן-97

MEANING From the point of view of the Divine, time is much more a matter of geography than of history. For a being not bound by the directional nature of time, as we are, the historical process must appear very different indeed. Perhaps if we could step outside time for a while and look at our past as a series of places, we would more easily recognize their similarity and then maybe reflect on why we have learned so little despite advancing so far. At an individual level, this dream is about the realization that you have a limited time in which to achieve your spiritual goals.

THE TREE OF LIFE The value of this dream is equivalent to the value of a Hebrew word meaning "architect." If buildings in dreams represent our personalities, then an architect represents that force within us that shapes our personalities. In recognizing that you have only so long in which to find some form of communion with the Divine, you are beginning to try to take on the role of that architect. This dream therefore sits on the path of Nun, since it is a path that is concerned with the deeper faith that comes in part from a thorough and honest examination of our own nature.

THE JOURNEY It is not easy to look at yourself honestly, and inevitably there will be memories and feelings that cause you sorrow and possibly a certain degree of regret that you did not act differently at certain times. The compression of this dream reminds you that the most important thing for you to do is to remain committed to the Great Work (Tzaddi). It also tells you that you should rely on the sword of rational analysis (Zayin) in order to help you make some sense out of your inner self as you begin investigating it. At a practical level, this dream reminds you that you should see time as an aid, not as your master. The closer we come to a spiritual understanding, the nearer we come to realizing that time does not need to control our lives to the extent that we tend to allow it to.

TITHE

*maaser-ma'ashr-*מעשר-610

MEANING The practice of tithing is now relatively rare. It meant essentially that a fixed portion of your income would go to a given institution. That may have been the church or a local landowner or an agent of royalty. The key point is that you paid a fixed proportion, rather like a tax. In spiritual terms, this could be seen as a symbol of the fact that you should set aside a certain amount of time each day to devote to spiritual pursuits.

THE TREE OF LIFE Traditionally, a tithe was one-tenth of your income, and some people still perform a form of tithing by donating that proportion of their income to charitable causes. This also has a spiritual analogy as it can be seen as a reference to the need to spend a certain amount of your time in the service of your community. Both of these forms of tithing share one thing in common in that they represent a form of self-sacrifice. The path of Mem is concerned with such altruistic acts, so it is on this path that we should position your dream.

THE JOURNEY The compression of this dream begins with the letter Mem in its final form. When we combine this with the fact that the spelling of the dream title also begins with the letter Mem, it is clear that you need to devote a considerable amount of your time to trying to help those in need. The final letter in the compression of your dream is the letter Yod. This letter stands for the Divine spark that exists within each of us. The suggestion here is that if you engage with this agenda of compassionate acts, you will be able to awaken the Divine spark that lies within you.

TOMB

*kever-qbr-*קבר-302

MEANING It would be a perfectly understandable reaction to see this dream as rather worrisome. Dreams about death put us in mind of our own mortality, and this is rarely a pleasant experience. However, the central letter in the spelling of this dream title is Beth, which means "house." The implication here is that in order to return to our spiritual home, we or at least a part of ourselves must die. That part of us that must be removed by one means or another is our ego-driven personality.

THE TREE OF LIFE The value of this dream is equivalent to the value of the Hebrew word meaning "to inquire into." This tells us that this dream is not so much about death as it is about looking closely into what a tomb actually signifies. On one hand, it certainly points to the end of your physical life. However, the value of this dream is also equivalent to a Hebrew word meaning "dawn," so a tomb also represents the beginning of a new life free of the fetters of the physical. It takes a very sophisticated and deep level of spiritual insight to fully internalize the truth of this message, so we should place your dream on the path of Beth.

THE JOURNEY You have already come to understand the necessity of mortality, since you have passed through the Sefirah of Gevurah in order to arrive on the path of Beth. What you must now learn is to fully accept this fact in terms of your individual life. The letter Shin, which begins the compression of the value of this dream suggests that you have sufficient raw spiritual energy to be able to deal with this challenging idea. It also seems very likely that you will be able to make the last leg of the journey, which leads to the spiritual home represented by the letter Beth.

TONGUE

*lashon-lshvn-*לישון-386

MEANING The tongue is one of the most sensitive organs in the human body. To dream of a tongue is a way for your higher self to indicate that you need to be sensitive to the smallest details in your life right now. The letter Nun stands out in this dream title as it appears in its final form. This tells us that one of the tasks before you in the next few weeks is to try to find ways in which you can deepen the strength of your faith in the spiritual quest. It is for this reason

that you need to be sensitive to the spiritual aspect of everything and everyone you encounter.

THE TREE OF LIFE It is tempting to place this dream on the path of Peh, since we would expect a dream about tongues to be concerned primarily with the act of communication. While the dream is indeed related to issues of communication, it is the more mental aspect of communication that is being highlighted. The letter Nun points to the need to communicate with yourself in a deeply reflective manner. The value of this dream is equivalent to the value of a title of a relatively complex form of Kabbalistic Gematria, and this also aligns this dream with the development of your mental alacrity. Consequently, the most appropriate location for this dream is within the Sefirah of Hod.

THE JOURNEY The central number in the value of this dream is the number 8. This refers both to eternity and to the task that is highlighted by the presence of the letter Nun in your dream title. The number 8 is also associated with the planet Mercury, which governs both communication and mental wit and is the number of the Sefirah of Hod. The letter Shin in the compression tells us that you have the mental energy needed to learn the lessons that Hod has to offer. The final letter, Vav, is a reminder that while it is good to be quick-witted, you also need to retain a willingness to spend time in quiet contemplation of the nature of the spiritual universe.

TOOL

*klee-kly-*כלי-60

MEANING There are those people who like to place the spiritual side of life in a very rarefied atmosphere. Such people believe that at least three types of incense and a bucketful of crystals are essential before any form of spiritual activity is attempted. There is at least a little bit of this sort of person in all of us, and we tend to react to the image of a tool as something that cannot have any truly profound spiritual significance. When we feel such things, we should remember that the key figures in the Jewish faith, whence the Kabbalah emerged, were pretty down-to-earth people who kept sheep or farmed or led armies as well as engaging in a direct relationship with the Divine.

THE TREE OF LIFE The value of this dream is equivalent to the Hebrew word meaning "tradition." The implication here is that you should be looking to the writings of the early Kabbalists for an inspiration in your spiritual quest. We can also see that the value of your dream is the same as the value of the letter Samech. The letter Samech literally means "prop," and the path of Samech is concerned with support and guidance in your quest for truth. Consequently, it is an ideal path on which to place your dream.

THE JOURNEY You should feel very encouraged by this dream. Its value is equivalent to the value of the Hebrew word meaning "excellence," and you should take this as a sign that you are progressing very well. The spelling of this dream title makes it clear that you will stand the best chance of benefiting from the support of the Divine if you are making a practical effort (Kaph). This effort should seek to put the results of your studies (Lamed) into a form of activity that can be useful to other people as well as help to awaken the Divine spark within you.

TOP
peesgah–psgh– פסגה‎-148

MEANING This dream analysis relates to any dream in which the predominant theme is of being on top. This could be on top of a mountain, or even on top of a bus. The key issue is your relative position. Symbolically, the notion of being on top relates to achievement, which could be of any kind, but in terms of your spiritual development this dream indicates that you are feeling enthusiastic and passionate about your future understanding of the Divine. The value of this dream reduces to 13, and this indicates that you are about to experience a major change in your life.

THE TREE OF LIFE The value of this dream is equivalent to the value of the Hebrew word meaning "victory." This association refers to the feeling that you have of making good progress with the Great Work. Additionally, this word is the title of the Sefirah of Netzach. This Sefirah is associated with the emotions and the drive to express yourself artistically. As the first letter of the spelling of this dream is Peh, which represents all forms of communication, this is an ideal location for your dream in a number of ways.

THE JOURNEY You have a significant level of confidence about your spiritual journey. However, the letter Qoph in the compression of this dream indicates that you have some worries about the future. However, the letter Mem, which follows, reminds you that you are being supported by the maternal aspect of the Divine. Further, the final letter, Cheth, relates to the protective force of the Divine, so you are in a very safe and secure position right now. This means that you can afford to fully explore your passion for the spiritual journey at this time.

TORCH
lapeed–lphyd– לפיד‎-124

MEANING When we start out on our spiritual quest we are facing the completely unknown, and in a sense we could picture this as a vast expanse of darkness. As we begin to learn more about ourselves and the nature of the Divine itself, the darkness gradually begins to be filled with an increasing number of points of light. The image of a torch indicates that you are about to find a means of illuminating the darkness of the unknown more fully and with greater ease.

THE TREE OF LIFE The initial letter in the spelling of this dream title is Lamed, and this tells you that in order to shine a bright light into the unfamiliar realm of the spiritual, you need to make sure that you are studying rigorously. When we reduce the value of this dream we find the number 7. This is the value of the letter Zayin, which literally means "sword." It is the path of Zayin that your dream sits on, as it represents the carefully analytical approach that you need to take to your spiritual development.

THE JOURNEY You might think that such a positive dream would leave you feeling extremely self-confident. However, we need to remember that the more encouraging a dream, the greater the perceived pressure to succeed. The anxiety that this perceived pressure creates is reflected by the letter Qoph in the compression of this dream. The subsequent letter, Kaph, indicates that you will help to build your confidence if you take some practical steps to put into practice in the material world the values and attitudes that you are beginning to develop.

TORPEDO
torpedo–tvrphdv– שורפדו‎-305

MEANING You are unlikely to wake up feeling particularly reassured about the state of your spiritual development after having a dream about a torpedo. It would seem that the only interpretation of this dream should be that you are either feeling violent or are at risk of suffering violence at the hands of someone else. However, this is only what the dream appears to be saying. After all, a torpedo is not just any weapon, it is a very specific weapon that travels at very high speed under water before exploding. As the element of Water relates to our emotions, we should see this dream as a warning that some long-hidden feelings are likely to come rushing to the surface very soon.

THE TREE OF LIFE When we reduce the value of this dream we find the number 8. This is the value of the Hebrew letter Cheth, which literally means "fence." This gives us a very strong clue as to why you are about to experience an explosive force of emotion. The letter Cheth refers to the protective force of the Divine, but it can also point to a defensive nature on the part of the dreamer. It is this latter meaning that is appropriate in the context of this dream. Your dream belongs on the path of Cheth since you are still repressing a number of emotions due to fear of what will happen if you allow them to surface.

THE JOURNEY It is important to remember that no matter how well we might weigh them down with the stones of fear, anxiety, and emotional pain, difficult memories and feelings will always ultimately come back up to the surface. This is about to happen to you, and in order to be able to move on spiritually you must face them and deal with them. The letter Shin in the compression of this dream's value makes it clear that this will take a great deal of energy. However, the final letter, Heh, is there to remind you that only by looking honestly at yourself will you be able to come to an understanding of the Divine.

TORRENT

*sheetafon-shytphvn-*שיטפון-455

MEANING Walking in the rain may be quite fun and walking in the rain with a partner can be extremely romantic. However, trying to walk in a torrent, no matter whom you are with, is simply not fun at all. This dream creates an image of being soaked in an unrelenting downpour. This suggests that the emotional feelings that you are experiencing at this time are likely to be overwhelming. Even though this points to a very testing time in your life, it may prove to be a valuable one once you emerge from the torrent.

THE TREE OF LIFE The first three letters in the spelling of this dream title all represent very strong energy of one kind or another. This emphasizes the

force with which the emotional torrent is likely to hit you. The letters Yod and Shin make it clear that there is a positive, Divinely inspired purpose behind this experience, while the letter Teth is there to urge you to stick with it no matter how difficult life gets in the process. The letter Nun appears in this dream in its final form, and it is to the path of Nun that we should assign this dream. This dream is about facing the range of difficult feelings that you have about yourself, the Divine, and the nature of the spiritual quest. It will ultimately lead to a deepening of your resolve to continue, which is exactly what the path of Nun is about.

THE JOURNEY When we reduce the value of this dream we find the number 5. This number refers to an individual who has brought the four elements within his personality under the control of the fifth element of Spirit. This is what you are currently attempting to achieve. It is never easy to take on such a challenge entirely by yourself. Admittedly, no one else can face this difficult period of time for you, but you should try to put yourself in touch with like-minded people with whom you can share your experiences and your concerns.

TORTURE

*eenooy-a'aynvy-*עינוי-146

MEANING Unless you have some very particular and quite unusual tastes, this dream is going to be deeply disturbing. It is the sort of dream where one cup of coffee is still not quite enough to dispel the feelings of disquiet that are there when you wake. Indeed, a dream of this nature might take a whole pot of coffee before you feel ready to face the day! Surprisingly, the spiritual significance of this dream is not terrible. In fact, the image of torture is more an expression of the extremity of your desire to achieve some kind of spiritual insight than an expression of any negative event that is due to occur. From a traditional Kabbalistic perspective, you should try to identify what it is in your practical life that is causing you to have such negative feelings.

THE TREE OF LIFE The value of this dream reduces to 11, which signifies that you are about to experience a moment of profound spiritual importance to you. The idea of torture actually relates to the absence of the Divine in your life, and you are beginning to feel it so strongly that it represents itself to your unconscious mind as a form of torture. The value of this dream is equivalent to the value of a Hebrew phrase meaning "the first gate." This suggests very clearly that you have yet to make a definite commitment to pursuing a spiritual path and that you are still languishing in the physical world of Malkut.

THE JOURNEY It may well be that this dream, as extreme in nature as it is, is just what you need to spur you on to making that leap of faith that will mark the beginning of your inner journey. The value of this dream is equivalent to the value of the Hebrew word meaning "adult," and we see the commencement of the Great Work very much as a coming-of-age in spiritual terms. As you have such a strong desire to feel a sense of the presence of the Divine, you should immediately engage in some practical activity to help bring this about. It would be an excellent idea for you to join a respected meditation class, since correct meditation can produce the most profound spiritual results.

TOURIST

*tayar-thyyr-*תייר-620

MEANING If we look at the idea of a tourist on a purely introspective level it points to a willingness to explore the depths of your personality. From a Kabbalistic point of view, this dream would also be seen as generally encouraging, but with slight reservations. The idea of a tourist can be seen as someone who never develops more than a partial understanding of the culture he is visiting. The danger of partial understanding in spiritual terms cannot be overstated, and it is referred to in the value of your dream, which is equivalent to the value of the Hebrew word *Shishak.* This word is spelled ShShK, and, by the use of a form of Kabbalistic analysis known as Temurah, it is related to the Hebrew word spelled BBL, or Babel to us. The Tower of Babel is, of course, on one level a symbol of the dangers involved in partially understanding the purpose or aim of the spiritual quest.

THE TREE OF LIFE Although, as we have said, there are certain reservations, this dream is generally positive in nature. The idea of a tourist indicates that at this stage you have little detailed knowledge about the nature of the Great Work. This means that we are looking at a position relatively low on the Tree of Life. The Sefirah of Yesod is the first staging point after the physical world of Malkut and is also concerned with the attractiveness and the mystery of spirituality. For these reasons, we should place your dream within the Sefirah of Yesod.

THE JOURNEY The value of this dream is equivalent to the value of a Hebrew word meaning "doors." The suggestion here is that you have opened the gateway to the spiritual. What you need to do now is make sure that you keep following the right path in order to gain a deeper insight into the spiritual nature of the universe. When we reduce the value of this dream we find the number 8, which is the value of the letter Cheth. In the context of this dream, this letter refers to a certain defensiveness on your part that may be partially responsible for why, up to now, you have immersed yourself in the Great Work like a tourist rather than as a local.

TOWER

*meegdal-mgdl-*מגדל-77

MEANING When we dream of a tower, a psychologist might argue that we are dreaming of being in a position of power over others. From a Kabbalistic point of view, though, this dream refers to your aspirations to rise higher up the Tree of Life and to come ever closer to an understanding of the Divine nature. The value of this dream is equivalent to the value of the Hebrew word that refers to the descending force form Keter. This makes it clear that while you are trying to build your way up toward the Godhead, the energy of the Divine is working its way down toward you. This dream also refers to those moments in your life when you feel a heightened sense of existence—the really key moments of bliss or deep understanding that come upon us from time to time.

THE TREE OF LIFE The value of this dream is also equivalent to the value of the Hebrew word meaning "he-goat." The path of Ayin is associated with the zodiac sign Capricorn, and this sign is represented by the image of a goat. The path of Ayin is very appropriate for your dream since it relates to the vigorous pursuit of your spiritual goals, and the image of a tower certainly suggests a vigorous approach to the Great Work.

THE JOURNEY You have every reason to feel optimistic about your current spiritual development. The number 7 is traditionally associated with good luck, and your dream's value consists entirely of the number 7. In the spelling of this dream title we see that as well as studying (Lamed), you should take some time to express your spirituality through caring for those around you who are in need (Mem). The central letters, Gimel and Daleth, tell you that if you continue to approach the Great Work in a creative manner, you will open the door to further levels of insight. You will certainly help your inner development if you make a point of actively seeking out those "peak" experiences referred to in this dream.

TOY

tsatsooa–tza'atzva'a– צעצוע *–326*

MEANING Many people would see this dream as expressing a desire within you to return to a state of childishness and perceive this to be negative, indicating that you are unwilling to take on the responsibilities of adulthood. However, you should see this dream as entirely positive since it associates the Great Work with something enjoyable. Additionally, the association with childhood can be seen simply as a sign that you are not being constrained by any cynicism in your attitude. It is important to remember that progress in the Great Work requires the ability to look at the world with an innocent outlook as well as a willingness to find the joy in experiencing a playful manner of interacting with the world around you.

THE TREE OF LIFE To a Christian Kabbalist, this dream would be particularly important since its value is equivalent to the Hebrew spelling of the name "Jesus." This spelling inserts the letter Shin into the standard spelling of the Divine name. Whether or not one accepts the Christian faith, this dream's value indicates that you are attempting to take the values represented by the Divine and live them within your day-to-day life. This requires a great deal of energy, and your dream should rightly be placed on the path of Shin.

THE JOURNEY When we reduce the value of this dream we find the number 11. This number tells us that you are close to having a significant spiritual insight. This may be related to the attitude with which you approach the spiritual quest. The idea of a toy suggests that you have something of the innocent faith of a child, and this is an ideal way in which to build your relationship with the Divine.

TRADE

meeskhar–mschr– מסחר *–308*

MEANING Commerce is not exactly the most spiritual of activities, so you might think that this dream should have a definitely negative feel to it. However, the fact that you are dreaming about trade does not mean that you are concerned only about the material side of life even in terms of your unconscious. On the contrary, it is your higher self that is advising

you that in your waking life you are allowing the material concerns of your life to dominate.

THE TREE OF LIFE When we reduce the value of this dream we find the number 11, which suggests that you are about to undergo a spiritually important experience. It is likely that this will relate to your realizing that you are not paying enough attention to your inner life. The path of Kaph, which is where your dream should be placed, is concerned with the practical, and it is also the eleventh letter in the Hebrew alphabet. In your case, this practical side is currently being misdirected into activities that do not have a spiritual dimension.

THE JOURNEY The letter Shin, which begins the compression of this dream's value, tells us that you have the energy to succeed once it is properly focused. The value of this dream is equivalent to the value of the Hebrew word meaning "daybreak," and this strongly suggests that you are about to have a sudden realization of how you should revise the priorities in your life. The final letter, Cheth, in the compression of this dream also reminds you that in attempting this rearrangement you will be under the protection of the Divine.

TRAFFIC

taavoorah–tha'abvrh– תעבורה *–683*

MEANING We tend to think of traffic as a modern phenomenon, but from the very first cities of Mesopotamia the human race has had to deal with traffic. Inevitably, traffic brings with it some very specific frustrations. The most annoying things that we associate with traffic are the facts that we have to go much slower than we would like and that we are simply one piece within a vast network of moving pieces. In spiritual terms, the dream of traffic refers to your desire to progress more quickly and to be able to fully express yourself in terms of your developing relationship with the Divine.

THE TREE OF LIFE Once you achieve a reasonable level of your spiritual progress, one of the things that you will learn is an increased measure of patience. The Great Work is not something that can be rushed, as it has to operate at the pace of the individual concerned. This may not always agree with the pace at which you would like to progress. As you are feeling rather frustrated with the pace at which you are increasing your insight into the spiritual realm, we should locate your dream on the path of Tav, as this is the first path leading out of Malkut.

THE JOURNEY The value of this dream is a prime number (a number that can be divided only by itself and by one). This is a reminder to you that even if you feel that you are not yet developing a personal relationship with the Divine through the agency of your higher self, you are a unique soul and it will happen in time. The central letter in the compression of the value of this dream is Peh. This letter literally means "mouth" and is concerned with all forms of communication. The message here is that although you may not be achieving any results, you should persist in your attempts to initiate a dialogue with your higher self.

TRAGEDY

tragedyah – trgdyh – תרגדיה *– 231*

MEANING We should not assume that a disaster is exactly the same as a tragedy. While a disaster is any kind of catastrophe, a tragedy, strictly speaking, requires a single weakness or flaw on the part of an individual that causes the ensuing problems. It is important to make this distinction because it has a bearing on the spiritual significance of this dream. To dream of a disaster might primarily indicate a concern for the welfare of others. To dream of a tragedy suggests a deep-seated fear that some flaw within yourself will cause your inner development to go awry.

THE TREE OF LIFE The value of this dream is equivalent to the value of the Hebrew name for the spiritual ruler of the element of Fire within the Western Mystery Tradition. This suggests that if you do have a hidden flaw, it is a certain rash quality in the way you make decisions. On the positive side, this dream's value is also equivalent to the value of the Hebrew phrase meaning "let there be light." This makes it clear that you are shortly about to gain an insight into the nature of your particular weakness. The letter Resh begins the compression of the value of this dream. The path of Resh is linked to the idea of light by its association with the Sun. Additionally, it represents a careful, rational, but optimistic level of introspection and thought. It is therefore an ideal location for your dream.

THE JOURNEY You should see this dream as encouraging, since everybody has his flaws but many people go through their whole lives without ever trying to deal with them. The letter Teth, which begins the spelling of this dream title, makes it very clear that it will take a lot of willpower to deal with your tendency to be overly hasty. However, if you apply yourself to the task at hand with the rigor suggested by the letter Lamed in this dream's compression, you will be sure to achieve success. One key meditation that you should consider is to focus on the probable source of your flaws and try to find ways in which to deal with them.

TRAIN

rakevet – rkbth – רכבת *– 622*

MEANING Dreams about different modes of transportation are always about the process of attempting to develop spiritually. The particular mode lets us know exactly how and sometimes also why you are attempting the spiritual journey. A dream of a train tells us that you are following a predetermined route. This means that your main focus within your spiritual work has been to study the ideas and methods of those who have gone before you. Additionally, since you will be a passenger on the train, it is likely that you would prefer to approach the Great Work as a member of a meditation or yoga class rather than as someone operating with total responsibility over the direction he takes.

THE TREE OF LIFE As you are metaphorically already on the train, we can infer that your spiritual quest has begun. However, the signs are that you have only just begun this voyage of discovery. The need to be driven, to have a fixed route and a preappointed destination, and the wish to travel with others all suggest the nervous anxiety of someone who is not yet entirely comfortable with spiritual matters. Consequently, we should place your dream on the path of Qoph, as this represents feelings of worry and concern.

THE JOURNEY The value of this dream is equivalent to the value of the Hebrew word meaning "blessings." This certainly bodes well for your inner journey. The letter Mem in its final form begins the compression of this dream's value and thus emphasizes the fact that you are operating under the maternal influence of the Divine. The central letter, Kaph, implies that to have the best chance of finding some way back to your spiritual home (Beth), you should engage in some form of spiritually enlivened practical activity.

TRAITOR

boged – bvgd – בוגד *– 15*

MEANING The idea that one could be a traitor to oneself may seem a little strange, but that is exactly what this dream is about. Since we do not have a single controlling and directing consciousness, it is perfectly possible for one element of our nature to behave in a way that is unhelpful for some other aspect. The value of this dream is equivalent to the value of the Hebrew word meaning "pride." This is certainly one quality that can lead us to behave in ways that are not genuinely in our own best interests. From a more traditional Kabbalist perspective, we would look at this dream as a warning that there may be someone around you at this time who may be seeking to harm you in some way.

THE TREE OF LIFE In order to progress up the Tree of Life, we need to be able to listen to the views of others even when they conflict with our initial perceptions of a situation. This is not something we can easily do if we are still beset by the problem of pride. The fact that you have had this dream indicates that you are now ready to do something about it. The value of this dream is equivalent to the value of the word *splendor* in Hebrew. This is, of course, the meaning of the Sefirah of Hod. The Sefirah of Hod is concerned in part with organizing the way in which we communicate with ourselves internally, so this is an ideal location for your dream.

THE JOURNEY When we reduce the value of this dream we find the number 6. This is the value of the letter Vav, which is present in order to reinforce the notion that you need to spend some time reflecting on your inner nature. While you may have some work to do in order to bring about an internal harmony between the competing elements that make up your personality, the suggestion is that you will succeed. The letter Yod in the compression of this dream's value tells us that the Divine spark is already burning within you, so you should not worry that you are going to be unable to resolve your current difficulty.

TRANSLATE
letargem – lthrgm – לתרגם *– 673*

MEANING There are two key issues that a good translator needs to bear in mind when dealing with a foreign text. The first and most important is that the content must be accurately transposed into the new language. Second, but in many ways equally or almost equally important, is the need to retain the tone or style of what has been written. To give a ridiculous example, a love poem translated so that the content remained but was conveyed in the style of an instruction manual would not only have lost its tone of voice but in the process would have suffered an altered or lost meaning. When we try to translate

the ideas and feelings we have as a result of our spiritual work into everyday language, it is very important that we retain a sense of the tone and context that surrounded those ideas.

THE TREE OF LIFE The initial letter in the spelling of this dream title is Lamed, which links with the idea of diligent study and so may seem an ideal path for this dream. However, while study is important, it is not the key to this dream's message. This dream is concerned far more with communication and the need for you to be as "tuned in" as possible to the insight that is being passed to you from your higher self. Consequently, we should place this dream on the path of Peh, as it is associated with all forms of communication.

THE JOURNEY As well as refer to the sense of understanding that you may receive almost unconsciously during meditation or other forms of spiritual practice, this dream can relate to the more down-to-earth process of reading spiritual texts. The central letter in the compression of this dream's value is Ayin. This indicates the importance of finding your individual understanding of the spiritual realm. In terms of reading texts, it means that here too you have to engage in a form of translation to ensure that what you read is set in the context of your approach to the Divine.

TRAP
malkodet – mlkvdth – מלכודת *– 500*

MEANING To dream of a trap may not seem particularly encouraging from a purely psychological reading of this dream, as it could be seen as suggesting unconscious desires to engage in the manipulation of others. However, if we see this dream in a spiritual context then it is entirely positive in nature. The idea of a trap is suggestive of someone who has realized the elusive nature of spiritual enlightenment and is determined to achieve some kind of insight by creating whatever circumstances are necessary to make this happen.

THE TREE OF LIFE It is important to remember that you are not dreaming of setting out to trap a person but are attempting to catch an idea or an understanding. One of the difficulties with the Great Work is that very often we can reach a level of insight during a meditation, but find that when we return to a normal waking state that insight has somehow dissolved. This dream is about the desire and the determination to ensure that you do not allow those insights to leave you once you have experienced them. It is your dogged will to succeed that places this dream on the path of Teth.

THE JOURNEY There are no hard and fast rules as to the best way in which to achieve a lasting level of inner wisdom. In many cases it is simply a matter of experience and time. The more you meditate and engage in spiritual practices, the longer the insights you gain will stay with you. The value of this dream is equivalent to the value of the letter Kaph. The letter Kaph is concerned with the practical expression of the spiritual. The suggestion here is that the more your spiritual work is linked to some practical activity the greater the likelihood of your being able to "trap" the results so that they stay in your consciousness. It is equally important that you accept the need to have a certain element of cleverness and strategy.

TRAVEL

*masa-msa'a-*מסע-170

MEANING In psychological terms, this dream refers to someone who is eager to explore the world around him. It may also be seen as an indication of an individual who finds it hard to settle in his career, his relationships, or where he lives. From the Kabbalistic standpoint, the notion of travel refers to the spiritual journey that takes us up out of Malkut and back toward the home of Keter, and as such this dream is seen as very positive.

THE TREE OF LIFE To be dreaming of travel suggests that you are already involved in the Great Work. This is because you are not dreaming about packing or booking a trip or even departing; this dream is about actively traveling. The value of this dream is equivalent to the value of the Hebrew word meaning "staff." Specifically, it is a reference to the staff of David, and it represents the supportive force of the Divine. The idea of protection from above is continued in the reduction of the value of this dream, which produces the number 8. This number is the value of the letter Cheth, which refers to the protective energy of the Divine. Consequently, we should place your dream on the path of Cheth.

THE JOURNEY While the central letter, Samech, in the spelling of this dream title indicates the guidance that you will receive in your travels, the letter Mem, which begins this dream title, suggests that in turn you should be careful to ensure that you behave in a compassionate and caring manner to those around you. While you have some doubts about your

future spiritual devlopment indicated by the letter Qoph in the compression of this dream, you should be feeling generally positive. The final letter, Ayin, in the compression tells us that you will be developing your unique approach to the Divine over the coming months. On a practical level, you should also prepare yourself for the possibility of some actual travel in the near future.

TREASURE

*otsar-avtzr-*אוצר-297

MEANING To someone who has no interest in the spiritual, this dream might offer the exciting potential of impending wealth. However, treasure comes in many forms, and the most valuable treasure is that which cannot be seen, because it sits within the soul. This is the treasure of wisdom and it is quite genuinely priceless. The value of this dream is equivalent to the value of the Hebrew word meaning "thesaurus." This association of words with treasure acts as a very strong clue to the fact that this dream is about intangible value rather than pots of gold or piles of cash. In Kabbalistic tradition, the idea of treasure has always been associated with spiritual rather than material wealth.

THE TREE OF LIFE Within the Kabbalah there are many different titles for the Divine, and they relate to the range of roles that the Divine force plays as it emerges into the universe. This dream's value is equivalent to the value of the Divine name that is associated with the Sefirah of Gevurah and that refers to the strength of the Creator. In terms of the search for the treasure of enlightenment, you too must have great strength of commitment to the Great Work. The letter Tzaddi appears within the spelling of this dream title and is the central letter in the compression of this dream's value. The path of Tzaddi relates to the commitment that one must have to the spiritual quest, so it is here that we should locate your dream.

THE JOURNEY When we reduce the value of this dream we find the number 9. This is the value of the letter Teth. The letter Teth literally means "serpent" and in its positive aspect it suggests a great strength of character and willpower on the part of the dreamer. It is this willpower that will help you to maintain your dedication to the spiritual quest even when you do not feel that you are making any progress. The final letter in the compression of this dream is Zayin, and this reminds you that you need to sift through a lot of low-grade material before you can hope to find any real treasure. It is very important that you always carefully analyze any spiritual ideas that you come across so that you retain only those ideas that will help you to move forward.

❧TREES
ets-a'atz-עץ-160

MEANING When we think of the world of plants, trees are the longest-lived and very often the most impressive examples that spring to mind. From a psychological point of view, this dream could be seen as referring to a very steady and solid personality. When we look at this dream from a more spiritually aware perspective, we find a different set of ideas. The key thing about a tree in spiritual terms is that a very large proportion of it, and it could be argued the most important part of it, consists of its roots, which are not visible but continue to grow regardless. The idea of a tree is a very positive one in the Kabbalah; the Torah itself is referred to as a Tree of Life, and of course the diagram known as the Tree of Life is central to this system of mysticism.

THE TREE OF LIFE The roots of the tree can be compared to the spiritual side of our nature, which, while unseen, is the part of our nature that truly holds us together and allows us to grow. At another level, the roots of the tree could be seen as that part of you that still holds on to the certainty of the earth while your more spiritual side is reaching up into the sky to seek out the Divine. The sense of being half wedded to the material and half yearning for the realm of the spiritual is present no matter which end of the Tree we see as representing which aspect of your nature. Consequently, we should place this dream on the path of Tav, as this is the first path to lead out of Malkut and so it is connected to the earth but reaches up to the Divine.

THE JOURNEY Images of trees are very common in spiritual literature. We have, of course, the Tree of Life, but there is also the Tree of the Norse religion, Ygdrassil, along with countless other tree symbols in other spiritual cultures. Although you have only just begun your spiritual journey, it is clear that you are already tapping in to the themes and symbols that underlie many religious systems. The spelling of this dream title is also very positive, telling us that you are both very committed (Tzaddi) and that you are able to formulate your own way of approaching (Ayin) the Divine.

See Zohar symbol, Tree.

TRENCHES
khafeerah-chphyrh-חפירה-303

MEANING When we have a symbolic dream, more often than not the symbol that presents itself to us will be of an item that has been existence in one form or another for a great many years. This is because it takes generations for an unconscious awareness of the symbolic value of an object to develop. The image of the trenches in the second World War is so hellish and horrific that it has acquired an enormous symbolic power within a mere generation. It is almost eerily predictive that the value of this dream is equivalent to the value of the Hebrew word meaning "did evil."

THE TREE OF LIFE When we consider the nature of a trench we should notice that it is a channel dug deep into the earth. Rather than climbing up toward the Divine, the image of a trench has us digging deeper into the world of the merely physical. This dream belongs in the Sefirah of Malkut, and it should be seen as something of a warning. The message within this dream is that the more you try to immerse yourself in the certainties of the material world, the further you move from the benign and encouraging influence of the Divine.

THE JOURNEY The image of the trenches makes it abundantly clear that there is nothing reassuring about a worldview that does not have room in it for a sense of humility before the Divine. You should take heart from the compression of this dream, which shows that you can climb your way out of your mental trench and begin the spiritual journey. The letter Shin tells us that you have untapped reserves of spiritual energy, while the letter Gimel advises you to try to find some creative way to awaken your faith in the spiritual dimension of the universe.

TRIAL
shfeetah-shphyth-שפיטה-404

MEANING To dream of being tried is not the most reassuring dream from which to wake. However, as is always the case, there is a valuable message and lesson for you hidden within the values and content of this dream. It is clear from the content of your dream that your higher self is trying to persuade you to spend more time focusing on the Great Work. You have placed yourself on trial in this dream as a way of pointing out to your waking self that you are not fully committing to the spiritual quest.

THE TREE OF LIFE The value of this dream is equivalent to the value of the Hebrew word meaning "to be awake." The relevance of this association is that right now, although you are engaging to some degree with spiritual issues, there is a sense in which it is still very low on your list of priorities. In order to be fully awake in a spiritual sense, you need to be more aware of the nature of the Divine, and this means that you need to spend more time rigorously studying. Consequently, we should place this dream on the path of Lamed. It is no coincidence that this path is also associated with the zodiac sign Libra, whose symbol is the Scales of Justice.

THE JOURNEY We can look at the value of this dream as a picture drawn with numbers. The central 0 represents the unity of the Divine, the concentration of the wisdom and understanding that you should be aiming for. It is flanked on both sides by the number 4. The number 4 represents the physical world, so we can see that it is your material concerns that are getting in the way of your making progress with the spiritual quest. The initial letter, Shin, in the spelling of this dream title tells us that you have the energy to commit to the Great Work, so all you need to do now is to find the willpower to maintain that commitment.

TRIANGLE

*meshoolash—mshvlsh—*משולש*‎-676*

MEANING In all mystical systems, geometrical figures are very important because they represent shorthand ways of displaying profound and complex ideas. The Kabbalah is no exception, and the image of a triangle is a very significant figure. The triangle points to the number 3, which is the number of creativity. This does not mean just the creativity of an artist or a musician but the ability of the Divine to genuinely create from nothing. When we look at the Tree of Life we see that the portion of the Tree that refers to the Divine level of existence consists of a triangle of three Sefirot known as the supernals. It is important that we do not confuse this with the idea of a trinity in the Christian faith. The Kabbalistic supernals are not Father, Son, and Spirit. Rather, they can be simplified as the pure existence of the Divine (Keter), the Father or the potential for creative force (Hokhmah), and the Mother or the potential for form (Binah).

THE TREE OF LIFE At an individual level, this dream indicates that you have made great strides in your spiritual understanding. The nature of the Divine is above the physical, and the fact that your

dream uses a geometrical figure instead of an object is one step closer to a nonphysical conception of the nature of the universe. The value of this dream reduces to 9. In the context of this dream, this number is important because it represents the number three multiplied by itself. This emphasizes some form of communication between the creative force of the Divine and the creative potential of your higher self. We should place this dream on the path of Gimel, as its value is 3 and it is the path that leads into the Sefirah of Keter.

THE JOURNEY It is very difficult to offer specific advice to someone who is at this level of spiritual understanding. The value of this dream is equal to the number that is produced when we multiply 26 by itself. The number 26 is the value of the main Hebrew title for the Divine. This suggests very strongly that you are approaching a point where you may be able to achieve a moment of communion with the creative force itself. The key thing to focus on is that you need to approach the Divine as the unique soul that you are, in your own individual manner. This is emphasized by the letter Ayin, which occupies the central position in the compression of this dream's value.

TROPHY

*mazkeret neetsakhon—mzkrth nytzchvn—*מזכרת ניצחון*‎-881*

MEANING Spiritual development is not a public affair; nobody but you will ever know what degree of insight you have into the spiritual reality behind the seemingly physical universe. It might seem strange, then, to be dreaming about a trophy, since its main purpose is to demonstrate to others your prowess and skill in a given field. However, in a dream the only audience consists of other aspects of your personality. The trophy in question is intended to demonstrate to your conscious self that you are indeed making progress in the Great Work.

THE TREE OF LIFE The value of this dream is equivalent to the value of the Hebrew word meaning "cranium." This serves to emphasize that the dream of a trophy relates to a need to demonstrate your achievement only to yourself and not to anyone else. The main goal of the first stage of the spiritual quest is to make contact with your higher self. This would certainly merit mentally giving yourself a trophy, so we should place this dream in the Sefirah of Tiferet. It is when you arrive in the Sefirah of Tiferet that you are able to begin a proper dialogue with your higher self.

THE JOURNEY When we reduce the value of this dream we find the number 8, which is the value of the Hebrew letter Cheth. This indicates that you are being protected by the Divine at this time, and you should make the most of this by trying to progress further up the Tree of Life. The letter Peh appears twice in the compression of this dream in both its standard and its final form. This tells you that the key task before you in the next months is to focus on opening up some line of communication with your higher self. The final letter, Aleph, is there as a promise of the ultimate unity of the Divine that you will be able to experience if you persist with your efforts.

LUGGAGE TRUNK

argaz meezvadah – argz mzvvdh – אַרְגַּז מִזְוָדָה *–279*

MEANING "Trunk" in the context of this dream refers to an old-fashioned container or chest rather than the storage compartment at the rear of a car. The idea of dreaming about a box seems fairly innocuous, but in fact there is a very definite warning within the values of this dream's title. An open trunk may suggest that you have a great store of spiritual insight on which you can draw if and when you need it. However, there is no suggestion of openness in this dream, so we can see that it indicates that you are locking yourself away in a metaphorical box.

THE TREE OF LIFE The value of this dream is equivalent to the value of the Hebrew word meaning "leprosy." The connection between the ancient scourge of leprosy and your dream is the idea of being cut off from society, the sense of self-exclusion because of an irreconcilable difference. In your case, this difference is not a disfiguring disease but is your commitment to spiritual development. The value of this dream can be reduced to 9, which is the value of the letter Teth. In its negative aspect the path of Teth is concerned with self-deception. Your dream belongs on the negative aspect of the path of Teth because you are laboring under the misconception that you should be shunning the company of others as a means of increasing your chances of spiritual success.

THE JOURNEY The universe was not created so that we should spend our time cloistered away, not wanting to engage in any form of interaction with others. It is important to remember that the spiritual quest is solitary only in the sense that no one but you can experience your particular relationship with the Divine. It is this individual approach to the Great Work that is implied by the letter Ayin in the center of the compression of this dream's value. In every other respect, though, you will greatly increase your chances of a deep understanding of the Divine if you participate with the world around you.

TRUST

meheymanoot – mhymnvth – מְהֵימָנוּת *–551*

MEANING Any good relationship counselor will tell you that the primary requirement in any relationship is that both people in that relationship trust each other. Without trust we have nothing. We can never be sure of a person's absolute and true nature without trust. In a spiritual context, the need for trust operates on two levels. First, we must have a trust in the Divine. If that is not there, then there is little point even in attempting to gain any kind of spiritual insight. Second, and equally important, is the need to trust our higher self.

THE TREE OF LIFE When we reduce the value of this dream we find the number 11. This number indicates that you are about to undergo a profoundly spiritual experience. In the context of this dream's title, that experience is likely to relate to your ability to trust your higher self. Our higher self tends to express itself through what we refer to as our intuition. Learning how to listen to that internal voice marks a very great step forward in your spiritual life. It will open a great many doors to deeper insights into the spiritual realm, so we should place this dream on the path of Daleth, which is concerned with the unlocking of avenues into the spiritual.

THE JOURNEY At the heart of the compression of this dream is the letter Nun. This is a reassurance that you are going to have this deep experience and that it will lead to a much stronger faith in the validity of your inner journey. The initial letter of the compression is the final form of Kaph, which tells us that you can help build up your trust of your intuition through practical activity. An ideal experiment would be to go for a walk and change direction only when advised to do so by your intuition; you should find that you have a very interesting and illuminating stroll.

TUNNEL

meenharah – mnhrh – מִנְהָרָה *–300*

MEANING Since tunnels are underground constructions, it would be understandable to see this dream as referring to an individual who is trying to dig himself deeper and deeper into the comfortable surroundings of a solely material world. However, the idea of a tunnel has a sense of direction about it that distinguishes a tunnel builder from someone who is merely trying to dig himself into a hole. Additionally, the values of this dream are far too positive to suggest that you are not engaging with the Great Work.

THE TREE OF LIFE The value of this dream is equivalent to the value of the Hebrew phrase meaning "the Spirit of the Divine." This spirit, or "Ruach," is the energizing spiritual force that moves within us and encourages us to take steps to try to climb our way back up the Tree of the Life toward Keter. The Ruach is associated with the path of Shin, and the value of this dream is the same as the value of the letter Shin. Consequently, we see that the path of Shin is the appropriate location for your dream.

THE JOURNEY When we begin our spiritual journey it is important that we start to look into our inner nature as well as looking up toward the Divine. The value of this dream is equivalent to the Hebrew word meaning "foundation," and it is this self-insight that represents the foundation of your future spiritual work. The image of tunneling refers to your attempts to get inside yourself to examine the unconscious drives, fears, and desires that motivate the way you behave and the way you perceive the world around you.

TWINE

khoot shazoor—chvt shzvr— **חוט שזור**‎ *-536*

MEANING For a very simple image, this dream has a very complex and profound significance. The idea of twine immediately suggests binding one or more items together. Additionally, twine is a type of rope or string that tends to be used primarily in gardening. This specific association adds in the idea that you are binding things together that they may grow more easily and more productively. In spiritual terms, this suggests that you are engaging in the business of linking different ideas or experiences in order to stimulate your spiritual growth. The image of twine also represents the process by which we can solidify our spiritual search through concrete actions.

THE TREE OF LIFE The value of this dream provides us with the two disparate ideas that you are linking or binding together. This dream's value is equivalent to the value of the Hebrew phrases refer-

ring to both "the sphere of the fixed stars" and "the world of the material." The implication here is that you are meditating on the relationship and interactions between the material world and the world of the spirit. The Sefirah of Yesod sits equidistant between the world of the material, or Malkut, and the point at which your nature becomes infused with the spiritual, or Tiferet, so we should place your dream on this Sefirah where the two aspects of the universe merge.

THE JOURNEY The sequence of numbers that makes up the value of this dream also describes a process of mediation between the human and the Divine or between the microcosmic consciousness and the macrocosmic consciousness. The number 5 represents the individual who has brought the four elements under the control of the fifth element of Spirit. The number 6 represents the Divine itself. Between the two lies the number 3, which stands for the creative energy that will allow you to make sense of the way in which these two states of consciousness relate to each other.

TWINS

teom—thavm— **תאום**‎ *-447*

MEANING It has always been assumed that there is a special bond between twins. Science seems to support this argument, but stops short of recognizing the level of mutual understanding that often exists and that cannot be explained without seriously altering some of our basic premises about the nature of communication and the capabilities of the human mind. In spiritual terms, this dream relates to the sense of a link that is emerging between you and your higher self.

THE TREE OF LIFE As soon as we start to think about the idea of twins in a more esoteric sense, we are likely to be reminded of the fact that the zodiac sign of Gemini is represented by the image of twins. In the Western Mystery Tradition, the sign of Gemini is attached to the path of Zayin. This path relates to analytical intelligence that allows us to separate out the useful from the misleading in terms of spiritual concepts. As your ability to communicate with your higher self increases, so too will your ability to analyze spiritual ideas, so this is an ideal path for your dream.

THE JOURNEY When we reduce the value of this dream we find the number 6. This is the value of the letter Vav and refers to the need for you to spend considerable time in quiet contemplation in order to fully develop your current understanding of the spiritual force behind the universe. The initial letter, Tav, in the compression of this dream indicates that you may still have some attachment to a material way of looking at the world. However, the letter Mem tells us that your sense of altruism and compassion will increasingly serve to emphasize the sense of the spiritual in the way that you approach the world and those around you.

UGLINESS

*keeoor-kya'avr-*כיעור-306

MEANING We live in a world that is almost obsessed by image, very often at the expense of any consideration of content. As long as something looks right, it must be good—this is the predominant attitude of our consumer culture. This has two worrisome consequences. The first is that we assume that a term about ugliness must refer to the physical appearance of an individual. Second, and more damning of our culture, is that we instantly regard the ugly as negative even though we are thinking only of it in terms of appearances.

THE TREE OF LIFE If a spiritual attitude can teach us anything, it should be that appearances are unimportant. It is interesting that the value of this dream is equivalent to the value of the Hebrew word meaning "honey." Nobody would dispute the sweetness of honey, but its appearance in its natural state is far from appealing, surrounded as it is by buzzing insects that can inflict a very nasty sting. The value of this dream reduces to 9, which is the value of the letter Teth. The path of Teth refers to strength of will and strength of character. Its negative aspect is concerned with the potential for self-deceit. The message of this dream is that you should not be deceived by mere appearance, so we should locate your dream on the path of Teth.

THE JOURNEY The compression of this dream consists of the letters Shin and Vav. When combined they produce the advice that you should meditate on the subject of this dream and allow the spirit of the Divine to inform you of the implications that it holds for your inner development. The letter Kaph at the beginning of the spelling of this dream title is also important. Kaph is concerned with practical applications, and its presence here is a reminder that in your day-to-day life as well as in your spiritual work you should look inside to see the sweetness and not be turned away by the metaphorical bees.

UMBRELLA

*meetreeyah-mtryyh-*מטרייה-274

MEANING In the real world, an umbrella is always a useful thing to have around. In spiritual terms, however, the image of an umbrella is not so positive. An umbrella's purpose is to protect us from getting wet, not because we will be harmed by rain but simply because it is uncomfortable. When we also remember that the element of Water is associated with our emotions, we can see that this dream relates to a desire to avoid the discomfort of tackling our emotions.

THE TREE OF LIFE Before we can begin to make any progress with the Great Work, we must first at least begin to examine our own nature. It is only by understanding ourselves that we can have any hope of understanding the Divine. The value of this dream reduces to 4, and this is the number of the physical world. All the associations point to this dream's being based in the Sefirah of Malkut. This is where you will stay until you have the confidence to put down your metaphorical umbrella and examine your emotions.

THE JOURNEY You should not be discouraged by this dream. The first step in any journey is always the biggest and the hardest to take. Given the nature of the spiritual journey, it is very common for people to take a while before making that great leap of faith. The value of this dream is equivalent to the value of the Hebrew word meaning "paths." The presence of this word is a reminder that there are many ways that you can follow that will lead you out of Malkut. The central letter, Ayin, in the compression of this dream makes it clear that whatever route you decide to follow should be one that you feel inwardly comfortable with as an individual.

UNATTACHED (SINGLE)

*lo kashoor-la qshvr-*לא קשור-637

MEANING Without the benefit of a Kabbalistic analysis, it would not be clear whether this dream indicates that you are unattached and quite happy with the situation since it leaves you more time to pursue the Great Work, or whether it suggests that you are alone and feeling lonely. In fact, this dream uses the imagery of emotional attachment as a symbol of your heightened spiritual understanding, as you have seen beyond the illusory nature of any attachments.

THE TREE OF LIFE It was the Buddha who pointed out that desire is the cause of all sorrow. The expression of desire is the forming of attachments, and these can be to people or places or even things. An attachment is not the same as a genuine love, since it carries with it ideas about control and ownership. It is when we are able to lose our attachments and seek to own nothing that we can catch a glimpse of the Divine. It is for the this reason that we position your dream on the path of Heh, as this path represents, among other things, a window onto the Divine.

THE JOURNEY It is worth noting that the Hebrew word for "nothing" is spelled LA, as found in the spelling of this dream. One of the common titles for the Divine in Hebrew is spelled AL, which is of course the reverse of the word for "nothing." This demonstrates the relationship between a lack of attachments and a closeness to the creative source itself. The central letter in the compression of this dream is Lamed, and this indicates that it takes a great deal of study to be able to achieve this level of enlightenment. Similarly, the reduction of this dream's value produces the number 7, which is the value of the letter Zayin. This letter reminds you of the analytical approach that will help you to maintain the high level of insight that this dream depicts.

UNDERWATER

tat maymee–thth mymy– תת מימי–900

MEANING From a psychological perspective, this dream would likely be interpreted as representing a desire to return to the womb. Consequently, the dreamer might be viewed as someone who is trying to avoid facing up to the reality of the adult world. However, the Kabbalistic interpretation of this dream puts a significantly more positive interpretation on the imagery. The element of Water represents the emotions, so this dream indicates that you have been able to fully immerse yourself in an exploration of your emotional makeup.

THE TREE OF LIFE The spelling of this dream title consists entirely of repeated letters, which is symbolic of the fact that you must examine the same feelings from a number of different angles in order to fully understand their significance. The letter Mem represents the element of Water, which permeates the entire dream, while the letter Yod indicates that your attempts to make sense of your inner nature are being carried out with the support of the Divine spark that burns within you. The letter Tav points to the fact that you will experience a certain amount of regret as you go about this task. The overall result will be to cause a deepening in the strength of your faith in the spiritual, so we should place this dream on the path of Nun.

THE JOURNEY You are now going through one of the most difficult phases in your spiritual development. Learning to face up to our inner nature is difficult enough when we have the support of a trained counselor or therapist to support us in our discoveries. The compression of this dream's value produces only one letter. This is the letter Tzaddi in its final form. Its presence in your dream serves to emphasize the need for complete commitment to the spiritual quest if you are to succeed in your current challenge.

UNDRESSING

leheetpashet–lhthphsht– להתפשט–824

MEANING There are two common associations that we would link with the idea of undressing. The first is that of preparing for bed, and the second is as a precursor to a medical examination. However, both of these associations are incorrect insofar as the spiritual interpretation of this dream is concerned. When we are undressed, we lose the trappings of any particular occupation or status that we have in life and become simply ourselves. This is the spiritual focus of your dream.

THE TREE OF LIFE As ever, we need to be careful to concentrate on the exact nature of the title of this dream. Dreaming about undressing should not be confused with actually being naked. This dream refers to the process that leads to our being able to face the Divine as we actually are, rather than already being in that position. The reduction value of this dream produces the number 5. This number relates to an individual who has managed to bring all the elements in his personality under the control of the fifth element of Spirit. This is a goal that you are working toward, so we should place your dream on the path of Samech since it leads into the Sefirah of Tiferet.

THE JOURNEY The image of undressing is about preparing yourself for an encounter with your higher self, an encounter for which you must be entirely yourself, without any external trappings. The compression of this dream provides some useful advice about how to approach this task. The initial letter, Peh, in its final form, makes it clear that above all you need to create a dialogue with your higher self. You will be able to do this more easily the more practically (Kaph) you bring your spiritual values into play in your day-to-day life. This is the best way for you to open the door (Daleth) that leads you to contact with your higher self.

UNIFORM

akheed-achyd-אחיד-23

MEANING We tend to think of uniforms as representations of conformity at best and as symbols of violence and oppression at worst. However, this says a lot more about the state of the world today than it does about the symbolic import of a uniform when it appears in your dream. The spelling of the dream title makes the spiritual implication of a uniform very clear. It represents unity (Aleph) and protection (Cheth) and denotes those who have awakened the Divine spark within themselves (Yod) and thereby opened the door (Daleth) to spiritual understanding.

THE TREE OF LIFE The value of this dream is equivalent to the value of the Hebrew word meaning "joy." We are looking for a position on the Tree of Life that indicates both joy and a much increased spiritual understanding. The ideal candidate is the Sefirah of Tiferet, as it is here that you have the opportunity to make some form of direct contact with your higher self. When we reduce the value of this dream we find the number 5. This number represents the individual who has successfully mastered the four elements within his personality through the control of his higher self, so this also supports the location of your dream in Tiferet.

THE JOURNEY It is very tempting once we arrive in Tiferet to see this as the end of our spiritual quest. However, there is never an end to the Great Work, and once you have contacted your higher self you should attempt to achieve a moment of communion with the Divine itself. The compression of this dream produces the letters Kaph and Gimel. These indicate that you need to be both down-to-earth and creative in your attempts to further develop your spiritual awareness.

UNKNOWN

lo yadooa-la ydva'a-לא ידוע-121

MEANING This dream's title has an immediate connection to the spiritual quest. Once we set foot on the path that ultimately leads back to Keter, we are permanently in a position of leaping into the

unknown. This is because as soon as we achieve one level of understanding, we have to push ourselves on to try to gain new insights into the nature of the Divine. The value of this dream is equivalent to the value produced when we multiply 11 by itself. Since the number 11 is associated with all things mystical, this implies that you are completely engrossed in the realm of the spiritual at this time.

THE TREE OF LIFE There is a certain ambivalence about this dream. On one hand, the value of this dream begins and ends with the number 1, which represents the unity and transcendence of the Divine. On the other, the value of this dream reduces to 4, which implies that you are still very much tied to the world of the physical. The value of this dream is equivalent to the value of the Hebrew word meaning "vain idols." This suggests that you are spending a lot of time examining the unknown and the anomalous, but that at this stage your interest is more in their mystery than in their value as a means to increase the depth of your understanding. Consequently, we should place your dream in the Sefirah of Yesod, as this is a stage where people are often attracted by the glamour rather than the value of the spiritual.

THE JOURNEY While the term *vain idols* may be harsh, it is important that you begin to engage with the spiritual in a completely open way with a view to developing a relationship with the Divine. The initial Qoph in the compression of this dream tells us that you are holding back due to a fear of failure. The subsequent Kaph advises you to take some practical steps to consolidate your commitment to the Divine (Aleph). An excellent idea would be to take meditation classes.

URINATING

lehashteen-lhshthyn-להשתין-795

MEANING If someone were to conduct a poll asking for suggestions for "the dream most likely to be used in a spiritually based book of dream analyses," it is highly unlikely that anyone would put forward a dream of urinating as a contender! However, urinating is no more or less human than eating or talking and is just as feasible as a subject for spiritual interpretation. The purpose of urination is quite straightforward: It removes liquid waste and in particular toxins from our bodies. In a spiritual context, we could see this dream as symbolizing the removal from your psyche of those attitudes and values that would be poisonous to any attempts at further spiritual development.

THE TREE OF LIFE When we look at the spelling of this dream title, the letter Nun stands out as it appears in its final form. The path of Nun is concerned with the business of deepening and strengthening our faith in the Divine. Very often this process has sorrowful and melancholic aspects since it inevitably requires you to deal with painful memories and feelings from your past. Once these have been dealt with, they can be removed, so the dream of urination sits very comfortably on the path of Nun.

THE JOURNEY When we reduce the value of this dream we find the number 3, which is associated with creativity in all its forms. Although it may seem bizarre to talk of creative urination, it is perfectly sensible to think of creative ways of dealing with difficult memories and feelings from your past. The central letter in the compression of this dream is Tzaddi, and this makes it clear that the key to success at this time is simply to maintain your commitment to the spiritual quest.

VACCINATE

leharkeev-lhrkyb- להרכיב-267

MEANING Mass inoculation is a relatively recent phenomenon, but it has already saved millions of lives. In order to understand the spiritual import of this dream, it is crucial that we have at least a basic understanding of how vaccination works. Essentially, the patient is given a medication that stimulates his body to produce just the right antigens to destroy the particular disease. In spiritual terms, we see this dream as symbolic of the development of your ability to protect yourself either from wrong behavior or from misleading spiritual frameworks.

THE TREE OF LIFE The value of this dream is equivalent to the value of the Hebrew word meaning "forbidden." We should not take this literally but see it as a reference to information or a level of understanding that is secret and therefore forbidden to those who have not made the spiritual effort to access it. When we reduce the value of this dream we find the number 6. This is the value of the letter Vav. The path of Vav is linked with the element of Air and refers to contemplation and meditation. These are the primary methods by which you will come to a deep understanding of the Divine, so it is here that we should locate your dream.

THE JOURNEY It is interesting that despite the fact that this dream refers to a very modern practice, the compression of the word's value not only describes the best way for you to approach your spiritual development but provides a good summary of the nature of vaccination. The letter Resh indicates the rational and optimistic use of your mental faculties as the means by which you will support (Samech) your attempts to separate (Zayin) those spiritual ideas that are useful from those that will ultimately harm your attempts to move up the Tree of Life.

VACUUM

reek-ryq- ריק-310

MEANING Scientifically, a pure vacuum is impossible to maintain for more than the briefest of moments, since physics does not allow for the existence of a complete absence of everything. In Kabbalistic theory, the Divine created a kind of spiritual vacuum moments before the emanation of the universe. The process known as Tzim Tzum involved the Divine's creating a momentary space within the Divine that paradoxically was not part of the Divine. In terms of your dream, the image of a vacuum also relates to an absence of the Divine in your life.

THE TREE OF LIFE The value of this dream is equivalent to the value of the Hebrew word meaning "to bind," and in the context of this dream it refers to the fact that you are currently bound to a purely physical conception of the world. This positions your dream firmly in the Sefirah of Malkut. However, you should take heart from the fact that your unconscious is already recognizing the fact that without the Divine you are living your life in a spiritual vacuum. This realization can be likened to a miniature human version of the process of Tzim Tzum. Once you have the awareness that there is an absence of the Divine, that absence begins to be filled with the energy of the Divine as you begin to reach up toward your higher self.

THE JOURNEY Even though you have yet to make the leap of faith that will lift you out of Malkut, it is already clear that this leap is about to happen. The value of this dream is equivalent to the value of the Hebrew word meaning "essence" or "being." This dream tells us that you are now realizing that your essence is dependent on a relationship with the Divine in order to be fully expressed. The final Yod in the compression of this dream's value also indicates that it will not be long before you have fully awakened the spark of the Divine within yourself.

VAGRANT

navad-nvvd- נווד-66

MEANING We live in a world where people are judged primarily on their wealth and position in society rather than on their nature as people. This is not because we are worse people now; it has almost always been the case that what we have speaks far louder than what we are. This largely comes down to our tendency to value what we can measure rather than to wonder about how we might measure those things that are truly valuable. Given the common attitudes about position and place, this dream would be seen as a veritable nightmare by a great many people. The Kabbalah tradition refers to the "Lamed Vav" or the "Thirty-six." These are saints who travel the globe, often disguised as vagrants, whose role is to sustain the spiritual well-being of the world.

THE TREE OF LIFE In a spiritual context, this dream is extremely positive, and it would be hard to find a dream that was more encouraging about your spiritual development. First of all, to dream of being a vagrant indicates a healthy lack of concern with the outward trappings of the material world. Additionally, the value of this dream is equivalent to the number that would be produced if we were to add together all the numbers between 1 and 11. The number 11 indicates that you are about to undergo a profound spiritual experience. The value of this dream consists of the number 6 repeated, and the number 6 is a symbolic representation of the Divine or macrocosm. Consequently, we should place your dream on the path of Aleph and infer that the impending profound experience is a moment of communion with the Divine itself.

THE JOURNEY You need very little in the way of advice since you have already climbed your way to the very pinnacle of the Tree of Life. When we reduce the value of this dream we find the number 12. This number is associated with themes of compassion and altruism, and this indicates that in order to progress to that moment of connection with the Divine force, you should ensure that you are engaging in some form of altruistic and compassionate activity in your day-to-day life.

VALLEY

emek-a'amq- עמק-210

MEANING In the natural world, valleys can be beautiful places and offer some of the most wonder-ful views that can be found anywhere. It might therefore seem reasonable to assume that this dream is wholly positive. However, the image of a valley has a very specific significance in spiritual terms. It represents the period of intense sorrow and possible despair that affects everyone at some point in their quest for truth. Most people are familiar with this image from the biblical line, "Yea, though I walk through the valley of the shadow of death, I will fear no evil. . . ."

THE TREE OF LIFE This dream may not be about the delightful scenery of a valley landscape but it is not negative in its overall perspective. You may be going through a very difficult time right now but you should not despair. The value of this dream is equivalent to the number that we find if we add together all the numbers between 1 and 20. The letter Kaph has a value of 20, and the path of Kaph, is concerned with finding practical applications for your spiritual development. We should locate your dream on the path of Kaph and you should see this as a sign that you will shortly be climbing out of your current feeling of despondency.

THE JOURNEY The value of this dream is equivalent to the value of the Hebrew word meaning "cycle." This association emphasizes the fact that you are simply passing through a common phase or cycle in your spiritual journey. The letter Resh, which commences the compression of this dream, reminds you to try to look at your situation in a rational and an optimistic way, while the letter Yod suggests that you will shortly be awakening the Divine spark within yourself. This experience alone should prove sufficiently reassuring to allow you to move on in your spiritual quest.

VAMPIRE

arpad-a'arphd- ערפד-354

MEANING Almost every culture has a vampire myth of some sort. In Europe, of course, there are the legends of Dracula and the Countess Bathory, while the Japanese have a well-established mythos of blood-drinking creatures. Other societies may not label their particular stories as vampire myths, but the essential characteristics are there. In Jewish folklore, for instance, it is Adam's mythical and demonic first wife, Lilith, who is supposed to suck the blood of newborn babies. What all these ideas have in common is the notion of draining the life force of another in order to grow stronger oneself. Traditional Kabbalah would suggest that you try to seek out the person in your life who is responsible for your feeling that you are being attacked in this way and that you then attempt to eliminate that person's influence.

THE TREE OF LIFE In terms of your personal spiritual development, this dream refers to a concern that you are increasing your understanding of the Divine but not giving anything back to your community. The sense of behaving in a parasitic manner is increased by the fact that much of your progress has been dependent on learning from those who have gone before you. The value of this dream is equivalent to value of the Hebrew word meaning to "grow fat." You wish to ensure that as your understanding increases so too does your level of altruism, so this dream belongs firmly on the path of Mem since it is concerned with all forms of compassionate and altruistic behavior.

THE JOURNEY While you are quite right to try to help those around you, the idea that you are growing fat on the efforts of others is accurate only in your own sense of yourself and is not something that you should worry about. The compression of this dream's value tells us that you have a lot of energy to give (Shin) to charitable causes and also points out that in doing so you will deepen your faith (Nun) while bringing happiness to the lives of others.

VASE
agartel–agrtl–אגרטל–243

MEANING This is another dream where it is very important that we pay attention not just to the general sense created by the image but to the exact nature of what is being described. A vase does suggest a receptacle in which to place flowers but it refers to an item that was made specifically for this purpose and is therefore an attractive item in its own right. In spiritual terms, we see the vase as yourself and the implied flowers as spiritual insight.

THE TREE OF LIFE At an individual level, this dream is about your attempts to make yourself a fitting vessel into which wisdom can be placed. Ideally, you should be in a position where you will be able to add something of your own to the wisdom that you receive, in the same way as a good vase will add something to the flowers that it holds. In terms of the Great Work, you will be able to add something of yourself to the insights that you gain by communicating both with your inner self and with your

higher self. For this reason, we should place your dream on the path of Peh.

THE JOURNEY Your task over the next few months is essentially to make yourself the best vase you can possibly be. You should always remember, to continue the metaphor, that the best bouquets need the most attractive vases. The value of this dream is equivalent to the value of the Hebrew word meaning "destroy." The presence of this associated word is to remind you that the process you are now going through is not just about the addition of new traits and values. In order to succeed, it will also be necessary for you to dispose of some traits and values that do not help in a spiritually based approach to the world.

VEHICLE
rekhev–rkb–רכב–222

MEANING Many spiritual systems talk about the physical body as a vehicle for the spirit while it is experiencing a life in the material world. The first thing that we notice about this dream is the fact that its value consists entirely of the number 2. In the context of this dream we can see the number 2 as representing the duality that permeates our physical life. On one hand, we have our "normal" day-to-day existence with our friends and colleagues. On the other hand, we have that aspect of ourselves that is seeking something more spiritual and eternal in nature.

THE TREE OF LIFE The value of this dream is equivalent to the value of the Hebrew phrase meaning "I will chase." This emphasizes the aspect of this dream's title that refers to traveling. In terms of the Great Work, what are you chasing is a moment of communion with the Divine itself. The fact that you are aware of the nature of the duality of existence implies that you have already climbed a considerable way up the Tree of Life. The letter Gimel literally means "camel," which is both an ancient form of transportation and a symbol of the journey up to Keter, so we should place your dream on the path of Gimel.

THE JOURNEY When we reduce the value of this dream we find the number 6, and in terms of this dream's content it should be seen as a symbol of the Divine. Its presence here is to act as a reminder that you are very close to achieving some form of direct insight into the nature of the creative force. The compression of this dream urges you to retain an optimistic frame of mind (Resh). It also makes it clear that if you find a practical means (Kaph) of demonstrating your spiritual awareness, you will have the best possible chance of entering the home (Beth) of the Divine.

VEIL

*tseeef-tza'ayph-*צעיף-250

MEANING It is tempting to interpret this dream purely in terms of a veil as an item of clothing worn by many women in Middle and Near Eastern cultures. However, the values within the dream push the analysis in a different direction. The value of this dream is equivalent to the value of the Hebrew word meaning "sleeping," so the suggestion is that the veil is symbolic of a separation from the waking world. In the Kabbalah, the idea of a veil represents the separation of the actual from the spiritual reality that lies beyond the world of the physical.

THE TREE OF LIFE This dream represents an attempt by your higher self to encourage you to draw aside the veil that separates you from the spiritual reality that lies beyond the physical universe. The value of this dream is equivalent to the value of the Hebrew word meaning "midday," and this implies that it is certainly time that you woke up! When we reduce the value of this dream we find the number 7. This is the value of the letter Zayin. The path of Zayin refers to the sword of analysis with which we can cut away the misleading and the illusory, so it is an ideal path on which to locate your dream.

THE JOURNEY The final letter in the spelling of this dream title is Peh in its final form. The letter Peh is concerned with communication in all its forms. The message here is that in order for you to see beyond the veil of the material, you need to build up a dialogue with your higher self. The compression of this dream indicates that you should be optimistic about the chances of this succeeding (Resh) and that your faith in the Divine will be much deeper (Nun) as a result. As you proceed along your spiritual path with this deepened faith, you will gradually be able to remove the veil that hides the true nature of the Divine.

VEIN

*vreed-vryd-*וריד-220

MEANING You might expect that a dream about a vein refers to a concern about the state of your physical health. From a spiritual point of view, this dream does indicate a concern, but not with your physical health. Within our bodies, the arteries carry oxygen around the body while the veins carry the blood that is no longer filled with life-giving oxygen. In a spiritual context, the oxygen represents the awareness of the Divine, so a dream of a vein indicates an absence of the life-giving force of the creative source in your life.

THE TREE OF LIFE It is a very encouraging sign that you are having this dream, as it tells us that at least at an unconscious level you are aware of an absence in your life. When we reduce the value of this dream we find the number 4. This number is associated with the world of the purely physical and so reinforces the idea that this dream belongs in the Sefirah of Malkut.

THE JOURNEY The value of this dream is equivalent to the value of the Hebrew word meaning "giants." The key feature about giants is that their material size is exaggerated while their souls and minds are of normal stature. This implies that you are making far too much of your material concerns. The prospects for your inner development look positive, though, as the compression of this dream's value begins with the letter Resh, encouraging you to have an optimistic outlook. Additionally, you should try to find some practical way (Kaph) of beginning to introduce a sense of the spiritual into your life.

VERTIGO

*sekharkhoret-schrchvrth-*סחרחורת-882

MEANING An initial response to this dream might be to assume that it relates to an individual who has made great progress in his spiritual work and has now reached a level that he finds disconcerting due to its distance from his previous regular existence. However, this dream uses the image of vertigo, and this is a fear of heights. There is no requirement to actually climb to any great height in order to have vertigo. In fact, many sufferers never put themselves in a position where they would have to suffer the ill effects of their condition.

THE TREE OF LIFE The title of this dream tells us that you have not been able to achieve any great spiritual insight due to your fear of the effects of committing fully to the Great Work. The letter Cheth appears twice in the spelling of this dream title, and this refers to your defensive outlook on the nature of the spiritual quest. However, the letter Resh also appears twice in the spelling of this dream title. The path of Cheth is concerned with a rational and optimistic approach to considerations of a spiritual nature. This is exactly the approach that you need to adopt, so we should locate your dream on the path of Resh.

THE JOURNEY Even though you have grave concerns about your suitability for a voyage of inner exploration, the overall message of this dream is a positive one. The letter Peh appears in both its standard and its final forms in the compression of this dream. This constitutes very definite advice that you need to engage in some communication about your spiritual development. This should certainly involve attempting to initiate a dialogue with your higher self. In addition to this, you should consider joining a meditation or yoga class so that you can share your worries and anxieties with like-minded people.

VEXATION
*rogez-rvgz-*רוגז*-*216

MEANING To be vexed is not exactly the same as to be angry. Vexation is a particular subset or type of anger. In order for you to be vexed, you must be not only annoyed but frustrated in some way. If someone pushed you on the street, you would be angry. If he pushed in front of you in a shopping line, you would be vexed since your attempt to get to the checkout had been temporarily frustrated. In spiritual terms, the dream of vexation indicates that you are attempting to make progress with the Great Work but are feeling blocked in some way.

THE TREE OF LIFE It is important that we remember that frustration only has to be felt, it does not have to be actual. When we reduce the value of your dream we find the number 9. This is the value of the letter Teth, and in its negative aspect the path of Teth indicates a capacity for self-deceit. It may be that you are believing yourself to be frustrated in your efforts rather than examining your inner nature to look for evidence of why you may not be progressing. Consequently, we should place this dream on the path of Teth. The path of Teth is associated with the zodiac sign Leo in the Western Mystery Tradition, and this placement is supported by the fact that the value of this dream is equivalent to the value of the Hebrew word meaning "lion."

THE JOURNEY We can discover the reason for your deciding that you are being blocked by examining the value of this dream. The value of the Hebrew word meaning "fear" is the same as the value of your dream. This tells us that it is your fear of failure that has persuaded your unconscious to create a sense of being frustrated. However, the central letter in the compression of this dream is Yod, and this indicates that you will soon be awakening the spark of the Divine within you. This release of spiritual awareness should help you to overcome your fear and begin to progress again.

VICE
*preetsoot-prytzvth-*פריצות*-*786

MEANING Dreaming of vice is not the same as having a sexual dream. If you have a dream that is sexual, or for that matter is centered on some other vice such as drinking or gambling, then it may simply be that you enjoy that particular activity and think about it sufficiently to also dream about it. To dream of vice implies that within the dream itself you regarded the activity as wrong and morally incorrect. This means that you are uncomfortable or unhappy with certain aspects of your nature and regard them as possible obstacles to your spiritual progress.

THE TREE OF LIFE It is important to remember that spiritual progress does not equate with ideal behavior. Your soul may be eternal but your personality is as much a temporary and organic element of existence as the grass at your feet. This means that although part of the Great Work is the translation of spiritual ideas into action, you may always have some substantial flaws in your behavior. At the moment, you are in danger of judging yourself far too harshly. The reduction of this dream's value produces the number 21. This corresponds to the twenty-first letter of the Hebrew alphabet, which is Shin. In its negative aspect the path of Shin refers in part to an excessive tendency to be judgmental, so we should position your dream on the path of Shin.

THE JOURNEY The initial letter in the spelling of this dream title is Peh. This letter is there to advise you to try to talk about your perceived flaws with other people who are also exploring their inner selves. You will find that you are not alone in being less than perfect. The compression of this dream also has the letter Peh at its center. The initial letter, Nun, makes it clear that if you find a balanced way of judging yourself, you will be more likely to relate more deeply to the Divine. The final letter, Vav, is a suggestion that quiet contemplation might be a much better option than self-condemnation.

VICTIM

*korban-qvrbn-*קורבן-358

MEANING We have, over the last decade or so, developed something of a victim culture. The idea of personal responsibility is increasingly giving way, and almost anything except the individual concerned can be held responsible. At the same time, we seem to regard more and more trivial events and situations as issues of terrible importance at the hands of which we are helpless victims. A few days' watching daytime chat shows more than demonstrates our gradual abandonment of responsibility. Almost all forms of spirituality and certainly the Kabbalah set great store by the fact that we must take responsibility for our actions and our lives in general. Consequently, we should not leap to assume that dreaming that you are a victim means that this is a correct interpretation of your position.

THE TREE OF LIFE The value of this dream is equivalent to the value of the Hebrew word *Nechesh*, which refers to the serpent in the garden of Eden. This suggests that your dream is about the capacity to transgress. Furthermore, the association with the original act of disobedience suggests that you are perceiving yourself as a victim because it is ingrained within human nature to go against the will of the Divine. However, the value of this dream is also equivalent to the value of the Hebrew word meaning "shame," and this suggests that you should recognize your errors as the result of your own free choice. There is a conflict in your mind between the Kabbalistic perspective and the view that you hold as a result of living in this particular historical context. This suggests that you are still very new to the Great Work, so we should place your dream on the path of Tav.

THE JOURNEY The spiritual path is not an easy one. It is certainly far more demanding in moral terms than the predominant culture in which we now live, and this takes a little time to adjust to. The compression of this dream tells us that you have the raw spiritual energy (Shin) to persist in your efforts. When you do realize that you are not a passive victim of the will of the Divine but a free individual making unique moral choices, you will find that your strength of faith in the validity of the spiritual quest will have deepened (Nun) considerably.

VICTORY

*neetsakh-ntzch-*נצח-148

MEANING If we did not look at this dream from a Kabbalistic perspective, we would be likely to assume that the dreamer was someone who had great confidence and quite possibly something of a competitive streak. However, from a spiritual perspective this dream is not about victory over anybody else; it refers to a developing mastery over your own nature. Indeed, the value of this dream is also equivalent to the value of the Hebrew word meaning to "withdraw." This makes it quite clear that you are not in any way a person who is looking for conflict or competition with others. This dream should be seen in a very positive light, as it represents the self-confidence and optimism that will carry you forward in your spiritual quest.

THE TREE OF LIFE The title of this dream is the same as the title of seventh Sefirah in the Tree of Life. While its name, Victory, makes perfect sense when one looks at the complex Kabbalistic theory underpinning the emanation of the universe, it can be slightly confusing to someone who has no Kabbalistic knowledge. In terms of your personal spiritual development, you should look at the Sefirah of Netzach, where this dream is placed, as the stage in your journey where you learn to reconcile your passions and your emotions with a spiritually based way of looking at the world.

THE JOURNEY When we reduce the value of this dream we find the number 13. This number indicates that great change is about to occur in your life, and this will be the result of the work that you do in Netzach. The initial letter, Qoph, in the compression of this dream tells us that you have some concerns about your future development. However, you should not be too anxious, as the letter Mem and the letter Cheth both indicate that the maternal and protective aspect of the Divine is with you at this time. Moreover, the title of this dream itself tells us that you should be feeling relatively confident about achieving positive results in your spiritual quest.

VINE

*gefen-gphn-*גפן-133

MEANING Thanks to the efforts of a range of temperance organizations, almost exclusively Christian in origin, we have developed a sense that somehow alcoholic drink is frowned upon by the Divine.

This is of course a possibility, but there is nothing in the Torah, or ironically enough in the New Testament, that would suggest this to be the case. Wine plays a very important part in Jewish culture and in expressions of appreciation to the Creator. The vine was therefore a very important part of the landscape, and it has often been used to symbolize the living nature of the universe, with our individual lives likened to the individual grapes.

THE TREE OF LIFE When we reduce the value of this dream we find the number 7. This is the value of the Hebrew word *Zayin*. The letter Zayin means "sword," and the path of Zayin is concerned with the process by which we cut away those ideas and thoughts that are not helpful to our future inner development. There is a relationship here to the symbolism of the vine. We make good wine by carefully removing any grapes that are not well ripened or are overly ripe. Similarly, to ferment a high level of wisdom within ourselves, we should focus only on those ideas that are properly formed and helpful.

THE JOURNEY The compression of this dream begins with the letter Qoph. This indicates a degree of anxiety on your part, which is understandable since nobody wants to discard a piece of information that ultimately proves to be extremely helpful. The subsequent letter, Lamed, makes it clear that the solution to your worries is to diligently apply yourself to your spiritual studies, while the final letter, Gimel, indicates that you also need to leave room for your creativity and unique approach to the Great Work.

VIOLENCE

*aleemoot-alymvth-*אלימות-487

MEANING In this dream, there is no sense of any purpose or justification for physical conflict. If you were dreaming of a war or a battle, it might be possible to see a reason behind the violence. However, to simply dream of violence in isolation is to symbolically represent the often directionless chaos that underlies our lives when we are not operating within a spiritual framework. Violence does not, of course, have to mean physically hitting an individual—it can refer to any form of significantly damaging behavior.

THE TREE OF LIFE The value of this dream is a prime number (a number that can be divided only by itself and by one). Such numbers are relatively rare and consequently should be seen as symbolic of uniqueness. The presence of a prime number in

this dream is to try to tell you that you need to find your own individuality in order to lift yourself out of your current state of inner turmoil. When we reduce the value of this dream we find the number 10. This is the number of the Sefirah of Malkut, and it is here that we should locate your dream.

THE JOURNEY The first two letters in the spelling of this dream title make up the spelling of one of the many Kabbalistic titles for the Divine. They are there to remind you of the possibility of finding a spiritual dimension to your life. Similarly, the initial letter, Tav, in the compression of the value of this dream represents the first path that is available to you as a route out of Malkut. The subsequent letter, Peh, suggests that you will stand the best chance of success if you try to discuss your interest in the Great Work with someone who has already begun to explore the realm of the spiritual.

VIOLIN

*keenor-kynvr-*כינור-286

MEANING Music has always been associated with the spiritual quest. From the earliest civilizations who used simple drumming techniques to raise their consciousness to the complex beauty of a piece such as Mozart's "Magic Flute," music has always had an effect not just on the emotions but on the soul of the listener. The violin is associated primarily with the melancholic and the highly melodic. It is a wonderfully expressive instrument and in spiritual terms it suggests an individual who is very capable when it comes to expressing his feelings. Music in general is regarded as very spiritual in nature within Kabbalistic tradition, and this dream represents that expressive and aesthetic aspect of your relationship to the Divine.

THE TREE OF LIFE The value of this dream is equivalent to the value of the Hebrew word meaning "high" or "lofty." This emphasizes the fact that your ability in terms of emotional expression will translate into an ability to progress well with your spiritual development. Additionally, your emotional sensitivity means that you can empathize with others who have difficulties. The initial letter, Kaph, in the spelling of this dream title suggests that you should make practical use of this ability. Consequently, we should place your dream on the path of Mem, as it refers to the compassionate and altruistic approach that you are being encouraged to adopt.

THE JOURNEY The compression of this dream's value indicates that you are likely to continue to make good progress up the Tree of Life. The initial Resh tells us that you have an optimistic but rational approach to the Divine. The subsequent letter, Peh, lets us know that you are already beginning to try to establish some form of dialogue with your higher self. The final letter, Vav, is there both to remind you of the need to reflect on your progress so far and as a promise of the communion with the Divine that ultimately awaits you.

VIRGIN

betoolah-bthvlh-בתולה-443

MEANING It is important to remember that there is no particular significance about the idea of a virgin within the Kabbalah. The fixation on virginity is an attitude specific to Christianity. The issue of virginity within Jewish culture was, as in most other early cultures, purely an issue in terms of marriage and was not a central theme in their spiritual framework. When we look at the idea of a virgin in a spiritual context, the most important association to focus on is the fact that a virgin has no practical experience. This suggests that your dream relates to the sense of being unschooled in the whole process of the Great Work. There is also a sense of purity about the image in this dream, which suggests that you have an admirable attitude toward the Great Work.

THE TREE OF LIFE The value of this dream reduces to 11, which suggests that you are on the brink of having a deeply significant spiritual experience. Consequently, although you are clearly new to the spiritual quest, it is likely that have you already made that initial commitment to pursue the possibility of spiritual truth. There is a sense of anxiety in the content of this dream. Of the lower paths on the Tree, the only one that fits the idea of anxiety and worry is the path of Qoph, and it is here that we should position your dream.

THE JOURNEY When we look at the compression of this dream we see that the initial letter, Tav, links you back to the Sefirah of Malkut, thus reiterating the idea that you are still very cautious about leaving behind the certainties of the material world. However, the subsequent letters, Mem and Gimel give you some specific advice as to how to let go of that sense of doubt. You should not focus so much on the overtly spiritual at this time. Rather, you should find a creative (Gimel) way in which you can offer some charitable help (Mem) to people who have significant needs that are not being addressed.

VISION

reeeyah-rayyh-ראייה-226

MEANING To be dreaming of a vision certainly indicates that you are very committed to the spiritual quest. It also tells us that you have aspirations to achieve a greatly heightened sense of spiritual awareness. If we look at the spelling of this dream title, we see that the central letters are Aleph and Yod repeated. This suggests that you have every reason to be aiming at such lofty achievements. The letter Aleph represents the transcendent unity of the Divine, while the letter Yod stands for the Divine spark that lives within each of us.

THE TREE OF LIFE The value of this dream is equivalent to the value of the Hebrew word meaning "profound" or "hidden." These associations make it clear that you do have the potential to penetrate the deeper mysteries of the spiritual universe. The final letter in the spelling of your dream title is Heh, which literally means "window." The path of Heh offers us the possibility of a glimpse of the nature of the supernal Sefirot. This is a level of insight that is usually hidden, and for this reason we should place your dream on the path of Heh.

THE JOURNEY You should feel extremely encouraged by this dream, particularly as its value reduces to 10. This number indicates the completion of an important cycle in your life, and this very strongly suggests that you are about to achieve your goal of finding some sense of communion with the Divine itself. You should make sure that you retain your optimistic outlook as well as find time both for practical expressions of your faith and for quiet contemplation.

VOICE

kol-qvl-קול-136

MEANING If you told a psychologist that you were dreaming of a voice, you might find yourself also being asked whether you heard that voice when you were awake or only in your sleep. From a spiritual point of view, this is a very auspicious dream. The idea of a voice suggests the potential of making direct contact with your higher self, and this is, of course, one of the main aims of the Great Work itself. In Kabbalistic tradition, the image of a voice is seen as symbolic of a communication from the Divine itself. Consequently, it is very important to discern the tone and content of the voice in your dream.

THE TREE OF LIFE When we reduce the value of this dream we find the number 10. This number refers to the completion of a major cycle in your life. In your case, this relates to the achievement of a contact with your higher self. This is deemed to occur in Tiferet. However, your dream is of a single voice rather than a conversation, and this suggests that you have not yet arrived in Tiferet itself. Consequently, we should locate your dream on the path of Samech, which leads into Tiferet.

THE JOURNEY Not surprisingly, you have a certain degree of anxiety about your spiritual future as you have the potential at this time to make a significant leap forward. This anxiety is represented by the letter Qoph in the compression of your dream's value. The subsequent letter, Lamed, indicates that you can avoid any possible pitfalls with your attempts to reach the insight represented by the Sefirah of Tiferet if you continue to a take a rigorous approach to your studies. If you do this, the final Vav tells you, you will be able to work toward a moment of communion with the Divine.

VOTING

*hatsbaah-htzba'ah-*הצבעה-172

MEANING Spiritual development is not something that can ever truly be taught or learned. We can pick up techniques and methods that might help us to get a little edge, but ultimately the spiritual cannot be taught or learned because it must be experienced firsthand. If it is not, then all you have are ideas rather than a moment of spirituality. If spirituality is about direct experience, then there would seem to be little room for the debate and argument that we associate with voting.

THE TREE OF LIFE The image of voting relates not so much to any spiritual process as to the mental process that you must go through before making the decision to pursue a spiritual path. The value of this dream is equivalent to the value of the Hebrew word meaning "divided." This refers to the division within yourself between the spiritual part of you and the side of your nature that is drawn to the certainties of the material world. Until this division is resolved you will remain in the Sefirah of Malkut.

THE JOURNEY The first step is always the hardest to take and this is certainly true when it comes to a decision as major as deciding whether or not to embark on a spiritual quest. The letter Qoph in the compression of this dream tells us that you have very strong anxieties about this leap into the unknown.

However, the subsequent letter, Ayin, encourages you to be as courageous as possible and pursue the spiritual with all the vigor you can muster. If you do so, then ultimately you may come to inhabit the house of the Divine as represented by the final letter, Beth.

VULGAR

*gas-gs-*גס-63

MEANING On the surface this does not appear to be a very reassuring dream. The idea of vulgarity does not sit well with our day-to-day aspirations, as the tendency is to regard vulgarity as evidence not just of poor manners but of low intelligence and low self-esteem. Additionally, it is hard to see how vulgarity could have any positive significance when viewed in a spiritual context. Indeed, the value of this dream is equivalent to the value of the Hebrew word meaning "dung." This all seems to point to a rather depressing picture, until we remember the fact that even the lowest aspect of creation is still part of the unifying force of the Divine.

THE TREE OF LIFE When you are fully engaged with the Great Work, your only concern should be whether your efforts are bringing you closer to the Divine. In this sense, the dream of being vulgar is actually a positive image. It indicates, albeit in an extreme way, that you do not have any interest in the perceptions of the outside world. The value of this dream is equivalent to the value of the Hebrew word meaning "fervor," and this points to the fact that you are vigorously enthusiastic about the spiritual quest. Consequently, we should place your dream on the path of Ayin.

THE JOURNEY The value of this dream reduces to the number 9, which is the value of the letter Teth. The letter Teth is present in your dream to represent the level of willpower that is needed in order to successfully pursue the spiritual reality underlying the universe. However, the letter Samech in the compression of this dream's value tells us that you will be supported and guided in your attempts by your higher self. The final letter, Gimel, is a promise of the hidden wisdom that will be yours if you persevere.

VULNERABILITY

*pageea-phgya'a-*פגיע-163

MEANING Many people might be inclined to look at the title of this dream and immediately assume it is negative in terms of its implications for your spiritual development. This is because people can often confuse vulnerability with weakness. In fact, this is a very encouraging dream because when you are capable of being genuinely vulnerable, you are able to be completely honest about your feelings. Honesty, especially with yourself, is a great asset when it comes to developing your relationship with the Divine.

THE TREE OF LIFE When we reduce the value of this dream we find the number 10. This number points to the completion of a major cycle in your life. The value of this dream is equivalent to the value of the Hebrew word meaning "woman." In terms of a woman with whom we can be entirely vulnerable, we would probably think of a mother figure. The Sefirah of Binah is often referred to as the Great Mother, and to reach this far up the Tree of Life would certainly indicate that you are entitled to a very real sense of having completed a major cycle in your life.

THE JOURNEY It takes a lot of courage to allow yourself to feel your essential vulnerability, so it is entirely understandable that the compression of this dream's value begins with the letter Qoph, which indicates your sense of anxiety. The subsequent letter, Samech, tells you that the support and guidance of the Divine will make it as easy as possible for you to find your way to the hidden wisdom that is represented by the final letter, Gimel, in the compression of this dream.

VULTURE

ozneeyah – a'avznyyh – עוזנייה –158

MEANING On the list of the world's most unpopular birds, the vulture would stand a good chance of getting the number-one spot. Not only do vultures manage to be the most ungraceful birds on the planet, but they are often startlingly unappealing to look at. However, most people dislike them primarily because they are scavenger birds. In spiritual terms, this dream suggests that you are finding different ways of looking at the nature of mortality. To most of us a dead animal on the highway is a sad sight—to a vulture it is lunch.

THE TREE OF LIFE When we reduce the value of this dream we find the number 5. In the context of this dream's content we should see this number as referring to the Sefirah of Gevurah, which is the fifth Sefirah on the Tree of Life. This Sefirah is concerned with the necessity of mortality and the inevitable decay and breakdown of all living things.

The value of this dream is equivalent to the value of the Hebrew word meaning "balances." It is the need for balance in the universe that makes the existence of Gevurah essential.

THE JOURNEY Recognizing that death is an essential part of the Divine framework of the universe is one of the hardest lessons that the Great Work has to offer you. It is especially hard when you have to accept that, like the vulture, we all, in one sense or another, feed off the dead. It is then hardly surprising that the letter Qoph, indicating anxiety and a degree of uneasiness, features in the compression of this dream. However, the final letter, Cheth, though, is there to reassure you that even in the presence of death the protective force of the Divine is still with you.

WADE

leheetkadem ba'atsaltayeem – lhthqdm ba'atzlthyym – להתקדם בעצלתיים –1231

MEANING Memories of beach holidays and rolled-up pant legs come to mind when one considers the image of wading. However, the spiritual implications of this dream are not quite as lighthearted as the memory of wading along the edge of the ocean looking for shellfish. From a spiritual perspective, the key point about wading is that one never gets deeply into the water; it is an activity that takes place right on the edge of the shore, where it is safest.

THE TREE OF LIFE The most important element in this dream is the element of Water. That is obvious both from the content and from the fact that both of the Hebrew words that make up the dream title end with the letter Mem in its final form. The letter Mem literally means "water," and the element of Water is associated with our emotions. The image of wading makes it clear that you are not ready to look closely at your emotional makeup but are merely skirting around the edges of the issues that you need to face. When we reduce the value of this dream we find the number 8, which is the value of the Hebrew letter Cheth. The path of Cheth in its negative aspect refers to a defensive attitude on the part of the dreamer, so this is where we should locate your dream.

THE JOURNEY This dream is trying to tell you that you have a number of emotional concerns that you need to deal with properly before you will be able to move forward in your spiritual life. The compression of this dream begins with the letter Qoph multiplied by a factor of 10, so we know that you are extremely anxious about examining your inner nature. You have no reason to be, and should instead feel quite optimistic (Resh) about the opportunity. If you make a point of diligently studying (Lamed) your own nature, the nature of the Divine (Aleph) will become far more comprehensible to you. From a traditional Kabbalistic viewpoint, this dream also urges you to take extra care of your personal safety at this time.

WAGER

*heetarvoot-htha'arbvth-*התערבות-1083

MEANING It is very important that we distinguish between a mere bet and a wager. While a bet can apply to any form of gambling, a wager is more involved. In a wager, at least one of the parties engaged in the wager must be gambling on his own ability to achieve something. This is a very important distinction in spiritual terms, since there is a difference between gambling on some other individual which is hard to fit into any kind of spiritual framework, and an individual taking a gamble with their own life and their own soul.

THE TREE OF LIFE In a sense, anyone who embarks on the Great Work is entering into a wager with himself. Nobody can predict how he is going to react to the range of ideas and concepts that have to be dealt with in order to secure an ever-increasing depth of spiritual understanding. It takes a great deal of inner courage to be willing to take such a leap into the dark. We should position your dream on the path of Daleth, both because it represents a doorway to a higher level of understanding and because you never know exactly what lies beyond the door.

THE JOURNEY Because of the nature of this dream, we would expect to see the letter Qoph in its compression, since a degree of anxiety is inevitable. The presence of the letter Peh advises you both to share your experiences with other people who are seeking the truth and to ensure that you are trying to initiate a dialogue with your higher self. The final letter, Gimel, is an encouragement to continue with your very creative approach to the Great Work.

WAGES

*sakhar-shkr-*שכר-520

MEANING This dream is not as simple as it might initially appear. It is certainly concerned with the material rather than the spiritual world, and it would seem to suggest that you are excessively con-

cerned with maximizing your income rather than the level of your spiritual understanding. However, in terms of the different words that could be used to signify payment, the word *wages* suggests the lowest possible level, compared, for instance, with the term *salary*. The implication of this dream is that you are seeking only the recompense that you need in order to live a reasonable life-style.

THE TREE OF LIFE The value of this dream is equivalent to the value of the Hebrew word meaning "tears." The presence of this word is to point out your sympathy for those who are in a worse material situation than you are. It is likely that you are engaging in some form of charitable activity for those in your community who have difficulties in their lives. The path of Kaph is related to the practical application of spiritual values, so it is here that we should position your dream. This is supported by the fact that the compression of your dream's value consists only of the letter Kaph in both its standard and final forms.

THE JOURNEY When we reduce the value of this dream we find the number 7. This is the value of the letter Zayin, which is concerned with the process whereby we analyze the relative merits of a situation or an idea. The implication here is that you need to ensure that when you are helping others you do not get so carried away with your generosity that you fail to look after your own needs.

WAGON

*agalah-a'aglh-*עגלה-108

MEANING The image of a wagon calls to mind the spirit of adventure and excitement that we associate with the wagon trains setting out to explore the West. This spirit of individualism and adventure is represented in the spelling of this dream title. The initial letter, Ayin, reflects the individualistic nature of the adventurous spirit, while the subsequent letter, Gimel, tells us that such a character must also be extremely creative in the way that he deals with the inevitable problems that he will meet along the way.

THE TREE OF LIFE From a spiritual perspective, the qualities that we associate with a wagon and that we find in the spelling of this dream title are also ideal for ensuring that you make good progress on your inner journey of self-exploration. When we reduce the value of this word we find the number 9. This is the value of the Hebrew letter Teth. The path of Teth refers to the great strength of character and willpower that is embodied in this dream, so it is here that we should locate your dream.

THE JOURNEY The value of this dream is equivalent to the value of the Hebrew word meaning "to love very much." It is important to remember that while we may be talking about qualities such as courage and willpower, the overwhelming force that drives the Great Work is the force of Love. Another word that shares its value with the value of this dream is the Hebrew word meaning "ears." This tells us that while it is very positive that you should strike out toward an understanding of the Divine on your own, you also need to ensure that you listen to the wisdom and advice of those who have gone before you.

WAIL

*yevavah-ybbh-*יבבה*-*19

MEANING Sometimes in order to move forward in a positive manner we have to have to go through a period of time where we feel anything but positive. The dream of wailing is suggestive of a very deep sense of loss and emotional distress. In spiritual terms, it indicates a feeling that you are somehow cut off from the loving force of the Divine. The value of this dream is equivalent to the value of the Hebrew word meaning "eve." This association emphasizes the sense of having lost the presence of the Divine.

THE TREE OF LIFE When we reduce the value of this dream we find the number 10. This number is associated with the Sefirah of Malkut, as this Sefirah is the tenth on the Tree of Life. Additionally, the number 10 represents completion and Malkut represents the completion of the emanation of the universe. The value of this dream is equivalent to the value of the Hebrew word meaning "to be black." This also links your dream with the Sefirah of Malkut, as this Sefirah is associated with the black earth since it represents the wholly material level of existence.

THE JOURNEY It is clear that the reason for your dream is that you are beginning to develop an awareness that there is more to life than the merely physical. Before we can take our first steps on the spiritual path, we must come to a definite conclusion that the Divine is a real force behind the universe that we wish to understand. The fact that you are dreaming of such distress suggests that you are very close to reaching that conclusion. Additionally, the compression of this dream's value tells us that you have the strength of will to begin the Great Work

(Teth). The initial letter, Yod, lets us know that you will shortly be able to awaken the spark of the Divine within yourself.

WAITING

*hamtanah-hmthnh-*המתנה*-*500

MEANING We all know the old adage that patience is a virtue. This may be a cliché but it still holds true. We live in a world where we are used to quick service in many areas of our lives. Our food is fast, our careers seem to be constantly changing, and the technological environment in which we live seems to become more advanced and more complex by the week. The spiritual quest operates on a much slower timetable, and one of the first things that you must learn when you begin the Great Work is that you have to wait and wait and then wait some more before you get any kind of tangible results.

THE TREE OF LIFE The content of this dream makes it clear that you have already learned the need for a stoic level of patience when engaging in the spiritual quest. The central letter in the spelling of this dream is Tav, and while it may point to a certain amount of melancholy, it also indicates a willingness on your part to do whatever is necessary to progress. Your dream's spelling begins and ends with the letter Heh. The letter Heh means "window," and the path of Heh relates to the possibility of approaching an understanding of the Divine through observation, so we should position this dream on the path of Heh.

THE JOURNEY When we reduce the value of this dream we find the number 5. This is present in your dream for two reasons. First, it is the value of the letter Heh, which is the path on which your dream sits. Second, it also relates to the pentagram, which is a symbol of the individual who has mastered the physical elements through the guiding force of his higher self. The compression of this dream produces the letter Kaph in its final form. This tells you that you should be taking some practical action to help increase your spiritual understanding. As you are supposed to be waiting for some form of insight, this activity refers not to yourself but to your getting involved in helping those around you.

WAKING

*leorer-la'avrr-*לעורר*-*506

MEANING It would be natural to assume that a dream about waking indicates simply that you are a restless sleeper. However, this dream does not refer to physically waking up but instead is a reference to the process of beginning the search for spiritual truth. You should see this dream as a positive sign that you are starting to make genuine progress that will eventually lead to your having the opportunity to achieve some kind of contact with your higher self.

THE TREE OF LIFE When we reduce the value of this dream we find the number 11. This number indicates that you are very close to achieving a moment of deep spiritual significance. As this is very early in your journey toward self-discovery, it is likely that this moment will be a point in the near future when you realize absolutely that you are convinced of the existence of a Divine force. The letter Resh appears twice in this dream title, and the path of Resh, on which this dream is placed, relates to a quietly optimistic attitude toward the Great Work.

THE JOURNEY The initial letter, Lamed, in the spelling of this dream title indicates that you need to spend a regular amount of time each day studying if you are to achieve the spiritual insight hinted at within the value of this dream. The compression of the dream's value tells us that you should also engage in some form of practical activity (Kaph) that will help to consolidate your spiritual beliefs. Since it should include a degree of contemplation (Vav), an ideal pursuit would be yoga. You could also consider following one of the Eastern martial arts such as aikido or tai chi.

See Zohar symbol, Waking Up.

WALKING

*tseeedah-tza'aydh-*צעירה*-*179

MEANING Usually when we go out walking the main thing on our minds is the destination. Perhaps we might go out with the intention of taking in the scenery. In any case, we tend not to focus on the act of walking itself. This dream encourages you to concentrate on the simple business of walking, as it is symbolic of your steady progress along the Tree of Life. When we reduce the value of this dream we find the number 8. This is the value of the letter Cheth, and this tells us that while your progress may be slow, you are walking in the protection of the Divine.

THE TREE OF LIFE There is no urgency to the Great Work, as the only thing that counts is that you

find a way to build a relationship with the Divine. It is not important how quickly or slowly you manage to develop that sense of understanding. It is significant, though, that you follow a path that you can relate to. The letter Ayin occupies a central position in the compression of this dream, and this letter relates to the vigorous pursuit of your individual approach to the Divine. This is the path on which we should locate your dream.

THE JOURNEY It takes a lot of courage to resolutely follow one's feelings in any walk of life. It is especially difficult when you are dealing with the development of your soul. The initial letter, Qoph, in the compression of this dream's value makes it clear that you have some anxieties about whether you are making the right choices to help increase your understanding of the spiritual reality behind the universe. The final letter, Teth, in the compression should be seen as a reassuring indication that you should rely on your strength of character to show you the way forward.

WALL

*keer-qyr-*קיר*-*310

MEANING To dream of a wall is a clear sign that you have a range of issues that at this moment you do not feel ready to face. The value of this dream is equivalent to the value of the Hebrew word meaning "to trample on." This association points to the fact that you have been actively repressing certain emotions and memories. This is not only unhealthy from a psychological point of view but will hinder your progress in the Great Work.

THE TREE OF LIFE The letter Cheth literally means "fence," and the path of Cheth is concerned with the protective force of the Divine. However, the image of a wall is not as protective as it might appear. Rather than act as a genuine defense, the wall that you have built within yourself acts simply as a means of keeping you from exorcising certain personal demons that, unless they are removed, will continually impact the way you live your life. Consequently, we should place your dream on the negative aspect of the path of Cheth.

THE JOURNEY The initial letter, Qoph, in the spelling of this dream title reveals the reason why you have built a wall around some of your more painful memories: It is because you have a real fear that in beginning to deal with them you will be unable to resolve them fully. The compression of this dream urges you to begin to pull down this wall, since you most definitely have the spiritual energy (Shin) to deal with your past. The final letter, Yod, in the compression of your dream tells us that if you persevere, you will shortly be able to awaken the Divine spark within yourself.

WANT

*tsorekh-tzvrk-*צורך-316

MEANING You should be greatly encouraged by this dream. In normal circumstances a positive dream would be one in which you achieved the object of your desires. However, there is no end to the spiritual quest, so a recognition of your state of wanting some form of contact is in itself extremely positive. The value of this dream is equivalent to the value of the Hebrew word meaning "to worship." This emphasizes the sincerity with which you are approaching the Great Work.

THE TREE OF LIFE When we look at the spelling of this dream title the first thing that we notice is the letter Kaph, because it appears in its final form. The path of Kaph is concerned with the practical application of your spiritual values. As a genuine seeker of truth and someone who is happy to actively worship the Divine, it is highly likely that you are living your life according to the principles of your spirituality, so we should place your dream on the path of Kaph.

THE JOURNEY The spelling of your dream title begins with the letter Tzaddi, which refers to the need for commitment and dedication to the spiritual quest. The initial Shin in the compression of your dream tells us that you certainly have the energized enthusiasm to maintain your commitment to your inner journey. This is no doubt due in part to the fact that the spark of the Divine (Yod) is already burning within you. Amid all this activity, though, it is equally important that you leave some time for quiet meditation (Vav) and reflection.

WAR

*meelkhamah-mlchmh-*מלחמה-123

MEANING No matter what the press or the movie industry may try to tell us, there is nothing glamorous, heroic, or laudable about warfare. Indeed, war is a sign of failure of the worst kind since it represents the absolute failure to communicate with mutual respect. While people may talk of victors

and the vanquished, in reality the outbreak of war is an admission of defeat on all sides. Thankfully, the image of war in your dream is somewhat less depressing in its implications.

THE TREE OF LIFE The dream of war indicates an inner conflict that you have been unable to resolve. When we look at the spelling of this dream we see the letters Lamed and Heh paired with the letter Mem. Lamed refers to rigorous study and hard work, while Heh indicates observation. There is a tension within you right now between the desire to study and the desire to engage in active spiritual practice. The letter Mem in each case represents the element of Water. The Sefirah of Hod is associated with the element of Water and is also concerned with the reconciliation of opposing ideas through communication. We should therefore position your dream in the Sefirah of Hod.

THE JOURNEY The fact that the value of this dream appears as the sequence of the first three numbers is in itself symbolic of the fact that you need to deal with this internal conflict step by step and as simply as possible. You are concerned as to how you will resolve matters as indicated by the letter Qoph in the compression of this dream's value. The following letter, Kaph, suggests that if you engage in some practical activity (Kaph) that is also creative (Gimel), you may find a way of combining study and practice at one time. For instance, you could try painting your inner responses to spiritual ideas.

WART

*yabelet-yblth-*יבלת-442

MEANING Warts have always had a quasi-supernatural air about them. This is in part because they have no obvious cause and can disappear and reappear seemingly at will. The removal of warts was one of the primary functions of the local wise woman before such practices were condemned as heresy and witchcraft. Warts cannot be easily removed, nor do they hurt, but they are very hard to ignore and can spread from one part of the body to another. In a spiritual sense, we could see a wart as a positive sign of an idea that you cannot shift out of your consciousness.

THE TREE OF LIFE When we reduce the value of this dream we find the number 10. This is the number of the Sefirah of Malkut and it is here that we should locate your dream. Although you have yet to make a definite commitment to the Great

Work, this dream's image tells us that the notion of a spiritual dimension to reality is one that you have been unable to shift. All the signs are that you will very shortly be making that first leap into the unknown.

THE JOURNEY At a practical level, it would be very helpful for you to find someone who has already made the decision to pursue a spiritually aware lifestyle, as he will be able to put your mind at rest about a number of worries that you may have. The spelling of the dream title tells us that the Divine spark (Yod) has encouraged you to begin to study (Lamed) with a view to possibly trying to return to your spiritual home (Beth). This will lead you soon enough to set foot on the path of Tav.

WASHING (LAUNDRY)
kveesah–kbysh–כבים–97

MEANING Psychologists will often point to the way in which dreams can hint at common phrases or proverbs as a way to communicate their message to your conscious mind. A dream of washing laundry has obvious connections to the idea of washing as a metaphor for examining one's emotional difficulties. This phrase usually ends "in public." The absence of any reference to the public in the value or content of this dream suggests that any emotional introspection is being carried out in the confines of your own mind.

THE TREE OF LIFE It is very healthy to take a very close look at your emotional makeup, and the better you know yourself the better chance you will have of being able to progress unhindered up the Tree of Life. The value of this dream is equivalent to the value of the Hebrew word meaning "architect." In the context of this dream, the suggestion is that you will be able to construct a new and more focused sense of self, following this introspective period. The path of Nun refers to the deepening of your faith and as such is an appropriate path on which to position your dream.

THE JOURNEY You are going through a very difficult period in your life and it may be tempting at times to simply turn your back on the spiritual quest and return to the relative comfort of the material world. However, it is important that you do persevere, as the end result of your efforts will be a much deeper understanding of yourself and the Divine. It is for this reason that the compression of this dream's value consists of the letter Tzaddi, which refers to the need for commitment and dedication,

and the letter Zayin, which advises you to view the world from an appropriately analytical perspective.

WASP
tseerah–tzra'ah–צרעה–365

MEANING People find it very difficult to feel friendly toward wasps. We tend to place them in the same category as bees, and they tend to do badly in comparison. Bees produce honey; they can also sting you but only once due to the fact that the act of stinging causes them to break off their stingers in your flesh. Wasps produce nothing that humans require and they can sting you as often as they like. Despite this, your dream is very positive in what it says about your inner development.

THE TREE OF LIFE As we develop further spiritually, we discover that all things, no matter how unpleasant to us, have a place in the Divinely created universe. Consequently, being able to see the value and even the beauty in a wasp indicates a high level of spiritual insight. When we reduce the value of this dream we find the number 5. This is a highly significant number in the Western Mystery Tradition as it represents the individual who has mastered the four elements within himself under the control of his higher self. It is in the Sefirah of Tiferet that we make contact with our higher self, and this is where we should locate your dream.

THE JOURNEY The value of this dream is also equivalent to the Hebrew spelling of one of the aspects of the Sefirah of Tiferet, while the compression of this dream advises you on how to create the best chance of making contact with your higher self. The initial letter, Shin, tells you that you still have a great amount of spiritual energy even though you will be helped by the supportive force (Samech) of the Divine. The final letter, Heh, meaning "window," is there to remind you that you need to observe all things around you and try to find within them evidence of the presence of the Divine.

WATCH (TIME PIECE)
shaon–sha'avn–שעון–426

MEANING We live in a world that is more and more dominated by the issue of time. Where news used to take weeks to arrive, now it can be broadcast to the world in a matter of minutes. Similarly, our jobs require us to be more and more conscious of time as the advance of technology demands greater and greater efficiency. The fact that you are dreaming of a watch indicates that you have allowed yourself to be excessively dominated by the time pressures of your day-to-day life. In spiritual terms, this dream suggests that you are in danger of losing out on some of the lessons of the Great Work through your sense of a deadline applying to all things, even to the spiritual quest.

THE TREE OF LIFE In the spelling of this dream title we see that you bring a lot of energy (Shin) to your spiritual work and that you are pursuing the possibility of a contact with your higher self with great vigor (Ayin). However, the final letter, Nun, emphasizes the need to be focused on the deepening of your understanding rather than on advancing up the Tree of Life in the least possible time. What you need to do is spend a little more time in quiet contemplation, as indicated by the letter Vav in the spelling of this dream, and it is the path of Vav on which we should locate your dream.

THE JOURNEY When we reduce the value of this dream we find the number 3, which is associated with the creative processes. The message here is that you should spend less time worrying about time and more time exploring the world around you in greater detail so that you have the space to develop your personal relationship with the Divine. The central letter in the compression of this dream's value is Kaph. This letter relates to the practical side of your spiritual life and reiterates the value that you will find from spending some time exploring the world and simply engaging with other people, since this is as much a part of the Great Work as any amount of studying. The content of this dream suggests that your life would benefit from a focus on time management.

WATER

mayeem-mym-מים-90

MEANING This is a very auspicious dream in terms of your progress in the Great Work. From a psychological point of view, a dream of a large body of water would be taken to represent a desire to return to the protective cocoon of the womb. While the Kabbalistic analysis would also focus on the emotional aspect of your personality, there is no suggestion of escapism in the spiritual interpretation of the dream of water.

THE TREE OF LIFE The element of Water is associated with the entire range of our emotions in the Western Mystery Tradition, and this dream's title is full of references to the element of Water.

The letter Mem literally means "water," and, as well as being the title of the dream, it appears twice in the spelling of the dream itself. The path of Mem is concerned with a compassionate and altruistic approach to life and to those in your community, and it is on the path of Mem that we should locate your dream.

THE JOURNEY The value of this dream is equivalent to the value of the Hebrew word meaning "silent." In the context of this dream, the significance of this associated word is that your emotional focus is on the needs of others rather than on your own emotional state. The compression of this dream produces the letter Tzaddi, which tells us that your commendably compassionate approach to those around you is a sign of your absolute commitment to the highest values of the spiritual quest.

WATERFALL

mapal mayeem-mphl mym-מפל מים-240

MEANING Waterfalls are very different depending on where we stand in relation to their awesome power. From a safe distance, they are an example of nature's raw but delicate beauty. Up close, they are an example of how the beauty of nature can pound you with such unrelenting force that you lose consciousness! In spiritual terms, this dream refers to our exposure to an emotional force that is both beautiful and powerful.

THE TREE OF LIFE The numerical value of this dream is equivalent to the value of the Hebrew word meaning "lofty." The association with ideas that are lofty tells us that we are looking for a position high on the Tree of Life. The Sefirah of Binah is one of the three Supernals and so certainly fits the definition of being "lofty." Additionally, it is the first Sefirah on the Tree that is linked with the element of Water. Consequently, we can see all the emotional force on the Tree initially pouring down out of the Great Mother, Binah. This makes it a very fitting location for your dream.

THE JOURNEY While your dream is located in Binah, you are not actually residing within the state of consciousness represented by this Sefirah. That would expose you to a level of emotional intensity that you would not likely be able to withstand. The Sefirah of Binah is also known as "Understanding," and we are not designed to experience such a totality of empathy with the created universe. It is, however, an appropriate aspiration. The final Mem in the compression of this dream's value tells you that you should make every effort to emulate the capacity for absolute understanding that is represented by the Great Mother.

WAVES
gal-gl-גל-33

MEANING We can all remember standing on the beach watching the waves roll in. There is something almost hypnotic in the repetition of wave after wave, all similar but each one slightly different. It is this similarity with a measure of difference that seems to encourage the mixed feelings of deep tranquility and a low-level excitement that watching the waves seems to promote. From a very broad spiritual perspective, this dream can be seen as a metaphor for the nature of human understanding in that there may be slight differences in the nature of belief, but each wave upon the shore of human consciousness has an enormous number of similarities.

THE TREE OF LIFE The value of this dream is equivalent to the value of the Hebrew word meaning "fountain." If the waves can be seen as representing the tide of changing human belief then the fountain can be seen as a symbol for the way in which a particular belief can spring to life within an individual. This dream indicates that you are relatively new to the Great Work and are at the stage of exploring the history of human belief as well as searching for your own approach to the Divine. This is a stage of development commonly associated with the Sefirah of Yesod and so it is here that we should locate your dream.

THE JOURNEY When we reduce the value of this dream we find the number 6, which is the value of the letter Vav. This letter is associated with reflection, and its presence in this dream is to encourage you to take your time in deciding which spiritual wave to catch a ride on. The spelling of this dream title makes it clear that you will need to study very hard (Lamed) to succeed in the Great Work, but that in time you may ultimately come to an understanding of the secret wisdom (Gimel) of the Divine.

WEATHER
mezeg aveer-mzg avvyr-מזג אוויר-273

MEANING The only thing that is certain about the weather is that we never know exactly what to expect. No matter how closely we watch the reports or how sophisticated our weather system tracking devices become, we can never be certain whether we really

can leave the umbrella at home! In spiritual terms, we can look at this dream as a symbol of the way in which we can never second-guess the Divine, that no matter how well we prepare we are always in the hands of the higher forces.

THE TREE OF LIFE The value of this dream is equivalent to the value of the Hebrew word meaning "the hidden light." This is a reference to the unseen and unknowable will of the Divine. This is the pure Divine will that emanates out of Keter along the path of Aleph. For much of our spiritual quest, we operate on the basis that if we study and meditate hard and long enough we may come to understand the Creator. It takes a very high level of insight to fully accept that we can only ever understand that part of the Divine that is shown to us, that much will always remain hidden. For this reason, we should place your dream on the path of Aleph.

THE JOURNEY The central letter, Ayin, in the compression of this dream confirms that you have pursued the spiritual path vigorously and in a manner that is sympathetic to your individual nature. You can afford to be optimistic about your future development as the letter Resh is also present, and all the signs are that you will be able to have sight of at least a portion of the hidden wisdom (Gimel) of the Divine.

WEAVING
leerog-larvg-לארוג-240

MEANING One of the benefits of the incredible advancement in technology over the last two hundred years is that we now have access to a whole range of cultural artifacts no matter where we live. We can watch American baseball while drinking German beer, eating Swiss chocolate, and wearing Italian clothes and English brogues. However, the more items we can access, the less we seem to be able to make for ourselves. The art of weaving, for instance, is one that has almost disappeared. So, while we can weave together cultures, we cannot begin to weave our own clothes. Similarly, while we can understand the complexity of I.T., we find it less urgent that we should understand the complexity of something as essential as our spiritual development.

THE TREE OF LIFE From a spiritual point of view, the image of weaving refers to the linking together in a workable manner all the different aspects of your inner nature. The value of this dream is equivalent to the value of the Hebrew word meaning "lofty." This emphasizes that the act of binding together the disparate elements within your personality requires a highly evolved state of consciousness. In fact, the unification of the four elements within yourself requires the intervention of your higher self, which places this dream in the Sefirah of Tiferet.

THE JOURNEY You should feel very pleased with your spiritual progress, since it is a rare achievement to make contact with your higher self. The compression of this dream's value makes it clear that you can also be optimistic about the future (Resh). This is in no small way thanks to the fact that you are being protected by the maternal aspect of the Divine, as represented by the final letter, Mem, in the compression.

WEB

maarag-marg-גראמ-244

MEANING For anybody under twenty-five who is reading this book, it might be worth pointing out that this is a dream about the handiwork of spiders and has nothing to do with URLs, dot-coms, or chat rooms! To dream of a web is to dream of being ensnared by something or someone. However, this does not mean that this dream should be seen in a negative light, as the values within the dream's title make it clear that this is a very encouraging dream from a spiritual point of view.

THE TREE OF LIFE When we reduce the value of this dream we find the number 10. The number 10 represents the sense of completion of a major cycle in your life. It is likely that this refers to your making the leap of faith that has led you to the Great Work. The sense of being caught in a web has very strong associations with the path of Tzaddi, whose literal significance suggests someone being "hooked." In broader terms, it refers to the dedication and commitment to the spiritual quest, and it is here that we should position your dream.

THE JOURNEY The value of this dream is equivalent to the value of the Hebrew phrase meaning "to be in a deep trance." This emphasizes the fact that you are completely hooked on the pursuit of spiritual advancement. The compression of this dream is very encouraging: You approach the inner journey with an optimistic and rational (Resh) mind. This attitude combined with your willingness to help those around you (Mem) will ensure that you are able to open the door (Daleth) to a new level of understanding.

WEDDING

khatoonah-chthvnh-הנותח-469

MEANING Everyone likes a wedding. The romantics enjoy the vows and the tears, the cynics enjoy the inevitable fight between the in-laws and the tears, while the rest of the guests enjoy the food and of course the tears. As you might expect, the spiritual significance of this dream relies on a much purer form of wedding than most of us are used to witnessing, as this dream is symbolic of the union between the spiritual and the material. In traditional Kabbalah, the image of a wedding signifies the union of a soul with the Divine, so this dream should be seen in a very positive light.

THE TREE OF LIFE You are not likely to contact your higher self until you reach the Sefirah of Tiferet. Any form of communion with the Divine itself is extremely rare. However, these are events that occur after the symbolic marriage of the spiritual and the material has occurred. After all, your spiritual quest only begins once you have made a commitment to the Great Work. It is that commitment that is symbolized here by the image of a wedding. The Sefirah of Malkut, which represents the physical and is the location for this dream is often referred to as the Bride of Keter, which is the Sefirah that is purely spiritual in nature. This dream merely plays out that particular symbolism.

THE JOURNEY As with any wedding, the only thing that is certain is that there will be cake. What happens thereafter is up to the couple themselves and is entirely unpredictable. However, the compression of this dream's value points to the path of Tav as your route out of Malkut. Additionally, you are advised that you will receive the support and guidance from your higher self (Samech) for as long as you continue to use all your will and strength of character (Teth) to progress up the Tree of Life. You should be greatly encouraged by the fact that the content of this dream points to a great potential for future spiritual achievement.

See Zohar symbol, Wedding.

WEDGE

treez-tryz-זיירט-226

MEANING Some words and ideas seem to seep spirituality; words like *grail, fountain,* and *dove* all have that quality about them. If the word *wedge* seems to have a quality, then it is one of solidity. If words wore clothes, "wedge" would be in sensible shoes and overalls. However, the values in this dream indicate that this dream relates to a significant level of spiritual understanding. The value of this word is, for instance, equivalent to the value of the Hebrew word meaning "profound" or "hidden."

THE TREE OF LIFE A wedge is anything that we can use to keep something open. In spiritual terms, we can see this as meaning some tool that holds open the possibility of spiritual advancement. The spelling of this dream title tells us that your strength of will (Teth) and your rational approach (Resh) have awakened the Divine spark (Yod) within you so that you can analyze (Zayin) the various ideas you have about the spiritual realm. It is likely that the tool that has enabled you to achieve this is rigorous studying, so we should position your dream on the path of Lamed.

THE JOURNEY The access that you now have to some of the profound wisdom of the Divine is thanks to your rational approach as indicated by the letter Resh in the compression of this dream's value. The subsequent letter, Kaph, suggests that you should now begin to explore practical ways of engaging with the realm of the spiritual. The final letter, Vav, points to the fact that an ideal avenue for you to explore would be some form of active meditation such as yoga or tai chi.

WEED

*esev shoteh–a'ashb shvth–*עשב שוטה*–692*

MEANING People often assume that there must be a class of plants that can be authoritatively referred to as weeds. This ignores the fact that the idea of a weed is related not to the species of genus of a given plant but to whether a particular individual wants that plant growing in his garden. This distinction is important when it comes to translating the image of a weed into a spiritual context. Rather than suggest that there are certain ideas that are universally unhelpful to spiritual growth, this dream suggests that you to need to make an individual decision about the merits of any given idea.

THE TREE OF LIFE When we reduce the value of this dream we find the number 8, which refers to the letter Cheth and indicates the protective force of the Divine. It is this force that is encouraging you to weed your spiritual garden. The letter Shin appears twice in the spelling of this dream, and this serves to emphasize the fact that you will need significant amounts of energy in order to accomplish this

process. More than anything, though, you must be able to distinguish between those ideas that will help and those that will hinder you. This is why we should place your dream on the path of Zayin, which is concerned with the ability to analyze possible spiritual routes.

THE JOURNEY The compression of this dream's value begins with the letter Mem in its final form. This tells us that you are being supported in your difficult task by the maternal aspect of the Divine. This force should help you to maintain your commitment (Tzaddi) to the Great Work so that you can ultimately come to the house of the Divine (Beth) and achieve a deep understanding of the realm of the spiritual. From a more practical and traditional Kabbalistic point of view, this dream would be seen as advice to seek out those aspects of your life that are choking and restricting you. Once discovered, you should take steps to remove negative influences from your life.

WEEPING

*bekheeyah–bkyyh–*בכייה*–47*

MEANING This is the sort of dream that one wakes up from with a vague but definite feeling of sorrow. It is very easy to spend the rest of the day trying to figure out the source of that emotional upset, since it is very difficult to see it as no more than the result of a dream. In spiritual terms, this dream also refers to a difficult period in your life but one that will ultimately prove to have been worthwhile. The value of this dream, interestingly enough, is equivalent to the value of the Hebrew word meaning "cloud," and of course every cloud has a silver lining.

THE TREE OF LIFE When we reduce the value of this dream we find the number 11. This is a number associated with an impending moment of great spiritual significance. Consequently, we really can claim that there is a silver lining to your currently cloudy perspective. The path of Nun is concerned with the process whereby we are able to achieve a great deepening in the level of our faith in the Divine and the validity of the spiritual quest. This process can often involve a degree of sorrow along the way because you have to examine your inner nature honestly and in detail, so we should place your dream on the path of Nun.

THE JOURNEY The letter Yod appears twice in the spelling of this dream title and you should see this as a reassurance that you have the strength of the Divine spark burning within you. This will enable you to make your way through this dark period in your spiritual life. Additionally, the letter Mem in the compression of this dream's value makes it clear that the maternal aspect of the Divine is with you at this time. This should give you the confidence and sense of support to continue with your inner journey. At a practical level, you should try to find out if there any aspects of your day-to-day life that are causing you to feel a sense of sadness.

WEIGHING

leeshkol-lshqvl- לשקול -466

MEANING At first, this seems to be a dream that is concerned mainly with matters of purely material significance. The need or the wish to measure things is an example of our desire to create a sense of control over the world by seeking to impose human definitions upon it. However, this is a very encouraging dream. The value of this dream is equivalent to the value of the Hebrew phrase that refers to the "World of Formation." This is a subdivision of the Tree of Life and indicates those paths and Sefirot that are immediately above Malkut.

THE TREE OF LIFE As this dream does not belong in the material world of Malkut, the theme of weighing must be being used in some symbolic capacity. Many religions talk of a person's soul being weighed as a means of determining its future after death. It could be that this dream refers to the fact that you are learning how your soul might be weighed. This would imply that you are engaging in a significant amount of study. As the letter Lamed appears twice in the spelling of this dream title, it is the most appropriate reading of this dream, so we should place your dream on the path of Lamed.

THE JOURNEY When we reduce the value of this dream we find the number 5. This number indicates a person who has brought the four elements under the control of his higher self. This is the state of consciousness to which you aspire and that is motivating your commendable level of study. The central letter, Samech, in the compression of this dream tells us that you are being supported in this by your higher self. The final letter, Vav, reminds you that study, to be truly valuable, must be accompanied by contemplation and reflection.

WELCOME

kabalat paneem-qblth phnym- קבלת פנים -712

MEANING There is not a great deal to say about the meaning of a dream that is as unequivocally positive as this one. To dream of being welcomed is a clear sign that you are gaining in confidence in your spiritual work. When we reduce the value of this dream we find the number 10, which indicates that you are on your way to completing a major cycle in your life. This adds a sense that you are being welcomed into a new level of insight or state of consciousness.

THE TREE OF LIFE If we look at the spelling of this dream title, it gives us a history of your spiritual development so far. Your anxieties (Qoph) about how to bring yourself closer to the house of the Divine (Beth) led you to study rigorously (Lamed) and leave Malkut by the path of Tav. By attempting to initiate a dialogue (Peh) with your higher self, you have deepened your faith (Nun) and awakened the Divine spark (Yod) within you. Your compassionate nature (Mem) means that you are also living out those spiritual lessons that you have learned. These qualities suggest an individual who is ready to enter the Sefirah of Tiferet, so we should place your dream on the path of Samech.

THE JOURNEY You should feel very pleased with your progress. The presence of the letter Nun in the compression of this dream's value makes it clear that you have a very deep faith and commitment to the Great Work. The central letter, Yod, indicates that you are guided in your efforts by the spark of the Divine that now burns within you. The final letter, Beth, is a promise that if you continue to persevere in your efforts, you will ultimately come to rest within the house of the Divine.

WELL

beer-bar- באר -203

MEANING In a world full of water-treatment plants, hot and cold running water, and advanced methods of water storage, the image of a well is somewhat quaint and carries all sorts of associations that would not have been present originally, when the symbolic significance of a well was first being defined. We need to try to look to the original importance of a well, and when we do this we find a resource that was crucial to the continuance of agriculture and therefore food and ultimately life itself. When we translate these associations into a spiritual framework, we see that this is a dream about the life-giving nature of the Divine itself.

THE TREE OF LIFE The value of this dream is equivalent to the value of the Hebrew words meaning "exotic" and "foreign." This tells us that at your current stage of inner development, the source of the Divine force is almost entirely alien to you. The image of a well adds to this idea in that the water of a well rarely lies near the surface but is down a long shaft. When we reduce the value of this dream we find the number 5, which, in the context of the content and other values, represents the letter Heh and indicates that you are constantly looking for evidence of the Divine. The novelty of the spiritual to you, combined with its importance in your view of the world, suggests that we should place this dream on the path of Tav.

THE JOURNEY Although you are new to the spiritual quest, you already have a very deep commitment to succeeding in the goals of the Great Work. The letter Resh, which begins the compression of this dream's value, tells us that you approach the inner journey with an optimistic but rational mind-set. The final letter, Gimel, suggests that while it is good to look for evidence of the Divine, you should also allow yourself to be creative in how you go about attempting to reach up to the Divine.

WHIP
shot-shvt-שום-315

MEANING Unless you like whips—and some of us do—this dream is unlikely to seem particularly encouraging in nature. We associate whips with punishment and coercion, so we might find it hard to fit this dream into a spiritual framework. However, when we look at this dream and remember that it refers to a process within your mind, it is easier to see its relevance to the Great Work. The suggestion of this dream is that you are whipping yourself. In other words, your higher self is trying to encourage you to make greater efforts to increase your understanding of the Divine.

THE TREE OF LIFE The value of this dream is equivalent to the value of the Hebrew word meaning "ice." This should be seen as symbolic of a certain coldness or lack of enthusiasm in your approach to the spiritual quest. When we reduce the value of this dream we find the number 9. This is the value of the letter Teth, which also occurs in the spelling of your dream. The path of Teth is concerned with the qualities of determination and willpower, which your higher self is trying to encourage within you, so this is the path where we should locate your dream.

THE JOURNEY When we look at the value of your dream's compression, we see that you certainly have

sufficient energy (Shin) to spur yourself on to greater efforts. The letter Yod tells us that you will shortly awaken the Divine spark within you, and this will definitely make a great difference to your approach. The value of this dream is equivalent to the value of a Hebrew phrase meaning "a splendid vision." The final letter of the compression is Heh, which means "window." The implication here is that you are soon going to have a revelatory moment that will serve to reignite your enthusiasm for the spiritual quest.

WHIRLPOOL
mearbolet-ma'arbvlth-מערבולת-748

MEANING This dream has a significance that is almost entirely dependent on the worldview of the individual who is analyzing its meaning. From a psychological standpoint, a whirlpool is a very visual representation of a sense of internal chaos and turmoil. As such, this dream might be seen as a worrisome indication of your state of mind. However, if we look at this same image in a spiritual context, the swirling energy of the whirlpool represents the awesome power of the Divine.

THE TREE OF LIFE Although it has the capacity to destroy, the power of the whirlpool when seen as a symbol of the energy of the Divine also has the capacity to entirely rearrange our perception of the world. The value of this dream is equivalent to the value of a Hebrew phrase meaning "the anointing oil." This association suggests that you have reached a point in your inner development where you are able to catch a glimpse of the nature of the Divine, and the whirlpool is how your unconscious presents this vision to your conscious mind. The path of Heh relates to the vision of the Divine nature, so it is here that we should locate your dream.

THE JOURNEY The compression of this dream's value supports the interpretation of this dream as relating to a vision of the Divine nature. The initial letter, Nun, appears in its final form and thus emphasizes the fact that you are going through a period in your life that will lead to a great deepening of your faith in the Divine. The letter Mem lets you know that while this vision may be rather overwhelming, the maternal aspect of the Divine will be with you along with the protective force (Cheth) of the Creator, so you should not let the intense power of your vision cause you any concern.

WHISPERING

lekheeshah–lchyshh–לחישה–353

MEANING It is a sad comment on our general nature that we tend to associate whispering with the quiet spreading of rumors far more than we would with any positive use of whispering. This dream is overwhelmingly positive in its message, and the content should be taken as a sign that while lies often need to shout to make themselves heard, a whisper of truth will still manage to find its way into the ears of those who are ready to listen.

THE TREE OF LIFE When we reduce the value of this dream we find the number 11. This number is a strong indication that you are about to undergo an experience of deep spiritual significance. This is emphasized by the fact that the value of this dream is equivalent to the value of the Hebrew word meaning "delight" or "joy." The path of Gimel is associated with access to the secret wisdom of the Divine. It certainly brings joy to those able to progress that far, and lessons of the path of Gimel need only to be whispered. Additionally, the value of the letter Gimel is 3, and this is the value with which this dream both begins and ends.

THE JOURNEY It takes a great deal of commitment and hard work to reach a level of spiritual insight that can be equated to the path of Gimel. The initial letter, Lamed, in the spelling of this dream title refers to the rigorous study that is required, while the initial letter, Shin, in the dream's compression points to your great spiritual energy. The letter Nun is central in the compression and represents the powerful effect on your faith in the validity of the Great Work that the experience of the path of Gimel will have. Finally, we have the letter Gimel itself, which not only refers to the path you are on but encourages you to try to take a creative view of how you should best approach the Divine.

WHISTLE

shreekah–shryqh–שריקה–615

MEANING There are certain sounds that seem to have the ability to cut through almost any amount of noise. Phrases like "drinks all around" certainly have the power to be heard above the rowdiest of crowds, and the sound of a whistle can penetrate through all but the most solid wall of background noise. In spiritual terms, the dream of a whistle is suggestive of a call that simply cannot be ignored, even if you try to drown it out with the comforting sounds of your day-to-day life.

THE TREE OF LIFE A whistle has always been an excellent way to get somebody's attention. In terms of this dream it is your higher self that is trying to get you to respond. The spelling of this dream title includes the letters that represent three of the five initial paths on the Tree of Life, and the suggestion is that you are being urged to leave the Sefirah of Malkut, where your dream is located, by way of one of the paths included in the dream.

THE JOURNEY The reduction of this dream produces the number 12, which is associated with a compassionate and altruistic mind-set. This is reflected in the initial letter, Mem, in the compression of this dream's value. It is clear that you already have a personality that would be more than suited to pursuing the spiritual dimension in your life. All you need to do is to make a leap of faith. The final letter, Heh, in the compression is there to remind you to take a close look at the world around you in the hope that you will begin to see evidence of the presence of the Divine.

WHITE

lavan–lbn–לבן–82

MEANING In many religious cultures and certainly in the symbolism of the Western Mystery Tradition the color white is used to represent the highest level of spiritual understanding and purity. This is because white is the brightest color and is an approximation of the light that emanates from the Sun, and, in a sense, because white has no hue it could be seen as the pure blank onto which the colors of the living universe were painted.

THE TREE OF LIFE The value of this dream is equivalent to the value of the Hebrew word meaning "righteous" and "kind." This serves to emphasize the advanced level of spiritual insight of the dreamer. White is the color of the topmost Sefirah in the Tree of Life, but you cannot be located within Keter itself, as this would be to equate an individual with the Divine force. We can reduce the value of this dream to 1, and in the context of the symbolism of the dream's content we should see this as referring to the path of Aleph, where your dream should be placed.

THE JOURNEY Now that you have reached such a significant level of understanding, you should try to encourage those around you to consider their own spiritual journeys. The initial letter, Peh, in the compression of this dream indicates that you ought to try to communicate something of your experiences to others so that they too may begin the Great Work. The value of this dream is equivalent to the value of the Hebrew word meaning "prayer." This tells us that you also need to try to communicate with the Divine in order to further increase your understanding so that ultimately you can enter the house of the Divine, as represented by the final letter, Beth, in this dream's compression.

WIDOW

*almanah-almnh-*אלמנה-126

MEANING It is unfortunate but true that we cannot always have cheerful dreams any more than we can always be happy in our lives. Moreover, sadness is just as essential to a full understanding of the spiritual dimension of your life as any amount of joy. If nothing else, without having experienced a sense of upset or emotional pain we would not be able to recognize the opposite of those feelings as positive states—they would simply be the norm.

THE TREE OF LIFE Few losses can be as painful as the loss of a loved partner. The value of this dream is equivalent to the value of the Hebrew word meaning "darkness," and this emphasizes the depth of the emotional pain indicated by this dream. We should remember that Malkut is known as the Bride of Keter. From a spiritual point of view, this dream refers to the fact that you are still in Malkut and are considering not pursuing a spiritual path at all. Your failure to undertake the spiritual quest would transform your consciousness from that of the bride to that of the widow.

THE JOURNEY While this dream is certainly depressing in nature, it does not mean that your life has to take a turn for the worse. You should see this dream as a warning. Its purpose is to try to give you a small sense of the regret that you will feel if you go through your whole life without exploring the world of the spiritual. When we reduce the value of this dream we find the number 9, which is the value of the letter Teth, meaning "serpent." It is its serpentine aspect that is relevant to this dream, as it indicates that your belief that you do not need to explore your inner self is a self-deceit that stems from an understandable fear of the unknown.

WIFE

*rayah-ra'ayh-*רעיה-285

MEANING It is important to note that the significance of this dream is the same whether you are a man or a woman. The distinction of gender in this dream should not be seen as a comment on the nature of wives in general. It should be seen as a purely symbolic use of the term that exploits certain archetypal associations with the nature of a wife in order to make a point about your future spiritual development. This dream uses the idea of a wife as a loyal and ever-present companion to symbolize the way in which you should seek to relate to your higher self.

THE TREE OF LIFE In very traditional conceptions of the role of a wife, it was very important that the wife should take her lead from her husband in terms of both thought and deed. While this may be a deeply inappropriate way for an actual marriage to operate, it does act as an ideal metaphor for the way in which you should try to allow your higher self to determine the direction that you take in your spiritual quest. When we reduce the value of this dream we find the number 6. This is the value of the letter Vav. The path of Vav is concerned with reflection and contemplation, and, since you need to engage in some serious reflection on your relationship to your higher self, it is the ideal path for your dream.

THE JOURNEY The fact that you are already in some form of relationship with your higher self is itself extremely positive. The letter Resh in the compression of this dream tells us that you have every reason to be optimistic about the future. The key thing for you to focus on in the next few months is to work on your dialogue (Peh) with your higher self. If you do so, you may eventually progress to a point where you can achieve the much-longed-for glimpse (Heh) of the nature of the Divine.

WIG

*peah nokhreet-phyah nvkryth-*פיאה נוכרית-782

MEANING We are all familiar with wigs as an object of comedy, but they do not seem particularly likely candidates for holding any deep spiritual significance. However, practically any item can hold an inner message. It is usually just a matter of getting to the core of any given object's purpose. In dreams, a wig is used not as a mere fashion accessory but as a psychological accessory. It hides those things that we are not comfortable with. and as a result we feel that we can face the world with much greater confidence.

THE TREE OF LIFE When we reduce the value of this dream we find the number 8. This is the value of the letter Cheth. The path of Cheth is concerned with the protective force of the Divine. At this point it is worth reflecting on the fact that whatever the wig wearer may think, those people around him would agree that not only was the wig visible but that the individual would look far more dignified without it. We can now see the image of a wig as a symbol of a level of self-defense that will not actually help your spiritual progress, so we place this dream on the negative aspect of the path of Cheth.

THE JOURNEY In the same way as we cannot fool our friends by wearing a wig, we cannot fool the Divine by trying to hide those aspects of our personality that we are not comfortable with. The letter Nun appears in its final form at the beginning of the compression of this dream. Its purpose here is to encourage you to examine your inner nature closely and honestly. It is only by communicating openly with yourself (Peh) that you will have any chance of entering the house of the Divine, represented by the final letter, Beth, in the compression of this dream.

WILDNESS
praoot-phravth- פראות-687

MEANING If we were to try to categorize the nature of the Divine and its opposite in quasi-scientific terms, the Divine would represent the tendency toward order and coherence, and the opposing force would represent chaos and disorder. These categories make sense in a commonsense world and are particularly appealing because we are frightened by our capacity for chaos, since this implies the potential for a loss of control.

THE TREE OF LIFE While the above definitions may be comforting, we need to consider the fact that without chaos there would be no creativity, and that the tendency for order in the universe, if left unchecked, would eventually lead to a steady state where absolutely nothing occurred or even existed. To be fully developed spiritual beings, we need both the sense of order and the wildness referred to in the title of this dream. The reduction value of this dream is 21. The path of Shin is the twenty-first path on the Tree of Life and also represents the raw spiritual power of this dream.

THE JOURNEY To be possessed of the energetic spirituality implied by the path of Shin is excellent for your spiritual development, as long as it is not operating in a vacuum. The initial letter in the compression of this dream is the final form of the letter Mem. Its presence here reminds you of the need to ensure that you are including a compassionate and empathetic approach to the world in the way that you pursue your spiritual quest. The letter Peh encourages you to try to find a way of reconciling through an inner dialogue both the caring and the energetic aspects of the Divine, and by analyzing (Zayin) both aspects carefully you should emerge with a fuller understanding of the nature of the spiritual realm.

WILL (LEGAL)
tsavaah-tzvvah- צוואה-108

MEANING Since your will only comes into its own once you are dead, it would be quite reasonable to see this dream as a reference to the need to adjust to and prepare for your ultimate demise. However, its spiritual significance is slightly more involved than that, and it refers very much to the way in which you should be living your life now, rather than to anything that may happen once you are dead.

THE TREE OF LIFE A will is a method by which we can dispose of our material possessions. Symbolically, this dream indicates that you are no longer tied to your physical environment and can happily conceive of giving away your goods. We can also see a will as a way of determining what should happen to you once your physical life is over. We can interpret this as referring not to death but to the end of the domination of your life by physical concerns. In this way, the dream of a will refers to the opportunity for your spiritual self to start planning the direction that you will take in life. This requires a great deal of willpower. The value of this dream reduces to 9, which is the value of the letter Teth. The path of Teth refers to the need for willpower and strength of character, so it is here that we should locate your dream.

THE JOURNEY It is not easy to allow the spiritual priorities in your life to take precedence over your material concerns. Not surprisingly, the letter Qoph appears in the compression of this dream's value and indicates the worries and anxieties that you are feeling at this time. However, you should not be unduly worried, since the letter Cheth also appears and this represents the fact that the protective force of the Divine is with you and will help you to make the right choices in your spiritual journey.

❧WIND

*rooach–rvch–*רוח*–*214

MEANING The human mind has a tendency to focus on extremes. Thus, when we see the word *wind* rather than think of the mild movement of a breeze we are far more inclined to visualize a roaring gust. In terms of this dream, we should not have any particular type of wind in mind since the dream content is general rather than definite. The focus of this dream is on the movement of air, not on the manner in which it is moving. You should also be aware that wind is symbolic of impending change in your life.

THE TREE OF LIFE In spiritual terms, the element of Air relates to the sphere of thoughts. This dream refers to your ability to turn spiritual ideas over in your mind, moving the ideas around in the attempt to reach a deeper level of understanding. The reduction of this dream's value produces the number 8. The Sefirah of Hod is the eighth Sephirah in the Tree of Life and is concerned with the process of internal communication and the attempt to reach an understanding of the world. Consequently, this would be the ideal location for your dream.

THE JOURNEY Understanding is not the same as knowing, and to achieve genuine understanding of even the tiniest piece of wisdom takes a great deal of time and effort. However, the image of wind suggests that you will be able to make the changes in your life needed to encourage your understanding. The letter Resh in the compression of this dream's value indicates that you are taking a rational but optimistic approach to your attempts at understanding. The effort itself is likely to awaken the Divine spark (Yod) within you, and this may lead you to being able to unlock the door (Daleth) that leads to the understanding you seek.

See Zohar symbol, Strong Wind.

WINDMILL

*takhnat rooakh–tchnth rvch–*טחנת רוח*–*681

MEANING Windmills belong to an era when we still built things with an eye to both their function and their appearance. Compare the appearance of any windmill to that of any modern milling installa-

tion and the contrast is immediately obvious. The purpose of most windmills was to grind grain into flour—to take the raw crop and transform it into potential food. The spiritual analogy for this process is, not surprisingly, the means by which you convert information or even the simple sensory data of your eyes and convert into wisdom that will feed your relationship to the Divine.

THE TREE OF LIFE While it is the milling of information into wisdom that is the key to this dream, we also need to remember that the dream image is of a windmill rather than of a modern industrial mill. Whereas a modern mill is powered by electrical machinery, the windmill relies only on the forces of nature. When translated into a spiritual context, this means that you should rely on your reflective powers to help you reach an inner understanding. When we reduce the value of this dream we find the number 6. This is the value of the letter Vav, and the path of Vav, on which this dream sits, is concerned with reflection and contemplation.

THE JOURNEY All natural processes take longer than those performed with the use of outside assistance, whether it is electrical machinery or the spiritual ideas of those who have gone before you. The initial letter, Mem, in the compression of this dream's value appears in its final form. This emphasizes the fact that the maternal aspect of the Divine is with you at this time. You should try to communicate (Peh) with your inner self in order to understand the spiritual ideas you are currently considering. This is the route that is most likely to bring you to a better understanding of the Divine (Aleph) itself.

WINDOW

*khalon–chlvn–*חלון*–*94

MEANING While the letter Heh literally means "window," the word used in the title of your dream is more common when referring to a window as a hole or a gap in a conversation or piece of text. There are obvious spiritual overtones to the image of a window, since it represents both the individual observing the world to try to understand the Divine and the potential for the Divine to observe you. The idea of being watched by the Divine is emphasized by the fact that the value of this dream is equivalent to the value of the Hebrew word meaning "children," and this is very much the nature of our relationship to the Divine. A traditional Kabbalistic interpretation would also emphasize the need for you to find new vistas in your life.

THE TREE OF LIFE When we reduce the value of this dream we find the number 13. This suggests that you are about to experience a major change in your life. It is highly likely that this will result from your observations of the world around you and indeed of yourself. The letter Nun stands out in the spelling of this dream title as it appears in its final form. The path of Nun refers to a great strengthening of your faith, often emerging from a long and difficult process of introspection, so this is where we should position your dream.

THE JOURNEY The compression of this dream tells you that as long as you maintain your commitment to the Great Work (Tzaddi), you will be able to open the door (Daleth) to increasingly higher levels of spiritual insight. You should remember that the image of a window is there to encourage you to seek new ideas and new ways of looking at the world to encourage your spiritual growth.

WINE

yayeen-yyn- יין*-*70

MEANING Many religions have failed to hold on to the notion that existence itself is a good reason to feel joyful. It is quite common for religion to promote the dour and the somber approach to life as somehow more pleasing to the Divine. Thankfully, there are some spiritual traditions that do not fall into this sanctimonious trap, and Judaism is among them. Wine is an absolute must in any such celebration, so at one level its symbolic significance is as a reminder of the essentially joyful nature of creation.

THE TREE OF LIFE The value of this dream is equivalent to the value of the Hebrew word meaning "secret." This spelling of the word *secret* is used when referring to the secret of the Lord. There is a deep mystical significance in the image of wine that relates to wisdom that is revealed to only those few who have entered into a covenant with the Divine. The value of this dream is also equivalent to the value of the letter Ayin. The path of Ayin refers to a very vigorous and active pursuit of the spiritual path, and this fits well with the themes of this dream, so it is here that we should locate your dream.

THE JOURNEY The spelling of this dream title indicates an abundance of Divine energy, since the letter Yod is repeated twice. The final form of the letter Nun, which follows, makes it clear that you have the opportunity at this time to significantly deepen your faith and your level of understanding.

If the vine can be seen as representing the flow of life itself and each individual life can be seen as a grape, then in order to approach a deeper understanding of the significance of wine we should begin by reflecting on the possible symbolism of a fermenting grape.

WINTER

*khoref-chvrph-*חורף*-*294

MEANING In wintertime, a good portion of the life in the world goes to sleep. The plants lose their blossoms and often their leaves, and generally it is a bleak time of year. Symbolically, winter represents a period in your life when it is hard to see the presence of the Divine or to believe in the purpose of the Great Work. It is particularly difficult to cope with since the image of winter suggests a faith that is fading rather than a faith that has never emerged. It is essential that you remember that the symbol of Winter urges patience and represents the still and unnoticed life that continues under the surface.

THE TREE OF LIFE When we look at the spelling of this dream title, the letter Peh is immediately noticeable because it appears in its final form. The path of Peh is concerned with all forms of communication. In order for you to be able to move out of your current state of despondency, you need to be able to talk about your concerns and your fears. Consequently, we should locate your dream on the path of Peh. This does not mean merely that you should try to find some like-minded people with whom to share your experiences; you should also try to establish a sense of dialogue with your higher self.

THE JOURNEY No matter how cold you feel on the inside, do not despair. This is the message of this dream. The initial letter, Resh, in the compression of this dream tells you that you should approach the Divine with a rational and as far as possible an optimistic approach. The central letter, Tzaddi, is there to remind you that if you can find some way to maintain your commitment to the spiritual quest, you will be able to find the doorway (Daleth) that leads you back to a sense of the Divine presence.

WIRE

*khoot matekhet-chvt mthkth-*תום מתכת*-*883

MEANING While it may not be the most inspiring of images, the dream of wire is nonetheless an encouraging one for you to have. When we think of wire we are likely to think of wire fences. This may seem like a negative association, but, although a wire fence may keep you from advancing, it does allow you to look beyond the confines of your current environment. In spiritual terms, this dream suggests that although you have yet to progress, you are certainly mentally preparing for that next step in your life.

THE TREE OF LIFE When we reduce the value of this dream we find the number 10, which indicates the Sefirah of Malkut, and this is where your dream should be located. However, all the signs indicate that you will shortly be able to move out of the wholly physical world and begin your spiritual journey. The value of this dream is equivalent to that of a Hebrew phrase meaning "the light out of the east." This refers to the dawning of your awareness that there is a spiritual reality for you to discover.

THE JOURNEY The letter Peh appears twice in the compression of this dream's value in both its standard and its final forms. Its presence here serves to emphasize the need for you to attempt to engage in communication with your higher self. Thanks to the metaphorical wire fence, you now have sight of the light that emanates from the Divine. What you must do now is begin trying to make contact with the source of that light.

WITNESS
ed-a'ad-עד-74

MEANING This dream should be seen as a very positive indication about your spiritual development. The content itself is indicative of someone who is paying very close attention to everything that is occurring around him. It is important that you do, since the value of this dream reduces to 11. This number indicates that you are on the verge of experiencing a moment of deep spiritual significance. It is therefore particularly important at this time that you examine every event in your life with a view to its potential spiritual significance.

THE TREE OF LIFE The value of this dream is equivalent to the value of the Hebrew word meaning "ox-goad." This is, of course, the literal meaning of the Hebrew letter Lamed. The path of Lamed is associated with rigorous study, and this is the path on which we should place your dream. It is through study that you will be able to learn to recognize events and signs that may be of symbolic and spiritual importance.

THE JOURNEY You are doing very well in terms of your inner development and have learned much from what you have read. It is, of course, very valuable to your continuing progress that you should maintain your diligent approach to studying matters of a spiritual nature. The compression of this dream's value produces the two letters Ayin and Daleth. Their purpose in this dream is to tell you that if you wish to open the door (Daleth) that leads to the highest levels of spiritual awareness, you will need to begin to formulate your personal (Ayin) understanding of and relationship with the Divine.

WOLF
zeev-zab-זאב-10

MEANING Wolves have an undeservedly bad reputation in most cultures. Even before we consider their association with lycanthropy we have to deal with the fact that they are erroneously regarded as man eaters and are considered loners. In fact, wolves are very social animals and are no better or worse than any other predator. Thankfully, this dream focuses on the genuine nature of wolves, so you should not see this dream as in any way negative.

THE TREE OF LIFE This dream refers to the ability not to only watch the world around you for clues as to the nature of the Divine but to analyze that information and determine which elements are useful and which are not. The letter Zayin, which begins the spelling of this dream title, represents this analytical skill, so it is here that we should position your dream.

THE JOURNEY The image of a wolf appears in this dream not because they are fierce or dangerous animals but because of their incredibly acute senses. It is this quality that you should be seeking to emulate. Additionally, the central letter in the spelling of this dream title refers to the absolute unity of the Divine and thus to the need for all people to see their essential links. This refers to the very social nature of the wolf. If at all possible, you should consider trying to work with like-minded people at this stage of your spiritual development.

WOMAN
eeshah-ayshh-אישה-316

MEANING Whenever we look at a dream where gender is an issue, we have to remember that the symbols that present themselves to our unconscious are based on ancient conceptions of what those genders represented. Even though we have, thankfully, moved on from those gender-based distinctions, we still have symbols that stem from that period. This is why we have the association by value of the word *woman* and the Hebrew word meaning "to bow down." In terms of the spiritual import of this dream, it is important for both men and women to adopt an attitude of appropriate humility before the Divine.

THE TREE OF LIFE When we reduce the value of this dream we find the number 12. This number is strongly associated with ideas about compassion and altruism. The path of Mem is concerned mainly with such values and it is also the path that reflects the maternal aspect of the Divine. While these may be stereotypical values to assign to a woman, they are very positive in terms of the development of all individuals who wish to deepen their understanding of the spiritual realm.

THE JOURNEY While this dream may be replete with ideas and concepts that it would be unthinkable to apply only to women in today's society, they are very valuable attitudes in their own right. Additionally, the compression of this dream's value indicates that you will need a great deal of energy in order to cope with the very demanding approach to the world that the path of Mem requires. The central letter, Yod, in the compression suggests that the spark of the Divine within you will ensure that you are able to achieve the goals set by your current position on the Tree of Life.

WOODLAND

*yaar-ya'ar-*יער-280

MEANING This dream relies partly on phrases for its meaning. The phrase "not being able to see the wood for the trees" is relevant to this dream since it refers to the difficulties you feel that you are having with making any progress in the Great Work. The value of this dream is equivalent to the Hebrew word meaning "terror." However, the image of trees is very positive in Kabbalistic symbolism, so this word association relates to your perception rather than the reality of your position. The dream of woodland is designed to make you see that you are surrounded by a number of trees and therefore by a great deal of positive energy.

THE TREE OF LIFE The value of this dream reduces to 10 and this is the number of the Sefirah of Malkut. This Sefirah is also indicated as the appropriate location for this dream in a number of other ways. The dream content itself links to the earthly associations of Malkut. In addition, the value of this dream is equivalent to the value of the Hebrew name for the archangel associated with the Sefirah of Malkut.

THE JOURNEY You have a deep-seated interest in the spiritual path, but your irrational fears are preventing you from taking any action to try to move yourself out of the solely physical world. The compression of this dream advises you that if you try to take a more rational and optimistic view (Resh) of the possible spiritual routes you could take out of Malkut, you will be able to begin the Great Work. The letter Peh points out that communication is crucial to reaching a position where you are able to begin the spiritual journey. Bearing in mind the title of this dream, it would also be useful for you to spend some time in the countryside learning to appreciate the Divine through an appreciation of the natural world.

WOOL

*tsemer-tzmr-*צמר-330

MEANING We don't expect wool to carry any exciting associations, but this dream is full of energy and indicates a person who is approaching the spiritual path with great vigor. To appreciate why such an innocuous substance as wool should be connected to a dream of great spiritual energy would require a very detailed explication of parts of the Kabbalistic *The Book of Concealed Mystery,* which deals with the nature of the Divine in a symbolic manner. From a traditional point of view, this dream would be seen as more comforting than energetic. Wool is associated with the docility of the sheep from which it comes, and in traditional Kabbalah it would function as a symbol of protective comfort for the soul.

THE TREE OF LIFE The value of this dream is equivalent to the value of the Hebrew word meaning "hurricane," and this is emblematic of the powerful energy that is found in your dream. The initial letter in the compression of this dream is Shin. The qualities of the path of Shin are reserves of fiery spiritual energy. Additionally, the letter Shin represents the spirit of God as it works through the world or the "Ruach Elohim." For these reasons, we should place your dream on the path of Shin.

THE JOURNEY You may be on an early path, but you have great reserves of energy and a great determination to succeed. The initial letter, Tzaddi, in the spelling of this dream title makes it clear that you are fully committed to the Great Work. When we reduce the value of this dream we find the number 6. This number is the value of the letter Vav and reminds you that it is also important to spend time in quiet contemplation as well as in vigorous pursuit of the Divine.

WORK

avodah-a'abvdh-עבודה-87

MEANING You could be forgiven for assuming that this dream must belong to the Sefirah of Malkut since it is concerned with work or labor. However, the work in question is not physical toil but the work of the spiritual quest. This does not mean that you will not have to put in any effort, though. The Great Work requires rigorous study and commitment. While the rewards are great, they can be achieved only with the right amount of work. The value of this dream is equivalent to the value of the Hebrew word meaning "moon." Its presence here is to emphasize the nonearthly focus of this dream, since the Moon is associated with all things spiritual and ethereal as well as being connected to the Sefirah of Yesod, which lies beyond the purely physical.

THE TREE OF LIFE While it may not relate to physical labor, this dream still implies a great deal of hard work. The value of this dream is equivalent to the value of the Hebrew word meaning "determined." This points to the high level of commitment that you have toward the Great Work. The path of Tzaddi is concerned with dedication to the spiritual quest, so it is here that we should locate your dream.

THE JOURNEY When we reduce the value of this dream we find the number 6. This is the value of the letter Vav and refers to the need for you to give yourself time to engage in quiet contemplation. The compression of this dream's value makes it clear that in order to be able to effectively separate out the useful spiritual information from the misleading (Zayin), you should try to find likeminded people with whom you can discuss (Peh) your progress.

WORLD

olam-a'avlm-עולם-146

MEANING This dream occurs very early in your spiritual development. It represents the first flush of enthusiasm and the desire to understand everything about the spiritual reality that lies beyond the physical universe. The value of this dream reduces to 11, and this implies very strongly that you will shortly be undergoing an experience that will be of great spiritual significance to you.

THE TREE OF LIFE The value of this dream is equivalent to the value of the Hebrew phrase meaning "the first gate." We can see this as a reference to the first path that takes you out of the world of the material. This is the path of Tav, and it is here that we should locate your dream. We now see that the deeply profound experience that awaits you is your arrival in the Sefirah of Yesod, which is the first staging point on the long journey back to the home of the Divine.

THE JOURNEY Although you are full of excitement at the prospect of the inner voyage that lies ahead, you have a number of understandable worries. These are referred to by the initial letter, Qoph, in the compression of this dream's value. The subsequent letter, Mem, makes it clear that the maternal aspect of the Divine is with you at this time in order to ease your initiation into the realm of the spiritual. Finally, we have the letter Vav, which functions in this dream as a promise of the potential link you may forge with the Divine or the macrocosm.

WORM

tolaat-thvla'ath-תולעת-906

MEANING There are some dreams that appear not to have any relevance to your spiritual progress, and this is one of them. We find it hard to associate something as lofty as the spiritual quest with something as poorly regarded as a worm. However, it is exactly the worm's lowly status that lies behind the spiritual message of this dream. From a wholly traditional Kabbalistic standpoint, this dream would be seen as rather negative. Worms feed on decaying matter, so this would be taken as a suggestion that you are too tied to the past or are failing to move on in your life.

THE TREE OF LIFE When we reduce the value of this dream we find the number 6. This is the value of the letter Vav, which refers to the need for contemplation and meditation. The letter Vav also appears in the compression of this dream's value, and it is the path of Vav on which we should locate your dream. The purpose of this dream is to encourage you include everything in your meditations, even the lowliest worm, as all things in the universe will help you to understand the Divine more when you understand them as fully as possible.

THE JOURNEY The central letter in the spelling of this dream title is the letter Lamed, which represents the need for you to engage in rigorous study in order to maintain your inner development. The compression of this dream begins with the letter Tzaddi in its final form. The final form serves to emphasize the message of the letter Tzaddi. That message is that the key to success is commitment and persistence. Study that has great gaps or contemplation that occurs only when the mood strikes you will not help you progress, whereas steady persistent effort will allow you to achieve all of your spiritual goals.

WOUND

*petsa-phtza'a-*פצע-240

MEANING The value of this dream is equivalent to the value of the Hebrew word meaning "myrrh." When we combine that with the fact that this is a dream about a wound, we may mistakenly think that the dreamer is heading for a dreadful time, especially given the associations with myrrh. However, the wound is purely symbolic and rather than suggesting that you are about to be wounded, it relates to your empathy for the pain of others rather than to any danger that you are literally facing.

THE TREE OF LIFE When we reduce the value of this dream we find the number 6. In the context of the other values in this dream, we should see this as a reference to the sixth Sefirah on the Tree of Life, or Tiferet. The value of this dream is equivalent to the value of the Hebrew word meaning "lofty," and this along with the other associated values points to the level of inner development that is best represented by the Sefirah of Tiferet. This indicates a significant achievement on your part and you should try to make some form of contact with your higher self.

THE JOURNEY The initial letter, Peh, in the spelling of this dream title is a reminder to you to try to make that contact with your higher self. The compression of the dream's value tells us that you can afford to be very optimistic (Resh) about your chances of achieving this aim. It also points out that as well as advancing your spiritual understanding, you are now in a position to try to assist others

(Mem), putting your feelings of compassion and empathy into practice.

WRECK

*khoorban-chvrbn-*חורבן-266

MEANING This dream could relate to any kind of wreck, from a shipwreck to a dilapidated building. The key theme is the sense of ongoing disrepair and decay. It would be reasonable to assume that this is a very negative dream—after all, destruction does not seem to fit very well with ideas of spirituality. However, although this dream has some difficult lessons for you to learn, it is ultimately one that will lead to a much greater level of awareness of the nature of the Divine.

THE TREE OF LIFE The value of this dream is equivalent to the value of the Hebrew word meaning "contraction." We should take this to refer to the general sense of reduction, as this dream is all about the tendency of all things to reduce, or decay, and ultimately to cease. The realization that the process of death and the decay of all forms is a part of the Divine nature of the universe occurs in the Sefirah of Gevurah, and it is here that we should locate your dream.

THE JOURNEY When we reduce the value of this dream we find the number 5. This serves to emphasize that this dream belongs in Gevurah, as it is the fifth Sefirah on the Tree of Life. Despite the difficult nature of this dream's message, the letter Resh in the compression of the dream's value indicates that you should maintain a rational outlook. If you do this, and rely on the support and guidance (Samech) of your higher self as well as careful meditation on the implication of this dream, you will come to a much closer sense of a relationship with the Divine.

WRINKLES

*kemet-qmt-*קמט-149

MEANING To dream of wrinkles suggests that you are dreaming of aging. In today's society, age is seen as something to be avoided at all costs. Every shopping mall is packed with products designed to smooth you down, tuck you in, and generally hide the fact that you have had the temerity to be alive for longer than some other people. In earlier cultures, age was respected and seen as a sign of great wisdom. The value of this dream is a prime number, and since prime numbers are considered signs of uniqueness, this should be seen as evidence that this dream takes a positive view of the issue of age.

THE TREE OF LIFE The value of this dream reduces to 5, and in the context of this dream it should be seen as a reference to the letter Heh, which has a value of 5. The path of Heh leads into the supernal Sefirah of Hokhmah, whose name and nature are "wisdom." Given the positive qualities of old age, this is an ideal path on which to place your dream. The meaning of the letter Heh is "window," and this suggests that you have developed the ability to see a great deal in the universe in terms of its underlying spiritual nature.

THE JOURNEY The spelling of this dream is exactly the same as the letters that are produced in its compression, and this tells us that the significance of each letter is thereby emphasized. The initial Qoph represents a level of concern and anxiety, not for yourself but for the welfare of those around you. The subsequent letter, Mem, with its associations with compassion and altruism, makes it clear that this is indeed the case. Finally, we have the letter Teth, which tells you that as long as you retain your strength of character you will continue to develop greater insight into the nature of the Divine.

WRITING
keteevah-kthybh-כתיבה-437

MEANING This dream does not necessarily mean that you are dreaming of writing; it could just as easily be a dream where you see writing that has been produced by someone else's hand. Writing had enormous power in the ancient world since the ability both to read and to write was restricted to a very small number of people. In spiritual terms, this dream refers to the attempt to access wisdom that is restricted or complex in nature.

THE TREE OF LIFE The central letter in the compression of this dream is Lamed. The path of Lamed relates to diligent and rigorous study. It is this level of study that will be required if you are to achieve the spiritual goals that you are setting for yourself. Consequently, we should place this dream on the path of Lamed.

THE JOURNEY When we reduce the value of this dream we find the number 5. This number refers to the individual who is able to master the four elements within himself under the mastery of the fifth element of Spirit. This is the work that takes place in the Sefirah of Tiferet and it is the ambition that

your higher self has set for you. The final letter, Zayin, in the compression of this dream tells you that you will need to very carefully analyze all the ideas that you encounter in order to select those that will help you to move forward along your path. It would be very helpful to your ability to analyze your progress if you make a point of keeping a journal in which you record your developing insights and understanding.

X-RAY
karney rentgen-qrny rntgn-קרני רנטגן-672

MEANING We find it much easier to see the spiritual relevance of images from the past—a candlestick or a goblet, for example—than of images that come right from the heart of our own culture. This is partly because we regard the world of the spiritual as separate and somehow alien. Consequently, it seems strange to find the Divine hiding among the letters that make up the word X-ray. In fact, this is not at all strange; the Divine force permeates the universe, so we should expect to find evidence of it everywhere.

THE TREE OF LIFE When we reduce the value of this dream we find the number 6. This is the value of the Hebrew letter Vav. The path of Vav is concerned with deep contemplation and meditation on the nature of the Divine. An X-ray is a scientific way of looking into the core of a person. Meditation is a spiritual way of looking into the core of the universe, so this is a very appropriate path on which to position your dream.

THE JOURNEY The compression of your dream begins with the letter Mem in its final form, and this emphasizes its significance as a sign that you are a deeply compassionate individual. The following letter, Ayin, tells you that you need to balance this concern for others with a similarly vigorous interest in pursuing your personal understanding of your relationship to the Divine. If you manage to achieve this delicate balance, you will be well on your way to returning to the home of the Divine as represented by the final letter, Beth.

YAWNING
lefahek-lphhq-לפהק-215

MEANING This dream suggests that you are not particularly enthusiastic about the spiritual quest. It could be seen as a suggestion that you feel rather apathetic about it, since this dream indicates that you are very close to sleep. The value of this dream is equivalent to the value of the Hebrew word meaning "a narrow way." This is a direct reference to the difficulty of the Great Work, and this implies that you are not so much bored as unable to progress at this point in you inner journey.

THE TREE OF LIFE When we reduce the value of this dream we find the number 8. This number is the value of the letter Cheth, and its literal meaning is "fence." The path of Cheth represents the protective force of the Divine. In its negative aspect this path refers to a defensive attitude. This attitude stems from a reluctance to examine the possible reasons for your lack of spiritual progress. This is the basis of your disinterest, so we should place your dream on the path of Cheth in its negative aspect.

THE JOURNEY You should not feel disheartened by the fact that you are finding the work difficult. This is very common. The value of this dream is equivalent to the value of a Hebrew word that refers to the rising of the light. This represents that if you try to remain optimistic, as indicated by the letter Resh in the compression of this dream's value, you will once again see the light of understanding begin to dawn. This will be due in part to the fact that you will be feeling the spark of the Divine (Yod) begin to burn within you.

YELLOW

tsahov-tzhvb- צהוב-103

MEANING We associate the color yellow with cowardice, so you might think that this dream indicates a person who lacks the courage to take a leap into the unknown and begin the spiritual quest. However, that association for the color yellow is relatively recent. Moreover, given the enormity of the Great Work, it would be foolish to embark on such a journey without engaging in some serious and extended consideration of the implications.

THE TREE OF LIFE When we reduce the value of this dream we find the number 4. This is the number of the physical world and suggests that we should place this dream in the Sefirah of Malkut. Additionally, the color yellow, or more precisely citrine, is one of the colors associated with this Sefirah. The value of this dream is equivalent to the value of the Hebrew word meaning "dust," so it seems quite conclusive that Malkut is the appropriate home for this dream.

THE JOURNEY The initial letter in the compression of this dream is Qoph, which refers to the kinds

of fear and anxiety that are perfectly natural for someone contemplating beginning the spiritual quest. The initial letter in the spelling of this dream title tells you that as long as you feel committed (Tzaddi) to the desire to understand the nature of the Divine, you will be able to make progress. The final letter, Gimel, in the compression serves as a promise of the secret wisdom that you may ultimately be able to unlock if you do make the leap of faith and set foot on the first stage of the inner journey.

YIELDING

leheekena-lhykna'a- להיכנע-185

MEANING We live not so much in a dog-eat-dog world as in a world of dog eat dog and then grind up the inedible bits for sale. This means that the idea of yielding to anyone or anything is not a popular one. However, if we are to progress in the Great Work, it is essential that we learn some humility in the face of the Divine. We may not recognize the authority of any person to determine our fate, but we must recognize the authority of the Divine.

THE TREE OF LIFE When we reduce the value of this dream we find the number 5. This is a very important number in the Western Mystery Tradition, since it indicates that you have managed to place the four elements of Fire, Earth, Air, and Water within your personality under the mastery of your higher self. This is a mirror image of your relationship to the Divine in that your lower instincts yield to your spiritual essence. This process takes place in the Sefirah of Tiferet, and it is here that we should locate your dream.

THE JOURNEY Achieving the mastery of your nature is a daunting task, as is the loss of the comforting certainties provided by your ego-based self. Consequently, it is no surprise to find the letter Qoph heading up the compression of this dream's value as a representation of your concerns. The subsequent letter, Peh, urges you to try to communicate with your higher self, since this will both ease your worries and enable to you to reach a clearer view (Heh) of the spiritual nature both of yourself and of the universe in general.

YOKE

ol-a'avl- עול-106

MEANING The idea of a yoke has been used so often that it has become a cliché in regard to particularly repressive regimes. We have often heard about one group or another being "under the yoke" of some dictatorship. Ironically, we are all under the yoke of an especially subtle dictator. That dictator is the ego-based side of ourselves, and we do not even realize that we are being driven along by it. When we reduce the value of this dream we find the number 7. This is the value of the letter Zayin, and it should be seen as an encouragement to you to try to analyze your behavior and cut out those aspects that are being determined by your lower instincts.

THE TREE OF LIFE The value of this dream is equivalent to the value of the letter Nun when spelled in full. The path of Nun relates to a process whereby we are able to significantly deepen and strengthen our faith in the Divine. To do so requires us to look honestly and sometimes painfully at our inner nature. This reveals the areas that are being led by our lower rather than by our higher self, so we should locate your dream on the path of Nun.

THE JOURNEY Looking so hard at your nature is not an easy task to take on, and this is why we find the letter Qoph, indicating a range of worries and anxieties, at the beginning of the compression of this dream. There is no easy way to rid yourself of these fears, since experiencing them is part of the work of the path of Nun. However, you can make sure that you give yourself lots of time to meditate on the implications of your emotional state, as indicated by the final letter Vav in the compression of this dream.

YOUNG

*tsaeer-tza'ayr-*צעיר-370

MEANING This is a very auspicious dream, and, despite what you might expect, it suggests that you have made great strides in terms of your spiritual development. In day-to-day life we are supposed to act like adults, and the irony is that we are all play-acting. Most of us go through adult life wondering if being "grown-up" came naturally to our parents, since we do not feel the same sense of confidence that they seemed to possess. Of course, our parents felt exactly the same, and so the charade goes on. In a spiritual life there is no clear injunction as to how we should feel or behave, so we are much freer to truly be ourselves.

THE TREE OF LIFE The value of this dream is equivalent to the value of the Hebrew word meaning "creation." This suggests that you have developed a very deep understanding of the Divine, since in terms of the Tree of Life the initial act of Creation occurs right at its very summit. When we reduce the value of this dream we find the number 1. This is the value of the path of Aleph. At an individual level, this path represents the innocence of the purely faithful, and it is here that we should locate your dream.

THE JOURNEY You may have the trusting innocence of the young when it comes to your relationship with the Divine, but the compression of this dream makes it clear that you also have an enormous amount of raw, fiery spiritual energy (Shin). The compression also tells you that in order to achieve that moment of longed-for communion with the Divine, you should remain true to your personal approach to the realm of the spiritual.

ZIPPER

*rokhsan-rvksn-*רוכסן-336

MEANING This seems a most unusual and potentially trivial dream to equate with anything remotely spiritual. However, it is its unusual nature that gives a clue to its inner meaning. On the surface, we can perhaps claim that since a zipper can be opened to reveal what lies within, so you are attempting to unzip the world of the physical in order to see the spiritual truth that lies within.

THE TREE OF LIFE When we reduce the value of this dream we find the number 3. This number is associated with creativity on all levels. Consequently, the slightly bizarre subject of this dream is in itself an example of your creative approach to the Divine. The Sefirah of Netzach is concerned with all forms of artistic endeavor, and, since you are especially passionate in the way that you express your spirituality, this is the ideal location for your dream.

THE JOURNEY The initial letter, Shin, in the compression of this dream points to the great store of spiritual energy that you have at your disposal. You also need to bear in mind the subsequent letter, Lamed, which indicates the need for you to be as diligent in your studies as you are in your enthusiasm for the Great Work. The final letter, Vav, reminds you of the importance of quiet contemplation to complement your active celebration of the Divine.

ZOO

*gan khayot-gn chyvth-*גן חיות 477

MEANING The image of a zoo might lead you to see this dream as belonging to the Sefirah of Malkut, since it is very definitely connected to a very physical and animalistic image. However, the dream of a zoo is more of a reflection on the nature of human society in general than on the animals themselves. Unless we take up the challenge of the Great Work, we all remain trapped in a very limited environment; we may believe ourselves to be living life to the full, but that is simply because we have not yet noticed the bars in the windows. A more traditional Kabbalistic analysis would see this dream as representing a danger that your inner nature is in some way being repressed or caged. It is important that you identify the source of this feeling and find a way to resolve it.

THE TREE OF LIFE To have this dream indicates that you have achieved a significant level of insight and are able to see the secular life for the gilded cage that it is. You are motivated by a desire for spiritual insight rather than material gain. When we reduce the value of this dream we find the number 9. This is the value of the letter Teth. The path of Teth refers to an individual who has great strength of character and willpower, so this seems to be an ideal position on which to place your dream.

THE JOURNEY You have already managed to master the elements within yourself and brought them under the control of your higher self, and you are now looking to attempt to achieve a moment of communion with the Divine itself. The compression of this dream indicates that you do have some sense of regret at having to leave behind some of the material world's certainties. However, the letters Ayin and Zayin tell us that you will continue to move forward spiritually, analyzing everything you experience in terms of its relevance to your inner voyage. Moreover, the approach that you take to the Divine will be one that is uniquely yours.